The Top 40 Latest and Greatest Quotes Harvested from a Bumper Crop of Praise for Previous Versions of *Macworld Photoshop Bible*

This was the best computer book I've ever read.
> — SM, Boulder, CO

The author's style is inviting and comfortable. He explains complex concepts in a very simple, familiar manner. Nothing else comes close.
> — TG, North Hollywood, CA

I read this book on vacation — and still had a good time!
> — DLG, Vanderbilt, Mississippi

This book has the most extensive coverage of Adobe Photoshop I've seen! Thanks for helping me realize the limitless potential of Photoshop!
> — DH, Big Sandy, Texas

. . . this encyclopedic effort ought to help both new and experienced users unleash the power of this multidimensional program. Nearly every feature is explored in detail — in McClelland's conversational style. . . . One imaging topic of importance among Photoshop disciples — Unsharp Masking — gets no less than seven pages in the *Bible*. It's as clear an explanation of USM as has ever been published, backed up with examples showing the effects achieved by varying the Amount, Radius, and Threshold settings. In fact, if you're looking for only one comprehensive Photoshop book, this may be the one.
> — *Photo District News*

It's a must have for every professional Photoshop user.
> — RC, London, England

I teach Photoshop; there would be no way for me to survive my first class without this book! Deke McClelland incorporates a funny way of explaining things, he's very thorough and tells you about "real-life" situations, not just what Adobe wants its customers to know.
> — CD, Addison, Texas

I thought I was an expert Photoshop user, but you should see how many pages I've marked in this book. Deke's presentation is one of the clearest and most accurate I've seen.

— CS, Fullerton, California

This book puts the Photoshop user manual to shame!

— DB, Toronto, Ontario, Canada

Deke is humorous, not a self-righteous "know everything" author. This book cuts straight to the usable information, without the typical hype or fluff of the manufacturer manuals.

— EV, Somerset, New Jersey

McClelland offers tons of tips, tricks and procedures. There are more insights than any one person will likely be able to digest, but even a few will prove invaluable for getting more out of the program. . . . One advantage of such a large book is that complicated subjects can be dealt with at length. McClelland takes full advantage of this in the special effects section, detailing how the different filters work, what the effects of the filters are, and how users can better control the results. . . . *Macworld Photoshop Bible* succeeds as a valuable tome for users of all levels. It will be helpful for beginners and relevant to advanced users.

— *Communication Arts*

I'm able to do more than I thought possible with Photoshop using this guide.

— DH, Lincoln, Nebraska

I liked the clear, concise, and practical application of each process in Photoshop. Especially the use of layers! WOW!

— MRB, Langley, Washington

It teaches me rather than trying to impress me with the knowledge of the author.

— BB, Porterville, California

I have every Photoshop book and this one is the best. It is the one I go to when I need an answer.

— EF, Boulder, Colorado

What I really like about the book is that Deke McClelland starts at the basics and takes you step by step as if you knew nothing about scanning or images. He takes nothing for granted, explaining in the introduction such fundamentals as when to use Photoshop and when to use a drawing program. . . So what does Photoshop do and how does this book help you in doing it? Mr. McClelland will answer both questions and every other question you can think of within the confines of the Macintosh and Photoshop.

> — *Work Place*, University College Dublin, Ireland

This is the first computer book I've read that is readable and interesting for its own sake, not just as a reference.

> — MAS, Commack, New York

No other book about Photoshop is as good as this one. It's the best!

> — JO, Garsfontein, South Africa

A truly wonderful book, jam packed with useful hints, tricks and basic procedures in Photoshop.

> — TW, Dubuque, Iowa

I had tough deadlines and had never used Photoshop before. This book added years to my life!

> — RB, Green Bay, Wisconsin

Great job McClelland! Many books are dull, but this one made me laugh out loud. It was easy to read the whole thing.

> — PM, Vallejo, California

I am laughing all day thinking about and reading this book.

> — SA, Barcelona, Spain

Given the technical nature of the topic and the depth of coverage, you might expect the writing to be rather dry — somewhat less than inspiring. Fortunately, Deke McClelland is as accomplished a writer as he is a Photoshop guru. He has managed to keep a potentially heavy topic from becoming too great a burden on the reader, while maintaining a strong flow of information. His wit and style show through repeatedly in every chapter. I strongly recommend this book to anyone who uses Adobe Photoshop on the Mac or PC.

> — *Flash*

This book is very reader friendly and easy to use. When I have a problem, I can find the answers quickly and I can understand what I'm reading!

— DS, San Diego, California

It has an answer waiting for every question I could possibly have about Photoshop.

— TL, Corona, California

This "Bible" brings all the comfort that the King James version no longer does — it's my new "Linus Blanket!" I have yet to find a topic that I can think of that isn't covered by the book, and it is stuffed full of topics that wouldn't have occurred to me.

— JC, London, England

I learn something new every time I open it.

— SRJ, Billerica, Massachusetts

It's a great book. . . definitely every Photoshop user's dream.

— CT, Brisbane, Australia

I like Deke McClelland's sense of humor! Plus I loved all the information he poured forth about every feature of Photoshop. I just think this book is excellent!

— TC, Augusta, Georgia

I think I love you, Deke McClelland! Thank you for continuing my ongoing quest!

— KW, Ocoee, Florida

This is a great book. I know Photoshop but I never realized you could do so much with it until I read this book.

— RLS, Whitestone, New York

It is easily understandable and very easy reading with as much information put together as I thought possible. It has everything!

— GKP, Eugene, Oregon

This book helped me to understand the thought processes the developers went through to build the program, which helps me to be a better user.

— JD, Arkansas City, Kansas

The best Photoshop book I've seen — I know; I'm a sixteen-year professional.
— CD, Hazelwood, Missouri

While reading this book it felt like a good friend was sitting over my shoulder letting me in on all the tips and tricks no one else would tell me about or knew about. Thanks!
— JO, San Marcos, Texas

I feel like Deke McClelland is right beside me explaining step by step.
— ECA, Ft. Lauderdale, Florida

Anyone involved with design knows about this book.
— TS, Philadelphia, Pennsylvania

This book has information on all aspects of Photoshop in non-technical, everyday language. It was enjoyable to read and I learned a lot.
— NI, Fairlawn, New Jersey

I was going to skim for information and ended up reading it cover to cover. It's awesome!
— KC, Kenmore, New York

Just picked up your book today and haven't been to stop reading it. A veritable gold mine of useful information that will stay right next to my mouse. Just wanted to say thank you for writing it.
— DC, Elizabeth, New Jersey

Macworld®
Photoshop® 4 Bible

Macworld®
Photoshop® 4 Bible

by Deke McClelland

**Foreword by
Mark Hamburg**

**Technical Review by
Ted Padova**

IDG Books Worldwide, Inc.
An International Data Group Company

Foster City, CA ♦ Chicago, IL ♦ Indianapolis, IN ♦ Southlake, TX

Macworld® Photoshop® 4 Bible

Published by
IDG Books Worldwide, Inc.
An International Data Group Company
919 E. Hillsdale Blvd.
Suite 400
Foster City, CA 94404

www.idgbooks.com (IDG Books Worldwide Web site)

Library of Congress Catalog Card No.: 96-79591

ISBN: 0-7645-4005-X

Printed in the United States of America

10 9 8 7 6 5 4 3 2 1

1B/SQ/RS/ZW/FC

Distributed in the United States by IDG Books Worldwide, Inc.

Distributed by Macmillan Canada for Canada; by Transworld Publishers Limited in the United Kingdom and Europe; by WoodsLane Pty. Ltd. for Australia; by WoodsLane Enterprises Ltd. for New Zealand; by Longman Singapore Publishers Ltd. for Singapore, Malaysia, Thailand, and Indonesia; by Simron Pty. Ltd. for South Africa; by Toppan Company Ltd. for Japan; by Distribuidora Cuspide for Argentina; by Livraria Cultura for Brazil; by Ediciencia S.A. for Ecuador; by Addison-Wesley Publishing Company for Korea; by Ediciones ZETA S.C.R. Ltda. for Peru; by WS Computer Publishing Company, Inc., for the Philippines; by Unalis Corporation for Taiwan; by Contemporanea de Ediciones for Venezuela. Authorized Sales Agent: Anthony Rudkin Associates for the Middle East and North Africa.

For general information on IDG Books Worldwide's books in the U.S., please call our Consumer Customer Service department at 800-762-2974. For reseller information, including discounts and premium sales, please call our Reseller Customer Service department at 800-434-3422.

For information on where to purchase IDG Books Worldwide's books outside the U.S., please contact our International Sales department at 415-655-3172 or fax 415-655-3295.

For information on foreign language translations, please contact our Foreign & Subsidiary Rights department at 415-655-3021 or fax 415-655-3281.

For sales inquiries and special prices for bulk quantities, please contact our Sales department at 415-655-3200 or write to the address above.

For information on using IDG Books Worldwide's books in the classroom or for ordering examination copies, please contact our Educational Sales department at 800-434-2086 or fax 817-251-8174.

For press review copies, author interviews, or other publicity information, please contact our Public Relations department at 415-655-3000 or fax 415-655-3299.

For authorization to photocopy items for corporate, personal, or educational use, please contact Copyright Clearance Center, 222 Rosewood Drive, Danvers, MA 01923, or fax 508-750-4470.

 is a trademark under exclusive license to IDG Books Worldwide, Inc., from International Data Group, Inc.

ABOUT IDG BOOKS WORLDWIDE

Welcome to the world of IDG Books Worldwide.

IDG Books Worldwide, Inc., is a subsidiary of International Data Group, the world's largest publisher of computer-related information and the leading global provider of information services on information technology. IDG was founded more than 25 years ago and now employs more than 8,500 people worldwide. IDG publishes more than 275 computer publications in over 75 countries (see listing below). More than 60 million people read one or more IDG publications each month.

Launched in 1990, IDG Books Worldwide is today the #1 publisher of best-selling computer books in the United States. We are proud to have received eight awards from the Computer Press Association in recognition of editorial excellence and three from *Computer Currents'* First Annual Readers' Choice Awards. Our best-selling *...For Dummies*® series has more than 30 million copies in print with translations in 30 languages. IDG Books Worldwide, through a joint venture with IDG's Hi-Tech Beijing, became the first U.S. publisher to publish a computer book in the People's Republic of China. In record time, IDG Books Worldwide has become the first choice for millions of readers around the world who want to learn how to better manage their businesses.

Our mission is simple: Every one of our books is designed to bring extra value and skill-building instructions to the reader. Our books are written by experts who understand and care about our readers. The knowledge base of our editorial staff comes from years of experience in publishing, education, and journalism — experience we use to produce books for the '90s. In short, we care about books, so we attract the best people. We devote special attention to details such as audience, interior design, use of icons, and illustrations. And because we use an efficient process of authoring, editing, and desktop publishing our books electronically, we can spend more time ensuring superior content and spend less time on the technicalities of making books.

You can count on our commitment to deliver high-quality books at competitive prices on topics you want to read about. At IDG Books Worldwide, we continue in the IDG tradition of delivering quality for more than 25 years. You'll find no better book on a subject than one from IDG Books Worldwide.

John J. Kilcullen

John Kilcullen
President and CEO
IDG Books Worldwide, Inc.

VIII
WINNER
Eighth Annual
Computer Press
Awards ≥1992

IX
WINNER
Ninth Annual
Computer Press
Awards ≥1993

X
WINNER
Tenth Annual
Computer Press
Awards ≥1994

XI
WINNER
Eleventh Annual
Computer Press
Awards ≥1995

IDG Books Worldwide, Inc., is a subsidiary of International Data Group, the world's largest publisher of computer-related information and the leading global provider of information services on information technology. International Data Group publishes over 275 computer publications in over 75 countries. Sixty million people read one or more International Data Group publications each month. International Data Group's publications include: **ARGENTINA:** Buyer's Guide, Computerworld Argentina, PC World Argentina; **AUSTRALIA:** Australian Macworld, Australian PC World, Australian Reseller News, Computerworld, IT Casebook, Network World, Publish, Webmaster; **AUSTRIA:** Computerwelt Osterreich, Networks Austria, PC Tip Austria; **BANGLADESH:** PC World Bangladesh; **BELARUS:** PC World Belarus; **BELGIUM:** Data News; **BRAZIL:** Annuário de Informática, Computerworld, Connections, Macworld, PC Player, PC World, Publish, Reseller News, Supergamepower; **BULGARIA:** Computerworld Bulgaria, Network World Bulgaria, PC & MacWorld Bulgaria; **CANADA:** CIO Canada, Client/Server World, ComputerWorld Canada, InfoWorld Canada, NetworkWorld Canada, WebWorld; **CHILE:** Computerworld Chile, PC World Chile; **COLOMBIA:** Computerworld Colombia, PC World Colombia; **COSTA RICA:** PC World Centro America; **THE CZECH AND SLOVAK REPUBLICS:** Computerworld Czechoslovakia, Macworld Czech Republic, PC World Czechoslovakia; **DENMARK:** Communications World Danmark, Computerworld Danmark, Macworld Danmark, PC World Danmark, Techworld Denmark; **DOMINICAN REPUBLIC:** PC World Republica Dominicana; **ECUADOR:** PC World Ecuador; **EGYPT:** Computerworld Middle East, PC World Middle East; **EL SALVADOR:** PC World Centro America; **FINLAND:** MikroPC, Tietoverkko, Tietoviikko; **FRANCE:** Distributique, Hebdo, Info PC, Le Monde Informatique, Macworld, Reseaux & Telecoms, WebMaster France; **GERMANY:** Computer Partner, Computerwoche, Computerwoche Extra, Computerwoche FOCUS, Global Online, Macwelt, PC Welt; **GREECE:** Amiga Computing, GamePro Greece, Multimedia World; **GUATEMALA:** PC World Centro America; **HONDURAS:** PC World Centro America; **HONG KONG:** Computerworld Hong Kong, PC World Hong Kong, Publish in Asia; **HUNGARY:** ABCD CD-ROM, Computerworld Szamitastechnika, Internetto online Magazine, PC World Hungary, PC-X Magazin Hungary; **ICELAND:** Tolvuheimur PC World Island; **INDIA:** Information Communications World, Information Systems Computerworld, PC World India, Publish in Asia; **INDONESIA:** InfoKomputer PC World, Komputek Computerworld, Publish in Asia; **IRELAND:** ComputerScope, PC Live!; **ISRAEL:** Macworld Israel, People & Computers/Computerworld; **ITALY:** Computerworld Italia, Macworld Italia, Networking Italia, PC World Italia; **JAPAN:** DTP World, Macworld Japan, Nikkei Personal Computing, OS/2 World Japan, SunWorld Japan, Windows NT World, Windows World Japan; **KENYA:** PC World East African; **KOREA:** Hi-Tech Information, Macworld Korea, PC World Korea; **MACEDONIA:** PC World Macedonia; **MALAYSIA:** Computerworld Malaysia, PC World Malaysia, Publish in Asia; **MALTA:** PC World Malta; **MEXICO:** Computerworld Mexico, PC World Mexico; **MYANMAR:** PC World Myanmar; **NETHERLANDS:** Computer! Totaal, LAN Internetworking Magazine, LAN World Buyers Guide, Macworld Netherlands, Net, WebWereld; **NEW ZEALAND:** Absolute Beginners Guide and Plain & Simple Series, Computer Buyer, Computer Industry Directory, Computerworld New Zealand, MTB, Network World, PC World New Zealand; **NICARAGUA:** PC World Centro America; **NORWAY:** Computerworld Norge, CW Rapport, Datamagasinet, Financial Rapport, Kursguide Norge, Macworld Norge, Multimediaworld Norge, PC World Ekspress Norge, PC World Nettverk, PC World Norge, PC World ProduktGuide Norge; **PAKISTAN:** Computerworld Pakistan; **PANAMA:** PC World Panama; **PEOPLE'S REPUBLIC OF CHINA:** China Computer Users, China Computerworld, China InfoWorld, China Telecom World Weekly, Computer & Communication, Electronic Design China, Electronics Today, Electronics Weekly, Game Software, PC World China, Popular Computer Week, Software Weekly, Software World, Telecom World; **PERU:** Computerworld Peru, PC World Profesional Peru, PC World SoHo Peru; **PHILIPPINES:** Click!, Computerworld Philippines, PC World Philippines, Publish in Asia; **POLAND:** Computerworld Poland, Computerworld Special Report Poland, Cyber, Macworld Poland, Networld Poland, PC World Komputer; **PORTUGAL:** Cerebro/PC World, Computerworld/Correio Informático, Dealer World Portugal, Mac*In/PC*In Portugal, Multimedia World; **PUERTO RICO:** PC World Puerto Rico; **ROMANIA:** Computerworld Romania, PC World Romania, Telecom Romania; **RUSSIA:** Computerworld Russia, Mir PK, Publish, Seti; **SINGAPORE:** Computerworld Singapore, PC World Singapore, Publish in Asia; **SLOVENIA:** Monitor; **SOUTH AFRICA:** Computing SA, Network World SA, Software World SA; **SPAIN:** Communicaciones World España, Computerworld España, Dealer World España, Macworld España, PC World España; **SRI LANKA:** Infolink PC World; **SWEDEN:** CAP&Design, Computer Sweden, Corporate Computing Sweden, Internetworld Sweden, it.branschen, Macworld Sweden, MaxiData Sweden, MikroDatorn, Nätverk & Kommunikation, PC World Sweden, PCAktiv, Windows World Sweden; **SWITZERLAND:** Computerworld Schweiz, Macworld Schweiz, PCtip; **TAIWAN:** Computerworld Taiwan, Macworld Taiwan, NEW ViSiON/Publish, PC World Taiwan, Windows World Taiwan; **THAILAND:** Publish in Asia, Thai Computerworld; **TURKEY:** Computerworld Turkiye, Macworld Turkiye, Network World Turkiye, PC World Turkiye; **UKRAINE:** Computerworld Kiev, Multimedia World Ukraine, PC World Ukraine; **UNITED KINGDOM:** Acorn User UK, Amiga Action UK, Amiga Computing UK, Apple Talk UK, Computing, Macworld, Parents and Computers UK, PC Advisor, PC Home, PSX Pro, The WEB; **UNITED STATES:** Cable in the Classroom, CIO Magazine, Computerworld, DOS World, Federal Computer Week, GamePro Magazine, InfoWorld, I-Way, Macworld, Network World, PC Games, PC World, Publish, Video Event, THE WEB Magazine, and WebMaster; online webzines: JavaWorld, NetscapeWorld, and SunWorld Online; **URUGUAY:** InfoWorld Uruguay; **VENEZUELA:** Computerworld Venezuela, PC World Venezuela; and **VIETNAM:** PC World Vietnam.   10/1/96

I am strangely fortunate to be unquestioningly loved by someone that I love without question. You're the sun in my sky, EP.

Foreword

If you are reading this foreword, it probably means that you've purchased a copy of Adobe Photoshop 4.0, and for that I and the rest of the Photoshop team at Adobe thank you.

If you own a previous edition of the *Macworld Photoshop Bible*, you probably know what to expect. If not, then get ready for an interesting trip.

I have long felt that the best way to learn Photoshop is through exploration. Rather than just offering a set of canned effects, it offers a broad collection of tools for a wide range of imaging tasks. Becoming a skilled Photoshop user involves getting to know those tools, how they interact, and when to use them. The best way I've found to do that is through use, exploration, and play.

On the other hand, since Photoshop allows one to do so much, it can be difficult to know where to begin. It's like opening a watch maker's tool chest: The screwdrivers are pretty obvious, but what about all these other strange and mysterious instruments?

In Photoshop 4.0, one of our main goals was to try to eliminate many of the inconsistencies and arcanum that had accreted in Photoshop over the years. At the expense of changing some of the ways in which people had become used to working — ways that we often felt were excessively awkward — we think we've come a long way. Those changes should make Photoshop easier to learn and use from the standpoint that what you learn in one place is more likely to apply in another. The program, however, still spans so much territory that it can be difficult to know where to begin.

This is where Deke McClelland comes in.

The *Macworld Photoshop 4 Bible* is a guided tour through Photoshop with a guide who has been over the territory many times. (I've been involved with Photoshop for six years, and for essentially as long as I can remember, I've had Deke looking over my shoulder.)

Deke takes you through most of Photoshop and covers a lot of areas in impressive depth. Not only does he show you the features in Photoshop — after all, you've got the manual to do that — he shows you how to use them to solve issues that look almost like real world problems. This is the *Photoshop Bible* not the *Photoshop Encyclopedia* and hence it tells stories rather than just presenting information.

Those stories take the form of looking at complex problems — like dealing with hair — and showing how you can use Photoshop's tools to solve those problems.

A second thing that you'll get from this book is a lot of commentary. Deke isn't shy about letting you know how he feels about various features. I don't always agree with Deke's opinions on these matters, but I think his openness about his opinions makes the book much richer. If you become a routine user of Photoshop, you will almost certainly develop your own opinions, some of which will probably match Deke's and some of which probably won't. It's valuable to get his opinions during the tour, however, because, even if you end up disagreeing with them, they give you more to think about.

Finally, the most invigorating aspect of this book is the enthusiasm Deke brings to the tour. You'll note that I included "play" in my list of strategies for coming to know Photoshop, and I think just having fun with the program is really one of the best things you can do when starting out. Deke almost relentlessly conveys that sense of excitement and fun, and for that I thank him.

So, fasten your seat belts, put on your pith helmets, and get ready. It's a fascinating trip ahead.

Mark Hamburg
Principal Scientist
and Architect for Adobe Photoshop
Adobe Systems Incorporated

Acknowledgments

Thank you to the following people and companies for their assistance in providing me with the information and product loans that I needed to complete this book.

Mark Hamburg, Russell Preston Brown, Sonya Schaefer, Patricia Pane, and Andrei Herasimchuk at Adobe Systems

Charles Smith at Digital Stock

Tom Hughes and Sophia McShea at PhotoDisc

John Palmer and Dan Patrick at Palmers

Kevin Hurst at Extensis

Sumeet Pasricha at Andromeda

Jeff Butterworth at Alien Skin Software

Paul Badger, Chris Cox, and Hugh Kawahara

Steve Zahm at DigitalThink

Burton Holmes at Burton Holmes Associates

Bruce Berkoff at Umax

and my excellent technical editor, Ted Padova at The Image Source

Additional kudos to the artists who contributed their work to this book: Jeff Brice, Steve Campbell, Christopher Ching, Kevin Curry, Diane Fenster, Larry Goode, Ranulfo Ponce, and Greg Vander Houwen.

A very special thank you to Amy Thomas, Wendy Sharp, Nancy Dunn, Marjorie Baer, Mark Collen, Denise McClelland, Russell McDougal, Julie King, John Kilcullen, and Matt Wagner.

Contents at a Glance

Table of Contents

Introduction

I have no idea where you are as you read this. You might be sitting down in front of your computer, lounging on a beach in Martinique, or curled up under the covers with a flashlight. But there's a chance that you're standing in a bookstore with a clerk behind you asking you if you need any help. If so, you're at what we in the book biz like to call the "point of purchase." From my perspective, the POP is a dangerous place, fraught with ambiguities and temptations. There's a chance — however infinitesimal — that you might put this book back where you found it and buy a competing title. I shudder just to think of it.

So for the benefit of you POPers, I'm about to lay it on a bit thick.

This book is not only the number-one selling guide to Adobe Photoshop, but one of the two or three most successful books on any electronic publishing topic ever printed. You can find localized translations in China, France, Japan, Korea, Poland, Russia, Spain, and the Netherlands. But my favorite story is the earliest: When the very first printing hit the market at the Boston Macworld Expo in August 1993, it sold an unprecedented 500 copies in three days — that's one book every three minutes.

Now, we all know that "best seller" doesn't necessarily translate to "best" — I needn't remind you that Air Supply sold a lot of albums in its day. But this book seems to have touched a chord. Based on the letters I've received over the years, most readers find the book informative, comprehensive, and entertaining. (Okay, there was that one woman who summed up the book as "violent, satanic, and blasphemous" — cross my heart, it's true — but now that we've taken out all the backward lyrics, I think we've addressed that problem.) The fact that people not only buy the book, but actually *read* it and find it pleasurable, gives me more satisfaction than I can say.

The driving philosophy behind the *Macworld Photoshop Bible* is that even the most intimidating topic can be made easy if it's explained properly. This goes double when the subject of the discussion is something as modest as a piece of software. Photoshop isn't some remarkable work of nature that defies our comprehension — it is nothing more than a commercial product designed by a bunch of regular people like yourself for the express purpose of being understood and put to use by a bunch of regular people like yourself. If I can't explain something that's already that inherently straightforward, then shame on me.

I've made it my mission to address each and every topic head on — no cop-outs, no apologies. Everything's here, from the practical benefits of creating accurate masks to the theoretical wonders of designing your own custom filters. Needless to say, I wasn't born with this knowledge, and there are times when I'm learning with you.

But if I don't know how something works, I research it and figure it out, sometimes discussing features directly with the programmers, sometimes taking advantage of other sources. My job is to find out the answers, make sure they make sense, and pass them along to you as clearly as I know how.

I also provide background, opinion, and humor. A dry listing of features followed by ponderous discussions of how they work doesn't mean squat unless I explain why the feature is there, where it fits into your workflow, and — on occasion — whether it's the best solution or not. I am alternatively cranky, excited, and just plain giddy as I explain Photoshop, and I make no effort to contain my criticisms or enthusiasm.

This book is me walking you through the program as subjectively as I would explain it to a friend.

But before I brag any more about the book, it's possible that you're not even sure what Photoshop is, much less why you'd need a book on the subject. Just so that we're all clear, let's take a little peek at the program.

What Is Photoshop?

Photoshop is software for Macintosh and Windows-based computers that enables you to edit photos and artwork scanned to disk and print out your results. Here's an example: Your job is to take a picture of Mr. High-and-Mighty CEO, touch up his crow's feet, and publish his smiling face on the cover of the annual report. No problem. Just shoot the photo, have it digitized to a Photo CD or some other high-tech gizmo, open Mr. H & M inside Photoshop, dab on the digital wrinkle cream, fix his toupee (and for heaven's sake, do *something* about those jowls), and there you go. The man looks presentable no matter how badly the company is doing.

Photoshop, then, is about changing reality. And it goes beyond just reducing the distance between two Giza pyramids on the cover of *National Geographic* or plopping a leaning Tom Cruise, photographed in Hawaii, onto the supportive shoulder of Dustin Hoffman, photographed in New York, for a *Newsweek* spread (both duller-than-fiction applications of photo-editing software). Photoshop brings you full-tilt creativity. Picture a diver leaping from the summit of Mount Everest, or a bright violet zebra galloping toward a hazel-green sunset, or an architectural rendering with wallpaper that looks exactly like the surface of the moon. Photoshop lets you paint snapshots from your dreams. The sky's the limit.

About This Book

If you're familiar with previous editions of this book, this one represents your everyday average humongous renovation. I've hacked out an interesting but long-winded chapter about compositing, and I added three chapters, one each for short-cuts and scripting, layering (which used to be peppered throughout the book), and Web graphics. I've also expanded my discussions of masking, transformations, color corrections, blend modes, and digital cameras.

 Naturally, I also devote much room to Photoshop 4's new capabilities, including the Navigator and Actions palettes, enhanced gradations, grids and guides, adjustment layers, and the more than 40 new filters. But the most significant change to Photoshop 4 is the interface. Frankly, if you're familiar with Versions 3 and earlier, you may find yourself a little lost and confused inside the new program. Not to worry. I explain every change, tell you why Adobe did it, and do everything within my power to make you more productive than you were in the past.

Images, color and otherwise

More than half of the figures and images in this book are new. If only for the sake of variety, I've taken out images that have been staples of previous editions and traded them for new photographs from stock-image vendors Digital Stock and PhotoDisc, as well as stuff that I've shot myself with the latest digital cameras.

As in the past, the book includes 32 pages of color images, with hundreds of color images and artwork available for your perusal on the CD. Of course, that still leaves a lot of grayscale images, which begs the question, why isn't this book printed in full-color throughout? The answer is a simple and irrefutable matter of economics. A full-color book of this size would cost nearly $150. With volume discounts, we could probably pull it off at something in the $85 to $90 range. But even so, that's a little steep for a book that's going to sit on your desk and get coffee stains and pen marks all over it, don't you think? We did, too, and so we opted to forego full-color throughout the book and concentrate on giving you what you really need: Tons of useful information at an affordable price.

That silver Frisbee in the back of the book

In the back of this book, you'll find a CD-ROM containing hundreds of pieces of original artwork and stock photography in full, natural color. I've included most of the pivotal images from this book so that you can follow along with my examples (if you see fit). The CD holds 650MB of data — and we took full advantage of it.

Wendy Sharp, formerly head of the reviews department at *Macworld* magazine, spent nearly as much time compiling the CD as I spent writing the book. Rather than limiting herself to the same old plug-ins that you find in every book, Wendy knocked herself out to make sure that this CD was valuable in and of itself. In addition to software from Adobe, Extensis, Alien Skin, Andromeda, Xaos Tools, DataStream Imaging, and others, you'll find shareware products from independent programmers Chris Cox, Paul Badger, and Hugh Kawahara. Also included are digital articles of direct interest to Photoshop users from *Macworld* magazine; stunning digital artwork from some of the best around, including Jeff Brice, Steve Campbell, Christopher Ching, Kevin Curry, Diane Fenster, Larry Goode, Ranulfo Ponce, and Greg Vander Houwen; and royalty-free stock photos from PhotoDisc and Digital Stock.

 Read Appendix C, "Using the CD-ROM," for a complete listing of the contents of the CD-ROM.

The Guts of the Book

Insofar as the actual pages in this massive tome are concerned, well, there are lots of them. But keep in mind that I don't cover every command or option available in Photoshop. That is the job of the Photoshop manual. My job is to explain the features that really count and explore capabilities that you won't easily glean on your own. I also look at Photoshop's place in the larger electronic design scheme and examine how to best approach Photoshop in ways that will yield the most efficient and accurate results.

 This is a big, fat book, so exercise caution. Those of you who like to read in-flight, remember to stow the book under the seat in front of you after you board the plane. It'll damage less luggage than if you try to stick it in the overhead compartment. If you plan on using the book for self-defense, be sure to spar with a partner armed with a volume of equal size. And please, take out the CD before using the book to prop up a youngster at the dinner table. That way, you can use the CD as a coaster in case of spills.

To enhance your enjoyment of Photoshop's mouth-watering capabilities, I sliced the task into five tasty parts and then diced those parts into a total of 18 digestible chapters. Bon appetite.

Part I: Welcome to Photoshop 4

Here's all the basic stuff you need to know about Photoshop. I explain the new Photoshop 4 interface, give you an overview of the low-level functions that have changed, and show you how to work with Photoshop from the keyboard. Whether you're new to Photoshop or an old hand, you'll find a lot you didn't know in these first three chapters.

 If you're experienced with Photoshop and you're familiar with the previous edition of this book, read the last section of Chapter 1, and all of Chapters 2 and 3. Then skip to the beginning of Part III and keep reading.

Chapter 1: Getting to Know Photoshop, explains how Photoshop fits into the larger experience of using the Mac to produce printed pages and on-screen presentations. I also list all the new features in Photoshop 4 in case you're trying to decide whether or not to upgrade.

Chapter 2: Inside Photoshop, introduces you to Version 4's revamped working environment and examines Photoshop's generous supply of tools, cursors, multi-paneled palettes, and preference settings.

Chapter 3: Shortcuts and Scripts, keeps you apprised of time-saving techniques and makes you more productive. Roughly half of Photoshop's key-based techniques have changed in Photoshop 4, as I explain in Table 3-1. This is also where I tell all about Photoshop 4's new Actions palette, which lets you design your own short-cuts and batch-process images.

Part II: Understanding Digital Imagery

This part of the book examines the core image editing process, taking you from composition and construction to color theory and output. You learn how to change the size and resolution of an image, how to define colors and navigate among color channels, and finally how to print the image to paper or film.

Chapter 4: Image Fundamentals, describes what it means to be a digitized image and how file formats such as TIFF and JPEG affect the content of an image and its size on disk. You also learn how to resample and crop images within Photoshop.

Chapter 5: Defining Colors, covers the fundamentals of editing colors on a computer screen. I explain how you can manipulate common color models to display predictable results. I also examine the differences and similarities between the commercial printing standards Pantone and Trumatch.

Chapter 6: Navigating Channels, looks at color channels, which are the building blocks of color images, and examines how they work. In a nutshell, channels are so important that even beginning Photoshop users should become comfortable with editing them.

Chapter 7: Printing Images, starts off with a glossary of printing terms that will help you better communicate with the folks at your service bureau or commercial print house. Following that, I explain how to print grayscale and color composites, four-color separations, and duotones, tritones, and quadtones.

Part III: Painting and Retouching Images

Every month or so, some fraudulent photo sparks a new flame of public scorn and scrutiny. Now it's your chance to give people something to talk about. These chapters show you how to exchange fact with a modicum of fantasy.

Chapter 8: Painting and Editing, shows you how to use Photoshop's brush tools to enhance and augment photographic images. It also explores ways to paint images from scratch using pressure-sensitive tablets. The chapter ends with an in-depth analysis of brush modes and how they add to everyday living.

Chapter 9: Filling and Stroking, shows how to paint the interiors and outlines of images with solid colors and gradations. It also steps you through the processes of creating drop shadows, halos, and translucent, gradient arrows (of all things). There's a lot more to Photoshop's straightforward fill and stroke functions than meets the eye.

Chapter 10: Duplicating and Reverting, details the operation of the rubber stamp tool, the most versatile and possibly the most frequently overlooked editing tool available to Photoshop users. In addition, you learn how to create seamless repeating patterns and textures in Photoshop for use with the rubber stamp and other tools. And finally, you learn how to revert images to their original appearance using the newly improved eraser tool.

Part IV: Selections, Layers, and Text

Selections are Photoshop's most important capability. They permit you to limit the area that you edit, as well as lift foreground images and combine them with other backgrounds. I also cover text in this section, because text in Photoshop is no more than character-shaped selection outlines.

Chapter 11: Selections and Paths, covers absolutely everything you ever wanted to know about the magic wand and the path tools, antialiasing and feathering, expanding, and growing. Also learn about the new role of the move tool, which is now the only way to move selections in Photoshop 4.

Chapter 12: Creating Masks, documents the inherent advantages of masks over the rest of the selection tools. I explain how to paint inside selection masks, how to work in the quick mask mode, how to generate selections automatically using the Color Range command, how to save masks to a separate channel, and how to create your own highly-accurate masks.

Chapter 13: Layers and Transformations, tells how layers work in Photoshop 4. Pasting, dragging and dropping, creating text, and several other operations now automatically result in new layers. You can also scale, rotate, and skew layers with more control than ever before. If you've shied away from layers in the past, read this chapter.

Chapter 14: Amazing Text Stuff, tells you how to create word art, including gradient text, characters with tiger stripes, raised letters, custom logos, and a whole mess of other effects guaranteed to make jaws drop and eyes boggle.

Part V: Filters and Special Effects

Making manual artistic enhancements is all very well and good, but it's easier to let your computer do the work. These chapters show ways to produce highly entertaining and effective results using fully automated operations.

Chapter 15: Corrective Filtering, covers how to get the most out of Photoshop's most commonly used filters, including Unsharp Mask, Gaussian Blur, Add Noise, and High Pass. I'll also explain how to clean up a photograph from a digital camera, and how to lessen the effects of a filter with the new Fade command.

Chapter 16: Full-Court Filtering, describes the old and new special effects filters available in Photoshop 4. I also document a series of specific applications for Photoshop's abundant supply of plug-in filters.

Chapter 17: Constructing Homemade Effects, investigates the exact workings of the Custom and Displace filters, which multiply and shift pixels to create user-definable effects. If you're really feeling brave, you can program your own effects using the Filter Factory.

Part VI: Corrections, Composites, and the Web

Here's where you learn what you can do with Photoshop's most powerful color correction commands, how to composite images using overlay modes and channel operations, and how to create images specifically for the World Wide Web.

Chapter 18: Mapping and Adjusting Colors, explores ways to change the color balance in scanned photographs to more accurately represent real life — or more radically depart from it. You learn how to make use of the straightforward Variations options, how to modify specific colors with Hue/Saturation, and how to adjust brightness values using Levels and Curves. I also document Photoshop's fantastic new adjustment layers.

Chapter 19: The Wonders of Blend Modes, describes everything you need to know about mixing images from different layers or even different windows. I answer such burning questions as how blend modes work, how to drop out colors in a layer and force through colors from underneath, and what you do when channel operations fail to provide sufficient control.

Chapter 20: Creating Graphics for the Web, tells you how to create images that you'll be proud to post on the World Wide Web. I explain how to account for differences in screen brightness, how to save progressive JPEG images, and how to downsize the color palette for GIF graphics. I also tell you all about the hottest new Web format, PNG.

Part VII: Appendixes

Three appendixes follow Chapter 20. The first explains how to install Photoshop onto your hard drive and offers some advice on which files you'll need to get the most out of this book. The second provides complete information about the photographers, image collections, and news services that contributed images to this book. And the third explains the expansive contents of the CD-ROM in the back of the book.

Last but not least is an astonishingly comprehensive index. It'll knock your socks off, should you happen to be wearing any.

Conventions

Every computer book seems to conform to a logic all its own, and this one's no exception. Although I try to avoid pig latin — ellway, orfay hetay ostmay artpay — I do subscribe to a handful of conventions that you may not immediately recognize.

Vocabulary

Call it computerese, call it technobabble, call it the synthetic jargon of propeller heads. The fact is, I can't explain Photoshop in graphic and gruesome detail without reverting to the specialized language of the trade. However, to help you keep up, I italicized vocabulary words (as in *random-access memory*) with which you may not be familiar or which I use in an unusual context. An italicized term is followed by a definition.

If you come across a strange word that is *not* italicized (that bit of italics was for emphasis), look it up in the index to find the first reference to the word in the book.

Commands and options

To distinguish the literal names of commands, dialog boxes, buttons, and so on, I capitalize the first letter in each word (for example, *click on the Cancel button*). The only exceptions are option names, which can be six or seven words long and filled with prepositions like *to* and *of.* Traditionally, prepositions and articles (*a, an, the*) don't appear in initial caps, and this book follows that time-honored rule, too.

When discussing menus and commands, I use an arrow symbol to indicate hierarchy. For example, *Choose File ⇨ Open* means to choose the Open command from the File menu. If you have to display a submenu to reach a command, I list the command used to display the submenu between the menu name and the final command. *Choose Image ⇨ Adjust ⇨ Invert* means to choose the Adjust command from the Image menu and then choose the Invert command from the Adjust submenu.

Version numbers

A new piece of software comes out every 15 minutes. That's not a real statistic, mind you, but I bet I'm not far off. As I write this, Photoshop has advanced to Version 4.0. But by the time you read this, the version number may be seven hundredths of a percentage point higher. So know that when I write *Photoshop 4*, I mean any version of Photoshop short of 5 (if that ever occurs).

Similarly, when I write *Photoshop 3*, I mean Versions 3.0, 3.0.1, 3.0.3, 3.0.4, and 3.0.5. *Photoshop 2.5* means 2.5 and 2.5.1; *Photoshop 2* means 2.0 and 2.01; and *Photoshop 1* means anything up to Version 1.0.7.

Icons

Like just about every computer book currently available on your green grocer's shelves, this one includes alluring icons that focus your eyeballs smack dab on important information. The icons make it easy for folks who just like to skim books to figure out what the heck's going on. Icons serve as little insurance policies against short attention spans. On the whole, the icons are self-explanatory, but I'll explain them anyway.

 The Caution icon warns you that a step you're about to take may produce disastrous results. Well, perhaps "disastrous" is an exaggeration. Inconvenient, then. Uncomfortable. For heaven's sake, use caution.

 The Note icon highlights some little tidbit of information I've decided to share with you that seemed at the time to be remotely related to the topic at hand. I might tell you how an option came into existence, why a feature is implemented the way it is, or how things used to be better back in the old days.

 The Photoshop 4 icon explains an option, command, or other feature that is brand spanking new to this latest revision. If you're already familiar with previous versions of Photoshop, you might just want to plow through the book looking for Photoshop 4 icons and see what new stuff is out there.

 This book is bursting with tips and techniques. If I were to highlight every one of them, whole pages would be gray with triangles popping out all over the place. The Tip icon calls attention to shortcuts that are specifically applicable to the Photoshop application. For the bigger, more useful power tips, I'm afraid you'll have to actually read the text.

 The New Technology icon highlights every one of those weird pieces of software and hardware that have managed to completely change the way we work. You may not have these products yet, but you might want to look into them.

The Cross-Reference icon tells you where to go for information related to the current topic. I included one a few pages back and you probably read it without thinking twice. That means you're either sharp as a tack or an experienced computer-book user. Either way, you won't have any trouble with this icon.

I thought of including one more icon that alerted you to every new bit of information — whether Photoshop 4-dependent or not — that's included in this book. But I found myself using it every other paragraph. Besides, that would have robbed you of the fun of discovering the new stuff yourself.

How to Bug Me

Even in its third edition, scanned by hundreds of thousands of readers' eyes and scanned about 60 times by the eyes of my editor, I'll bet someone, somewhere will still manage to locate errors and oversights. If you notice those kinds of things and you have a few spare moments, please let me know what you think. I always appreciate readers' comments.

If you want to share your insights, comments, or corrections, please contact me over the Internet at `dekemc@internetMCI.com`. Or try me on America Online at plain old `DekeMc`. (Sorry, my old CompuServe account is *fini*.) Don't fret if you don't hear from me for a few days, or months, or ever. I read every letter and try to implement nearly every idea anyone bothers to send me.

I also urge you to visit my Web site, the infamous `http://www.dekemc.com`. There you'll find news and excerpts about my books, tips for various graphics products, and other goofy online stuff. Let me know what you think.

Now, without further ado, I urge you to turn the page and advance forward into the great untamed frontier of image editing. But remember, this book can be a dangerous tool if wielded unwisely. Don't set it on any creaky card tables or let your children play with it without the assistance of a stalwart adult, preferably an All-Star Wrestler or that guy who played the Incredible Hulk on TV. And no flower pressing. The little suckers would be pummeled to dust by this monstrously powerful colossus of a book.

Welcome to Photoshop 4

PART

I

Getting to Know Photoshop

In This Chapter

- An introduction to Photoshop
- The difference between painting and drawing programs
- How Photoshop fits into the bigger Macintosh design scheme
- The many uses of Photoshop
- The new features in Photoshop 4

What Is Photoshop?

Adobe Photoshop is the most popular image-editing application available for the Macintosh. Despite hefty competition from programs such as Macromedia xRes, Live Picture, and others, Adobe Systems, Inc., reports that Photoshop's sales account for more than 80 percent of the image-editing market. (The estimate includes Fractal Design Painter, an image-creation program that does not strictly compete with Photoshop.) This makes Photoshop four times more popular than all of its competitors combined.

The term *application* — as in *image-editing application* — is just another word for *computer program*. Photoshop satisfies a specific purpose, so programmers abuse the language by calling it an application. I also use the word in the conventional sense throughout the book, as in "Photoshop has many applications." Hopefully, you won't become hopelessly confused.

If you're already familiar with Photoshop and you just want to scope out its new capabilities, skip to the section "Fast Track to Version 4."

Photoshop's long-term advantage

Photoshop's historically lopsided sales advantage provides Adobe with a clear incentive to reinvest in Photoshop and regularly enhance — even overhaul — its capabilities. Meanwhile, other vendors have had to devote smaller resources to playing catch-up. Though competitors xRes and Live Picture provide interesting and sometimes amazing capabilities, the sums of their parts remain inferior to Photoshop.

As a result, Photoshop rides a self-perpetuating wave of industry predominance. It hasn't always been the best image editor, nor was it the earliest. But its deceptively straightforward interface combined with a few terrific core functions made it a hit from the moment of its first release. More than half a decade later — thanks to substantial capital injections and highly creative programming on the part of Adobe's staff and Photoshop originators Thomas and John Knoll — it has evolved into the most popular program of its kind.

A brief history of image-editing

For those history buffs in the audience, Macintosh image-editing software went through its infancy in the late 1980s. The first was ImageStudio, a grayscale program from Fractal Design, creators of ColorStudio and Painter. The first Macintosh image editor to feature color was an Avalon Development Group entry called PhotoMac, which is now all but forgotten. Rumor had it that the *best* photo editor during this time was Lumena from Time Arts, a DOS-based program that ran on IBM PCs and compatibles.

Meanwhile, Photoshop began as Tom Knoll's graduate school project. If brother John hadn't quickly put it to work within the hallowed walls of George Lucas's Industrial Light and Magic, it's unlikely the program would have ever seen the light of day, much less become the dominant player in computer graphics. Even when Adobe purchased the product in 1990, Photoshop was viewed as a modest-selling companion piece for the company's bread and butter, Illustrator. Little did anyone guess that the tail would end up wagging the dog, with Illustrator, Macromedia FreeHand, and every other drawing program on the planet scurrying to ride the coattails of Photoshop.

Image-Editing Theory _____

Having used mirrors, dry ice, and some rather titillating industry analysis to convince you of Photoshop's prowess, I will now answer that burning question: What the heck does Photoshop *do*?

Like any *image editor,* Photoshop enables you to alter photographs and other scanned artwork. You can retouch an image, apply special effects, swap details between photos, introduce text and logos, adjust color balance, and even add color to a grayscale scan. Photoshop also provides the tools you need to create images from scratch. These tools are fully compatible with pressure-sensitive tablets, so you can create naturalistic images that look for all the world like watercolors and oils.

Bitmaps versus objects

Image editors fall into the larger software category of *painting programs.* In a painting program, you draw a line, and the application converts it to tiny square dots called *pixels.* The painting itself is called a *bitmapped image,* but *bitmap* and *image* are equally acceptable terms. Every program I've discussed so far is a painting program. Other examples include Color It, PixelPaint, and the recent and most surely doomed, Corel Artisan.

Photoshop uses the term *bitmap* exclusively to mean a black-and-white image, the logic being that each pixel conforms to one *bit* of data, 0 or 1 (off or on). In order to avoid ad hoc syllabic mergers like *pix-map* — and because forcing a distinction between a painting with exactly two colors and one with anywhere from four to 16 million colors is entirely arbitrary — I use the term bitmap more broadly to mean any image composed of a fixed number of pixels, regardless of the number of colors involved.

What about other graphics applications, such as Adobe Illustrator and Macromedia FreeHand? Illustrator, FreeHand, CorelDraw, and others fall into a different category of software called *drawing programs.* Drawings comprise *objects,* which are independent, mathematically-defined lines and shapes. For this reason, drawing programs are sometimes said to be *object-oriented.* Some folks prefer the term *vector-based,* but I really hate that one because *vector* implies the physical components, direction and magnitude, which generally are associated with straight lines. Besides, my preference suggests an air of romance, as in, "Honey, I'm bound now for the Object Orient."

Illustrator and FreeHand are sometimes called *illustration programs,* though this is more a marketing gimmick — you know, like Father's Day — than a legitimate software category. The idea is that Illustrator and FreeHand provide a unique variety of features unto themselves. In reality, their uniqueness extends little beyond more reliable printing capabilities and higher prices.

The ups and downs of painting

Painting programs and drawing programs each have their strengths and weaknesses. The strength of a painting program is that it offers an extremely straightforward approach to creating images. For example, although many of Photoshop's features are complex — *exceedingly* complex on occasion — its core painting tools are as easy to use as a pencil. You alternately draw and erase until you reach a desired effect, just as you've been doing since grade school. (Of course, for all I know, you've been using computers since grade school. If you're pushing 20, you probably managed to log in many happy hours on paint programs in your formative years. Then again, if you're under 20, you're still in your formative years. Shucks, we're *all* in our formative years. Wrinkles, expanding tummies, receding hairlines. . . if that's not a new form, I don't know what is.)

In addition to being simple to use, each of Photoshop's core painting tools is fully customizable. It's as if you have access to an infinite variety of crayons, colored pencils, pastels, airbrushes, watercolors, and so on, all of which are entirely erasable. Doodling on the phone book was never so much fun.

The downside of a painting program is that it limits your *resolution* options. Because bitmaps contain a fixed number of pixels, the resolution of an image — the number of pixels per inch — is dependent upon the size at which the image is printed, as demonstrated in Figure 1-1. Print the image small, and the pixels become tiny, which increases resolution; print the image large, and the pixels grow, which decreases resolution. An image that fills up a standard 13-inch screen (640 × 480 pixels) prints with smooth color transitions when reduced to, say, half the size of a postcard. But if you print that same image without reducing it, you may be able to distinguish individual pixels, which means that you can see jagged edges and blocky transitions. The only way to remedy this problem is to increase the number of pixels in the image, which dramatically increases the size of the file on disk.

 Bear in mind that this is a very simplified explanation of how images work. For a more complete description that includes techniques for maximizing image performance, refer to the "How Images Work" section of Chapter 4.

Figure 1-1
When printed small, a painting appears smooth (left). But when printed large, it appears jagged (right).

The downs and ups of drawing

Painting programs provide tools reminiscent of traditional art tools. A drawing program, on the other hand, features tools that have no real-world counterparts. The process of drawing might more aptly be termed *constructing,* because you actually build lines and shapes point by point and stack them on top of each other to create a finished image. Each object is independently editable — one of the few structural advantages of an object-oriented approach — but you're still faced with the task of building your artwork one chunk at a time.

Nevertheless, because a drawing program defines lines, shapes, and text as mathematical equations, these objects automatically conform to the full resolution of the *output device,* whether it's a laser printer, imagesetter, or film recorder. The drawing program sends the math to the printer and the printer *renders* the math to paper or film. In other words, the printer converts the drawing program's equations to printer pixels. Your printer offers far more pixels than your screen — a 300 dots-per-inch (dpi) laser printer, for example, offers 300 pixels per inch (dots equal pixels) whereas most screens offer 72 pixels per inch. So the printed drawing appears smooth and sharply focused regardless of the size at which you print it, as shown in Figure 1-2.

Another advantage of drawings is that they take up relatively little room on disk. The file size of a drawing depends on the quantity and complexity of the objects the drawing contains. Thus, the file size has almost nothing to do with the size of the printed image, which is just the opposite of the way bitmapped images work. A thumbnail drawing of a garden that contains hundreds of leaves and petals consumes several times more disk space than a poster-sized drawing that contains three rectangles.

Figure 1-2
Small or large, a drawing prints smooth, but it's a pain to create. This one took more than an hour out of my day, and as you can see, I didn't even bother with the letters around the perimeter of the design.

When to use Photoshop

Thanks to their specialized methods, painting programs and drawing programs fulfill distinct and divergent purposes. Photoshop and other painting programs are best suited to creating and editing the following kinds of artwork:

- ⌣ Scanned photos, including photographic collages and embellishments that originate from scans

- ⌣ Realistic artwork that relies on the play between naturalistic highlights, midranges, and shadows

- ⌣ Impressionistic-type artwork and other images created for purely personal or aesthetic purposes

- ⌣ Logos and other display type featuring soft edges, reflections, or tapering shadows

- ⌣ Special effects that require the use of filters and color enhancements you simply can't achieve in a drawing program

- ⌣ Just about any graphic or photograph that you intend to post on the World Wide Web

When to use a drawing program

You're probably better off using Illustrator, FreeHand, or some other drawing program if you're interested in creating more stylized artwork, such as the following:

- ⌣ Poster art and other high-contrast graphics that heighten the appearance of reality

- Architectural plans, product designs, or other precise line drawings

- Business graphics, such as charts and other "infographics" that reflect data or show how things work

- Traditional logos and text effects that require crisp, ultrasmooth edges (Drawing programs are unique in that they enable you to edit character outlines to create custom letters and symbols)

- Brochures, flyers, and other single-page documents that mingle artwork, logos, and standard-sized text (such as the text you're reading now)

If you're serious about computer graphics, you should own at least one painting program and one drawing program. If I had to rely exclusively on two graphics applications, I would probably choose Photoshop and Illustrator. Both are Adobe products, and the two function together almost without a hitch. Much to its credit, however, FreeHand also works remarkably well in combination with Photoshop.

The Computer Design Scheme___

If your aspirations go beyond image editing into the larger world of computer-assisted design, you'll soon learn that Photoshop is just one cog in a mighty wheel of programs used to create artwork, printed documents, and presentations.

The natural-media paint program Fractal Design Painter emulates real-world tools such as charcoal, chalk, felt-tip markers, calligraphic pen nibs, and camel-hair brushes as deftly as a synthesizer mimics a thunderstorm. Three-dimensional drawing applications such as Specular Infini-D, Strata StudioPro, and Ray Dream Designer enable you to create hyper-realistic objects with depth, lighting, shadows, surface textures, reflections, refractions — you name it. These applications can import images created in Photoshop as well as export images that you can then enhance and adjust with Photoshop.

Page-layout programs such as Adobe PageMaker and QuarkXPress from Quark, Inc., let you integrate images into newsletters, reports, books (such as this one), and just about any other kind of document you can imagine. If you prefer to transfer your message to slides, you can use Adobe Persuasion or Microsoft PowerPoint to add impact to your images through the use of charts and diagrams.

With Adobe Premiere and After Effects, you can merge images with video sequences recorded in the QuickTime format. You even can edit individual frames in Premiere movies with Photoshop. Macromedia Director makes it possible to combine images with animation, QuickTime movies, and sound to create multimedia presentations you can show on a screen or record on videotape.

The latest rage in screen design is the World Wide Web. Using Adobe PageMill, Claris Home Page, or Netscape Navigator, you can create Web pages that include lots of fast-loading screen images. The Web is single-handedly breathing new life and respectability into low-resolution images.

Photoshop Scenarios

All the programs just described run on the Macintosh computer and many — including Painter, PageMaker, QuarkXPress, PowerPoint, and Premiere — also run on Windows. But the number of programs you decide to purchase and how you use them is up to you. The following list outlines a few specific ways to use Photoshop alone and in tandem with other products:

- After scanning and adjusting an image inside Photoshop, use PageMaker or QuarkXPress to place the image into your monthly newsletter and then print the document from the page-layout program.

- After putting the finishing touches on a lovely tropical vista inside Photoshop, import the image for use as an eye-catching background inside PowerPoint. Then save the document as a self-running screen presentation or print it to overhead transparencies or slides from the presentation program.

- Capture an on-screen image (by pressing ⌘-Shift-3 or using a screen capture utility such as Mainstay's Capture). Then open the screen shot and edit it in Photoshop. Place the corrected image into Illustrator or FreeHand, annotate the screen shot using arrows and labels, and print it from the drawing program.

- Paint an original image inside Photoshop using a Wacom pressure-sensitive tablet. Use the image as artwork in a document created in a page-layout program or print it directly from Photoshop.

- Snap a photo with a digital camera such as Kodak's DC50 or Epson's PhotoPC. Correct the focus and brightness in Photoshop (as explained in Chapters 15 and 18). Then add the photo to your personal Web site using PageMill or a similar program.

- Scan a surface texture such as wood or marble into Photoshop and edit it to create a fluid repeating pattern (as explained in Chapter 10). Import the image for use as a texture map in a three-dimensional drawing program. Render the 3D graphic to an image file, open the image inside Photoshop, and retouch as needed.

- Create a repeating pattern, convert it to the system software's built-in 256-color palette inside Photoshop, and apply it as a desktop pattern at Finder level, using a utility such as ResEdit or Wallpaper.

- Take a problematic Illustrator EPS file that keeps generating errors when you try to print it, open it inside Photoshop, and render it as a high-resolution bitmap. Then place the image in a document created in a page-layout program or print it directly from Photoshop. Many top drawing programs, including FreeHand and CorelDraw, support the Illustrator format.

- Start an illustration in a drawing program and save it as an Illustrator EPS file. Open the file in Photoshop and use the program's unique tools to add textures and tones that are difficult or impossible to create in a vector-based drawing program.

- Record a QuickTime movie in Premiere and export it to the FilmStrip format. Open the file inside Photoshop and edit it one frame at a time by drawing on the frame or applying filters. Finally, open the altered FilmStrip file in Premiere and convert it back to the QuickTime format.

Obviously, few folks have the money to buy all these products and even fewer have the energy or inclination to implement every one of these ideas. But quite honestly, these are just a handful of projects I can list off the top of my head. There must be hundreds of uses for Photoshop that involve no outside applications whatsoever. In fact, so far as I've been able to figure, there's no end to the number of design jobs you can handle in whole or in part using Photoshop.

Simply put, this is a versatile and essential product for any designer or artist who currently uses or plans to purchase a Macintosh or Windows-based computer. I, for one, wouldn't remove Photoshop from my hard drive for a thousand bucks. (Of course, that's not to say I'm not willing to consider higher offers. For $1,500, I'd gladly swap it to a Jaz cartridge.)

Fast Track to Version 4 _____

If it seems like you've been using Photoshop 3 for the better part of your professional career and you're itching to strap on the new version and ride, the following list explains all. Here I've compiled a few of the most prominent features that are new to Photoshop 4, in rough order of importance. I also point you to the chapter where you can rocket on to more information.

- **Enhanced navigation capabilities (Chapter 2):** Photoshop 4 adds new keyboard shortcuts for magnifying and reducing your image on screen. It also introduces the Navigator palette, which lets you scroll and zoom very large images by dragging inside a miniature thumbnail. And if that doesn't satisfy your needs, you can zoom with 0.1-percent accuracy.

- **Hot link to Adobe's Web site (Chapter 2):** Click on the Adobe logo in the splash screen (which you access by choosing Apple ➪ About Photoshop) to open an HTML file that Photoshop automatically installs on your hard disk. If you have a live connection to the Internet, you can then click on the hypertext (underlined text) in the HTML page to link to various pages in Adobe's Web site. It's a great way to find information about the latest Photoshop upgrades and documentation.

- **Revised interface (Chapter 2):** Photoshop 4 is packed with little interface enhancements that go a long way toward making the program more consistent. For example, you can tab through option boxes in the palettes and even jump from one palette to the next. You can adjust values in the Colors palette numerically, access all tools from the toolbox, hide and show paths, and bring up context-sensitive pop-up menus by Control-clicking. The downside is that a lot of this housekeeping comes at the expense of age-old techniques that are second nature for many of us. For the experienced user, Photoshop 4.0 takes some serious getting used to.

- **Scripting and batch processing (Chapter 3):** The Commands palette has spun a cocoon and metamorphosed into the Actions palette. The new palette not only lets you assign keyboard shortcuts to commands, but also group commands into repeatable sequences. You can even have Photoshop batch-process entire folders full of images while you go out for lunch. The Actions palette isn't perfect, but it's easy to use and it's a heck of an improvement over its predecessor.

- **More amenable sanitation service (Chapter 3):** You can now click on the trash can icon in the Layers, Channels, Paths, and Actions palettes to delete the selected item. Photoshop displays an alert box to make sure your click wasn't a mistake. To bypass the message, Option-click on the trash icon.

- **Improved gradients (Chapter 9):** Now you can create custom gradients that contain three or more colors, much as in sibling Illustrator. You can also assign transparency to a gradient, something you've only been able to do with third-party plug-ins in the past. The new gradients aren't as robust as those in, say, Kai's Power Tools, but they come close.

- **The more prominent move tool (Chapter 11):** It used to be the move tool was just for moving whole layers. Now you have to use the move tool to move or clone *any* pixel, whether in a selection or on a layer. You can temporarily access the move tool when another tool is active by pressing the ⌘ key. But this upsets old ⌘-key tasks — such as subtracting from a selection outline — which have mutated into Option-key tasks. It's *extremely* confusing at first, but it ultimately makes a good deal of sense. I walk you through the entire thorny issue in Chapter 11.

↪ **Good-bye floating selections (Chapter 13):** Photoshop 3 introduced layers, but Version 4 forces you to use them. The type tool creates a new layer, the Paste command creates a new layer, even ⌘-J creates a new layer. In fact, floating selections are for all practical purposes dead. Taking their place are a host of layer management and merging capabilities that make working with layers a whole lot easier.

↪ **Advanced transformation capabilities (Chapter 13):** Photoshop's rotation and resizing capabilities used to be so lame that I didn't even bother to document them in this book. But that changes with Photoshop 4. You can experiment with moving, scaling, and rotating a selection all at the same time without making permanent changes to the image. You can even apply numerical transformations. It's about time.

↪ **Better layer masks (Chapter 13):** Most Photoshop users don't pay much attention to layer masks, but you have new reasons to check them out in Photoshop 4. First of all, some commands — such as Paste Inside — automatically generate layer masks. Second, adjustment layers use masks to determine which areas are affected and which are not. Third, you can now create layer masks with the click of a button. And fourth, you can load layer masks as selection outlines, and convert selections to masks. I'm not normally one for predictions, but I'm guessing layer masks are going to be bigger than the "Macarena."

↪ **Grids and guides (Chapter 13):** Also look to lucky Chapter 13 for the straight dope on Photoshop's new grids and guides. You can drag guides from the ruler, specify a grid, and otherwise establish a structured working environment. And don't be thinking they're just for looks — these grids and guides snap like turtles.

↪ **Stacking order shortcuts (Chapter 13):** You can now send layers forward and backward using keyboard shortcuts and menu commands. You can still drag layer names up and down in the Layers palette, but the shortcuts are much more convenient. And you never know — these same keystrokes might pop up in Illustrator and PageMaker.

↪ **Linking layers (Chapter 13):** You've always been able to move two or more layers together. But now you can link layers together so that they rotate, resize, flip, skew, distort, and otherwise transform as a group. (Don't confuse this new linking feature with the confusingly named Group command, which merely creates a clipping group.)

↪ **New type mask tool (Chapter 14):** In Photoshop, text is just a bunch of filled selection outlines in the shape of familiar characters. Now you can bag the fill and create the selection outlines directly. Just use the new type mask tool, available in the type tool pop-up menu.

- **Fading filters (Chapter 15):** I've been yammering about the benefits of mixing a filtered image with the unfiltered original for years now, and I guess someone at Adobe decided to listen. After you apply a filter like Unsharp Mask or Gaussian Blur, you can mix the result with the original by choosing Filter ➪ Fade (or pressing ⌘-Shift-F). You gotta love it.

- **Improved distortion previews (Chapter 16):** The distortion filters — under the Filter ➪ Distort submenu — were the first Photoshop filters to offer previews. But after the other filters added previews in Photoshop 3, the puny little zoomed-out distortion thumbnails appeared comically inaccurate, providing only a hint of the effect you could expect to achieve. This changes in Photoshop 4. Though you can't preview an effect in the image window, the dialog box previews are finally up to snuff.

- **Adjustment layers (Chapter 18):** In the old days, you had to color-correct each layer independently. But in Photoshop 4, you can create an adjustment layer that affects every layer under it. This means you can modify the brightness, contrast, and color balance of multiple layers at a time. Plus, these modifications are temporary, so you can come back and revise the settings any time you like. You can even paint in affected and protected areas using a layer mask. It's a little bit of Live Picture in Photoshop.

- **Expanded support for Web graphics (Chapter 20):** According to Adobe, more than half of Photoshop artists use the program to create Web graphics, and that number is only growing. That's why Photoshop 4 provides built-in support for Mac, Windows, and Web color palettes. You can also save images in a variety of Web formats — including interlaced GIF, progressive JPEG, PNG, and PDF — using the standard Save command. Chapter 20 of this book is your guide to creating Web graphics in Photoshop.

For you special effects nuts, Version 4 integrates the 48 filters from the old Gallery Effects collection (as I explain in Chapter 16). You also get three new blend modes (covered in Chapters 8 and 19), a few handy Delete-key techniques (Chapter 9), a new image caching scheme (Chapter 2), and a special polygonal lasso tool to make up for the wacky revisions to Option-clicking (Chapter 11).

Frankly, this isn't the most dramatic upgrade to Photoshop, but it may be the most bewildering. Instead of a few big modifications, we have gobs and gobs of little ones. Look out for the Photoshop 4.0 icon in this book to get you over the hump and back into the image-editing groove again.

Inside Photoshop

- -

In This Chapter

➠ A tour of the updated Photoshop 4 desktop

➠ Brief introductions to Photoshop's tools, cursors, and control icons

➠ Working with Photoshop 4's revised palettes

➠ Zooming in 0.1-percent increments

➠ Scrolling from the keyboard

➠ The new Navigator palette

➠ Expanded coverage of Photoshop's preference settings

➠ Captions, copyrights, and other image annotations

- -

The New Look and Feel of Photoshop 4

This chapter introduces Photoshop's tools, palettes, and other interface ingredients. Normally, I'd recommend these pages as essential reading to new Photoshop users. (In fact, if you are a new user, skip to "The Photoshop Desktop" section and dive right in.) But I'd tell experienced folks to browse through the "Customizing the Interface" section only when trying to decipher some weird new preference setting like the Use Cache for Histograms check box.

However, Photoshop 4 is not your typical upgrade. This is one version of the program that's likely to challenge experienced users nearly as much as their novice counterparts. Photoshop 4 offers a numerical magnification option, three new zoom commands, and a full-blown Navigator palette. The crop tool is now grouped with the marquee tools, the path tools have moved into the toolbox, and there are two variations for each of the lasso and type tools. A menu has disappeared, another has moved, and two new ones have sprouted up. The cursors have changed, the Swatch palette is dead, and the Preferences dialog box is completely revamped. In short, your Photoshop world has turned upside-down.

Adobe has restructured Photoshop from the ground up, sometimes bravely forging ahead for the long-term good, sometimes recklessly trampling over time-honored techniques. But whatever your take on the new version, it is the way it is. Adobe is unlikely to go back to the old ways — regardless of the inevitable grumbling — because of its internal mandate to homogenize features among Photoshop, Illustrator, and PageMaker. You can go back to Photoshop 3 — and undoubtedly some will — but don't expect things in Photoshop 5, 6, or 7 to return to the old ways.

In this regard, Photoshop 4 is less an enhancement than an immutable force of nature. Do what you would do if your work was interrupted by a power outage or a similar inconvenience. Buck up and adapt. Start by skimming this chapter, keeping an eye out for the Photoshop 4 icon. Then proceed to Chapter 3 and read it too. (If you think the interface has changed, wait until you get a load of the keyboard modifiers. The shortcuts are shaken, not stirred.) When you finish, your head may still be spinning, but at least the initial seasickness will have gone away.

The Photoshop Splash Screen ___

Shortly after you launch Photoshop, the Photoshop *splash screen* appears. Shown at the top of Figure 2-1, the splash screen explains the launching process by telling you which plug-in modules are loading. Any time while running Photoshop, you can access the splash screen by choosing the About Photoshop command from the Apple menu.

 If you can't find the Photoshop application icon, it may be because you haven't installed it yet. Check out Appendix A for information about how to install Photoshop 4.

 I know no one cares about the splash screen. In fact, the only reason I even mention it is because Photoshop 4 offers a few splash screen-related tips and tricks:

    ➭ If it's too much effort to choose Apple ⇨ About Photoshop, you can display the splash screen by clicking on that little icon at the top of the toolbox (highlighted in Figure 2-1).

- If you ⌘-click on the toolbox icon, you display the double-secret Big Electric Cat screen. (You can also press ⌘ when choosing the About Photoshop command.)

- ⌘-click on the cat's nose to make him burp. This is easily the most essential productivity tip in all of Photoshop 4. (My sources tell me you can customize the way the cat burps — use Apple's ResEdit utility to add more sounds to the BLCH resource in the Photoshop application file — but then you're *really* wasting your time.)

- Click on the Adobe icon in the upper left corner of the splash screen to open the Adobe Web page in your favorite browser (most likely Netscape Navigator). If you have Internet access, you can navigate from the page into Adobe's online Web site.

Figure 2-1
The splash screen from Photoshop 4, as well as its hidden companions.

Click here

If you choose the About Photoshop command and wait a moment, the list of programmers and copyright statement at the bottom of the splash screen begins to scroll. Press the Option key to make the list scroll more quickly. The final line of the scrolling message thanks *you*, of all people, for being "one of our favorite customers."

After the credits start to scroll a second time, click in the empty area just above the credits in the standard splash screen (or just above the Big Electric Cat graphic on the alternative screen) to cycle through a series of strange and entertaining quotes. Wait for the top 10 list if you're intent upon seeing it through to the bitter end.

To make the splash screen go away, click on it or press the Return key.

The Photoshop Desktop

After the launch process is complete, the Photoshop desktop consumes the foreground. Figure 2-2 shows the Photoshop 4 desktop as it appears when an image is open and all palettes are visible.

Many of the elements that make up the Photoshop desktop are well known to folks familiar with the Macintosh computer. They work just like the elements of the Finder desktop and the standard application window. For example, the menu bar provides access to menus and commands. You can drag the title bar to move the image window. And the scroll bars let you view hidden portions of the image.

Other elements of the Photoshop desktop work as follows:

- **Image window:** You can open as many images in Photoshop as RAM and virtual memory allow. Each open image resides inside its own window. The lower left corner of the window features a magnification box, which tells you the current view size, and a preview box, which lists the size of the foreground image in memory.

  For complete information on the magnification box, read the "Navigating Inside Photoshop 4" section later in this chapter. I explain the preview box in the very next section.

- **Toolbox:** The toolbox offers 20 tool icons. The tools are organized into logical groups, starting with the selection tools on top; then the painting and editing tools; the path, type, and fill tools; and the two navigation tools at the bottom. To select a tool, click on its icon. Then use the tool by clicking or dragging with it inside the image window.

  The lower third of the toolbox features three sets of controls. The color controls let you change the colors with which you paint; the mask controls let you enter and exit the quick mask mode; and the image window controls let you change the state of the foreground window on the desktop.

↬ **Floating palettes:** Photoshop 4 offers several floating palettes: Brushes, Color, Layers, and so on. The term "floating" refers to the fact that each palette is independent of the image window and of other palettes. Four palettes contain multiple panels, which offer related but independent options. For example, the Layers palette contains the Layers, Channels, and Paths panels. Read "The floating palettes" section later in this chapter for a brief overview of each of these palettes and their panels.

Figure 2-2
The Photoshop 4 desktop in all its glory.

The preview box

By default, the preview box contains two numbers divided by a slash. The first number is the size of the base image in memory. Photoshop calculates this value by multiplying the height and width of the image (both in pixels) by the *bit depth* of the image, which is the size of each pixel in memory. A full-color RGB image takes up three bytes per pixel; a grayscale image takes up one byte per pixel; and a black-and-white image consumes one bit (or ¹/₈ byte) per pixel. This means a 640 × 480-

pixel RGB image takes up $640 \times 480 \times 3$ = 921,600 bytes, which is exactly 900K. (There are 1,024 bytes in one kilobyte, and 1,024K in one megabyte.)

The number after the slash takes into account any additional layers in your image. Photoshop measures the opaque pixels in each layer only; transparent pixels are ignored. If you transfer a 160×320-pixel selection of an RGB image to a new layer, for example, that layer consumes only $160 \times 320 \times 3$ = 153,600 bytes = 150K, even if the base image is much larger. If the image contains one layer only, the numbers before and after the slash are the same.

Click and hold on the preview box to display a pop-up window that shows the placement of the image on the printed page. The preview even shows the approximate placement of crop marks and other elements requested in the Page Setup dialog box (File ⇨ Page Setup).

     Press Option and mouse down on the preview box to view the size and resolution of the image.

You can also ⌘-click on the preview box to see the tile sizes. Photoshop uses tiles to calculate pixel manipulations. If you confine your work to a single tile, it will probably go faster than if you slop a little over into a second tile. But who cares? Unless you're some kind of tile-reading robot, this technical information is rarely of any practical use.

Click and hold on the right-pointing arrowhead next to the preview box to display a pop-up menu of four options. The first option — Document Sizes — is selected by default. It displays the image size values described above.

The following sections explain how the three remaining options work.

Scratch sizes

When you select Scratch Sizes, Photoshop changes the values in the preview box to represent memory consumption and availability. The first value is the amount of room required to hold all open images in RAM. This value is generally equal to about 3 $1/2$ times the sum total of all images, including layers. However, the value constantly updates depending on the operations that you perform, growing as large as five times the image size when floating images and complex operations are involved.

The second preview box value indicates the amount of RAM space available to images after the Photoshop application is loaded. This value does not change unless you quit Photoshop and change the amount of RAM dedicated to the application (as explained in Appendix A).

If the value before the slash in the preview box is larger than the value after the slash, Photoshop has to take advantage of *virtual memory* in order to display the open images. Virtual memory makes Photoshop run more slowly because the program has to swap portions of the image on and off your hard disk. To speed up the application, close one or more images until the first value is smaller than the second value. (If this isn't possible, don't sweat it. Virtual memory is an occasional fact of life when using Photoshop.)

Efficiency

When you select the Efficiency option, Photoshop lists the amount of time it spends running operations in RAM compared with swapping data back and forth between the hard disk. A value of 100 percent is the best-case scenario. It means that Photoshop never has to rely on virtual memory. Low values indicate higher reliance on the hard disk, and as a result, slower operations. Adobe recommends that if the value falls below 75 percent, you should either assign more memory to Photoshop or purchase more RAM for your computer.

The Efficiency option is a reality check. If it seems that Photoshop is dragging its feet — and you hear it writing a little too often — you can refer to the Efficiency rating to see if things are as bad as you suspect. Bear in mind that hearing Photoshop occasionally write to disk is not in and of itself cause for concern. All versions of Photoshop since 3.0 automatically copy open images to a disk buffer just in case virtual memory is later warranted. In fact, this is the reason Adobe added the Efficiency option to Version 3.0.1 — to quash fears that a few sparks from your hard drive indicated anything less than peak performance.

 If you're using an AV Mac or a Power Mac, an asterisk (*) may appear next to the efficiency value in the preview box. This indicates that your primary hard disk supports *asynchronous file-handling*, which permits Photoshop greater flexibility and improved performance when trading data between RAM and the hard disk. A hard disk that supports asynchronous file-handling — as most drives formatted in the last two to three years do — is operating at the top of its form. An asterisk, therefore, is a mighty good thing.

If you don't see an asterisk, you're either using an older model Mac or you need to update the drivers for your hard disk. You can update the drivers for an external SCSI drive using the Apple HD SC Setup utility (Version 7.3 or later), which is included with your original system CD. Updating an internal hard disk may prove a little more difficult, and even mean reformatting the drive. Contact your hard disk manufacturer or the dealer that sold you your computer for more information.

 If you run up against a brick wall, don't worry about the asterisk. Asynchronous file-handling will save you time in the long run, but it isn't a do-or-die issue. Sad to say, one must occasionally live with imperfection.

Or better yet, add more RAM. Nothing speeds up Photoshop like RAM, and RAM is fairly inexpensive as I write this. If you can get the Efficiency rating up to 100 percent, it doesn't matter how fast your hard drive is (except when opening and saving files).

Timing

The final option, Timing, is new to Photoshop 4. When selected, it tells how long Photoshop took to perform the last operation (including background tasks, such as transferring an image to the system Clipboard). Adobe may have added this option to help testing facilities, such as Macworld Lab, run their Photoshop tests. But built-in timing helps you as well.

For example, suppose that you're trying to decide whether to purchase a new computer. You read a magazine article comparing the newest super-fast Power Mac system (such as that intriguing and insightful "Ultimate Performance Mac" feature in the December, 1996 *Macworld*). You can run the same filters with the same settings on your computer and see how much slower your results are, all without picking up a stop watch.

At the risk of starting inter-office feuding, the Timing option also provides you with a mechanism for testing your computer against those of coworkers and friends. The Timing option serves as a neutral arbitrator, permitting you and an associate to test identical operations over the phone. Like Efficiency, Timing is a reality check. If you and your associate own similarly configured computers and your Timing values are vastly different, something's wrong.

The tools

The new Photoshop 4 toolbox shows only 20 of its 33 tools at any one time. The other tools are hidden inside pop-up menus. Any tool icon that includes a tiny right-pointing triangle harbors a pop-up menu with one or more alternate tools. As demonstrated in Figure 2-3, just drag on a tool to display the pop-up menu.

You can also Option-click on a tool icon to switch to the next tool in the pop-up menu.

Also, when you hover your cursor over a tool, Photoshop 4 tells you the name of the tool and how to select it from the keyboard. For example, *Marquee tool (M)* means that you can press the M key to get the marquee tool. I explain more about keyboard shortcuts in Chapter 3.

Figure 2-3
Drag from any tool icon with a
triangle to display a pop-up
menu of alternates.

Drag from
tool...

...to display pop-up menu

 If you find the tool tips irritating, you can turn them off using File ➪ Preferences ➪ General (⌘-K). I explain more about this and other preference settings in the "General preferences" section later in this chapter.

Despite the cosmetic changes to the toolbox, most of the tools work just as they did in Photoshop 3. The exceptions are the selection tools, which have changed fairly dramatically thanks to the new role of the move tool. I hint at the differences in the following brief descriptions, but for a complete analysis, read Chapter 11.

 I've catalogued each tool in the following lengthy list, with tool icons, pithy summaries, and the chapter to which you can refer for more information. There's no need to read the list word for word; just use it as a reference to get acquainted with the new program. Incidentally, unless otherwise noted, each of the following descriptions tells how to use the tool inside the image window. For example, if an item says *drag,* you click on the tool's icon to select the tool and then drag in the image window; you don't drag on the tool icon itself.

⌷ **Rectangular marquee (Chapter 11):** Drag with this tool to enclose a portion of the image in a rectangular *marquee,* which is a pattern of moving dash marks that indicates the boundary of a selection.

 Shift-drag to add to a selection; Option-drag to delete from a selection (versus ⌘-drag in Photoshop 4). The same goes for the other marquee tools as well as the lasso and magic wand.

○ **Elliptical marquee (Chapter 11):** Drag with the elliptical marquee tool to enclose a portion of the window in an oval marquee.

⠶ **Single-row marquee (Chapter 11):** Click with this tool to select an entire horizontal row of pixels that stretches all the way across the image. You can also drag with the tool to position the selection. You'll rarely need it.

╏ **Single-column marquee (Chapter 11):** Same as the Single-row marquee, except it selects an entire vertical column of pixels. Again, not a particularly useful tool.

⌗ **Crop (Chapter 4):** Drag with the crop tool to enclose the portion of the image you want to retain in a rectangular boundary. The crop boundary sports several square handles that you can drag to resize the cropped area.

 Drag outside the boundary to rotate it. Drag inside the boundary to move it. Press Return to crop away the portions of the image that lie outside the boundary; press Escape to cancel.

▶₊ **Move (Chapter 11):** Drag to move the selected portion of an image. If no portion of the image is selected, dragging with the move tool moves the entire layer.

 In Photoshop 4, the move tool is the exclusive means for moving and cloning selected portions of an image. (You can also ⌘-drag selections with other tools, but only because ⌘ temporarily accesses the move tool.)

♐ **Lasso (Chapter 11):** Drag with the lasso tool to select a free-form portion of the image. You can also Option-click with the lasso to create a straight-sided selection outline.

⋎ **Polygonal lasso (Chapter 11):** Click hither and yon with this tool to draw a straight-sided selection outline (just like Option-clicking with the standard lasso). Each click sets a corner point in the selection.

⤬ **Magic wand (Chapter 11):** Click with this tool to select a contiguous area of similarly colored pixels. To select discontiguous areas, click in one area and then Shift-click in another.

✐ **Airbrush (Chapter 8):** Drag with the airbrush tool to spray diffused strokes of color that blend into the image, just the thing for creating shadows and highlights.

∥ **Paintbrush (Chapter 8):** Drag with the paintbrush tool to paint soft lines that aren't as jagged as those created with the pencil but not as fluffy as those created with the airbrush.

⌀ **Eraser (Chapter 10):** Drag with the eraser tool to paint in the background color, or erase areas in a layer to reveal the layers below. Option-drag to access the "magic" eraser, which changes portions of the image back to the way they appeared when last saved.

There are four styles of erasers in all — paintbrush, airbrush, pencil, and square (called "block"). You can cycle through them by Option-clicking on the eraser tool icon in the toolbox.

Pencil (Chapter 8): Drag with the pencil tool to paint jagged lines.

Rubber stamp (Chapter 10): This tool serves many functions, but you usually use it to copy one portion of the image onto another. Option-click on the part of your image that you want to clone, then drag to clone that area to another portion of the image.

 You also can use the rubber stamp tool to paint with a pattern or to change portions of an image to the way they looked when last saved. To cycle through the seven alternative settings, Option-click on the rubber stamp tool icon in the toolbox.

Smudge (Chapter 8): Drag with this tool to smear colors inside the image.

Blur (Chapter 8): Drag with the blur tool to diffuse the contrast between neighboring pixels, which blurs the focus of the image. You can also Option-drag to sharpen the image.

Sharpen (Chapter 8): Drag with this tool to increase the contrast between pixels, which sharpens the focus. Option-drag when this tool is active to blur the image.

Dodge (Chapter 8): Drag with the dodge tool to lighten pixels in the image. Option-drag to darken the image.

Burn (Chapter 8): Drag with the burn tool to darken pixels. Option-drag to lighten.

Sponge (Chapter 8): Drag with the sponge tool to decrease the amount of saturation in an image, so the colors appear dimmer and eventually gray. You can also increase color saturation by changing the setting of the first pop-up menu in the Toning Tool Options palette.

Pen (Chapter 11): Once available only from the Paths palette, the pen tool and its cohorts are now included in the toolbox. Use the pen tool by clicking and dragging to set points in the image window. Photoshop draws an editable path outline — much like a path in Illustrator — that you can convert to a selection outline or stroke with color.

Direct selection (Chapter 11): Use this tool — which I generally call the arrow tool — to edit a path drawn with the pen tool. You can drag points or control handles. Option-click on a path to select all of its points and move the path as a whole.

Insert point (Chapter 11): Click on a segment with this tool to insert a point in the path.

Remove point (Chapter 11): Click on a point to remove the point without interrupting the outline of the path. Photoshop automatically draws a new segment between the neighboring points.

Convert point (Chapter 11): Points in a path come in different varieties, some indicating corners and others indicating smooth arcs. The convert point tool lets you change one kind of point to another. Drag on a point to convert it from a corner to an arc. Click on a point to convert it from an arc to a sharp corner.

T **Type (Chapter 14):** Click with the type tool to display the Type Tool dialog box, which lets you enter and format text. Note that you can't use the type tool to edit existing text as you would in a page-layout or drawing program. (Like any other image, type is just a bunch of colored dots. If you misspell a word, you have to erase it and try again.)

 In Photoshop 4, the type tool invariably creates text on a new layer. This way, you can edit the text and adjust the letter spacing using the selection tools without harming other parts of the image.

Type mask (Chapter 14): As with the standard type tool, clicking with the mask type tool brings up the Type Tool dialog box. But when you exit the dialog box, Photoshop creates the letters as transparent selection outlines. If you don't want to add a new layer, this is the type tool to use.

Line (Chapter 9): Drag with the line tool to create a straight line. Click on the Start or End option in the Line Tool Options palette to add arrowheads.

Gradient (Chapter 9): Drag with this tool to fill a selection with a gradual transition of colors, commonly called a gradient.

 By default, the gradient fades from the foreground color to the background color. But in Photoshop 4, you can create custom gradients by clicking on the Edit button in the Gradient Tool Options palette.

Paint bucket (Chapter 9): Click with the paint bucket tool to fill a contiguous area of similarly colored pixels with the foreground color or a predefined pattern.

Eyedropper (Chapter 5): Click with the eyedropper tool on a color in the image window to make that color the foreground color. Option-click on a color in the image to make that color the background color.

Hand (Chapter 2): Drag an image with the hand tool to scroll the window so that you can see a different portion of the image. Double-click on the hand tool icon to magnify or reduce the image so that it fits on the screen in its entirety.

Zoom (Chapter 2): Click with the zoom tool to magnify the image so that you can see individual pixels more clearly. Option-click to step back from the image and take in a broader view. Double-click on the zoom tool icon to restore the image to 100 percent view size.

 You can modify the performance of the active tool by adjusting the settings in the Options palette. To display this palette, double-click on the tool icon in the toolbox. Or just press the Return key. Only the type tools lack palette options.

The cursors

Every version of Photoshop witnesses a cursor explosion, and Photoshop 4 is no exception. The cursor population has grown from a little over 50 in Photoshop 3 to nearly 100 in the current version. Most of these cursors are related to selection actions. A few correspond to a specific tool. And every one of them conveys special meaning.

You may think that reading about each and every cursor amounts to a big waste of time. And certainly my descriptions don't qualify as literary treats. But you have to realize that the cursor is Photoshop's way of communicating with you. Each cursor is a different visual cue in the program's on-screen vocabulary.

So don't read the entire list if you don't want to, but keep it close by as a handy reference. If you can't figure out what Photoshop is trying to say, you have only to look here to get the gist.

Arrow: The left-pointing arrow appears any time the cursor is outside of the image window. You can select a tool, set palette options, or choose a command when this cursor is visible.

Marquee: The cross appears when any of the marquee tools is active and the cursor is outside the selected area. If a marquee tool is active and no part of the image is selected, Photoshop shows you this cursor no matter what keys you press.

Add marquee: When you press the Shift key to add to a selection with one of the marquee tools, you get this cursor.

Subtract marquee: Press the Option key and drag with one of the marquee tools to subtract from a selection.

Intersect marquee: When you Shift-Option-drag with a marquee tool, you find the intersection of the dragged area and the previous selection outline. I explain this in more detail in Chapter 11.

Lasso: The lasso cursor works the same way as the marquee cursor, except that it indicates that the lasso tool is selected.

Add lasso: Shift-drag with the lasso tool to get this cursor. It tells you that Photoshop intends to add to your selection.

Subtract lasso: Option-drag with the lasso tool to carve bits out of a selection.

Intersect lasso: Shift-Option-drag with the lasso tool to find the intersection of the dragged area and the previous selection outline.

Polygonal lasso: When the polygonal lasso tool is selected and the cursor is positioned outside a selection, you get this cursor. It tells you that Photoshop is ready to draw a new selection outline.

Add polygonal lasso: Shift-click with the polygonal lasso tool to add to a selection.

Subtract polygonal lasso: Option-click with the polygonal lasso tool to clip away selected portions of the image.

Intersect polygonal lasso: Shift-Option-click with the polygonal lasso tool to find the intersection of the enclosed area and the previous selection outline.

Close polygonal lasso: When you position the polygonal lasso cursor over the first point in the shape — the point at which you first clicked — you get this cursor. It tells you that clicking now will close the shape and finish off the selection outline.

Wand: This cursor tells you that Photoshop is ready to start a new magic wand selection the moment you click. Naturally, the magic wand tool must be selected and the cursor must be positioned over a deselected area in the image.

Add wand: Shift-click with the magic wand tool to add an area of contiguous color to a selection.

Subtract wand: Option-click with the magic wand tool to remove a chunk from the selection.

Intersect wand: When you Shift-Option-click with the magic wand, Photoshop selects an area of contiguous color that falls inside the previous selection.

Move selection outline: If you're familiar with previous versions of Photoshop, this may be the first of the new cursors to catch your attention. You get it when you used to get the right arrow — that is, when a selection tool is active and you move the cursor inside a selected portion of the image. But rather than moving the selected area, dragging with this cursor moves just the selection outline and leaves the image unchanged. You have to use the move tool to modify the image.

Float and move: This is the cursor that you want to see when preparing to move a selected area in an image. Either select the move tool, or press the ⌘ key along with one of the other tools. Drag with this cursor to move the selection so it floats in front of some other portion of the image.

Move floater: Once the selection is floating, you can drag it with the move tool or any of the selection tools. This cursor tells you that it's safe to drag. Don't click, however, or you'll defloat the selection. (You also get this cursor when moving points in a path.)

Clone: Option-drag with the move tool to clone the selected portion of an image. If some other tool is selected, ⌘-Option-drag. (This cursor also appears when cloning a path by Option-dragging it with the arrow tool.)

Move layer: If you position the move tool cursor over a deselected portion of an image, you get this cursor. It tells you that Photoshop is prepared to drag the selection or — if no portion of the image is selected — the entire layer.

Crop: This cursor appears when the crop tool is selected and remains on-screen until you marquee the portion of the image that you want to retain.

Scale vertical: After you draw the crop boundary, you can change its size by dragging one of the square handles. Drag the top or bottom handle to scale the boundary vertically. (This cursor and the three that follow also appear when scaling a selection using Layer ⇨ Free Transform.)

Scale horizontal: Drag the left or right handle to scale the crop boundary horizontally.

Scale top left/bottom right: Drag the top left or bottom right handle to scale the crop boundary horizontally and vertically at the same time.

Scale top right/bottom left: You can also scale the crop boundary both horizontally and vertically by dragging the top right or bottom left handle.

Rotate from right: Position the cursor outside the crop boundary to get one of 12 rotate cursors. This one appears when the cursor is to the right of the boundary. Drag up to rotate counter-clockwise; drag down to rotate clockwise. (All 12 rotate cursors also appear when rotating a selection using Layer ⇨ Free Transform.)

Rotate from bottom right: Again, this cursor appears when you position the crop tool outside the boundary, this time under the bottom right corner. Drag to rotate.

Rotate from bottom: This cursor appears when you move the crop tool under the boundary. Drag left to rotate clockwise; drag right to rotate counter-clockwise.

Rotate from bottom left: I'm guessing. . .

ζ **Rotate from left:** . . . that by now. . .

↲ **Rotate from top left:** . . . you're beginning. . .

↶ **Rotate from top:** . . . to get. . .

↳ **Rotate from top right:** . . . the idea.

▶ **Distort:** Photoshop 4's new Free Transform command lets you scale, rotate, move, skew, and otherwise distort a selection or layer in one continuous operation. After choosing Layer ⇨ Free Transform, ⌘-drag a corner handle to get this cursor. Photoshop distorts the image.

▶↕ **Skew vertical:** Press the ⌘ key and drag the left or right handle of the transformation boundary to skew the image vertically.

▶↔ **Skew horizontal:** You might care to ⌘-drag the top or bottom handle of the transformation boundary to skew the image horizontally.

▶↖ **Skew top left/bottom right:** After a few skews and distorts, the transformation boundary may get pretty twisted around. What was once a top side becomes a diagonal edge. But no matter — Photoshop updates the skew cursor to keep up with the new inclination.

▶↗ **Skew top right/bottom left:** Here's yet another wacky skew cursor that you may spy when ⌘-dragging a transformation boundary.

I **Type:** The common I-beam cursor indicates that the type tool is selected and ready to use. You also get this cursor when using the type mask tool. Click to display the Type Tool dialog box.

I+ **Add type mask:** So far as Photoshop is concerned, the type mask tool is just another selection tool. Shift-click with the tool to add the character outlines to the previous selection.

I- **Subtract type mask:** Option-click with the type mask tool to carve letter-shaped holes out of the previous selection.

I× **Intersect type mask:** You can also Shift-Option-click with the type mask tool to find the intersection of a few characters and the previous selection outline.

✒ **Pen:** This cursor appears when the pen tool is selected, enabling you to start a new path or add points to the current path.

✒+ **Insert point:** When a small plus sign accompanies the pen cursor, you can click on a segment in a path to insert a point.

✒- **Remove point:** When this cursor is active, click on a point in a path to delete it. A new segment joins the remaining points to prevent a break in the path.

Close path: When you position your cursor over the first point in an open path, this cursor appears. Click with the cursor to close the path.

Arrow: Press the ⌘ key when using the pen tool to access the arrow cursor, which lets you move a point or adjust a control handle. This cursor also appears when the direct selection tool is active.

Convert point: Use this cursor to convert a corner in a path to an arc or an arc to a corner. Just click on a point to change it to a corner; drag from a point to change it to an arc.

Hand: The hand cursor appears when you select the hand tool or when you press the spacebar with some other tool selected. Drag to scroll the image inside the image window.

Zoom in: This cursor appears when you select the zoom tool or press ⌘-spacebar when some other tool is selected. Click or drag to magnify the image on-screen.

Zoom out: The zoom out cursor appears when you press Option with the zoom tool selected or press Option-spacebar with some other tool selected. Click to reduce your view of the image.

Zoom limit: This cursor appears when you're at the end of your zoom rope. You can't zoom in beyond 1,600 percent or out beyond 0.2 percent (depending on image size). You also see this cursor when ⌘-dragging inside the Navigator palette.

Airbrush: Assuming the Standard cursor option is selected in the Preferences dialog box (as it is by default), you see this cursor when you paint with the airbrush.

Paintbrush: When you select the paintbrush, this cursor appears (again, by default).

Pencil: This is the cursor that greets you when you paint with the pencil tool.

Soft eraser: This cursor appears when you select the eraser tool and one of the soft brush settings — Paintbrush, Airbrush, or Pencil — in the Eraser Options palette.

Soft magic eraser: When you Option-drag with the soft eraser, Photoshop displays this cursor to show you that any dragging will change the image back to the way it looked when last saved.

Block eraser: You get this cursor when you select the eraser tool along with the old-style Block option in the Eraser Options palette.

Block magic eraser: This cursor appears when you press the Option key while using the eraser tool set to the Block mode. You then drag to change portions of the image to the way they looked when last saved.

Stamp: This cursor shows you that the rubber stamp tool is active.

Stamp pickup: When you press the Option key while using the rubber stamp tool, you see this cursor. You then click to specify which portion of an image you want to clone.

Smudge: This cursor appears when the smudge tool is selected.

Blur: When you use the blur tool, you see this cursor.

Sharpen: This cursor appears when you press the Option key in combination with the blur tool or when you select the sharpen tool from the toolbox.

Dodge: This cursor appears when you select the dodge tool. Drag to lighten an image.

Burn: If you prefer to darken portions of an image, press the Option key while using the dodge tool or select the burn tool from the toolbox. Either way, you get this handy cursor.

Sponge: Drag with the sponge tool cursor to decrease or increase the saturation of colors in the image.

Brush size: This cursor varies in size to show you the exact diameter of the brush that you're using when dragging with any of the paint or edit tools, from the airbrush to the sponge. You can request this special cursor by selecting the Brush Size radio button in the Preferences dialog box, as I explain later in this chapter.

Crosshair: You see this cursor when you press the Caps Lock key while using any selection, painting, or editing tool. Caps Lock is a particular blessing when using the rubber stamp or smudge tool, since otherwise the big cursors can prevent you from seeing what you're doing.

Line/gradient: This cursor appears when you select either the line or gradient tool. Drag with the cursor to determine the angle and length of a prospective straight line or gradient fill.

Paint bucket: This cursor appears when the paint bucket tool is selected. Click to fill an area with the foreground color.

Eyedropper: This cursor appears when you select the eyedropper tool, or when you press Option while using the type tool, paint bucket tool, gradient tool, or any of the painting tools except the eraser. Click to lift a color from the image window.

Crosshair pickup: If the eyedropper cursor prevents you from seeing what you're doing, press the Caps Lock key to display a crosshair cursor that zeroes in on an exact pixel. This specific crosshair appears when you use the eyedropper tool or when you Option-click with the rubber stamp tool while Caps Lock is down.

Black eyedropper: This cursor and the two that follow are available only when you work in the Levels and Curves dialog boxes. Click on a color in the image window to change that color to black.

Gamma eyedropper: Click on a color with this cursor to change the color to medium gray (sometimes called the *gamma*).

White eyedropper: Use this cursor to click on a color in the image window and change it to white.

Eyedropper plus: This cursor and the next are available only when using the Color Range and Replace Color commands. Click with this cursor to add colors to the temporary mask. For complete information about these commands, read Chapters 12 and 18, respectively.

Eyedropper minus: Click with this cursor to remove colors from the temporary mask in the Color Range and Replace Color dialog box.

Palette hand: This cursor appears when working in the Layers, Channels, or Paths palette. Drag with the cursor to move a selected item above or below other items listed in the palette.

Palette selection: In Photoshop 4, you can convert a layer, channel, or path to a selection outline by ⌘-clicking on it. When you do, you see this cursor.

Add palette selection: If you can convert layers, channels, and paths to selections, it only makes sense that you can add the new selection outline to the previous one. Just ⌘-Shift-click on an item to see this cursor.

Subtract palette selection: When you ⌘-Option-click on a palette item, you subtract it from the previous selection.

Intersect palette selection: You can also ⌘-Shift-Option-click on a layer, channel, or path name to find the intersection of the item with the previous selection.

Move palette item: When you drag a layer, channel, or path, the palette hand changes to the move palette item cursor.

Vertical guide: Drag from the vertical ruler into the image window to create a vertical guide in Photoshop 4. When creating or moving a vertical guide, you see this cursor.

Horizontal guide: Drag from the horizontal ruler along the top of the image window to create a horizontal guide.

Group layers: Press the Option key and position the cursor over the horizontal line between two layers in the Layers palette to get this cursor. Then click to group the layers divided by that line.

Ungroup layers: When two layers are grouped, the horizontal line between them becomes dotted. Option-click on the dotted line to ungroup the two layers.

Not available: If you try to click on a palette icon that is not applicable to the current state of affairs, Photoshop tells you the icon is off limits with this cursor.

Watch: The watch cursor is the universal Macintosh symbol for hurry up and wait. When you see this cursor inside Photoshop, you can either sit on your idle hands, waiting for the devil to start playing with them, or you can switch to another application and try to get some work done.

The toolbox controls

You have to love lists. They're fun to write and they're a joy to read.

All right, so I'm lying. Making your way through lists of information is a monstrous chore, whether you're on the giving or receiving end. But these particular lists happen to contain essential reference information. So on we go with the most astonishing list yet — the one that explains the controls at the bottom of the toolbox.

 Foreground color: Click on the foreground color icon to bring up the Color Picker dialog box. Select a color and press Return to change the foreground color, which is used by all painting tools except the eraser.

 I'm not sure why, but many users make the mistake of double-clicking on the foreground or background color icons when they first start using Photoshop. A single click is all that's needed.

Background color: Click on the background color icon to display the Color Picker and change the background color, which is used by the eraser and gradient tools. Photoshop also uses the background color to fill a selected area on the background layer when you press the Delete key.

Switch colors: Click on the switch colors icon to exchange the foreground and background colors.

Default colors: Click on this icon to automatically change the foreground color to black and the background color to white.

 At any time, you can quickly make the foreground color white by clicking on the default colors icon and then clicking on the switch colors icon.

Marching ants: Click on this icon to exit Photoshop's quick mask mode and view selection outlines as animated dotted lines that look like marching ants, hence the name. (Adobe calls this the "standard" mode, but I think marching ants mode better describes how it works.)

 Quick mask: Click here to enter the quick mask mode, which allows you to edit selection boundaries using painting tools. The marching ants vanish and the image appears half covered by a translucent layer of red, like a rubylith in traditional paste-up. The red layer covers the deselected — or masked — portions of the image. Paint with black to extend the masked areas, thereby subtracting from the selection. Paint with white to erase the mask, thereby adding to the selection.

The quick mask mode is too complex a topic to sum up in a few sentences. If you can't wait to find out what it's all about, check out Chapter 12.

Standard window: Click on this icon to display the foreground image in a standard window, as shown earlier in Figure 2-2. By default, every image opens in the standard window mode.

Full screen with menu bar: If you can't see enough of your image inside a standard window, click on this icon. The title bar and scroll bars disappear, as do all background windows, but the menu bar and palettes remain visible, as in Figure 2-4. (You can still access other open images by choosing their names from the Window menu.) A light gray background fills any empty area around the image.

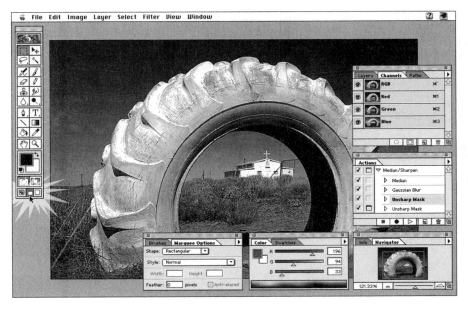

Figure 2-4
Click on the full screen with menu bar icon to hide
the title bar, scroll bars, and preview box.

☐ **Absolute full screen:** If you still can't see enough of your image — or the light gray area in the image is too distracting — click on the rightmost of the image window icons to see the photo set against a neutral black background. The menu bar disappears, limiting your access to commands (though you still can choose some commands using keyboard shortcuts). Only the toolbox and palettes remain visible, as shown in Figure 2-5.

If the palettes get in your way when you're viewing an image in full screen mode, you can hide all palettes — including the toolbox — by pressing the Tab key. To bring the toolbox back into view, press Tab again.

In Photoshop 4, you can hide the palettes but leave the toolbox up on screen by pressing Shift-Tab. Press Shift-Tab again to bring the palettes back. (Pressing Tab while the palettes are gone hides the toolbox.)

Figure 2-5
Click on the absolute full screen icon to hide everything but the toolbox, floating palettes, and image.

The floating palettes

The palettes in Photoshop 4 have seen their fair share of changes, but they include the same basic elements as their predecessors from Version 3. That is to say, the palettes offer most or all of the elements labeled in Figure 2-6. (Some panels lack scroll bars, others lack size boxes.)

Many palette elements are miniature versions of the elements that accompany any window. For example, the close box and title bar work identically to their image-window counterparts. The title bar lacks a title, but you can still drag it to move the palette to another location on-screen. Photoshop automatically snaps palettes into alignment with other palettes.

 To snap a palette to the edge of the screen, just Shift-click on its title bar. You can also Shift-drag the title bar to move the palette around the perimeter of the screen, or to snap the palette from one edge of the screen to the other. (This tip also works with the toolbox.)

Figure 2-6
Most palettes include the same basic elements as the Brushes palette, shown here.

Four elements are unique to floating palettes:

- ➤ **Palette options:** Each floating palette offers its own collection of options. These options may include tools, icons, pop-up menus, slider bars, you name it.

- ➤ **Palette menu:** Drag from the right-pointing arrowhead icon to display a menu of commands specific to the palette. These commands enable you to manipulate the palette options and adjust preference settings.

- ➤ **Panel tabs:** Click on a panel tab to switch from one panel to another inside a palette. (You can also switch panels by selecting the palette commands from the Window menu, but it's more convenient to click on a tab.)

- ➤ **Collapse box:** Click on the collapse box to decrease the on-screen space consumed by the palette. If you previously enlarged the palette by dragging the size box, your first click reduces the palette back to its default size. After that, clicking on the collapse box hides all but the most essential palette options.

In most cases, collapsing a palette hides all options and leaves only the panel tabs visible. But in the case of the Options, Color, and Layers palettes, clicking on the collapse box leaves a sliver of palette options intact, as demonstrated in the middle example of Figure 2-7. To eliminate all options for these panels — as in the last example — Option-click on the collapse box. You can also double-click on one of the panel tabs, or in the empty area to the right of the tabs. These tricks work even if you've enlarged the palette by dragging the size box.

Figure 2-7
The Options palette shown at full size (top), partially collapsed (middle), and fully collapsed (bottom).

Click here

Option-click here

or double-click here

Tabbing through the options

I mentioned earlier how you can hide the palettes by pressing Shift-Tab, or hide both palettes and toolbox by pressing Tab. But this keyboard trick doesn't work if an option box is active.

For example, suppose you click inside the R option box in the Color palette. This activates the option. Now press Tab. Rather than hiding the palettes, Photoshop advances you to the next option box in the palette. You can keep pressing Tab to advance from one option box to the next, even if the next option is in another palette. You can even advance to the magnification option in the bottom left corner of the image window. To move backward through the options, press Shift-Tab.

To apply an option box value and return focus to the image window, press Return. This deactivates the palette options. This is very important. If an option box remains active, certain keyboard tricks — such as pressing a key to select a tool — won't work properly. Photoshop will either ignore the shortcut or it will beep at you for pressing a key that the option box doesn't like. For more information on shortcuts, read Chapter 3.

You can also return focus to the palette options from the keyboard by pressing the Return key. When you press Return, Photoshop displays the Options palette for the active tool. Assuming the Options palette for that tool offers an option box, Photoshop highlights the contents of the option. Then you can tab around to the option that you want to change, enter a new value, and press Return to get out.

Shuffling panels

Photoshop lets you separate and group panels into palettes as you see fit. To separate a panel into its own palette, just drag the panel tab away from the palette, as demonstrated in Figure 2-8. To combine a panel with a different palette, drag the panel tab onto the palette so that the palette becomes highlighted, and then release. The middle and right examples in the figure show off this technique.

Figure 2-8
Dragging a panel off a palette (left) results in a new panel (middle). Dragging a panel onto another palette (middle) adds that panel to the palette (right).

If you ever completely muck up the palettes — or a palette somehow gets stuck under the menu bar — press ⌘-K and click on the Reset Palette Locations to Default button in the Preferences dialog box. For more information, read the "General preferences" section later in this chapter.

Navigating Inside Photoshop 4

All graphics and desktop publishing programs provide a variety of navigational tools and functions that enable you to scoot around the screen, visit the heartlands and nether regions, examine the fine details, and take in the big picture. And

Photoshop is no exception. In fact, Photoshop's navigation tools would make Magellan drool (were he inclined to edit an image or two).

 The truth is, Photoshop 3 provided more navigational tricks per square pixel than just about any other graphics program, and the navigation controls have just about doubled in Version 4. So hold onto your hats, folks. We're going to be zooming and scrolling with a fair amount of gusto in the next few pages.

The view size

You can change the *view size* — the size at which an image appears on-screen — so that you can either see more of an image or concentrate on individual pixels. Each change in view size is expressed as a *zoom ratio,* which is the ratio between screen pixels and image pixels. Photoshop 4 displays the zoom ratio as a percentage value in the title bar. The 100 percent zoom ratio shows one image pixel for each screen pixel, and is therefore equivalent to the old 1:1 zoom ratio in Photoshop 3. A 200 percent zoom ratio doubles the size of the image pixels on-screen, and so on.

Actual pixels

 Photoshop 4 calls the 100 percent zoom ratio the "actual-pixels" view. This happens to be the most accurate view size because you can see the image as it really is. Reduced view sizes drop pixels; magnified view sizes stretch pixels. Only the actual-pixels view displays each and every pixel without a trace of screen distortion.

You can switch to this most accurate of view sizes at any time using one of the following techniques:

    ☞ Choose View ⇨ Actual Pixels.

    ☞ Press ⌘-Option-0. (That's a zero, not the letter O.)

    ☞ Double-click on the zoom tool icon in the toolbox.

Fit on screen

When you first open an image, Photoshop displays it at the largest zoom ratio (up to 100 percent) that permits the entire image to fit on-screen. Assuming that you don't change the size of the image, you can return to this "fit-on-screen" view size in one of the following ways:

    ☞ Choose View ⇨ Fit on Screen.

cⱷ Press ⌘-0.

cⱷ Double-click on the hand tool icon in the toolbox.

 Strangely, any of these techniques may magnify the image beyond the 100 percent view size. When working on a very small image, for example, Photoshop 4 enlarges the image to fill the screen, even if that means maxing out the zoom to 1,600 percent. Personally, I prefer to use the fit-on-screen view only when working on very large images.

 If you've become thoroughly accustomed to pressing ⌘-0 to switch to the color composite view, as in earlier versions of Photoshop, try to make a mental note that this shortcut now zooms the window. To switch to the color composite view, you have to press ⌘-tilde (the ~ key in the upper left corner of the keyboard). Old habits die hard.

Print size

 You can switch to yet another predefined view size by choosing View ⇨ Print Size. New to Photoshop 4, this command displays the image on-screen at the size it will print. (You set the print size using Image ⇨ Image Size, as I explain in Chapter 4.)

That's the theory, anyway. In practice, the "print-size" view isn't particularly reliable. Photoshop assumes your monitor displays exactly 72 pixels per inch. Though this is the most common setting, monitor resolutions simply aren't that dependable. High-end monitors — such as the Radius PressView series and others — let you change screen resolutions without Photoshop even noticing.

The long and the short is this: Don't expect to hold up your printed image and have it exactly match the print-size view on screen. It's just a rough approximation, designed to show you how the image will look when imported into QuarkXPress, PageMaker, or some other publishing program.

The zoom tool

Obviously, these aren't the only zoom ratios available to you. You can zoom in as close as 1,600 percent and zoom out to 0.2 percent.

The easiest way to zoom in and out of your image is to use the zoom tool:

cⱷ Click in the image window with the zoom tool to magnify the image in preset increments — from 33.33 percent to 50 to 66.67 to 100 to 200 and so on.

Photoshop tries to center the zoomed view at the point where you clicked (or come as close as possible).

⤳ Option-click with the zoom tool to reduce the image incrementally — 200 to 100 to 66.67 to 50 to 33.33 and so on. Again, Photoshop tries to center the new view on the click point.

⤳ Drag with the zoom tool to draw a rectangular marquee around the portion of the image you want to magnify. Photoshop magnifies the image so that the marqueed area fits just inside the image window. (If the horizontal and vertical proportions of the marquee do not match those of your screen — for example, if you draw a tall, thin marquee or a really short, wide one — Photoshop favors the smaller of the two possible zoom ratios to avoid hiding any detail inside the marquee.)

⤳ If you like, you can instruct Photoshop to resize the window when you click with the zoom tool. Press Return when the zoom tool is active to display the Zoom Options palette, then select the Resize Windows to Fit check box. (Turn this option off to zoom without resizing the window, as in Photoshop 3 and earlier.)

To temporarily access the zoom tool when some other tool is selected, press and hold the ⌘ and spacebar keys. Release both keys to return control of the cursor to the selected tool. To access the zoom out cursor, press Option with the spacebar. These keyboard equivalents work from inside many dialog boxes, permitting you to modify the view of an image while applying a filter or color correction.

The zoom commands

You can also zoom in and out using the following commands and keyboard shortcuts:

⤳ Choose View ⇨ Zoom In or press ⌘-plus (+) to zoom in. This works exactly like clicking with the zoom tool except that you can't specify the center of the new view size. Photoshop merely centers the zoom in keeping with the previous view size.

⤳ Choose View ⇨ Zoom Out or press ⌘-minus (-) to zoom out.

⤳ Photoshop's Zoom commands resize the window as they magnify. To override this, press the Option key. Press ⌘-Option-plus to zoom in without resizing and ⌘-Option-minus to zoom out without resizing.

In Photoshop 3, the Option-key shortcuts would zoom to the maximum and minimum view sizes, respectively. No one seemed to find these operations terribly useful, so they're now extinct.

The magnification box

Another way to zoom in and out without changing the window size is to enter a value into the magnification box, located in the lower left corner of the image window. Select the magnification value, enter a new one, and press Return. Photoshop zooms the view without zooming the window.

In Figure 2-9, I started with a specially sized window at actual-pixels view. I then entered two different zoom ratios into the magnification box — 156.7 percent and 60.4 percent — alternately enlarging and reducing the image within the confines of a static window.

Figure 2-9
To zoom an image without changing the window size, enter a zoom ratio into the magnifica-tion box and press Return

Magnification box

If you later decide you want to change the dimensions of the window to exactly fit the image, click on the zoom box in the upper right corner of the title bar. Or just press ⌘-plus or ⌘-minus to zoom image and window together.

Here are a couple of other things you might like to know about the magnification box:

↪ Pressing Shift-Return: When you press Return after entering a magnification value, Photoshop changes the view size and returns focus to the image window. If you aren't sure exactly what zoom ratio you want to use, try pressing Shift-Return instead. This changes the view size while keeping the magnification value active; this way you can enter a new value and try again.

↪ Nudging the zoom ratio: Press the up and down arrow keys to raise or lower the magnification value in 0.01-percent increments. Press Shift with an arrow key to raise or lower the value in 0.1-percent increments.

When trying to precisely zoom an image, I find it especially helpful to do a few Shift-arrows in a row and then press Shift-Return to try out the new value. If it isn't quite right, Shift-arrow and Shift-Return again.

Creating a reference window

In the old days, paint programs provided a cropped view of your image at the actual-pixels view size to serve as a reference when you worked in a magnified view. Because it's so doggone modern, Photoshop does not, but you can easily create a second view of your image by choosing View ➪ New View. Use the new window to maintain a 100 percent view of your image while you zoom and edit inside the original window. Both windows track the changes to the image. For example, the paintbrush strokes applied to the leaves in Figure 2-10 appear in both windows.

Scrolling inside the window

In the standard window mode, you have access to scroll bars, just as you do in the vast majority of Macintosh applications. But as you become more proficient with Photoshop, you'll use the scroll bars less and less. One way to bypass the scroll bars is to use the keyboard equivalents listed in Table 2-1. If you're using a Mac without an extended keyboard — such as a PowerBook — try out the Control key equivalents in the third column.

Figure 2-10
You can create multiple windows to track the changes made to a single image by choosing the New View command from the View menu.

Table 2-1	Scrolling from the Keyboard	
Scrolling Action	*Extended Keyboard*	*Other Keyboard*
Up one screen	Page Up	Control-K
Up slightly	Shift-Page Up	Control-Shift-K
Down one screen	Page Down	Control-L
Down slightly	Shift-Page Down	Control-Shift-L
To upper left corner	Home	Control-A
To lower right corner	End	Control-D

Unfortunately, you can't scroll exclusively left or right from the keyboard. But who cares? You won't be scrolling from the keyboard that often anyway. Most of the time, you'll use the hand tool.

To temporarily access the hand tool when some other tool is selected, press and hold the spacebar. Releasing the spacebar returns the cursor to its original appearance. This keyboard equivalent even works from inside many dialog boxes.

The Navigator palette

I've saved the best for last. Shown in Figure 2-11, the Navigator palette is the best thing to happen to zooming and scrolling since Photoshop was first introduced. If you routinely work on large images that extend beyond the confines of your relatively tiny screen, you'll want to get up and running with this palette as soon as possible.

Figure 2-11
The Navigator palette is the best thing to happen to zooming and scrolling since Photoshop 1.0.

If the Navigator palette isn't visible, choose Window ⇨ Show Navigator. You can then use the palette options as follows:

- **View box:** Drag the red view box inside the image thumbnail to reveal some hidden portion of the photograph. Photoshop dynamically tracks your adjustments in the image window. Isn't it great?

But wait, it gets better. Press ⌘ to get a zoom cursor in the Navigator palette. Then ⌘-drag to resize the view box and zoom the photo in the image window. Awesome!

You can change the color of the zoom box by choosing the Palette Options command from the palette menu. My favorite setting is yellow, but it ultimately depends on the colors in your image. You ideally want something that stands out. To lift a color from the image itself, move the cursor outside the dialog box and click in the image window with the eyedropper.

- **Magnification box:** This value works just like the one in the lower left corner of the image window. Just enter a new zoom ratio and press Return.

- **Zoom out:** Click on the zoom out button to reduce the view size in the same predefined increments as the zoom tool. The difference is that this button doesn't alter the size of the image window. So it works like the zoom tool used to work.

- ✎ **Zoom slider:** Give the slider triangle a yank and see where it takes you. Drag to the left to zoom out, drag rightward to zoom in. Again, Photoshop dynamically tracks your changes in the image window. Dang, it's nice to be able to zoom on the fly.

- ✎ **Zoom in:** Click on the big mountains to incrementally magnify the view of the image without altering the window size.

 As it turns out, the Navigator palette originated outside Adobe. A developer named Extensis created a Photoshop plug-in called PhotoNavigator and gave it away as a promotional piece back in the summer of 1996. The Adobe folks liked the idea so much that they integrated it into Photoshop 4. Lucky for us. Though PhotoNavigator was pretty good, Adobe's reworking is significantly better.

By the way, if you come across PhotoNavigator online, don't bother downloading it. It's a fine addition to Photoshop 3, but it's merely redundant in Version 4.

Customizing the Interface_____

Every program gives you access to a few core settings so that you can modify the program to suit your personal needs. These settings are known far and wide as *preferences.* Photoshop ships with certain recommended preference settings already in force — known coast-to-coast as *factory defaults* — but just because they're recommended doesn't mean they're right. In fact, I disagree with quite a few of them. But why quibble when you can change the preferences according to your merest whim?

You can modify preference settings in two ways. You can make environmental adjustments using File ➪ Preferences ➪ General, or you can change the operation of specific tools by adjusting settings in the Options palette. Photoshop remembers environmental preferences, tool settings, and even the file format under which you saved the last image by storing this information to a file called *Adobe Photoshop 4.0 Prefs* in the Preferences folder inside the System Folder.

 To restore Photoshop's factory default settings, delete the Adobe Photoshop 4.0 Prefs file when the application is *not* running. The next time you launch Photoshop, it creates a new preferences file automatically.

Deleting the preferences file is also a good idea if Photoshop starts acting funny. Photoshop's preference file has always been highly susceptible to corruption, possibly because the application writes to it so often. Whatever the reason, if Photoshop starts behaving erratically, quit the program, delete the Adobe Photoshop 4.0 Prefs file, and relaunch Photoshop. You'll have to reset your preferences, but a smooth-running program is worth the few minutes of extra effort.

After you get your preferences set just the way you like them, you can prevent Photoshop from altering them any further by locking the file. Go to the Finder desktop, select the Adobe Photoshop 4.0 Preferences file, and choose File ➪ Get Info (⌘-I). Then select the Locked check box inside the Info dialog box. From now on, Photoshop will start up with a consistent set of default settings.

Personally, I don't use the previous tip because I periodically modify settings and I want Photoshop to remember the latest and greatest. Instead, I make a backup copy of my favorite settings. After a couple of weeks of working in the program and getting things to a more or less acceptable level, copy the Adobe Photoshop 4.0 Preferences file to a separate disk. Or just stick a copy in the Goodies folder (which resides in the same folder as the Photoshop application file). Then, if the preference file becomes corrupt, you can replace it with your backup.

The preference panels

Photoshop 4 now includes a long list of commands in the File ➪ Preferences submenu. As it turns out, you never need choose any of these commands if you'll remember a simple keyboard shortcut — ⌘-K. This brings up the Preferences dialog box, which provides access to eight panels of options, representing every one of the File ➪ Preferences commands. Just select the desired panel from the pop-up menu in the upper left corner of the dialog box, as demonstrated in Figure 2-12. Or press the ⌘ key equivalent for the panel as listed in the pop-up menu. You can also click on the Prev and Next buttons to cycle from one panel to the next.

Figure 2-12
Select a panel of options from the pop-up menu, or click on the Prev and Next buttons to advance from one panel to the next.

Photoshop always displays the first panel, General, when you press ⌘-K. If you prefer to go to the panel that you were last using, press ⌘-Option-K.

To accept your settings and exit the Preferences dialog box, press the Return key. Or press Escape or ⌘-period to cancel your settings. Okay, so you already knew that, but here's one you might not know: Press and hold the Option key to change the Cancel button to Reset, then click on the button to restore the settings that were in force before you entered the dialog box. You can also press Option-Escape or ⌘-Option-period.

The following sections examine each of the Preferences panels, in the order they appear in the Figure 2-12 pop-up menu. Out of context like this, Photoshop's preference settings can be a bit confusing. In future chapters, I'll try to shed some additional light on the settings you're likely to find most useful.

General preferences

The General panel, shown in Figure 2-13, contains a miscellaneous supply of what are arguably the most important Preferences options. In the following list, I explain how each option works. I also include what I consider to be the optimal setting in parentheses:

➥ **Color Picker (Photoshop):** When you click on the foreground or background color control icon in the toolbox, Photoshop displays one of two color pickers, its own or the one provided by the Apple system software. If you are familiar with other Macintosh graphics programs but new to Photoshop, the system software's Color Picker dialog box may be more familiar to you. However, Photoshop's color picker is more versatile.

Figure 2-13
The General panel provides access to the most important environmental preference settings.

Preferences
General ▼
Color Picker: Photoshop ▼
Interpolation: Bicubic (Better) ▼
Options
☒ Anti-alias PostScript   ☐ Beep When Done
☒ Export Clipboard   ☒ Dynamic Color Sliders
☒ Short PANTONE Names   ☒ Save Palette Locations
☒ Show Tool Tips
Reset Palette Locations to Default
OK
Cancel
Prev
Next

↪ **Interpolation (Bicubic):** When you resize an image using Image ➪ Image Size or transform it using Layer ➪ Free Transform, one of the commands in the Layer ➪ Transform submenu, Photoshop has to make up — or *interpolate* — pixels to fill in the gaps. You can change how Photoshop calculates the interpolation by choosing one of three options from the Interpolation submenu.

If you select Nearest Neighbor, Photoshop simply copies the next-door pixel when creating a new one. This is the fastest setting, but it invariably results in jagged effects.

The second option, Bilinear, smoothes the transitions between pixels by creating intermediate shades. Photoshop averages the color of each pixel with four neighbors — the pixel above, the one below, and the two to the left and right. It takes more time, but typically, the softened effect is worth it.

Still more time-intensive is the default setting, Bicubic, which averages the color of a pixel with its eight closest neighbors — one up, one down, two on the sides, and four in the corners. This setting boosts the amount of contrast between pixels in order to offset the blurring effect that generally accompanies interpolation.

The moral is this: Select Bicubic to turn Photoshop's interpolation capabilities on, and select Nearest Neighbor to turn them off. The Bilinear setting is a poor compromise between the two, too slow for roughing out effects but too remedial to waste your time with.

↪ **Anti-alias PostScript (on):** Photoshop lets you import object-oriented graphics from Illustrator and 3D drawing program Adobe Dimensions (included with Illustrator 6). Either copy the objects in Illustrator or Dimensions and paste them into Photoshop, or drag the objects from Illustrator and drop them into an open Photoshop image window. Either way, the Anti-alias PostScript option softens the edges of PostScript objects. If you prefer jagged edges, turn this check box off.

↪ **Export Clipboard (off):** When selected, this option tells Photoshop to transfer a copied image from the program's internal Clipboard to the system's Clipboard whenever you switch applications. This permits you to paste the image into any program that supports PICT images. Turn this option off if you plan to use copied images only within Photoshop and you want to reduce the lag time that occurs when you switch from Photoshop to another program. Even with this option off, you can paste images copied from other programs into Photoshop.

↪ **Short Pantone Names (on):** Generally speaking, Photoshop doesn't support Pantone-brand spot colors. In fact, you can assign Pantone colors only when printing a grayscale image as a duotone (as explained in Chapter 7). Otherwise, feel free to completely ignore this option.

For those of you who will be creating duotones, Photoshop supports the most recent Pantone naming conventions. This is great for printing duotones directly from Photoshop, but if you plan to import a Pantone duotone into a desktop publishing or drawing package, you need to select the Short Pantone Names check box to ensure that the receiving application properly recognizes the color names. (Actually, naming conventions vary from one application to the next — PageMaker 6 and FreeHand 7 default to long names, for example — but since all programs support the short names, short is safest.)

↪ **Show Tool Tips (on):** When on, this option displays little labels and keyboard shortcuts when you hover your cursor over a tool or palette option. The tool tips don't impede Photoshop's performance, so I see no reason to turn this option off.

↪ **Beep When Tasks Finish (off):** You can instruct Photoshop to beep at you whenever it finishes an operation that displays a Progress window. This option may be useful if you find yourself dozing off during particularly time-consuming operations. But I'm a firm believer that computers should be seen and not heard.

↪ **Dynamic Color Sliders (on):** When selected, this option instructs Photoshop to preview color effects within the slider bars of the Color palette. When the option is turned off, the slider bars show the same colors regardless of your changes. Unless you're working on a Mac II or some other old-model machine, leave this option on. It takes a fraction of a second longer to calculate, but it's worth it.

↪ **Save Palette Locations (on):** When this option is selected, Photoshop remembers the location of the toolbox and floating palettes from one session to the next. If you turn this check box off, Photoshop restores the default palette positions next time you restart the program.

↪ **Reset Palette Locations to Default:** Every once in a while, palettes go haywire. They can get stuck under menu bars. And if you change monitor resolutions, a palette can even disappear off the screen. If this happens, click on this button and Photoshop will restore the palettes to their original "safe" positions.

Saving files

When in the Preferences dialog box, press ⌘-2 to advance to the Saving Files panel, shown in Figure 2-14. Every one of these options affects how Photoshop saves images to disk. The following list explains how the options work, and the recommended settings:

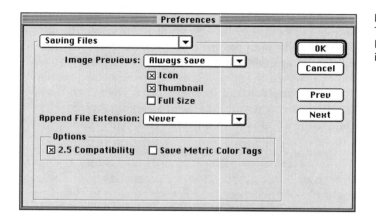

Figure 2-14
The Saving Files options tell
Photoshop how to save your
images to disk.

∞ **Image Previews (thumbnail only):** Photoshop saves previews so that you can see what an image looks like before opening or importing it. You can select as many as three kinds of image previews:

  • The Icon option creates a tiny preview icon that you can view from the Finder desktop. In my opinion, this option is hardly worth the extra disk space, and too many custom icons can cause problems with your system software.

  • The more useful Thumbnail option creates a larger preview that displays inside the Open dialog box when you select a file. Always leave this option on.

  • The third option, Full Size, creates a 72-dpi preview that can be used for placement inside a page-layout program.

If you want to decide which previews to assign when saving a file, select the Ask When Saving option from the pop-up menu above the check boxes. All three Image Preview options then appear at the bottom of the Save dialog box.

∞ **Append File Extension (Ask When Saving):** This option appends a three-character extension to the end of a file name to make your images compatible with Windows and DOS programs. For example, a layered composition saved in the Photoshop format gets a .PSD extension. I personally like to set this option to Ask When Saving; that way, I can decide whether or not to include a PC-style extension from inside the Save dialog box on a file-by-file basis.

∞ **2.5 Compatibility (off):** This option permits backward compatibility between Photoshop 4 and Photoshop 2.5, but it comes at a steep price. Here's the story: The only file format that retains layers is the Photoshop format. Even though Photoshop 2.5 does not support layers, it can open a flattened version of the image in which all the layers are fused together, so long as the 2.5 Compatibility check box is on. This is because Photoshop inserts an additional flattened version of the image into the file, which takes up a considerable amount of disk space. On the other hand, if you don't need to open your images in Photoshop 2.5, you can reduce the file size by as much as 50 percent by turning this check box off. Granted, old versions of Photoshop won't be able to open the image, but unless you're working with folks who are behind the times, backward compatibility doesn't matter.

↪ **Save Metric Color Tags (off):** If you use EFI's EfiColor for Photoshop to help with screen and printer calibration, and you import and print most of your images inside QuarkXPress, turn this option on. Photoshop then references the active EfiColor separation table when saving an image in the TIFF or EPS file format, making the table available to XPress and thus maintaining consistent color between the two applications. If you don't use EfiColor, as most folks don't, leave the option off.

Display & Cursors

Press ⌘-3 to saddle up to the Display & Cursors options, which appear in Figure 2-15. These options affect the way colors and cursors appear on-screen. Here's how the options work, along with recommended settings:

↪ **CMYK Composites (Faster):** Your monitor mixes red, green, and blue light to create colors on-screen. This is the RGB color mode. An opposite color mode known as CMYK (cyan, magenta, yellow, and black) is used to print colors on paper. As a result, when you edit a CMYK image, Photoshop has to convert the colors to their RGB equivalents.

For those who spend a lot of time editing CMYK images, Photoshop lets you dictate the accuracy of the CMYK-to-RGB conversion. If you select the Smoother option, Photoshop preserves the actual CMYK color values and converts them on the fly to your RGB display — a precise but slow process. If you opt instead for the Faster option, Photoshop cheats by converting the colors in an image to their nearest RGB equivalents according to a predefined look-up table (known as an LUT), which speeds up the screen display but sacrifices a very small amount of color accuracy.

Unless your monitor is precisely calibrated, the Smoother option isn't likely to do you much good. And if you do own a calibrated monitor (such as a Radius PressView), you may also want to invest in a piece of CMYK acceleration hardware, (such as a Radius Thunder board). This makes the Smoother option run nearly as fast as Faster. Otherwise, select the Faster radio button and enjoy the speed savings.

✑ **Color Channels in Color (off):** An individual color channel contains just 8 bits of data per pixel, which makes it equivalent to a grayscale image. Photoshop provides you with the option of colorizing the channel according to the primary color it represents. For example, when this option is turned on, the red color channel looks like a grayscale image viewed through red acetate. However, most experts agree that the effect isn't very helpful and does more to obscure your image than make it easier for you to see what's going on. Leave this check box turned off, and read Chapter 6 for more information.

Figure 2-15
The Display & Cursors options control the way images and cursors look on-screen.

✑ **Use System Palette (off):** If you're working on an 8-bit monitor that displays no more than 256 colors at a time — as when using Photoshop on a PowerBook — then this option matters to you. Otherwise, give it the slip.

To simulate the 16 million-color spectrum on a 256-color screen, Photoshop automatically jumbles colored pixels using a technique called *dithering*. By default, Photoshop selects 256 colors that are best suited to your image. In doing so, however, it must switch to a new set of 256 colors every time you bring a new document to the foreground. If you want all open documents to conform to the same set of colors — namely, the so-called "system palette" built into the Macintosh operating system — select this check box. But for the most accurate display, leave the option turned off and live with the periodic screen fluctuations.

✑ **Use Diffusion Dither (on):** Here's another option for you folks working on 8-bit screens. Where the previous option controls the colors that are used, this option controls the pattern of dithered pixels. Photoshop offers a naturalistic "diffusion" dither that looks very nice on-screen. But because the diffusion dither follows no specific pattern, you sometimes see distinct edges between selected and deselected portions of your image after applying a filter or some other effect. You can get rid of these edges and resort to a more geometric dither pattern by turning this check box off.

Turning off the Use Diffusion Dither check box is an awfully drastic (not to mention ugly) solution. The better way to eliminate the occasional visual disharmony is to force Photoshop to redraw the entire image. You can press ⌘-Option-0 or perform some other zoom function.

♺ **Video LUT Animation (off):** If you've ever worked inside one of Photoshop's color correction dialog boxes — such as Levels or Curves — and turned off the Preview check box, you've seen Photoshop's video look-up table animation in progress. Photoshop changes the LUT on the fly according to your specifications, in effect applying the color correction to the entire screen. It's not a real preview — in fact, it's pretty lousy. Video LUT animation doesn't account for selections, and it doesn't properly preview CMYK images. I go into more detail on this option in Chapter 18, but for now, turn it off.

Those of you familiar with previous editions of this book may notice that I've changed my assessment of this option 180 degrees. Well, live and learn. I had previously deferred to Adobe's judgment on this option. But two additional years of experience and a few heated conversations with colleagues has shed new light — Video LUT Animation sacrifices essential color accuracy with little discernible benefit.

The *only* reason to keep Video LUT Animation on is to view black and white clipping from the Levels dialog box. And if you know how to read a histogram, I argue that even this function is unnecessary. To find out way more than you ever wanted to learn about this topic, read Chapter 18.

♺ **Painting Cursors (Brush Size):** When you use a paint or edit tool, Photoshop can display one of three cursors. The default Standard cursor looks like a paintbrush, airbrush, finger, or whatever. These cursors are great if you have problems keeping track of what tool you selected, but otherwise they border on childish.

The Precise and Brush Size options are more functional. Precise displays crosshairs, the same ones that appear when you press the Caps Lock key (as explained back in "The cursors" section earlier in this chapter).

Brush Size shows the actual size of the brush up to 300 screen pixels in diameter. This means that if the zoom ratio is 50 percent and the brush size is 500 pixels wide, the brush only appears 250 pixels wide on-screen. But if you switch to the actual-pixels view, the brush size is too large to display, and the standard cursor appears instead. In the final analysis, the Brush Size option is the setting of choice.

When Standard or Brush Size is selected, pressing the Caps Lock key displays the precise crosshair cursors. But when Precise is selected, pressing Caps Lock displays the actual brush size.

↪ **Other Cursors (Standard):** Again, you can select Standard to get the regular cursors or Precise to get crosshairs. I prefer to leave this option set to Standard, because you can easily access the crosshairs by pressing Caps Lock. The Precise option locks you into crosshairs whether you like it or not.

Transparency & Gamut

Press ⌘-4 to switch to the Transparency & Gamut panel shown in Figure 2-16. The options in this panel change how Photoshop displays two conceptual items — transparent space behind layers, and RGB colors that can't be expressed in CMYK printing.

Figure 2-16
The options in this panel affect how Photoshop represents transparency and out-of-gamut colors on-screen.

The options are arranged into two groups — Transparency Settings and Gamut Warning — as explained in the following sections.

Transparency settings

Just as the Earth spins around in empty space, a Photoshop image rests on a layer of absolute transparency. By default, Photoshop represents this transparency as a gray checkerboard pattern. (What better way to demonstrate nothingness? I might have preferred a few lines from a Jean-Paul Sartre play, but no matter.) You get a brief glimpse of this checkerboard when you first open an image or switch to Photoshop from another application.

When viewing a layer independently of others, Photoshop fills the see-through portions of the layer with the checkerboard. So it is essential that the checkerboard stand out from the layer itself. You can customize the size of the checkers and the color of the squares using the Grid Size and Grid Colors pop-up menus. You can also click on the color swatches to define your own colors.

To lift colors from the image window, move your cursor outside the Preferences dialog box to get the eyedropper. Click on a color to change the color of the white checkers; Option-click to change the gray ones.

If you own a TrueVision NuVista+ board or some other 32-bit device that permits chroma keying, you can select the Use Video Alpha check box to view a television signal in the transparent area behind a layer. Unless you work in video production, you don't need to worry about this option.

Gamut warning

If Photoshop can display a color on-screen, but it can't accurately print the color, the color is said to be "out of gamut." You can choose View ⇨ Gamut Warning to coat all out-of-gamut colors with gray. I'm not a big fan of this command — View ⇨ CMYK Preview is much more useful — but if you use it, you don't have to accept gray as the out-of-gamut coating. Change the color by clicking on the Color swatch, and lower the Opacity value to request a translucent coating.

Units & Rulers

The fifth Preferences panel is Units & Rulers, and hence you reach the panel by pressing ⌘-5. Shown in Figure 2-17, the options in this panel allow you to change the predominant system of measurement used throughout the program.

Figure 2-17
Go to the Units & Rulers panel to change the system of measurement.

 Whenever the rulers are visible, the Units & Rulers panel is just a double-click away. Choose View ⇨ Show Rulers (⌘-R) to see the rulers on-screen, then double-click on either the horizontal or vertical ruler.

Rulers

Start by selecting the desired unit of measure from the Units pop-up menu. When you're first learning Photoshop, it's tempting to go with inches or picas, but experienced Photoshop artists use pixels. Because you can change the resolution of an image at any time, the only constant is pixels. An image measures a fixed number of pixels high by a fixed number of pixels wide — you can print those pixels as large or as small as you want. (To learn more about resolution, read Chapter 4.)

Column size

The Column Size options allow you to size images according to columns in a newsletter or magazine. Just enter the width of your columns and the size of the gutter better columns into the Width and Gutter option boxes. Then use File ⇨ New or Image ⇨ Image Size to specify the number of columns assigned to the width of the image. I explain these commands in more detail in Chapter 4.

Point/pica size

The last option in the Units & Rulers panel may be the most obscure of all Photoshop options. In case you aren't familiar with points and picas, there are exactly 12 points in a pica, and about 6.06 picas in an inch.

Well, because picas are almost evenly divisible into inches, the folks who came up with the PostScript printing language decided to bag the difference and define a pica as exactly $1/6$ inch. This makes a point exactly $1/72$ inch.

But a few purists didn't take to it. They found that their new electronic documents weren't quite matching their old paste-up documents, and — well, I guess life pretty much lost its meaning. So Adobe had to go back and add the Traditional (72.7 points/inch) option to keep everyone happy.

I happen to prefer the nontraditional PostScript definition of points. This way, a pixel on screen translates to a point on paper when you print an image at 72 ppi (the standard screen resolution). Call me a soulless technodweeb, but computer imaging makes more sense when you can measure points and pixels without resorting to a calculator. The old ways are dead; long live the $1/72$-inch point.

Guides & Grid

Someone at Adobe said, "Let the preference settings continue." And, lo, there was Guides & Grid, which could be accessed by all who pressed ⌘-6, and viewed by all who cast an eye on Figure 2-18. This panel lets you modi-

fy the colors of Photoshop 4's new guides, and specify the size of
Photoshop 4's new grid.

Figure 2-18
Use these options to adjust
the size of the grid, and the
way both the grid and ruler
guides appear on-screen.

 You can display the Preferences dialog box and go directly to the Guides &
Grid panel by ⌘-double-clicking on a guide. (To create a guide, drag from
the horizontal or vertical ruler into the image.)

I explain these options in more detail in Chapter 13, but for the moment, here are
some very brief descriptions.

Guides

Select a color for horizontal and vertical ruler guides from the Color pop-up menu.
To list a color from the image, move your cursor outside the Preferences dialog box
and click in the image window with the eyedropper. You can also view guides as
solid lines or dashes by selecting an option from the Style pop-up menu.

Grid

Select a color for the grid from the Color menu, or Option-click in the image window to lift a color from the image. Then decide how the grid lines look by selecting
a Style option. The Dots setting is the least intrusive.

The Gridline Every value determines the increments for the visible grid marks on
screen. But the Subdivision value sets the real grid. For example, if you request a
grid mark every two inches with four subdivisions — as in Figure 2-18 — Photoshop
snaps selections and layers in half-inch increments (two inches divided by four).

Plug-ins & Scratch Disk

Press ⌘-7 to advance to the panel shown in Figure 2-19. Each time you launch Photoshop, the program searches for plug-in modules and identifies a scratch disk. You have to tell Photoshop where the plug-ins can be found and where the temporary scratch files should go.

The settings in this panel don't take affect until the next time you launch Photoshop. This means you have to quit Photoshop and restart the program.

Figure 2-19
Tell Photoshop where to find plug-ins and where to put scratch files using these options.

Plug-ins folder

By default, the plug-ins are located in a folder called Plug-ins that resides in the same folder as the Photoshop application. But you can rename the folder and put it anywhere you like. You can even organize your plug-ins into multiple folders, loading one folder of plug-ins one day, and another folder the next.

If you do change the location of the plug-ins, tell Photoshop where to find them by clicking on the Choose button and locating the desired folder on disk. When you find the folder, select it (don't enter it) and click on the Select button at the bottom of the Open dialog box. Click on the None button to turn all plug-ins off.

You can tell Photoshop to select a different plug-ins folder before it starts up by pressing and holding ⌘ and Option during the launch cycle. This eliminates the need to restart the program because you're telling Photoshop where to find the plug-ins before it launches.

Scratch disks

By default, Photoshop assumes that you have just one hard disk. It therefore stores its temporary virtual memory documents — called *scratch files* — on the same disk that contains your system software. However, if you have more than one drive available, you might want to tell Photoshop to look elsewhere.

For example, my Mac is equipped with two internal hard drives, one 1GB drive that contains the system, and a 4GB drive that contains applications and workaday files. The 4GB drive is partitioned into two 2GB segments, called PowerShrine.1 and PowerShrine.2. (Let's face it, I spend most of my time praying that my computer will work, so I decided to make it official.) Because PowerShrine.1 has the most free space, I selected it from the Primary pop-up menu. On the off chance that my images get so huge that Photoshop has to look for another drive, I selected PowerShrine.2 from the Secondary pop-up menu.

Photoshop is very good about freeing up disk space when you close images, and it completely deletes the scratch files when you quit the program. It even has a con-tingency plan for those occasional times when you crash. After your computer starts backup, you'll notice that the Trash icon is full. Just choose Special ⇨ Empty Trash to throw the old useless scratch file away.

Adobe advises against using removable media such as SyQuest and Zip dri-ves as a scratch disk. Removable media is typically less reliable and slower than a permanent drive. If you must use a SyQuest or Zip drive, you're bet-ter off saving your images to the cartridge and using a hard disk for the scratch files.

You have to restart Photoshop before the new scratch disks take effect. But as with the plug-ins folder, you can reassign a scratch disk during startup by pressing ⌘ and Option. The trick is to press the keys at the right time. When launching Photoshop, keep an eye on the start-up screen. Near the beginning, you'll see the message *Scanning for plug-ins*. Wait until the indi-vidual plug-in names start flashing by, then press and hold the ⌘ and Option keys. In a few seconds — after the *Initializing* message — Photoshop displays a small dialog box that lets you assign new scratch disks. Just select the disks and press Return; there's no need to restart the program.

Image cache

Ever since Photoshop 3 came out, Adobe has received a fair amount of flack from high-end users who demand faster image handling. Programs like Live Picture and xRes take seconds to apply complex operations to super-huge photographs, while

Photoshop putters along for a minute or more. Granted, Live Picture and xRes aren't nearly as capable as Photoshop, but they are faster.

 Unfortunately, Photoshop 4 isn't quite the speed breakthrough that many had hoped it would be. In fact, rumor has it that the big speed bump awaits us in Version 5. But while we wait, Photoshop 4 has made modest improvements. The program sports a new caching scheme that speeds up operations at reduced view sizes. You can adjust this feature by pressing ⌘-8 in the Preferences dialog box. This displays the Image Cache panel, shown in Figure 2-20.

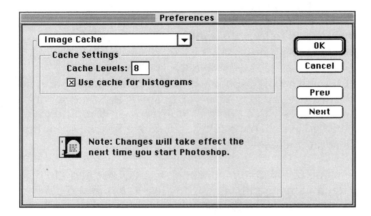

Figure 2-20
Photoshop's new caching capabilities speed up the processing of very large images.

Cache levels

Photoshop has been criticized for its lack of a "pyramid-style" file format, such as Live Picture's IVUE or xRes' LRG. Both IVUE and LRG store an image several times over at progressively smaller and smaller image sizes, which are called *downsamplings*. For example, the program would save a full view of the image, a 50-percent view, a 25-percent view, and so on. Live Picture or xRes can then load and edit just the portion of the image that's visible on screen, greatly accelerating functions.

Photoshop's alternative is *image caching*. Rather than saving the downsamplings to disk, Photoshop generates the reduced images in RAM. By default, the Cache Levels value is set to 4, the medium value. This means Photoshop can cache up to four downsamplings — at 100, 50, 33, and 25 percent — which permits the program to apply operations more quickly at reduced view sizes. For example, if you choose a color correction command at the 50 percent view size, it previews much faster than normal because Photoshop has to modify a quarter as many pixels on screen.

The downside is that Photoshop has to cache downsamplings in RAM, which takes away memory that could be used to hold the image. If you have lots of RAM (60MB or more) and you frequently work on large images (20MB or larger), then you'll probably want to raise the value to the maximum, 8. The lost memory is worth the speed boost. However, if you have little RAM (say, 16MB or less) and you usually work on small images (4MB or smaller), you may want to reduce the Cache Levels value. When files are small, RAM is better allocated to storing images rather than caching them.

Use cache for histograms

The Use Cache for Histograms check box tells Photoshop whether to generate the histograms that appear in the Levels and Threshold dialog boxes based on the cached sampling or the original image. As I explain in Chapter 18, a *histogram* is a bar graph of the colors in an image. When you choose a command like Image ⇨ Adjust ⇨ Levels, Photoshop has to spend a few seconds graphing the colors. If you turn the Use Cache for Histograms check box on, Photoshop graphs the colors in the reduced screen view, which takes less time but is also less accurate. Turn the check box off for slower, more accurate histograms.

Generally speaking, I say leave the option on. A histogram is just a visual indicator — most folks will be unable to judge the difference between a downsampled histogram and a fully accurate one.

Again, if you're working in very large images and you have the Cache Levels value maxed out at 8, you should probably leave this check box selected. But if you have to reduce the Cache Levels value, turn the check box off. Histograms are the first thing that can go.

Annotating an Image

If you work for a stock agency or you distribute your work by some other means, you'll be interested in Photoshop's image annotation feature. You can attach captions, credits, bylines, photo location and date, copyright, and other information, as prescribed by the IPTC (International Press Telecommunications Council). We're talking official worldwide guidelines here.

Choose File ⇨ File Info to display the six-paneled File Info dialog box. You switch from one panel to another by pressing ⌘-1 through ⌘-6. All six panels appear in Figure 2-21.

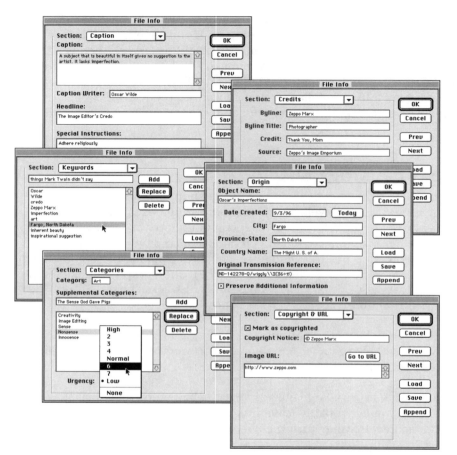

Figure 2-21
You can document your image in encyclopedic detail using the wealth of options in the File Info dialog box.

Though sprawling with options, this dialog box is pretty straightforward. For example, if you want to create a caption, enter it into the Caption option box, which can hold up to 2,000 characters. The Keywords panel allows you to enter a list of descriptive words that will help folks find the image if it's part of a large electronic library. Just enter the desired word and press Return (or click on the Add button) to add it to the list. Alternatively, you can replace a word in the list by selecting it and pressing Return (or clicking on Replace). Browser utilities such as Fetch from Extensis let you search images by keyword, as do some dedicated image servers.

The Categories panel may seem foreign to anyone who hasn't worked with a news service. Many large news services use a system of three-character categories to file and organize stories and photographs. If you're familiar with this system, you can enter the three-character code into the Category option box and even throw in a few supplemental categories up to 32 characters long. Finally, use the Urgency pop-up menu to specify the editorial timeliness of the photo. The High option tells editors around the world to hold the presses and holler for their copy boys. Low is for celebrity mug shots that can be tossed in the morgue to be hauled out only if the subject of the photograph decides to do something diverting like lead police on a nail-biting tour of the Los Angeles freeway system.

 The new Copyright & URL panel lets you add a copyright notice to your image and include a World Wide Web address (if you have one). Then, if a person has your image open in Photoshop 4, he or she can come to this panel, click on the Go to URL button, and find out more information about your stuff (whatever your stuff may be).

File information is saved with an image regardless of the format you use. Photoshop merely tacks the text on to the image as a resource. Because you cannot format the text in the File Info dialog box, it consumes very little space on disk — one byte per character — which means that all the text in Figure 2-20 doesn't even take up 1K.

You can also save the information from the File Info dialog box by clicking on the Save button. Or open information saved to disk previously by clicking on Load. To add the information from a saved file to the information you've already entered into the File Info dialog box, click on the Append button.

Shortcuts and Scripts

In This Chapter

- Selecting tools from the keyboard
- A few fantastic palette shortcuts
- Comprehensive shortcut table comparing Photoshop 4 with Version 3
- Recording scripts in the Actions palette
- Editing and playing recorded commands
- Batch-processing entire folders of images

Keystrokes and Modifiers

Unlike most graphics programs, Photoshop invests a lot of its capabilities in the keyboard. There are literally hundreds of functions that are available exclusively at the press of a key. For example, Photoshop offers no command that adds the next selection outline you draw to the previous one. There is no command that fills just the opaque areas of a selection with the background color, nor is there a command that brings up the last-used color correction settings. In fact, every one of these options is out of your reach if you don't know the right key. The keyboard may seem like an unlikely artistic tool, but it is a powerful and essential ally in Photoshop.

There are two basic varieties of keyboard tricks. Some keystroke combinations produce immediate effects. For example, pressing ⌘ and Delete together fills the selection with the background color. Other keys change the behavior of a tool or command. Pressing Shift while dragging with the lasso tool adds the lassoed area to the previous selection. As a result, Shift, Option, ⌘, and Control are known collectively as *modifiers*.

Photoshop 4.0 offers one more kind of keyboard trick that you'll want to check out. *Scripts* are collections of commands that Photoshop can play over and over again in a specified order and with specified settings. You create scripts using the new Actions palette, which I explain at length later in this chapter. After creating a script, you can assign a keyboard equivalent to it, or you can play the script by ⌘-double-clicking on it. Even the shortcuts have shortcuts.

But wonderful as all this may sound, I feel compelled to share one pretty significant bit of bad news that might cast something of a cloud on your otherwise sunny day. If you're familiar with previous versions of Photoshop, much of what you know is wrong. It's an exaggeration to say that *every* technique involving the ⌘ or Option key has changed, but it's not far from the truth. For example, when using the marquee tool, you now Option-drag to subtract from a selection, ⌘-drag to move the selection, and ⌘-Option-drag to clone the selection. Photoshop 4 has gone and turned our worlds upside-down.

But never fear. This chapter addresses new and old users alike. If you're having problems making the keyboard transition to Photoshop 4, skim through this chapter, practice a few of the techniques, and then take a much-deserved rest in your favorite Barco-Lounger. After a few hours of uninterrupted downtime, the initial shock should pass, and you'll be ready to tackle the rest of the book with an open mind.

Hidden Shortcuts and Modifiers

Shortcuts enable you to initiate operations without resorting to the laborious task of choosing commands from menus or clicking on some tool icon until your arm falls off. Many shortcuts are fairly obvious. For example, Photoshop lists keyboard equivalents for its commands next to the command in the menu. You can choose File ⇨ New by pressing ⌘-N, choose Edit ⇨ Undo by pressing ⌘-Z, choose Select ⇨ All by pressing ⌘-A, and so on. But most of Photoshop's shortcuts are hidden. And, wouldn't you know it, the hidden ones are the most essential.

Control-clicking

 The best hidden trick in Photoshop 4 is Control-clicking. Press the Control key, then press and hold the mouse button in the image window. You get a pop-up menu of commands. For example, if you Control-click with the lasso tool while a selection is active, you get the list of commands that are shown in Figure 3-1. Though there are certainly other commands you can apply to a selection, these are some of the most common.

Figure 3-1
If you get stuck, Control-click to bring up a pop-up menu of helpful commands. It's more productive than praying to your computer.

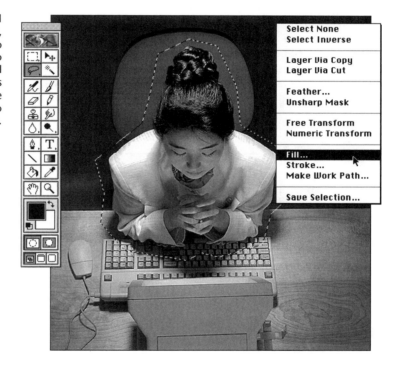

The Control-click pop-up menu is *context-sensitive*, which means that it changes to suit the active tool and the current state of the image (selected or not). You can also Control-click on items such as brushes and layers in the palettes.

Interestingly enough, Adobe developed this feature to satisfy the typical Windows 95 user, who is armed with a two-button mouse. When you click the right mouse button in Photoshop 4 and other Windows 95 programs, you see a pop-up menu.

If you envy this right mouse button action — it is admittedly easier than Control-clicking — you can purchase a two-button mouse from a company like Kensington or Mouse Systems and set the second mouse button to Control-click. There are even keyboards that have two-button touchpads built into them.

My favorite solution is the one most likely to appeal to artists. The ArtPad II is a drawing tablet from Wacom that now includes a four-button stylus — the pen nib, two side switches, and an eraser. As shown in Figure 3-2, you can modify the performance of either of the side switches. I personally set one switch to "click lock," which locks down the mouse button, making it easier to select commands from a pop-up menu. And I set the other to Control-click.

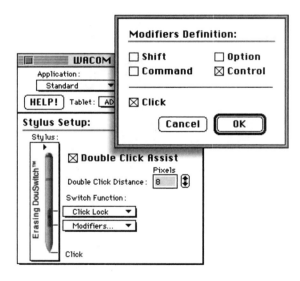

Figure 3-2
You can set the switch of a Wacom stylus to Control-click so you don't have to waste your valuable time pressing Control manually.

Toolbox shortcuts

Usability has always been one of Photoshop's great strengths. One of the ways Photoshop expedites your workflow is to permit you to select tools from the keyboard. This way, you can use one tool, press a key, and immediately start in with another tool without losing your place in the image.

 Best of all, the shortcuts work even when the toolbox is hidden. The only reason I even look at the toolbox is to monitor which tool is selected so I don't get mixed up.

Figure 3-3 tells the whole, wonderful story. Just press the appropriate key, as shown in the figure — no ⌘, Option, or other modifiers required. Many of the shortcuts make sense. *M* selects the marquee tool, *L* is for lasso tool. But then there are the weird ones, like *K* for paint bucKet, *O* for dOdge, *U* for smUdge, and my favorite, *I* for I-dropper. The only alphabetical key that goes unused is *J*.

If you're used to Photoshop 3, you'll notice three changes to Version 4: The Y, T, and P keys have changed. Y used to select the type tool, now it's *T*. T used to select the pen tool, now it's *P*. And P used to select the pencil, now it's *Y*. Is it possible someone at Adobe is using a pYncYl?

Figure 3-3
Press these keys to select tools and activate controls in Photoshop 4.

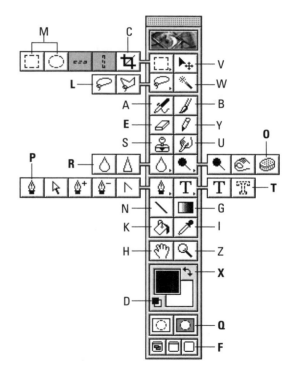

The keys that appear in bold type in Figure 3-3 act as toggles. For example, if you press M once, you get the last marquee tool used (rectangular by default). Press M again to select the other marquee tool. Other toggles work as follows:

    ∞ **L** switches between the standard lasso tool that we all know and love from the ancient days of MacPaint, and the new polygonal lasso tool.

  ✐ **E** changes between the four styles of eraser — paintbrush, airbrush, pencil, and block. You can monitor the active style by pressing Return to display the Eraser Options panel.

  ✐ **R** switches between the blur and sharpen tools.

  ✐ **O** toggles between the dodge, burn, and sponge tools.

  ✐ **P** switches between the five paths tools — from the pen tool to the arrow tool and so on down the list.

  ✐ **T** selects the standard type tool or the new type mask tool.

  ✐ **X** swaps the foreground and background colors and then swaps them back again.

  ✐ **Q** enters the quick mask mode and then exits it.

  ✐ **F** takes you from one window mode to the next.

Palette shortcuts

Photoshop also lets you access a few palette options from the keyboard. I've documented these options in Figure 3-4. But the figure is sufficiently peculiar that I thought I'd back it up with the following list. And as with the tool keys, each of these shortcuts works even when the palette is hidden:

  ✐ Press the bracket keys [and] to respectively decrease and increase the brush shape when a paint or edit tool is selected.

  ✐ Press Shift-[to select the first brush shape (generally the single-pixel brush). Press Shift-] to select the last brush shape.

  ✐ When a paint, edit, or fill tool is selected, press a number key to change the Opacity, Pressure, or Exposure setting assigned to that tool in the Options palette. Lowered values let you create translucent strokes and fills. Press 1 to change the value to 10 percent, 2 for 20 percent, all the way up to 0 for 100 percent. Or enter the exact value — such as 15 percent — by typing 1-5 right in a row.

  ✐ When any other tool is selected — whether a selection, navigation, type, or eyedropper tool — pressing a number key changes the Opacity value assigned to a floating selection or layer. Again, press one number to modify the Opacity setting in 10-percent increments; press two numbers to specify an exact Opacity setting.

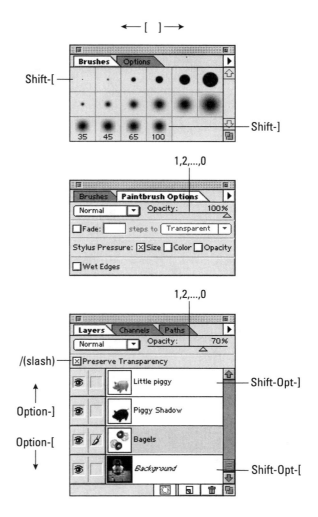

Figure 3-4
You can take advantage of these palette shortcuts even when the palettes themselves are hidden.

↩ Press the forward slash key (/) to turn on and off the Preserve Transparency check box. This is easily one of the least known shortcuts in all of Photoshop. But it's very useful, as I explain further in Chapter 13.

↩ Press Option-] to ascend through the layers. Press Option-[to descend. (Experienced users should note that the old Photoshop 3 shortcuts — ⌘-] and ⌘-[— now change the order of the active layer.)

↩ Press Shift-Option-] to activate the top layer in the image. Press Shift-Option-[to go all the way down to the background layer.

The Great Grandmother of All Shortcut Tables

As I write this, Saddam Hussein is back in the news. No doubt he's in the news as you're reading this, too. He's a compulsive invader. I mean, can you imagine living next door to the guy? You'd wake up one day and find out he'd taken over your garage. Anyway, I know he's not a very popular fellow — what with being a blood-thirsty dictator and all — but you have to give him credit for that "mother of all battles" thing. He really added to our language. I'm sure we'll be joking about the mothers of all this and that for years to come.

 But still, the phrase doesn't quite do justice to Table 3-1. Here's a list that covers every keystroke and modifier available to Photoshop 4. So far, we've just barely scratched the surface — there are tons of shortcuts left to discuss. Add to it that about half of these shortcuts are new to Photoshop 4, and we face a monumental challenge. So I've done something that you probably won't find in any other book. I've created a table that tells you both the old Photoshop 3 keyboard shortcut and the new Photoshop 4 equivalent. If the shortcut has changed in Version 4, I've indicated it in **bold type** so you can more quickly scan the list.

Now, keep in mind, a shortcut isn't liable to make much sense if you aren't familiar with the feature it facilitates. I explain both features and their shortcuts in context in later chapters. The intent of the table is to serve as a reference that you can revisit over and over as your knowledge of Photoshop grows. The more you learn, the more useful the table becomes.

So fold the corner of this page, tag it with a sticky note, or stab it with a bayonet. This isn't your everyday average mother of all shortcuts table. This table is so huge and all-encompassing that it skips two whole generations. Table 3-1 is a great grandmother — and you know how powerful grandmothers can be!

Table 3-1	Photoshop's Hidden Shortcuts and Modifiers	
Operation	*Old Photoshop 3 shortcut*	*New Photoshop 4 shortcut*
	Menu commands	
Actual Pixels	*new command*	⌘-**Option-zero (0)**
Auto Levels	*none*	⌘-**Shift-L**
Brightness/Contrast	⌘-B	*none*

Operation	Old Photoshop 3 shortcut	New Photoshop 4 shortcut
Menu commands		
Bring Layer Forward	*new command*	⌘-]
Bring Layer to Front	*new command*	⌘-**Shift-]**
Clear	Delete	Delete
Close	⌘-W	⌘-W
CMYK Preview	*none*	⌘-**Y**
Color Balance	⌘-Y	⌘-**B**
Color Balance, with last settings	⌘-Option-Y	⌘-**Option-B**
Copy	⌘-C	⌘-C
Copy Merged	*none*	⌘-**Shift-C**
Curves	⌘-M	⌘-M
Curves, with last settings	⌘-Option-M	⌘-Option-M
Cut	⌘-X	⌘-X
Desaturate	*none*	⌘-**Shift-U**
Defloat	⌘-J	⌘-**E**
Equalize	⌘-E	*none*
Fade Filter	*new command*	⌘-**Shift-F**
Feather Selection	*none*	⌘-**Shift-D**
Fill	Shift-Delete	Shift-Delete
Filter, repeat last	⌘-F	⌘-F
Filter, repeat with new settings	⌘-Option-F	⌘-Option-F
Fit on Screen	*new command*	⌘-**zero (0)**
Float Selection	⌘-J	⌘-**Option-arrow**
Free Transform	*new command*	⌘-**T**
Gamut Warning	*none*	⌘-**Shift-Y**
Grid, show or hide	*new command*	⌘-**quote (")**
Group with Previous Layer	*new command*	⌘-**G**
Grow Selection	⌘-G	*none*
Guides, show or hide	*new command*	⌘-**semicolon (;)**
Hide Edges	⌘-H	⌘-H
Hide Path	*new command*	⌘-**Shift-H**
Hue/Saturation	⌘-U	⌘-U
Hue/Saturation, with last settings	⌘-Option-U	⌘-Option-U
Inverse Selection	*none*	⌘-**Shift-I**
Invert	⌘-I	⌘-I

(continued)

Table 3-1 *(continued)*

Operation	Old Photoshop 3 shortcut	New Photoshop 4 shortcut
Menu commands		
Layer Via Copy	*new command*	⌘-**J**
Layer Via Cut	*new command*	⌘-**Shift-J**
Levels	⌘-L	⌘-L
Levels, with last settings	⌘-Option-L	⌘-Option-L
Lock Guides	*new command*	⌘-**Option-semicolon (;)**
Merge Down	*none*	⌘-**Shift-E**
Merge Visible	*none*	⌘-**E**
New	⌘-N	⌘-N
New, with default settings	⌘-Option-N	⌘-Option-N
Numeric Transform	*new command*	⌘-**Shift-T**
Open	⌘-O	⌘-O
Page Setup	*none*	⌘-**Shift-P**
Paste	⌘-V	⌘-V
Paste Into	*none*	⌘-**Shift-V**
Preferences	⌘-K	⌘-K
Preferences, last panel	*none*	⌘-**Option-K**
Print	⌘-P	⌘-P
Quit	⌘-Q	⌘-Q
Redo	⌘-Z	⌘-Z
Rulers, show or hide	⌘-R	⌘-R
Save	⌘-S	⌘-S
Save As	*none*	⌘-**Shift-S**
Save a Copy	*none*	⌘-**Option-S**
Select All	⌘-A	⌘-A
Select None	⌘-D	⌘-D
Send Layer Backward	*new command*	⌘-**[**
Send Layer to Back	*new command*	⌘-**Shift-[**
Snap to Grid	*new command*	⌘-**Shift-quote (")**
Snap to Guides	*new command*	⌘-**Shift-semicolon (;)**
Threshold	⌘-T	*none*
Undo	⌘-Z	⌘-Z
Ungroup Layers	*new command*	⌘-**Shift-G**

Operation	Old Photoshop 3 shortcut	New Photoshop 4 shortcut
Menu commands		
Zoom In	⌘-plus (+)	⌘-plus (+)
Zoom In, all the way	⌘-Option-plus (+)	**None**
Zoom Out	⌘-minus (−)	⌘-minus (−)
Zoom Out, all the way	⌘-Option-minus (−)	⌘-Option-minus (−)
Navigation		
Scroll image with hand tool	spacebar-drag	spacebar-drag **or drag in Navigator palette**
Scroll up or down one screen	press Page Up or Page Down	press Page Up or Page Down
Scroll up or down slightly	Shift-Page Up or Shift-Page Down	Shift-Page Up or Shift-Page Down
Scroll up or down exactly one frame in FilmStrip file	Shift-Page Up or Shift-Page Down	Shift-Page Up or Shift-Page Down
Switch to upper left corner	press Home key	press Home key
Switch to lower right corner	press End key	press End key
Zoom in without changing window size	⌘-spacebar-click	⌘-spacebar-click **or ⌘-Option-plus (+)**
Magnify to custom zoom ratio	⌘-spacebar-drag	⌘-spacebar-drag **or ⌘-drag in Navigator palette**
Zoom in and change window size to fit	⌘-plus (+)	⌘-plus (+)
Zoom out without changing window size	Option-spacebar-click	Option-spacebar-click **or ⌘-Option-minus (−)**
Zoom out and change window size to fit	⌘-minus (−)	⌘-minus (−)
Zoom to 100%	double-click on zoom tool icon	**⌘-Option-zero (0)** or double-click on zoom tool icon
Fit image on screen	double-click on hand tool icon	**⌘-zero (0)** or double-click on hand tool icon
Apply zoom value but keep magnification box active	*new feature*	**Shift-Return**
Painting and editing		
Display Options palette	Return	Return
Display crosshair cursor	Caps Lock	Caps Lock
Revert image with magic eraser	Option-drag with eraser	Option-drag with eraser
Cycle through eraser styles	Option-click on eraser tool icon or press E key	Option-click on eraser tool icon or press E key

(continued)

Table 3-1 (continued)

Operation	Old Photoshop 3 shortcut	New Photoshop 4 shortcut
		Painting and editing
Specify an area to clone	Option-click with rubber stamp	Option-click with rubber stamp
Cycle through rubber stamp options	none	**Option-click on rubber stamp tool icon or press S key**
Dip into the foreground color when smearing	Option-drag with smudge tool	Option-drag with smudge tool
Cycle through focus tools	Option-click on focus tool icon or press R key	Option-click on focus tool icon or press R key
Sharpen with the blur tool or blur with the sharpen tool	Option-drag	Option-drag
Cycle through toning tools	Option-click on toning tool icon or press O key	Option-click on toning tool icon or press O key
Darken with the dodge tool or lighten with the burn tool	Option-drag	Option-drag
Paint or edit in a straight line	click and then Shift-click	click and then Shift-click
Change opacity, pressure, or exposure in 10% increments	press number key (1 through 0)	press number key (1 through 0)
Change opacity, pressure, or exposure in 1% increments	none	**press two number keys in a row**
Change brush mode	select mode from Options palette	select mode from Options palette **or Control-drag in image window**
Display or hide Brushes palette	F5	F5
Cycle through brush shapes	press bracket key, [or]	press bracket key, [or]
Switch to first shape in Brushes palette	Shift-[	Shift-[
Switch to last shape in Brushes palette	Shift-]	Shift-]
Delete shape from Brushes palette	⌘-click on brush shape	⌘-click on brush shape
Create new brush shape	click in empty area of palette	click in empty area of palette
Edit brush shape	double-click on brush shape	double-click on brush shape

Operation	Old Photoshop 3 shortcut	New Photoshop 4 shortcut
Applying colors		
Lift foreground color from image	Option-click with paint tool or click with eyedropper	Option-click with paint tool or click with eyedropper
Lift background color from image	Option-click with eyedropper	Option-click with eye dropper
Lift foreground color from color bar at bottom of Color palette	click color bar	click color bar
Lift background color from color bar	Option-click color bar	Option-click color bar
Display or hide Color palette	F6	F6
Cycle through color bars	Shift-click on color bar	Shift-click on color bar
Specify new color bar	⌘-click on color bar	⌘-click on color bar
Lift foreground color from Swatches palette	click on swatch	click on swatch
Lift background color from Swatches palette	Option-click on swatch	Option-click on swatch
Delete swatch from palette	⌘-click on swatch	⌘-click on swatch
Replace swatch with foreground color	Shift-click on swatch	Shift-click on swatch
Add new swatch to palette	click in empty area of palette or Shift-Option-click on swatch	click in empty area of palette or Shift-Option-click on swatch
Fill selection or layer with foreground color	Option-Delete	Option-Delete
Fill layer with foreground color but preserve transparency	*none*	**Shift-Option-Delete**
Fill selection on background layer with background color	Delete	Delete
Fill selection on *any* layer with background color	*none*	**⌘-Delete**
Fill layer with background color but preserve transparency	*none*	**Shift-⌘-Delete**
Display Fill dialog box	Shift-Delete	Shift-Delete
Display Stroke dialog box	*none*	**Control-drag to Stroke command with selection tool**

(continued)

Table 3-1 *(continued)*

Operation	Old Photoshop 3 shortcut	New Photoshop 4 shortcut
Selections		
Select everything	⌘-A	⌘-A
Deselect everything	⌘-D	⌘-D
Hide or show marching ants	⌘-H	⌘-H
Feather the selection	*none*	**⌘-D**
Reverse the selection	*none*	**⌘-Shift-I**
Draw out from center with marquee tool	Option-drag	Option-drag
Constrain marquee to square or circle	press Shift while drawing shape	press Shift while drawing shape
Move shape with marquee tool	*none*	**press spacebar while drawing shape**
Draw straight-sided selection outline	Option-click with lasso tool	Option-click with lasso tool **or press L to switch to polygonal lasso tool**
Add to selection	Shift-drag or Shift-click with selection tool	Shift-drag or Shift-click with selection tool
Subtract from selection	⌘-drag or ⌘-click with selection tool	**Option-drag or Option-click with selection tool**
Retain intersected portion of selection	Shift-⌘-drag or Shift-⌘-click with selection tool	**Shift-Option-drag or Shift-Option-click with selection tool**
Temporarily access magic wand	press Control when selection tool is active	*none*
Add character outlines to a selection	*new feature*	**Shift-click with type mask tool**
Cut letter-shaped holes into a selection	*new feature*	**Option-click with type mask tool**
Retain areas where character outlines and selection intersect	*new feature*	**Shift-Option-click with type mask tool**
Temporarily access move tool	*none*	*none*
Move selection	drag with selection or move tool	drag with move tool **or ⌘-drag with other tool**
Constrain movement vertically or horizontally	press Shift while dragging selection	press Shift while dragging selection
Move selection in 1-pixel increments	press any arrow key	**⌘-arrow key**
Move selection in 10-pixel increments	Shift-arrow key	**⌘-Shift-arrow key**

Operation	Old Photoshop 3 shortcut	New Photoshop 4 shortcut
	Selections	
Clone selection	Option-drag with selection or move tool	Option-drag with move tool **or ⌘-Option-drag with other tool**
Clone selection in 1-pixel increments	Option-arrow key	**⌘-Option-arrow key**
Clone selection in 10-pixel increments	Shift-Option-arrow key	**⌘-Shift-Option-arrow key**
Clone selection to different image	drag selection from one window and drop it into another	**⌘-drag selection from one window and drop it into another**
Move selection outline independently of its contents	⌘-Option-drag with selection or move tool	**drag with selection tool**
Move selection outline in 1-pixel increments	⌘-Option-arrow key	**press any arrow key when selection tool is active**
Move selection outline in 10-pixel increments	⌘-Shift-Option-arrow key	**Shift-arrow key when selection tool is active**
Copy empty selection outline to different image	*none*	**drag selection from one window into another with selection tool**
Float selection in place	⌘-J	**⌘-Option-up arrow then press the down arrow key**
Drop floating selection	⌘-J	**⌘-E**
Drop fragment of floating selection	⌘-drag with type tool	*none*
Change opacity of floating selection in 10% increments	press number key (1 through 0) when selection tool is active	press number key (1 through 0) when selection tool is active
Change opacity of floating selection in 1% increments	*none*	**press two number keys in a row when selection tool is active**
Paste image into selection	*none*	**⌘-Shift-V**
Paste image behind selection	press Option and choose Edit ⇨ Paste Into	**⌘-Shift-Option-V**
	Layers	
Display or hide Layers palette	F7	F7
View single layer by itself	Option-click on eyeball icon in Layers palette	Option-click on eyeball icon in Layers palette
Create new empty layer	click on new layer icon at bottom of Layers palette	click on new layer icon at bottom of Layers palette

(continued)

Table 3-1 *(continued)*

Operation	Old Photoshop 3 shortcut	New Photoshop 4 shortcut
Layers		
Clone selection to new layer	none	⌘-J
Convert selection to new layer and leave hole behind	none	⌘-Shift-J
Convert floating selection to new layer	double-click on Floating Selection item in Layers palette	double-click on Floating Selection **or ⌘-Shift-J**
Clone entire layer to new layer	drag layer name onto page icon	drag layer name onto page icon **or ⌘-A, ⌘-J**
Ascend one layer	⌘-]	**Option-]**
Descend one layer	⌘-[	**Option-[**
Ascend to top layer	⌘-Option-]	**Shift-Option-]**
Descend to background layer	⌘-Option-[	**Shift-Option-[**
Go directly to layer that contains specific image	⌘-click on image with move tool	**⌘-Control-Option-click on image with any tool**
Preserve transparency of layer	press slash (/) key	press slash (/) key
Convert layer's transparency mask to selection outline	⌘-Option-T	**⌘-click on layer name in Layers palette**
Add transparency mask to selection	none	**⌘-Shift-click on layer name**
Subtract transparency mask from selection	none	**⌘-Option-click on layer name**
Retain intersection of transparency mask and selection	none	**⌘-Shift-Option-click on layer name**
Move entire layer	drag with move tool	drag with move tool **or ⌘-drag with other tool**
Move entire layer in 1-pixel increments	press any arrow key when move tool is active	**⌘-arrow key**
Move entire layer in 10-pixel increments	Shift-arrow key when move tool is active	**⌘-Shift-arrow key**
Bring layer forward one level	drag layer name in palette	⌘-]
Bring layer to front of file	drag layer name in palette	⌘-Shift-]
Send layer backward one level	drag layer name in palette	⌘-[
Send layer to back, just above the background layer	drag layer name in palette	⌘-Shift-[

Operation	Old Photoshop 3 shortcut	New Photoshop 4 shortcut
Layers		
Link layer with active layer	click in front of layer name	click in front of layer name
Change opacity of active layer in 10% increments	press number key (1 through 0) when selection tool is active	press number key (1 through 0) when selection tool is active
Change opacity of active layer in 1% increments	none	**press two number keys in a row when selection tool is active**
Edit blend options for layer	double-click on layer name in Layers palette	double-click on layer name in Layers palette
Adjust "fuzziness" in Layer Options dialog box	Option-drag slider triangle	Option-drag slider triangle
Merge layer with next layer down	none	**⌘-E**
Merge linked layers	none	**⌘-E**
Merge all visible layers	none	**⌘-Shift-E**
Copy merged version of selection to Clipboard	none	**⌘-Shift-C**
Clone contents of layer into next layer down	none	**⌘-Option-E**
Clone contents of linked layers to active layer	none	**⌘-Option-E**
Clone contents of all visible layers to active layer	Option-choose Merge Layers from Layers palette menu	**⌘-Shift-Option-E**
Group neighboring layers	Option-click on horizontal line in Layers palette	Option-click on horizontal line **or press ⌘-G**
Ungroup neighboring layers	Option-click on dotted line in Layers palette	Option-click on dotted line **or press ⌘-Shift-G**
Create adjustment layer	new feature	**⌘-click on page icon at bottom of Layers palette**
Save flattened copy of layered image	none	**⌘-Option-S**
Channels and masks		
Switch between independent color and mask channels	⌘-1 through ⌘-9	⌘-1 through ⌘-9
Switch to composite color channel	⌘-zero (0)	**⌘-tilde (~)**

(continued)

Table 3-1 *(continued)*

Operation	Old Photoshop 3 shortcut	New Photoshop 4 shortcut
Channels and masks		
Activate or deactivate color channel	Shift-click on channel name in Channels palette	Shift-click on channel name in Channels palette
Create channel mask from selection outline	click on mask icon at bottom of Channels palette	click on mask icon at bottom of Channels palette
View channel mask and image together	click on eyeball in front of hidden channel	click on eyeball in front of hidden channel
Convert channel mask to selection outline	press ⌘ and Option with number key or Option-click on name in Channels channel palette	press ⌘ and Option with number key **or ⌘-click on channel name in Channels palette**
Add channel mask to selection	Shift-Option-click on channel name	**⌘-Shift-click on channel name**
Subtract channel mask from selection	⌘-Option-click on channel name	⌘-Option-click on channel name
Retain intersection of channel mask and selection	⌘-Shift-Option-click on channel name	⌘-Shift-Option-click on channel name
Enter or exit quick mask mode	press Q key	press Q key
Toggle quick mask color over masked or selected area	Option-click on quick mask icon in toolbox	Option-click on quick mask icon in toolbox
Change quick mask color overlay	double-click on quick mask icon in toolbox	double-click on quick mask icon in toolbox
View quick mask independently of image	click on topmost eyeball in Channels palette	click on topmost eyeball in Channels palette
Create layer mask filled with white	choose Add Layer Mask from Layers palette menu	**click on mask icon at bottom of Layers palette**
Create layer mask filled with black	*none*	**Option-click on mask icon**
Create layer mask from selection outline	*none*	**click on mask icon**
Create layer mask that hides selection	*none*	**Option-click on mask icon**
Switch focus from layer mask to image	⌘-zero (0)	**⌘-tilde (~)**
Switch focus from image to layer mask	⌘-tilde (~)	**⌘-backslash (\)**

Operation	Old Photoshop 3 shortcut	New Photoshop 4 shortcut
Channels and masks		
View layer mask independently of image	Option-click on layer mask thumbnail in Layers palette	Option-click on layer mask thumbnail in Layers palette
View layer mask and image together	Shift-click on layer mask thumbnail	**Shift-Option-click on layer mask thumbnail**
Disable layer mask	⌘-click on layer mask thumbnail	**Shift-click on layer mask thumbnail**
Toggle link between layer and layer mask	*none*	**click between layer and mask thumbnails in Layers palette**
Convert layer mask to selection outline	⌘-Option-tilde (~)	**⌘-Option-backslash (\) or ⌘-click on layer mask thumbnail**
Add layer mask to selection	*none*	**⌘-Shift-click on layer mask thumbnail**
Subtract layer mask from selection	*none*	**⌘-Option-click on layer mask thumbnail**
Retain intersection of layer mask and selection	*none*	**⌘-Shift-Option-click on layer mask thumbnail**
Transformations		
Select crop tool	press C key	press C key
Move cropping boundary	⌘-drag boundary handle	**drag inside boundary**
Resize cropping boundary	drag boundary handle	drag boundary handle
Rotate cropping boundary	Option-drag boundary handle	**drag outside boundary**
Accept crop	click inside boundary	**press Return**
Cancel crop	click outside boundary	**press Escape**
Transform selection or layer numerically	*new feature*	**⌘-Shift-T**
Freely transform selection or layer	*new feature*	**⌘-T**
Move transformation boundary	*new feature*	**drag inside boundary**
Resize transformation boundary	*new feature*	**drag boundary handle**
Rotate transformation boundary	*new feature*	**drag outside boundary**
Distort transformation boundary	*new feature*	**⌘-drag boundary handle**
Symmetrically distort adjacent corners	*new feature*	**⌘-Option-drag boundary handle**

(continued)

Table 3-1 *(continued)*

Operation	Old Photoshop 3 shortcut	New Photoshop 4 shortcut
Filters		
Repeat filter with last-used settings	⌘-F	⌘-F
Repeat filter with different settings	⌘-Option-F	⌘-Option-F
Scroll preview box in corrective filter dialog boxes	drag in preview box or click in image window	drag in preview box or click in image window
Zoom preview box in corrective filter dialog boxes	⌘-spacebar-click and Option-spacebar-click	⌘-spacebar-click and Option-spacebar-click
Increase selected option-box value by 1 (or 0.1)	up arrow	up arrow
Decrease value by 1 (or 0.1)	down arrow	down arrow
Increase value by 10 (or 1)	Shift-up arrow	Shift-up arrow
Decrease value by 10 (or 1)	Shift-down arrow	Shift-down arrow
Adjust Angle value (where offered) in 15° increments	Shift-drag in Angle wheel	Shift-drag in Angle wheel
Reset options inside corrective filter dialog boxes	Option-click on Cancel button or press Option-Escape	Option-click on Cancel button or press Option-Escape
Specify numerical location of flare in Lens Flare dialog box	Option-click on flare	Option-click on flare
Clone light in Lighting Effects dialog box	Option-drag light	Option-drag light
Delete Lighting Effects light	press Delete key	press Delete key
Adjust size of footprint without affecting angle of light	Shift-drag handle	Shift-drag handle
Adjust angle of light without affecting size of footprint	⌘-drag handle	⌘-drag handle
Paths		
Select pen tool	press T key	**press P key**
Cycle between path tools	*none*	**press P key**
Move selected points	drag point with arrow tool or ⌘-drag with pen tool	drag point with arrow tool or ⌘-drag with pen tool
Select multiple points in path	Shift-click on point with arrow or ⌘-Shift-click with pen	Shift-click on point with arrow or ⌘-Shift-click with pen
Select entire path	Option-click on path with arrow or ⌘-Option-click with pen	Option-click on path with arrow or ⌘-Option-click with pen

Operation	Old Photoshop 3 shortcut	New Photoshop 4 shortcut
Paths		
Clone path	Option-drag path with arrow or ⌘-Option-drag with pen	Option-drag path with arrow or ⌘-Option-drag with pen
Convert corner to arc or arc to corner	Control-drag point with arrow or ⌘-Control-drag with pen	Control-drag point with arrow or ⌘-Control-drag with pen
Convert arc to cusp	Control-drag handle with arrow or ⌘-Control-drag with pen	Control-drag handle with arrow or ⌘-Control-drag with pen
Insert point in path	⌘-Option-click on segment with arrow tool or Control-click with pen tool	⌘-Option-click on segment with arrow tool or Control-click with pen tool
Remove point from path	⌘-Option-click on point with arrow tool or Control-click with pen tool	⌘-Option-click on point with arrow tool or Control-click with pen tool
Convert path to selection outline	press Enter when selection or path tool is active	press Enter when selection or path tool is active **or ⌘-click on path name in Paths palette**
Add path to selection	Shift-Enter when selection or path tool is active	Shift-Enter **or ⌘-Shift-click on path name**
Subtract path from selection	⌘-Enter when selection or path tool is active	**Option-Enter or ⌘-Option-click on path name**
Retain intersection of path and selection	⌘-Shift-Enter when selection or path tool is active	**Shift-Option-Enter or ⌘-Shift-Option-click on path name**
Apply brushstroke around perimeter of path	press Enter when paint or edit tool is active	press Enter when paint or edit tool is active
Revert around perimeter of path	press Option-Enter when eraser tool is active	press Option-Enter when eraser tool is active
Save path for future use	double-click on Work Path item in Paths palette	double-click on Work Path item in Paths palette
Hide path (it remains active)	*none*	**⌘-Shift-H**
Deactivate path	click in empty portion of Paths palette	click in empty portion of Paths palette

(continued)

Operation	Old Photoshop 3 shortcut	New Photoshop 4 shortcut
Table 3-1 *(continued)*		
	Rulers and guides	
Display or hide rulers	⌘-R	⌘-R
Display or hide Info palette	F8	F8
Change unit of measure	drag from X,Y pop-up in Info palette	drag from X,Y pop-up in Info palette **or double-click on ruler**
Display or hide guides	*new function*	**⌘-semicolon (;)**
Create guide	*new function*	**drag from ruler**
Move guide	*new function*	**drag guide with move tool or ⌘-drag with other tool**
Toggle horizontal guide to vertical or vice versa	*new function*	**press Option while dragging guide**
Snap guide to ruler tick marks	*new function*	**press Shift while dragging guide**
Toggle guide magnetism	*new function*	**⌘-Shift-semicolon (;)**
Lock or unlock guides	*new function*	**⌘-Option-semicolon (;)**
Display or hide grid	*new function*	**⌘-quote (")**
Toggle grid magnetism	*new function*	**⌘-Shift-quote (")**
Edit guide color and grid increments	*new function*	**double-click on guide with move tool or ⌘-double-click with other tool**
	Miscellaneous	
Display or hide all palettes, including toolbox	Tab	Tab
Display or hide all palettes, except toolbox	*none*	**Shift-Tab**
Hide just the toolbox	Option-Tab	**Tab, Shift-Tab**
Move a panel out of a palette	drag panel tab	drag panel tab
Snap palette to edge of screen	Shift-click on palette title bar	Shift-click on palette title bar
Fully collapse palette	Option-click on collapse box or double-click on panel tab	Option-click on collapse box or double-click on panel tab
Delete item in Layers, Channels, Paths, or Actions palette	drag item to trash icon at bottom of palette	**Option-click on trash icon at bottom of palette**
Preview how image sits on printed page	click on preview box	click on preview box
View size and resolution of image	Option-click on preview box	Option-click on preview box

Operation	Old Photoshop 3 shortcut	New Photoshop 4 shortcut
Miscellaneous		
Change the preference settings	⌘-K	⌘-K
Display last used Preferences dialog box panel	*none*	**⌘-Option-K**
Bring up dialog box with last-used settings	Option-choose command from Image ⇨ Adjust submenu	Option-choose command from Image ⇨ Adjust submenu
Duplicate image and bypass dialog box	press Option and choose Image ⇨ Duplicate	press Option and choose Image ⇨ Duplicate
Display tiny option names in Calculations dialog box	press Option and choose Image ⇨ Calculations	press Option and choose Image ⇨ Calculations
Exit Type Tool dialog box	Enter	Enter
Activate Don't Save button	press D key	press D key
Cancel the current operation	⌘-period or Escape	⌘-period or Escape

Creating Scripts

So much for the shortcuts that are built into Photoshop 4. But while Table 3-1 may be the longest shortcuts list you've ever seen in your life, it's very possible that it's not long enough. There are still quite a few common commands that you have to choose from the menus. Image Size, Unsharp Mask, Variations, CMYK Color, and Color Range are just a few of the commands that I dearly wish included keyboard equivalents. Frankly, I used all five a heck of a lot more often than Show Rulers, Color Balance, and Gamut Warning, all of which Photoshop has endowed with shortcuts.

Back in Version 3, Photoshop provided the nifty Commands palette, which permitted you to assign function-key shortcuts to as many as 30 commands. Photoshop 4 has dispensed with this palette and substituted the Actions palette, which is at once better and worse than its predecessor.

The Actions palette is an improvement in that it permits you to create *scripts*, which are sequences of operations that you can apply en masse. You can also *batch-process* images, which means to apply a script to an entire folder of files while you go off and have one of those power lunches you've heard so much about. If you spend much of your time performing repetitive tasks, scripts can help you automate your workaday routine so you can devote your creative energies to something more important, like a nap.

If you took advantage of the Commands palette in Photoshop 3, then the bad news boils down to a lack of continuity. The Actions palette can't open Version 3 Commands palette files, so you'll have to create your old shortcuts from scratch. And the Actions palette lacks many of the modifiers that made the Commands palette so easy to use.

In fact, the only similarity between the Actions and Commands palette is the keystrokes that you can assign to your scripts. You can assign the function keys F1 through F15, as well as these same keys with Shift. So like Version 3 before it, Photoshop 4.0 tops out at 30 user-defined shortcuts. Frankly, I think this artificial limitation is stupid — I for one could use twice as many custom shortcuts — but nobody asked me.

 For examples of real scripts, read Chapters 15 and 18. Both chapters contain recipes for correcting pictures that you've shot with a digital camera or downloaded from the Web.

Recording a script

Choose Window ⇨ Show Actions to view the Actions palette. The icons along the bottom of the palette — labeled in Figure 3-5 — permit you to record commands and manage your recorded scripts. A script can include just a single command, as in the case of the Grayscale and RGB Color items listed near the top of the palette in the figure. Or you can record many commands in a row, as in the case of the Digital Pix Fix example. Photoshop divides one script from the next with a horizontal line.

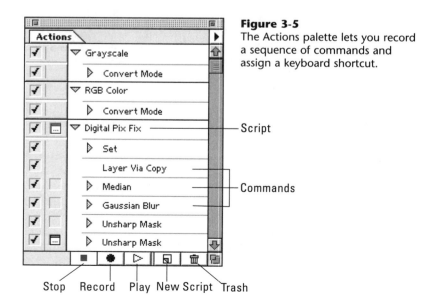

Figure 3-5
The Actions palette lets you record a sequence of commands and assign a keyboard shortcut.

If you've ever used a macro editor like QuicKeys or Tempo, the Actions palette isn't much different. (If you've never even heard of these utilities, not a problem. No experience required.) Here's a basic rundown of how you record a script.

STEPS   **Recording a Script**

Step 1.   **Create a new script.** Click on the new script icon — the one that looks like a little page — at the bottom of the Actions palette. Photoshop responds with the New Action dialog box, shown in Figure 3-6.

If you don't care about naming your script and assigning a function key, you can Option-click on the new script icon to skip the dialog box in Figure 3-6 and proceed directly to Step 4.

Figure 3-6
You can assign a name, func-tion key, and color to a new script.

> **New Action**
>
> Name: My new script   Record
>
> Function Key: None ▼ ☐ Shift   Cancel
>
> Color: ☐ None ▼

Step 2.   **Enter a name for your script.** You can also assign a function key, with or without Shift, and a color. Don't get too worked up about this stuff. You can always go back and change the name, function key, and color later on.

Step 3.   **Press Return to start recording.** The circular record icon at the bottom of the Actions palette turns red to show you that Photoshop is now observing your every action.

There are two things to bear in mind as you proceed into the next steps. First, if you mess up, just keep going. Photoshop lets you insert and reorder commands later on. Second, there's no rush. You can take all day to figure out what you're doing. You can start to choose a command and then change your mind. You can even enter a dialog box and cancel out of it. Photoshop ignores your hesitations and false starts. All it cares about are commands.

Step 4.   **Choose a command. If a dialog box comes up, enter some settings and press Return.** Just about any command will do, but you have to work with commands, or use shortcuts that access commands. For example, Photoshop records you if you press ⌘-A because that's the same as choosing Select ⇨ All. But it ignores you if you change the opacity of a layer or paint with the airbrush because neither of these operations requires a command.

At this point, some of you automation enthusiasts — especially you folks who are familiar with AppleScript — might be grumbling that this is pretty lame scripting. And in truth, it is. The Actions palette is easy to use, but it's not very powerful. Sometimes, you have to be creative to get around its limitations.

After you complete the command, Photoshop adds it to the Actions palette. The program constantly keeps you apprised of what it's recording. If you perform an action and Photoshop doesn't add it to the palette, you have just officially been ignored.

Step 5. **Choose a few more commands.** Add as many as you like. Just remember to keep an eye on the Actions palette so you know that Photoshop is keeping up.

 If Photoshop ignores a command — as it may well do on occasion — don't fret. You can force Photoshop to add an uncooperative command after you finish recording the script. I'll show you how shortly.

Step 6. **Click on the square stop icon at the bottom of the Actions palette.**

That's it, you've now successfully recorded a script.

 Photoshop not only records your commands in the Actions palette, it also applies them to whatever image you have open. (If you open an image while recording, Photoshop adds the Open command to the script.) For this reason, it's usually a good idea to have a dummy image open. When you're finished recording, you can choose File ⇨ Revert to restore the original, unmolested image.

If your script includes a Save operation, try to use File ⇨ Save As or File ⇨ Save a Copy. That way, the original file will remain intact.

 Oh, and one other thing: If you assigned a color to the script back in Step 2, you'll notice its conspicuous absence in the Actions palette. The color is visible only in the button mode, which I discuss in the "Playing scripts and commands" later in this chapter.

Editing a script

You probably have about a 50/50 chance of recording your script right the first time. But no matter, Photoshop offers the following options to help you get it exactly right:

⊛ **Adding more commands:** To add on more commands at the end of a script, just select the script — or any command name in the script — and click on the round record icon. Then start choosing those commands. When you finish, click again on the stop icon. Photoshop automatically adds the new commands to the end of the script.

⊛ **Moving a command:** To change the order of a command, drag the command up or down in the list. You can even drag a command from one script into another if you like.

⊛ **Copying a command:** To make a copy of a command, Option-drag it to a different location. Again, you can Option-drag commands between scripts.

⊛ **Investigating a command:** If you can't remember what setting you entered in a dialog box — or you don't recognize what a command name like Set means — click on the triangle before the command name to expand it. Figure 3-7 shows an example of a Set command expanded to show that Photoshop has *Set* the *selection* to *all*. This is Actions palette code for Select ⇨ All.

Dialog box

Figure 3-7
Click on the little triangles
to expand the commands
and view their settings.

On/off

Expanded
command

⊛ **Changing a setting:** If the command name includes an embossed square to the left of it — in the column marked *Dialog box* in Figure 3-7 — then the command brings up a dialog box. When you expand the command, Photoshop tells you the settings entered into that dialog box. In the case of the Median item in the figure, for example, the Radius value in the Median dialog box has been set to 3. To change the setting, double-click on the command name to display the dialog box, then revise the settings and press Return.

Photoshop will go ahead and apply the settings to your image. If this is a problem, just press ⌘-Z to undo the command. This reverses the settings applied to the image, but has no effect on the changed settings in the script. The Actions palette ignores Edit ➪ Undo.

↪ **Leaving a setting open:** Not all images are alike, and not all images will need the same settings applied to them. If you want to be able to enter your own settings as the script plays, click on the faint square in front of the command name in the dialog box column. A little dialog box icon appears, showing you that you have to be on hand when the script is played. In Figure 3-7, for example, a dialog box icon appears before the Gaussian Blur item. When I later play the script, Photoshop will leave the Gaussian Blur dialog box up on-screen until I enter a setting and press Return. Then the program will continue playing the script through to completion.

Option-click in front of a command name in the dialog box column to display a dialog box icon in front of that one command and hide all others. To bring up dialog boxes for everybody, Option-click on that same dialog box icon again, or click on the red dialog box icon in front of the script name.

↪ **Forcing Photoshop to record a command:** If Photoshop ignored one of the commands you tried to record, choose Insert Menu Item from the Actions palette menu (the right-pointing triangle below the title bar). Photoshop displays the dialog box shown in Figure 3-8, which asks you to choose a command. Go ahead and do it — the dialog box won't interfere with your progress. Then press Return to add the command to the script. If the command brings up a dialog box, the Actions palette will probably ignore it, requiring you to manually enter settings and press Return when you play back the script.

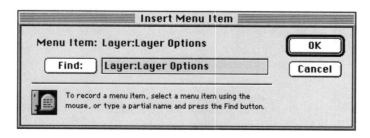

Figure 3-8
This dialog box forces Photoshop to record your command, whether it likes it or not.

↪ **Inserting a stop:** A *stop* is a pause in the action. You can't do anything when the script is paused — not in Photoshop anyway. You can switch to a different application, but Photoshop's options are off limits until you cancel or complete the script. The only real purpose of a stop is to give you the chance to see how the commands have progressed so far. To add a stop, choose the Insert Stop command from the Actions palette menu. Then enter the message that you want to appear when the stop occurs. Select the Allow Continue check box to permit you to continue the script during playback.

- ☞ **Changing the name and function key:** To change the name, shortcut, or color assigned to a script, double-click on the script name. Up comes the Action Options dialog box, which contains the same options as appeared back in Figure 3-6. Change the settings as you like. Any function keys that are assigned to other scripts appear dimmed.

- ☞ **Deleting a command:** To delete a command, drag it to the trash icon at the bottom of the Actions palette. Or easier still, select the command you want to delete, then Option-click on the trash icon. (You can also merely click on the icon, but Photoshop will display an irritating alert message. Option-clicking skips the message.)

Playing scripts and commands

When it comes time to play your script, you can play all of it, or just a single command. The simplest way to play back an entire script is to press the function key you assigned to it.

If you don't like to fill your brain with ephemeral nonsense like what function key does what, you might prefer to switch to the button mode. To do so, choose the Button Mode command from the Actions palette menu, as demonstrated in Figure 3-9. You can now see the colors you assigned to the scripts, as well as the function keys. Just click on the button for the script you want to play.

Figure 3-9
Choose the Button Mode command to view each script as an independent button.

But the button mode has its drawbacks. All you can do is click on buttons. You can't edit scripts, you can't change the order of scripts, you can't assign new function keys to scripts, and you can't play individual commands. This is a great mode if you want to protect your scripts from less adept users, but it's an awful mode if you want to modify your scripts and create new ones.

So, choose the Button Mode command to return to the normal palette setup. Then try out some of these less restrictive script-playing techniques:

∽ To play a selected script, click on the play icon at the bottom of the palette. You can also play a script by ⌘-double-clicking on the script name.

∽ To play a script from a certain command on, select that command name in the palette, then click on the play icon.

∽ To play a single command, and no more, drag the command name onto the play icon. Or ⌘-double-click on the command name.

∽ You can tell Photoshop which commands to play and which to skip using the check marks in the on/off column (labeled back in Figure 3-7). Click on a check mark to turn the corresponding command off.

∽ Option-click on a check mark to turn that one command on and the rest off. To turn all the commands in the script on again, Option-click on the check mark again, or click on the red check mark by the script name.

Batch-Processing Images _____

Batch-processing is one of those scary terms that you hear bandied about by experts on a fairly regular basis. But it's actually relatively easy, especially with Photoshop 4's Batch command.

The following steps walk you through the task of batch-processing a bunch of files. This isn't the only way to batch-process files — Photoshop offers a couple of additional variations you can experiment with on your own. But these steps represent the best way.

STEPS Batch-Processing Files

Step 1. **Create the script that you want to apply.** The last step in the script should be File ➪ Save As. This saves the completed image to disk without saving over the original. Use whatever format you like (as discussed in Chapter 4).

Step 2. **Round up the images that you want to apply the script to.**

You can put all the images in a single folder. Or if you own a digital camera from which Photoshop can open images directly — anything from the $3,000 Polaroid PDC-2000 to the $300 Kodak DC20 — you should plug the camera into your Mac and turn it on.

Step 3. **Create a folder to collect the images once Photoshop is done processing them.** If you're opening images from a folder, you *can* have Photoshop save to the same folder, but that will save over the original files (even with File ⇨ Save As). It's a good precaution to save the files elsewhere so you can refer back to the originals if you're not pleased with the scripted results.

Step 4. **Choose the Batch command from the Actions palette menu.** Photoshop displays the dialog box shown in Figure 3-10. It offers a lot of options, but it's really a peach once you get to know it.

Figure 3-10
Here I have the Batch command all set up to import images from a Polaroid PDC-2000, run the Digital Pix Fix script, and save the images in a folder on my hard drive.

Step 5. **Select a source for the images.** Select Import from the Source pop-up menu if you want to acquire the images from a digital camera. Then select the acquire module that you generally use to communicate with the camera from the From pop-up menu.

To open images from a folder, select Folder from the Source pop-up menu. Then click on the Choose button and locate the folder on disk.

Step 6. **Select your script from the Action pop-up menu.** Photoshop selects the active script by default, but you can select any script you like.

Step 7. **Select the destination folder.** First, select the Folder option from the Destination pop-up menu. Then click on the Choose button and locate the destination folder on disk.

The Destination pop-up menu offers two other options — None, which collects the images on-screen without saving them, and Save and Close, which saves the images over the originals and closes them. One clogs up the RAM and slows performance while the other eliminates your backup images. Boo to both.

You can also select a check box to ignore any saving instructions included in your script. But your Save As command is exactly what the doctor ordered, so there's no sense in deactivating it. Go ahead and leave the check box turned off.

Step 8.   **Turn on the Override Action "Save In" Commands check box.** If you worked all day, I don't think you could come up with a more confusing name for a check box. (Why didn't Adobe just name it Jibberish and have done with it?) But it has an important purpose. It overrides the folder destination and file name included with the Save As command in your script. The script instead retains the original name of the image and saves it to the folder you requested in the last step. However, Photoshop still saves the image in the file format you specified with the Save As command.

Step 9.   **Press the Return key.** Photoshop begins batch-processing your images, starting with the first images in alphabetical order.

You might want to watch the first image from start to finish to make sure everything goes smoothly, particularly the save operation. (Photoshop should close each image after it finishes saving it.) But after the first image, you should probably leave Photoshop and your Mac alone to work their wonders. A watched pot never boils, and a watched batch defeats the purpose. You're supposed to be out there engaging in interesting carbon-based activities while Photoshop slaves away in your absence. So get out of here!

Understanding Digital Imagery

II PART

Image Fundamentals

CHAPTER 4

In This Chapter

- How to scale an image for the printer and for the screen
- Four ways to create an image in Photoshop
- Tips for savings images to disk
- Explanations of every image format supported by Photoshop
- The inner workings of the JPEG format
- How to render object-oriented EPS and PICT images
- Ways to change the number of pixels in an image

How Images Work

Think of a bitmapped image as a mosaic made out of square tiles of various colors. When you view the mosaic up close, it looks like something you might use to decorate your bathroom. You see the individual tiles, not the image itself. But if you back a few feet away from the mosaic, the tiles lose their definition and merge together to create a recognizable work of art, presumably Medusa getting her head whacked off or some equally appetizing thematic classic.

Similarly, images are colored pixels pretending to be artwork. If you enlarge the pixels, they look like an unrelated collection of colored squares. Reduce the size of the pixels, and they blend together to form an image that looks to all the world like a standard photograph. Photoshop deceives the eye by borrowing from an artistic technique older than Mycenae or Pompeii.

Of course, there are differences between pixels and ancient mosaic tiles. Pixels come in 16 million distinct colors. Mosaic tiles of antiquity came in your basic granite and sandstone varieties, with an occasional chunk of lapis lazuli thrown in for good measure. Also, you can resample, color separate, and crop electronic images. We know from the time-worn scribblings of Dionysius of Halicarnassus that these processes were beyond the means of classical artisans.

But I'm getting ahead of myself. I won't be discussing resampling, cropping, or Halicarnassus for several pages. In the meantime, I'll address the inverse relationship between image size and resolution.

Size versus resolution

If you haven't already guessed, the term *image size* describes the physical dimensions of an image. *Resolution* is the number of pixels per linear inch. I say *linear* because you measure pixels in a straight line. If the resolution of an image is 72 *ppi* — that is, *pixels-per-inch* — you get 5,184 pixels per-square-inch (72 pixels wide × 72 pixels tall = 5,184).

Assuming that the number of pixels in an image is fixed, increasing the size of an image decreases its resolution and vice versa. Therefore, an image that looks good when printed on a postage stamp probably will look jagged when printed as an 11 × 17-inch poster.

Figure 4-1 shows a single image printed at three different sizes and resolutions. The smallest image is printed at twice the resolution of the medium-sized image, and the medium-sized image is printed at twice the resolution of the largest image.

One inch in the smallest image includes twice as many pixels vertically and twice as many pixels horizontally as an inch in the medium-sized image, for a total of four times as many pixels per square inch. Therefore, the smallest image covers one-fourth of the area of the medium-sized image.

The same relationships exist between the medium-sized image and the largest image. An inch in the medium-sized image comprises four times as many pixels as an inch in the largest image. Consequently, the medium-sized image consumes one-fourth of the area of the largest image.

Figure 4-1
These three images
contain the same
number of pixels
but are printed at
different resolutions.
Doubling the
resolution of an
image reduces it
to 25 percent of
its original size.

Changing the printing resolution

When printing an image, a higher resolution translates to a sharper image with greater clarity. Photoshop allows you to change the resolution of a printed image in one of two ways:

> ✑ Choose Image ➪ Image Size to access the controls that let you change the pixel dimensions and resolution of an image. Then enter a value into the Resolution option box, either in pixels per inch or pixels per centimeter.

It's a good idea (although not essential) to turn off Resample Image, as demonstrated in Figure 4-2. If you leave it on, Photoshop may add or subtract pixels, as discussed in the "Resampling and Cropping" section later in this chapter.

↪ Alternatively, you can instruct Photoshop to scale an image during the print cycle by choosing File ➪ Page Setup (⌘-Shift-P) and entering a percentage value into the Reduce or Enlarge option box.

Figure 4-2
Turn off the Resample Image check box to maintain a constant number of pixels in an image and change only the printed resolution.

Both the Resolution and Reduce or Enlarge settings are saved with an image. Together, the two determine the printed resolution. Photoshop divides the Resolution value in the Image Size dialog box by the Reduce or Enlarge percentage in the Page Setup dialog box. For example, if the image resolution is set to 72 ppi and you reduce the image to 48 percent, then the final printed image has a resolution of 150 ppi (72 divided by .48).

At the risk of boring some folks, I'll briefly remind the math haters in the audience that whenever you use a percentage in an equation, you first convert it to a decimal. For example, 100 percent is 1.0, 64 percent is .64, 5 percent is .05, and so on.

To avoid confusion, most folks rely exclusively on the Resolution value and leave Reduce or Enlarge set to 100 percent. The only exception is when printing proofs. Because proof printers offer lower-resolution output, you may find it helpful to print images larger so you can see more pixels. Raising the Reduce or Enlarge value permits you to accomplish this without upsetting the Resolution value. Just be sure to restore the Reduce or Enlarge value to 100 percent after printing the proof.

Changing the page-layout resolution

The Reduce or Enlarge setting has no affect on the size and resolution of an image imported into an object-oriented application, such as QuarkXPress or Illustrator. But these same applications do observe the Resolution setting.

Specifying the resolution in Photoshop is a handy way to avoid resizing operations and printing complications in your page-layout program. For example, I preset the resolution of all the images in this book so that the production team had only to import the images and print away.

Always remember: Photoshop is as good or better at adjusting pixels than any other program that you work with. Therefore, prepare an image as completely as possible in Photoshop before importing the image into another program. Ideally, you should never have to resize, rotate, or crop an image in any other program.

Screen resolution

Regardless of the Resolution and Reduce or Enlarge values, Photoshop displays each pixel on-screen according to the zoom ratio (as discussed in Chapter 2). If the zoom ratio is 100 percent, for example, each image pixel takes up a single screen pixel. Zoom ratio and printer output are unrelated.

When creating an image for a screen presentation or display, you want the image size to fit inside the prospective monitor at the 100 percent zoom ratio. I say *prospective* monitor because although you may use a 17-inch monitor when you create the image, you may want to display the final image on a 13-inch monitor. In that case, you would set the image size no larger than 640 × 480 pixels (the standard resolution of a 13-inch monitor) with no concern for the size it appears on your 17-inch monitor.

Many monitors conform to specific default resolutions, as listed in Table 4-1. But more and more graphics cards — especially on the PC side of the aisle — let you change the resolution of the monitor so that a 640 × 480-pixel image may shrink or grow on-screen. For this reason, many Web and screen artists prepare for the worst-case scenario, typically 640 × 480. (Old-model Macs have lower screen resolutions, but it's safe to say that few folks who are still using Classics are out surfing the Web.)

I discuss Web graphics in more detail in Chapter 20. In the meantime, Table 4-1 lists a few common Macintosh and DOS-based PC screen sizes. If you care, flag the pages as a resource. If you don't, rip them out and wrap a few fish.

Table 4-1	Macintosh and PC Monitor Standards	
Monitor	*Pixels wide*	*Pixels tall*
Macintosh		
Old-model PowerBooks	640	400
Monochrome Plus, SE, Classic screens	512	342
10-inch Color Classic screens	512	384
12-inch LC screens	512	384
Post-1994 PowerBooks	640	480
13-inch screens	640	480
15-inch portrait screens	640	870
17-inch screens	832	624
19-inch screens	1024	768
21-inch (two-page) screens	1152	870
High-end graphics cards	1360	1024
Professional-level cards	1600	1200
IBM compatibles		
Old monochrome Hercules cards	720	348
16-color EGA cards	640	350
Old MCGA cards	640	480
VGA and XGA cards	640	480
SuperVGA	800	600
8514/a or TIGA cards	1024	768
High-end graphics cards	1280	1024
Professional-level cards	1600	1200

Keep in mind, these are just a representative few of the kinds of monitors and graphics cards that exist. And modern video cards permit you to switch between different resolutions. For example, the S3 Vision card installed in my current Pentium PC can accommodate 640 × 480, 800 × 600, 1024 × 768, or 1280 × 1024 pixels, depending on how many colors I want to display.

Even so, the values in Table 4-1 are indicative of the basic resolution settings available and the inherent differences between platforms. Both Macs and PCs support 640 × 480 and 1,024 × 768. But while the medium Mac setting is 832 × 624, the medium PC setting is 800 × 600. This small discrepancy can mean the difference between an image fitting on-screen or cutting short.

How to Open, Duplicate, and Save Images

Before you can work on an image in Photoshop — whether you're creating a brand new document or opening an image from disk — you must first load the image into an image window. Here are the four basic ways to create an image window:

- **File ➪ New:** Create a new window by choosing File ➪ New (⌘-N). After you fill out the desired size and resolution specifications in the New dialog box, Photoshop confronts you with a stark, white, empty canvas. You then face the ultimate test of your artistic capabilities — painting from scratch. Feel free to go nuts and cut off your ear.

- **File ➪ Open:** Open an image saved to disk or CD-ROM by choosing File ➪ Open (⌘-O). Of the four ways to create an image window, you most likely will use this method most frequently. You can open images scanned in other applications, images purchased from stock photo agencies, slides and transparencies digitized to a Kodak Photo CD, or an image you previously edited in Photoshop.

- **Edit ➪ Paste:** Photoshop automatically adapts a new image window to the contents of the Clipboard (provided those contents are bitmapped). So if you copy an image inside a different application or in Photoshop and then choose File ➪ New, Photoshop enters the dimensions and resolution of the image into the New dialog box. All you have to do is accept the settings and choose Edit ➪ Paste (⌘-V) to introduce the image into a new window. This technique is useful for editing screen shots captured to the Clipboard and for testing out filtering effects on a sample of an image without harming the original.

 Photoshop 4 automatically pastes an image to a new layer. This means you can save the resulting file exclusively in the native Photoshop format (as I explain later in this chapter). To flatten the pasted image so you can save it in some other format, choose Layer ➪ Merge Down or press ⌘-E.

- **File ➪ Import:** If you own a scanner or digital camera, it may include a plug-in module that lets you transfer an image directly into Photoshop. Just copy the module into Photoshop's Plug-ins folder and then run or relaunch the Photoshop application. To initiate a scan or load an image into Photoshop, choose the plug-in module from the File ➪ Import submenu.

For example, to load an image from my Polaroid PDC-2000 — the best camera under $5,000 as I write this — I cable the camera to my Mac's SCSI port. Then I turn the camera on and choose File ➪ Import ➪ PDC-2000. A dialog box appears showing thumbnails of all the images I've shot, as in Figure 4-3. I select the images I want to edit, click on the Transfer button, and the images open directly inside Photoshop.

Figure 4-3
The Polaroid PDC-2000 module lets me view images stored in the camera's memory and open them up directly inside Photoshop.

Creating a new image

Whether you're creating an image from scratch or transferring the contents of the Clipboard to a new image window, choose File ➪ New or press ⌘-N to bring up the New dialog box shown in Figure 4-4. If the Clipboard contains an image, the Width, Height, and Resolution option boxes show the size and resolution of that image. Otherwise, you can enter your own values in one of five units of measurement: pixels, inches, centimeters, picas, or points. If you're not sure exactly what size image you want to create, enter a rough approximation. You can always change your settings later.

But while Photoshop matches the contents of the Clipboard by default, you can also match the size and resolution of other images:

- ➣ Press the Option key when choosing File ➪ New, or press ⌘-Option-N to override the contents of the Clipboard. Photoshop displays the size and resolution of the last image you created, whether it came from the Clipboard or not. Use this technique when creating many same-sized images in a row.

- ➣ You can also match the size and resolution of the new image to any other open image. While the New dialog box is open, choose the name of the image that you want to match from the Window menu. It's that simple.

Figure 4-4
Use the New dialog box to specify the size, resolution, and color mode of your new image.

Units of measure

The Width and Height pop-up menus contain the five common units of measure mentioned above — pixels, inches, centimeters, points, and picas. But the Width pop-up menu offers one more, called Columns. If you want to create an image that fits exactly within a certain number of columns when it's imported into a desktop publishing program, select this option. You can specify the width of a column and the gutter between columns by pressing ⌘-K and ⌘-5 for the Units & Rulers preferences. Then enter values into the Column Size option boxes.

The Gutter value affects multiple-column images. Suppose that you accept the default setting of a 15-pica column width and a 1-pica gutter. If you specify a one-column image in the New dialog box, Photoshop makes it 15 picas wide. If you ask for a two-column image, Photoshop adds the width of the gutter to the width of the two columns and creates an image 31 picas wide.

The Height pop-up menu in the New dialog box lacks a Column option because vertical columns have nothing to do with an image's height.

You can change the default unit of measure that appears in the Width and Height pop-up menus by pressing ⌘-K, ⌘-5, and selecting a different option from the Units pop-up menu. Easier still, bring up the Info palette by pressing the F8 key. Then drag on the little cross icon in the palette's lower left corner. Up comes a pop-up menu of units, as demonstrated in Figure 4-5.

Figure 4-5
You can select a default unit of measure from the coordinates pop-up menu in the lower left corner of the Info palette.

New image size

In most cases, the on-screen dimensions of an image depend on your entries in the Width, Height, and Resolution option boxes. If you set both the Width and Height values to 10 inches and the Resolution to 72 ppi, the new image will measure 720 × 720 pixels. The exception occurs if you choose pixels as your unit of measurement, as in Figure 4-4. In that case, the on-screen dimensions depend solely on the Width and Height options, and the Resolution value determines the size at which the image prints.

Color mode

Use the Mode pop-up menu to specify the number of colors that can appear in your image. Choose Bitmap to create a black-and-white image and choose Grayscale to access only gray values. RGB Color, CMYK Color, and Lab Color all provide access to the full range of 16 million colors, although their methods of doing so differ.

RGB stands for red-green-blue; CMYK for cyan-magenta-yellow-black; and Lab for luminosity and two abstract color variables, *a* and *b*. To learn how each of these color modes works, read the "Working in Different Color Modes" section of Chapter 5.

Background color

The New dialog box also provides three Contents radio buttons that allow you to change the color of the background for the new image. You can fill the new image with white, with the current background color (assuming, of course, that the background color is something other than white), or with no color at all. This last setting, Transparent, results in a floating layer with no background image whatsoever, which can be useful when editing one layer independently of the rest of an image, or when preparing a layer to be composited with an image. (For an in-depth examination of the more nitty-gritty aspects of layering, see Chapter 13.)

If you do select a transparent background, you'll have to later flatten the layer by choosing Layer ⇨ Flatten Image if you want to save the image to any format other than native Photoshop. The advantage of the Transparent setting, however, is that Photoshop doesn't create a new layer when you press ⌘-V to paste the contents of the Clipboard. Not that it makes much difference in the long run — you still have to flatten the image before saving it — but at least you don't have to fuss around with two layers, one of which is completely empty.

Naming the new image

The New dialog box provides a Name option. If you know what you want to call your new image, enter the name now. Or don't. It doesn't matter. Either way, when you choose File ⇨ Save, Photoshop asks you to specify the location of the file and confirm the file's name, just as in previous versions. So don't feel compelled to name your image anything. The only real reason for this option is to help you keep your images organized on-screen. Lots of folks create temporary images that they never save; Photoshop offers a way to assign temporary images more meaningful names than *Untitled-4, Untitled-5, Untitled-6,* and so on.

Opening an existing image

If you want to open an image stored on disk, choose File ⇨ Open or press ⌘-O to display the Open dialog box. Despite its new three-dimensional look, the Open dialog box behaves just like the ones in other Macintosh applications, with a folder bar, Desktop button, and other standard navigation options. You can also use standard navigational shortcuts. Press ⌘-left and right arrow to change drives, ⌘-up and down arrow to exit and enter folders, and ⌘-D to switch to the desktop view.

But Photoshop's Open dialog box goes the extra mile by offering a few options that other Open dialog boxes lack. It sports a couple of check boxes, a thumbnail preview of the selected image on the left side of the scrolling list, and two Find buttons on the right. The following sections explain how these unusual options work.

Opening elusive files

The scrolling list contains the names of documents Photoshop recognizes that it can open. If you cannot find a desired document, it may be because Photoshop does not recognize the document's four-character *type code*. The type code for a document created or last edited on a Macintosh computer corresponds to the file format under which the image was saved (as explained in the upcoming "File Format Roundup" section).

For example, TIFF is the type code for a TIFF image, JPEG is the type code for a JPEG image, and so on. However, if you transferred a document from another platform, such as an IBM-compatible PC or UNIX workstation, it likely lacks a type code. In the absence of a type code, Photoshop looks for a three-character extension at the end of the file name, such as *.tif* or *.jpg*. But if the extension is so much as a character off — as in *.tff* or *.jpe* — Photoshop won't know the file from Adam.

To see *all* documents regardless of type code or extension, select the Show All Files check box inside the Open dialog box. When you click on a document in the scrolling list, Photoshop displays the format that it thinks the file is saved in — if it has any thoughts to offer — in the Format option. If you disagree, select a different format file from the pop-up menu, as demonstrated in Figure 4-6. If the desired document conforms to the selected format option, Photoshop opens the image after you click on the Open button or press Return. If Photoshop displays an error message instead, you need to either select a different format option or try to open the document in a different application.

Incidentally, you can view and modify the type code for a document using PrarieSoft's DiskTop or Apple's ResEdit, both of which are distributed separately.

Viewing the thumbnail

Turn on the Show Thumbnail check box to display a thumbnail preview of the selected image on the left side of the dialog box. If you deselect the option, the preview disappears and the Open dialog box collapses to save screen space.

Figure 4-6
Select the
Show All Files
option to access
any document
regardless of its
four-character
type code.

A preview appears only if the Thumbnail check box in the Preferences dialog box was selected when you saved the image to disk (as discussed back in the "Saving Files" section of Chapter 2). If no preview appears, you may be able to create a preview on the fly by clicking on the Create button. However, QuickTime must be running for this button to function, and even then, the button only applies to PICT images. If the image is saved in any other file format — TIFF, JPEG, EPS, and so on — you can generate a preview only by opening the image, pressing ⌘-K and ⌘-2, selecting the Thumbnail check box, and resaving the image to disk. So much for convenience, eh?

The thumbnail preview is only visible when the Show Thumbnail check box is selected *and* QuickTime is running. If the Show Thumbnail check box is dimmed, chances are QuickTime did not load when you started up your Mac. See Appendix A for information about installing QuickTime with Photoshop.

Finding lost files

If you know the name of a file — or at least part of the name — but you can't remember where you put it, you can look for it using the Find button. Just click on the button or press ⌘-F, enter some text in the resulting option box, and press the Return key. Photoshop searches the disk in a fairly random fashion and takes you to the first file name that contains the exact characters you entered.

If the first file name isn't the one you're looking for, click on the Find Again button or press ⌘-G to find the next file name that contains your text. If you want to search for a different string of characters, press ⌘-F and enter some different text.

Duplicating an image

Have you ever wanted to try out an effect without permanently damaging an image? Certainly, you can undo the last action performed in Photoshop (by choosing Edit ⇨ Undo), but what if the technique involves multiple steps? And what if you want to apply two or more effects to an image independently and compare them side by side? And later maybe even merge them? This is a job for image duplication.

To create a new window with an independent version of the foreground image, choose Image ⇨ Duplicate. A dialog box appears requesting a name for the new image. Just like the Name option in the New dialog box, the option is purely an organizational tool that you can use or ignore. If your image contains multiple layers, Photoshop will by default retain all layers in the duplicate document. Alternatively, you can merge all visible layers into a single layer by selecting the Merged Layers Only check box. (Hidden layers remain independent.) Press Return to create your new, independent image. (This image is unsaved; you need to choose File ⇨ Save to save any changes to disk.)

If you're happy to let Photoshop automatically name your image and you don't care what it does with the layers, press the Option key while choosing Image ⇨ Duplicate. This bypasses the Duplicate Image dialog box and immediately creates a new window.

Saving an image to disk

The first rule of storing an image on disk is to save it frequently. If the foreground image is untitled, as it is when you work on a new image, choosing File ⇨ Save (⌘-S) displays the Save dialog box, enabling you to name the image, specify its location on disk, and select a file format. After you save the image once, choosing the Save command updates the file on disk without bringing up the Save dialog box.

Choose File ➪ Save As or press ⌘-Shift-S to change the name, location, or format of the image stored on disk. By the way, if your only reason for choosing the Save As command is to change the file format, it's perfectly acceptable to overwrite (save over) the original document, assuming that you no longer need the previous copy of the image. Granted, your computer could crash during the Save As operation, in which case you would lose both the new document and the original. But the chance of crashing during a Save As is extremely remote — no more likely than crashing during any other save operation.

To speed up the save process, I usually save an image in Photoshop's native format until I'm finished working on it. Before I close the image, I choose File ➪ Save As and save the image in the compressed TIFF or JPEG format. By using this method, I only compress each image once during a session.

Naming an image for the PC

When creating an image that you intend to distribute over the Web or to a colleague on another platform, you have to observe special naming conventions. Windows 3.1 and DOS limit you to eight-character (or fewer) names with three-character extensions, divided by a period, as in *bobby.tif*. You can't use spaces, slashes, commas, or other punctuation (beyond the one period). If you want to divide two words, use an underscore or a hyphen, as in *my_brain.jpg*.

Windows 95, NT, and UNIX-based Web names can be longer, but spaces are still forbidden on the Web, and you still need the three-character extension (or four-character, in the case of UNIX). No platform but the Mac supports the four-character type codes (discussed earlier in the "Opening elusive files" section), so the only way non-Mac programs can recognize image files is by their extensions.

Rather than remembering all those extensions — like *.psd* for the native Photoshop format and *.tif* for TIFF — you can ask Photoshop to append them automatically. Just press ⌘-K and ⌘-2 to display the Saving Files preferences. Then select the Ask When Saving option from the Append File Extension pop-up menu. Now whenever you save a new image, Photoshop presents you with a check box in the Save dialog box. Select the check box whenever the file is bound for a different platform.

Saving a copy

The final save command — File ➪ Save a Copy (⌘-Option-S) — allows you to save a copy of the current image without changing that special relationship between the image and its original on disk. It's like duplicating the image, saving it, and closing the duplicate all in one step.

The whole purpose of the Save a Copy command is to save a flattened version of a layered image, or dump the extra channels in an image that contains masks. Just select the file format you want to use and let Photoshop do the flattening and dumping automatically.

When you choose the Save a Copy command, Photoshop displays two extra check boxes at the bottom of the standard Save dialog box, as shown in Figure 4-7.

- **Flatten Image**: Photoshop activates this check box whenever you select a format other than the native Photoshop format. Since no other format supports layers, the check box has to turn on to show that the layers will fuse together when the image is saved. Not to worry, however. Because you're only saving a copy of the image, the layers remain available to you on-screen.

- **Don't Include Alpha Channels**: "Alpha channel" is Photoshop's techy name for a mask. As discussed in Chapter 12, a mask is a method for defining highly accurate selections. But only a few formats — Photoshop, TIFF, and Raw — support masks. Other formats abandon them. Again, Photoshop automatically activates this check box when you select a no-mask format.

Figure 4-7
Choose the Save a Copy command to save a separate flattened copy of a layered image. This way, you can continue to adjust the layers in the future.

The Save a Copy command is perfect for those times when you want to export a layered image for use in another program. A page-layout application like QuarkXPress doesn't support Photoshop's native format, but you don't want to flatten the image and lose your layers for good either. So here's your compromise. Keep one copy with layers in the Photoshop format, and create a flattened copy for QuarkXPress.

The whole issue of formats is too big to discuss here. In fact, it takes up the majority of this chapter, starting with the "File Format Roundup" section coming up shortly.

Disabling the Save command

If you use CE Software's QuicKeys or some other scripting program, you can disable the Save command's standard ⌘-S shortcut. Why in the world would you want to do that? To avoid accidentally saving over perfectly good data.

Saving in Photoshop is a delicate balance. Because the program offers just one level of undo, you learn to use the saved version of the image as a backup that you can return to in case something goes wrong. Instead of saving every two or three minutes — as in a word processor — you're better off saving about once every ten minutes, and then only if you have everything exactly the way you want it.

If you work from the keyboard a lot, you probably spend a lot of time pressing ⌘-D to deselect an image. You may even occasionally press ⌘-A to select the entire image. But if you're like me, you get sloppy sometimes and you press ⌘-S (which lies between A and D) instead. Back in the old days, you had time to realize your mistake and press ⌘-period to cancel the operation before it was too late. But today's Power Macs are just too fast. Before you know what you've done, the file is saved.

In my opinion, saving is too important to be left to ⌘-S. So here's what I do in QuicKeys:

- ↝ Set ⌘-S to play a sound. This will alert you that you pressed ⌘-S instead of ⌘-D or ⌘-A, and get you in the habit of using your new Save shortcut.

- ↝ Set ⌘-Option-S to alias the ⌘-S shortcut. From now on, ⌘-Option-S — not ⌘-S — saves your image. There is no ⌘-Option-D or ⌘-Option-A so you're less likely to flub it.

- ↝ Set ⌘-Shift-Option-S to alias ⌘-Option-S. This turns ⌘-Shift-Option-S into the shortcut for File ⇨ Save a Copy. It's not a very convenient shortcut, but you probably don't use the Save a Copy command that much anyway.

If you're a careful typist, you probably think I'm nuts for even suggesting this tip. But if you're sloppy like me, you know that prevention is the best cure.

File Format Roundup

As you might have noticed back in Figure 4-6, Photoshop 4 supports more than 20 file formats from inside its Open and Save dialog boxes. It can support even more through the addition of plug-in modules, which attach commands to the File ⇨ Import and File ⇨ Export submenus.

File formats represent different ways to save a file to disk. Some formats provide unique image *compression schemes,* which save an image in a manner that consumes less space on disk. Other formats enable Photoshop to trade images with different applications on the Mac and on different platforms.

The native formats

Photoshop 4 offers two *native formats* — that is, formats that are optimized for Photoshop's particular capabilities and functions. One native format supports layers, the other does not:

    ⅆ The straight Photoshop format saves every attribute you can apply in Photoshop, including layers, and is compatible with Versions 3 and later of the program. This is a very useful format.

 It's also worth noting that Photoshop 4 can open and save in its native format more quickly than in any other format. This format offers image compression missing from the Photoshop 2.0 format. Like TIFF's compression, it does *not* result in any loss of data.

    ⅆ The Photoshop 2.0 format is compatible with older versions, but since it doesn't support layers, the format is virtually useless. The TIFF format supports everything that the Photoshop 2.0 format does, and TIFF is an industry standard compatible with hundreds of applications on both the Mac and PC platforms. So the chances you'll ever need to use the Photoshop 2.0 format are about the same as the chances you'll be abducted by space aliens. The format is there merely for backward compatibility.

Where does Photoshop 2.5 fit into this picture? Well, it turns out that the newer Photoshop format is compatible with Photoshop 2.5 *if* the 2.5 Compatibility check box is selected inside the Preferences dialog box (which you reach by pressing ⌘-K and then ⌘-2). If this check box is turned off, Photoshop 2.5 will *not* be able to open a layered image saved in the modern Photoshop format.

After that explanation, it may come as surprise when I tell you that I leave the 2.5 Compatibility check box turned off. Now that we're two versions beyond Photoshop 2.5, it's safe to assume the overwhelming majority of folks have upgraded at least as far as Version 3. More importantly, you save disk space by turning the 2.5 Compatibility option off, particularly if your image involves layers.

Cross-platform formats

Photoshop 4 provides nine formats for saving an image that you want to transfer to a different computer or post on the World Wide Web. If your clients or coworkers use computers other than Macs, you'll find these formats essential.

 The GIF, PDF, and PNG formats have special significance for Web designers. I discuss all three — as well as compression champ JPEG — in Chapter 20.

Amiga's IFF and HAM

Every time I talk about the Amiga — a computer created by the now-dead typewriter developer Commodore — I feel compelled to share my opinion on what a botched effort it was. You could perform some major video editing with NewTek's Video Toaster, but beyond that, the Amiga was a hunk of junk. Unfortunately, this perfectly reasonable assessment invariably ruffles the feathers of some Amiga enthusiasts, of which there seem to be about five in all the world. According to one fellow I talked to, an ex-member of the Doobie Brothers really has it out for me. Sadly, he didn't tell me which Doobie it is. (Weren't there about 17 of them in all?) But if I see some guy with long hair and a bushy mustache following me home one night, I'll know I'm in trouble.

But while we wait for the Amiga to gasp its last dying breaths, you can trade images using IFF (*Interchange File Format*). IFF is the Amiga's all-around graphics format, serving much the same function as PICT on the Mac. IFF is even supported by a few aging DOS applications, most notably DeluxePaint from Electronic Arts. Photoshop also supports a compressed variation of IFF called HAM (*Hold and Modify*). You can open HAM images with up to 256 colors and IFF images with up to 16 million colors.

To save a HAM image, choose File ⇨ Export ⇨ Amiga HAM. Unfortunately, HAM is generally useless for images that don't conform to one of two standard image sizes — 320 × 200 pixels or 320 × 400 pixels. Most Amiga applications treat nonstandard images as having rectangular as opposed to square pixels, thus stretching the image out of proportion. You can account for some of this by enlarging the image horizontally before exporting it — as recommended in the Photoshop documentation — but even then, you'll notice some distortion. Mac and Amiga pixels are simply different animals. And, yes, the Mac is better.

Microsoft Paint's BMP

BMP (*Windows Bitmap*) is the native format for Microsoft Paint (included with Windows) and is supported by a variety of Windows, DOS, and OS/2 applications. Photoshop supports BMP images with up to 16 million colors. You also can use RLE (*Run-Length Encoding*), a lossless compression scheme specifically applicable to the BMP format.

 The term *lossless* refers to compression schemes such as BMP's RLE and TIFF's LZW (*Lempel-Ziv-Welch*) that enable you to save space on disk without sacrificing any data in the image. The only reasons *not* to use lossless compression are that it slows down the open and save operations and it may prevent less-sophisticated applications from opening an image. *Lossy* compression routines, such as JPEG, sacrifice a user-defined amount of data to conserve even more disk space.

CompuServe's GIF

Originally, CompuServe supported GIF (pronounced *jiff*, short for *Graphics Interchange Format*) as a means of compressing files so that you could quickly transfer photographs via modem to and from the company's commercial bulletin board service. Like TIFF, GIF uses LZW compression, but unlike TIFF, GIF can't handle more than 256 colors.

However, with the advent of the World Wide Web, GIF graphics have become more sophisticated. There are currently two varieties of GIF, known by the helpful codes 87a and 89a. GIF87a supports strictly opaque pixels, while GIF89a permits some pixels to be transparent. You can open either kind of image using File ➪ Open. You can save an image to the GIF87a format by choosing File ➪ Save and selecting CompuServe GIF from the Format pop-up menu. To save a GIF89a file with transparent pixels, choose File ➪ Export ➪ GIF89a Export.

 Before saving a GIF image, it's always a good idea to use Image ➪ Mode ➪ Indexed Color to lower the number of colors to 256 or fewer. For complete information about creating and saving GIF images for the Web, see Chapter 20.

PC Paintbrush's PCX

PCX doesn't stand for anything. Rather, it's the extension that PC Paintbrush assigns to images saved in its native file format. Though the format is losing favor, there are still a lot of PCX images in use today, largely due to the fact that PC Paintbrush is the oldest painting program for DOS. Photoshop supports PCX images with up to 16 million colors.

Adobe's paperless PDF

The *Portable Document Format* (PDF) is a variation on the PostScript printing language that permits you to view electronically produced documents on screen. This means you can create a publication in QuarkXPress or PageMaker, export it to PDF, and distribute it without worrying about color separations, binding, and other printing costs. Using a program called Adobe Acrobat, you can open PDF documents, zoom in and out of them, and follow hypertext links by clicking on highlighted words. Adobe distributes both Mac and Windows versions of the Acrobat Reader for free, so just about anyone with a computer can view your stuff in full, natural color.

Photoshop offers only limited support for the PDF format. You can't open full PDF documents created in QuarkXPress or PageMaker; you can only open and save PDF images. And frankly folks, there's very little reason to save an image to PDF. Although the PDF format supports JPEG compression, you have no way to change the amount of compression applied (as you do when saving JPEG images, discussed later in the "JPEG" section of this chapter). Unless you want to save an image for use in Acrobat Exchange — which is restricted to PDF images — then you'll probably want to use some other format instead.

Pixar workstations

Pixar has created some of the most memorable computer-animated movies and commercials in recent memory. Examples include the desk lamps playing with a beach ball from *Luxo, Jr.;* the run-amok toddler from the Oscar-winning *Tin Toy;* and the commercial adventures of a Listerine bottle that boxes Gingivitis one day and swings Tarzan-like through a spearmint forest the next. But Pixar really made the grade with the feature-length *Toy Story*, which provided Disney with enough merchandising options to last a lifetime.

Pixar works its 3D magic using mondo-expensive workstations. Photoshop enables you to open a still image created on a Pixar machine or save an image to the Pixar format so you can integrate it into a 3D rendering. The Pixar format supports grayscale and RGB images.

PNG for the Web

Pronounced *ping*, the PNG format permits you to save 16 million-color images without compression for use on the Web. As I write this, only a few browsers support PNG, including Netscape Navigator 3.0. But for those folks who want full-color images without the pesky visual compression artifacts that you get with JPEG, PNG may well be a big player in the future.

PNG was invented for the World Wide Web, and I've never seen anyone use it for a purpose other than the Web. So like all things Webby, you'll find more information about it in Chapter 20.

Scitex image-processors

Some high-end commercial printers use Scitex printing devices to generate color separations of images and other documents. Photoshop can open images digitized with Scitex scanners and save the edited images to the *Scitex CT* (*Continuous Tone*) format. Because you need special hardware to transfer images from the Mac to a Scitex drive, you'll probably want to consult with your local Scitex service bureau technician before saving to the CT format. It's very possible that the technician will prefer that you submit images in the native Photoshop, TIFF, or JPEG format. The Scitex CT format supports grayscale and CMYK images.

TrueVision's TGA

TrueVision's Targa and NuVista video boards let you overlay Macintosh graphics and animation onto live video. The effect is called *chroma keying* because typically, a key color is set aside to let the live video show through. TrueVision designed the TGA (*Targa*) format to support 32-bit images that include 8-bit *alpha channels* capable of displaying the live video. Though support for TGA is scarce among Macintosh applications, it is widely implemented among professional-level color and video applications on the PC.

Interapplication formats

In the name of interapplication harmony, Photoshop supports a few software-specific formats that enable you to trade files with programs that run on the Mac, including such popular object-oriented programs as Illustrator and QuarkXPress. Photoshop can also trade images directly with two painting pioneers, MacPaint and PixelPaint. And finally, you can use Photoshop to edit frames from a QuickTime movie created with Adobe Premiere.

Rasterizing an Illustrator or FreeHand file

Photoshop supports object-oriented files saved in the EPS format. EPS is specifically designed for saving object-oriented graphics that you intend to print to a PostScript output device. Every drawing program and most page-layout programs permit you to save EPS documents.

Prior to Version 4, Photoshop could interpret only a small subset of EPS operations supported by Illustrator. But Photoshop 4 now offers a full-blown EPS translation engine, capable of interpreting EPS illustrations created in FreeHand, Canvas, CorelDraw, and more. You can even open EPS drawings that contain imported images, something else Photoshop 3 could not do. This is one of those extremely important but little-known advances that should make your life *much* easier in the future.

When you open an EPS illustration, Photoshop *rasterizes* (or *renders*) the artwork — that is, it converts it from a collection of objects to a bitmapped image. During the open operation, Photoshop presents the Rasterize Generic EPS Format dialog box (see Figure 4-8), which enables you to specify the size and resolution of the image, just as you can in the New dialog box. Assuming the illustration contains no imported images, you can render it as large or as small as you want without any loss of image quality.

Figure 4-8
You can specify the size and resolution at which Photoshop renders an EPS illustration.

If the EPS illustration does contain an imported image or two, you'll need to know the resolution of the images and factor this information into the Rasterize Generic EPS Format dialog box. Select anything but Pixels from both the Width and Height pop-up menus, and leave the suggested values unchanged. Then enter the setting for the highest-resolution imported image into the Resolution option box. (If all the images are low-rez, you may want to double or triple the Resolution value to ensure that the objects render smoothly.)

You should always select the Anti-aliased check box unless you're rendering a very large image — say, 300 ppi or higher. *Antialiasing* blurs pixels to soften the edges of the objects so that they don't appear jagged. When you're rendering a very large image, the difference between image and printer resolution is less noticeable, so antialiasing is unwarranted.

Photoshop renders the illustration to a single layer against a transparent background. Before you can save the rasterized image to a format other than native Photoshop, you have to eliminate the transparency by choosing Layer ⇨ Flatten Image. Or save a flattened version of the image to a separate file by choosing File ⇨ Save a Copy.

Rendering an EPS illustration is an extremely useful technique for resolving printing problems. If you regularly work in Illustrator or FreeHand, you no doubt have encountered *limitcheck errors,* which occur when an illustration is too complex for an imagesetter or other high-end output device to print. If you're frustrated with the printer and you're tired of wasting your evening trying to figure out what's wrong (sound familiar?), use Photoshop to render the illustration at 300 ppi and print it. Nine out of ten times, this technique works flawlessly.

If Photoshop can't *parse* the EPS file — which is a techy way of saying that Photoshop can't break down the individual objects — it attempts to open the PICT (Mac) or TIFF (Windows) preview. Most of the time, this exercise is totally useless, but you may occasionally want to take a quick look at an illustration in order to, say, match the placement of elements in an image to those in the drawing.

Placing an EPS illustration

If you want to introduce an EPS graphic into the foreground image rather than rendering it into a new image window of its own, choose File ⇨ Place. Unlike other File menu commands, Place supports only EPS illustrations.

After you import the EPS graphic, it appears inside a box with a great big X across it. Photoshop lets you move, scale, and rotate the illustration into position before rasterizing it to pixels. Drag a corner handle to resize the image, drag outside the image to rotate it. You can also nudge the graphic into position by pressing the arrow keys. When you get everything the way you want it, press the Return key to rasterize the illustration. Or double-click inside the box. If the placement isn't perfect, not to worry. The graphic appears on a separate layer so you can move it with complete freedom. To cancel the Place operation, press Escape instead of Return.

Saving an EPS image

Illustrator 6 now supports a wide range of file formats, including TIFF (finally). But it's implementation is pretty awful, especially where large images are concerned. If you import an image saved in any format but EPS, it takes forever to import, it takes forever to print, and it swells the size of your illustration like a balloon. Unlike

FreeHand, which smartly tags a TIFF file on disk, Illustrator insists on importing every pixel. And Illustrator is not adept at dealing with pixels.

So if you want to import an image into Illustrator, your best bet remains EPS. Illustrator tags EPS images on disk, so they don't slow down the program, and they print very quickly. Unfortunately, EPS is not a particularly efficient format for saving images. An EPS image may be three to four times larger than the same image saved to the TIFF format with LZW compression. It's the price we pay.

To save an image in the EPS format, choose Photoshop EPS from the Format pop-up menu in the Save dialog box. After you press Return, Photoshop displays the dialog box shown in Figure 4-9. The options in this dialog box work as follows:

⤷ **Preview:** Technically, an EPS document comprises two parts: a pure Post-Script-language description of the graphic for the printer, and a bitmapped preview that enables you to see the graphic on-screen. Select the Macintosh (8 bits/pixel) option from the Preview pop-up menu to save a 256-color PICT preview of the image. Or select the Macintosh (JPEG) option for a 24-bit preview (which in most cases takes up less room on disk, thanks to the JPEG compression). If you want to import the image into Illustrator 4 or some other Windows application, select TIFF (8 bits/pixel). The 1-bit options provide black-and-white previews only, which are useful if you want to save a little room on disk. Select the None option to include no preview and save even more disk space.

Figure 4-9
When saving an image in the EPS format, you can specify the type of preview and tack on some printing attributes.

⤷ **Encoding:** If you're exporting an image for use with Illustrator, QuarkXPress, or some other established program, select the Binary encoding option (also known as *Huffman encoding*), which compresses an EPS document by substituting shorter codes for frequently used characters. The letter *a*, for example, receives the 3-bit code *010* rather than its standard 8-bit ASCII code, *01100001* (the binary equivalent of what we humans call *97*). Some programs don't recognize Huffman encoding, in which case you must select the ASCII option. (*ASCII* stands for *American Standard Code for Information Interchange,* which is fancy jargon for *text-only.* In other words, you can open and edit an ASCII EPS document in a word processor, provided you know how to read and write PostScript.)

Only select one of the JPEG options if you'll be printing your final artwork to a PostScript Level 2 printer. Earlier PostScript devices do not support EPS artwork with JPEG compression. JPEG compression results in smaller files on disk, but it also degrades the quality of the image. Select JPEG (Maximum Quality) to invoke the least degradation. For more information, read the "JPEG" section later in this chapter.

∽ **Clipping Path:** These options allow you to select a path that you created using the path tool and saved in the Paths panel of the Layers palette. You can then use that path to mask the contents of the EPS image. For complete information about clipping paths, see the final section in Chapter 11.

∽ **Include Halftone Screen:** EPS does have one significant advantage over other image formats: It can retain printing attributes. If you specified a custom halftone screen using the Screen button inside the Page Setup dialog box, you can save this setting with the EPS document by selecting the Include Halftone Screen check box. For information on halftone screens, see Chapter 7.

∽ **Include Transfer Function:** As described in Chapter 7, you can change the brightness and contrast of a printed image using the Transfer button inside the Page Setup dialog box. To save these settings with the EPS document, select the Include Transfer Function check box.

∽ **Transparent Whites:** When saving black-and-white EPS images in Photoshop, the two check boxes above drop away, replaced by Transparent Whites. Select this option to make all white pixels in the image transparent.

Although Photoshop EPS is the only format that offers the Transparent Whites option, many programs — including Illustrator 6 — treat white pixels in black-and-white TIFF images as transparent as well.

QuarkXPress DCS

Quark developed a variation on the EPS format called *DCS (Desktop Color Separation).* When you work in QuarkXPress, this format enables you to print color separations of imported artwork. If you save a CMYK image in the EPS format, Photoshop displays the additional Desktop Color Separation options shown in Figure 4-10. When you save to the DCS format, Photoshop creates five files on disk: one master document plus one file each for the cyan, magenta, yellow, and black color channels. Select Off (Single File) to save the image as a single standard EPS document. Select one of the three On options to save the separations as five independent DCS files.

Figure 4-10
Photoshop offers four
DCS options when you
save a CMYK image in
the EPS format.

Photoshop also gives you the option of saving a 72 ppi PostScript-language version of the image inside the DCS master document. Independent from the bitmapped preview — which you specify as usual by selecting a Preview option — the 72 ppi *composite* image enables you to print a low-resolution version of a DCS image imported into QuarkXPress or PageMaker to a consumer-quality printer such as a LaserWriter. If you're using a black-and-white printer, select the 72 pixel/inch grayscale option; if you're using a color printer, select the final option. Note that the composite image significantly increases the size of the master document on disk.

You convert an image to the CMYK mode by choosing Image ⇨ Mode ⇨ CMYK Color. Do not choose this command casually. Converting back and forth between RGB and CMYK results in a loss of color information. Only use the CMYK Color command if you want to convert an image to CMYK color for good. For more information, see Chapter 5.

Premiere Filmstrip

Adobe Premiere is the foremost QuickTime movie-editing application for the Mac. The program is a wonder when it comes to fades, frame merges, and special effects, but it offers no frame-by-frame editing capabilities. For example, you can't draw a mustache on a person in the movie, nor can you make brightly colored brush strokes swirl about in the background — at least, not inside Premiere.

However, you can export the movie to the Filmstrip format, which is a file-swapping option exclusive to Photoshop and Premiere. A Filmstrip document organizes frames in a long vertical strip, as shown on the left side of Figure 4-11. The right side of the figure shows the movie after each individual frame was edited in ways not permitted by Premiere. (I believe it's in the Constitution somewhere that a brother has the right to edit his sister's face in bizarre and unusual ways.)

Figure 4-11
Four frames from a QuickTime movie as they appear in the Filmstrip format before (left) and after (right) editing the frames in Photoshop.

A gray bar separates each frame. The number of each frame appears on the right; the *SMPTE (Society of Motion Picture and Television Engineers)* time code appears on the left. The structure of the three-number time code is *minutes:seconds:frames,* with 30 frames per second.

If you change the size of a Filmstrip document inside Photoshop in any way, you cannot save the image back to the Filmstrip format. Feel free to paint and apply effects, but stay the heck away from the Image Size and Canvas Size commands.

 I don't really delve into the Filmstrip format anywhere else in this book, so I want to pass along a couple of quick Filmstrip tips right here and now:

⇝ First, you can scroll up and down exactly one frame at a time by pressing Shift-Page Up or Shift-Page Down, respectively.

⇝ Second, you can move a selection exactly one frame up or down by pressing ⌘-Shift-up arrow or ⌘-Shift-down arrow.

⇝ If you want to clone the selection as you move it, press ⌘-Shift-Option-up arrow or ⌘-Shift-Option-down arrow.

And finally — here's the great one — you can select several sequential frames and edit them all at once by following these steps:

STEPS   **Selecting Sequential Frames in a Movie**

Step 1.   **Select the first frame you want to edit.** Select the rectangular marquee tool by pressing the M key. Then drag around the area you want to edit in the movie. (This is the only step that takes any degree of care or coordination whatsoever.)

Step 2.   **Switch to the quick mask mode by pressing the Q key.** The areas around the selected frame are overlaid with pink.

Step 3.   **Set the magic wand Tolerance value to 0.** Double-click on the magic wand tool icon in the toolbox to display the Magic Wand Options panel in the Brushes palette. Enter 0 for the Tolerance value and deselect the Anti-aliased check box.

Step 4.   **Click inside the selected frame (the one that's not pink) with the magic wand tool.** This selects the unmasked area inside the frame.

Step 5.   **Press ⌘-Shift-Option-down arrow to clone the unmasked area to the next frame in the movie.** When you exit the quick mask mode, both this frame and the one above it will be selected.

Step 6.   **Repeat several times.** Keep ⌘-Shift-Option-down arrowing until you've gotten rid of the pink stuff on all the frames that you want to select.

Step 7.   **Exit the quick mask mode by pressing the Q key again.** All frames appear selected.

Step 8.   **Edit the frames to your heart's content.**

If you're new to Photoshop, half of those steps, if not all of them, probably went sailing over your head like so many extraterrestrial spaceships. If you want to learn more about selections and cloning, see Chapter 11. In Chapter 12, I explore the quick mask mode and other masking techniques in depth. After you finish reading those chapters, you can come back to this section and see if it doesn't make a little more sense.

The process of editing individual frames as just described is sometimes called *roto-scoping,* named after the traditional technique of combining live-action film with animated sequences. You also can try out some *scratch-and-doodle* techniques, which is where an artist scratches and draws directly on frames of film. As if that's not enough, you can emulate *xerography,* in which an animator makes Xerox copies of photographs, enhances the copies using markers or whatever else is convenient, and shoots the finished artwork, frame by frame, on film. In a nutshell, Photoshop extends Premiere's functionality by adding animation to its standard supply of video-editing capabilities.

You can save an image in the Filmstrip format only if you opened the image as a Filmstrip document and did not change the size of the image. To do so, just press ⌘-S.

MacPaint

MacPaint was the first painting program for the Mac. In fact, MacPaint and MacWrite preceded all other Macintosh applications and shipped with the first 128K Mac. Last updated in 1987, MacPaint 2.0 is severely lacking by today's standards. The good news is, it's no longer for sale.

The MacPaint format accommodates 1-bit (black-and-white) images on vertically-oriented, 7.5 × 10.5-inch pages. End of story. It's no wonder that Photoshop can open MacPaint images but can't save to the MacPaint format. What would be the point? If you dig, you can find truckloads of old clip art in the MacPaint format, which is the only reason Photoshop bothers to support it at all.

PixelPaint

PixelPaint from Pixel Resources was the first color painting application for the Mac. In its day, it was a show-stopper, easily as remarkable as Photoshop is now. In fact, PixelPaint's demise started about the same time that Photoshop arrived on the scene. Some coincidence, huh?

Photoshop supports the old 8-bit PixelPaint format, the native format for the standard PixelPaint 1.0 and 2.0. PixelPaint Professional offers a 24-bit format that Photoshop does not support. I guess Adobe figures that most of its users gave up on PixelPaint when Photoshop became available. Yet the most recent upgrade, PixelPaint Professional 3, didn't sell well, but it provided a number of capabilities that Photoshop is still trying to catch up with, including a scripting option for recording operations and more flexible channel operations. To trade an image with PixelPaint Professional 3, save it in the TIFF or PICT format.

The mainstream formats

The formats discussed so far are mighty interesting, and they all fulfill their own niche purposes. But the following formats — JPEG, PICT, and TIFF — are the all-stars of Macintosh imagery. You'll use these formats the most because of their outstanding compression capabilities and almost universal support among Macintosh graphics applications.

JPEG

Photoshop supports the JPEG format, named after the folks who designed it, the Joint Photographic Experts Group. JPEG is the most efficient and essential compression format currently available and is likely to be the compression standard for years to come. It is a *lossy* compression scheme, which means that it sacrifices image quality to conserve space on disk. However, you can control how much data is lost during the save operation.

When you save an image in the JPEG format, Photoshop displays the dialog box in Figure 4-12, which offers a total of 11 compression settings. (That's seven more than Photoshop 3 offered, and two more than Photoshop 2.5.) Just select an option from the Quality pop-up menu or drag the slider triangle from 0 to 10 to specify the quality setting. Of the named options, Low takes up the least space on disk but distorts the image rather severely; Maximum retains the highest amount of image quality but consumes more disk space. Of the numbered options, 0 is the most severe compressor and 10 does the least damage.

Figure 4-12
The new JPEG Options dialog box provides a total of 11 compression settings, ranging from 0 (heaviest compression) to 10 (best quality), as well as some new Web options.

JPEG evaluates an image in 8 × 8-pixel blocks, using a technique called *Adaptive Discrete Cosine Transform* (or ADCT, as in "Yes, I'm an acronym ADCT"). It averages the 24-bit value of every pixel in the block (or 8-bit value of every pixel in the case of a grayscale image). It then stores the average color in the upper left pixel in the block and assigns the remaining 63 pixels smaller values relative to the average.

Next, JPEG divides the block by an 8 × 8 block of its own called the *quantization matrix,* which homogenizes the pixels' values by changing as many as possible to zero. It's this process that saves the majority of disk space and loses data. When Photoshop opens a JPEG image, it can't recover the original distinction between the zero pixels, so the pixels become the same or similar colors. Finally, JPEG applies lossless Huffman encoding to translate repeating values to a single symbol.

In most instances, I recommend that you use JPEG only at the Maximum quality setting (8 or higher), at least until you gain some experience with it. The smallest amount of JPEG compression saves more space on disk than any non-JPEG compression format and still retains the most essential detail from the original image. Figure 4-13 shows a grayscale image saved at each of the four compression settings.

The samples are arranged in rows from highest image quality (upper left) to lowest quality (lower right). Below each sample is the size of the compressed document on disk. Saved in the only moderately compressed native Photoshop format, the image consumes 116K on disk. From 116K to 28K — the result of the lowest-quality JPEG setting — is a remarkable savings, but it comes at a price.

I've taken the liberty of sharpening the focus of strips in each image so that you can see more easily how JPEG averages neighboring pixels to achieve smaller file

Figure 4-13
Four JPEG settings applied to a single image, with the highest image quality setting illustrated at the upper left and the lowest at bottom right.

Maximum   66K   High   50K

Medium   33K   Low   28K

sizes. The first strip in each image appears in normal focus, the second strip is sharpened once by choosing Filter ⇨ Sharpen ⇨ Sharpen More, and the third strip is sharpened twice. I've also adjusted the gray levels to make the differences even more pronounced. You can see that although the lower image quality setting leads to a dramatic saving in file size, it also gums up the image excessively. The effect, incidentally, is more obvious on-screen. And believe me, after you familiarize yourself with JPEG compression, you'll be able to spot other people's overly compressed JPEG images a mile away. It's not something that you want to exaggerate in your images.

To see the impact of JPEG compression on a full-color image, check out Color Plate 4-1. The original image consumes 693K in the native Photoshop format, but 116K when compressed at the JPEG module's Maximum setting. To better demonstrate the differences between different settings, I enlarged one portion of the image and oversharpened another.

JPEG is a *cumulative compression scheme,* meaning that Photoshop recompresses an image every time you save it in the JPEG format. There's no disadvantage to repeatedly saving an image to disk during a single session, because JPEG always works from the on-screen version. But if you close an image, reopen it, and save it in the JPEG format, you inflict a small amount of damage. Therefore, use JPEG sparingly. In the best of all possible worlds, you should only save to the JPEG format after you finish *all* work on an image. Even in a pinch, you should apply all filtering effects before saving to JPEG, because these have a habit of exacerbating imperfections in image quality.

JPEG is best used when compressing *continuous-tone* images (images in which the distinction between immediately neighboring pixels is slight). Any image that includes gradual color transitions, as in a photograph, qualifies for JPEG compression. JPEG is not the best choice for saving screen shots, line drawings (especially those converted from EPS graphics), and other high-contrast images. These are better served by a lossless compression scheme such as TIFF with LZW. The JPEG format is available when you are saving grayscale, RGB, and CMYK images.

Occupying the bottom half of the JPEG Options dialog box are three radio buttons, designed to optimize JPEG images for the World Wide Web. When creating images for print media, select the first option, Baseline ("Standard"). For information on the other two radio buttons, see Chapter 20.

PICT

PICT (*Macintosh Picture*) is the Macintosh system software's native graphics format. Based on the QuickDraw display language that the system software uses to convey images on-screen, PICT is one of the few file formats that handles object-oriented artwork and bitmapped images with equal aplomb. It supports images in any bit depth, size, or resolution. It even supports 32-bit images, so you can save a fourth masking channel when working in the RGB mode.

If you've installed QuickTime, you can subject PICT images to JPEG compression. After you select PICT File from the Format pop-up menu in the Save dialog box, Photoshop offers the compression options shown in Figure 4-14. Although this dialog box appears to provide many of the same compression settings as the one from

Figure 4-12, QuickTime's JPEG compression is actually somewhat inferior to that provided by Photoshop's JPEG format. The difference becomes especially noticeable if you open the file and again save it to disk, effectively reapplying the compression.

Figure 4-14
If QuickTime is installed, Photoshop provides JPEG compression options when you save an image in the PICT format.

In most cases, you'll want to use the JPEG format instead of PICT when compressing images. JPEG images are compatible with the World Wide Web; PICT images are not. Also, more Windows applications recognize JPEG than PICT, and it's extremely difficult to find a Windows program that can handle PICT files with QuickTime JPEG compression (particularly since only about three Windows machines in the western hemisphere are equipped with QuickTime).

In fact, the only reason to use PICT is to prepare an image for a non-PostScript printing device — such as a film recorder — or to ensure low-end compatibility. If you're trying to save an image in a format that your mom can open on her Mac, PICT is a better choice than JPEG. Heck, you can open PICT files inside a word processor, including everything from SimpleText to Microsoft Word. Just be sure mom has QuickTime loaded on her machine.

TIFF

Developed by Aldus back in the early days of the Mac to standardize an ever-growing population of scanned images, TIFF (*Tag Image File Format*) is the most widely supported image printing format across both the Macintosh and PC platforms. Unlike PICT, it can't handle object-oriented artwork and it doesn't support JPEG compression. But it's otherwise unrestricted. In fact, TIFF offers a few tricks of its own that are worth mentioning. When you save an image in the TIFF format, Photoshop displays the TIFF Options dialog box (see Figure 4-15), which offers these options:

↦ **Byte Order:** Leave it to Photoshop to name a straightforward option in the most confusing way possible. Byte Order? No, this option doesn't have anything to do with how you eat your food. Rather, because Macintosh TIFF and PC TIFF are two slightly different formats, this option permits you to specify whether you want to use the image on the Mac or on an IBM PC-compatible machine. I'm sure it has something to do with the arrangement of 8-bit chunks of data, but who cares? You want Mac or you want PC? It's that simple.

Figure 4-15
Photoshop lets you save TIFF files in either the Mac or PC format and compress the image using LZW.

↦ **LZW Compression:** Like Huffman encoding (described earlier in the "Saving an EPS image" section), the LZW (Lempel-Ziv-Welch) compression scheme digs into the computer code that describes an image and substitutes frequently used codes with shorter equivalents. But instead of substituting characters, as Huffman does, LZW substitutes strings of data. Because LZW doesn't so much as touch a pixel in your image, it's entirely lossless. Most image editors and desktop publishing applications — including FreeHand, PageMaker, and QuarkXPress — import LZW-compressed TIFF images, but a few still have yet to catch on.

If names like Huffman and LZW ring a faint bell, it may be because these are the same compression schemes used by Aladdin's StuffIt, Salient's Auto-Doubler, Bill Goodman's Compact Pro, and other compression utilities. For that reason, there's no sense in using an additional utility to compress a TIFF image that was already compressed using LZW. Neither do you want to compress a JPEG image, because JPEG takes advantage of Huffman encoding. You may shave off a couple of K, but it's not enough space to make it worth your time and effort.

In Photoshop, the TIFF format supports up to 24 channels, which is the maximum number permitted in any image. In fact, TIFF is the only format other than "raw" and the native Photoshop format that can save more than four channels. To save a TIFF file without extra mask channels, choose File ⇨ Save a Copy and select the Don't Include Alpha Channels check box. (For complete information on channels, read Chapter 6.)

If you have limited RAM or you're working with a very large TIFF image, you can open up an isolated detail of the image using File ➭ Import ➭ Quick Edit. Photoshop displays a small preview of the image. Drag in the preview to select the area you want to open and press Return. Photoshop opens just that isolated portion of the file. To save the detail back into the larger TIFF image, choose File ➭ Export ➭ Quick Edit.

I must admit that I have a love/hate thing going with Quick Edit. I appreciate the fact that it lets you open small chunks of an image at a time. But I hate the fact that you can open uncompressed TIFF images only, and that Quick Edit doesn't support any format other than TIFF. It doesn't even support the native Photoshop format. What a stinker.

The oddball formats

Can you believe it? After plowing through a half million formats, I still haven't covered them all. The last three are the odd men out. Few programs other than Photoshop support these formats, so you won't be using them to swap files with other applications. Also, these formats don't let you compress images, so you can't use them to conserve disk space. What can you do with these formats? Read the following sections and find out.

Photo CD YCC images

Photoshop can open Eastman Kodak's Photo CD and Pro Photo CD formats directly. This is not an essential capability because a Photo CD contains compressed PICT versions of every image in each of the five scan sizes provided on Photo CDs — from 128×192 pixels (72K) to $2,048 \times 3,072$ pixels (18MB). However, these PICT files are RGB images. The Photo CD format uses the *YCC color model,* a variation on the CIE (Commission Internationale de l'Eclairage) color space discussed in the next chapter. YCC provides a broader range of color — theoretically, every color your eye can see.

The Pro Photo CD format can accommodate each of the five sizes included in the regular Photo CD format, plus one additional size — $4,096 \times 6,144$ pixels (72MB) — that's four times as large as the largest image on a regular Photo CD. As a result, Pro Photo CDs hold only 25 scans; standard Photo CDs hold 100. Like their standard Photo CD counterparts, Pro Photo CD scanners can accommodate 35mm film and slides. But they can also handle

70mm film and 4×5-inch negatives and transparencies. The cost might knock you out, though. While scanning an image to a standard Photo CD costs between $1 and $2, scanning it to a Pro Photo CD costs about $10. It just goes to show you; once you gravitate beyond consumerland, everybody expects you to start coughing up the big bucks.

By opening Photo CD files directly, you can translate the YCC images directly to Photoshop's Lab color mode, another variation on CIE color space that ensures no color loss. The Photo CD files are found inside the IMAGES folder in the PHOTO_CD folder, as shown in Figure 4-16. The PICT images are located inside the Photos folder.

 For more information on the relationship between YCC, Lab, and every other color mode you ever thought you might want to learn about, see Chapter 5.

Figure 4-16
On a Photo CD disk, the YCC documents are in the IMAGES folder inside the PHOTO_CD folder.

Photoshop 4 includes the latest Kodak Color Management Software (CMS), which tweaks colors in Photo CD images based on the kind of film from which they were scanned. When you open a Photo CD image, Photoshop displays the dialog box shown in Figure 4-17. Here you can specify the image size you want to open by selecting an option from the Resolution pop-up menu. The dialog box even shows you a preview of the image. But the options that make a difference are the Source and Destination buttons:

⊷ **Source:** Click on this button to specify the kind of film from which the original photographs were scanned. You can select from two specific Kodak brands — Ektachrome and Kodachrome — or settle for the generic Color Negative Film option. Your selection determines the method by which Photoshop transforms the colors in the image.

↪ **Destination:** After clicking on this button, select an option from the Device pop-up menu to specify the color model you want to use. Select Adobe Photoshop RGB to open the image in the RGB mode; select Adobe Photoshop CIELAB to open the image in the Lab mode.

A CMYK profile can be purchased separately from Kodak. Some stock photo agencies also include special color profiles. For example, Digital Stock currently provides its excellent image library on Photo CDs. The company offers a source profile for its particular drum scanning technology as well as CMYK destination profiles.

Figure 4-17
Use these options to select a resolution and calibrate the colors in the Photo CD image.

To access Photo CD images, you need a single-session or multi-session CD-ROM device and the proper CD extensions from Apple. If you purchased your CD-ROM drive in the last three years, you're probably set; older drives may not be compatible.

Photoshop cannot save to the Photo CD format. And frankly, there's little reason you'd want to do so. Photo CD is strictly a means for transferring slides and film negative onto the world's most ubiquitous and indestructible storage medium, the CD-ROM.

PICT resource (startup screen)

If you really want to open a *PICT resource,* such as the splash screen included with Photoshop or the contents of the Scrapbook, choose File ➪ Import ➪ PICT Resource, as described in the upcoming "Lifting PICT resources" section. The PICT Resource option provided by the Open and Save dialog boxes is useful only for opening, editing, and saving *startup screens.*

What is a startup screen? Well, when you boot your computer, a message appears welcoming you to the great big wonderful Macintosh experience. This is the default startup screen included with the system software. However, you can change the startup screen by creating an image and saving it in the PICT Resource file format under the name *StartupScreen* in the root directory of your System Folder. When I recently changed over to a Power Mac 7100, I decided that the old startup screen must die and a new startup screen must dawn. Hence, Figure 4-18. I'm so proud of the darn thing — it shows off a host of third-party filters, many of which are included for your perusal on the CD — that I decided to include a full-color version of it in Color Plate 4-2.

Figure 4-18
An example of a custom startup screen saved as a PICT resource file.

To save an image as a startup screen, first make sure the resolution of the image is set to 72 ppi in the Image Size dialog box (as explained earlier in this chapter). Then choose File ⇨ Save, select the PICT Resource option from the Format pop-up menu, name the image *StartupScreen*, and save it in your System Folder. The PICT Resources Options dialog box appears (as in Figure 4-19), asking you to enter a four-character Name code. The secret code is *SCRN*.

Figure 4-19
Be sure to set the Resolution to 72, the Name to SCRN, and the Compression to None when saving a custom startup screen.

If you're saving a 24-bit startup screen, the PICT Resources Options dialog box offers a bunch of QuickTime compression options. *Don't select any of them!* Because QuickTime isn't built into the ROM of your computer, it won't be available when the startup screen appears, and therefore a weird-looking, stretched error message will appear on-screen instead. To avoid this, select None from the Compression options.

For best results, create a startup screen that conforms to the exact dimensions of your screen. If you're unsure what those dimensions are, consult Table 4-1 near the beginning of this chapter.

Opening a raw document

A *raw document* is a plain binary file stripped of all extraneous information. It contains no compression scheme, it specifies no bit depth or image size, and it offers no color mode. Each byte of data indicates a brightness value on a single color channel, and that's it. Photoshop offers this function specifically so that you can open images created in undocumented formats, such as those created on mainframe computers.

To open an image of unknown origin, choose File ➪ Open and select the Show All Files check box. Then select the desired image and choose Raw from the Format pop-up menu. After you press Return, the dialog box shown in Figure 4-20 appears, featuring these options:

- ☞ **Width, Height:** If you know the dimensions of the image in pixels, enter the values in these option boxes.

- ☞ **Swap:** Click on this button to swap the Width value with the Height value.

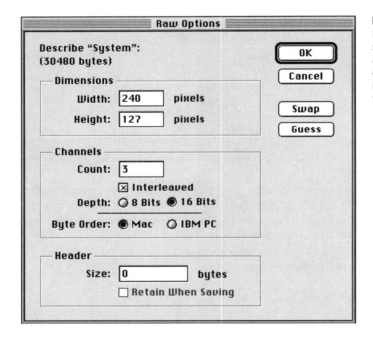

Figure 4-20
Photoshop requires you to specify the size of an image and the number of color channels when you open an image that does not conform to a standardized file format.

- ☞ **Count:** Enter the number of color channels in this option box. If the document is an RGB image, enter 3; if it is a CMYK image, enter 4.

- ☞ **Interleaved:** Select this value if the color values are stored sequentially by pixels. In an RGB image, the first byte represents the red value for the first pixel, the second byte represents the green value for that pixel, the third the blue value, and so on. If you turn this check box off, the first byte represents the red value for the first pixel, the second value represents the red value for the second pixel, and so on. When Photoshop finishes describing the red channel, it describes the green channel and then the blue channel.

- **Depth:** Select the number of bits per color channel. Most images contain 8 bits per channel, but scientific scans from mainframe computers may contain 16.

- **Byte Order:** If you specify 16 bits per channel, you have to tell Photoshop whether the image comes from a Mac or a PC.

- **Header:** This value tells Photoshop how many bytes of data at the beginning of the file comprise header information that it can ignore.

- **Retain Header When Saving:** If the Header value is greater than zero, you can instruct Photoshop to retain this data when you save the image in a different format.

- **Guess:** If you know the Width and Height values but you don't know the number of bytes in the header — or vice versa — you can ask Photoshop for help. Fill in either the size or header information and then click on the Guess button to ask Photoshop to take a stab at the unknown value. Photoshop estimates all this information when the Raw Options dialog box first appears. Generally speaking, if it doesn't estimate correctly the first time around, you're on your own. But hey, the Guess button is worth a shot.

If a raw document is a CMYK image, it opens as an RGB image with an extra masking channel. To correctly display the image, choose Image ⇨ Mode ⇨ Multichannel to free the four channels from their incorrect relationship. Then recombine them by choosing Image ⇨ Mode ⇨ CMYK Color.

Saving a raw document

Photoshop also allows you to save to the raw document format. This capability is useful when you create files that you want to transfer to mainframe systems or output to devices that don't support other formats, such as the Kodak XL7700.

Do not save 256-color indexed images to the raw format, or you will lose the color lookup table and therefore lose all color information. Be sure to first convert such images to RGB or one of the other full-color modes before saving.

When you save an image in the raw document format, Photoshop presents the dialog box shown in Figure 4-21. The dialog box options work as follows:

- **File Type:** Enter the four-character file type code (TIFF, PICT, and so on) in this option box. (You may want to check the documentation for the application you plan to use to open the raw document.) If you plan to use this file on a computer other than a Mac, you can enter any four characters you like; only Macs use this code.

Figure 4-21
When saving a raw document, enter file type and creator codes and specify the order of data in the file.

∞ **File Creator:** Enter the four-character *creator code,* which tells the system software which application created the file. By default, the creator code is 8BIM, Photoshop's code. Ignore this option unless you have a specific reason for changing it — for example, to open the image in a particular Macintosh application. (You won't hurt anything by changing the code, but you will prevent Photoshop from opening the image when you double-click on the document icon at the Finder desktop.)

∞ **Header:** Enter the size of the header in bytes. If you enter any value but zero, you must fill in the header using a data editor such as Norton Disk Editor or Central Point Software's MacTools.

∞ **Save Image In:** Select the Interleaved Order option to arrange data sequentially by pixels, as described earlier. To group data by color channel, select Non-interleaved Order.

How to import PICT elements

Right about now, you're probably hoping against hope that you never see another format again. Personally, I thought my brain was going to dissolve during that last section. Talk about your raw topics! Anyway, on to bigger and better things, including — do you believe it? — more formats! But these last few formats are more interesting. I promise.

The first topic of discussion is importing PICT images into Photoshop via the File ➪ Import submenu. You can do this using two different methods. These functions enable you to open Canvas and MacDraw Pro documents and extract PICT images from places where you never expected to find them.

Rendering a PICT drawing

As I mentioned back in "The mainstream formats" section, Apple designed the PICT format to handle both images and object-oriented drawings. In fact, if you use Canvas, ClarisDraw, or some other QuickDraw drawing program, you probably save a fair amount of your images to the PICT format. Photoshop provides a plug-in module that lets you render an object-oriented PICT file and convert it to an antialiased image, just as you can render an EPS graphic.

Choose File ➪ Import ➪ Anti-aliased PICT, select the desired drawing, and click on the Open button or press Return. Photoshop displays the Anti-aliased PICT dialog box, which allows you to specify the size of the image. The drawing is object-oriented, so you can render it as large or as small as you want without any loss of image quality. Select the Constrain Proportions check box to preserve the width-to-height ratio of the drawing. You also can change the colors in the drawing to gray values or open the drawing as an RGB image. Photoshop automatically antialiases objects to give them soft edges.

Photoshop renders PICT drawings remarkably well, especially compared to other applications that import PICT — mostly notably PageMaker and QuarkXPress, both of which do a pretty lousy job. However, Photoshop does not support bitmapped patterns in a PICT drawing. Any patterns render to solid color.

Lifting PICT resources

When you choose File ➪ Import ➪ PICT Resource, Photoshop lets you open an application or other resource file on disk and browse through any PICT images it may contain. Figure 4-22 shows the dialog box that appears after you select a file to open. You use the double arrow symbols to advance from one PICT image to the next. Click on the Preview button to display the image in the preview box.

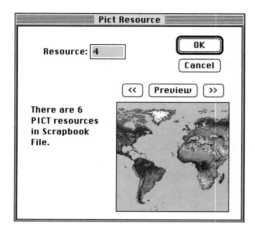

Figure 4-22
Choose File ⇨ Import ⇨ PICT Resource to browse through the PICT images inside an application or other file that contains a resource fork, such as the Scrapbook.

The best use for File ⇨ Import ⇨ PICT Resource is to open images directly from the Scrapbook. In fact, this function becomes phenomenally practical if you use a commercial or shareware screen-capture utility (such as Mainstay's Capture) that can store screens in the Scrapbook, as demonstrated in Figure 4-23. You can process your screen shots en masse at your leisure. In fact, this is how I created many of the screen shots in this book.

Figure 4-23
Use a commercial or shareware screen-capture utility to save your screen shots to the Scrapbook and then use Photoshop to process them in a single sitting.

Back in previous Photoshop manuals, Adobe used to suggest that you try to open the Photoshop application using File ⇨ Import ⇨ PICT Resource. But this meant trying to force Photoshop to open itself, which is a very dangerous operation. So now the one and only application that File ⇨ Import ⇨ PICT Resource *can't* open is Photoshop.

If you're feeling like wasting a little time, and you have DiskTop or ResEdit handy, there is a way around this little problem that's safe as milk. First, duplicate the Photoshop application by Option-dragging it to a new location at the Finder level. Then change the four-character creator code to something meaningless like XXXX. (You'll need DiskTop or ResEdit for this operation.) Finally, open the dummy application with File ⇨ Import ⇨ PICT Resource. There's some amusing stuff in there, including the graphics from both splash screens.

Still can't get that file open?

If you have problems opening or saving any of the formats listed in this chapter — particularly the PC-type formats, such as BMP, GIF, PCX, and others — you may want to try out DeBabelizer from Equilibrium. Absolutely the best format converter bar none, DeBabelizer handles every format Photoshop handles, as well as Dr. Halo's CUT, Fractal Design Painter's RIFF, the animation formats PICS, FLI, and ANM, as well as UNIX workstation formats for Silicon Graphics, Sun Microsystems, and others.

Resampling and Cropping___

After you bring up an image — whether you created it from scratch or opened an existing image stored in one of the five billion formats discussed in the preceding pages — its size and resolution are established. However, neither size nor resolution is set in stone. Photoshop provides two methods for changing the number of pixels in an image: resampling and cropping.

Resizing versus resampling

Typically, when folks talk about *resizing* an image, they mean enlarging or reducing it without changing the number of pixels in the image, as demonstrated back in Figure 4-1. By contrast, to *resample* an image is to scale it so that it contains a larger or smaller number of pixels. With resizing, there is an inverse relationship between size and resolution — size goes up when resolution goes down, and vice versa. But resampling affects either size or resolution independently. Figure 4-24 shows an image resized and resampled to 50 percent of its original dimensions. The resampled and original images have identical resolutions, while the resized image has twice the resolution of its companions.

Figure 4-24
An image (top) resized (bottom left) and resampled (bottom right) down to 50 percent. The resized image sports a higher resolution; the resampled one contains fewer pixels.

Resized   Resampled

Resizing an image

To resize an image, use one of the techniques discussed in the "Changing the printing resolution" section near the beginning of this chapter. To briefly recap, the best method is to choose Image ⇨ Image Size, turn off the Resample Image check box, and enter a value into the Resolution option box. See Figure 4-2 to refresh your memory.

Resampling an image

You also use Image ⇨ Image Size to resample an image. The difference is that you leave the Resample Image check box turned on, as shown in Figure 4-25. As its name implies, the Resample Image check box is the key to resampling.

Figure 4-25
With the Resample
Image check box
turned on, you can
modify the number of
pixels in your image.

When Resample Image is selected, the Resolution value is independent of both sets of Width and Height values. (The only difference between the two sets of options is that the top options work in pixels, and the bottom options work in relative units of measure like percent and inches.) You can increase the number of pixels in an image by increasing any of the five values in the dialog box, or decrease the number of pixels by decreasing any value. Photoshop stretches or shrinks the image according to the new size specifications.

At all times, you can see the new number of pixels that Photoshop will assign to the image, as well as the increased or decreased file size. In Figure 4-25, for example, the Pixel Dimensions value at the top of the dialog box reads *362K (was 1.13M)*, which shows that the file size has decreased. You can also look to the Print Size values, which are set to 56 percent. All of these indicators show that I'm about to dump pixels.

To calculate the pixels in the resampled image, Photoshop must use its powers of interpolation, as explained back in the "General preferences" section of Chapter 2. Quite handily, you can now modify the interpolation setting right inside the Image Size dialog box. Simply select the desired method from the Resample Image pop-up menu. Bicubic results in the smoothest effects. Bilinear is faster. And Nearest Neighbor turns off interpolation so Photoshop merely throws away the pixels it doesn't need or duplicates pixels to resample up.

Here are a few more random items you should know about resampling with the Image Size dialog box:

∞ This may sound odd, but you generally want to avoid adding pixels. When you resample up, you're asking Photoshop to make up detail out of thin air, and the program isn't that smart. Simply put, an enlarged image almost never looks better than the original, it merely takes up more disk space and prints slower.

∞ Resampling down, on the other hand, is a very useful technique. It permits you to smooth away photo grain, halftone patterns, and other scanning artifacts. One of the most tried and true rules of thumb is to scan at the maximum resolution permitted by your scanner, and then resample the scan down to, say, 72 or 46 percent (with the interpolation set to Bicubic, naturally). By selecting a round value other than 50 percent, you force Photoshop to jumble the pixels into a regular, homogenous soup. You're left with fewer pixels, but these remaining pixels are better. And you have the added benefit that the image takes up less space on disk.

∞ To make an image tall and thin, or short and fat, you must first turn off the Constrain Proportions check box. This permits you to edit the two Width values entirely independently of the two Height values.

∞ You can resample an image to precisely match the size and resolution of any other open image. While the Image Size dialog box is open, choose the name of the image you want to match from the Window menu.

If you ever get confused inside the Image Size dialog box and you want to return to the original size and resolution settings, press the Option key to change the Cancel button to Reset. Then click on the Reset button to start from the beginning. You can also press Option-Escape or ⌘-Option-period.

Cropping

Another way to change the number of pixels in an image is to *crop* it, which means to clip away pixels around the edges of an image without harming the remaining pixels. (The one exception occurs when you rotate a cropped image, in which case Photoshop has to interpolate pixels to account for the rotation.)

Cropping enables you to focus in on an element in your image. For example, Figure 4-26 shows a bit of urban graffiti from a Digital Stock CD. I like this fellow's face — good chiaroscuro — but I can't quite figure out what's going on with this guy. I mean, what is with the screw. And is that a clown hat or what? All I do is crop around the guy's head to delete all the extraneous image elements and focus right in on his sleepy features, as shown in Figure 4-27.

Figure 4-26
This image contains too much extraneous information. Where should my eye go? I'm so confused.

Figure 4-27
Cropping allows you to clean up the background junk and focus in on the essential foreground image.

Changing the canvas size

One way to crop an image is to choose Image ⇨ Canvas Size, which displays the Canvas Size dialog box shown in Figure 4-28. The options in this dialog box enable you to scale the imaginary *canvas* on which the image rests separately from the image itself.

Figure 4-28
Choose Image ➪ Canvas Size to crop an image or add empty space around the perimeter of an image.

If you enlarge the canvas, Photoshop surrounds the image with a white background (assuming that the background color is white). If you reduce the canvas, you crop the image.

Click inside the Anchor grid to specify the placement of the image on the new canvas. For example, if you want to add space to the bottom of an image, enlarge the canvas size and then click inside the upper middle square. If you want to crop away the upper left corner of an image, create a smaller canvas size and then click on the lower right square. Photoshop 4 offers new little arrows to show how the canvas will shrink or grow.

Using the crop tool

Generally speaking, the Canvas Size command is most useful for enlarging the canvas or shaving a few pixels off the edge of an image. If you want to crop away a large portion of an image, using the crop tool is a better choice.

To crop the image, select the crop tool by pressing the C key. (Selecting the tool manually is quite inconvenient in Photoshop 4, so get used to pressing C.) Then drag with the crop tool to create a rectangular marquee that surrounds the portion of the image you want to retain.

As you drag, you can press the spacebar to temporarily move the crop boundary on the fly. To stop moving the boundary and return to resizing it, release the spacebar. This excellent technique is new to Photoshop 4.

If you don't get the crop marquee right the first time, you can move, scale, or rotate it at will. These operations have been changed in Photoshop 4, significantly for the better in my opinion. But they may come as a bit of a shock to Version 3 users. Here's what you do:

- ↝ Drag inside the crop marquee to move it.

- ↝ Drag one of the square handles to resize the marquee. You can Shift-drag a handle to scale the marquee proportionally (the same percentage vertically and horizontally).

- ↝ Drag outside the crop marquee to rotate it. This may strike you as weird at first, but it works wonderfully.

When the marquee surrounds the exact portion of the image you want to keep, press the Return key or double-click inside it. This action clips away all pixels except those that lie inside and along the border of the crop marquee.

Rotating the crop marquee

As I said, you can rotate an image by dragging outside the crop marquee. Straightening out a crooked image can be a little tricky, however. I wish I had a certified check for every time I thought that I had the marquee rotated properly, only to find that the image was still crooked after I pressed Return. If that happens to you, choose Edit ⇨ Undo (⌘-Z) and try again. Do *not* try using the crop tool a second time to rotate the already rotated image. If you do, Photoshop sets about interpolating between already interpolated pixels, resulting in more lost data. Every rotation gets farther away from the original image.

A better solution is to do it right the first time. Locate a line or general axis in your image that should be straight up and down. Rotate the crop marquee so that it aligns *exactly* with that axis. In Figure 4-29, I've rotated my crop marquee so that one edge bisects the graffiti guy's egg-shaped head. Don't worry that this isn't how you want to crop the image — you're just using the line as a reference. After you arrive at the correct angle for the marquee, then drag the handles to properly size and position the boundary. So long as you don't drag outside the marquee, its angle remains fixed throughout.

Crop marquee   Handles

Rotate cursor

Figure 4-29
Align the crop marquee with an obvious axis in your image to determine the proper angle of rotation.

Cropping an image to match another

There are two ways to crop an image so that it matches the size and resolution of another:

∞ Bring the image that you want to crop forward and choose Image ⇨ Canvas Size. Then, while inside the Canvas Size dialog box, select the name of the image that you want to match from the Window menu.

This method doesn't give you much control when cropping an image, but it's a great way to enlarge the canvas and add empty space around an image.

∞ Better yet, use the crop tool. First, bring the image that you want to match to the front. Then select the crop tool and press Return to display the Cropping Tool Options palette, pictured in Figure 4-30. Select the Fixed Target Size check box, and click on the Front Image button. Photoshop loads the size and resolution values into the palette's option boxes.

Now bring the image that you want to crop to front and drag with the crop tool as normal. Photoshop constrains the crop marquee to the proportions of the targeted image. After you press Return, it crop, resamples, and rotates the image as necessary.

Figure 4-30
Bring the image that you want to target to front, and
click on each of the two options at the top of the
Cropping Tool Options palette.

Cropping a selection

Another way to crop an image is to create a rectangular selection and then choose
Image ⇨ Crop. One of the advantages of this technique is that you don't have to
switch back and forth between the marquee and crop tools. One tool is all you need
to select and crop. (If you're as lazy as I am, the mere act of selecting a tool can
prove more effort than it's worth.) And as with the crop tool, you can now press
the spacebar while drawing a marquee to move it on the fly. It's no trick to get the
placement and size exactly right — the only thing you can't do is rotate.

Another advantage of the Crop command is flexibility. You can draw a selection,
switch windows, apply commands, and generally use any function you like prior to
choosing Image ⇨ Crop. The crop tool, by contrast, is much more demanding. After
drawing a cropping marquee, you can't do *anything* but adjust the marquee until
you press Return to accept the crop or Escape to dismiss it.

And finally, Image ⇨ Crop lets you crop the canvas to the boundaries of an
image pasted from the Clipboard or dragged and dropped from another
image window. As long as the boundaries of the pasted image are rectangular, as in the case of an image copied from a different application, you can

choose Edit ⇨ Paste, ⌘-click on the new layer in the Layers palette to regain the selection outline, and then choose Image ⇨ Crop. This both replaces the former image and crops the window to fit the new image.

Defining
Colors

5 CHAPTER

....

In This Chapter

➠ How to use the color controls in the toolbox

➠ How to select and define colors in the Color Picker dialog box

➠ In-depth examinations of the RGB, HSB, CMYK, and Lab color models

➠ How to create grayscale and black-and-white images

➠ Introductions to the Trumatch and Pantone color standards

➠ How to use the Color palette and eyedropper

....

Selecting and Editing Colors ____

Every once in a while, the state of Macintosh graphics technology reminds me
of television in the early 1950s. Only the upper echelon of Photoshop artists can
afford to work exclusively in the wonderful world of color. The rest of us print most
of our images in black and white.

Some of you might be thinking, "Wait a second, what about the equalizing
force of the Internet? It brings color to all of us!" Well, I must concur whole-
heartedly. So read on, yon color user, paying special attention to RGB and
little to CMYK. Then advance to Chapter 20, and learn how you can reduce
color palettes and otherwise prepare your images for the bold new chal-
lenges of the World Wide Web.

Regardless of who you are — print person or Web head — color is a prime concern.
Even gray values, after all, are colors. Many folks have problems accepting this
premise — I guess we're all so used to separating the worlds of grays and other colors in our minds that never the two shall meet. But the fact is, gray values are just
variations on what Noah Webster used to call "The sensation resulting from stimu-
lation of the retina of the eye by light waves of certain lengths." (Give the guy a few
drinks and he'd spout off 19 more definitions, not including the meanings of the

transitive verb.) Just as black and white represent a subset of gray, gray is a subset of color. In fact, you'll find that using Photoshop involves an awful lot of navigating through these and other colorful subsets.

Specifying colors

First off, Photoshop provides four color controls in the toolbox, as shown in Figure 5-1. These icons work as follows:

- **Foreground color:** The foreground color icon indicates the color you apply when you use the type, paint bucket, line, pencil, airbrush, or paintbrush tool or if you Option-drag with the smudge tool. The foreground color also begins any gradation created with the gradient tool. You can apply the foreground color to a selection by choosing Edit ⇨Fill or Edit ⇨Stroke or by pressing Option-Delete. To change the foreground color, click on the foreground color icon to display the Color Picker dialog box or click in an open image window with the eyedropper tool.

Figure 5-1
The color controls provided with Photoshop (along with keyboard shortcuts in parentheses, where applicable).

Switch colors (X)

Foreground color

Background colors

Default color (D)

⮡ **Background color:** The active background color indicates the color you apply with the eraser tool. The background color also ends any gradation created with the gradient tool. You can apply the background color to a selection by pressing the Delete key. To change the background color, click on the background color icon to display the Color Picker dialog box or Option-click in any open image window with the eyedropper tool.

⮡ **Switch colors:** Click on this icon (or press the X key) to exchange the foreground and background colors.

⮡ **Default colors:** Click on this icon (or press the D key) to make the foreground color black and the background color white, according to their factory default settings.

Using the Color Picker

When you click on the foreground or background color icon, Photoshop displays the Color Picker dialog box. (This assumes that Photoshop is the active option in the Color Picker pop-up menu in the General Preferences dialog box. If you select the Apple option, the generic Apple Color Picker appears, as described in the "HSB" section later in this chapter.) Figure 5-2 labels the wealth of elements and options in the Color Picker dialog box, which work as follows:

⮡ **Color slider:** Use the color slider to home in on the color you want to select. Drag up or down on either of the *slider triangles* to select a color from a particular 8-bit range. The colors represented inside the slider correspond to the selected radio button. For example, if you select the H (Hue) radio button, which is the default setting, the slider colors represent the full 8-bit range of hues. If you select S (Saturation), the slider shows the current hue at full saturation at the top of the slider, down to no saturation — or gray — at the bottom of the slider. If you select B (Brightness), the slider shows the 8-bit range of brightness values, from solid color at the top of the slider to absolute black at the bottom. You also can select R (Red), G (Green) or B (Blue), in which case the top of the slider shows you what the current color looks like when subjected to full-intensity red, green, or blue (respectively), and the bottom of the slider shows every bit of red, green, or blue subtracted.

For a proper introduction to the HSB and RGB color models, including definitions of specific terms such as hue, saturation, and brightness, read the "Working in Different Color Modes" section later in this chapter.

Figure 5-2
Use the elements and options in the Color Picker dialog box
to specify a new foreground or background color from the
16-million-color range.

↦ **Color field:** The color field shows a 16-bit range of variations on the current
slider color. Click inside it to move the *color selection marker* and thereby
select a new color. The field graphs colors against the two remaining attributes *not* represented by the color slider. For example, if you select the H (Hue)
radio button, the field graphs colors according to brightness vertically and
saturation horizontally, as demonstrated in the first example of Figure 5-3.
The other examples show what happens to the color field when you select
the S (Saturation) and B (Brightness) radio buttons.

Likewise, Figure 5-4 shows how the field graphs colors when you select the R
(Red), G (Green), and B (Blue) radio buttons. Obviously, it would help a lot
to see these images in color, but you probably wouldn't have been able to
afford this big, fat book if we had printed it in full color. Therefore, I recommend that you experiment with the Color Picker inside your version of
Photoshop or refer to Color Plate 5-1 to see how the dialog box looks when
the H (Hue), S (Saturation), and B (Brightness) options are selected.

 Slider and field always work together to represent the entire 16-million-
color range. The slider displays 256 colors, and the field displays 65,000
variations on the slider color; 256 times 65,000 is 16 million. Therefore, no

matter which radio button you select, you have access to the same colors. It's just that your means of accessing them changes.

Figure 5-3
The color field graphs colors against the two attributes that are not represented in the slider. Here you can see how color is laid out when you select (top to bottom) the H (Hue), S (Saturation), and B (Brightness) radio buttons.

Figure 5-4
The results of selecting (top to bottom) the R (Red), G (Green), and B (Blue) radio buttons.

⌐◦ **Current color:** The color currently selected from the color field appears in the top rectangle immediately to the right of the color slider. Click on the OK button or press Return to make this the current foreground or background color (depending on which color control icon in the toolbox you clicked to display the Color Picker dialog box in the first place).

- **Previous color:** The bottom rectangle just to the right of the color slider shows how the foreground or background color — whichever one you are in the process of editing — looked before you displayed the Color Picker dialog box. Click on the Cancel button or press Escape to leave this color intact.

- **Alert triangle:** The alert triangle appears when you select a bright color that Photoshop can't print using standard process colors. The box below the triangle shows the closest CMYK equivalent, which is invariably a duller version of the color. Click either on the triangle or box to bring the color into the printable range.

Entering numeric color values

In addition to selecting colors using the slider and color field, you can enter specific color values in the option boxes in the lower right region of the Color Picker dialog box. Novices and intermediates may find these options less satisfying to use than the slider and field. However, the options enable artists and print professionals to specify exact color values, whether to make controlled adjustments to a color already in use or to match a color used in another document. These options fall into one of four camps:

- **HSB:** These options stand for hue, saturation, and brightness. Hue is measured on a 360-degree circle. Saturation and brightness are measured from 0 to 100 percent. These options permit access to more than 3 million color variations.

- **RGB:** You can change the amount of the primary colors red, green, and blue by specifying the brightness value of each color from 0 to 255. These options permit access to more than 16 million color variations.

- **Lab:** This acronym stands for *luminosity,* measured from 0 to 100 percent, and two arbitrary color axes, *a* and *b,* whose brightness values range from -128 to 127. These options permit access to more than 6 million color variations.

- **CMYK:** These options display the amount of cyan, magenta, yellow, and black ink required to print the current color. In fact, when you click on the alert triangle, these are the only values that don't change, because these are the values that make up the closest CMYK equivalent.

In my opinion, the numerical range of these options is extremely bewildering. For example, numerically speaking, the CMYK options enable you to create 100 million unique colors, whereas the RGB options permit the standard 16 million variations, and the Lab options permits a scant 6 million. Yet in point of fact, Lab is the largest color space, theoretically encompassing all colors from both CMYK and RGB. The printing standard CMYK provides by far the fewest colors, just the opposite of what you might expect. What gives? Misleading numerical ranges. How do these weird color models work? Keep reading and you'll find out.

Working in Different Color Modes

The four sets of option boxes inside the Color Picker dialog box represent *color models* — or, if you prefer, *color modes* (one less letter, no less meaning, perfect for you folks who are trying to cut down in life). Color models are different ways to define colors both on-screen and on the printed page.

Outside the Color Picker dialog box, you can work inside any one of these color models by choosing a command from the Modes menu. In doing so, you generally change the colors in your image by dumping a few hundred or even thousand colors that have no equivalents in the new color model. The only exception is Lab, which in theory encompasses every unique color your eyes can detect.

Rather than discuss the color models in the order in which they occur in the Modes menu, I cover them in logical order, starting with the most common and widely accepted color model, RGB. Also note that I don't discuss the duotone or multichannel modes at this time. Image ⇨ Mode ⇨ Duotone represents an alternative method for printing grayscale images, and is therefore discussed in Chapter 7. The multichannel mode, meanwhile, is not even a color model. Rather, Image ⇨ Mode ⇨ Multichannel enables you to separate an image into entirely independent channels which you then can swap around and splice back together to create special effects. For more information, see the "Using multichannel techniques" section of Chapter 6.

RGB

RGB is the color model of light. It comprises three *primary colors* — red, green, and blue — each of which can vary between 256 levels of intensity (called *brightness values,* as discussed in previous chapters). The RGB model is also called the *additive primary model,* because a color becomes lighter as you add higher levels of red, green, and blue light. All monitors, projection devices, and other items that transmit or filter light, including televisions, movie projectors, colored stage lights, and even stained glass, rely on the additive primary model.

Red, green, and blue light mix as follows:

- **Red and green:** Full-intensity red and green mix to form yellow. Subtract some red to make chartreuse; subtract some green to make orange. All these colors assume a complete lack of blue.

- **Green and blue:** Full-intensity green and blue with no red mix to form cyan. If you try hard enough, you can come up with 65,000 colors in the turquoise/jade/sky blue/sea green range.

- **Blue and red:** Full-intensity blue and red mix to form magenta. Subtract some blue to make rose; subtract some red to make purple. All these colors assume a complete lack of green.

- **Red, green, and blue:** Full-intensity red, green, and blue mix to form white, the absolute brightest color in the visible spectrum.

- **No light:** Low intensities of red, green, and blue plunge a color into blackness.

Insofar as image editing is concerned, the RGB color model is ideal for editing images on-screen because it provides access to the entire range of 24-bit screen colors. Furthermore, you can save an RGB image in every file format except GIF that is supported by Photoshop. As shown in Table 5-1, the only other color mode that is compatible with a wider range of file formats is grayscale.

Table 5-1	File-Format Support for Photoshop 4's Color Models						
	Bitmap	*Grayscale*	*Duotone*	*Indexed*	*RGB*	*Lab*	*CMYK*
Photoshop	yes	yes	yes	yes	yes	yes	yes
BMP	yes	yes	no	yes	yes	no	no
EPS	yes	yes	yes	yes	yes	yes	yes
GIF	yes	yes	no	yes	no	no	no
JPEG	no	yes	no	no	yes	no	yes
PCX	yes	yes	no	yes	yes	no	no
PICT	yes	yes	no	yes	yes	no	no
PNG	yes	yes	no	yes	yes	no	no
Scitex CT	no	yes	no	no	yes	no	yes
TIFF	yes	yes	no	yes	yes	yes	yes

Table 5-1 lists color models in the order they appear in the Image ➪ Modes submenu. Again, I left out the multichannel mode because it is not a color model. (Also, the multichannel mode can only be saved in the Photoshop and raw formats.) The native Photoshop format, not listed in the table, supports all color models.

On the negative side, the RGB color model provides access to a wider range of colors than you can print. Therefore, if you are designing an image for full-color printing, you can expect to lose many of the brightest and most vivid colors in your image. The only way to entirely avoid such color loss is to scan your image and edit it in the CMYK mode, which can be an exceptionally slow proposition. The better solution is to scan your images to Photo CDs and edit them in the Lab mode, as explained in the upcoming "CIE's Lab" section.

HSB

Back in Photoshop 2, the Modes menu provided access to the HSB — hue, saturation, brightness — color model, now relegated to the Color Picker dialog box and the Color palette (discussed later in this chapter). *Hue* is pure color, the stuff rainbows are made of, measured on a 360-degree circle. Red is located at 0 degrees, yellow at 60 degrees, green at 120 degrees, cyan at 180 degrees (midway around the circle), blue at 240 degrees, and magenta at 300 degrees. It's basically a pie-shaped version of the RGB model at full-intensity.

 To see a fair approximation of what the hue circle looks like, press ⌘-K to display the Preferences dialog box, select Apple from the Color Picker pop-up menu, and press Return. Then click on the foreground or background color icon in the toolbox to display the modular System 7.5 Apple Color Picker dialog box shown in Figure 5-5. If you set the Lightness value to 50 percent or higher, the perimeter of the color wheel shows each and every hue at full saturation. The center of the wheel represents lowest saturation. To close the Apple Color Picker, press Return.

Lightness slider bar   Color wheel

Figure 5-5
The Apple Color Picker dialog box graphically demonstrates the HSL color model.

Saturation represents the purity of the color. A zero saturation value equals gray. White, black, and any other colors you can express in a grayscale image have no saturation. Full saturation produces the purest version of a hue.

Brightness is the lightness or darkness of a color. A zero brightness value equals black. Full brightness combined with full saturation results in the most vivid version of any hue.

 The Apple Color Picker uses a slightly different measurement called *lightness*. A zero lightness value still equals black, but a value of 100 percent turns any hue or saturation value to white. Therefore, medium lightness — 50 percent — is required to produce the most vivid version of any hue.

CMYK

In nature, our eyes perceive pigments according to the *subtractive color model*. Sunlight contains every visible color found on earth. When sunlight is projected on an object, the object absorbs (subtracts) some of the light and reflects the rest. The reflected light is the color that you see. For example, a fire engine is bright red because it absorbs all non-red — meaning all blue and green — from the white-light spectrum.

Pigments on a sheet of paper work the same way. You can even mix pigments to create other colors. Suppose you paint a red brush stroke, which absorbs green and blue light, over a blue brush stroke, which absorbs green and red light. You get a blackish mess that has only a modicum of blue and red light left, along with a smidgen of green because the colors weren't absolutely pure.

But wait — every child knows that red and blue mix to form purple. So what gives? What gives is that what you learned in elementary school is only a rude approximation of the truth. Did you ever try mixing a vivid red with a canary yellow only to produce an ugly orange-brown gloop? The reason you didn't achieve the bright orange you wanted is obvious if you stop and think about it. The fact that red starts out darker than bright orange means that you have to add a great deal of yellow before you arrive at orange. And even then, it had better be an incredibly bright lemon yellow, not some deep canary yellow that already has a lot of red in it.

Commercial subtractive primaries

The subtractive primary colors used by commercial printers — cyan, magenta, and yellow — are for the most part very light. Cyan absorbs only red light, magenta absorbs only green light, and yellow absorbs only blue light. Unfortunately, on their own, these colors don't do a very good job of producing dark colors. In fact, at full intensities, cyan, magenta, and yellow all mixed together don't get much beyond a muddy brown. That's where black comes in. Black helps to accentuate shadows, deepen dark colors, and, of course, print real blacks.

In case you're wondering how colors mix in the CMYK model, it's basically the opposite of the RGB model. However, because pigments are not as pure as primary colors in the additive model, there are some differences:

- **Cyan and magenta:** Full-intensity cyan and magenta mix to form a deep blue with a little violet in it. Subtract some cyan to make purple; subtract some magenta to make a dull medium blue. All these colors assume a complete lack of yellow.

- **Magenta and yellow:** Full-intensity magenta and yellow mix to form a brilliant red. Subtract some magenta to make vivid orange; subtract some yellow to make rose. All these colors assume a complete lack of cyan.

- **Yellow and cyan:** Full-intensity yellow and cyan mix to form a bright green with a hint of blue in it. Subtract some yellow to make a deep teal; subtract some cyan to make chartreuse. All these colors assume a complete lack of magenta.

- **Cyan, magenta, and yellow:** Full-intensity cyan, magenta, and yellow mix to form a muddy brown.

- **Black:** Black pigmentation added to any other pigment darkens the color.

- **No pigment:** No pigmentation results in white (assuming that white is the color of the paper).

Editing in CMYK

If you're used to editing RGB images, editing in the CMYK mode can require some new approaches, especially when editing individual color channels. When you view a single color channel in the RGB mode (as discussed in the following chapter), white indicates high-intensity color, and black indicates low-intensity color. It's just the opposite in CMYK. When you view an individual color channel, black means high-intensity color, and white means low-intensity color.

This doesn't mean that RGB and CMYK color channels look like inverted versions of each other. In fact, because the color theory is inverted, they look pretty much the same. But if you're trying to achieve the full-intensity colors mentioned in the preceding section, you should apply black to the individual color channels, not white as you would in the RGB mode.

Should I edit in CMYK?

RGB doesn't accurately represent the colors you get when you print an image, because RGB allows you to represent many colors — particularly very bright colors — that CMYK can't touch. That's why when you switch from RGB to CMYK, the colors appear duller. (If you're familiar with painting, RGB is like oils and CMYK is like acrylics. The latter lacks the depth of color provided by the former.)

For this reason, lots of folks advocate working in the CMYK mode. I, however, do not. While working in CMYK eliminates color disappointments, it is also much slower because Photoshop has to convert CMYK values to your RGB screen on the fly. (One way to accelerate the CMYK mode is to purchase a CMYK video accelerator, such as the Thunder card from Radius. It makes the CMYK mode as fast as editing in the RGB mode.)

Furthermore, your scanner and monitor are RGB devices. No matter how you work, a translation from RGB to CMYK color space must occur at some point in time. If you pay the extra bucks to purchase a commercial drum scan, for example, you simply make the translation at the beginning of the process — Scitex has no option but to use RGB sensors internally — rather than at the end. In fact, every color device on earth is RGB *except* the printer.

Therefore, you should wait to convert to the CMYK mode until right before you print. After your artwork is finalized, choose Image ⇨ Mode ⇨ CMYK and make whatever edits you deem necessary. For example, you might want to introduce a few color corrections, apply some sharpening, and even retouch a few details by hand. Photoshop applies your changes more slowly in the CMYK mode, but at least you're only slowed down at the end of the job, not throughout the entire process.

 Before converting an image to the CMYK color space, it's a good idea to make sure that Photoshop is aware of the monitor that you're using and the printer that you intend to use. These two items can have a pronounced effect on how Photoshop generates a CMYK image. I discuss how to set up monitor and printer in the "Creating Color Separations" section of Chapter 7.

Previewing the CMYK color space

This is not to say that you can't edit in the RGB mode and still get a picture of what the image will look like in CMYK. If you choose View ⇨ CMYK Preview or press ⌘-Y, Photoshop displays colors in the CMYK color space on-screen while allowing you to continue to work in the larger world of RGB.

View ⇨ Gamut Warning (⌘-Shift-Y) is a companion command that covers so-called "out-of-gamut" colors — RGB colors that have no CMYK equivalents — with gray. I personally find this command less useful because it demonstrates a problem without suggesting a solution. You can desaturate the grayed colors with the sponge tool (which I explain in Chapter 8), but this merely accomplishes what Photoshop will do automatically. A CMYK preview is much more serviceable and representative of the final CMYK image.

 You can choose both the CMYK Preview and Gamut Warning commands while inside Photoshop's Color Picker dialog box. CMYK Preview shows how all colors will appear in the CMYK color space, regardless of which options you use to define the color. And Gamut Warning takes on new meaning, permitting you to mask out colors that won't print. It's also an excellent way to glean a little color theory.

CIE's Lab

RGB isn't the only mode that responds quickly and provides a bountiful range of colors. Photoshop's Lab color space comprises all the colors from RGB and CMYK and is every bit as fast as RGB. Many high-end users prefer to work in this mode, and I certainly advocate it if you're brave enough to take it on.

Whereas the RGB mode is the color model of your luminescent computer screen and the CMYK mode is the color model of the reflective page, Lab is independent of light or pigment. Perhaps you've already heard the bit about how in 1931, an international color organization called the *Commission Internationale d'Eclairage* (CIE) developed a color model that in theory contains every single color the human eye can see. (Gnats, iguanas, fruit bats, go find your own color models; humans, you have CIE. Mutants and aliens — maybe CIE, maybe not, too early to tell.) Then, in 1976, the significant birthday of our nation, the CIE celebrated by coming up with two additional color systems. One of those systems was Lab, and the other was shrouded in secrecy. Well, at least *I* don't know what the other one was. Probably something that measures how it is that the entire visible spectrum of color can bounce off your retina when using flash photography and come out looking the exact shade of red one normally associates with lab (not Lab) rabbits. But that's just a guess.

The beauty of the Lab color model is that it fills in gaps in both the RGB and CMYK models. RGB, for example, provides an overabundance of colors in the blue-to-green range, but is stingy on yellows, oranges, and other colors in the green-to-red range. Meanwhile, the colors missing from CMYK are enough to fill the holes in Albert Hall. Lab gets everything just right.

Understanding Lab anatomy

The Lab mode features three color channels, one for luminosity and two others for color ranges known simply by the initials *a* and *b*. (The Greeks would have called them *alpha* and *beta*, if that's any help.) Upon hearing *luminosity,* you might think, "Ah, just like HSL." Well, just to make things confusing, Lab's luminosity is just like HSB's brightness. White indicates full-intensity color.

Meanwhile, the *a* channel contains colors ranging from deep green (low brightness values) to gray (medium brightness values) to vivid pink (high brightness values). The *b* channel ranges from bright blue (low brightness values) to gray to burnt yellow (high brightness values). As in the RGB model, these colors mix together to produce lighter colors. Only the brightness values in the luminosity channel darken the colors. Therefore, you can think of Lab as a two-channel RGB with brightness thrown on top.

To get a glimpse of how it works, try the following simple experiment.

STEPS   **Testing Out the Lab Mode**

Step 1.   **Create a new image in the Lab mode — say, 300 × 300 pixels.**

Step 2.   **Press the D key to return the default colors to the toolbox.** The foreground color is now black and the background color is white.

Step 3.   **Press ⌘-2.** This takes you to the *a* channel.

Step 4.   **Double-click on the gradient tool in the toolbox.** Make sure that you see the words *Normal, Foreground to Background,* and *Linear* in the Gradient Tool Options panel of the Brushes palette. If these words aren't visible, select them from the first, second, and third pop-up menus, respectively.

Step 5.   **Shift-drag with the gradient tool from the top to the bottom of the window.** This creates a vertical black-to-white gradation.

Step 6.   **Press ⌘-3.** This takes you to the *b* channel.

Step 7.   **Shift-drag from left to right with the gradient tool.** Photoshop paints a horizontal gradation.

Step 8.   **Press ⌘-tilde (~) to return to the composite display.** Now you can see all channels at once. If you're using a 24-bit monitor, you should be looking at a window filled with an incredible array of super bright colors. In theory, these are the brightest shades of all the colors you can see. In practice, however, the colors are limited by the display capabilities of your RGB monitor.

Step 9.   **Just for laughs, compare this color circle to the one included in the Apple Color Picker dialog box.** Press ⌘-K to bring up the Preferences dialog box. Select Apple from the Color Picker pop-up menu and press Return. Then click on the foreground color icon in the tool box. Change the Lightness value to 50 percent and check out the difference with the image in the background. You can see that although it appears slightly rotated, the Lab color space contains the same basic colors as in the hue/saturation circle, but far more of them. Or, at least, far more colors that are discernible to your eye, and that's what ultimately counts.

Step 10.   **If you really want a sobering sight, choose View ⇨ CMYK Preview and watch those bright colors disappear.** Aagh, isn't it pitiful? Luckily, CMYK is capable of doing a slightly better job than this. Choose Image ⇨ Adjust ⇨ Auto Levels (or press ⌘-Shift-L). That's better — quite a bit better, in fact — but it's still very much muted compared with its Lab counterpart.

Using Lab

Because it's device independent, you can use the Lab mode to edit any image. Editing in the Lab mode is as fast as editing in the RGB mode and several times faster than editing in the CMYK mode. If you plan on printing your image to color separations, you may want to experiment with using the Lab mode instead of RGB, because Lab ensures that no colors are altered when you convert the image to CMYK, except to change colors that fall outside the CMYK range. In fact, any time you convert an image from RGB to CMYK, Photoshop automatically converts the image to the Lab mode as an intermediate step.

 If you work with Photo CDs often, open the scans directly from the Photo CD format (as opposed to the PICT format) as Lab images. Kodak's proprietary YCC color model is nearly identical to Lab, so you can expect an absolute minimum of data loss; some people claim there is no loss whatsoever.

Grayscale

Grayscale is possibly my favorite color mode. It frees you from all the hassles and expense of working with color and provides access to every bit of Photoshop's power and functionality. Anyone who says you can't do just as much with grayscale as you can with color missed out on *Citizen Kane, L'Aventura, To Kill a Mockingbird,* and *Raging Bull.* You can print grayscale images to any laser printer, reproduce them in any publication, and edit them on nearly any machine. Besides, they look great, they remind you of old movies, and they make a hefty book like this one affordable. What could be better?

Other than extolling its virtues, however, there isn't a whole lot to say about grayscale. You can convert an image to the grayscale mode regardless of its current mode, and you can convert from grayscale to any other mode just as easily. In fact, choosing Image ⇨ Mode ⇨ Grayscale is a necessary step in converting a color image to a duotone or black-and-white bitmap.

Search your channels before converting

When you convert an image from one of the color modes to the grayscale mode, Photoshop normally weights the values of each color channel in a way that retains the apparent brightness of the overall image. For example, when you convert an image from RGB, Photoshop weights red more heavily than blue when computing dark values because red is a darker-looking color than blue (much as that might seem contrary to popular belief).

However, if you choose Image ⇨ Mode ⇨ Grayscale while viewing a single color channel, Photoshop retains all brightness values in that channel only and abandons the data in the other channels. This can be an especially useful technique for rescuing a grayscale image from a bad RGB scan.

Therefore, before switching to the grayscale mode, be sure to take a look at the individual color channels — particularly the red and green channels (the blue channel frequently contains substandard detail) — to see how each channel might look on its own. To browse the channels, press ⌘-1 for red, ⌘-2 for green, and ⌘-3 for blue. Or ⌘-1 for cyan, ⌘-2 for magenta, ⌘-3 for yellow, and ⌘-4 for black. Or even ⌘-1 for luminosity, ⌘-2 for *a*, and ⌘-3 for *b*. Chapter 6 describes color channels in more detail.

Dot gain interference

You should be aware of a little item that might throw off your gray value calculations. If the Use Dot Gain for Grayscale Images check box in the Printer Inks Setup dialog box (File ⇨ Color Settings ⇨ Printer Inks Setup) is turned on, Photoshop figures in *dot gain* when calculating the lightness and darkness of grayscale images.

Dot gain is more thoroughly discussed in the "Printer calibration" section of Chapter 7, but the basic concept is this: Printed images are made up of tiny dots of ink called *halftone cells*. During the printing process, the halftone cells expand — it's sort of like what happens to drops of water plopped onto a paper towel. The Use Dot Gain for Grayscale Images check box lightens the gray values in an image, which reduces the size of the halftone cells, thereby giving the dots some room to bleed.

Suppose that you click on the foreground color icon and change the B (Brightness) value in the Color Picker dialog box to 50 percent. Later, after applying the 50 percent gray to the current image, you move your cursor over some of the medium gray pixels while the Info palette is displayed. You notice that the Info palette interprets the pixels to be 56 percent gray, six percentage points darker than the color you specified. This happens because Photoshop automatically darkens the colors in your image to reflect how they will print subject to the dot gain specified in the Printing Inks Setup dialog box.

 At this point, I need to insert two bits of information to avoid (or perhaps enhance) confusion. First, as long as the S (Saturation) value is 0, the B (Brightness) value is the only Color Picker option you need to worry about when editing grayscale images. Second, although the B (Brightness) value measures luminosity, ranging from 0 percent for black to 100 percent for white, the K value in the Info dialog box measures ink coverage, thus reversing the figures to 100 percent for black and 0 percent for white. Ignoring dot gain for a moment, this means that a 50 percent brightness translates to 50 percent ink coverage, a 40 percent brightness translates to 60 percent ink coverage, a 30 percent brightness translates to 70 percent ink coverage, and so on.

In theory, automatic dot gain compensation is a good idea, but in practice, it frequently gets in the way. Fortunately, this option is turned off by default. But you never know when the person using Photoshop ahead of you might go in there and snap it on.

Black and white (bitmap)

Choose Image ⇨ Mode ⇨ Bitmap to convert a grayscale image to exclusively black-and-white pixels. This may sound like a pretty boring option, but it can prove useful for gaining complete control over the printing of grayscale images. After all, output devices such as laser printers and imagesetters render grayscale images as a series of tiny dots. Using the Bitmap command, you can specify the size, shape, and angle of those dots.

When you choose Image ⇨ Mode ⇨ Bitmap, Photoshop displays the Bitmap dialog box, shown in Figure 5-6. Here you specify the resolution of the black-and-white image and select a conversion process. The options work as follows:

↪ **Output:** Specify the resolution of the black-and-white file. If you want control over every single pixel available to your printer, raise this value to match your printer's resolution. As a rule of thumb, try setting the Output value somewhere between 200 to 250 percent of the Input value.

↪ **50 Percent Threshold:** Select this option to make every pixel that is darker than 50 percent gray black and every pixel that is 50 percent gray or lighter white. Unless you are working toward some special effect — for example, overlaying a black-and-white version of an image over the original grayscale image — this option most likely isn't for you. (And if you're working toward a special effect, Image ⇨ Adjust ⇨ Threshold is the better alternative.)

Figure 5-6
The Bitmap dialog box
converts images from
grayscale to black and
white.

↪ **Pattern Dither:** To *dither* pixels is to mix them up to emulate different colors. In this case, Photoshop mixes up black and white pixels to produce shades of gray. The Pattern Dither option dithers an image using a geometric pattern. Unfortunately, the results are pretty ugly, as demonstrated in the top example in Figure 5-7. And the space between dots has a tendency to fill in, especially when you output to a laser printer.

↪ **Diffusion Dither:** Select this option to create a mezzotint-like effect, as demonstrated in the second example in Figure 5-7. Again, because this option converts an image into thousands of stray pixels, you can expect your image to darken dramatically when output to a low-resolution laser printer and when reproduced. So be sure to lighten the image with something like the Levels command (as described in Chapter 18) before selecting this option.

Figure 5-7
The results of selecting the Pattern Dither option (top) and the much more acceptable Diffusion Dither option (bottom).

↪ **Halftone Screen:** When you select this option and press Return, Photoshop displays the dialog box shown in Figure 5-8. These options permit you to apply a dot pattern to the image, as demonstrated in Figure 5-9. Enter the number of dots per inch in the Frequency option box and the angle of the dots in the Angle option box. Then select a dot shape from the Shape pop-up menu. Figure 5-9 shows examples of four shapes, each with a frequency of 24 lines per inch.

 I cover screen patterns and frequency settings in more depth in the "Changing the halftone screen" section of Chapter 7.

Figure 5-8
This dialog box appears when you select the Halftone Screen option in the Bitmap dialog box.

Figure 5-9
Four random examples of halftone cell shapes. In all cases, the Frequency value was set to 24.

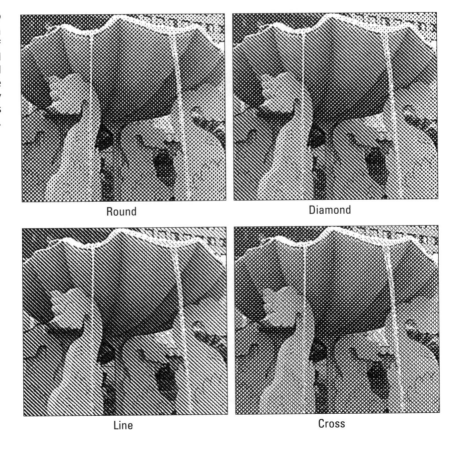

Round

Diamond

Line

Cross

∞ **Custom Pattern:** If you have defined a repeating pattern by choosing Edit ⇨ Define Pattern, you can use it as a custom dither pattern. Figure 5-10 shows two custom examples. The first pattern was created using the Twirl Pattern file, which you'll find in the Displacement Maps folder inside the Plug-Ins folder included with your Photoshop application. I created the second pattern manually using the Add Noise, Emboss, and Ripple filters (as discussed in the "Creating texture effects" section of Chapter 17).

For a complete guide to creating and defining patterns in Photoshop, see the "Applying Repeating Patterns" section of Chapter 10.

Figure 5-10
Two examples of employing repeating patterns (created with Edit ⇨ Define Pattern) as custom halftoning patterns.

Photoshop lets you edit individual pixels in the so-called bitmap mode, but that's about the extent of it. After you go to black-and-white, you can't perform any serious editing, nor can you expect to return to the grayscale mode and restore your original pixels. So be sure to finish your image editing before choosing Image ⇨ Mode ⇨ Bitmap. More importantly, be sure to save your image before converting it to black-and-white. Frankly, saving is a good idea when performing any color conversion.

Using Photoshop's Other Color Selection Methods

In addition to the Color Picker dialog box, Photoshop provides a handful of additional techniques for selecting colors. The sections that finish out this chapter explain how to use the Custom Colors dialog box, the Colors palette, and the eyedropper tool. None of this information is terribly exciting, but it will enable you to work more efficiently and more conveniently.

Predefined colors

If you click on the Custom button inside the Color Picker dialog box, Photoshop displays the Custom Colors dialog box shown in Figure 5-11. In this dialog box, you can select from a variety of predefined colors by choosing the color family from the Book pop-up menu, moving the slider triangles up and down the color slider to specify a general range of colors, and ultimately selecting a color from the color list on the left. If you own the swatchbook for a color family, you can locate a specific color by entering its number on the keyboard.

Figure 5-11
The Custom Colors dialog box enables you to select predefined colors from brand-name libraries.

The color families represented in the Book pop-up menu fall into six brands: ANPA (now NAA), DIC, Focoltone, Pantone, Toyo, and Trumatch, all of which get a big kick out of capitalizing their names in dialog boxes. I honestly think that one of these companies would stand out better if its name *weren't* capitalized. Anyway, at the risk of offending a few of these companies, you're likely to find certain brands more useful than others. The following sections briefly introduce the brands in order of their impact on the American market — forgive me for being ethnocentric in this regard — from smallest impact to greatest.

 The number-one use for predefined colors in Photoshop is in the creation of duotones, tritones, and quadtones (described in Chapter 7). You can also use predefined colors to match the colors in a logo or some other important element in an image to a commercial standard.

Focoltone, DIC, and Toyo

Focoltone, Dianippon Ink and Chemical (DIC), and Toyo fall into the negligible impact category. All are foreign color standards with followings abroad. Focoltone is an English company; not English-speaking — although they probably do — but English-living, as in commuting-to-France-through-the-Chunnel England. DIC and Toyo are popular in the Japanese market, but have next to no subscribers outside Japan.

Newspaper Association of America

ANPA — *American Newspaper Publishers Association* — recently changed its name to NAA, which stands for *Newspaper Association of America,* and updated its color catalog. NAA provides a small sampling of 33 *process colors* (mixes of cyan, magenta, yellow, and black ink) plus 5 *spot colors* (colors produced by printing a single ink). The idea behind the NAA colors is to isolate the color combinations that reproduce most successfully on inexpensive newsprint and to provide advertisers with a solid range of colors from which to choose without allowing the color choices to get out of hand. You can purchase a Pocket Tint Chart from NAA for $175. Members pay only $100.

Trumatch

Trumatch remains my personal favorite process-color standard. Designed entirely using a desktop system and created especially with desktop publishers in mind, the Trumatch Colorfinder swatchbook features more than 2,000 process colors, organized according to hue, saturation, and brightness. Each hue is broken down into 40 tints and shades. Tints are created by reducing the saturation in 15 percent increments; shades are created by adding black ink in 6 percent increments. The result is a guide that shows you exactly which colors you can attain using a desktop system. If you're wondering what a CMYK blend will look like when printed, you need look no farther than the Trumatch Colorfinder.

As if the Colorfinder weren't enough, Trumatch provides the ColorPrinter Software utility, which automatically prints the entire 2,000-color library to any PostScript-compatible output device. The utility integrates EfiColor and PostScript Level 2, thereby enabling design firms and commercial printers to test out the entire range of capabilities available to their hardware. Companies can provide select clients with swatches of colors created on their own printers, guaranteeing that what you see is darn well what you'll get.

Pantone

On the heels of Trumatch, Pantone released a 3,006-color Process Color System Guide (labeled *Pantone Process* in the Book pop-up menu) priced at $75, $10 less than the Trumatch Colorfinder. Pantone also produces the foremost spot color swatchbook, the Color Formula Guide 1000. Then there's the Process Color Imaging Guide, which enables you to quickly figure out whether you can closely match a Pantone spot color using a process-color blend or whether you ought to just give it up and stick with the spot color.

Pantone spot colors are ideal for creating duotones, as discussed in Chapter 7. Furthermore, Pantone is supported by every computer application that aspires to the color prepress market. As long as the company retains the old competitive spirit, you can most likely expect Pantone to remain the primary color printing standard for years to come.

The Color palette

Another means of selecting colors in Photoshop is to use the Color palette, shown in Figure 5-12. If you're willing to sacrifice on-screen real estate for the convenience of being able to define colors on the spot — without having to call up the Color Picker dialog box — the Color palette is a useful tool indeed.

Figure 5-12
The Color and Swatches palettes let you edit colors without having to display the Color Picker dialog box.

To display the palette, choose Window ⇨ Show Color. You then can use the elements and options inside the palette as follows:

- **Foreground color/background color:** Click on the foreground or background color icon in the Color palette to specify the color that you want to edit. If you click on the foreground or background color icon when it's already highlighted — as indicated by a double-line frame — Photoshop displays the Color Picker dialog box.

- **Slider bars:** Drag the triangles in the slider controls to edit the highlighted color. By default, the sliders represent the red, green, and blue primary colors. You can change the slider bars by choosing a different color model from the palette menu.

 In Photoshop 4, you can also enter numerical values into the option boxes to the right of the sliders. It's about time! Press Tab to advance from one option box to the next; press Shift-Tab to go to the previous option.

- **Alert triangle:** Photoshop displays the alert triangle when a color falls outside the CMYK color gamut. The color swatch to the right of the triangle shows the closest CMYK equivalent. Click on the triangle or the color swatch to replace the current color with the CMYK equivalent.

- **Color bar:** The bar along the bottom of the Color palette displays all colors contained in the CMYK spectrum. Click or drag inside the color bar to lift a color and make it the current foreground or background color (depending on whether the foreground or background icon is selected above). The sliders update as you drag. Option-click or drag to lift the background color if the foreground icon is selected or the foreground color if the background color is selected.

- **Color Bar option:** You don't have to accept the CMYK spectrum in the color bar. To change to a different spectrum, select the Color Bar command from the palette menu. The resulting dialog box lets you change to the RGB spectrum or select a black-to-white gradation (Grayscale Ramp). If you select Foreground to Background, the color bar is filled with a gradation from the current foreground color to the current background color. Unless you select the Lock to Current Colors check box, the color bar continuously updates to represent the newest foreground and background colors.

 Here are a couple of neat shortcuts that let you change color bars without going to all the trouble of choosing the Color Bar command from the palette menu. Just ⌘-click on the color bar to bring up the Color Bar dialog box. Or better yet, Shift-click on the bar to cycle from one color bar to the next.

You can hide and show the Color palette from the keyboard by pressing the F6 key. (This assumes you haven't assigned F6 to a script in the Actions palette, as explained in Chapter 3.)

The Swatches palette

As shown in Figure 5-12, the Color palette offers an additional panel called Swatches. (A third panel, Scratch, was dropped from Photoshop 4 because of a complete lack of user interest in the function.) The Swatches palette lets you collect colors for future use, sort of like a favorite color reservoir.

Here's how to use the swatches in the reservoir:

- ☞ To select a color from the reservoir, click on it.

- ☞ To add the current foreground color to the reservoir, Shift-click on an existing color swatch to replace the old color or click in an empty swatch to append the new color. In either case, your cursor temporarily changes to a paint bucket.

- ☞ To insert a color anywhere in the palette, Shift-Option-click on a swatch. The other colors scoot over to make room.

- ☞ To delete a color from the panel, ⌘-click on a color swatch. Your cursor changes to a pair of scissors and cuts the color away.

You can also save and load color palettes on disk using options in the pop-up menu. The Load Swatches option replaces the colors in the panel with the colors in the file; the Append Swatches option tacks the colors on to the end of the palette. The Color Palettes folder, located inside the same folder that contains the Photoshop application, contains palettes for the major color libraries from Pantone, Trumatch, and others. When one of these palettes is loaded, positioning your cursor over a color swatch makes the name of that color appear in place of the word *Swatches* in the panel tab.

The eyedropper tool

The eyedropper tool — which you can select by pressing the I key — provides the most convenient and most straightforward means of selecting colors in Photoshop. It's so straightforward, in fact, that it's hardly worth explaining. But very quickly, here's how it works:

↪ **Selecting a foreground color:** To select a new foreground color, click on the desired color inside any open image window with the eyedropper tool. (This assumes that the foreground icon in the Color palette is selected. If the background icon is selected, Option-click with the eyedropper tool to lift the foreground color.) You can even click inside a background window to lift a color without bringing that window to the foreground.

↪ **Selecting a background color:** To select a new background color, Option-click on the desired color with the eyedropper tool. (Again, this assumes that the foreground icon is selected in the Color palette. If the background icon is selected, click with the eyedropper to lift the background color.)

↪ **Skating over the color spectrum:** You can animate the foreground color control box by dragging with the eyedropper tool in the image window. As soon as you achieve the desired color, release your mouse button. To animate the background color icon, Option-drag with the eyedropper tool. The icon color changes as you move the eyedropper tool.

↪ **Sampling multiple pixels:** Normally, the eyedropper tool selects the color from the single pixel on which you click. However, if you prefer to average the colors of several neighboring pixels, double-click on the eyedropper icon in the toolbox and select a different option from the Sample Size pop-up menu in the Eyedropper Options palette. Or Control-click with the eyedropper to bring up a convenient pop-up menu of sampling options.

 To temporarily access the eyedropper tool when using the type, paint bucket, gradient, line, pencil, airbrush, or paintbrush tool, press the Option key. The eyedropper cursor remains in force for as long as the Option key is down. The eyedropper lifts whatever color is active in the Color palette (foreground or background). To lift the other color, you have to switch to the eyedropper tool by pressing the I key and then Option-click in an image window.

Navigating Channels

- -

In This Chapter

➡ Putting channels in perspective and understanding how they work

➡ Viewing the contents of independent color channels within a full-color image

➡ Using channel editing commands in the Channels palette menu

➡ Improving the appearance of poorly scanned images

➡ Editing channels to achieve special effects

- -

Introducing Color Channels_____

Have you ever seen a set of separated CMYK transparencies? Certainly print professionals see these things all the time, but even if you're an absolute beginner, you may have come in contact with them — perhaps on that grade school field trip to the print shop. Some nebulous adult — life was a stream of nebulous adults back then — held up four sheets of acetate. One sheet showed a cyan picture, another showed the same picture in magenta, a third showed it in yellow, and the last depicted the scene in a rather washed-out black. By themselves, the pictures appeared exceedingly light and rather sparse in the detail department. But when they were put together — one layered in front of another — you saw a full-color picture. Pretty cool stuff.

Sound familiar? Whether it does or not — hey, I can't spend all day conjuring up these little slices of nostalgia — those sheets of acetate have a functional equivalent inside Photoshop: *channels*. In a CMYK image, for example, there is one cyan channel, one magenta channel, one yellow channel, and one black channel. They mix on-screen to form a full-color image. The RGB mode features a red channel, a green channel, and a blue channel. Because RGB is the color model of light, the three images mix together like three differently colored slides in different projectors aimed at the same screen. In other words, regardless of color mode, channels are distinct planes of primary color.

Channels frequently correspond to the structure of an input or output device. Each channel in a CMYK image, for example, corresponds to a different printer's plate when the document goes to press. The cyan plate is inked with cyan, the magenta plate is inked with magenta, and so on. Each channel in an RGB image corresponds to a pass of the red, green, or blue scanner sensor over the original photograph or artwork. Only the Lab mode is device independent, so its channels don't correspond to any piece of hardware.

Why you should care

But so what, right? Who cares how many planes of color an image comprises? You want to edit the photograph, not dissect it. "Dammit, Jim, I'm an artist, not a doctor!" Well, even if you don't like to rebuild car engines or poke preserved frog entrails with sharp knives, you'll get a charge out of editing channels. The fact is, channels provide you with yet another degree of selective control over an image.

Consider this example: Your client scanned an image that he wants you to integrate into some goofy ad campaign for his car dealership. Unfortunately, the scan is downright rotten. Maybe it looked good on his computer, but on your screen it looks like dried. . . well, perhaps I shouldn't get too graphic here. Still, you don't want to offend the guy. The image is a picture of his favorite daughter, after all (come on, I'm making this up as I go along), so you praise him on his fine scan and say something to the effect of, "No problem, boss." But after you take it back to your office and load it into Photoshop, you break out in a cold sweat. You try swabbing at it with the edit tools, applying a few filters, and even attempting some scary-looking color correction commands, but the image continues to look like the inside of a garbage disposal. (Not that I've ever seen the inside of a garbage disposal, but it can't be attractive.)

Suddenly, it occurs to you to look at the channels. What the heck, it can't hurt. With very little effort, you discover that the red and green channels look okay, but the blue channel looks like it's melting. Big gobs of gooey detail slide off the kid's face like some kind of mobile acne. Her mouth is sort of mixed in with her teeth, her eyes look like an experiment in expressionism, and her hair has taken on a slightly geometric appearance. (If you think that this is a big exaggeration, take a look at a few blue channels from low-end scanners. They're frequently ripe with tattered edges, random blocks of color, stray pixels, and other so-called *digital artifacts*.)

The point is, you've located the cancer, Doctor. You don't have to waste your time trying to perform surgery on the entire image; in fact, doing so may very well harm the channels that are in good shape. You merely have to fix this one channel. A wave of the Gaussian Blur filter here, an application of the Levels command there, and some selective rebuilding of missing detail borrowed from the other channels — all of which I'll get to in future sections or chapters — result in an image that resembles a living, breathing human being. It may not be absolute perfection, but it's solid enough to pass muster.

How channels work

Photoshop devotes 8 bits of data to each pixel in each channel, thus permitting 256 brightness values, from 0 (black) to 255 (white). Therefore, each channel is actually an independent grayscale image. At first, you may be thrown off by this. If an RGB image is made up of red, green, and blue channels, why do all the channels look gray?

Photoshop provides an option in the Display & Cursors panel of the Preferences dialog box (⌘-K, then ⌘-3) called Color Channels in Color. When selected, this function displays each channel in its corresponding primary color. But although this feature can be reassuring — particularly to novices — it's equally counterproductive.

When you view an 8-bit image composed exclusively of shades of red, for example, it's easy to miss subtle variations in detail that may appear obvious when you print the image. You may have problems accurately gauging the impact of filters and tonal adjustments. I mean, face it, red isn't a friendly shade to stare at for a half hour of intense editing. So leave the Color Channels in Color option off and temporarily suspend your biological urge for on-screen color. With a little experience, you'll be able to better monitor your adjustments and predict the outcome of your edits in plain old grayscale.

 Just because you're editing a single channel doesn't mean that you have to work with blinders on. At any time, you can see how your changes affect the full-color image. Simply create a new view of your image by choosing View ⇨ New View. Leave this window set to the standard composite view (presumably RGB, but it could be CMYK, Lab, or any other color mode) and edit away on the individual channel in the first image. (Don't worry, I explain how to switch channels in the very next section.)

Images that include 256 or fewer colors can be expressed in a single channel and therefore do not include multiple channels that you can edit independently. A grayscale image, for example, includes a single channel. A black-and-white image permits only one bit of data per pixel, so a single channel is more than enough to express it. Duotones are the really weird ones. Though they may contain two, three, or four plates of color, Photoshop treats them as a single channel of 8-bit color. I explain duotones in detail in Chapter 7.

You can add channels above and beyond those required to represent a color or grayscale image for the purpose of storing masks, as described in Chapter 12. But even then, each channel is typically limited to 8 bits of data per pixel — meaning that it's just another grayscale image. Mask channels do not affect the appearance of the image on-screen or when it is printed. Rather, they serve to save selection outlines, as Chapter 12 explains.

How to switch and view channels

To access channels in Photoshop, display the Channels palette by choosing Window ⇨ Show Channels. Every channel in the image appears in the palette — including any mask channels — as shown in Figure 6-1. Photoshop even shows little thumbnail views of each channel so that you can see what it looks like.

Figure 6-1
Photoshop displays tiny thumbnails of each color and mask channel in the Channels palette.

To switch to a different channel, click on a channel name in the Channels palette. The channel name becomes gray — like the Mask channel in Figure 6-1 — showing that you can now edit it independently of other channels in the image.

To edit more than one channel at a time, click on one channel name and then Shift-click on another. You can also Shift-click on an active channel to deactivate it independently of any others.

When you select a channel, Photoshop normally displays the channel that you want to edit on-screen. However, you can view additional channels beyond those that you want to edit. To specify which channels appear on-screen, click in the far left column of the Channels palette. Click on an eyeball icon to make it disappear and hence hide that channel. Click where there is no eyeball to create one and thus display the channel.

When only one channel is visible, that channel appears as a grayscale picture in the image window (possibly colorized in accordance with the Color Channels in Color check box in the Preferences dialog box). However, when more than one channel is visible, you always see color. If both the blue and green channels are visible, for example, the image appears blue-green. If the red and green channels are visible, the image has a yellow cast, and so on. If a mask channel and some other channel are visible, the mask appears by default as a pink overlay. (The color of the mask can be changed.) For more information on viewing two or more individual channels simultaneously — and why in the world you'd want to do so — read the "Viewing mask and image" section of Chapter 12.

In addition to the individual channels, Photoshop provides access to a *composite view* that displays all colors in an RGB, CMYK, or Lab image at once. (The composite view does not show mask channels; you have to specify their display separately.) The composite view is listed first in the Channel palette and is displayed by default. Notice that when you select the composite view, all the names of the individual color channels in the Channels palette turn gray along with the composite channel. This shows that all the channels are active. The composite view is the one in which you will perform the majority of your image editing.

Press ⌘ plus a number key to switch between color channels. Depending on the color mode you're working in, ⌘-1 takes you to the red (RGB), cyan (CMYK), or luminosity (Lab) channel; ⌘-2 takes you to the green, magenta, or *a* channel; and ⌘-3 takes you to the blue, yellow, or *b* channel. In the CMYK mode, ⌘-4 displays the black channel. Other ⌘-key equivalents — up to ⌘-9 — take you to mask channels (if there are any).

New to Photoshop 4, ⌘-tilde (~) takes you to the composite view. (That's the key to the left of 1.) You should get out of pressing ⌘-0 — the old shortcut — pretty darn fast. It now zooms the image to fit on screen.

The shortcuts are slightly different when you're working on a grayscale image. You access the image itself by pressing ⌘-1. ⌘-2 and higher take you to the mask channels.

Don't freak or in any way feel inadequate if your images don't contain mask channels. You have to create masks manually, and as I mentioned earlier, we won't be talking about masks until Chapter 12. In the meantime, I'm just trying to make sure that I don't leave any stone unturned as I explain the many nuances of this many-splendored topic.

Trying Channels on for Size _____

Feeling a little mystified? Need some examples? Fair enough. Color Plate 6-1 shows a woman in a bright yellow swim suit on a bright red floatation device set against a bright green ocean beneath a bright blue sky. These colors — yellow, red, green, and blue — cover the four corners of the color spectrum. Therefore, you can expect to see a lot of variation between the images in the independent color channels.

RGB channels

Suppose that the sunbathing woman is an RGB image. Figure 6-2 compares a grayscale composite of this same image (created by choosing Image ⇨ Mode ⇨ Grayscale) compared with the contents of the red, green, and blue color channels from the original color image. The green channel is quite similar to the grayscale composite because green is an ingredient in all colors in the image, except for the red of the raft. The red and blue channels differ more significantly. The pixels in the red channel are lightest in the swimsuit and raft because they contain the highest concentrations of red. The pixels in the blue channel are lightest in the sky and water because — you guessed it — the sky and water are rich with blue.

Notice how the channels in Figure 6-2 make interesting grayscale images in and of themselves? The red channel, for example, looks like the sky darkening above our bather, even though the sun is blazing down.

I mentioned this as a tip in the previous chapter, but it bears a bit of casual drumming into the old noggin. When converting a color image to grayscale, you have the option of calculating a grayscale composite or simply retaining the image exactly as it appears in one of the channels. To create a grayscale composite, choose Image ⇨ Mode ⇨ Grayscale when viewing all colors in the image in the composite view, as usual. To retain a single channel only, switch to that channel and then choose Image ⇨ Mode ⇨ Grayscale. Instead of the usual *Discard color information?* message, Photoshop displays the message *Discard other channels?* If you click on the OK button, Photoshop chucks the other channels into the electronic abyss.

Figure 6-2
A grayscale
composite of the
image from Color
Plate 6-1 followed by
the contents of the
red, green, and blue
color channels.

Grayscale composite

Red

Green

Blue

CMYK channels

In the name of fair and unbiased coverage, Figures 6-3 and 6-4 show the channels
from the image after it was converted to other color modes. In Figure 6-3, I converted the image to the CMYK mode and examined its channels. Here, the predominant
colors are cyan (sky and water) and yellow (in the swimsuit and raft). Because this
color mode relies on pigments rather than light, as explained in the "CMYK" section
of Chapter 5, dark areas in the channels represent high color intensity. For that reason, the sky in the cyan channel is dark, whereas it's light in the blue channel back
in Figure 6-2.

Cyan

Magenta

Yellow

Black

Figure 6-3
The contents of the cyan, magenta, yellow, and black channels from the image shown in Color Plate 6-1.

Notice how similar the cyan channel in Figure 6-3 is to its red counterpart in Figure 6-4. Same with the magenta and green channels, and the yellow and blue channels. The CMY channels have more contrast than the RGB pals, but the basic brightness distribution is the same. Here's another graphic demonstration of color theory. In a perfect world, the CMY channels would be identical to the RGB channels — one color model would simply be the other turned on its head. But because this is not a perfect world (you might have noticed that as you've traveled life's bitter highway), Photoshop has to boost the contrast of the CMY channels and throw in black to punch up those shadows.

Lab channels

To create Figure 6-4, I converted the image in Color Plate 6-1 to the Lab mode. The image in the luminosity channel looks very similar to the grayscale composite because it contains the lightness and darkness values for the image. The *a* channel maps the greens and magentas, while the *b* channel maps the yellows and blues, so both channels are working hard to provide color information for this photograph. Certainly there are differences — the *a* channel is hotter in the raft, while the *b* channel offers more cloud detail — but the two channels carry roughly equivalent amounts of color information.

Figure 6-4
The grayscale composite followed by the contents of the luminosity channel and the *a* and *b* color channels after converting the image shown in Color Plate 6-1 to the Lab mode.

Grayscale Composite   Luminosity

a (black is green, white is magenta)   b (black is blue, white is yellow)

You can achieve some entertaining effects by applying commands from the Image ⇨ Adjust submenu to the *a* and *b* color channels. For example, if I go to the *a* channel in Figure 6-4 and reverse the brightness values by choosing Image ⇨ Adjust ⇨ Invert (⌘-I), the water turns a sort of salmon red and the raft turns green, as demonstrated in the first example of Color Plate 6-2. If I apply Image ⇨ Adjust ⇨ Auto Levels (⌘-Shift-L) to the *b* channel, the sky lights up with brilliant blue without altering so much as a color in the woman or her raft, as in the second example. The third example in Color Plate 6-2 shows what happens when I apply both Invert and Auto Levels to both the *a* and *b* channels. Now there's the way I want to vacation — on a different planet!

Other Channel Functions

In addition to viewing and editing channels using any of the techniques discussed in future chapters of this book, you can choose commands from the Channels palette menu and select icons along the bottom of the palette (labeled back in Figure 6-1). The following items explain how the commands and icons work.

 You'll notice that I say "see Chapter 12" every so often when explaining these options, because many of them are specifically designed to accommodate masks. This list is designed to introduce you to *all* the options in the Channels palette, even if you'll need more background to use a few of them. After I introduce the options, we'll revisit the ones that have a direct affect on managing the colors in your image.

⟿ **Palette Options:** Even though this is the last command in the menu, it's the easiest, so I'll start with it. When you choose Palette Options, Photoshop displays four Thumbnail Size radio buttons, enabling you to change the size of the thumbnail previews that appear along the left side of the Channels palette. Figure 6-5 shows the four thumbnail settings — nonexistent, small, medium, and large.

 Press the Option key when choosing the Palette Options command to see a little picture of Merlin. Isn't that terribly amusing? Adobe programmers are always hard at work, folks.

Figure 6-5
The Channels Palette Options dialog box lets you select between four thumbnail preview options.

✑ **New Channel:** Choose this command to add a mask channel to the current image. The Channel Options dialog box appears, enabling you to name the channel. You also can specify the color and translucency that Photoshop applies to the channel when you view it with other channels. I explain how these options work in the "Changing the red coating" section of Chapter 12. An image can contain no more than 24 total channels, regardless of color mode.

You can also create a new channel by clicking on the new channel icon at the bottom of the Channels palette. (It's the one that looks like a little page.) Photoshop creates the channel without displaying the dialog box. To force the dialog box to appear on-screen, Option-click on the page icon.

✑ **Duplicate Channel:** Choose this command to create a duplicate of the selected channel, either inside the same document or as part of a new document. (If the composite view is active, the Duplicate Channel command is dimmed, because you can only duplicate one channel at a time.) The most common reason to use this command is to convert a channel into a mask. Again, you can find real-life applications in Chapter 12.

You can also duplicate a channel by dragging the channel name onto the new channel icon. No dialog box appears; Photoshop merely names the channel automatically. To copy a channel to a different document, drag the channel name and drop it into an open image window. Photoshop automatically creates a new channel for the duplicate.

✑ **Delete Channel:** To delete a channel from an image, click on the channel name in the palette and choose this command. You can delete only one channel at a time. The Delete Channel command is dimmed when any essential color channel is active, or when more than one channel is selected.

If choosing a command is too much effort, just drag the channel onto the delete channel icon (which is the little trash icon in the lower right corner of the Channels palette). In Photoshop 4, you can also merely click on the trash icon, in which case Photoshop asks you if you really want to delete the channel. To bypass this warning, Option-click on the trash icon.

✑ **Channel Options:** Choose this command or double-click on the channel name in the palette's scrolling list to change the name, color, and translucency settings of a mask channel, as described in the "Viewing mask and image" section of Chapter 12. The Channel Options command is dimmed when any of the color channels is active. It is applicable to mask channels only.

✑ **Split Channels:** When you choose this command, Photoshop splits off each channel in an image to its own independent grayscale image window. As demonstrated in Figure 6-6, Photoshop automatically appends the channel color to the end of the window name. The Split Channels command is useful as a first step in redistributing channels in an image prior to choosing Merge Channels (as demonstrated later in this chapter).

Figure 6-6
When you choose the Split Channels command, Photoshop relocates each channel to an independent image window.

⌐☞ **Merge Channels:** Choose this command to merge several images into a single multichannel image. The images you want to merge must be open, they must be grayscale, and they must be absolutely equal in size — the same number of pixels horizontally and vertically. When you choose Merge Channels, Photoshop displays the Merge Channels dialog box, shown in Figure 6-7. It then assigns a color mode for the new image based on the number of open grayscale images that contain the same number of pixels as the foreground image.

Figure 6-7
The two dialog boxes that appear after you choose Merge Channels enable you to select a color mode for the merged image (top) and to associate images with color channels (bottom).

You can override Photoshop's choice by selecting a different option from the Mode pop-up menu. (Generally, you won't want to change the value in the Channels option box because doing so causes Photoshop to automatically select Multichannel from the Mode pop-up menu. I explain multichannel images in the upcoming "Using multichannel techniques" section.)

After you press Return, Photoshop displays a second dialog box, which also appears in Figure 6-7. In this dialog box, you can specify which grayscale image goes with which channel by choosing options from pop-up menus. When working from an image split with the Split Channels command, Photoshop automatically organizes each window into a pop-up menu according to the color appended to the window's name. For example, Photoshop associates the window *Sunbathe.Cyan* with the Cyan pop-up menu.

☞ **Convert selection:** Click on the channel-to-selection icon — the one in the bottom left corner of the Channels palette — to convert a selected channel to a selection outline. You can also click on the next icon to the right to convert a selection outline to a new mask channel. For the complete story on these options, read Chapter 12.

Color Channel Effects

Now that you know how to navigate among channels and apply commands, permit me to suggest a few reasons for doing so. The most pragmatic applications for channel effects involve the restoration of bad color scans. If you use a color scanner, know someone who uses a color scanner, or just have a bunch of color scans lying around, you can be sure that some of them look like dog meat. (Nothing against dog meat, mind you. I'm sure that Purina has some very lovely dog meat scans in their advertising archives.) With Photoshop's help, you can turn those scans into filet mignon — or at the very least, into an acceptable Sunday roast.

Improving the appearance of color scans

The following are a few channel editing techniques you can use to improve the appearance of poorly scanned full-color images. Keep in mind that these techniques don't work miracles, but they can retrieve an image from the brink of absolute ugliness into the realm of tolerability.

Don't forget that you can choose View ⇨ New View to maintain a constant composite view. Or you can click on the eyeball icon in front of the composite view in the Channels palette to view the full-color image, even when editing a single channel.

- **Aligning channels:** Every so often, a scan may appear out of focus even after you use Photoshop's sharpening commands to try to correct the problem, as discussed in Chapter 15. If, on closer inspection, you can see slight shadows or halos around colored areas, one of the color channels probably is out of alignment. To remedy the problem, switch to the color channel that corresponds to the color of the halos. Then select the move tool (by pressing the V key) and use the arrow keys to nudge the contents of the channel into alignment. Use the separate composite view (created by choosing View ⇨ New View) or click on the eyeball in front of the composite channel to monitor your changes.

- **Channel focusing:** If all channels seem to be in alignment (or, at least, as aligned as they're going to get), one of your channels may be poorly focused. Use the ⌘-key equivalents to search for the responsible channel. When and if you find it, use the Unsharp Mask filter to sharpen it as desired. You may also find it helpful to blur a channel, as when trying to eliminate moiré patterns in a scanned halftone. (For a specific application of these techniques, see the "Cleaning up Scanned Halftones" section in Chapter 15.)

- **Bad channels:** In your color channel tour, if you discover that a channel is not so much poorly focused as simply rotten to the core — complete with harsh transitions, jagged edges, and random brightness variations — you may be able to improve the appearance of the channel by overlaying the other channels on top of it. Suppose that the blue channel is awful, but the red and green channels are in fairly decent shape. First, save your image to disk in case this technique does more to harm the image than help it. Then switch to the red channel (⌘-1), select the entire image (⌘-A), and copy it (⌘-C). Switch back to the blue channel (⌘-3) and paste the contents of the Clipboard (⌘-V). Photoshop pastes the channel as a floating selection, permitting you to mix it with the underlying pixels. Change the opacity of the floating red channel to somewhere in the neighborhood of 30 to 50 percent by adjusting the Opacity slider bar in the Layers palette. Next, switch to the green channel (⌘-2) and repeat the process. The colors in the composite view will change slightly or dramatically depending on the range of colors in your image. But if you can live with the color changes, the appearance of the image will improve dramatically.

As discussed in Chapter 19, Image ⇨ Calculations serves as an alternate method for blending one channel with another. At first glance, the dialog box might appear sufficiently complicated to make you feel a mild twinge of panic. But if you give it a chance, you'll find that it works faster than transferring images via the Clipboard, particularly when editing very large images. In the meantime, don't worry about it. Chapter 19 will come soon enough.

Using multichannel techniques

The one channel function I've so far ignored is Image ⇨ Mode ⇨ Multichannel. When you choose this command, Photoshop changes your image so that channels no longer have a specific relationship to one another. They don't mix to create a full-color image; instead, they exist independently within the confines of a single image. The multichannel mode is generally an intermediary step for converting between different color modes without recalculating the contents of the channels.

For example, normally when you convert between the RGB and CMYK modes, Photoshop maps RGB colors to the CMYK color model, changing the contents of each channel as demonstrated back in Figures 6-2 and 6-3. But suppose, just as an experiment, that you want to bypass the color mapping and instead transfer the exact contents of the red channel to the cyan channel, the contents of the green channel to the magenta channel, and so on. You convert from RGB to the multichannel mode and then from multichannel to CMYK as described in the following steps.

STEPS   Using the Multichannel Mode as an Intermediary Step

Step 1.   Open an RGB image. If the image is already open, make sure that it is saved to disk.

Step 2.   Choose Mode ⇨ Multichannel. This eliminates any relationship between the formerly red, green, and blue color channels.

Step 3.   Click on the new channel icon at the bottom of the Channels palette. Or choose the New Channel command from the palette menu and press Return to accept the default settings. Either way, you add a mask channel to the image. This empty channel will serve as the black channel in the CMYK image. (Photoshop won't let you convert from the multichannel mode to CMYK with less than four channels.)

Step 4.   Press ⌘-I. Unfortunately, the new channel comes up black, which would make the entire image black. To change it to white, press ⌘-I or choose Image ⇨ Adjust ⇨ Invert.

Step 5. **Choose Mode ⇨ CMYK.** The image looks washed out and a tad bit dark compared to its original RGB counterpart, but the overall color scheme of the image remains more or less intact. This is because the red, green, and blue color channels each have a respective opposite in the cyan, magenta, and yellow channels.

Step 6. **Press ⌘-Shift-L.** Or choose Image ⇨ Adjust ⇨ Auto Levels. This punches up the color a bit by automatically correcting the brightness and contrast.

Step 7. **Convert the image to RGB, and then back to CMYK again.** The problem with the image is that it lacks any information in the black channel. So although it may look okay on-screen, it will lose much of its definition when printed. To fill in the black channel, choose Image ⇨ Mode ⇨ RGB Color, then choose Image ⇨ Mode ⇨ CMYK Color. Photoshop automatically generates an image in the black channel in keeping with the standards of color separations (as explained in Chapter 7).

Keep in mind that these steps are by no means a recommended procedure for converting an RGB image to a CMYK image. Rather, they are merely intended to suggest one way to experiment with channel conversions to create a halfway decent image. You can likewise experiment with converting between the Lab, multichannel, and RGB modes, or Lab, multichannel, and CMYK.

Replacing and swapping color channels

If you truly want to abuse the colors in an RGB or CMYK image, there's nothing like replacing one color channel with another to produce spectacular effects. Color Plate 6-3 shows a few examples applied to an RGB image. In the first example, I copied the image in the blue channel (⌘-3, ⌘-A, ⌘-C) and pasted it into the red channel (⌘-1, ⌘-V). The result is a green woman floating in a green sea under a purple sky. To achieve the next example (starting again from the original RGB image), I copied the red channel and pasted it into the green channel. The result this time is a yellow woman against a deep blue background. To create the purple woman in a green world on the right side of Color Plate 6-3, I copied the red channel and pasted it into the blue channel.

 Again, instead of copying and pasting, you can transfer images between channels without upsetting the contents of the Clipboard by choosing Image ⇨ Calculations. I discuss this and other applications for this command in Chapter 19.

You can create more interesting effects by swapping the contents of color channels. For example, in the lower left example of Color Plate 6-3, I swapped the contents of the red and blue channels to create a blue woman on a green sea under an orange sky. To accomplish this, I chose the Split Channels command from the Channels palette menu. I then chose the Merge Channels command and accepted the default settings in the Merge Channels dialog box. When the Merge RGB Channels dialog box appeared, I selected the blue channel from the Red pop-up menu and the red channel from the Blue pop-up menu.

The next two examples along the bottom of Color Plate 6-3 show the results of swapping the red and green channels (for a bright green woman) and the green and blue channels. Because the green and blue channels contain relatively similar data, this produces the most subtle effect, mostly switching the sea and sky colors and turning the swimsuit pink.

 When experimenting, it's a good idea to keep the original contents of each color channel close at hand just in case you don't like the results. I recommend using the Duplicate Channel command to save each color channel in the image to a separate mask channel. For example, when editing an RGB image, create three duplicates, one each for duplicates of the red, green, and blue channels, for a total of six channels in the image. You then can replace channels with impunity, knowing that you have backups if you need them.

Printing Images

In This Chapter

➥ Terms you need to know to communicate with your commercial printer

➥ How to print grayscale and color composites

➥ A complete guide to the Page Setup dialog box

➥ The theory behind halftone screens

➥ How to assign transfer functions to distribute brightness values

➥ A discussion of the color-separation process

➥ How to apply color trapping

➥ How to convert a grayscale image into a duotone, tritone, or quadtone

➥ Some advice on adding spot-color highlights to a CMYK image

Welcome to Printing

On one hand, printing can be a very straightforward topic. You choose the Print command, press the Return key, wait for something to come out of your printer, and admire yet another piece of forestry that you've gone and destroyed. On the other hand, printing can be a ridiculously complicated subject, involving dot gain compensation, hardware calibration, under color removal, toxic processor chemicals, separation table generation, and so many infinitesimal color parameters that you're liable to spend half your life trying to figure out what's going on.

This chapter is about finding a middle ground. Although it is in no way intended to cover every possible facet of printing digitized images, it walks you through the process of preparing and printing the three major categories of output: composites, color separations, and duotones. By the end of the chapter, you'll be familiar with all of Photoshop's printing options. You'll also be prepared to communicate with professionals at your service bureau or commercial printer, if need be, and to learn from their input and expertise.

Understanding Printing Terminology

I'm not a big believer in glossaries. Generally, they contain glib, jargony, out-of-context definitions that are about as helpful in gaining understanding of a concept as a seminar in which all the presenters speak in pig latin. But before I delve into the inner recesses of printing, I thought I should introduce, in a semi-logical, sort of random order, a smattering of the printing terms you'll encounter. Ood-gay uck-lay:

- **Service bureau:** A service bureau is a shop filled with earnest young graphic artists (at least they were young and earnest when *I* worked there), printer operators, and about a billion dollars worth of hardware. A small service bureau is usually outfitted with a few laser printers, photocopiers, and self-service computers. Big service bureaus offer scanners, imagesetters, film recorders, and other varieties of professional-quality input and output equipment.

- **Commercial printer:** Generally speaking, a commercial printer takes up where the service bureau leaves off. Commercial printers reproduce black-and-white and color pages using offset presses, web presses, and a whole bunch of other age-old technology that I don't cover in this mini-glossary (or anywhere else in this book, for that matter). Suffice it to say, the process is less expensive than photocopying when you're dealing with large quantities — say, more than 100 copies — and it delivers professional-quality reproductions.

- **Output device:** This is just another way to say *printer.* Rather than writing *Print your image from the printer,* which sounds repetitive and a trifle obvious, I write *Print your image from the output device.* Output devices also include laser printers, imagesetters, film recorders, and a whole bunch of other machines.

- **Laser printer:** A laser printer works much like a photocopier. First, it applies an electric charge to a cylinder, called a *drum,* inside the printer. The charged areas, which correspond to the black portions of the image being printed, attract fine, petroleum-based dust particles called *toner.* The drum transfers the toner to the page, and a heating mechanism fixes the toner in place. Most laser printers have resolutions of 300 dots (or *printer pixels*) per inch. A few offer higher resolutions, such as 600 and 1,200 dots per inch (*dpi*).

↷ **Color printers:** Color printers fall into three categories. Generally speaking, *ink-jet* and *thermal-wax* printers figure in at the low end and *dye-sublimation* printers occupy the high end. Ink-jet printers deliver colored dots out of disposable ink cartridges. Thermal-wax printers apply wax-based pigments to a page in multiple passes. Both kinds of printers mix cyan, magenta, yellow, and, depending on the specific printer, black dots to produce full-color output. If you want photographic quality prints — the kind you'd be proud to hang on your wall — you must migrate up the price ladder to dye-sublimation printers. Dye-sub inks permeate the surface of the paper, literally dying it different colors. Furthermore, the cyan, magenta, yellow, and black pigments mix in varying opacities from one dot to the next, resulting in a continuous-tone image that appears nearly as smooth on the page as it does on-screen.

↷ **Imagesetter:** A typesetter that is equipped with a graphics page-description language such as PostScript is called an *imagesetter*. Unlike a laser printer, an imagesetter prints photosensitive paper or film by exposing the portions of the paper or film that correspond to the black areas of the image. The process is a lot like exposing film with a camera, but an imagesetter only knows two colors, black and white. The exposed paper or film collects in a light-proof canister. In a separate step, the printer operator develops the film in a *processor* that contains two chemical baths — developer and fixer — a water bath to wash away the chemicals, and a heat dryer to dry off the water. Developed paper looks like a typical glossy black-and-white page. Developed film is black where the image is white and transparent where the image is black. Imagesetters typically offer resolutions between 1,200 and 3,600 dpi. But the real beauty of imageset pages is that blacks are absolutely black (or transparent), as opposed to the irregular gray you get with laser-printed pages.

↷ **Film recorder:** This device transfers images to full-color 35mm and 4 by 5 slides that are perfect for professional presentations. Slides also can be useful as a means for providing images to publications and commercial printers. Many publications can scan from slides, and commercial printers can use slides to create color separations. So if you're nervous that a color separation printed from Photoshop won't turn out well, ask your service bureau to output the image to a 35mm slide. Then have your commercial printer reproduce the image from the slide.

↷ **PostScript:** The PostScript page-description language was the first project developed by Adobe, the same folks who sell Photoshop, and is now a staple of hundreds of brands of laser printers, imagesetters, and film recorders. A *page-description language* is a programming language for defining text and graphics on a page. PostScript specifies the locations of points, draws line segments between them, and fills in areas with solid blacks or *halftone cells* (dot patterns that simulate grays). PostScript Level 2, an updated version of the original PostScript, speeds up output time and provides improved halftoning options, better color separations, automated antialiasing of jagged images, and direct support for Lab images (discussed in the "CIE's Lab" section of Chapter 5).

- ↫ **QuickDraw:** QuickDraw is a competing page-description language developed by Apple. It is the language that displays images on any Macintosh screen. It is also built into a few laser printers, including the old LaserWriter SC. QuickDraw GX automates kerning and other typographic functions, provides better printer spooling, offers new graphics capabilities previously exclusive to PostScript, and integrates Apple's ColorSync color-matching technology to ensure smooth transitions from scanner to screen to printer. But Adobe currently has no plans to support QuickDraw GX, and the professional market in general has ignored its presence.

- ↫ **Spooling:** Printer *spooling* allows you to work on an image while another image prints. Rather than communicating directly with the output device, Photoshop describes the image to the system software. Under System 7, this function is performed by a program called PrintMonitor. When Photoshop finishes describing the image — a relatively quick process — you are free to resume working while the system software prints the image in the background.

- ↫ **Calibration:** Traditionally, *calibrating* a system means to synchronize the machinery. However, in the context of Photoshop, it means to adjust or compensate for the color displays of the scanner, monitor, and printer so that what you scan is what you see on-screen, which in turn is what you get from the printer. Colors match from one device to the next. Empirically speaking, this is impossible; a yellow image in a photograph won't look exactly like the on-screen yellow or the yellow printed from a set of color separations. But calibrating is designed to make them look as much alike as possible, taking into account the fundamental differences in hardware technology. Expensive hardware calibration solutions seek to change the configuration of scanner, monitor, and printer. Less expensive software solutions, including those provided by Photoshop, manipulate the image to account for the differences between devices.

- ↫ **Brightness values/shades:** As described at length in Chapter 5, there is a fundamental difference between the way your screen and printer create gray values and colors. Your monitor shows colors by lightening up an otherwise black screen; the printed page shows colors by darkening an otherwise white piece of paper. Therefore, on-screen colors are measured in terms of *brightness values*. High values equate to light colors; low values equate to dark colors. On the printed page, colors are measured in percentage values called *shades,* or if you prefer, *tints*. High percentage values result in dark colors, and low percentage values result in light colors.

↝ **Composite:** A *composite* is a page that shows an image in its entirety. A black-and-white composite printed from a standard laser printer or imagesetter translates all colors in an image to gray values. A color composite printed from a color printer or film recorder shows the colors as they actually appear. Composites are useful any time you want to proof an image or print a final grayscale image from an imagesetter, an overhead projection from a color printer, or a full-color image from a film recorder.

↝ **Proofing:** To *proof* an image is to see how it looks on paper in advance of the final printing. Laser printers are considered low-end proofing devices because they lack sufficient quality or resolution to output final images. Color printers aren't necessarily proofing devices because commercial printers can't reproduce from any color composite output except slides. (Well, they *can* reproduce from other kinds of color composites, but you don't get the same quality results.) Professional-level proofing devices include the 3M Rainbow dye-sublimation printer, which prints images of photographic quality, and the IRIS, which uses a special variety of ink-jet technology to create arguably the most accurate electronic proofs in the business.

↝ **Bleeds:** Simply put, a *bleed* is an area outside the perimeter of a page that can be printed. You use a bleed to reproduce an image all the way to the edge of a page, as in a slick magazine ad. By way of example, this book includes bleeds. Most of the pages — like the page you're reading — are encircled by a uniform two-pica margin of white space. This margin keeps the text and figures from spilling off into oblivion. However, a few pages — including the parts pages and the color plates in the middle of the book — print all the way to the edges. In fact, the original artwork goes two picas beyond the edges of the paper. This ensures that if the paper shifts when printing — as it invariably does — you don't see any thin white edges around the artwork. This two picas of extra artwork is the bleed. In Photoshop, you create a bleed by clicking on the Bleed button in the Page Setup dialog box.

↝ **Color separations:** To output color reproductions, commercial printers require color separations (or slides, which they can convert to color separations for a fee). A color-separated image comprises four printouts, one each for the cyan, magenta, yellow, and black primary printing colors. The commercial printer transfers each printout to a *plate* that is used in the actual reproduction process.

↝ **Duotone:** A grayscale image in Photoshop can contain as many as 256 brightness values, from white on up to black. A printer can convey significantly fewer shades. A typical laser printer, for example, provides 26 shades at most. An imagesetter typically provides from 150 to 200 shades, depending on resolution and screen frequency. And that's assuming perfect printing conditions. You can count on at least 30 percent of those shades getting lost in the reproduction process. A *duotone* helps to retain the depth and clarity of detail in a grayscale image by printing with two inks. Suddenly, the number of shades available to you jumps from 150 to 22,000 (150^2). Photoshop also permits you to create *tritones* (three inks) and *quadtones* (four inks). Note, however, that using more inks translates to higher printing costs. Color Plate 7-1 shows a quadtone.

Printing Composites

Now that you've picked up a bit of printer's jargon, you're ready to learn how to put it all together. This section explores the labyrinth of options available for printing composite images. Later in this chapter, I cover color separations and duotones.

Like any Macintosh application, Photoshop can print composite images to just about any output device you hook up to your Mac. Assuming that your printer is turned on, properly attached, and in working order, printing a composite image from Photoshop is a five-step process, as outlined below.

The following sections describe each of these steps in detail.

STEPS   **Printing a Composite Image**

Step 1.   **Choose your printer.** Use the Network control panel and Chooser desk accessory to select the output device to which you want to print. If your computer is not part of a network that includes multiple printers, you probably rely on a single output device, in which case you can skip this step.

Step 2.   **Choose File ⇨ Page Setup (⌘-Shift-P).** This permits you to specify the page size and the size and orientation of the image on the page. You can also use Image ⇨ Image Size to control the size of the image by changing its resolution, as explained in the "Changing the printing resolution" section of Chapter 4.

Step 3.   **Adjust the halftone screens, if needed.** Click on the Screens button to change the size, angle, and shape of the halftone screen dots. This step is purely optional, useful mostly for creating special effects.

Step 4.   **Adjust the transfer function, again if needed.** Click on the Transfer button to map brightness values in an image to different shades when printed. This step is also optional, though frequently very useful.

Step 5.   **Choose File ⇨ Print (⌘-P).** Photoshop prints the image according to your specifications.

Choosing a printer

If you are connected to more than one network, you may need to choose Apple ⇨ Control Panels ⇨ Network to display the Network control panel and select the connection that you want to use. After that, choose the Chooser desk accessory from the list of desk accessories under the Apple menu. The Chooser dialog box appears, as shown in Figure 7-1. The dialog box is split in two, with the left half devoted to a scrolling list of printer driver icons and network zones, and the right half to specific printer options.

Figure 7-1
Use the Chooser desk accessory to select the desired output device.

Select the printer driver icon that matches your model of printer. *Printer drivers* help the Macintosh hardware, system software, and Photoshop translate the contents of an image to the printer hardware and the page-description language it uses. If you intend to use a PostScript-compatible printer, you'll generally want to select the LaserWriter or PSPrinter driver. (They're really the same thing — LaserWriter comes from Apple and PSPrinter comes from Adobe.)

If the network at your office (or, heaven forbid, at your home) is divided up into multiple zones, you'll see two scrolling lists on the left side of the Chooser dialog box, as in Figure 7-1. Select the zone that contains the desired printer from the lower list. The figure shows how zones are laid out in the vast network at the *Macworld* magazine complex. I gained access remotely — just as might be an option at your workplace — using Apple Remote Access. Once connected, my Chooser can access printers thousands of miles away from my office. (I'm in Boulder, Colorado; *Macworld* is in San Francisco.) Of course, this slows the printing down a bit, and I have to hop aboard a plane to go fetch the page, but it's great for sending a message to some staff member. For example, if I wanted to say hello to *Macworld* editor-in-chief Adrian Mello, I'd select the printer *Adrian's NTR-Do Not Use.* In fact, I plan on printing my electronic book version of *Alice in Wonderland* for him this very afternoon. He'll get a kick out of it.

After you select the required printer driver and, if necessary, gain access to the proper zone, you can select the name of your printer from the scrolling list on the right side of the Chooser dialog box. When using a PostScript printer, you see two sets of radio buttons, Background Printing and AppleTalk. The latter refers to the kind of cabling required to hook up PostScript printers. If you turn it off, you won't be able to access your printer anymore, so by all means leave it turned on. Background Printing, on the other hand, is not so cut and dried. When on, this option lets you print an image in the background while you continue to work in Photoshop or some other application. This enables you to take advantage of *spooling*, as defined earlier in this chapter.

Spooling can interrupt foreground tasks and increase the likelihood of printing errors. Photoshop images are particularly prone to spooling problems. For example, a half inch across the middle of the image may print out of alignment with the rest of the image. For perfect image printing, turn off the Background Printing option.

Any PostScript printer driver beyond LaserWriter 8 includes support for *PostScript printer description* (*PPD*) files. A single driver can't account for the myriad differences between different models of PostScript printers, so each PPD serves as a little guidance file, customizing the driver to accommodate a specific printer model. After selecting a printer from the right-hand scrolling list, you can access the proper PPD by clicking on the Setup button. (Or just double-click on the printer name in the list.) The dialog box shown in Figure 7-2 appears. It contains several buttons — you can display all the ones shown in Figure 7-2 by clicking on the More Choices button — but the most important one is Auto Setup. Click on this button to instruct the system software to automatically select the correct PPD for your printer. If the system fails or if it selects the Generic option, click on the Select PPD button and try to locate the proper PPD files inside the Printer Descriptions folder in the Extensions folder in your System Folder.

Figure 7-2
Use this dialog box to select the proper PPD file for your specific brand of PostScript printer.

Current Printer Description File (PPD) Selected:
"LaserWriter Pro 630 v2010.130"

[Select PPD...] [Configure] [Printer Info] [Help]

[Fewer Choices] [Auto Setup] [Cancel] [OK]

If your printer does not require AppleTalk-protocol cabling, as is generally the case with ImageWriters, StyleWriters, and other low-end devices, the right-hand scrolling list contains two icons: one for the printer port, and the second for the modem port. Select the icon that corresponds to the serial port in the back of your Mac that connects to your printer.

When you finish selecting options in the Chooser dialog box, click on the close box in the upper left corner of the title bar to return to the Photoshop desktop.

Setting up the page

The next step is to define the relationship between the current image and the page on which it prints. Assuming that you're using a PostScript output device, choosing File ➪ Page Setup (or pressing ⌘-Shift-P) displays the LaserWriter Page Setup dialog box shown in Figure 7-3.

Assuming that you're using LaserWriter driver 8 or later, this dialog box provides the following options:

> ➥ **Paper:** Select the option from the Paper pop-up menu that corresponds to the size of the paper loaded into your printer's paper tray. The paper size you select determines the *imageable area* of a page — that is, the amount of the page that Photoshop can use to print the current image. For example, the US Letter option calls for a page that measures 8.5 × 11 inches, but only 7.7 × 10.2 inches is imageable.

Figure 7-3
Use this dialog box to specify the relationship between the printed image and the page on which it appears.

To slightly enlarge the imageable area of a page without changing paper sizes, click on the Options button to display the LaserWriter Options dialog box and select the Larger Print Area check box, as shown in Figure 7-4. For example, when you print to a letter-sized page, this option increases the size of the imageable area from 7.7 × 10.2 inches to 8.0 × 10.8 inches. The dotted line in the page preview on the left side of the dialog box enlarges slightly to demonstrate the option's effect.

Figure 7-4
Select the Larger Print Area check box to enlarge the size of the imageable area of a page printed from a laser printer.

∞ **Layout:** This option allows you to print more than one page per each sheet of paper. For example, if you wanted to proof the layout of a 16-page QuarkXPress document, you could select the 4 Up option to print four quarter-sized versions of each page per each piece of paper. You save paper, kill fewer trees, and even waste a little less time. However, because there is no such thing as a multipage document in Photoshop, this option serves no purpose. If you select the 4 Up option, for example, you simply get one image reduced to 25 percent its normal size in the upper left corner of the printed page. So always leave this option set to 1 Up when printing from Photoshop.

∞ **Reduce or Enlarge:** Enter a percentage value into this option box to enlarge or reduce the size of the image when printed. For more information on this option, see Chapter 3.

∞ **Orientation:** You can specify whether an image prints upright on a page (called the *portrait setting*) or on its side (called the *landscape setting*) by selecting the corresponding Orientation icon. The landscape setting is useful when an image is wider than it is tall.

After specifying the Reduce or Enlarge percentage and Orientation icon, you can check to see how the image fits on the page. To do so, press Return to exit the LaserWriter Page Setup dialog box and click and hold on the preview box in the lower left corner of the image window. The rectangle with the inset X that appears inside the pop-up window represents the image on the page. If the rectangle extends outside the page, you need to further reduce the image or change the page orientation.

Nearly every Macintosh application offers the options described so far because they're a function of the Macintosh system software. However, it's a different story when you descend below the dotted line to the options at the bottom of the LaserWriter Page Setup dialog box. These options are specific to Photoshop. First I'll describe how to use the buttons on the left and then I'll explain the check boxes on the right:

- ⌦ **Screen:** Click on this button to enter a dialog box that allows you to change the size, angle, and shape of the printed halftone cells, as described in the upcoming "Changing the halftone screen" section.

- ⌦ **Transfer:** The dialog box that appears when you click on this button allows you to redistribute shades in the printed image, as explained in the upcoming "Specifying a transfer function" section.

- ⌦ **Background:** To assign a color to the area around the printed image, click on this button and select a color from the Color Picker dialog box, which is described in more detail in Chapter 4. This button and the one that follows (Border) are designed specifically for use when printing slides from a film recorder.

- ⌦ **Border:** To print a border around the current image, click on this button and enter the thickness of the border into the Width option box. The border automatically appears in black.

- ⌦ **Bleed:** This button allows you to print outside the imageable area of the page when outputting to an imagesetter. (Imagesetters print to huge rolls of paper or film, so you can print far outside the confines of standard page size. Most other printers use regular old sheets of paper; any bleed — were the printer to even acknowledge it — would print off the edge of the page.) Click on the Bleed button and enter the thickness of the bleed into the Width option box. Two picas (24 points) is generally a good bet. (Bleeds are defined in the "Understanding Printing Terminology" glossary at the beginning of this chapter.)

Now for the check boxes in the lower middle and right-hand sections of the dialog box. Most of these options — all except Negative, Emulsion Down, and Interpolation — append special labels and printer marks to the printed version of the image. These labels and marks are demonstrated in Figure 7-5.

 By the way, Figure 7-5 shows the actual labels and marks exactly as they print. This may not sound like much, but in the past, such printer's marks have been very difficult to capture because there was no way to save them in a reliable file format. A book writer like me either had the option of printing the file to disk as an EPS file — which might or might not print accurately when placed into a page-layout program — or simply printing the page independently and manually pasting it up into the book. But thanks to the fact that Illustrator 6 opens EPS files created in any application, I was able to create an editable version of the printed image.

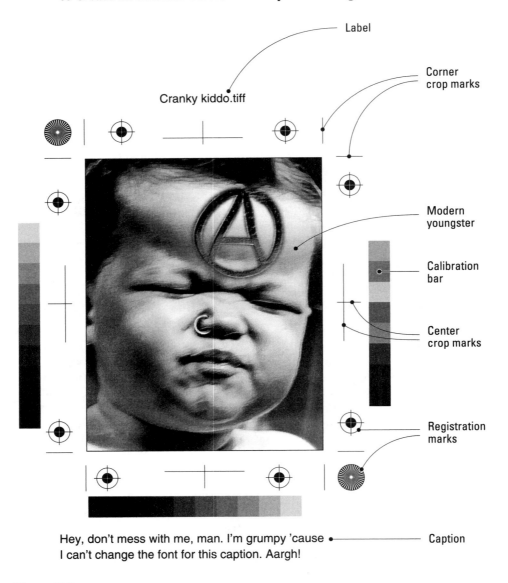

Label

Cranky kiddo.tiff

Corner
crop marks

Modern
youngster

Calibration
bar

Center
crop marks

Registration
marks

Hey, don't mess with me, man. I'm grumpy 'cause ●————————— Caption
I can't change the font for this caption. Aargh!

Figure 7-5
An image printed with nearly all the Page Setup check
boxes turned off.

In the name of full disclosure — my job is to pass along information, not store up trade secrets — here's how I accomplished this smallish feat: I first printed the Photoshop image to disk as an EPS file (as described in the "Printing pages" section later in this chapter) — labels, printer's marks, and all. I then used Illustrator to open the EPS file and assign the callouts — which are those little labels like "Calibration bar" and "Modern youngster."

Here's how the check box options work:

- **Caption:** To print a caption beneath the image, select this option. Then press the Return key to exit this dialog box, choose File ➪ File Info, and enter a caption into the File Info dialog box. The caption prints in 9-point Helvetica. It's strictly an image-annotation feature, something to help you 17 years down the road, when your brain starts to deteriorate and you can't remember why you printed the darn thing. (You might also use the caption to keep images straight in a busy office where hundreds of folks have access to the same images, but I don't like this alternative as much because I can't make fun of it.)

- **Calibration Bars:** A calibration bar is a 10-step grayscale gradation that starts at 10 percent black and ends at 100 percent black. The function of the calibration bar is to ensure that all shades are distinct and on target. If not, the output device isn't properly calibrated, which is a fancy way of saying that the printer's colors are out of whack and need realignment by a trained professional armed with a hammer and hacksaw. When you print color separations, the Calibration Bars check box instructs Photoshop to print a gradient tint bar and progressive color bar, also useful to printing professionals.

- **Registration Marks:** Select this option to print eight crosshairs and two star targets near the four corners of the image. Registration marks are absolutely imperative when you print color separations because they provide the only reliable means for ensuring exact registration of the cyan, magenta, yellow, and black printing plates. When printing a composite image, however, you can ignore this option.

- **Corner Crop Marks:** Select this option to print eight hairline *crop marks* — two in each of the image's four corners — which indicate how to trim the image in case you anticipate engaging in a little traditional paste-up work.

- **Center Crop Marks:** Select this option to print four pairs of hairlines that mark the center of the image. Each pair forms a cross. Two pairs are located on the sides of the image, one is above the image, and the fourth is below.

- **Labels:** When you select this check box, Photoshop prints the name of the image and the name of the printed color channel in 9-point Helvetica. If you process lots of images, you'll find this option extremely useful for associating printouts with documents on disk.

- **Negative:** When you select this option, Photoshop prints all blacks as white and all whites as black. In-between colors switch accordingly. For example,

20 percent black becomes 80 percent black. Imagesetter operators use this option to print composites and color separations to film negative.

- **Emulsion Down:** The *emulsion* is the side of a piece of film on which an image is printed. When the Emulsion Down check box is turned off, film prints from an imagesetter emulsion side up; when the check box is turned on, Photoshop flips the image so that the emulsion side is down. Like the Negative option, this option is useful only when you print film from an imagesetter and should be set in accordance with the preferences of your commercial printer.

- **Interpolation:** If you own an output device equipped with PostScript Level 2, you can instruct Photoshop to antialias the printed appearance of a low-resolution image by selecting this option. The output device resamples the image up to 200 percent and then reduces it to its original size using bicubic interpolation (as described in the "General preferences" section of Chapter 2), thereby creating a less jagged image. This option has no effect on older-model PostScript devices.

Changing the halftone screen

Before I go any farther, let me explain a bit more about how printing works. To keep costs down, commercial printers use as few inks as possible to create the appearance of a wide variety of colors. Suppose that you want to print an image of a pink flamingo wearing a red bow tie. Your commercial printer could print the flamingos in one pass using pink ink, let that color dry, and then load the red ink and print all the bow ties. But why go to all that trouble? After all, pink is just a lighter shade of red. Why not imitate the pink by lightening the red ink?

Well, unfortunately, with the exception of dye-sublimation printers, very high-end ink jets, and film recorders, output devices can't print lighter shades of colors. They recognize only solid ink and the absence of ink. So how do you print the lighter shade of red necessary to represent pink?

The answer is *halftoning*. The output device organizes printer pixels into spots called *halftone cells*. Because the cells are so small, your eyes cannot quite focus on them. Instead, the cells appear to blend with the white background of the page to create a lighter shade of an ink. Figure 7-6 shows a detail of an image enlarged to display the individual halftone cells.

The cells grow and shrink to emulate different shades of color. Large cells result in dark shades; small cells result in light shades. Cell size is measured in printer pixels. The maximum size of any cell is a function of the number of cells in an inch, called the *screen frequency*.

Figure 7-6
A detail from an image (left)
enlarged so you can see the
individual halftone cells
(right).

Figure 7-6
A detail from an image (left) enlarged so you can see the individual halftone cells (right).

For example, the default frequency of the Apple LaserWriter is 60 halftone cells per linear inch. Because the resolution of the LaserWriter is 300 printer pixels per linear inch, each halftone cell must measure 5 pixels wide by 5 pixels tall ($300 \div 60 = 5$), for a total of 25 pixels per cell (5^2). When all pixels in a cell are turned off, the cell appears white; when all pixels are turned on, you get solid ink. By turning on different numbers of pixels — from 0 up to 25 — the printer can create a total of 26 shades, as demonstrated in Figure 7-7.

Figure 7-7
5×5-pixel halftone cells with different numbers of pixels activated, ranging from 25 (top left) to 0 (bottom right). Each cell represents a unique shade from 100 to 0 percent black.

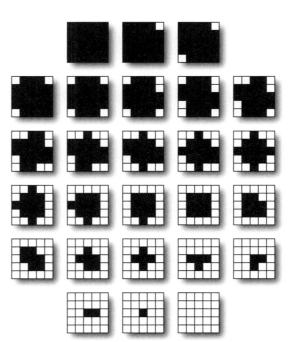

Photoshop lets you change the size, angle, and shape of the individual *halftone cells* used to represent an image on the printed page. To do so, click on the Screens button in the LaserWriter Page Setup dialog box. The Halftone Screens dialog box shown in Figure 7-8 appears.

Figure 7-8
Use the Halftone Screens dialog box to edit the size, angle, and shape of the halftone cells for any one ink.

In the dialog box, you can manipulate the following options:

- **Use Printer's Default Screens:** Select this check box to accept the default size, angle, and shape settings built into your printer's ROM. All other options in the Halftone Screens dialog box automatically become dimmed to show they are no longer in force.

- **Ink:** If the current image is in color, you can select the specific ink that you want to adjust from the Ink pop-up menu. When you work with a grayscale image, no pop-up menu is available.

- **Frequency:** Enter a new value into this option box to change the number of halftone cells that print per linear inch. A higher value translates to a larger quantity of smaller cells; a smaller value creates fewer, larger cells. Frequency is traditionally measured in *lines-per-inch,* or *lpi* (as in lines of halftone cells), but you can change the measurement to lines per centimeter by selecting Lines/cm from the pop-up menu to the right of the option box.

Higher screen frequencies result in smoother-looking printouts. However, raising the Frequency value also decreases the number of shades an output device can print because it decreases the size of each halftone cell and likewise decreases the number of printer pixels per cell. Fewer printer pixels means fewer shades. You can calculate the precise number of printable shades using the following formula:

Number of shades = (printer resolution ÷ frequency)^2 +1

⌦ **Angle:** To change the orientation of the lines of halftone cells, enter a new value into the Angle option box. In the name of accuracy, Photoshop accepts any value between negative and positive 180 degrees.

When printing color composites to ink-jet and thermal-wax printers and when printing color separations, Photoshop calculates the optimum Frequency and Angle values required to print seamless colors. In such a case, you should change these values only if you know *exactly* what you're doing. Otherwise, your printout may exhibit weird patterning effects. When printing grayscale images, however, you can edit these values to your heart's content.

⌦ **Shape:** By default, most PostScript printers rely on roundish halftone cells. You can change the appearance of all cells for an ink by selecting one of six alternate shapes from the Shape pop-up menu. For a demonstration of four of these shapes, see Figure 5-9 in the "Black and white (bitmap)" section of Chapter 5. If you know how to write PostScript code, you can select the Custom option to display a text-entry dialog box and code away.

⌦ **Use Accurate Screens:** If your output device is equipped with PostScript Level 2, select this option to subscribe to the updated screen angles for full-color output. Otherwise, don't worry about this option.

⌦ **Use Same Shape for All Inks:** Select this option if you want to apply a single set of size, angle, and shape options to the halftone cells for all inks used to represent the current image. Unless you want to create some sort of special effect, leave this check box deselected. The option is not available when you are printing a grayscale image.

⌦ **Auto:** Click on this button to display the Auto Screens dialog box shown in Figure 7-9, which automates the halftone editing process. Enter the resolution of your output device in the Printer option box. Then enter the screen frequency you would like to use in the Screen option box. After you press the Return key to confirm your change, Photoshop automatically calculates the optimum screen frequencies for all inks. This technique is especially useful when you print full-color images; because Photoshop does the work for you, you can't make a mess of things.

Figure 7-9
To automate the halftone editing process, enter the resolution of the output device and the screen frequency you want to use into the Auto Screens dialog box.

Auto Screens		
Printer: `2400`	`dots/inch` ▼	**OK**
Screen: `133`	`lines/inch` ▼	Cancel
☐ **Use Accurate Screens**		

◅ **Load/Save:** You can load and save settings to disk in case you want to reapply the options to other images. These buttons are especially useful if you find a magic combination of halftone settings that results in a really spectacular printout.

 You can change the default size, angle, and shape settings that Photoshop applies to all future images by Option-clicking on the Save button. When you press Option, the Save button changes to read ⇨*Default*. To restore the default screen settings at any time, Option-click on the Load button (⇦ *Default*).

 The Halftone Screens dialog box settings don't only apply to printing images directly from Photoshop. You can export these settings along with the image for placement in QuarkXPress or some other application by saving the image in the Photoshop EPS format. Just be sure to turn on the "Include Halftone Screen" check box in the EPS Format dialog box, as discussed in the "Saving an EPS image" section of Chapter 4. This also applies to transfer function settings, explained in the next section.

 If you do decide to include the halftone screen information with your EPS file, be sure that the settings are compatible with your intended output device. You don't want to specify a low Frequency value such as 60 lpi when printing to a state-of-the-art 3,600-dpi imagesetter, for example. If you have any questions, be sure to call your service bureau or printer before saving the image. The last thing you want is a last-minute surprise, and a hefty bill to boot.

Specifying a transfer function

A *transfer function* enables you to change the way on-screen brightness values translate — or *map* — to printed shades. By default, brightness values print to their nearest shade percentages. A 30 percent gray on-screen pixel (which equates to a brightness value of roughly 180) prints as a 30 percent gray value.

Problems arise, however, when your output device prints lighter or darker than it should. For example, in the course of using my LaserWriter NTX over the last five years or so — I know it's going to die one day, but it still keeps on chugging along — I've discovered that all gray values print overly dark. Dark values fill in and become black; light values appear a dismal gray, muddying up any highlights. The problem increases if I try to reproduce the image on a photocopier.

To compensate for this over-darkening effect, I click on the Transfer button in the LaserWriter Page Setup dialog box and enter the values shown in Figure 7-10. Notice that I lighten 30 percent on-screen grays to 10 percent printer grays. I also lighten 90 percent screen grays to 80 percent printer grays. The result is a smooth, continuous curve that maps each gray value in an image to a lighter value on paper.

Figure 7-10
The transfer function curve lets you map on-screen brightness values to specific shades on paper.

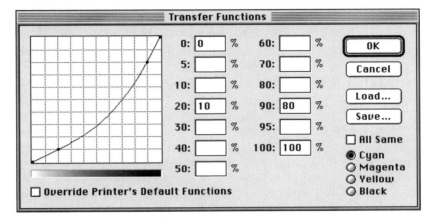

The options in the Transfer Functions dialog box work as follows:

- **Transfer graph:** The *transfer graph* is where you map on-screen brightness values to their printed equivalents. The horizontal axis of the graph represents on-screen brightness values; the vertical axis represents printed shades. The *transfer curve* charts the relationship between on-screen and printed colors. The lower left corner is the origin of the graph — the point at which both on-screen brightness value and printed shade are white. Move to the right in the graph for darker on-screen values; move up for darker printed shades. Click in the graph to add points to the line. Drag up on a point to darken the output; drag down to lighten the output.

 For a more comprehensive explanation of how to graph colors on a curve, read about the incredibly powerful Curves command, covered in Chapter 18.

- **Percentage option boxes:** The option boxes are labeled according to the on-screen brightness values. To lighten or darken the printed brightness values, enter higher or lower percentage values in the option boxes. Note that there is a direct correlation between changes made to the transfer graph and the option boxes. For example, if you enter a value in the 50 percent option box, a new point appears along the middle line of the graph.

- **Override Printer's Default Functions:** As an effect of printer calibration, some printers have custom transfer functions built into their ROM. If you have problems making your settings take effect, select this check box to instruct Photoshop to apply the transfer function you specify regardless of the output device's built-in transfer function.

╼ **Load/Save:** Use these buttons to load and save settings to disk. Option-click on the buttons to retrieve and save default settings.

╼ **Ink controls:** When you print a full-color image, five options appear in the lower right corner of the Transfer Functions dialog box. These options enable you to apply different transfer functions to different inks. Select the All Same check box to apply a single transfer function to all inks. To apply a different function to each ink, select one of the radio buttons and edit the points in the transfer graph as desired.

Printing pages

When you finish slogging your way through the mind-numbingly extensive Page Setup options, you can initiate the printing process by choosing File ⇨ Print (⌘-P). The Printer dialog box or its equivalent appears, shown in its RGB and CMYK forms in Figure 7-11.

Figure 7-11
The Print dialog box as it appears when printing an RGB (top) and CMYK (bottom) image.

Most of the options of this dialog box are a function of the Macintosh system software, but a few at the bottom of the dialog box are exclusive to Photoshop. The options work as follows:

╼ **Copies:** Enter the number of copies you want to print in this option box. You can print up to 999 copies of a single image, although why you would want to do so is beyond me.

╼ **Pages:** There is no such thing as a multipage document in Photoshop, so you can ignore the All, From, and To options.

╼ **Paper Source:** If you want to print your illustration on a letterhead or other special piece of paper, select the Manual Feed radio button. If you're using the LaserWriter driver 8 or later, select the First From radio button and then select Manual Feed from the accompanying pop-up menu. LaserWriter 8 lets you print the first page to different paper than other pages in the document. However, because Photoshop images are never more than one page long, you can pretty well ignore this option.

∞ **Destination:** This option allows you to generate a PostScript-language definition of the file on disk rather than printing it directly to your printer. Select the Printer option to print the image to an output device as usual. Select File to write a PostScript-language version of the image to disk. Because Photoshop offers its own EPS option via the Save dialog box, you'll probably want to ignore this option. In fact, the only reason to select File is to capture printer's marks, as I did back in Figure 7-5. If you select File, a second dialog box appears, asking you where you want to save the EPS file. You can navigate just as in the Open and Save dialog boxes. For the best results, select the Binary radio button.

∞ **Print Selected Area:** Select this option to print the portion of an image that is selected with the rectangular marquee tool. You can use this option to divide an image into pieces when it's too large to fit on a single page.

∞ **Print In:** Select one of these radio buttons to specify the type of composite image Photoshop prints. Select the first radio button to print the image as a grayscale composite. Select the second radio button to let the printer translate the colors from the current color mode to CMYK, or to print an image to an RGB film recorder. Select the third radio button to instruct Photoshop to convert the image to CMYK colors during the print process. These options are not available when you print a grayscale image. (When printing a CMYK image, the Print In options change to a single Print Separations check box, which is described in the next section.)

Relying on the output device to translate colors can result in printing errors, thanks to the low memory capabilities of most printers. If an image refuses to print, try selecting either the Gray or CMYK radio button. Use the first option when you print to black-and-white devices such as laser printers and imagesetters; use the last option when printing to color printers.

∞ **Encoding:** If your network doesn't support binary encoding, select the ASCII option to transfer data in the text-only format. The printing process takes much longer to complete, but at least it's possible.

The Options button is another little item you can ignore. It brings up a dialog box with three options. The first lets you print a cover page, which is a ridiculous waste of paper in the context of Photoshop. The second option, Print, lets you convert color images to grayscale. Photoshop is not only capable of printing both grayscale and color composites without the assistance of the system software, it actually accomplishes the task more quickly and more expertly than the system. Leave this option set to Black & White unless you want the system's assistance. The final option is the only one that's remotely useful, allowing you to display PostScript printing errors on-screen. My advice is to set this option to Summarize On Screen. Then close the dialog box and never return to it.

Press Return inside the Printer dialog box to start the printing process on its merry way. To cancel a print in progress, click on the Cancel button or Escape. If Photoshop ignores you, keep pressing away on those keys. I never have figured out if it does any good, but at least you feel like you're doing everything you can.

Creating Color Separations

If printing a composite image is moderately complicated, printing color separations is a terrific pain in the behind. Printer manufacturers and software developers are working to simplify this process, but for the present, Photoshop requires you to stagger through a maze of variables and obtuse options. The upcoming steps explain how to muddle your way through the color-separation process. You'll recognize many of the steps from the process described for printing a grayscale or color composite.

STEPS   Printing CMYK Color Separations

Step 1.   **Choose your printer.** If your computer is part of a network that includes many printers, use the Chooser desk accessory to select the printer to which you want to print, as described previously in the "Choosing a printer" section.

Step 2.   **Calibrate your system.** Make sure your monitor and printer are in sync using File ➪ Color Settings ➪ Monitor Setup and File ➪ Color Settings ➪ Printing Inks Setup. You only need to complete this step once for each time you switch hardware. If you always use the same monitor and printer combination, you need to repeat this step very rarely, say once every six months, to account for screen and printer degradation.

Step 3.   **Adjust the CMYK separation setting.** Use File ➪ Color Settings ➪ Separation Setup to control how Photoshop converts RGB and Lab colors to CMYK color space. Again, you need to perform this step only when you want to compensate for a difference in the output device or if you simply want to fine-tune Photoshop to create better separations.

Step 4.   **Convert the image to the CMYK color space.** Choose Image ➪ Mode ➪ CMYK Color to convert the image from its present color mode to CMYK. The CMYK mode is explained in the "CMYK" section of Chapter 5.

Step 5. **Adjust the individual color channels.** Switching color modes can dramatically affect the colors in an image. To compensate for color and focus loss, you can edit the individual color channels as described in the "Color Channel Effects" section of Chapter 6.

Step 6. **Trap your image, if necessary.** If your image features many high-contrast elements and you're concerned that your printer might not do the best job of registering the cyan, magenta, yellow, and black color plates, you can apply Image ⇨ Trap to prevent your final printout from looking like the color funnies.

Step 7. **Turn on a few essential printer marks.** Choose File ⇨ Page Setup to specify the size of the pages and the size and orientation of the image on the pages, as described earlier in this chapter. Also be sure to select — at the very least — the Calibration Bars, Registration Marks, and Labels check boxes.

Step 8. **Adjust the halftone and transfer functions as needed.** Click on the Screens and Transfer buttons to modify the halftone screen dots and map brightness values for each of the CMYK color channels, as described earlier in the "Changing the halftone screen" and "Specifying a transfer function" sections. This step is optional.

Step 9. **Choose File ⇨ Print (⌘-P).** Select the Print Separations check box in the lower left corner of the dialog box (see Figure 7-11). Photoshop then prints the color separations according to your specifications.

Steps 1 and 7 through 9 are repeats of concepts explained in earlier sections of this chapter. To fully understand Steps 4 and 5, read the larger color theory discussions contained in Chapters 5 and 6. That leaves Steps 2, 3, and 6, which I describe in detail in the following sections.

You also can create color separations by importing an image into a desktop publishing program like PageMaker or QuarkXPress. To do so, convert the image to the CMYK color space, then export the image in the DCS format, as described in the "QuarkXPress DCS" section of Chapter 4. Then print the separations directly from the desktop publishing program. Because DCS is a subset of the EPS format, it enables you to save halftone screen and transfer function settings.

Monitor calibration

Choose File ⇨ Color Settings ⇨ Monitor to display the Monitor Setup dialog box shown in Figure 7-12. Along with the Gamma control panel, which offers the added capability of adjusting specific red, green, and blue color intensities, this dialog box represents the extent of Photoshop's monitor-calibration capabilities. However, unlike Gamma, the Monitor Setup dialog box provides options that directly affect the conversion of scanned colors to their CMYK equivalents. These options advise Photoshop that certain on-screen color distortions are in effect and instruct the program to make accommodations when converting between the RGB and CMYK color modes.

Figure 7-12
The options in the Monitor Setup dialog box tell Photoshop how to compensate for on-screen colors when preparing color separations.

The options in the Monitor Setup dialog box work as follows:

↪ **Monitor:** In the best of all possible worlds, you can select your exact model of monitor from this pop-up menu. Photoshop automatically changes the settings in the Monitor Parameters box — Gamma, White Point, and Phosphors — in accordance with the recommendations of the monitor's manufacturer. If you can't find your exact model, look for a model that is made by the same manufacturer and whose *only* difference from your model is screen size. If you can't find a suitable model, select the Other option.

Do *not* assume that all monitors from the same vendor are basically alike. Most vendors sell screens manufactured by different companies. For example, the SuperMac 16-inch Trinitron (listed in the pop-up menu) is manufactured by Sony, while the SuperMac 19-inch Color may come from Hitachi or Ikegami. More importantly, the two screens use different technology (Trinitron versus shadow-masked tridot). Do not select a monitor other than the one you use unless the only difference in the name is screen size.

↪ **Gamma:** This value represents the brightness of medium colors on-screen. Low values down to 0.75 darken the printed image to compensate for an overly light screen; high values up to 3.00 lighten the image to compensate for an overly dark screen. Generally speaking, 1.8 is the ideal value for

Macintosh RGB screens. When you use an NTSC television monitor — as when editing video images using TrueVision's NuVista+ or RasterOps' ProVideo32 — set Gamma to 2.2.

∞ **White Point:** This value represents the temperature of the lightest color your screen can produce. Measured on the Kelvin temperature scale, it refers to the heat at which a so-called "black body" would turn to white. So theoretically, if you took the Maltese Falcon and heated it to 6,500 degrees Kelvin, it would turn white (if it didn't catch on fire first). The only way to achieve the correct value for this option is to consult the technical support department for your make of monitor or use a hardware testing device such as DayStar's Colorimeter 24.

∞ **Phosphors:** This pop-up menu lets you select the kind of screen used in your monitor. About half the monitors used with Macintosh computers — including most monitors sold by Apple — use Trinitron screens. (You can recognize Trinitron screens by the fact that they bow slightly outward horizontally but are flat vertically.) Select the NTSC option if you are using a television monitor. Otherwise, consult your vendor's technical support department. The technician may be willing to supply you with precise chromacity coordinates, which you enter by choosing the Custom option.

∞ **Ambient Light:** Select the amount of light in your office or studio from this pop-up menu. In a dark room, Photoshop slightly darkens the image. In a light room, Photoshop lightens it so that you can see it clearly despite the ambient light.

If you use a professional-level monitor that offers a hardware calibrator, such as the Radius PressView series, you can probably save a monitor color profile that you can load into Photoshop. In the case of the PressView, you run the ProSense utility (pictured in Figure 7-13) and stick a suction-cup calibrator to the screen. The software automatically measures the red, green, and blue phosphors and adjusts for any variance from absolute perfection. When you quit, ProSense saves a Photoshop monitor profile. To load the profile, you merely choose File ⇨ Color Settings ⇨ Monitor Setup inside Photoshop, click on the Load button, and open the profile (which appears as PressView 21SR.5500.AMS in Figure 7-12).

When you finish messing with the Monitor Setup options, press Return to close the dialog box. Photoshop takes a moment or two to recalculate the display of any CMYK images open on-screen.

Figure 7-13
The ProSense software from Radius works in combinations with a hardware calibrator to precisely adjust the colors on a PressView SR monitor.

Printer calibration

To prepare an image that is to be reproduced on a commercial offset or web press, choose File ➪ Color Settings ➪ Printing Inks Setup to display the Printing Inks Setup dialog box shown in Figure 7-14.

Figure 7-14
Use the options in the Printing Inks Setup dialog box to prepare an image for printing on a commercial offset or web press.

Like the Monitor Setup options, these settings are very technical and can be properly set only with the assistance of your commercial printer. But just so you have an inkling about inks, here's how the options work:

↪ **Ink Colors:** Select the specific variety of inks and paper stock that will be used to reproduce the current image. (Consult your commercial printer for this information.) Photoshop automatically changes the settings of the Dot Gain and Gray Balance options to the most suitable values.

↪ **Dot Gain:** Enter any value from -10 to 40 percent to specify the amount by which you can expect halftone cells to shrink or expand during the printing process, a variable known as *dot gain.* When printing to newsprint, for example, you can expect halftone cells to bleed into the page and expand by about 30 percent. When you convert to the CMYK color mode, Photoshop automatically adjusts the brightness of colors to compensate for the dot gain.

↪ **Gray Balance:** Assuming that the inks are up to snuff, equal amounts of cyan, magenta, yellow, and black ink should produce gray. But inks can fade and become impure over time. To compensate for this, you can vary the amount of ink that mixes to produce medium gray by entering values from 0.50 to 2.00 in the Gray Balance option boxes. Think of it as a recipe — 0.75 parts cyan mixed with 1.50 parts magenta and so on. Again, consult with your commercial printer before changing these values.

↪ **Use Dot Gain for Grayscale Images:** When this option is turned off, the Dot Gain value only affects the creation and editing of CMYK images. If you select this check box, however, you also can apply the value to grayscale images. Then, any time you select a gray value, Photoshop automatically treats it as if it were lighter or darker depending on whether the Dot Gain value is negative or positive, respectively.

Rather than getting 50 percent gray when you select 50 percent gray, for example, you might get 58 percent gray. This can cause problems when you want to create displacement maps, create precise gradations, or simply achieve exact brightness values. I strongly recommend that you turn this check box off unless you have some specific reason for turning it on, like you've suddenly taken leave of your senses.

How to prepare CMYK conversions

Now that you've told Photoshop how to compensate for the foibles of your screen and commercial printer, you need to explain what kind of separation process you intend to use. To do this, choose File ➪ Color Settings ➪ Separation Setup to display the Separation Setup dialog box, shown in Figure 7-15. Unlike the options in the Printing Inks Setup dialog box, which describe the specific press belonging to your commercial printer, these options describe a general printing process. Even so, you'll probably find it helpful to consult with your commercial printer before changing the settings.

The options in the Separation Setup dialog box work as follows:

- **Separation Type:** When the densities of cyan, magenta, and yellow inks reach a certain level, they mix to form a muddy brown. The GCR (*gray component replacement*) option avoids this unpleasant effect by overprinting these colors with black to the extent specified with the Black Generation option. If you select the UCR (*under color removal*) option, Photoshop removes cyan, magenta, and yellow inks where they overlap black ink. Generally speaking, GCR is the setting of choice except when you're printing on newsprint.

- **Black Generation:** Available only when the GCR option is active, the Black Generation pop-up menu lets you specify how dark the cyan, magenta, and yellow concentrations have to be before Photoshop adds black ink. Select Light to use black ink sparingly and Heavy to apply it liberally. The None option prints no black ink whatsoever, while the Maximum option prints black ink over everything. You may want to use the UCA Amount option to restore cyan, magenta, and yellow ink if you select the Heavy or Maximum option.

- **Black Ink Limit:** Enter the maximum amount of black ink that can be applied to the page. By default, this value is 100 percent, which is solid ink coverage. If you raise the UCA Amount value, you'll probably want to lower this value by a similar percentage to prevent the image from over-darkening.

- **Total Ink Limit:** This value represents the maximum amount of all four inks permitted on the page. For example, assuming that you use the default Black Ink Limit and Total Ink Limit values shown in Figure 7-14, the darkest printable color contains 100 percent black ink. Therefore, the sum total of cyan, magenta, and yellow inks is 200 percent. (You subtract the Black Ink Limit value from the Total Ink Limit value to get the sum total of the three other inks.)

☞ **UCA Amount:** The opposite of UCR, UCA stands for *under color addition,* which lets you add cyan, magenta, and yellow inks to areas where the concentration of black ink is highest. For example, a value of 20 percent raises the amount of cyan, magenta, and yellow inks applied with black concentrations between 80 and 100 percent. This option is dimmed when the UCR radio button is active.

The Gray Ramp graph demonstrates the effects of your changes to any option in the Separation Setup dialog box. Four lines, one in each color, represent the four inks. Though you can't edit the lines in this graph by clicking and dragging on them, as you can in the Transfer Functions dialog box, you can observe the lines to gauge the results of your settings.

Color trapping

If color separations misalign slightly during the reproduction process (a problem called *misregistration*), the final image can exhibit slight gaps between colors. Suppose that an image features a 100 percent cyan chicken against a 100 percent magenta background. (Pretty attractive image idea, huh? Go ahead, you can use it if you like.) If the cyan and magenta plates don't line up exactly, you're left with a chicken with a white halo around it. Yuck.

A *trap* is a little extra bit of color that fills in the gap. For example, if you choose Image ➚ Trap and enter 4 into the Width option box, Photoshop outlines the chicken with an extra 4 pixels of cyan and the background with an extra 4 pixels of magenta. Now the registration can be off a full 8 pixels without any halo occurring.

Continuous-tone images, such as photographs and natural-media painting, don't need trapping because there are no harsh color transitions. In fact, trapping will actually harm such images by thickening up the borders and edges, smudging detail, and generally dulling the focus.

Therefore, the only reason to use the Trap command is to trap rasterized Illustrator drawings. Some state-of-the-art prepress systems trap documents by first rasterizing them to pixels and then modifying the pixels. Together, Photoshop and Illustrator constitute a more rudimentary but nonetheless functional trapping system. When you open an Illustrator document in Photoshop, the latter converts the illustration into an image according to your size and resolution specifications, as described in the "Rasterizing an Illustrator or FreeHand file" section of Chapter 4. Once the illustration is rasterized, you can apply Image ➚ Trap to the image as a whole. Despite the command's simplicity, it handles nearly all trapping scenarios, even going so far as to incrementally reduce the width of the trap as the colors of neighboring areas grow more similar.

If you plan on having a service bureau trap your files for you, do *not* apply Photoshop's Trap command. You don't want to see what happens when someone traps an image that's already been trapped. If you're paying the extra bucks for professional trapping, leave it to the pros.

Printing Duotones

It's been a few pages since the "Understanding Printing Terminology" section, so here's a quick recap: A *duotone* is a grayscale image printed with two inks. This technique expands the depth of the image by allowing additional shades for highlights, shadows, and midtones. If you've seen one of those glossy Calvin Klein magazine ads, you've seen a duotone. Words like *rich, luxurious,* and *palpable* come to mind.

Photoshop also allows you to add a third ink to create a *tritone* and a fourth ink to create a *quadtone.* Color Plate 7-1 shows an example of an image printed as a quadtone. Figure 7-16 shows a detail from the image printed in its original grayscale form. See the difference?

Figure 7-16
This salute to all-around athlete Jim Thorpe by artist Mark Collen looks pretty good, but if you want to see great, check out the quadtone in Color Plate 7-1.

Creating a duotone

To convert a grayscale image to a duotone, tritone, or quadtone, choose Image ⇨ Mode ⇨ Duotone. Photoshop displays the Duotone Options dialog box shown in Figure 7-17. By default, Duotone is the active Type option, and the Ink 3 and Ink 4 options are dimmed. To access the Ink 3 option, select Tritone from the Type pop-up menu; to access both Ink 3 and Ink 4, select Quadtone from the pop-up menu.

Figure 7-17
The Duotone Options dialog box allows you to apply multiple inks to a grayscale image.

You specify the color of each ink you want to use by clicking on the color box associated with the desired ink option. Select a color from the Custom Colors dialog box as described in the "Predefined colors" section of Chapter 5. (You can also have Photoshop display the Color Picker dialog box, described in the "Using the Color Picker" section of that same chapter.)

When creating duotones, tritones, and quadtones, prioritize your inks in order from darkest at the top to lightest at the bottom when you specify them in the Duotone Options dialog box. Because Photoshop prints inks in the order that they appear in the dialog box, the inks will print from darkest to lightest. This ensures rich highlights and shadows and a uniform color range.

After selecting a color, you can use either of two methods to specify how the differently colored inks blend. The first and more dependable way is to click on the transfer function box associated with the desired ink option. Photoshop then displays the Transfer Functions dialog box, described back in the "Specifying a transfer function" section of this chapter. This enables you to emphasize specific inks in different portions of the image according to brightness values.

For example, Figure 7-17 shows the inks and transfer functions assigned to the quadtone in Color Plate 7-1. The Navy Blue color is associated only with the darkest brightness values in the image; Rose peaks at about 80 percent gray and then descends; Teal covers the midtones in the image; and Dull Orange is strongest in the light values. The four colors mix to form an image whose brightness values progress from light orange to olive green to brick red to black.

The second method for controlling the blending of colors is to click on the Overprint Colors button. An Overprint Colors dialog box appears, showing how each pair of colors will mix when printed. Other color swatches show how three and four colors mix, if applicable. To change the color swatch, click on it to display the Color Picker dialog box.

The problem with this second method is that it complicates the editing process. Photoshop doesn't actually change the ink colors or transfer functions in keeping with your new specifications; it just applies the new overprint colors without any logical basis. Secondly, you lose all changes made with the Overprint Colors dialog box when you adjust any of the ink colors or any of the transfer functions.

To go back and change the colors or transfer functions, choose Image ➪ Mode ➪ Duotone again. Instead of reconverting the image, the command now enables you to edit the existing duotone, tritone, or quadtone.

Reproducing a duotone

If you want a commercial printer to reproduce a duotone, tritone, or quadtone, you must print the image to color separations, just like a CMYK image. However, because you already specified which inks to use and how much of each ink to apply, you don't have to mess around with all those commands in the File ➪ Color Settings submenu. Just take the following familiar steps:

STEPS   **Printing a Duotone, Tritone, or Quadtone**

Step 1.   **Choose the printer you want to use.** Select a printer with the Chooser desk accessory, as described previously in the "Choosing a printer" section.

Step 2.   **Turn on the printer marks.** Choose File ➪ Page Setup (⌘-Shift-P) to specify the size of the pages and the size and orientation of the image on the pages, as described earlier in this chapter in the "Setting up the page" section. Be sure to select the Registration Marks option.

Step 3. **Adjust the halftone screens, if desired.** If you're feeling inventive, click on the Screens button to change the size, angle, and shape of the halftone screen dots for the individual color plates, as described previously in the "Changing the halftone screen" section.

Step 4. **Choose File ⇨ Print (⌘-P).** Select the Print Separations check box in the lower left corner of the dialog box to print each ink to a separate sheet of paper or film.

To prepare a duotone to be imported into QuarkXPress, Illustrator, or some other application, save the image in the EPS format, as described in the "Saving an EPS image" section of Chapter 4. As listed back in Table 5-1 of Chapter 5, EPS (and its DCS variation) is the only file format other than the native Photoshop format that supports duotones, tritones, and quadtones.

If you'll be printing your duotone using CMYK colors, and you can't quite get the effect you want inside the Duotone Options dialog box, you can convert the duotone to the CMYK mode (by choosing Image ⇨ Mode ⇨ CMYK). Not only will all the duotone shades remain intact, but you'll have the added advantage of being able to tweak colors and even add color using Photoshop's standard color correction commands and editing tools. You can even edit individual color channels, as described in the previous chapter.

Spot-Color Separations _____

Photoshop 4 offers no new capability that accommodates spot-color printing. Photoshop is, after all, designed for creating and editing continuous-tone images; and although spot colors work well for printing duotones, they more often lend themselves to high-contrast artwork created in drawing and page-layout programs.

But what if you want to add a spot-color highlight to an image? For example, suppose that you have a full-color image of a jet ski. The logo along the side of the boat is fully visible, just as the client wants it to be, but the color is off. Normally, the logo appears in Pantone 265 purple. But the CMYK equivalent for this color looks about three shades darker, four shades redder, and several times muddier. The only solution is to assign the proper spot color — Pantone 265 — to the logo. But how do you do it? Here are your options:

⇨ Paint over the logo in the actual image. Then import the image into Illustrator or FreeHand and recreate the logo as object-oriented text. Then assign the text Pantone 265 and export the document in the EPS format or print it directly from the drawing program. The logo will appear on its own separation.

⊷ Select the logo using the magic wand tool (or some more exacting method, as described in Chapters 11 and 12) and remove it using Edit ⇨ Cut (⌘-X). Then create a new channel by choosing the New Channel command from the Channels palette menu. After the Channel Options dialog box appears, click on the Color swatch and change it to a color that matches Pantone 265 as closely as possible. Press Return twice to create the new channel and then press ⌘-I to invert the channel and make it white. Paste in the logo art (Edit ⇨ Paste or ⌘-V). As long as your selection outline is still intact, the logo is pasted in the exact same position as in the original image. To see logo and image together, click on the eyeball icon in front of the CMYK composite view to show all channels at once. The logo will automatically appear in the purple color that you selected in the Channel Options dialog box. Edit the CMYK image and logo as desired.

If you opt for the second option, you can print the image directly from Photoshop in two passes. First, you switch to the CMYK composite view (⌘-tilde) and print the traditional four-color separation. Then you switch to the logo channel (⌘-5) and print this channel independently.

However, you cannot import the image into QuarkXPress or some other publishing program. Photoshop doesn't offer any file formats that support more than four color channels, except the native Photoshop format (which most other programs don't support and certainly not for the purpose of printing quality separations). If you were to save the image to the EPS or DCS format, for example, Photoshop would simply jettison the logo channel.

 That's where Lowly Apprentice's PlateMaker comes in. This $300 plug-in allows you to export CMYK images with up to 16 additional spot-color channels to the DCS format. When you choose File ⇨ Export ⇨ PlateMaker, the plug-in treats each mask channel as a separate plate of spot color. The product supports clipping paths (defined in Chapter 11) and allows you to assign custom halftone screens. The manual even contains instructions for editing the plug-in inside ResEdit to assign different default settings. Certainly, $300 is a lot to spend on what is essentially no more than an export module, and the DCS file doesn't display the spot color correctly inside QuarkXPress, PageMaker, or any other program, but if you're a print professional, this may be your only solution.

Painting and Retouching Images

Painting and Editing

■ ■

CHAPTER 8

In This Chapter

➼ Explanations of Photoshop's paint and edit tools

➼ How to paint straight and perpendicular lines

➼ The smudge tool in action

➼ Everything you want to know about the new sponge tool

➼ A thorough explanation of the Brushes palette

➼ How to save any selection as a custom brush

➼ How to paint lines that gradually fade away or taper to a point

➼ An introduction to pressure-sensitive drawing tablets

➼ Thorough examinations of all 18 paint tool brush modes (including three new modes in Photoshop 4)

■ ■

Paint and Edit Tool Basics

Here it is, Chapter 8 and I'm finally getting around to explaining how to use Photoshop's painting tools. You must feel like you're attending some kind of martial arts ritual where you have to learn to run away, cry, beg, and attempt bribery before you get to start karate chopping bricks and kicking your instructor. "The wise person journeys through the fundamentals of image editing before painting a single brushstroke, Grasshoppa." *Wang, wang, wang.* (That's a musical embellishment, in case you didn't recognize it. Man, I hate to have to explain my jokes. Especially when they're so measly.) Now that you've earned your first belt or tassel or scouting patch or whatever it is you're supposed to receive for slogging this far through the book, you're as prepared as you'll ever be to dive into the world of painting and retouching images.

You may be thinking that these tools require artistic talent. In truth, each tool provides options for just about any level of proficiency or experience. Photoshop offers get-by measures for novices who just want to make a quick edit and put the tool down before they make a mess of things. If you have a few hours of experience with other painting programs, you'll find that Photoshop's tools provide at least as much functionality and in many cases more. (The one exception is Painter, which is several times more capable than Photoshop in the painting department.) And if you're a professional artist — well, come on now — you'll have no problems learning how to make Photoshop sing. Suffice it to say that no matter who you are, you'll find electronic painting and editing tools to be more flexible, less messy, and more forgiving than their traditional counterparts.

If you screw something up in the course of painting your image, stop and choose Edit⇨Undo (or press ⌘-Z). If that doesn't work, try one of the reversion techniques described in the "Selectively Undoing Changes" section of Chapter 10. So long as a previous version of the image is saved on disk, you have a way out.

Meet your tools

Photoshop provides three paint tools: the pencil, paintbrush, and airbrush. You also get six edit tools: smudge, blur, sharpen, burn, dodge, and sponge. Figure 8-1 shows all these tools. The keyboard equivalent for each tool appears in parentheses.

In case you're wondering about all the other tools, Figure 8-2 segregates tools by category and lists the chapter in which you can find more information.

The paint tools

The paint tools apply paint in the foreground color. In this and other respects, they work like their counterparts in other painting programs, but there are a few exceptions:

   ∽ **Pencil:** The pencil has been a Macintosh standard since the first version of MacPaint. Unlike pencil tools found in most other painting programs — which paint lines one pixel thick — Photoshop's pencil paints a hard-edged

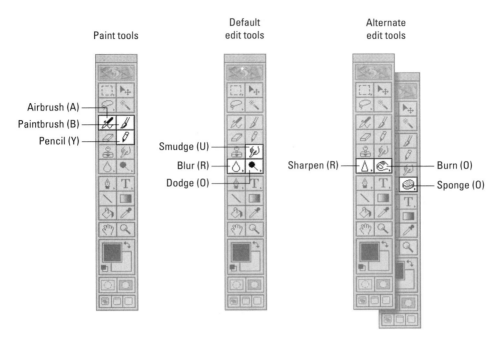

Figure 8-1
The three paint tools; the three edit tools that appear in
the toolbox by default; and the three alternative edit tools.

Figure 8-2
The rest of
Photoshop's
tools fall into
the categories
listed above
each toolbox.
The chapter in
which I discuss
each category
of tools appears
in parentheses.

line of any thickness. Figure 8-3 compares the default single-pixel pencil line with a fatter pencil line, a paintbrush line, and an airbrush line.

If you're used to selecting the pencil tool by pressing the P key, get used to being confused. You now select the pencil by pressing Y.

Thin pencil line   Thick pencil line   Paintbrush line   Paintbrush with wet edes   Airbrush line

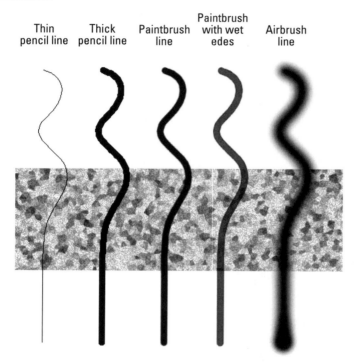

Figure 8-3
Five lines painted in black with the pencil, paintbrush, and airbrush tools. The Wet Edges option (second from right) causes the line to appear translucent. Notice that I held the airbrush tool in place for a few moments at the end of the rightmost line.

↪ **Paintbrush:** The paintbrush works just like the pencil tool, except that it paints an antialiased line that blends in with its background.

The paintbrush offers a Wet Edges option. (Double-click on the paintbrush tool icon in the toolbox and you'll see the Wet Edges check box in the bottom left corner of the Paintbrush Options palette.) When this option is turned on, the paintbrush creates a translucent line with darkened edges, much as if you were painting with watercolors. Soft brush shapes produce more naturalistic effects. An example of this effect is shown in Figure 8-3.

↪ **Airbrush:** It's tempting to dismiss Photoshop's airbrush tool as a softer version of the paintbrush, because it uses a softer brush shape by default. Photoshop's default settings also call for a lighter pressure, so the airbrush paints a translucent line. But unlike the paintbrush, which applies a continuous stream of color and stops applying paint when you stop dragging, the airbrush applies a series of colored dollops and continues to apply these dollops as long as you press the mouse button. Figure 8-3 shows the dark glob of paint that results from pressing the mouse button while holding the mouse motionless at the end of the drag.

The edit tools

The edit tools don't apply color; rather, they influence existing colors in an image. Figure 8-4 shows each of the five edit tools applied to a randomized background. The tools work as follows:

- **Smudge:** The smudge tool smears colors in an image. The effect is much like dragging your finger across wet paint.

- **Blur:** The first of the two focus tools, the blur tool blurs an image by lessening the amount of color contrast between neighboring pixels.

Figure 8-4
The effects of dragging with each of Photoshop's edit tools. The boundaries of each line are highlighted so you can clearly see the distinctions between line and background.

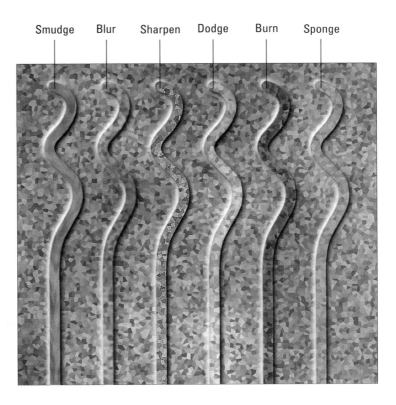

Smudge Blur Sharpen Dodge Burn Sponge

- **Sharpen:** The second focus tool selectively sharpens by increasing the contrast between neighboring pixels. Generally speaking, both the blur and sharpen tools are less useful than their command counterparts in the Filters menu. They provide less control and usually require scrubbing at an image. Maybe I've been using a computer too long, but my wrist starts to ache when I use these tools. If, unlike me, you like the basic principle behind the tools but you want to avoid Carpel Tunnel Syndrome, you can achieve consistent, predictable results without scrubbing by using the tools in combination with the Shift key, as described in the next section.

- **Dodge:** The first of three toning tools, the dodge tool lets you lighten a portion of an image by dragging across it. Named after a traditional film exposure technique, the dodge tool is supposed to look like a little paddle thingie — you know, like one of those spoons you put over your eye at the optometrist's — that you wave over an image to diffuse the amount of light that gets to the film and therefore lighten the print. Thank golly we no longer have to wave little paddle thingies in our modern age.

- **Burn:** The burn tool enables you to darken a portion of an image by dragging over it. The effect is similar to burning a film negative, which you apparently do by holding your hand in a kind of O shape in an effort to focus the light, kind of like frying a worker ant using a magnifying glass (except not quite so smelly). At least, that's what they tell me. Sadly, I've never had the pleasure of trying it out.

- **Sponge:** The final toning tool, the sponge tool, robs an image of both saturation and contrast. Alternately, you can set the tool so that it boosts saturation and adds contrast. For more information, stay tuned for the upcoming section "Mopping up with the sponge tool."

To temporarily access the sharpen tool when the blur tool is selected, press and hold the Option key while using the tool. The sharpen tool remains available only as long as you press the Option key. You also can press Option to access the blur tool when the sharpen tool is selected; to access the burn tool when the dodge tool is selected; and to access the dodge tool when the burn tool is selected. (If the sponge tool is active, pressing the Option key has no effect, except maybe to give your finger a cramp.)

You can replace the blur tool with the sharpen tool in the toolbox by Option-clicking on the tool's icon. To *toggle* (switch) back to the blur tool, Option-click on the sharpen icon. Likewise, you can Option-click on the dodge tool icon to toggle between the dodge, burn, and sponge tools.

As explained in Chapter 3, the keyboard equivalents also toggle between the tools. When the blur tool is selected, press R to toggle to the sharpen tool. Another tap of the R key takes you back to blur. When the dodge tool is selected, press O to toggle to the burn tool, then press O again to get the sponge. Press O one more time to take the trail back to dodge. (What dodge tool discussion would be complete without at least one *Gunsmoke* joke?)

 To modify the performance of a tool, double-click on its icon in the toolbox to display the customized Options palette. Alternatively, you can simply press the Return key while the tool is selected. I discuss the options inside the various Options palettes throughout the remainder of this chapter.

Basic techniques

I know several people who claim that they can't paint, and yet they create beautiful work in Photoshop. Even though they don't have sufficient hand-eye coordination to write their names on-screen, they have unique and powerful artistic sensibilities and they know lots of tricks that enable them to make judicious use of the paint and edit tools. I can't help you in the sensibilities department, but I can show you a few tricks that will boost your ability and inclination to use the paint and edit tools.

Painting a straight line

You're probably already aware that you can draw a straight line with the line tool. If not, try it out. The line tool is that diagonal line on the left side of the toolbox. After selecting the tool, drag with it inside the image window to create a line. Pretty hot stuff, huh? Well, no, it's actually pretty dull. In fact, the only reason I ever use this tool is to draw arrows like those shown in the upcoming Figure 8-6. If you don't want to draw an arrow, you're better off using Photoshop's other means for creating straight lines: the Shift key.

 To add an arrowhead to a line drawn with the line tool, double-click on the line tool icon in the toolbox and select the Start or End check box inside the Line Tool Options palette. These options are explained in the "Applying Strokes and Arrowheads" section of Chapter 9.

To draw a straight line with any of the paint or edit tools, click on one point in the image and then press Shift and click on another point. Using the current tool, Photoshop draws a straight line between the two points.

To create free-form polygons, continue to Shift-click with the tool. Figure 8-5 features a photograph and a tracing that I made on a separate layer (as explained in Chapter 13) exclusively by Shift-clicking with the paintbrush tool. As an academic exercise, I never dragged with the tool, I never altered the brush size, and I used just two colors, black and gray.

Figure 8-5
Starting from an image by photographer Barbara Penoyar (left), I created a stylized tracing (right) by clicking and Shift-clicking with the paint-brush tool on a separate layer.

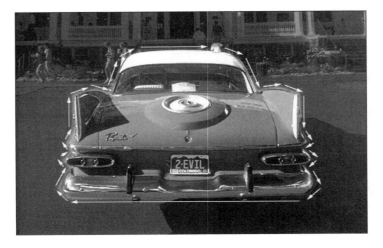

Figure 8-6
It takes one click and 24 Shift-clicks to soften or accentuate the edges around this car using the blur or sharpen tool.

The Shift key makes the blur and sharpen tools halfway useful. Suppose that you want to edit the perimeter of the car shown in Figure 8-6. The arrows in the figure illustrate the path your Shift-clicks should follow. Figure 8-7 shows the effect of Shift-clicking with the blur tool; Figure 8-8 demonstrates the effect of Shift-clicking with the sharpen tool.

Figure 8-7
The results of blurring the car's perimeter with the pressure set to 50 percent (top) and 100 percent (bottom). You set the pressure using the slider bar in the Focus Tools Options palette.

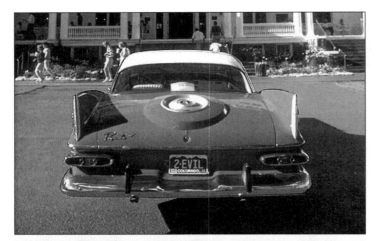

Figure 8-8
The results of sharpening the car with the pressure set to 50 percent (top) and 100 percent (bottom).

Painting a perpendicular line

To draw a perpendicular line — that is, one that is either vertical or horizontal — with any of the paint or edit tools, press and hold the mouse button, press the Shift key, and begin dragging in a vertical or horizontal direction. Don't release the Shift key until you finish dragging or until you want to change the direction of the line, as demonstrated in Figure 8-9. Notice that pressing the Shift key in mid-drag snaps the line back into perpendicular alignment.

One way to exploit the Shift key's penchant to snap to the perpendicular is to draw "ribbed" structures. Being left-handed, I dragged from right to left with the paintbrush to create both of the central outlines around the skeleton that appears at the top of

Figure 8-9
Pressing the Shift key after you start to drag with a paint or edit tool results in a perpendicular line for as long as the key is pressed.

Press mouse button, press Shift, begin drag

Release Shift

Press Shift again. . .

. . . to snap line back to perpendicular

Release mouse button, release Shift

Figure 8-10. I painted each rib by pressing and releasing the Shift key as I dragged with the paintbrush tool. Pressing Shift snapped the line to the horizontal axis, whose location was established by the beginning of the drag.

Figure 8-10
To create the basic structure for our bony pal, I periodically pressed and released the Shift key while dragging with the paintbrush (top). Then I embellished the fish using the paintbrush and pencil (middle). Finally, I applied the Emboss filter to transform fish into fossil (bottom).

In the figure, I represented the axis for each line in gray. After establishing the basic skeletal form, I added some free-form details with the paintbrush and pencil tools, as shown in the middle image in Figure 8-10. I then selected a general area around the image and chose Filter ⇨ Stylize ⇨ Emboss to create the finished fossil image. Nobody's going to confuse my painting with a bona fide fossil — "Hey Marge, look what I done tripped over in the back forty!" — but it's not half bad for a cartoon.

It's no accident that Figure 8-10 features a swordfish instead of your everyday round-nosed carp. In order to snap to the horizontal axis, I had to establish the direction of my drag as being more horizontal than vertical. If I had instead dragged in a fish-faced convex arc, Photoshop would have interpreted my drag as vertical and snapped to the vertical axis.

Painting with the smudge tool

Lots of first-time Photoshop artists misuse the smudge tool to soften color transitions. In fact, softening is the purpose of the blur tool. The smudge tool *smears* colors by shoving them into each other. The process bears more resemblance to the finger painting you did in grade school than to any traditional photographic editing technique.

In Photoshop, the performance of the smudge tool depends in part on the settings of the Pressure and Finger Painting options. Both reside in the Smudge Tool Options palette (see Figure 8-11), which you access by pressing Return when the smudge tool is active. These two options work as follows:

- **Pressure:** Measured as a percentage of the brush shape, this option determines the distance that the smudge tool drags a color. Higher percentages and larger brush shapes drag colors farthest. A Pressure setting of 100 percent equates to infinity, meaning that the smudge tool drags a color from the beginning of your drag until the end of your drag, regardless of how far you drag. Cosmic, Daddy-O.

Figure 8-11
Combined with brush shape, the Pressure and Finger Painting options are the most important considerations when using the smudge tool.

∞ **Finger Painting:** The folks at Adobe used to call this effect *dipping,* which I think more accurately expressed how the effect works. When you select this option, the smudge tool begins by applying a smidgen of foreground color, which it eventually blends in with the colors in the image. It's as if you dipped your finger in a color and then dragged it through an oil painting. Use the Pressure setting to specify the amount of foreground color applied. If you turn on Finger Painting and set the Pressure to 100 percent, the smudge tool behaves exactly like the paintbrush tool.

You can reverse the Finger Painting setting by Option-dragging. If the option is off, Option-dragging dips the tool into the foreground color. If Finger Painting is turned on, Option-dragging smudges normally.

For some examples of the smudge tool in action, take a look at Figure 8-12. The figure shows the effects of using the smudge tool set to four different Pressure percentages and with the Finger Painting option both off and on. In each instance, the brush shape is 13 pixels in diameter and the foreground color is set to black.

Figure 8-12
Eight drags with the smudge tool subject to different Pressure and Finger Painting settings.

The third option highlighted in Figure 8-11 — Sample Merged — instructs the smudge tool to grab colors in all visible layers and smudge them into the current layer. Whether the option is on or off, only the current layer is affected; the background and other layers remain intact.

For example, suppose that the inverted eyes of the woman at the top of Figure 8-13 are on a different layer than the rest of the face. If I use the smudge tools on the eyes layer with Sample Merged turned off, Photoshop ignores the face layer when smudging the eyes. As a result, details like the nose and teeth remain unsmudged, as you can see in the lower left example. If I turn Sample Merged on, Photoshop lifts colors from the face layer and mixes them in with the eyes layer, as shown in the lower right example.

Figure 8-13
The original image (top) features inverted eyes on a layer above the rest of the face. I first smudged the eyes with Sample Merged turned off (lower left) and then with the option turned on (lower right).

Note that all of this activity occurs exclusively on the eyes layer. Just to give you a better look, the two lower examples on the eyes layer are shown independently of those on the face layer in Figure 8-14. You can now clearly see the proliferation of face details mixed into the eyes in the right example. Meanwhile, the face layer remains absolutely unaffected.

Figure 8-14
The eyes layer from the previous figure shown by itself.

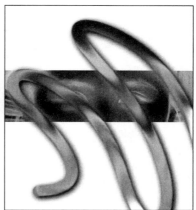

Incidentally, in case you're wondering where the heck the option name Sample Merged comes from, Photoshop is saying that it will *sample* — that is, lift colors — as if all layers are merged into one. For more information about setting up and merging layers, read Chapter 13.

Mopping up with the sponge tool

The sponge tool is actually a pretty darn straightforward tool, hardly worth expending valuable space in a book as tiny as this one. But I'm a compulsive explainer, so here's the deal: Press Return when the sponge tool is active to gain access to the Toning Tool Options palette. In the upper left corner of the palette is a pop-up menu that offers two options, Desaturate and Saturate. When set to the former, as by default, the tool reduces the saturation of the colors over which you drag. When editing a grayscale image, the tool reduces the contrast. If you select the Saturate option, the sponge tool increases the saturation of the colors over which you drag or increases contrast in a grayscale image. Higher Pressure settings produce more dramatic results.

Consider Color Plate 8-1. The upper left example shows the original PhotoDisc image. The upper right example shows the result of applying the sponge tool set to Desaturate. I dragged with the tool inside the pepper and around in the corner area. The Pressure was set to 100 percent. Notice that the affected colors are on the wane, sliding toward gray. In the lower right example, the effect is even more pronounced. Here I applied the sponge tools with great vim and vigor two additional times. There's hardly any hint of color left in these areas now.

To create the lower left example in Color Plate 8-1, I applied the sponge tool set to Saturate. This is where things get a little tricky. If you boost saturation levels with the sponge tool in the RGB or Lab color modes, you can achieve colors of absolutely neon intensity. However, these high-saturation colors don't stand a snowball's chance in a microwave of printing in CMYK. Therefore, I recommend that you choose Image ⇨ Mode ⇨ CMYK Preview before boosting saturation levels with the sponge tool. This way, you can accurately view the results of your edits. After you're finished, choose Image ⇨ Mode ⇨ CMYK Preview to turn off the CMYK preview and return to the RGB view.

Figure 8-15 shows the yellow channel from Color Plate 8-1. Because yellow is the most prevalent primary color in the image, it is the most sensitive to saturation adjustments. When I boosted the saturation in the lower left example, the yellow brightness values deepened, adding yellow ink to the CMYK image. When I lessened the saturation in the two right-hand examples, the amount of ink diminished.

Figure 8-15
The yellow channel from Color Plate 8-1 shows the greatest amount of variation when reducing and boosting the saturation with the sponge tool.

One of Adobe's recommended purposes of the sponge tool is to reduce the saturation levels of out-of-gamut RGB colors before converting an image to the

CMYK mode. I'm not too crazy about this use of the tool for the simple reason that it requires a lot of scrubbing. It's generally easier to select the out-of-gamut area and reduce the colors using more automated controls (as discussed in Chapter 16). Instead, you might prefer to use the sponge tool when a more selective, personal touch is required, as when curbing a distracting color that seems to be leaping a little too vigorously off the screen or boosting the saturation of a detail in the CMYK mode.

Brush Shape and Opacity

So far, I mentioned the words *brush shape* several times and I have yet to explain what the Sam Hill I'm talking about. Luckily, it's very simple. The brush shape is the size and shape of the tip of your cursor when you use a paint or edit tool. A big, round brush shape paints or edits in broad strokes. A small, elliptical brush shape is useful for performing hairline adjustments.

Though it is not set up this way by default, Photoshop is capable of displaying a cursor whose outline reflects the selected brush shape. To access this incredibly useful cursor, press ⌘-K to bring up the Preferences dialog box and press ⌘-3 for the Display & Cursors panel. Then select Brush Size from the Painting Cursors radio buttons. Photoshop now shows the actual size of the brush you're using, up to 300 pixels in diameter. If the brush is bigger — as when you zoom in on the image while using a large brush — the standard tool cursor appears instead.

When using very small brushes, as when using the single-pixel pencil to do very precise retouching, the cursor includes four dots around its perimeter, making the cursor easier to locate. If you need a little more help, press the Caps Lock key to access the more obvious crosshair cursor.

The Brushes palette

You access brush shapes by choosing Window ⇨ Palettes ⇨ Show Brushes to display the Brushes palette. Or you can press the F5 key. Figure 8-16 shows the Brushes palette with pop-up menu wide open for your viewing pleasure.

Figure 8-16
Photoshop's Brushes palette lets you select a predefined brush shape or create one of your very own.

You can switch brush shapes from the keyboard without displaying the Brushes palette. Press the left-bracket key, [, to select the previous brush shape in the palette; press the right-bracket key,], to select the next brush shape. You can also press Shift-[to select the first brush shape in the palette and Shift-] to select the last shape.

Editing a brush shape

To edit a brush shape in the Brushes palette, select the brush you want to change and choose Brush Options from the palette menu (as in Figure 8-16). To create a new brush shape, choose New Brush. Either way, the dialog box shown in Figure 8-17 appears. (If you choose the New Brush command, the title bar is different but the options are the same.)

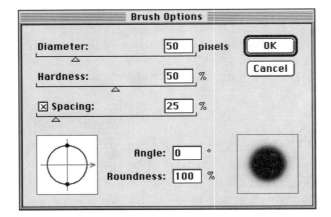

Figure 8-17
The Brush Options dialog box lets you change the size, shape, and hardness of the brush shape.

If you hate menus — and who doesn't? — you can more conveniently edit a brush shape by simply double-clicking on it. To create a new brush shape, click once on an empty brush slot, as shown in the first example in Figure 8-18. (Incidentally, you can also delete a brush from the palette. To do so, press the ⌘ key to display the scissors cursor — as in the second example in Figure 8-18 — then click. It's a great little housekeeping tip.)

Figure 8-18
Clicking on an empty brush slot (left) brings up the New Brush dialog box so you can create a new brush shape. ⌘-clicking on a brush shape (right) deletes it from the palette.

Whether you're editing an existing brush or creating a new one, you have the following options at your disposal:

⌦ **Diameter:** This option determines the width of the brush shape. If the brush shape is elliptical instead of circular, the Diameter value determines the longest dimension. You can enter any value from 1 to 999 pixels. Brush shapes with diameters of 30 pixels or higher are too large to display accurately in the Brushes palette and instead appear as circles with inset Diameter values.

⌦ **Hardness:** Except when you use the pencil tool, brush shapes are always antialiased. However, you can further soften the edges of a brush by dragging the Hardness slider bar away from 100 percent. The softest setting, 0 percent, gradually tapers the brush from a single solid color pixel at its center to a ring of transparent pixels around the brush's perimeter. Figure 8-19 demonstrates how low Hardness percentages expand the size of a 100-pixel brush beyond the Diameter value (as demonstrated by the examples set against black). Even a 100 percent hard brush shape expands slightly because it is antialiased. The Hardness setting is ignored when you use the pencil tool.

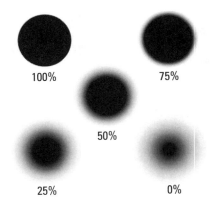

Figure 8-19
A 100-pixel diameter brush shown as it appears when set to a variety of Hardness percentages. Below, I changed the background pixels from white to black so you can see the actual diameter of each brush shape. The tick marks indicate 10-pixel increments.

100%

75%

50%

25%

0%

102 pixels

120 pixels

132 pixels

150 pixels

166 pixels

∞ **Spacing:** The Spacing option controls how frequently a tool affects an image as you drag, measured as a percentage of the brush shape. Suppose that the Diameter of a brush shape is 12 pixels and the Spacing is set to 25 percent (the setting for all default brush shapes). For every 3 pixels (25 percent of 12 pixels) you drag with the paintbrush tool, Photoshop lays down a 12-pixel wide spot of color. A Spacing of 1 percent provides the most coverage, but may also slow down the performance of the tool. If you deselect the Spacing check box, the effect of the tool is wholly dependent on the speed at which you drag, which can be useful for creating nonuniform or splotchy lines. Figure 8-20 shows examples.

∞ **Angle:** This option enables you to pivot a brush shape on its axes. However, it won't make a difference in the appearance of the brush shape unless the brush is elliptical.

Figure 8-20
Examples of lines drawn with different Spacing values in the Brush Options dialog box. Gaps or ridges generally begin to appear when the Spacing value exceeds 30 percent. The final line was created by turning off the Spacing option.

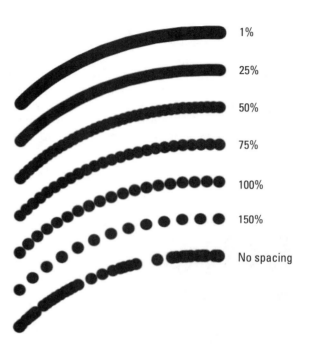

1%

25%

50%

75%

100%

150%

No spacing

↪ **Roundness:** Enter a value of less than 100 percent into the Roundness option to create an elliptical brush shape. The value measures the width of the brush as a percentage of its height, so a Roundness value of 5 percent results in a long, skinny brush shape.

You can adjust the angle of the brush dynamically by dragging the gray arrow inside the box to the left of the Angle and Roundness options. Drag the handles on either side of the black circle to make the brush shape elliptical, as demonstrated in Figure 8-21.

Figure 8-21
Drag the gray arrow or the black handles to change the angle or roundness of a brush, respectively. The Angle and Roundness values update automatically, as does the preview of the brush in the lower right corner of the dialog box.

Brush Options		
Diameter:	40 pixels	OK
Hardness:	70 %	Cancel
☒ Spacing:	25 %	
	Angle: 46 °	
	Roundness: 48 %	

I heartily recommend that you take a few moments one of these days to experiment at length with the Brush Options dialog box. By combining paint and edit tools with one or more specialized brush shapes, you can achieve artistic effects unlike anything permitted via traditional techniques. Starting with a PhotoDisc image lightened and filtered to serve as a template, I painted Figure 8-22 using the flat, 45-pixel brush shape shown in the dialog box. (For a color version of the effect, take a look at Color Plate 8-2.) No other brush shape or special effect was applied. Think of what you can accomplish if you don't limit yourself as ridiculously as I did.

Figure 8-22
Just to show off, I painted over a scanned image with the paintbrush tool, using the brush shape shown in the dialog box at top.

Creating and using custom brushes

You can define a custom brush shape by selecting a portion of your image that you want to change to a brush and choosing the Define Brush command from the Brushes palette pop-up menu.

In addition to giving you the flexibility to create a brush out of some element in your image, Photoshop ships with a file called Assorted Brushes that contains all kinds of little symbols and doodads you can assign as custom brush shapes. You can load the contents of the Assorted Brushes file into the Brushes palette by choosing the Load Brushes command from the palette menu (or Append Brushes if you don't want to lose the brush shapes that currently occupy the palette). You'll find Assorted Brushes inside the Brushes and Patterns folder, which resides in the same folder as the Photoshop application. Figure 8-23 shows an inspirational image I created using Photoshop's predefined custom brushes.

Figure 8-23
Yes, it's Boris, the sleeping custom-brush guy. If you suspect that this image is meant to suggest that custom brushes are more amusing than utilitarian, you're right. The brushes from the Assorted Brushes file appear on the right.

In Photoshop, you can adjust the performance of a custom brush in the following ways:

↪ **Brush options:** Choose the Brush Options command from the palette menu or double-click on the custom brush in the Brushes palette to bring up the dialog box shown in Figure 8-24. Here you can adjust the spacing of the brush shape and specify whether Photoshop antialiases (softens) the edges or leaves them as is. If the brush is sufficiently large, the Anti-aliased check box appears dimmed. All custom brushes are hard-edged when you use the pencil tool.

Figure 8-24
The dialog box that appears when
you double-click on a custom brush.

- **Brush color:** The foreground color affects a custom brush just as it does a standard brush shape. To erase with the brush, select white as the foreground color. To paint in color, select a color.

- **Opacity and brush modes:** The setting of the Opacity slider bar and the brush modes pop-up menu also affect the application of custom brushes. For more information on these options, keep reading this chapter.

You can achieve some unusual and sometimes interesting effects by activating the smudge tool's Finger Painting option and painting in the image window with a custom brush. At high Pressure settings, say 80 to 90 percent, the effect is rather like applying oil paint with a hairy paintbrush, as illustrated in Figure 8-25.

Figure 8-25
I created this organic, expressive image by combining the smudge tool's dipping capability with four custom brushes. I don't know what those finger-like growths are, but they'd probably feel right at home in an aquarium.

To restore the factory-default brush shapes, just choose Reset Brushes from the Brushes palette menu.

Opacity, pressure, and exposure

The brush shapes in the Brushes palette affect two tools other than the paint and edit tools, these being the eraser and the rubber stamp, both discussed in Chapter 10. But the slider bar in the upper right corner of the Options palette additionally affects the paint bucket, gradient, and line tools. Photoshop assigns one of three labels to this slider bar, illustrated in Figure 8-26.

☞ **Opacity:** The Opacity slider bar determines the translucency of colors applied with the paint bucket, gradient, line, pencil, paintbrush, eraser, or rubber stamp tool. At 100 percent, the applied colors appear opaque, completely covering the image behind them. (The one exception is the paintbrush with Wet Edges active, which is always translucent.) At lower settings, the applied colors mix with the existing colors in the image.

Figure 8-26
The slider bar in the upper right corner of the Brushes palette assumes one of these functions, depending on the selected paint or edit tool.

☞ **Pressure:** The Pressure slider bar affects different tools in different ways. When you use the airbrush tool, the slider bar controls the opacity of each spot of color the tool delivers. The effect appears unique because the airbrush lays each spot of color onto the previous spot, mixing them together. This results in a progressive effect. Meanwhile, the paintbrush and pencil tools are not progressive, so that their spots blend to form smooth lines.

When you use the smudge tool, the slider bar controls the distance that the tool drags colors in the image. And in the case of the blur, sharpen, or sponge tool, the slider bar determines the degree to which the tool changes the focus or saturation of the image, 1 percent being the minimum and 100 percent being the maximum.

☞ **Exposure:** If you select the dodge or burn tool, the slider bar title changes to *Exposure.* A setting of 100 percent applies the maximum amount of lightening or darkening to an image, which is still far short of either absolute white or black.

The factory default setting for all Exposure and Pressure slider bars is 50 percent; the default setting for all Opacity sliders is 100 percent.

As long as one of the tools listed in this section is selected, you can change the Opacity, Pressure, or Exposure setting in 10 percent increments by pressing a number key on the keyboard or keypad. Press 1 to change the setting to 10 percent, press 2 for 20 percent, and so on, all the way up to 0 for 100 percent.

In Photoshop 4, you can go one better. Press two keys in a row to change the Opacity, Pressure, or Exposure setting in 1 percent increments. Press 4 twice for 44 percent, 0 and 7 for 7 percent, and so on. This tip and the previous one work whether or not the Options palette is visible. Get in the habit of using the number keys and you'll thank yourself later.

Tapered Lines

Photoshop provides two ways to create tapering lines that are reminiscent of brush strokes created using traditional techniques. You can specify the length over which a line fades by entering a value into the Fade option box, as described in the next section. Or, if you own a pressure-sensitive drawing tablet, you can draw brush strokes that fade in and out automatically according to the amount of pressure you apply to the stylus. Both techniques enable you to introduce an element of spontaneity into what otherwise seems at times like an absolute world of computer graphics.

Fading the paint

All three paint tools offer Fade check boxes in their respective Options palettes that enable you to create lines that gradually fade away as you drag. Figure 8-27 shows the Fade option as it appears in the Paintbrush Options palette, along with some examples of the effect.

After selecting the Fade check box, enter a value into the option box to specify the distance over which the color fading should occur. The fading begins at the start of your drag and is measured in brush shapes.

Figure 8-27
The Fade check box as it appears in the Paintbrush Options palette, along with four examples.

Fade to transparent

Fade to background

Fade to transparent with wet edges

Fade to background with wet edges

For example, assume that the foreground color is black. If you enter 40 into the Fade option box — as in Figure 8-27 — Photoshop paints 40 brush shapes, the first in black and the remaining 39 in increasingly lighter shades of gray.

In Photoshop, you can paint gradient lines by selecting the To Background radio button. Photoshop fades the line from the foreground color to the background color, much the same way that the gradient tool fades the interior of a selection. For more information on the gradient tool, see the "Applying Gradient Fills" section of Chapter 9.

Fading and spacing

The physical length of a fading line is dependent both on the Fade value and on the value entered into the Spacing option box in the Brush Options dialog box, discussed back in the "Editing a brush shape" section earlier in this chapter.

To recap, the Spacing value determines the frequency with which Photoshop lays down brush shapes, and the Fade value determines the number of brush shapes laid down. Therefore, as demonstrated in Figure 8-28, a high Fade value combined with a high Spacing value creates the longest line.

1%

12%

25%

37%

50%

Figure 8-28
Five fading lines drawn with the paintbrush tool. In each case, the Fade option is set to 36 brush shapes. I changed the Spacing value incrementally from 1 to 50 percent, as labeled.

Creating sparkles and comets

Fading lines may strike you as pretty ho-hum, but they enable you to create some no-brainer, cool-mandoo effects, especially when combined with the Shift key techniques discussed earlier, in the "Painting a straight line" section.

Figures 8-29 and 8-30 demonstrate two of the most obvious uses for fading straight lines: creating sparkles and comets. The top image in Figure 8-29 features two sets of sparkles, each made up of 16 straight lines emanating from the sparkle's center. To create the smaller sparkle on the right, I set the Fade value to 60 and drew each of the four perpendicular lines with the paintbrush tool. I changed the Fade value to 36 before drawing the four 45-degree diagonal lines. The eight very short lines that occur between the perpendicular and diagonal lines were drawn with a Fade value of 20. I likewise created the larger sparkle on the left by periodically adjusting the Fade value, this time from 90 to 60 to 42.

For comparison's sake, I used different techniques to add a few more sparkles to the bottom image in Figure 8-29. To achieve the reflection in the upper left corner of the image, I chose Filter ⇨ Stylize ⇨ Lens Flare and selected 50-300mm Zoom from the Lens Type options. (Lens Flare works exclusively in the RGB mode, so I had to switch to RGB to apply the filter, even though Figure 8-29 is a grayscale image.)

I created the two tiny sparkles on the right edge of the bumper using a custom brush shape. I merely selected the custom brush, set the foreground color to white,

Figure 8-29
I drew the sparkles in the top image using the paintbrush tool. The second image features a reflection applied with the Lens Flare filter (upper left corner) and two dabs of a custom brush shape (right edge of the bumper).

and clicked once with the paintbrush tool in each location. So many sparkles make for a tremendously shiny image.

In Figure 8-30 — a nostalgic tribute to the days when gas was cheap and the whole family would pile in the Plymouth for a Sunday drive through space — I copied the car and pasted it on top of a NASA photograph of Jupiter. I then went nuts clicking and Shift-clicking with the paintbrush tool to create the comets — well, if you must know, they're actually cosmic rays — that you see shooting through and around the car. It's so real, you can practically hear the in-dash servo unit warning, "Duck and cover!"

Figure 8-30
To create the threatening cosmic rays, I set the Fade option to 110 and then clicked and Shift-clicked on opposite sides of the image with the paintbrush tool.

After masking portions of the image (a process described at length in Chapter 12), I drew rays behind the car and even one ray that shoots up through the car and out the spare tire. The three bright lights in the image — above the left fin, above the roof, and next to the right turn signal — are more products of the Lens Flare filter in the RGB mode.

I drew all the fading lines in Figures 8-29 and 8-30 with the paintbrush tool, using a variety of default brush shapes. Because I didn't edit any brush shape, the Spacing value for all lines was a constant 25 percent.

Setting up pressure-sensitive tablets

The pressure-sensitive tablet has to be the single most useful piece of optional hardware available to computer artists. Not only can you draw with a pen-like *stylus* instead of a clunky mouse, you also can dynamically adjust the thickness of lines and the opacity of colors by changing the amount of pressure you apply to the stylus. As I write this, several vendors manufacture pressure-sensitive tablets, but my favorite continues to be Wacom.

Of these, my favorite is Wacom's $200 ArtPad II, a handy little tablet that plugs into your Mac's ADB port, which is the same port that accommodates the keyboard and mouse. Measuring a diminutive 7 × 7.25 inches (with an active area of 4 × 5 inches), this thing is smaller than a standard mouse pad.

The tablet offers 256 levels of pressure and a resolution of thousands of lines per inch. (Like any digital tracking device, a tablet uses pixels to communicate the location of your stylus. The higher the resolution, the smoother your mouse movements.)

Wacom's cordless stylus comes in several different varieties — illustrated in Figure 8-31 — each of which weighs less than an ounce. All of them feature both a pressure-sensitive nib and at least one side switch for double-clicking or choosing macros. My favorite stylus is the WideBody, which actually includes pencil lead or ink. This way, you can see what you're drawing both on paper and on-screen. Oh, what miracles the modern age brings!

Figure 8-31
Wacom boasts the largest pressure-sensitive stylus library of any tablet vendor. You can customize the settings for your particular stylus from a pop-up menu in the central control panel.

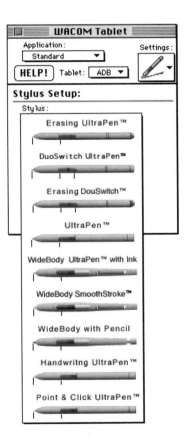

If you're an artist and you've never experimented with these or any other pressure-sensitive tablet, I recommend that you do so at your earliest convenience. You'll be amazed at how much it increases your range of artistic options. Thirty minutes after I installed my first tablet back in 1990, I had executed the cartoon you see in Figure 8-32 (and in Color Plate 8-3) with nothing more than a Macintosh IIci, a 13-inch monitor, and Photoshop 1.0.7. Whether you like the image or not — I'll admit there is a certain troglodyte quality to the slope of his forehead, and that jaw could bust a coconut — it shows off the tablet's ability to paint tapering lines and accommodate artistic expression.

Figure 8-32
Though I painted this caricature years ago, it still demonstrates the range of artistic freedom provided by a pressure-sensitive tablet.

Undoing pressure-sensitive lines

Pressure-sensitive lines are hard to undo (especially when you have just one level of undo at your disposal, as in Photoshop). Because a Wacom or other stylus is so sensitive to gradual pressure, you can unwittingly let up and repress the stylus during what you think is a single drag. If, after doing so, you decide you don't like the line and choose Edit ➪ Undo, Photoshop deletes only the last portion of the line, because it detected a release midway through. As a result, you're stuck with half a line that you don't want or, worse, that visually mars your image.

Problems are even more likely to occur if you use a stylus with a side switch, as all of the modern ones do. It's very easy to accidentally press your thumb or forefinger against the switch as you drag. If you have the switch set to some separate operation, such as double-clicking, you interrupt your line. This not only creates an obvious break but also makes the error impossible to undo.

To prepare for this eventuality — and believe me, it *will* happen — make sure to save your image at key points when you're content with its appearance. Or better yet, paint on a separate layer in your image (as discussed in Chapter 13). Then, if you find yourself stuck with half a line, you can remove the line by Option-dragging with the eraser tool— or by simply erasing within the layer — as discussed in the "Selectively Undoing Changes" section of Chapter 10.

Pressure-sensitive options

All paint and edit tools, as well as the eraser and rubber stamp, provide three check boxes for controlling Photoshop's reaction to stylus pressure (see Figure 8-33). Available from the Options palette only when a pressure-sensitive tablet is hooked up to your computer, these options include the following:

☞ **Size:** If you select the Size check box, Photoshop varies the thickness of the line. The more pressure you apply, the thicker the line. The Size check box is selected by default. Figure 8-34 shows three paintbrush lines drawn with the Size option selected. I drew the first line using a hard brush, the second with a soft brush, and the third with a hard brush and with the Wet Edges check box selected.

Figure 8-33
Photoshop provides three check boxes for interpreting the signals from a pressure-sensitive tablet.

☞ **Color:** Select this option to create custom gradient lines. Full pressure paints in the foreground color; very slight pressure paints in the background color; medium pressure paints a mix of the two.

☞ **Opacity:** This option paints an opaque coat of foreground color at full pressure that dwindles to transparency at very slight pressure.

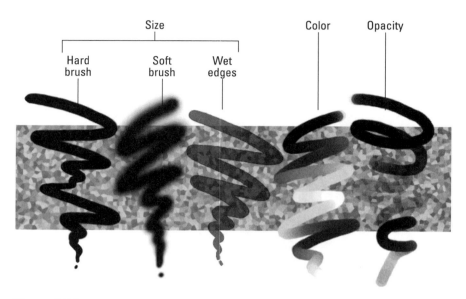

Figure 8-34
The effects of the Size, Color, and Opacity options on
lines drawn with the paintbrush tool and a pressure-
sensitive tablet.

Because Photoshop presents its pressure options as check boxes, you can select
more than one option at a time. For example, you can select both Size and Color to
instruct Photoshop to change both the thickness and color of a line as you bear
down or lift up on the stylus.

Brush Modes

When a painting or editing tool is active, the pop-up menu in the Options palettes
provides access to Photoshop's *brush modes,* which control how the colors applied
by the tools affect existing colors in the image. Figure 8-35 shows which brush
modes are available when you select various tools.

With the exception of the specialized brush modes provided for the dodge,
burn, and sponge tools, brush modes and the blend modes described in
Chapter 19, are varieties of the same animal. Read this section to get a brief
glimpse of brush modes; read Chapter 19 for a more detailed account that
should appeal to brush-mode aficionados.

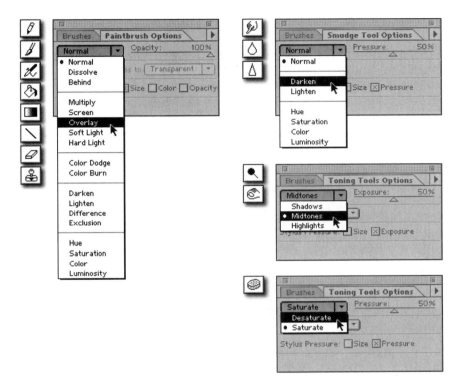

Figure 8-35
The number of options in the brush modes pop-up
menu varies depending on whether you select a paint
tool (left), an edit tool (top right), the dodge or burn
tool (middle right), or the sponge tool (bottom right).

The 18 paint tool modes

Photoshop 4 provides a whopping 18 brush modes when you're using the pen-cil,
paintbrush, airbrush, or any of the other tools shown along the left side of Figure
8-35. To give you an idea of what these brush modes look like when applied to an
image, Color Plates 8-4, 8-5, and 8-6 illustrate all 18 of them. In each case, I used
the paintbrush tool to apply a bit of green graffiti to a work of 14th-century
religious iconography. Who among us hasn't been tempted with the primal urge
to paint "Kilroy" on something old and priceless? Now, thanks to the miracle of
digital imagery, you need resist this temptation no longer.

The 18 standard brush modes work as follows:

- **Normal:** Choose this mode to paint or edit an image normally. A paint tool coats the image with the foreground color and an edit tool manipulates the existing colors in an image according to the setting of the Opacity or Pressure slider bar.

- **Dissolve:** This mode and the six that follow are not applicable to the edit tools (though I wonder why — the Dissolve mode would be especially useful with the smudge tool). Dissolve scatters colors along the edge of a brush-stroke randomly throughout the course of your drag. The Dissolve mode produces the most pronounced effects when used with soft brushes and the airbrush tool.

- **Behind:** This one is applicable exclusively to layers with transparent back-grounds. When Behind is selected, the paint tool applies color behind the image on the active layer, showing through only in the transparent and translucent areas. In Color Plate 8-4, for example, I have painted over the Madonna's head, and yet the brush stroke appears behind her head because she is positioned on an independent layer. When you're working on an image without layers or on the background layer of a multilayered image, the Behind mode is dimmed.

- **Multiply:** The Multiply mode combines the foreground color with an existing color in an image to create a third color that is darker than the other two. Using the multiply analogy, red times white is red, red times yellow is orange, red times green is brown, red times blue is violet, and so on. As discussed in Chapter 5, this is subtractive (CMYK) color theory at work. The effect is almost exactly like drawing with felt-tipped markers, except that the colors don't bleed. Check out the first Kilroy in Color Plate 8-5 to see the Multiply mode in action.

The multiply mode has no effect on the paintbrush when it's set to Wet Edges; the Wet Edges brush already multiplies.

- **Screen:** The inverse of the Multiply mode, Screen combines the foreground color with each colored pixel you paint over to create a third color that is lighter than the other two. Red on white is white, red on yellow is off-white, red on green is yellow, and red on blue is pink. The Screen mode uses additive (RGB) color theory. If the effect has a traditional counterpart, it's like some impossibly bright, radioactive Uranium-238 highlighter hitherto used only by G-Men to mark the pants cuffs of Communist sympathizers.

Since the Wet Edges option always multiplies, combining it with the Screen mode must render the brush invisible. If the paintbrush tool isn't working, this could be your problem.

  ➥ **Overlay:** Overlay, Soft Light, and Hard Light are cousins. Each mode multiplies the dark pixels in an image and screens the light pixels as you lay down color with a paint tool. But while related, the three are not variations on an identical theme. In other words, you can't emulate the Soft Light mode by simply applying the Hard Light mode at 70 percent or some similar Opacity.

      Of the three modes, Overlay is the kindest. It always enhances contrast and it always boosts the saturation of colors in an image. In fact, it works rather like a colored version of the sponge tool set to Saturate. It mixes the colors in the image with the foreground color to come up with a vivid blend that is almost always visually pleasing. This may be the most interesting and downright useful brush mode of the bunch.

  ➥ **Soft Light:** This mode applies a subtle glazing of color to an image. In fact, Soft Light is remarkably similar to painting a diluted acrylic wash to a canvas. It never completely covers up the underlying detail — even black or white applied at 100 percent Opacity does no more than darken or lighten the image — but it does slightly diminish contrast.

  ➥ **Hard Light:** This mode might better be named *Obfuscate*. It's as if you were applying a thicker, more opaque wash to the image. You might think of Hard Light as Normal with a whisper of underlying detail mixed in.

      For examples of Overlay, Soft Light, and Hard Light, check out the middle brushstrokes in Color Plate 8-5.

  ➥ **Color Dodge:** New to Photoshop 4, this brush mode lightens the pixels in an image according to the lightness or darkness of the foreground color. Color Dodge produces a harsher, chalkier effect than the Screen mode, and is designed to act like a dodge tool that also adds color. At 100 percent Opacity, even painting with black has a lightening effect.

  ➥ **Color Burn:** If Color Dodge is like drawing with chalk, Color Burn is like drawing with coal. It darkens pixels according to the lightness or darkness of the foreground color, and is designed to simulate a colored version of the burn tool. For examples of Color Dodge and Color Burn, look to the last two Kilroys in Color Plate 8-5.

  ➥ **Darken:** Ah, back to the old familiars. If you choose the Darken mode, Photoshop applies a new color to a pixel only if that color is darker than the present color of the pixel. Otherwise, the pixel is left unchanged. The mode works on a channel-by-channel basis, so it might change a pixel in the green channel, for example, without changing the pixel in the red or blue channel. I used this mode to create the first brushstroke of Color Plate 8-6.

⤷ **Lighten:** The opposite of the previous mode, Lighten ensures that Photoshop applies a new color to a pixel only if the color is lighter than the present color of the pixel. Otherwise, the pixel is left unchanged. On or off — either you see the color or you don't.

⤷ **Difference:** When a paint tool is set to the Difference mode, Photoshop subtracts the brightness value of the foreground color from the brightness value of the pixels in the image. If the result is a negative number, Photoshop simply makes it positive. The result of this complex-sounding operation is an inverted effect. Black has no effect on an image; white inverts it completely. Colors in between create psychedelic effects. In the third example of Color Plate 8-6, for example, the Difference mode inverts the green paint to create a red brushstroke.

Because the Difference mode inverts an image, it results in an outline around the brush stroke. You can make this outline thicker by using a softer brush shape. For a really trippy effect, select the paintbrush tool, turn on Wet Edges, and apply the Difference mode with a soft brush shape.

⤷ **Exclusion:** Recently, I e-mailed Mark Hamburg, lead programmer for Photoshop 4 about this new brush mode. He kindly explained — and I quote — "Exclusion applies a probabilistic, fuzzy-set-theoretic, symmetric difference to each channel." Don't think about it too long — your frontal lobe will turn to boiled squash. When Mark remembered that he was communicating with a lower life form, he explained that Exclusion inverts an image in much the same way as Difference, except that colors in the middle of the spectrum mix to form medium gray. Exclusion typically results in high-contrast effects with less color saturation than Difference. My suggestion is that you try out the Difference mode first. If you're looking for something a little different, press ⌘-Z and try Exclusion instead. (Both Difference and Exclusion brushstrokes appear in Color Plate 8-6.)

⤷ **Hue:** Understanding the next few modes requires a color theory recap. Remember how the HSL color model calls for three color channels? One is for *hue,* the value that explains the colors in an image; the second is for *saturation,* which represents the intensity of the colors; and the third is for *luminosity,* which explains the lightness and darkness of colors. Therefore, if you choose the Hue brush mode, Photoshop applies the hue from the foreground color without changing any saturation or luminosity values in the existing image.

None of the HSL brush modes — Hue, Saturation, Color, or Luminosity — is available when painting within grayscale images.

∞ **Saturation:** If you choose this mode, Photoshop changes the intensity of the colors in an image without changing the colors themselves or the lightness and darkness of individual pixels. In Color Plate 8-6, it has the effect of breathing new life into those ancient egg-tempura colors.

∞ **Color:** This mode might be more appropriately titled *Hue and Saturation*. It enables you to change the colors in an image and the intensity of those colors without changing the lightness and darkness of individual pixels.

The Color mode is most often used to colorize grayscale photographs. Open a grayscale image and then choose Image ➪ Mode ➪ RGB Color to convert it to the RGB mode. Then select the colors you want to use and start painting. The Color mode ensures that the details in the image remain completely intact.

∞ **Luminosity:** The opposite of the Color mode, Luminosity changes the lightness and darkness of pixels but leaves the hue and saturation values unaffected. Frankly, this mode is rarely useful. But its counterpart — the Luminosity blend mode — is exceptionally useful when applied to layers. Read Chapter 19 to find out more.

The three dodge and burn modes

Phew, that takes care of the brush modes available to the paint tools, the smudge tool, and the two focus tools. I already explained the Desaturate and Saturate modes available to the sponge tool (back in the "Mopping up with the sponge tool" section of this chapter). That leaves us with the three brush modes available to the dodge and burn tools:

∞ **Shadows:** Along with the Midtones and Highlights modes (described next), Shadows is unique to the dodge and burn tools. When you select this mode, the dodge and burn tools affect dark pixels in an image more dramatically than they affect light pixels and shades in between.

∞ **Midtones:** Select this mode to apply the dodge or burn tools equally to all but the very lightest or darkest pixels in an image.

∞ **Highlights:** When you select this option, the dodge and burn tools affect light pixels in an image more dramatically than they affect dark pixels and shades in between.

Dodge

Burn

Shadows / Highlights
Midtones

Shadows \ Highlights
Midtones

Figure 8-36
The dodge and burn tool applied at 100 percent Exposure settings subject to each of the three applicable brush modes.

Selecting Shadows when using the dodge tool or selecting Highlights when using the burn tool has an equalizing effect on an image. Figure 8-36 shows how using either of these functions and setting the Exposure slider bar to 100 percent lightens or darkens pixels in an image to very nearly identical brightness values.

Filling and Stroking

In This Chapter

- Applying color with the paint bucket tool and Fill command
- New Delete key tricks in Photoshop 4
- Creating an antique framing effect with the paint bucket
- Adjusting settings in the Gradient Tool Options palette
- Compensating for banding in printed gradations
- Designing your own multicolor gradation in Photoshop 4
- Using the gradient tool with the Dissolve brush mode
- Creating outlines and borders
- Attaching an arrowhead to any stroke

Filling Portions of an Image

No explanation of filling and stroking would be complete without a definition, so here goes: To *fill* a selection or layer is to put color inside it; to *stroke* a selection or layer is to put color around it. Simple stuff, actually. Lots of you already knew it and are getting plenty hot under the collar that you had to waste valuable seconds of your day reading such a flat-out obvious sentence. And you're getting even more steamed that you have to read sentences like these that don't add much to your overall understanding of Photoshop. And this sentence here, well, it's sufficient reason to write the publisher and burst a blood vessel.

In fact — he said, miraculously veering off the shoulder of the road and back onto the highway of the main story — Photoshop's fill and stroke functions are so straightforward that you may have long since dismissed them as wimpy little tools with remarkably limited potential. But the truth is, you can do a world of stuff with them. In this chapter, for example, I'll show you how to fill selections in five different ways using the Delete key, how to create an antique framing effect, how to make the most of Photoshop 4's new gradient editor, and how to add an arrowhead to a curving line, all in addition to the really basic stuff that many Photoshop users already know. Actually, come to think of it, you might even want to read about the basic stuff on the off chance that you missed some golden nugget of information in your Photoshopic journeys thus far.

Filling an Area with Color

You can fill an area of an image with color in four ways:

- ➣ **The paint bucket tool:** You can apply the foreground color or a repeating pattern to areas of related color in an image by clicking in the image window with the paint bucket tool (known in some circles as the fill tool). For example, if you want to turn all midnight blue pixels in an image into red pixels, you just set the foreground color to red and then click on one of the blue pixels.

- ➣ **The Fill command:** Select the portion of the image that you want to color and then fill the entire selection with the foreground color or a repeating pattern by choosing Edit ➪ Fill.

 To choose the Fill command without so much as moving the mouse, press Shift-Delete.

- ➣ **Delete-key techniques:** After selecting part of the single layer image — or part of the Background layer — you can fill the selection with the background color by pressing the Delete key. On any other layer, press ⌘-Delete (new to Photoshop 4). To fill the selection with the foreground color, press Option-Delete.

- ➣ **The gradient tool:** Drag across the image with the gradient tool to fill it with a multicolor gradation. Newly revamped in Photoshop 4, the gradient tool is now as powerful as the ones included with high-end drawing programs Illustrator and FreeHand. It's still so special and wide-ranging in its capabilities, in fact, that I devote several pages to the topic in the section "Applying Gradient Fills" later in this chapter.

The following sections discuss each of these options in depth.

The paint bucket tool

Unlike remedial paint bucket tools in other painting programs, which apply paint exclusively within outlined areas or areas of solid color, the Photoshop paint bucket tool offers several useful adjustment options. To explore them, double-click on the paint bucket icon in the toolbox to display the Paint Bucket Options palette, shown in Figure 9-1. (Alternatively, you can press the K key to select the paint bucket tool and then press Return to display the Options palette.)

Figure 9-1
The Paint Bucket Options palette governs the performance of the paint bucket tool.

The brush mode's pop-up menu and the Opacity slider bar work just like their counterparts in the Paintbrush Options palette, which I covered at length in the previous chapter. But just in case you need a recap, here's how these and other options work, in the order they appear in the palette:

- **Brush modes:** Select an option from the brush modes pop-up menu to specify how and when color is applied. For example, if you select Darken, the paint bucket tool affects a pixel in the image only if the foreground color is darker than that pixel. If you select Color, the paint bucket colorizes the image without changing the brightness value of the pixels.

 In Color Plate 9-1, for example, I used the Color mode to change a couple of oranges to blue and the background to green, all by clicking at five different spots with the paint bucket tool. I then touched up the stray pixels that the paint bucket didn't catch with the paintbrush and airbrush tools.

- **Opacity:** Drag the Opacity slider or press a number key to change the translucency of a color applied with the paint bucket.

- **Tolerance:** You can raise or lower the Tolerance value to increase or decrease the number of pixels affected by the paint bucket tool. The Tolerance value represents a range in brightness values, as measured from the pixel on which you click with the paint bucket.

Immediately after you click on a pixel, Photoshop reads the brightness value of that pixel from each color channel. Next, the program calculates a color range based on the Tolerance value — which can vary from 0 to 255. It adds the Tolerance to the brightness value of the pixel on which you clicked to determine the top of the range, and subtracts the Tolerance from the pixel's brightness value to determine the bottom of the range. For example, if the pixel's brightness value is 100 and the Tolerance value is 32, the top of the range is 132 and the bottom is 68.

After establishing a Tolerance range, Photoshop applies the foreground color to any pixel that both falls inside the range and touches some other affected pixel. (This way, the paint bucket fills an isolated area, rather than seeping out into every similarly colored pixel in the image.)

Figure 9-2 shows the result of clicking on the same pixel three separate times, each time using a different Tolerance value. In Color Plate 9-1, I raised the Tolerance to 120. But even with this high setting, I had to click several times to recolor all the nooks and crannies of the oranges. The moral is, don't get too hung up on getting the Tolerance exactly right — no matter how you paint it, the bucket is not a particularly precise tool.

↪ **Anti-aliased:** Select this option to soften the effect of the paint bucket tool. As demonstrated in the left-hand example of Figure 9-3, Photoshop creates a border of translucent color between the filled pixels and their unaffected neighbors. If you don't want to soften the transition, turn off the Anti-aliased check box. Photoshop then fills only those pixels that fall inside the Tolerance range, as demonstrated in the right example of the figure.

Figure 9-2
The results of applying the paint bucket tool to the exact same pixel after setting the Tolerance value to 16 (top), 32 (middle), and 64 (bottom). In each case, the foreground color is light gray.

Paint bucket cursor

Figure 9-3
The results of turning on (left) and off (right) the Anti-aliased check box prior to using the paint bucket tool. It all depends on whether you want cottage cheese or little spiky coral edges.

⌦ **Contents:** You can either apply the foreground color or a repeating pattern created using Edit ➪ Define Pattern. The Define Pattern command is covered in the "Applying Repeating Patterns" section of Chapter 10.

⌦ **Sample Merged:** Select this option to make the paint bucket see beyond the current layer. When the option is selected, the tool takes all visible layers into account when calculating the area to be filled. Mind you, it only fills the active layer, but the way it fills an area is dictated by all layers.

For an example of Sample Merged, look no further than Figure 9-4. The dog sits on one layer and the fire hydrant rests on another layer directly below. If I were to click on the fire hydrant when the dog layer was active *and* the Sample Merged check box was turned off, I'd fill everything around the dog. The paint bucket wouldn't be able to see the hydrant; all it could see is the transparent area of the dog layer, so it would try to fill that. To avoid this, I selected Sample Merged and then clicked on the hydrant. With Sample Merged on, the paint bucket could see all layers, so it contained its fill within the hydrant, as in the second example of the figure.

Because the fill and hydrant were on separate layers, I could edit the two independently of each other. I used the airbrush to alternatively paint inside and behind the fill (using the Behind brush mode, discussed in the previous chapter). I painted the teeth and eyes with the paintbrush, and used the smudge tool to mix colors around the white fill. (Naturally, I had to turn on the Sample Merged check box inside the Smudge Tool Options palette as well.) As a result, all the bizarre alterations you see in the bottom example of Figure 9-4 were applied to the dog layer. I didn't change a single pixel in the hydrant layer (which is a good thing — in light of my changes, I might like to get that hydrant back).

Figure 9-4
Although dog and hydrant are on separate layers (top), I can mix them together with Sample Merged. This option lets me fill an area of the hydrant (middle), even though the dog layer is active. Then I paint in front of and behind the fill without harming the hydrant (bottom).

To limit the area affected by the paint bucket, select a portion of the image before using the tool. As when using a paint or edit tool, the region outside the selection outline is protected from the paint bucket. To see an interesting application of this, skip ahead to the "Using the paint bucket inside a selection" section later in this chapter.

When working on a layer, you can likewise protect pixels by turning on the Preserve Transparency check box in the Layers palette. For everything you ever wanted to know about layers, read Chapter 13.

The Fill command

The one problem with the paint bucket tool is its lack of precision. Though undeniably convenient, the effects of the Tolerance value are so difficult to predict that you typically have to click with the tool, choose Edit ➪ Undo when you don't like the result, adjust the Tolerance value, and reclick with the tool several times more before you fill the image as desired. For my part, I rarely use the paint bucket for any purpose other than filling same-colored areas. On my machine, the Tolerance option is nearly always set to 0 and Anti-alias is generally off, which puts me right back in the all-the-subtlety-of-dumping-paint-out-of-a-bucket camp.

A better option is to select the area that you want to fill and choose Edit ➪ Fill or press Shift-Delete. In this way, you can define the exact area of the image you want to color using the entire range of Photoshop's selection tools, which are so extensive they consume all four chapters in Part IV. For example, instead of putting your faith in the paint bucket tool's Anti-aliased option, you can draw a selection outline that features hard edges in one area, antialiased edges elsewhere, and downright blurry edges in between.

When you choose the Fill command, Photoshop displays the Fill dialog box shown in Figure 9-5. In this dialog box, you can apply a translucent color or pattern by entering a value into the Opacity option box and you can choose a brush mode option from the Mode pop-up menu. In addition to its inherent precision, the Fill command maintains all the functionality of the paint bucket tool — and then some.

Figure 9-5
The Fill dialog box combines the Opacity and brush mode options from the Paint Bucket Options palette with an expanded collection of Contents options.

If you display the Contents pop-up menu, as shown in the lower example in Figure 9-5, you'll see a collection of things you can use to fill the selected area. Foreground Color and Pattern perform the same functions they do with the paint bucket tool. You can also fill a selection with the Background Color and such monochrome options as Black, White, and 50% Gray. Black and White are useful if the foreground and background colors have been changed from their defaults; 50% Gray allows you to access the absolute medium color without having to mess around with the Color palette. Saved and Snapshot allow you to revert the selected area to a previous appearance, as I discuss at length in the "Reverting selected areas" section of Chapter 10.

The Preserve Transparency check box works exactly like the identically named option in the Layers palette (discussed in Chapter 13). When the option is turned on, you can't fill the transparent pixels in the active layer. When Preserve Transparency is turned off, you can fill the selection outline uniformly. (The option is dimmed when you're working on the background layer or when the Preserve Transparency check box in the Layers palette is already turned on.)

Delete-key techniques

Of all the fill techniques, the Delete key is by far the most convenient and, in most respects, every bit as capable as the others. The key's only failings are that it can't fill a selection with a repeating pattern, nor can it revert a selection to its last-saved appearance. But with the exception of those two items, you can rely on the Delete key for the overwhelming majority of your fill needs.

Here's how to get a ton of functionality out of the Delete key:

- **Background color, method 1:** To fill a selection on the background layer with solid background color, press Delete. The selection outline remains intact.

- **Background color, method 2:** The problem with pressing Delete is that it's not very reliable. If the selection is floating, as I explain in Chapter 11, the Delete key actually deletes it. Delete also deletes pixels on a layer. So there's no time like the present to get in a new habit — press ⌘-Delete instead. ⌘-Delete fills the selection with the background color, no matter where it is.

- **Foreground color:** To fill a selection with solid foreground color, press Option-Delete. You can fill floating and nonfloating selections alike by pressing Option-Delete.

- **Black or white:** To fill an area with black, press D to get the default foreground and background colors and then press Option-Delete. To fill it with white, press D for defaults and then ⌘-Delete.

- **Preserve transparency:** Photoshop 4 adds two more Delete-key tricks that will make more sense when you read Chapter 13. (Don't worry, I'll repeat the tricks then.) You can fill just the opaque pixels in a layer — whether Preserve Transparency is turned on or not — by pressing Shift. Press Shift-Option-Delete to fill a selection with the foreground color while preserving transparency. Press ⌘-Shift-Delete to fill the opaque pixels with the background color. This is a great technique for drop shadows, as I explain in Chapter 13.

Using the paint bucket inside a selection

So far, I've come up with two astounding generalizations: the paint bucket tool is mostly useless, and you can fill anything with the Delete key. Well, just to prove that you shouldn't believe everything I say — some might even suggest that you dismiss *everything* I say — the following steps explain how to create an effect that you can perform only with the paint bucket tool. Doubtless, it's the only such example you'll ever discover using Photoshop — after all, the paint bucket *is* mostly useless and you *can* fill anything with the Delete key — but I'm man enough to eat my rules just this once.

The steps explain how to create an antique photographic frame effect like the one shown in Figure 9-6.

STEPS   Creating an Antique Photographic Frame

Step 1. **Use the rectangular marquee tool to select the portion of the image that you want to frame.** Make sure that the image extends at least 20 pixels outside the boundaries of the selection outline. And be sure to use a photo — this effect won't look right against a plain white background.

Step 2. **Choose Select ⇨ Feather (⌘-Shift-D).** Then specify a Radius value somewhere in the neighborhood of 6 to 12 pixels. I've found that these values work for just about any resolution of image. (If you enter too high a value, the color you'll add in a moment with the paint bucket will run out into the image.)

Step 3. **Choose Select ⇨ Inverse (⌘-Shift-I).** This exchanges the selected and deselected portions of the image.

Step 4. **Press the D key to make sure that the background color is white.** Then press ⌘-Delete to fill the selected area with the background color.

Step 5. **Select the paint bucket tool and press Return to display the Paint Bucket Options palette.** Enter 20 to 30 in the Tolerance option box and turn on the Anti-aliased check box. (You can also experiment with turning this option off.)

Step 6. **Click inside the feathered selection to fill it with black.** The result is an image fading into white and then into black, like the edges of a worn slide or photograph, as shown in Figure 9-6.

Figure 9-6
I created this antique frame effect by filling a feathered selection with the paint bucket tool.

Figure 9-7 shows a variation on this effect that you can create using the Dissolve brush mode. Rather than setting the Tolerance value to 20, raise it to something in the neighborhood of 60. Then, after selecting the paint bucket tool, select the Dissolve option from the brush modes pop-up menu in the Paint Bucket Options palette. When you click inside the feathered selection with the paint bucket tool, you create a frame of random pixels, as illustrated in the figure.

Figure 9-7
Select Dissolve from the Brushes palette pop-up menu to achieve a speckled frame effect.

Applying Gradient Fills_____

 In the previous edition of this book — the one for Photoshop 3 — I berated the application for its lousy gradient tool. You could create a smooth transition of shades from the foreground color to the background color, or cycle through an HSB-style color wheel, but that was about it. It just goes to show you how incredibly influential this immense tome is. Oh sure, Adobe has been ignoring my complaints about Illustrator, PageMaker, and half a dozen other products for years. But when I diss the gradient tool in Photoshop, it gets fixed. I tell you, I'm crazy with power!

The gradient tool itself gives no hint of its new capabilities. And the Gradient Tool Options palette seems hardly changed at all. But click on the Edit button, and your world comes alive. You can now add up to 32 colors to a gradient. You can name gradients, and save them to disk for later use. But best of all, you can adjust the transparency of colors, so that they fade in and out over the course of the gradient fill, mixing in with the original colors in the image. The bad news is that you're still limited to linear and radial fills — no conical fills or gradients along a path — but I for one can live with these limitations.

 If you're used to using gradients in a drawing program — like Illustrator or FreeHand — Photoshop is better. Because Photoshop is a pixel editor, it lets you blur and mix colors in a gradation if they start *banding* — that is, if you can see a hard edge between one color and the next when you print the image. And Photoshop's gradations will never choke the printer or slow it down, no matter how many colors you add. While each band of color in an object-oriented gradation is expressed as a separate shape — so that one gradation can contain hundreds or even thousands of objects — gradations in Photoshop are just plain old colored pixels, the kind we've been editing for eight and a half chapters.

Using the gradient tool

First, the basics. A *gradation* (also called a *gradient fill*) is a progression of colors that fade gradually into one another, as demonstrated in Figure 9-8. You specify a few key colors in the gradation, and Photoshop automatically generates the hundred or so colors in between to create a smooth transition.

Figure 9-8
Dragging with the gradient tool within a single selection (left) and across multiple selections (right).

You apply gradations using the gradient tool (just above the eyedropper on the right side of the toolbox). Unlike the paint bucket tool, which fills areas of similar color according to the Tolerance setting, the gradient tool affects all colors within a selection. If you don't select a portion of your image, Photoshop applies the gradation to the entire layer.

To select the gradient tool, press the G key. To use the tool, drag inside the selection, as shown in the left example of Figure 9-8. The point at which you begin dragging (upper left corner in the figure) defines the location of the first color in the gradation. The point at which you release (lower right corner) defines the location of the last color. If multiple portions of the image are selected, the gradation fills all selections continuously, as demonstrated by the right example of Figure 9-8.

Gradient tool options

To master the gradient tool, you have to fully understand how to modify its performance. Press Return when the gradient tool is active to display the Gradient Tool Options palette, shown in Figure 9-9. This palette allows you to specify the colors in a gradation as well as the arrangement of those colors by using the following options:

☞ **Brush mode and Opacity:** These options work the same way they do in the paint and edit tool Options palettes, in the Paint Bucket Options palette, in the Fill dialog box, and everywhere else that they pop up. Select a different brush mode to change how colors are applied; lower the Opacity value to make a gradation translucent. In both cases — as with all the other options in this palette — you have to adjust the options before using the gradient tool. They do not affect existing gradations.

Figure 9-9
The Gradient Tool Options palette provides access to the all-important Edit button, which lets you create custom gradations.

Gradient preview

☞ **Gradient:** The new Gradient pop-up menu provides access to gobs of factory predefined gradations. When you select a gradation, Photoshop displays it in the gradient preview (labeled in Figure 9-9). The first three factory gradations are dependent on the current foreground and background colors. The others contain specific colors that bear no relationship to the colors specified in the toolbox. If you create and name your own custom gradations, they will also show up in this menu.

☞ **Type:** Select Linear or Radial from this pop-up menu to specify the variety of gradation you want to create. A *linear gradation* progresses in bands of color in a straight line between the beginning and end of your drag, like the gradation shown back in Figure 9-8. A *radial gradation* progresses outward from a central point in concentric circles, as in Figure 9-10. The point at which you begin dragging defines the center of the gradation; the point at which you release defines the outermost circle. This means that the first color in the gradation appears in the center of the fill. So to create the gradation on the right side of Figure 9-10, you have to set white to the foreground color and black to the background color.

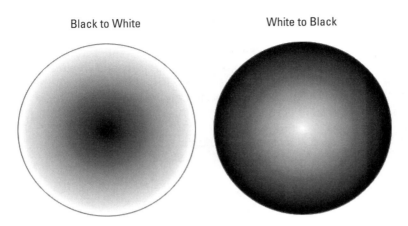

Black to White

White to Black

Figure 9-10
With Foreground to Background selected from the Gradient pop-up menu, set the foreground and background colors to their defaults to get the left-hand gradation. Press X to swap the colors for the gradation on the right.

- **Mask:** You can now specify different levels of opacity throughout a gradation in Photoshop 4. For example, the Transparent Stripes effect (available from the Gradient pop-up menu) lays down a series of alternately black and transparent stripes. But you don't have to use this transparency information. If you prefer to apply a series of black and white stripes instead, you can make all portions of the gradation equally opaque by turning off the Mask check box.

  For example, in Figure 9-11, I applied Transparent Stripes as a radial gradation in two separate swipes, at top and bottom. Both times, I changed the Opacity setting to 50 percent so as never to obscure dog and hydrant. (The Opacity setting works independently of the gradation's built-in transparency, providing you with additional flexibility.) In the top gradation, the Mask check box is on, so the white stripes are completely transparent. In the bottom gradation, Mask is turned off, so the white stripes become 50 percent opaque (as prescribed by the Opacity setting).

- **Dither:** In the old days, Photoshop drew its gradients one band at a time. Each band was filled with an incrementally different shade of color. The potential result was banding, in which you could clearly distinguish the transition between two or more bands of color. The Dither check box helps to eliminate this problem by mixing up the pixels between bands (much as Photoshop dithers pixels when converting a grayscale image to black-and-white). You should leave this option turned on unless you want to use the banding to create a special effect.

Eliminating gradient banding

Despite the helpful effect of the Dither check box, banding is not necessarily completely eliminated. If you do experience banding, this section describes how to get rid of it.

As explained in Chapter 15, the Add Noise filter randomizes pixels in a selection. Therefore, when you apply Filter ⇨ Noise ⇨ Add Noise to a gradation, it randomly mixes the bands of color, very much like a variable dithering function. In fact, it allows you to out-dither the Dither check box.

The first column in Figure 9-12 shows linear and radial gradations. In the second column, I applied the Add Noise filter three times in a row to both gradations. To make the effect as subtle as possible — you don't want the noise to be obvious — I specified an Amount value of 8 and selected the Uniform radio button inside the Add Noise dialog box. Multiple repetitions of a subtle noise effect are preferable to a single application of a more radical effect.

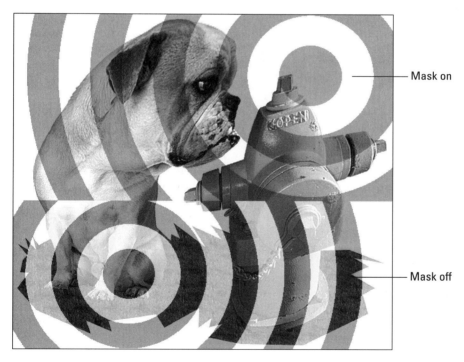

Figure 9-11
With the Opacity slider set to 50 percent, I applied the Transparent Stripes gradation with Mask on (top) and off (bottom). When Mask is off, the white stripes obscure our view of the underlying image.

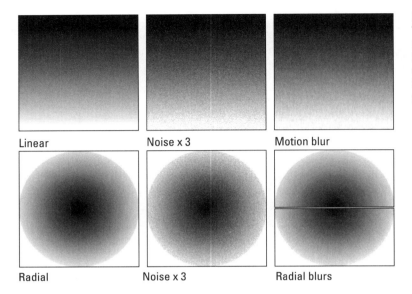

Figure 9-12
The results of applying noise (middle column) and directional blur effects (right column) to linear and radial gradations.

Linear   Noise x 3   Motion blur

Radial   Noise x 3   Radial blurs

If noise isn't enough or if the noise appears a little too obvious, you can further mix the colors in a gradation by applying a directional blur filter. To blur a linear gradation, apply the Motion Blur filter in the direction of the gradation. In the top right example of Figure 9-12, I applied Filter ➪ Blur ➪ Motion Blur with an Angle value of 90 degrees (straight up and down) and a Distance value of 3 pixels.

To blur a radial gradation, apply the Radial Blur filter (Filter ➪ Blur ➪ Radial Blur). To mix the noise around the center of the gradation, select the Spin option in the Radial Blur dialog box. To blend color in the bands, select the Zoom option. The lower right example in Figure 9-12 is divided into two halves. To create the top half, I applied the Spin option with an Amount value of 10; to create the bottom half, I applied Zoom with an Amount value of 20. (If you can barely see any difference between the two — that's the idea when it comes to gradations — look closely at the perimeter of the gradients. The top one, created with the Spin option, is smooth; the one created with the Zoom option is rougher.)

To further de-emphasize color bands in a horizontal linear gradation, you can apply the Wind filter (Filter ➪ Stylize ➪ Wind). Color Plate 9-2 shows three sample gradations subject to the Add Noise, Wind, and Motion Blur filters. In each case, I applied the Add Noise filter three times (just as in Figure 9-18), the Blast option in the Wind dialog box twice (once in each direction), and the Motion Blur filter in a horizontal direction at 10 pixels.

You can get a sense of what the Add Noise, Motion Blur, Radial Blur, and Wind filters do just by experimenting with them for a few minutes. If you want to learn even more, I discuss all four in Chapter 15.

Creating custom gradations

The only remaining option in the Gradient Tool Options palette is the Edit button. Click on this button to create your own custom gradation or edit one of the factory presets. Photoshop answers your request with the Gradient Editor dialog box, pictured in Figure 9-13. Because this dialog box has so much going on in it, I've lifted the most essential options and labeled them in Figure 9-14.

Figure 9-13
Click on the Edit button in the Gradient Tool Options palette to bring up this dialog box, which allows you to design your own custom gradations.

Figure 9-14
This small handful of options are actually quite powerful. Despite the array of buttons available in the Gradient Editor dialog box, these controls are where it's all at.

Select a named gradation that interests you from the scrolling list. Then click on the Duplicate button to design a new gradation based on the selected one. Photoshop asks you to name the new gradient. Do so, then press Return.

Positioning colors and midpoint markers

Below the scrolling list is the *fade bar* (labeled in Figure 9-13). The starting color appears as a house-shaped *color stop* on the left; the ending color appears on the far right. Positioned between each pair of color stops along the top of the fader bar is a diamond-shaped *midpoint marker*, which represents the spot where the two colors mix in exactly equal amounts. You can change the location of any stop or marker by dragging it. Or you can click on a stop or marker to select it and then enter a value into the Location option box below the fade bar. The selected stop or marker appears black.

∽ When numerically positioning a selected color stop, a value of 0 percent indicates the left end of the fade bar; 100 percent indicates the right end. Even if you add more color stops to the gradation, the values represent absolute positions along the fade bar.

∽ When repositioning a midpoint marker, the initial setting of 50 percent is smack dab between the two color stops; 0 percent is all the way over to the left stop and 100 percent is all the way over to the right. Midpoint values are therefore measured relative to color stop positions. In fact, when you move a color stop, Photoshop moves the midpoint marker along with it to maintain the same relative positioning. Figure 9-15 shows four radial gradations subjected to different midpoint settings, ranging from the minimum to maximum allowed values. (If you enter a value below 13 percent or over 87, Photoshop politely ignores you.)

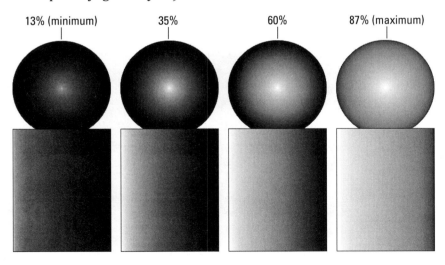

Figure 9-15
Four sets of white-to-black gradations — radial on top and linear at bottom — subject to different midpoint settings.

It's tempting to press the Return key after you enter a value into the Location option box, but don't do it. Pressing Return takes you out of the Gradient Editor dialog box. Instead, press the Tab key. Tab advances you from one marker to the next — from color stop to midpoint marker to the next color stop and so on. Press Shift-Tab to move to the previous marker.

Adjusting the colors in a gradation

You can change the colors in a gradation by selecting a color stop and clicking in the stop color box (immediately to the left of the Location option box). Photoshop displays the Color Picker dialog box. Select the desired color and press Return.

 That's the hard way. The easy way is to lift a color from the image window. When you move the cursor outside the dialog box into the image window, it changes to an eyedropper. Just click on the color in the image that you want to use.

If you want a color stop to vary with the active foreground color, select the color stop and click on the little *F* icon in the stop types area (on the left side of the dialog box, labeled back in Figure 9-14). To use the background color, select a stop and click on the little *B* icon.

Adding and deleting color stops

Here are three last items you should know about color stops:

- As I mentioned earlier, you can add as many as 32 colors per gradation. To add a color stop, click anywhere along the bottom of the fade bar. A new stop appears right where you click. Photoshop also adds a midpoint marker between the new color stop and its neighbor.

 - To duplicate a color stop, Option-drag it to a new location along the fade bar.

- To remove a color stop, drag the stop away from the fade bar. The stop icon vanishes and the fade bar automatically adjusts as defined by the remaining color stops.

Adjusting the transparency mask

 Photoshop 4 allows you to include a *transparency mask* with each gradation that determines where the colors are opaque and where they fade into translucency, or even transparency. You create and edit this mask independently of the colors in the gradation, and you can turn it on and off using the Mask check box in the Gradient Tool Options palette (as explained earlier).

To create a transparency mask, click on the Transparency radio button in the Gradient Editor dialog box. The fade bar changes to reflect the transparency settings (if any), as in Figure 9-16. As when editing colors, you click under the fade bar to add *transparency stops*, drag the stops to move them, and edit the Location value to position a selected stop numerically.

Figure 9-16
Click on the Transparency radio button to switch to a different fade bar that controls how the gradation fades in and out of sight.

The difference is that instead of changing the color of the stops, you modify their opacity. By default, each new stop is 100 percent opaque. You can modify the transparency by selecting a stop and changing the Opacity value. The preview along the bottom of the dialog box updates to reflect your changes. A checkerboard pattern represents the underlying image.

Color Plate 9-3 demonstrates the effect of applying a three-color gradation to a photograph. The gradation fades from red to transparency to green to transparency and finally to blue. In the first example in the color plate, I dragged over a standard checkerboard pattern with the gradient tool, from the lower left corner to the upper right. The second example shows the photograph prior to applying the gradation. In the last example, I applied the gradient — again from lower left to upper right — using the Overlay brush mode. Previously, you haven't been able to achieve this effect in Photoshop without the help of a third-party plug-in.

Gradations and brush modes

Overlay isn't the only brush mode you can use with gradations. All 18 of the standard brush modes are available, and they make a tremendous impression on the performance of the gradient tool. This section examines yet another way to apply a brush mode in conjunction with the tool. Naturally, it barely scrapes the surface of what's possible, but possibly it'll inspire you to experiment and discover additional effects on your own.

The following steps tell you how to use the Dissolve mode in combination with a radial gradation to create a supernova explosion. (At least, it looks like a supernova to me — not that I've ever seen one up close, mind you.) Figures 9-17 through 9-19 show the nova in progress. In addition to allowing you to experiment with a brush mode setting, the steps offer some general insight into creating radial gradations.

 These steps involve the use of the elliptical marquee tool. Generally speaking, it's a very easy tool to use. But if you find that you have problems making it work according to my instructions, you may want to quickly read the "Geometric selection outlines" section of Chapter 11. It's only a couple of pages long.

STEPS   Creating a Gradient Supernova

Step 1.   **Create a new image window.** Make it 500×500 pixels. A grayscale image is fine for this exercise.

Step 2.   **Click with the pencil tool at the apparent center of the image.** Don't worry if it's not the exact center. This point is merely intended to serve as a guide. If a single point is not large enough for you to easily identify, draw a small cross.

Step 3.   **Option-drag from the point with the elliptical marquee tool to draw the marquee outward from the center.** You can select the elliptical marquee tool by pressing the M key twice in a row. While dragging with the tool, press and hold the Shift key to constrain the marquee to a circle. Release Shift after you release the mouse button. Draw a marquee that fills about $^3/_4$ of the window.

Step 4.   **Choose Image ➪ Adjust ➪ Invert (⌘-I).** This fills the marquee with black and makes the center point white.

Step 5.   **Choose Select ➪ None (⌘-D) to deselect the circle.**

Step 6.   **Again Option-drag from the center point with the elliptical marquee tool.** And again press Shift to constrain the shape to a circle. Create a marquee roughly 20 pixels larger than the black circle.

Step 7.   **Option-drag from the center point with the elliptical marquee tool.** This subtracts a hole from the selection. After you begin dragging, release the Option key (but keep that mouse button down). Then press and hold both Shift and Option together and keep them down. Draw a marquee roughly 20 pixels smaller than the black circle. Then release the mouse button and finally release the keys. The result is a doughnut-shaped selection — a large circle with a smaller circular hole — as shown in Figure 9-17.

Figure 9-17
The result of creating a black circle and two circular marquees, all centered about a single point.

Step 8.   **Choose Select ⇨ Feather and enter 10 for the Radius value.** Then press Return to feather the section outline.

Step 9.   **Press the D key, then press X.** This makes the foreground color white and the background color black.

Step 10.   **Select the gradient tool and press Return to display the Options palette.** Select Foreground to Background from the Gradient pop-up menu. Also select the Radial option from the Type pop-up menu.

Step 11.   **Select Dissolve from the brush modes pop-up menu on the left side of the Gradient Tool Options palette.**

Step 12.   **Drag from the center point in the image window to anywhere along the outer rim of the largest marquee.** The result is the fuzzy gradation shown in Figure 9-18.

Figure 9-18
The Dissolve brush mode option randomizes the pixels around the feathered edges of the selection outlines.

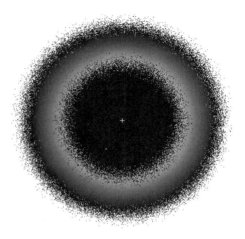

Step 13. **Choose Select ➪ None (⌘-D) to deselect the image.**

Step 14. **Choose Image ➪ Map ➪ Invert (⌘-I) to invert the entire image.**

Step 15. **Press the D key to restore black and white as foreground and background colors respectively.** Then use the eraser tool to erase the center point. The finished supernova appears in Figure 9-19.

Figure 9-19
By inverting the image from the previous figure and erasing the center point, you create an expanding series of progressively lighter rings dissolving into the black void of space, an effect better known to its friends as a supernova.

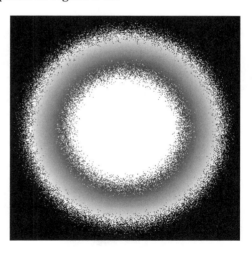

Applying Strokes and Arrowheads

Photoshop is nearly as adept at drawing lines and outlines as it is at filling selections. The following sections discuss how to apply a border around a selection outline — which is practical, if not terribly exciting — and how to create arrowheads — which can yield more interesting results than you might think.

Stroking a selection outline

Stroking is useful for creating frames and outlines. Generally speaking, you can stroke an image in Photoshop in three ways:

- **Using the Stroke command:** Select the portion of the image that you want to stroke and choose Edit ⇨ Stroke to display the Stroke dialog box shown in Figure 9-20. Enter the thickness of the stroke in pixels into the Width option box. Select a Location radio button to specify the position of the stroke with respect to the selection outline. The Stroke dialog box also includes Opacity, Mode, and Preserve Transparency options that work just like those in the Fill dialog box.

Figure 9-20
Use the options in the Stroke dialog box to specify the thickness of a stroke and its location with respect to the selection outline.

When in doubt, select Inside from the Location radio buttons. This ensures that the stroke is entirely inside the selection outline in case you decide to move the selection. If you select Center or Outside, Photoshop may apply part or all of the stroke to the deselected area around the selection outline.

- **Using the Border command:** Select a portion of the image and choose Select ⇨ Modify ⇨ Border to retain only the outline of the selection. Specify the size of the border by entering a value in pixels into the Width option box and press Return. To fill the border with the background color, press ⌘-Delete. To fill the border with the foreground color, press Option-Delete. To apply a repeating pattern to the border, choose Edit ⇨ Fill and select the Pattern option from the Use pop-up menu. You can even apply a command under the Filter menu or some other special effect.

- **Framing the image:** Okay, so this is a throwaway, but it's pretty useful just the same. To create an outline around the entire image, change the background color (yes, the background color) to the color that you want to apply to the outline. Then choose Image ⇨ Canvas Size and add twice the desired border thickness to the Width and Height options in pixels. For example, to create a 1-pixel border, add 2 pixels to the Width value (1 for the left side and 1 for the right) and 2 pixels to the Height value (1 for the top edge and 1 for the bottom). When you press Return, Photoshop enlarges the canvas size according to your specifications and fills the new pixels around the perimeter of the image with the background color. Simplicity at its best.

Applying arrowheads

The one function missing from all the operations in the previous list is applying arrowheads. The fact is, in Photoshop, you can only apply arrowheads to straight lines drawn with the line tool. To create an arrowhead, double-click on the line tool icon in the toolbox (or press N to select the line tool and then Return) to display the Line Tool Options palette shown in Figure 9-21. Enter a value into the Line Width option box to specify the thickness of the line — better known as the line's *weight* — and then use the Arrowheads options as follows:

- **Start:** Select this check box to append an arrowhead to the beginning of a line drawn with the line tool.

- **End:** Select this check box to append an arrowhead to the end of a line. (Like you needed me to tell you *that*.)

- **Shape:** Click on the Shape button to display the Arrowhead Shape dialog box, which also appears in Figure 9-21.

Figure 9-21
Click on the Shape button in the Line Tool Options palette (top) to display the Arrowhead Shape dialog box (bottom). The line tool remains the only way to create arrowheads in Photoshop.

The Arrowhead Shape dialog box contains three options that let you specify the size and shape of the arrowhead as a function of the line weight:

⌐ **Width:** Enter the width of the arrowhead in pixels into this option box. The width of the arrowhead is completely independent of line weight.

⌐ **Length:** Enter the length of the arrowhead, measured from the base of the arrowhead to its tip, into this option box. Again, length is measured in pixels and is independent of line weight.

⌐ **Concavity:** You can specify the shape of the arrowhead by entering a value between negative and positive 50 percent into the Concavity option box. Figure 9-35 shows examples of a few Concavity settings applied to an arrowhead 50 pixels wide and 100 pixels long.

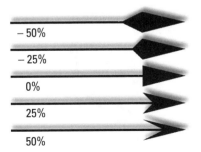

Figure 9-22
Examples of a 50 × 100-pixel arrowhead subject to five different Concavity values.

Appending arrowheads to curved lines

Applying arrowheads to straight lines is a simple matter. Double-click on the line tool icon, select a few choice options, and draw a line with the line tool. Applying an arrowhead to a stroked selection outline is a little trickier, but still possible. The following steps explain the process.

STEPS   **Adding an Arrowhead to a Free-form Stroke**

Step 1.   **Create a new layer.** Display the Layers palette by pressing the F7 key. Then click on the little page icon to create a new layer.

Step 2.   **Draw and stroke a selection.** Draw any selection outline you like and stroke it by choosing Edit ⇨ Stroke and applying whatever settings strike your fancy. Remember the value you enter into the Width option. In Figure 9-23, I drew a wiggly line with the lasso tool and applied a 4-pixel black stroke at 30 percent Opacity.

Figure 9-23
Here, I created a new layer, drew a free-form shape with the lasso tool, and stroked it with a 4-pixel black outline at 30 percent Opacity.

Step 3.   **Press ⌘-D.** Or choose Select ⇨ None to deselect all portions of the image.

Step 4.   **Erase the portions of the stroke that you don't need.** Select the eraser tool by pressing the E key. Then drag to erase through the stroke layer without harming the layer below. Erase away the areas of the stroke at which you want to add arrowheads. I wanted to add an arrowhead behind the fly, so I erased around the fly.

Step 5.   **Double-click on the line tool icon.** Up comes the Line Tool Options palette.

Step 6. **Specify the arrowhead settings.** Enter the line weight that you used when stroking the selection outline into the Line Width option box (in my case, 4 pixels). Then select the End check box and deselect the Start check box if necessary. Then click on the Shape button and specify the width, length, and concavity of the arrowhead as desired.

Step 7. **Set the foreground color as needed.** I applied a black stroke at 30 percent Opacity, so I set the foreground color to 30 percent gray.

Step 8. **Zoom in on the point in the image at which you want to add the arrowhead.** You have to get in close so you can see what you're doing, as in Figure 9-24.

Step 9. **Draw a very short line exactly the length of the arrowhead at the tip of the stroke.** Figure 9-24 illustrates what I mean. This may take some practice to accomplish. Make sure to start the line a few pixels in from the end of the stroke to make sure the base of the arrowhead fits snugly. If you mess up the first time, choose Edit ➪ Undo (⌘-Z) and try again.

Figure 9-24
Use the line tool to draw a line no longer than the arrowhead to append the arrow to the end of the stroke. The view size of this image is magnified 300 percent.

That's all there is to it. From there on, you can continue to edit the stroke as you see fit.

Figure 9-25
I finished up by erasing dashes into the line and softening the end of the trail with a large, fuzzy eraser.

In Figure 9-25, I erased a series of scratches across the stroke to create a dashed-line effect, all the rage for representing cartoon fly trails. I then set the eraser brush size to the largest, fuzziest setting and erased the end of the stroke (above the dog's head) to create a gradual trailing off. That crazy fly is distracting our hero from his appointed rounds.

Duplicating and Reverting

CHAPTER 10

In This Chapter

- ❖ A complete description of the rubber stamp tool and its many settings
- ❖ Touching up blemishes and eliminating elements from an image
- ❖ Painting a repeating pattern with the rubber stamp tool
- ❖ A step-by-step guide to creating seamless patterns and textures
- ❖ Using the Undo and Revert commands
- ❖ Reverting portions of an image with the eraser and rubber stamp tools
- ❖ Using the Take Snapshot command

Introducing the Amalgamated Rubber Stamp

This chapter is primarily about just one tool: the rubber stamp tool. Although the eraser figures into the reversion discussion in this chapter (and I even include a small reference to the pencil tool), the main ingredient — after you boil it down at your local editorial content refinery — is the rubber stamp tool. This tool provides four loosely related but distinct capabilities, every one of which deserves to be split off into a tool of its own.

The name *rubber stamp* is pretty misleading because this particular tool has nothing to do with rubber stamps. First of all, no tree sap is involved — let's get that sticky issue resolved right off the bat. Secondly, you don't use it to stamp an image. When I think of rubber stamps, I think of those things you see in stationery stores that plunk down laudatory exclamations and smiley faces and Pooh bears. Elementary school teachers and little girls use rubber stamps. I've never seen a professional image editor walking around with a rubber stamp in my life.

So put rubber stamps entirely out of your mind for the moment. To discover exactly what the stamp tool does, select the tool and press Return to display the Rubber Stamp Options palette. Photoshop then displays the Rubber Stamp Options palette, shown in Figure 10-1. In addition to the standard brush modes pop-up menu, Opacity slider, Stylus Pressure options, and Sample Merged check box provided with half a dozen paint and edit tools (see Chapter 8 if your memory's getting a tad fuzzy), the Rubber Stamp Options palette includes an Option pop-up menu. The real heart of the tool, this pop-up menu includes the following options:

- **Cloning:** Select one of the two Clone options to duplicate portions of an image by dragging over it. Option-click with the tool to specify a point of reference and then drag in a different area of the image to begin cloning. (Don't worry, I cover the difference between the two Clone options in the upcoming "Aligned and non-aligned cloning" section.)

Figure 10-1
Select an option from the Option pop-up menu to define the way the rubber stamp tool works.

- **Pattern application:** Select one of the two Pattern options to paint an image with a repeating pattern rather than the standard foreground color. Before using this option, you must establish a pattern by selecting a portion of the image and choosing Edit ➪ Define Pattern.

- **Reversion:** The From Snapshot option lets you use the rubber stamp tool to revert portions of your image to the way they appeared when you last chose Edit ➪ Take Snapshot. From Saved enables you to revert portions of an image to the way they appeared when you last saved the image.

- **Impressionist:** The last option, Impressionist, retrieves the last saved version of the image and sort of smears it around to create a gooey, unfocused effect. You can achieve some mildly interesting and halfway useful effects — and I'm being generous here — by combining this function with the Overlay, Hard Light, or Soft Light brush modes, but it wouldn't be my first choice for any job. This is my nomination for the least useful of the rubber stamp settings, and this is the last time I'll mention it.

 If there is a tie that binds the rubber stamp's various capabilities, it is the fact that most enable you to paint with images. When you clone with the rubber stamp tool, for example, you paint with a displaced version of the image itself. When you paint a pattern, you paint with an image fragment. When you revert, you paint with the saved version of the image. Even Impressionist paints with the saved image in its own skewed sort of way. (Ah, man, I wasn't going to mention that option again.)

As you can see, a better name for the rubber stamp tool might be the "clone/pattern/revert/stupid effects tool" or maybe the "junk-drawer tool." Then again, the "mother of all mixed-up tools" has a certain ring to it. In any case, the remainder of this chapter explores every one of the rubber stamp's capabilities.

 In Photoshop 4, you needn't visit the Rubber Stamp Options palette to switch between one Option pop-up menu and the next. Just press the S key. Each press of S cycles from one option to the next — for example, from Clone (Aligned) to Clone (Non-aligned) to Pattern (Aligned) and so on, and eventually back to the beginning again. Because there are so many options, it's generally helpful to keep the Rubber Stamp Options palette up on-screen so you can see which one is active.

Cloning Image Elements_____

Although my take on the rubber stamp tool may sound a bit derogatory, most of its capabilities can come in very handy. All except that dumb Impressionist option — which I swear, really, I'm going to stop mentioning.

Take cloning, for example. As any died-in-the-wool Photoshop user will tell you, the rubber stamp is an invaluable tool for touching up images, whether you want to remove dust fragments, hairs, and other blotches scanned with a photo or to eliminate portions of an image.

You also can use the rubber stamp to duplicate specific elements in an image, like flowers and umbrellas, as described in the Photoshop manual. But by all accounts, this is an inefficient use of the tool. If you want to duplicate an element, you'll have better luck if you select it and clone it, as explained in Chapter 11. By taking that approach, you can specify the exact boundaries of the element, the softness of its edges, and the precise location of the clone. Cloning an element with the rubber stamp is more of an ordeal, because it's easy to accidentally clone areas around the element and to begin a clone in the wrong location.

The cloning process

To clone part of an image, double-click on the rubber stamp tool icon and select either the Clone (Aligned) or Clone (Non-aligned) option. (The upcoming section explains the difference between the two.) Option-click in the image window to specify a point of reference in the portion of the image you want to clone. Then click or drag with the tool in some other region of the image to paint a cloned spot or line.

In Figure 10-2, for example, I Option-clicked just above and to the right of the bird's head, as demonstrated by the appearance of the stamp pickup cursor. I then painted the line shown inside the white rectangle. The rubber stamp cursor shows the end of my drag; the cross-shaped clone reference cursor shows the corresponding point in the original image.

Stamp pickup cursor

Rubber stamp cursor

Clone reference cursor

Figure 10-2
After Option-clicking at the point indicated by the stamp pickup cursor, I dragged with the rubber stamp tool to paint with the image. (The only reason I painted inside the white rectangle was to set off the line so that you can see it better.)

Photoshop lets you clone not only from within the image you're working on, but also from an entirely separate image window. This technique enables you to merge two different images together, as demonstrated in Figure 10-3. To achieve this effect, Option-click in one image, bring a second image to the foreground, and then drag with the rubber stamp tool to clone from the first image.

Figure 10-3
I merged the area around horse and rider with a water image from another open window (see the upcoming Figure 10-6). The translucent effects were created by periodically adjusting the Opacity slider bar to settings ranging from 50 to 80 percent.

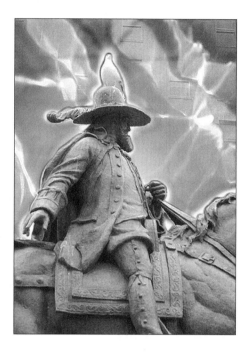

Aligned and non-aligned cloning

Now that I've explained how to use the tool, I'll return to the options in the Rubber Stamp Options palette:

- ⟿ **Clone (Aligned):** To understand how this option works, think of the locations where you Option-click and begin dragging with the rubber stamp tool as opposite ends of an imaginary straight line, as illustrated in the top half of Figure 10-4. The length and angle of that imaginary line remains fixed until you Option-click a second time. As you drag, Photoshop moves the line, cloning pixels from one end of the line and laying them down at the other. Regardless of how many times you start and stop dragging with the stamp tool, all lines match up as seamlessly as pieces in a puzzle.

↪ **Clone (Non-aligned):** If you want to repeatedly clone from a single portion of an image, select this option. The second example in Figure 10-4 shows how the length and angle of the imaginary line change every time you paint a new line with the rubber stamp tool.

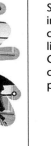

Figure 10-4
Select the Clone (Aligned) option to instruct Photoshop to clone an image continuously, no matter how many lines you paint (top). If you select Clone (Non-aligned), Photoshop clones each new line from the point at which you Option-click.

Stamp differences

When cloning, the Photoshop 4 rubber stamp tool works just like the Version 3 rubber stamp, which is different than the Version 2 stamp. I only mention this because I personally liked the Version 2 setup better. In Version 2, the rubber stamp cloned the image as it existed before you start using the tool. Even when you drag over an area that contains a clone, the tool references the original appearance of the image to prevent recloning. This keeps you from creating more than one clone during a single drag and produces the effect in the first example of Figure 10-5.

In Photoshop 4, however, any changes you make to the image affect the tool as you use it, which can result in the repeating patterns like those shown in the second example of the figure. Although you can create some interesting effects, avoid cloning and recloning areas when retouching, because it can result in obvious patterns that betray your adjustments.

Figure 10-5
Photoshop 2's rubber stamp tool cloned the image as it existed before you started using the tool (top). In Version 4, the tool clones and reclones images during a single drag (bottom).

To avoid recloning areas in Photoshop 4, clone from a duplicate of the image. Begin by choosing Image ⇨ Duplicate to create a copy of the current image (as explained back in Chapter 4). Option-click with the rubber stamp tool somewhere in the duplicate window. Then switch to the original image and drag freely with the tool to clone from the duplicate. Because your changes don't affect the duplicate image, there's no chance of recloning.

Touching up blemishes

One of the best uses for the rubber stamp tool is to touch up a scanned photo. Figure 10-6 shows a Photo CD image that desperately needs the stamp tool's attention. Normally, Kodak's Photo CD process delivers some of the best consumer-quality scans money can buy. But this particular medium-resolution image looks like the folks at the lab got together and blew their respective noses on it. It's a little late to go back to the service bureau and demand that they rescan the photo, so my only choice is to touch it up myself.

The best way to fix this image — or any image like it — is to use the rubber stamp over and over again, repeatedly Option-clicking at one location and then clicking at another. Begin by selecting a brush shape that's a little larger than the largest blotch. Of the default brushes, the hard-edged varieties with diameters of 5 and 9 pixels generally work best. (The soft-edged brush shapes have a tendency to incompletely cover the blemishes.)

Figure 10-6
This appallingly bad Photo CD image is riddled with blotches and big hurky wads of dust that didn't exist on the original 35mm slide.

Option-click with the stamp tool at a location that is very close to the blemish and features similarly colored pixels. Then click — do not drag — directly on the blemish. The idea is to change as few pixels as possible.

If the retouched area doesn't look quite right, choose Edit ➪ Undo (⌘-Z), Option-click at a different location, and try again. If your touch-up appears seamless — *absolutely* seamless — move on to the next blemish, repeating the Option-click and click routine for every dust mark on the photo.

This process isn't necessarily time-consuming, but it does require patience. For example, although it took more than 40 Option-click and click combinations (not counting 10 or so undos) to arrive at the image shown in Figure 10-7, the process itself took less than 15 minutes. Boring, but fast.

It's a little trickier to retouch hairs than dust and other blobs. That's because a hair, although very thin, can be surprisingly long. However, the retouching process is the same. Rather than dragging over the entire length of the hair, Option-click and click your way through it, bit by little bit. The one difference is brush shape. Because you'll be clicking so many times in succession and because the hair is so thin, you'll probably achieve the least conspicuous effects if you use a soft brush shape, such as the default 9-pixel model in the second row of the Brushes palette.

Figure 10-7
The result of Option-clicking and clicking more than 40 times on the photo shown in Figure 10-6. Notice that I also cropped the image and added a border.

At this point you might wonder, "Why go to all this work to remove dust and scratches when Photoshop provides the automated feature Filter ⇨ Noise ⇨ Dust & Scratches?" The reason is, quite frankly, the Dust & Scratches filter stinks. No offense to the designers of this filter — they're wonderful people, every one of them — but it doesn't produce the effect it advertises. It mucks up the detail in your image by averaging neighboring pixels, and that simply isn't an acceptable solution. Do your photograph a favor — fix its flaws manually (not to mention lovingly) with the rubber stamp tool.

Eliminating distracting background elements

Another way to apply the stamp tool's cloning capabilities is to eliminate background action that competes with the central elements in an image. For example, Figure 10-8 shows an absolutely wonderful news photo shot by Michael Probst for the Reuters image library. Although the image is well-photographed and historic in its implications — in case you missed the last century, that's Comrade V. I. Lenin (Vlad to his mom) — that rear workman doesn't contribute anything to the scene and in fact draws your attention away from the foreground drama. I mean, hail to the worker and everything, but the image would be better off without him. The following steps explain how I eradicated the offending workman from the scene.

Keep in mind as you read the following steps that deleting an image element with the rubber stamp tool is something of an inexact science; it requires some trial and error. So regard the following steps as an example of how to approach the process of editing your image rather than a specific procedure that works for all images. You may need to adapt the process slightly depending upon your image.

Figure 10-8
You have to love that old Soviet state-endorsed art. So bold, so angular, so politically intolerant. But you also have to lose that rear workman.

STEPS   Eliminating Distracting Elements from an Image

Step 1. I began by cloning the area around the neck of the statue with a soft brush shape. Abandoning the controlled clicks I recommended in the last section, I allowed myself to drag with the tool because I needed to cover relatively large portions of the image. The apartment building (or whatever that structure is) behind the floating head is magnificently out of focus, just the thing for hiding any incongruous transitions I might create with the rubber stamp. So I warmed up to the image by retouching this area first. Figure 10-9 shows my progress.

Notice that I covered the workman's body by cloning pixels from both his left and right sides. I also added a vertical bar where the workman's right arm used to be to maintain the rhythm of the building. Remember that variety is the key to using the rubber stamp tool: If you consistently clone from one portion of the image, you create an obvious repetition that the viewer can't help but notice.

Figure 10-9
Cloning over the background
worker's upper torso was fairly
easy because the background
building is so regular and out of
focus, providing a wealth of
material from which to clone.

Step 2. The next step was to eliminate the workman's head. This was a little tricky because it involved rubbing up against the focused perimeter of Lenin's neck. I had to clone some of the more intricate areas using a hard-edged brush. I also ended up duplicating some of the neck edges to maintain continuity. In addition, I touched up the left side of the neck (your left, not Lenin's) and removed a few of the white spots from his face. You see my progress in Figure 10-10.

Step 3. Now for the hard part: eliminating the worker's legs and lower torso. See that fragment of metal that the foreground worker is holding? What a pain. Its edges were so irregular that there was no way I could restore it with the rubber stamp tool if I messed up while trying to eradicate the background worker's limbs. So I lassoed around the fragment to select it and chose Select ⇨ Inverse (⌘-Shift-I) to protect it. I also chose Select ⇨Feather (⌘-Shift-D) and gave it a Radius value of 1 to slightly soften its edges. This prevented me from messing up the metal no matter what edits I made to the background worker's remaining body parts.

Figure 10-10
I eliminated the workman's head and touched up details around the perimeter of the neck.

Step 4. From here on out, it was just more cloning. Unfortunately, I barely had anything to clone from. See that little bit of black edging between the two "legs" of the metal fragment? That's it. That's all I had to draw the strip of edging to the right of the fragment that eventually appears in Figure 10-11. To pull off this feat, I pressed the S key to switch to the Clone (Non-aligned) option. Then I Option-clicked on the tiny bit of edging and click, click, clicked my way down the street.

Step 5. Unfortunately, the strip that I laid down in Step 4 appeared noticeably blobular — it looked for all the world like I clicked a bunch of times. Darn. To fix this problem, I clicked and Shift-clicked with the smudge tool set to about 30 percent pressure. This smeared the blobs into a continuous strip, but again, the effect was noticeable. It looked as if I had smeared the strip. So I went back and cloned some more, this time with the Opacity slider bar set to 50 percent.

Figure 10-11
After about 45 minutes worth of monkeying around with the rubber stamp tool — a practice declared illegal during Stalin's reign — the rear workman is gone, leaving us with an unfettered view of the dubious one himself.

Step 6. To polish the image off, I chose Select ➪ None (⌘-D) and ran the sharpen tool along the edges of the metal fragment. This helped to hide the fact that I retouched around it and further distinguished the fragment from the unfocused background. I also cropped away 20 or so pixels from the right side of the image to correct the balance of the image.

What I hope I demonstrated in this section is that cloning with the rubber stamp tool requires that you alternate between patching and whittling away. There are no rights and wrongs, no hard and fast rules. Anything you can find to clone is fair game. As long as you avoid mucking up the foreground image, you can't go wrong (so I guess there is *one* hard and fast rule). If you're careful and diligent, no one but you is going to notice your alterations.

Any time you edit the contents of a photograph, you tread on very sensitive ground. Though some have convincingly argued that electronically retouching an image is theoretically no different than cropping a photograph, a technique that has been available and in use since the first daguerreotype, photographers have certain rights under copyright law that cannot be ignored. A photographer may have a reason for including an element that you wish to eliminate. So before you edit any photograph, be sure to get permission either from the original photographer or from the copyright holder (as I did for this photo).

Applying Repeating Patterns____

Before you can use the rubber stamp tool to paint with a pattern, you must define a pattern by selecting a portion of the image with the rectangular marquee tool and choosing Edit ⇨ Define Pattern. For the Define Pattern command to work, you must use the rectangular marquee — no other selection tool will do. In addition, the selection cannot be feathered, smoothed, expanded, or in any other way altered. If it is, the command is dimmed.

Figure 10-12 shows an example of how you can apply repeating patterns. I selected the single apartment window (surrounded by marching ants) and chose Edit ⇨ Define Pattern. I then applied the pattern with the rubber stamp tool at 80 percent opacity over the horse and rider statue.

 Like the Clipboard, Photoshop can retain only one pattern at a time and remembers the pattern throughout a single session. Any time you choose Edit ⇨ Define Pattern, you delete the previous pattern as you create a new one. Photoshop also deletes the pattern when you quit the program. Therefore, each time you launch Photoshop, you must define the pattern from scratch.

Figure 10-12
After marqueeing a single window (top) and choosing Edit ➪ Define Pattern, I painted a translucent coat of the pattern over the statue with the rubber stamp tool (bottom).

Pattern options

To paint with a pattern, double-click on the rubber stamp tool icon and select either the Pattern (Aligned) or Pattern (Non-aligned) option from the Option pop-up menu in the Rubber Stamp Options palette. These options work as follows:

- **Pattern (Aligned):** Select this option to align all patterns you apply with the stamp tool, regardless of how many times you start and stop dragging. The two left examples in Figure 10-13 show the effects of selecting this option. The elements in the pattern remain exactly aligned throughout all the lines.

I painted the top image with the Opacity slider bar set to 50 percent, which is why the lines darken when they meet.

↩ **Pattern (Non-aligned):** To allow patterns in different lines to align randomly, select this option. The positioning of the pattern within each line is determined by the point at which you begin dragging. I dragged from right to left to paint the horizontal lines and from top to bottom to paint the vertical lines. The two right examples in Figure 10-13 show how nonaligned patterns overlap.

Figure 10-13
Select the Pattern (Aligned) option to align the patterns in all brush strokes painted with the stamp tool (left). If you select Pattern (Non-aligned), Photoshop aligns each pattern with the beginning of the line (right).

After you select Pattern (Aligned) or Pattern (Non-aligned), you're free to start dragging with the stamp tool. You don't need to Option-click or make any other special provisions, as you do when cloning.

As discussed in Chapter 9, you can also apply a pattern to a selected portion of an image by choosing Edit ⇨ Fill and selecting the Pattern option from the Use pop-up menu. Photoshop offers another function that lets you load an image from disk and apply it as a repeating pattern throughout the selection. Choose Filter ⇨ Render ⇨ Texture Fill to open any image saved in the native Photoshop format and then repeat it as many times as the selection will permit.

How to create patterns

The biggest difficulty with painting patterns is not figuring out the rubber stamp tool, but creating the patterns in the first place. Ideally, your pattern should repeat continuously, without vertical and horizontal seams. Here are some ways to create repeating, continuous patterns:

> ∞ **Load a displacement map:** Photoshop offers a Displacement Maps folder inside the Plug-ins folder. This folder contains several images, each of which represents a different repeating pattern, as illustrated in Figure 10-14. To use one of these patterns, open the image, choose Select ➪ All (⌘-A), and choose Edit ➪ Define Pattern. (For more information on displacement maps, see Chapter 15.)

Figure 10-14
The 12 patterns contained in the Displacement Maps folder included with Photoshop.

12-sided   Cees   Crumbles   Fragment layers

Honeycomb   Mezzo effect   Pentagons   Random strokes

Rectangular tiles   Schnable effect   Streaks pattern   Twirl pattern

> ∞ **Illustrator patterns:** Sunk deep inside the PostScript Patterns folder inside the Brushes & Patterns folder in the Goodies folder are 22 Illustrator EPS files that contain repeating object patterns. The patterns, some of which appear in Figure 10-15, are all seamless repeaters. You can open them and rasterize them to any size you like. Then press ⌘-A, choose Edit ➪ Define Pattern, and you have your pattern.

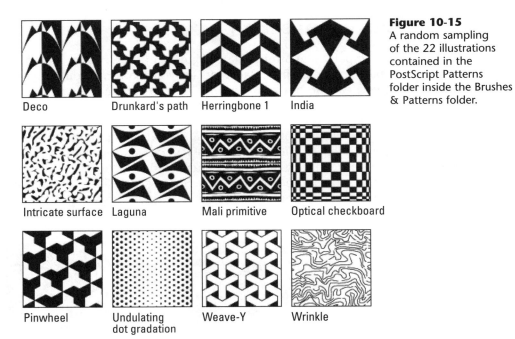

Figure 10-15
A random sampling of the 22 illustrations contained in the PostScript Patterns folder inside the Brushes & Patterns folder.

Deco   Drunkard's path   Herringbone 1   India

Intricate surface   Laguna   Mali primitive   Optical checkboard

Pinwheel   Undulating dot gradation   Weave-Y   Wrinkle

↪ **Using filters:** As luck would have it, you can create your own custom textures without painting a single line. In fact, you can create a nearly infinite variety of textures by applying several filters to a blank document. To create the texture shown in the bottom right box in Figure 10-16, for example, I began by selecting a 128 × 128-pixel area. I then chose Filter Noise ⇨ Add Noise, entered a value of 32, and selected the Gaussian radio button. I pressed ⌘-F twice to apply the noise filter two more times. Finally, I chose Filter ⇨ Stylize ⇨ Emboss and entered 135 into the Angle option box, 1 into the Height option box, and 100 percent into the Amount option box. The result is a bumpy surface that looks like stucco. This is merely one example of the myriad possibilities filters afford. There's no end to what you can do, so experiment away.

For more information on using Add Noise, see Chapter 15. For information about Emboss and other filter commands, see Chapter 16.

Figure 10-16
To create a stucco texture, apply Filter ⇨ Noise ⇨ Add Noise three times in a row (upper left, upper right, lower left). Then choose Filter ⇨ Stylize ⇨ Emboss and enter a Height value of 1 (lower right).

☞ **Marquee and clone:** You can use the rectangular marquee and rubber stamp tools to transform a scanned image into a custom pattern. Because this technique is more complicated as well as more rewarding than the others, I explain it in the upcoming section, "Steps: Building a Repeating Pattern from a Scanned Image."

The following steps describe how to change a scanned image into a seamless, repeating pattern. To illustrate how this process works, Figures 10-17 through 10-20 show various stages in a project I completed. You need only two tools to carry out these steps: the rectangular marquee tool and the rubber stamp tool with the Clone (Aligned) option active.

 Even so, these steps do involve a few selection and layering techniques that I haven't yet discussed (for those of you reading sequentially). If you become confused, you can find out more about selecting, moving, and cloning images in Chapter 11.

STEPS   Building a Repeating Pattern from a Scanned Image

Step 1. **Begin by marqueeing a portion of your scanned image and copying it to the Clipboard.** For best results, specify the exact size of your marquee by double-clicking on the rectangular marquee icon in the toolbox, selecting Fixed Size from the Style pop-up menu (in the Marquee Options palette), and entering specific values into the Width and Height option boxes. This way, you can easily reselect a portion of the pattern in the steps that follow and use the fixed-size marquee to define the pattern when you are finished. To create the patterns shown in the example, I set the marquee to 128×128 pixels.

Step 2. **Choose File ⇨ New (⌘-N) and triple the values Photoshop offers as the default image dimensions.** In my case, Photoshop offered 128×128 pixels because that was the size of the image I copied to the Clipboard. Therefore, I changed the image size to 384×384 pixels.

Step 3. **Paste the marqueed image into the new image window.** When you press ⌘-V, Photoshop pastes the image smack dab in the center of the window, which is exactly where you want it. This image will serve as the central tile of your repeating pattern. Unfortunately, Photoshop 4 pastes the image on a new layer. So you have to recover the selection outline and flatten the image. The following steps tell how.

Step 4. **⌘-click on the item labeled Layer 1 in the Layers palette.** This brings back the selection outline. Hooray.

Step 5. **Press ⌘-E.** This merged the layer with the background, in effect flattening it. You can alternatively choose Layer ⇨ Flatten Image. Either way, the selection outline remains intact.

Step 6. **Clone the selection by ⌘-Option-dragging it a total of eight times.** The idea is to fill the window with a 3 × 3-tile grid, as shown in Figure 10-17. First, ⌘-Option-drag up, then keep going around the perimeter of the image. Incidentally, it's important that you make the edges match up exactly, so take care when cloning. Feel free to use the arrow keys to nudge the selection if necessary.

Step 7. **Press ⌘-D to deselect the image.** Once you clone the image a few times, you need to deselect it so you can clone freely with the rubber stamp.

Figure 10-17
To build the repeating pattern shown in Figure 10-20, I started by creating a grid of nine image tiles. As you can see, the seams between the tiles in this grid are harsh and unacceptable.

Step 8. **Drag the title bar of the new image window to position it so that you can see the portion of the image you copied in the original image window.** If necessary, ⌘-drag the title bar of the original image window to reposition it as well. (⌘-dragging a window is an old Mac trick that lets you move the window without bringing it to the foreground.) This way, you can clone from the original image without switching back and forth between windows.

Step 9. **Select the Clone (Non-aligned) option.** First select the rubber stamp by pressing the S key. Then press Return to display the Rubber Stamp Options palette. If Clone (Non-aligned) is not selected in the Option pop-up menu, press the S key until it is.

Step 10. **Specify the image you want to clone by Option-clicking in the original image window.** No need to switch out of the new window. Option-click on an easily identifiable pixel that belongs to the portion of the image you copied. The *exact* pixel you click is very important. If you press the Caps Lock key, you get the crosshair cursor, which allows you to narrow in on a pixel. In my case, I clicked on the corner of the Buddha's mouth. (At least, I assume that's Buddha. What a narrow-minded, Western-bred ignoramus I must be.)

Step 11. **Now click with the stamp tool on the matching pixel in the central tile of the new window.** If you've clicked on the correct pixel, the tile should not change one iota. If it shifts at all, press ⌘-Z (Edit ➪ Undo) and try again. Because Clone (Non-aligned) is the active stamp setting, you can keep undoing and clicking over and over again without resetting the clone-from point in the original image.

Step 12. **Switch the Option setting to Clone (Aligned).** Once you click in the image without seeing any shift, select the Clone (Aligned) option from the pop-up menu in the Rubber Stamp Options palette to lock in the alignment between clone-from and clone-to points.

Step 13. **Use the stamp tool to fill in portions of the central tile.** For example, in Figure 10-18, I extended the Buddha's cheek and neck down into the lower row of tiles. I also extended the central forehead to meet the Buddha on the left.

Figure 10-18
I used the rubber stamp's cloning capability to extend the features in the central face toward the left and downward.

Step 14. **After you establish one continuous transition between two tiles in any direction — up, down, left, or right — select a portion of the image with the rectangular marquee tool and clone the selection repeatedly to fill out a single row or column.** In my case, I managed to create a smooth transition between the central and bottom tiles. Therefore, I selected a region that includes half of the central tile and half of the tile below it. Because I fixed the rectangular marquee to a 128 × 128-pixel

square, I only had to click on an area to select it. (Drag to position the marquee exactly where you want it.) I then cloned that selection along the entire width of the image.

Step 15.   **Press ⌘-D to deselect the image.** Again, you need to deselect the image so you can clone freely.

Step 16.   **If you started by creating a horizontal transition, use the rubber stamp tool to now create a vertical transition.** Likewise, if you started vertically, now go horizontally. You may very well need to press the S key to again switch to the Clone (Non-aligned) setting. This permits you to change the location of the clone-to point and build on one of the perimeter tiles. In my case, I shifted the clone-to point several times — alternatively building on the central Buddha, the right-hand one, and the middle one in the bottom row. Each time you get the clone-to point properly positioned, select the Clone (Aligned) option again to lock in the alignment. Then clone away.

As long as you get the clone-from and clone-to points properly aligned, you really can't make a mistake. If you change your mind, just realign the clone points and try again. In my case, I cloned the long, droopy earlobe down into the face of the Buddha below. (What's a long, droopy earlobe between identical cousins?). I also cloned the god's chin onto the forehead of the one to the right, ultimately achieving the effect shown in Figure 10-19.

Figure 10-19
After completing a smooth transition between the central tile and the tiles below and to the right of it, I selected a portion of the image and chose Edit ⇨ Define Pattern.

Step 17.   **After you build up one set of both horizontal and vertical transitions, you can select a portion of the image and choose Edit ⇨ Define**

Pattern. Figure 10-19 shows where I positioned my 128 × 128-pixel selection boundary. It includes parts of each of four neighboring heads, including the all-important droopy earlobe. (Didn't Buddha realize that once the droopy earlobe fad passed, he was going to be stuck with it for the rest of his life?) Don't worry that the image doesn't appear centered inside the selection outline. What counts is that the selection repeats seamlessly when placed beside itself.

Step 18. **Select the Pattern (Aligned) option inside the Rubber Stamp Options palette.** To confirm that the pattern is indeed seamless and every bit as lovely as you had hoped, drag around inside the current image with the rubber stamp tool and a large brush shape. Figure 10-20 shows the seamless results of my dragging. If you see any flaws, cover them up some more with the Clone (Aligned) and Clone (Non-aligned) settings, as explained previously.

Step 19. **Press ⌘-S to save your completed image.** You don't want to go to all this trouble for nothing.

Figure 10-20
This Eastern montage is the result of applying the Buddha pattern. He sure looks serene and comfortable, especially considering that he's resting on his own head.

Selectively Undoing Changes ____

Welcome to the second act of this chapter. It's a short act — more like a scene, really — so you'll have to forgo the intermission.

Now that I've explained the cloning and related patterning attributes of the rubber stamp tool, it's time to turn your attention — come on, turn, turn, just a little more, there you go — to a new topic. The rest of this chapter deals with *reversion,* which is a fancy word for returning your image to the way it looked before you went and made an unholy mess of it.

Using the traditional undo functions

Before I dive into the rubber stamp's reversion capabilities, allow me to introduce the more traditional reversion functions that are found in nearly all paint applications, including Photoshop:

   ☞ **Undo:** To restore an image to the way it looked before the last operation, choose Edit ➪ Undo (⌘-Z). You can undo the effect of a paint or edit tool, a change made to a selection outline, or a special-effect or color-correction command. You can't undo disk operations, such as opening or saving. However, Photoshop does let you undo an edit after printing an image. You can test out an effect, print it, and then undo it if you think it looks awful.

Photoshop still offers just one level of Undo. This is fast becoming unacceptable. Hopefully, Adobe will remedy this most obvious of all possible oversights in the next version. If it doesn't — well, I'm going to be plenty steamed, that's all.

   ☞ **Revert:** Choose File ➪ Revert to reload an image from disk. Most folks think of this as the last-resort function, the command you choose after everything else has failed. But really, it's quite useful as a stop-gap measure. Suppose that you're about to embark on a series of filtering operations that may or may not result in the desired effect. You're going to perform multiple operations, so you can't undo them if they don't work. Before choosing your first filter, choose File ➪ Save. Now you're ready for anything. You can wreak a degree of havoc on your image that no user in his or her right mind would dare. If everything doesn't go exactly as you planned or hoped, you can simply choose File ➪ Revert and you're back in business.

   ☞ **The eraser tool:** Drag with the eraser tool to paint in white or some other background color. This allows you to revert portions of your image back to bare canvas.

Actually, that's just the beginning of the eraser tool's capabilities. Once a piddly little tool of little consequence, the eraser has grown muscles over the years. That's why I explain it in so much detail in the next section.

Using the eraser tool

Select the eraser tool by pressing the E key, then press Return to display the Eraser Options palette. As shown in Figure 10-21, the palette offers a pop-up menu of eraser styles. Block is the old 16 × 16-pixel square eraser that's great for hard-edged touch-ups. The other options work exactly like the tools for which they're named.

 You don't have to go to the trouble of selecting the options from the pop-up menu. When the eraser is selected, pressing the E key cycles through the different eraser styles.

Figure 10-21
The eraser tool can now paint like the paintbrush, the airbrush, the pencil, or the old eraser (Block). The only question is, why didn't Adobe do this a long time ago?

As if that weren't enough, the eraser is pressure-sensitive, it responds to Opacity settings, and you can create fading eraser strokes. For cryin' in a bucket, you even have access to the Wet Edges check box described back in Chapter 8. The only thing missing is the brush modes menu, which I'm afraid you'll just have to live without.

Here are a few things to know and love about the eraser:

⌦ **Erasing on a layer:** By now, some of you are probably thinking, "You know, why does Photoshop even have an eraser? If all it does is paint in the background color, who needs it? You can do that with any paint tool just by pressing the X key." What makes Photoshop's eraser tool unique is layers. When working on a layer with the Preserve Transparency check box turned off, the eraser tool actually removes paint and exposes portions of the underlying image. Suddenly, the eraser tool performs like a *real* eraser.

 If the Preserve Transparency check box is turned on, Photoshop won't let the eraser bore holes in the layer and instead paints in the background color. For more information on Preserve Transparency and its other pals in the Layers palette, read Chapter 13.

↺ **Erasing lightly:** Change the Opacity setting in the Eraser Options palette to make portions of a layer translucent in inverse proportion to the Opacity value. For example, if you set the Opacity to 90 percent, you remove 90 percent of the opacity from the layer and therefore leave 10 percent of the opacity behind. The result is a nearly transparent stroke through the layer.

↺ **The eraser compared with layer masks:** As described in the "Creating layer-specific masks" section of Chapter 13, you can also erase holes in a layer using a layer mask. But unlike the eraser — which gets rid of pixels for good — a layer mask doesn't do any permanent damage. On the other hand, using the eraser tool doesn't increase the size of your image, as a layer mask does. It's a trade-off.

↺ **Erasing everything:** In case you're curious, you now restore the entire image window to the background color by clicking on the Erase Image button in the Eraser Options palette. When you're working on a layer, the button changes to Erase Layer and erases the current layer only. Considering how often most folks need to start over at square one — that is, never — this isn't a function you're likely to use very often.

↺ **Erasing with the pencil:** If you double-click on the pencil icon in the toolbox and select the Auto Erase check box in the Pencil Options palette, the pencil draws in the background color any time you click or drag on a pixel colored in the foreground color. This can be very useful when you're drawing a line against a plain background. Set the foreground color to the color of the line; set the background color to the color of the background. Then use the pencil tool to draw and erase the line until you get it just right.

 Unlike the eraser, the pencil always draws either in the foreground or background color, even when used on a layer.

Reverting to the last saved image

The traditional reversion functions just described are all very well and good. But they don't hold a candle to Photoshop's *selective reversion* functions, which allow you to restore specific portions of an image to the way they looked when you last saved the image to disk.

The most convenient selective reversion function is the magic eraser tool. To access the magic eraser, press the Option key while using the standard eraser tool. (You can also select the Erase to Saved check box in the Eraser Options palette, in which case dragging with the eraser reverts and Option-dragging paints in the background color.) A tiny page icon appears behind the eraser cursor. Option-drag with the magic eraser to paint with the last saved image or, if you prefer to think of it in a different way, to scrape away paint laid down since the last time you saved the image to disk. The process is demonstrated in Figure 10-22.

Figure 10-22
After making a dreadful mistake (top), I Option-dragged with the eraser tool to restore the image to the way it looked when I last saved it (bottom).

Before Photoshop can begin to selectively revert an image, it must load the last saved version of the image into memory. This operation takes a little time — the same amount of time, in fact, that it took Photoshop to open the image in the first place. You probably won't want to hold the mouse button down for the entire time. Therefore, if this is the first time you've selectively reverted inside the current image, Option-click with the eraser tool and then wait for Photoshop to load the image. Your click won't effect the image in the slightest. After the load operation is completed, Option-drag with the eraser as described earlier.

Reverting with the rubber stamp tool

Thanks to the improved performance of the eraser tool in Photoshop 3.0, the rubber stamp tool offers only two advantages over the magic eraser. The first is that you can take advantage of brush modes. By choosing a different brush mode from the pop-up menu in the upper left corner of the Rubber Stamp Options palette, you can mix pixels from the changed and saved images to achieve interesting and sometimes surprising effects.

The other advantage is that you can revert to one of two different images. Either choose From Saved from the Options pop-up menu in the Rubber Stamp Options palette to revert to the last image saved to disk, or choose From Snapshot to revert to the last image stored in memory as a *snapshot*.

To store the current version of an image in memory, choose Edit ⇨ Take Snapshot. The operation takes no time to complete because the image is already in memory. By choosing the Take Snapshot command, you merely instruct Photoshop not to get rid of this image.

There's no waiting when you use the tool either. When you drag with the rubber stamp tool set to From Snapshot, you don't have to wait for the image to load into memory as you do when reverting to a saved version, because it's already there. The function works instantaneously.

 Photoshop can remember only one snapshot at a time. Therefore, when you choose the Take Snapshot command, you not only capture the current image, you abandon any snapshot previously stored in memory. You cannot undo the Take Snapshot command, so be careful how you use it.

Reverting selected areas

As I explained briefly in the previous chapter, you can also revert selected areas of an image. After selecting the portion of the image you want to revert, choose Edit ⇨ Fill (or press Shift-Return) to display the Fill dialog box. Then select the Saved or Snapshot option from the Use pop-up menu and press the Return key. The selected area reverts to the saved image or snapshot, according to your choice.

Because you're actually filling the selected area with the saved image or snapshot, all the selection operations that I mention in Chapter 11 are equally applicable to reversions. You can revert a feathered or antialiased selection; you can revert an area selected with the pen tool; you can even revert the contents of a layer and apply overlay modes from the Layers palette. (The Fill dialog box offers its own Mode pop-up menu, but it's easier to apply the overlay modes from the Layers palette because you can preview the results as they occur.)

Reversion limitations

Photoshop doesn't allow you to selectively revert an image from disk if you have in any way changed the number of pixels in the image since it was last saved. Neither the Fill command nor the eraser and rubber stamp will revert if you have chosen Image ⇨ Image Size or Image ⇨ Canvas Size or if you have used the crop tool or Edit ⇨ Crop command.

Photoshop also can't revert an image if you haven't yet saved the image or if it can't read the document from disk (as when the image is saved in a format that requires conversion or can only be opened by means of a plug-in module).

You can, however, work around the image size problem by taking the following steps.

STEPS   Selectively Reverting a Resized Image

Step 1.   **Select the entire image and copy it to the Clipboard.**

Step 2.   **Option-click on the preview box in the lower left corner of the window to view the size of the document in pixels.** Write this information down or assign it to memory (the memory in your head, that is).

Step 3.   **Choose File ⇨ Revert.** Photoshop loads the last-saved version of the image into the image window.

Step 4.   **Choose Image ⇨ Canvas Size.** Resize the image to the dimensions you noted when Option-clicking the preview box in Step 2.

Step 5.   **Save the image to disk.**

Step 6.   **Paste the copied changes back into the image window.** Then use the rubber stamp or magic eraser to selectively revert the image.

That's all there is to it. In fact, it's so simple that Photoshop should be able to revert from a resized image without your help. Sometimes, computers are so stupid. But what can you do? I guess that's why it's a good thing we're here to occasionally help them out. We're lucky really. The day they're smart enough to take care of themselves, we'll all be obsolete.

Color Plate 4-1
This little warlock shows off the differences between the four different JPEG compression settings, from maximum quality, minimum compression (upper left) to minimum quality, maximum compression (lower right). Inspect the enlarged eye and sharpened staff for subtle erosions in detail.

Maximum   116K

High   66K

Medium   50K

Low   46K

Color Plate 4-2
My personal 1024 × 768-pixel startup screen features effects created with Kai's Power Tools, Xaos Paint Alchemy, Xaos Terrazzo, Gallery Effects, and Alien Skin's Black Box (now Eye Candy).

Color Plate 5-1
The colors inside the field and slider in the Color Picker dialog box change to reflect the selection of the H (Hue), S (Saturation), and B (Brightness) radio buttons.

Color Plate 6-1
This colorful image is the basis for an awful lot of channel discussions in Chapter 6. Right about now, I wish I was in that inner tube instead of editing it.

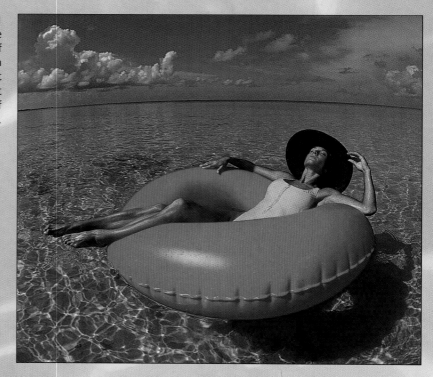

Color Plate 6-2
One of the wonderful things about the Lab mode is that it allows you to edit the colors in an image independently of the brightness values. Here I've inverted and boosted the contrast of the a and b color channels to produce some startling effects, all without harming a smidgen of detail.

Invert a

Auto Levels b

Invert and Auto Levels a and b

Replace red with blue

Replace green with red

Replace blue with red

Color Plate 6-3
You can wreak some pretty interesting havoc on the colors in an image by copying the image from one channel and pasting it into another, or by swapping the contents of two color channels.

Swap red and blue

Swap red and green

Swap green and blue

Color Plate 7-1
I converted this grayscale piece by Seattle-based artist Mark Collen to a quadtone using the colors navy blue, rose, teal, and dull orange. All colors were defined and printed using CMYK pigments.

Color Plate 8-1
Starting with an image of typical saturation (upper left), I applied the sponge tool set to Desaturate to the inside of the pepper and the corn in the background (upper right). I then repeated the effect two more times to make the areas almost gray (lower right). Returning to the original image, I then selected the Saturate option and again scrubbed inside the pepper and in the corn to boost the colors (lower left).

Color Plate 8-2
To create this image, I traced an image from the PhotoDisc library using the paintbrush tool and a flat brush shape. Although Photoshop offers automated filters that you can use to create similar effects, nothing is so versatile and precise as a simple paintbrush.

Color Plate 8-3
If you've picked up a previous edition of this book, you've seen this image before. But I keep it in because it's the first thing I ever drew with a pressure-sensitive tablet. Within an hour of plugging a Wacom SD-510 tablet into my Mac, I had rendered this image as you see it in Photoshop 1.0.7. If I can do it, so can you.

Behind

Dissolve

Normal

Color Plate 8-4
Here I've gone and desecrated a pivotal work of European iconography by scribbling the name of America's patron saint of graffiti. Reading up from the bottom, the Normal brush mode applies paint normally. The Dissolve mode scattered pixels along the fuzzy edge of the brushstroke. And the Behind mode paints behind the current layer, in this case, a layer containing the Madonna's head.

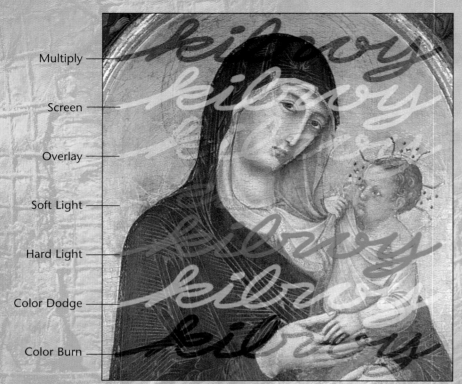

Multiply

Screen

Overlay

Soft Light

Hard Light

Color Dodge

Color Burn

Color Plate 8-5
Here I've painted green lines using the seven brush modes in the middle of the Options palette pop-up menu. Multiply darkens uniformly and Screen lightens uniformly. (In fact, Multiply and Screen are direct opposites.) Overlay, Soft Light, and Hard Light all multiply the darkest pixels and screen the lightest ones to produce different contrast-enhancing effects. New to Photoshop 4, Color Dodge and Color Burn work like dodge and burn tools that also add color to an image.

Color Plate 8-6
Here are the effects of the final eight entries in Photoshop 4's enormous arsenal of brush modes. Darken and Lighten are opposites, Difference and Exclusion are very closely related, and the last four apply different bits and pieces of the HSL color model. Because many of these modes produce slight effects—particularly the Saturation and Luminosity modes— I have added dark halos around the brushstrokes to offset them slightly from the background. Naturally, the halos feel right at home.

Darken

Lighten

Difference

Exclusion

Hue

Saturation

Color

Luminosity

Color Plate 9-1

Here I've used the paint bucket to colorize two oranges (top) with bright blue. First, I set the Tolerance value in the Paint Bucket Options palette to 120 and changed the brush mode to Color. Then I clicked at each of the four points marked with blue arrows (middle). After that, I changed the foreground color to green and clicked just once in the lower right corner of the image (marked with the green arrow). Unfortunately, the paint bucket isn't very precise, so I had to touch up the dimples and edges with the paintbrush, also set to the Color mode. Finally, I used the airbrush—set to the Color Burn mode—to deepen some of the blue shadows inside the fruit.

Noise × 3

Blast and Motion Blur

Color Plate 9-2

The results of filtering the three horizontal gradations, first by applying the Add Noise filter three times in a row (top) and then blasting the gradations with the Wind filter and applying the Motion Blur filter (bottom).

I started by designing a three-color gradient that fades twice into transparency, as demonstrated by the checkerboard background (left). Such a gradation is meant to be blended with an image, such as the piano keys (middle). So I selected the Overlay brush mode from the Gradient Tool Options palette and tickled my gradation across the ivories (right).

Color Plate 11-1
If you attempt to select this whimsical sign with the magic wand tool, you end up selecting old little fragments of the yellow areas one at a time. However, by switching to the blue channel—in which both sign and Sasquatch appear black against a relatively light background—you can easily select both portions of the sign in two easy clicks. I then inverted the sign (right) by pressing ⌘-I. The effect isn't perfect, but it's as good as it gets with the magic wand.

Color Plate 12-1

Two selections (top left and right) followed by their equivalent masks (middle). Here the mask is represented as a transparent red overlay, permitting you to see mask and image at the same time. Red-tinted areas are masked, representing deselected areas in the image; untinted areas are unmasked, and represent selected areas. In the final examples, I inverted the selected areas to demonstrate the full extent of the selection outlines.

Color Plate 12-2
In the left example, I drew a black-to-white gradation in the quick mask mode, extending from the base of the top row of pillars to the top of the flagpole. Then I applied the Add Noise filter to jumble up the pixels a little. Finally, I exited the quick mask mode to convert the mask to a selection, and ⌘-dragged the Capitol into the lava image (right).

Color Plate 12-3
Which twin has the Toni? With the help of a very precise mask, I dragged this girl in from her old environment into this new one. But despite the mask's accuracy, I managed to bring in some blue from her prior background (left). To fix this problem, I brushed in some color from the new background, and erased a few of the overly dark hairs (right).

Color Plate 13-1

After filling my layered drop shadow with a reddish orange (top), I chose the Multiply option from the blend mode pop-up menu in the Layers palette to mix the drop shadow with the underlying image (middle). Then I changed the Opacity setting to 70 percent (bottom) to create the finished colored drop shadow.

Color Plate 13-2

The popular cartoon character Neutron Mammal—what, you've never heard of Neutron Mammal?—is the result of applying both the haloing and spotlighting effects described in Chapter 13 and then setting the whole thing against an inverted background.

Color Plate 13-3

Here I've used a clipping group to fill some characters of type with a water pattern. I started by adding a couple of pool images that I shot with a digital camera to a layer above my text—which is itself on an independent layer—as demonstrated on the left. Then I just Option-clicked on the horizontal line between the two layers in the Layers palette. Photoshop automatically assigned the type layer's transparency mask to the pool layer, filling the letters.

Unsharp Mask

Dust & Scratches

Smart Blur

High Pass

Color Plate 15-1

Shown here are the results of four corrective filters. Normally, the High Pass (last example) filter takes the saturation out of an image, leaving many areas gray. To restore the colors, I chose Filter⇨Fade High Pass (⌘-Shift-F) and selected Luminosity mode in the Fade dialog box.

Color Plate 15-2

Here are the effects of four destructive filters from the Filter⇨ Distort, Pixelate, Render, and Stylize submenus. Every one of these filters has a dramatic impact on the color and detail of an image. From a pixel's perspective, destructive filters are dynamite, so use with care and moderation.

ZigZag

Mezzotint

Difference Clouds

Find Edges

Red

Green

Blue

Color Plate 15-3
The results of applying the Unsharp Mask filter to independent color channels in an RGB image. In each case, the Amount value was 300, the Radius value was 1.0, and the Threshold was 0. In each case, I applied the filter twice.

Red & green

Green & blue

Blue & red

Color Plate 15-4
Again, I applied Unsharp Mask to the independent color channels, but this time with an exaggerated Radius value, 10.0, a more moderate Amount value, 100, and the default Threshold, 0. Rather than pinpointing the sharpening effect, as in Color Plate 15-3, the high Radius value allows the colors to bleed as they are strengthened by the Amount value.

Red

Green

Blue

Red & green

Green & blue

Blue & red

Red

Green

Blue

Red & green

Green & blue

Blue & red

Color Plate 15-5
The results of applying Image⇨Other⇨High Pass with a Radius value of 10.0 to each channel and pair of channels in an RGB image. To boost the color values in the images slightly, I applied the Levels command (⌘-L) after each application of High Pass.

Color Plate 15-6
After applying the Gaussian Blur filter with a Radius of 8.0, I used the Fade Gaussian Blur command to mix the filtered image with the original. The labels tell the blend mode and Opacity setting applied to each image.

Normal, 60%

Luminosity, 50%

Darken, 80%

Lighten, 80%

Color Plate 15-7
An image scanned from an old issue of *Macworld* magazine shown as it appears in the normal RGB mode (top right) and when each channel is viewed separately (top left). The middle images show the affects of the Dust & Scratches filter set to a Radius of 2 and a Threshold of 20. The bottom images show how the channels look after suppressing the moiré patterns with the Gaussian Blur, Median, and Unsharp Mask filters.

Color Plate 16-1
The result of applying the Extrude filter to the lower left rose from Color Plate 15-4. If you select the Blocks and Solid Front Faces options, the filter transforms the image into mosaic tiles and shoves the tiles out at you in 3D space.

Color Plate 16-2
Here I applied Filter⇨Sketch⇨ Charcoal with the foreground color set to dark green and the background color light blue (as demonstrated in the upper left inset). Then I used the Fade Charcoal command to change the blend mode to Overlay.

Color Plate 16-3
I applied the Mezzotint filter set to the Long Strokes effect in each of the RGB, Lab, and CMYK color modes (top row). After each application of the filter, I pressed ⌘-Shift-F and faded the filtered image into the original using the Overlay mode and an Opacity setting of 40 percent (bottom row).

RGB   Lab   CMYK

Color Plate 16-4
In both examples, I applied the Emboss filter armed with an Angle of 135 degrees, a Height value of 2, and an Amount of 300 percent. To create the left image, I used the Fade command to mix embossed and original images together using the Luminosity blend mode and an Opacity setting of 80 percent. To get the psychedelic effect on right, I selected the Difference mode and reduced the Opacity value to 40 percent.

Color Plate 16-5
After selecting an image from the PhotoDisc library (top left), I layered the image, blurred it, applied the Find Edges filter, and darkened it with the Levels command (top middle). I then composited the image using the Overlay mode and an Opacity setting of 80 percent (top right). The bottom row shows the results of applying three effects filters set to the Luminosity mode and 80 percent Opacity settings.

Original

Blur and Find Edges

Overlay, 80%

Bas Relief

Plastic Wrap

Chrome

Selections, Layers, and Text

IV

PART

Selections and Paths

In This Chapter

- ➔ Special tricks that work only with the rectangular and elliptical marquee tools
- ➔ What's up with the new polygonal lasso tool
- ➔ How the magic wand's Tolerance setting works
- ➔ Selecting brightness values inside a single color channel
- ➔ Manual and automatic methods for editing selection outlines
- ➔ Using the Option key to subtract from a selection in Photoshop 4
- ➔ An in-depth look at the Feather command
- ➔ How to move and clone selections and selection outlines
- ➔ Floating selections in Photoshop 4
- ➔ A discussion of Photoshop's path tools
- ➔ The hows and whys of painting along an open path
- ➔ Exporting paths for use in Illustrator 6 (and later)
- ➔ Creating and saving clipping paths

Selection Fundamentals

Selections direct and protect. If it weren't for Photoshop's selection capabilities, you and I would be flinging paint on the canvas for all we're worth, like so many Jackson Pollock and Vasily Kandinsky wannabes, without any means to constrain, discriminate, or otherwise regulate the effects of our actions. Without selections, there'd be no filters, no color corrections, and no layers. In fact, we'd all be dangerously close to real life, that dreaded environment we've spent so much time and money to avoid.

That's the first reason this chapter is one of the most important in the book. The other reason is everything changes under Photoshop 4. If you're familiar with previous versions of the mighty image editor, get ready to see your world change.

 This is a classic domino effect. To forge greater consistency with other Adobe applications (Illustrator, PageMaker, and the like), you now must use the move tool — previously used only with layers — to move and clone selections. Because this is such a pain in the keister, Photoshop 4 lets you temporarily access the move tool by pressing and holding the ⌘ key (the same key used to access the arrow tool in Illustrator). This means old techniques that used to involve ⌘-dragging — such as subtracting from selection outlines — have been reassigned to the Option key. Old Option key techniques change to ⌘-Option, and old ⌘-Option techniques change to. . . well, it gets pretty gnarly.

If the last paragraph went by a little quickly, not to worry. I will explain every selection technique — new or old — in the following pages. Just be aware that if you try to sit down and select images in Photoshop 4 the same way you used to select them in Version 3, you're likely to encounter quite a few surprises. My suggestion is that you read through this chapter before you attempt anything important. Or at least skim the next few pages for the telltale Photoshop 4 icon.

How selections work

Before you can edit a portion of an image, you must first *select* it, which is computerese for marking the boundaries of the area you want to edit. To *select* part of an image in a painting program, you must surround it with a *selection outline* or *marquee;* this tells Photoshop where to apply your editing instructions. The selection outline appears as a moving pattern of dash marks, lovingly termed *marching ants* by doughheads who've been using the Mac too long. (See Figure 11-1 for the inside story.)

Figure 11-1
A magnified view of a dash mark in a selection outline reveals a startling discovery.

Photoshop 4 provides eight tools for drawing selection outlines, which are described in the following list. You can access most of the tools from the keyboard, as noted in the parentheses:

- **Rectangular marquee (M):** The rectangular marquee tool has been a staple of painting programs since the earliest MacPaint. This tool lets you select rectangular or square portions of an image.

- **Elliptical marquee (M again):** The elliptical marquee tool works just like the rectangular marquee except that it selects elliptical or circular portions of an image. (Pressing the M key switches between the rectangular and elliptical marquee tools.)

 - **Single-row/single-column:** The single-row and single-column tools let you select a single row or column of pixels that stretches the entire width or height of the image. These are the only tools in all of Photoshop that you can't access from the keyboard.

- **Lasso (L):** Another hand-me-down from MacPaint, the lasso tool lets you select a free-form portion of an image. You simply drag with the lasso tool around the area you want to edit. However, unlike the lasso tools in most Macintosh painting programs, which shrink selection outlines to disqualify pixels in the background color, Photoshop's lasso tool selects the exact portion of the image you enclose in your drag.

 - **Polygonal lasso (L again):** Click at different points in your image to set corners in a straight-sided selection outline. This is a great way to select free-form if you're not good at wielding the mouse, or your wrists are getting a tad sore. (You can achieve this same effect by Option-clicking with the lasso tool, but I'll explain this more in the "Free-form outlines" section later in this chapter.)

- **Magic wand (W):** First introduced by Photoshop, this tool enables you to select a contiguous region of similarly colored pixels by clicking inside it. For example, you might click inside the boundaries of a face to isolate it from the hair and background elements. Novices tend to gravitate toward the magic wand because it seems like such a miracle tool, but, in fact, it's the least predictable and ultimately least useful of the bunch.

- **Pen (P):** Now available in the main toolbox, the pen tool is both the most difficult to master and the most accurate and versatile of the selection tools. You use the pen tool to create a *path,* which is a special breed of selection outline. You click and drag to create individual points in the path. You can edit the path after the fact by moving, adding, and deleting points. You can even transfer a path via the Clipboard to or from Illustrator 6 or FreeHand 7. For a discussion of the pen tool, read the "How to Draw and Edit Paths" section later in this chapter.

Technically, Photoshop 4's new type mask tool also is a selection tool because Photoshop converts each character of type to a selection outline. But type involves a bunch of other issues that would merely confuse the content of this chapter, which is why I've awarded type its own chapter later in the book (Chapter 14).

If this were all you needed to know to use the selection tools in Photoshop, the application would be on par with the average paint program. Part of what makes Photoshop exceptional, however, is that it provides literally hundreds of little tricks to increase the functionality of every selection tool.

Furthermore, all of Photoshop's selection tools work together in perfect harmony. You can exploit the specialized capabilities of all eight tools (and the type mask tool as well) to create a single selection boundary. After you understand which tool best serves which purpose, you'll be able to isolate any element in an image, no matter how complex or how delicate its outline.

Geometric selection outlines

The default tool in the upper left corner of the toolbox is the rectangular marquee tool. You can access the elliptical marquee tool by Option-clicking on the marquee tool icon or by pressing the M key when the rectangular marquee tool is already selected. Pressing M again takes you back to the rectangular marquee tool. Option-clicking cycles through the single-row and single-column tools.

The marquee tools are more versatile than they may appear at first glance. You can adjust the performance of each tool as follows:

- **Constraining to a square or circle:** Press and hold Shift *after* beginning your drag to draw a perfect square with the rectangular marquee tool or a perfect circle with the elliptical marquee tool. (Pressing Shift *before* dragging also works if no other selection is active; otherwise, this adds to a selection, as I explain later in the "Ways to Change Selection Outlines" section.)

- **Drawing a circular marquee:** When perusing an online forum a while back, someone asked how to create a perfect circular marquee. Despite more than a month of helpful suggestions — some highly imaginative — no one offered the easiest suggestion of all (well, I ultimately did, but I'm a know-it-all). So remember to press Shift after you begin to drag and you'll be one step ahead of the game.

- **Drawing out from the center:** Press and hold the Option key after you begin dragging to draw the marquee from the center outward instead of from corner to corner. (Again, pressing Option before dragging works if no selection outline is active; otherwise, this subtracts from the selection.) This technique is especially useful when you draw an elliptical marquee. Frequently, it's easier to locate the center of the area you want to select than one of its corners — particularly because ellipses don't have corners.

⤳ **Moving the marquee on the fly:** Here's the slickest addition to marquees in Photoshop 4. While drawing a marquee, press and hold the spacebar to move the marquee rather than resize it. When you get the marquee in place, release the spacebar and keep dragging to modify the size. The spacebar is most helpful when drawing elliptical selections or when drawing a marquee out from the center — this eliminates the guesswork so you can position your marquees exactly on target.

⤳ **Selecting a single-pixel line:** Use the single-row and single-column tools to select a single row or column of pixels. Then choose the Single Row or Single Column option from the Shape pop-up menu. I use this option to fix screwups such as a missing line of pixels in a screen shot, to delete random pixels around the perimeter of an image, or to create perpendicular lines within a fixed space.

⤳ **Constraining the aspect ratio:** If you know you want to create an image that conforms to a certain height/width ratio — called an *aspect ratio* — you can constrain either a rectangular or an elliptical marquee so the ratio between height and width remains fixed, no matter how large or small a marquee you create. To accomplish this, press Return when the marquee tool is active to display the Marquee Options palette, shown in Figure 11-2. Then select Constrained Aspect Ratio from the Style pop-up menu. Enter the desired ratio values into the Width and Height option boxes. For example, if you want to crop an image to the ratio of a 640 × 480-pixel screen, you would enter 4 and 3 respectively into the Width and Height option boxes, and press Return to confirm your changes. Then select the area of the image that you want to retain and choose Image ➪ Crop.

Figure 11-2
Select the Constrained Aspect Ratio option in the Marquee Options palette to constrain the width and height of a marquee.

- ✎ **Sizing the marquee numerically:** If you're editing a screen shot or some other form of regular or schematic image, you may find it helpful to specify the size of a marquee numerically. To do so, select the Fixed Size option from the Style pop-up menu and enter size values into the Width and Height option boxes. To match the selection to a 640 × 480-pixel screen, for example, just change the Width and Height values to 640 and 480.

- ✎ **Drawing feathered selections:** A Feather option box is available when you use either of the marquee tools. To *feather* a selection is to blur its edges beyond the automatic antialiasing afforded to most tools. For more information on feathering, refer to the "Softening selection outlines" section later in this chapter.

- ✎ **Creating jagged ellipses:** By default, elliptical selection outlines are antialiased. If you don't want antialiasing — you might prefer harsh edges when editing screen shots or designing screen interfaces — deselect the Anti-aliased check box. (This option is dimmed when you use the rectangular marquee because antialiasing is always off for this tool. Perpendicular lines are smooth without the help of antialiasing.)

Frequently, Photoshop's lack of geometric shape tools throws novices for a loop. In fact, such tools do exist — you just don't recognize them. To draw a rectangle or ellipse in Photoshop, draw the shape as desired using the rectangular or elliptical marquee tool. Then choose Edit ➪ Fill or Edit ➪ Stroke, respectively, to color the interior or outline of the selection. You can also fill the selection using the Delete-key techniques discussed in Chapter 9. It's that easy.

Free-form outlines

In comparison to the rectangular and elliptical marquee tools, the lasso tool provides a rather limited range of options. Generally speaking, you just drag in a free-form path around the image you want to select. The few special considerations are as follows:

- ✎ **Feathering and antialiasing:** To adjust the performance of the lasso tool, press Return while the lasso tool is selected to display the Lasso Options palette shown in Figure 11-3. Just as you can feather rectangular and elliptical marquees, you can feather selections drawn with the lasso tool. You can also soften the edges of a lasso outline by selecting the Anti-aliased check box.

Be aware that although you can adjust the feathering of any selection after you draw it by choosing Select ➪ Feather, you must specify antialiasing before you draw a selection. Unless you have a specific reason for doing otherwise, leave the Anti-aliased check box turned on (as it is by default).

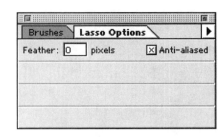

Figure 11-3
Double-click on the lasso tool icon to access the veritable truckload of options shown here.

↪ **Drawing polygons:** If you press and hold the Option key, the lasso tool works like a standard polygon tool. (*Polygon,* incidentally, just means a shape with multiple straight sides.) With the Option key down, you click to specify corners in a free-form polygon, as shown in Figure 11-4. If you want to add curves to the selection outline, just drag with the tool while still pressing the Option key. Photoshop closes the selection outline the moment you release both the Option key and the mouse button.

You can extend a polygon selection outline to the absolute top, right, or bottom edges of an image. To do so, Option-click with the lasso tool on the scroll bar or the title bar of the image window, as illustrated by the gray lines and squares in Figure 11-4.

This technique does not work on the left side of an image because the left side lacks a scroll bar or a title bar. To extend a selection to the absolute left edge of an image, drag out beyond the left edge of the image. Be sure to keep the mouse button down—don't click outside the window or you'll switch to some background application.

↪ **The polygonal lasso tool:** If you don't want to bother with pressing the Option key, you can simply use Photoshop 4's new polygonal lasso tool instead. Press the L key when the lasso is active to switch to the polygonal lasso tool. Then click inside the image to set corners in the selection. Click on the first point in the selection or double-click with the tool to complete the selection outline.

To create free-form curves with the polygonal lasso tool, press the Option key and drag.

Adobe added the polygonal lasso to Photoshop 4 because of the new role of the Option key. If no portion of the image is selected, it's no trick to Option-click with the standard lasso to draw a straight-sided selection. But if some area in the image is selected, pressing Option tells Photoshop that you want to subtract from the selection outline. For this reason, it's often easier to use the polygonal lasso (although you still can make it work by pressing Option *after* you click with the lasso tool, as I explain in the "Ways to Change Selection Outlines" later in this chapter).

Figure 11-4
Option-click with the lasso tool to create corners in a selection outline, shown as black squares in the bottom image. Drag to create free-form curves. Surprisingly, you can Option-click on the scroll bar to add corners outside the boundaries of the image window.

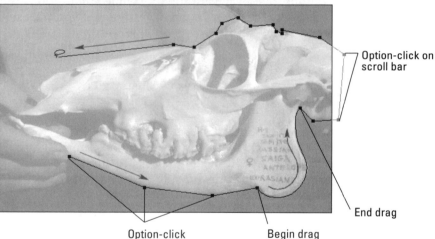

Option-click on scroll bar

End drag

Option-click

Begin drag

The world of the wand

Using the magic wand tool is a no-brainer, right? You just click with the tool and it selects all the neighboring colors that fall within a selected range. The problem, however, is getting the wand to recognize the same range of colors you see on-screen. For example, if you're editing a photo of a red plate against a pink table-cloth, how do you tell the magic wand to select the plate and leave the tablecloth alone?

Sadly, adjusting the performance of the wand is pretty tricky and unsatisfying. If you press Return when the magic wand is active, you'll see three options inside the Magic Wand Options palette, as shown in Figure 11-5. The Anti-aliased option softens the selection, just as it does for the lasso tool. The Tolerance value determines the range of colors the tool selects when you click with it in the image window. And the Sample Merged check box allows you to take all visible layers into account when defining a selection.

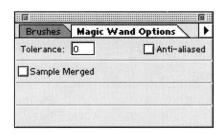

Figure 11-5
Use these options to specify the range of colors you want to select the next time you use the magic wand tool.

Adjusting the tolerance

By now you already understand what's up with the Anti-aliased option, so I'll start with Tolerance. You may have heard the standard explanation for adjusting the Tolerance value: You can enter any number from 0 to 255 in the Tolerance option box. Enter a low number to select a small range of colors; increase the value to select a wider range of colors.

Nothing is wrong with that explanation — it's accurate in its own small way — but it doesn't provide one iota of information you couldn't glean on your own. The fact is, if you really want to understand this option, you must dig a little deeper.

When you click on a pixel with the magic wand tool, Photoshop first reads the brightness value assigned to that pixel by each of the color channels. If you're working with a grayscale image, Photoshop reads a single brightness value from the one channel only; if you're working with an RGB image, it reads three brightness values, one each from the red, green, and blue channels; and so on. Because each color channel permits 8 bits of data, brightness values range from 0 to 255.

Next, Photoshop applies the Tolerance value, or simply *tolerance,* to the pixel. The tolerance describes a range that extends in both directions — lighter and darker — from each brightness value.

Suppose you're editing a standard RGB image. The tolerance is set to 32 (as it is by default); you click with the magic wand on a turquoise pixel, whose brightness values are 40 red, 210 green, and 170 blue. Photoshop adds and subtracts 32 from each brightness value to calculate the magic wand range, which in this case is 8 to 72 red, 178 to 242 green, and 138 to 202 blue. Photoshop selects any pixel that both falls inside this range *and* can be traced back to the original pixel via an uninterrupted line of other pixels that also fall within the range.

From this information, you can draw the following basic conclusions about the magic wand tool:

- ✐ **Creating a contiguous selection:** The magic wand selects a contiguous region of pixels emanating from the pixel on which you click. If you're trying to select land masses on a globe, for example, clicking on St. Louis selects everything from Juneau to Mexico City; it doesn't select London, though, because the cities are separated by an ocean of water that doesn't fall within the tolerance range.

- ✐ **Clicking midtones maintains a higher range:** Because the tolerance range extends in two directions, you cut off the range when you click on a light or dark pixel, as demonstrated in Figure 11-6. Consider the two middle gradations. In both cases, the tolerance is set to 60. In the top gradation, I clicked on a pixel with a brightness of 140, so Photoshop calculated a range from 80 to 200. But when I clicked on a pixel with a brightness value of 10, as in the bottom gradation, the range shrank to 0 to 70. Clicking on a medium-brightness pixel, therefore, permits the most generous range.

- ✐ **Selecting brightness ranges:** Many people have the impression that the magic wand selects color ranges. In fact, the magic wand selects brightness ranges within color channels. So, if you want to select a flesh-colored region — regardless of shade — set against an orange or red background that is roughly equivalent in terms of brightness values, you probably should use a different tool.

- ✐ **Selecting from a single channel:** If the magic wand repeatedly fails to select a region of color that appears unique from its background, try isolating that region inside a single-color channel. You'll probably have the most luck isolating a color on the channel that least resembles it. For example, to select the yellow Sasquatch Xing sign shown in Color Plate 11-1, I switched to the blue channel (⌘-3). Because yellow contains no blue and the brambly background contains quite a bit of blue — as demonstrated in the last example of Figure 11-7 — the magic wand can distinguish the two relatively easily. Experiment with this technique and it will prove more and more useful over time.

Making the wand see beyond a single layer

The final option in the Magic Wand Options palette, the Sample Merged option, lets you create a selection based on pixels from different layers (see Chapter 13). For example, returning to my previous land mass example, suppose that you set Europe on one layer and North America on the layer behind it. The two countries overlap. Normally, if you clicked inside Europe with the magic wand tool, the wand would select an area inside Europe without extending out into the area occupied by North America. This is because the wand doesn't even see the contents of other layers; anything outside Europe is just an empty void. We're talking pre-Columbus Europe here.

Figure 11-6
The results of clicking on a pixel with a brightness value of 140 (top row) and a brightness value of 10 (bottom row) with the tolerance set to three different values.

Figure 11-7
Because the yellow Sasquatch sign contains almost no blue, it appears most clearly distinguished from its background in the blue channel. This is, therefore, the easiest channel in which to select the sign with the magic wand.

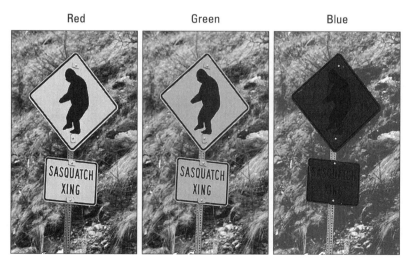

If you select the Sample Merged option, however, things change. Suddenly, the wand can see all the layers you can see. If you click on Europe, and if North America and Europe contain similar colors, the wand selects across both shapes.

Mind you, the Sample Merged option does *not* permit the wand to select images on two separate layers. Strange as this may sound, no selection tool can pull off this feat. Every one of the techniques explained both in this chapter and in all of Part III is applicable to just one layer at a time. Sample Merged merely allows the wand to draw selection outlines that appear to encompass colors on many layers.

What good is this? Well, suppose you want to apply an effect to both Europe and North America. With the help of Sample Merged, you can draw a selection outline that encompasses both countries. After you apply the effect to Europe, you can switch to the North America layer — the selection outline remains intact — and then reapply the effect.

Ways to Change Selection Outlines

If you don't draw a selection outline correctly the first time, you have two options. You can either draw it again from scratch, which is a real bore, or you can change your botched selection outline, which is likely to prove the more efficient solution. You can deselect a selection, add to a selection, subtract from a selection, and even select the stuff that's not selected and deselect the selected stuff. (If this sounds like a load of nonsense, keep reading.)

Quick changes

Some methods of adjusting a selection outline are automatic: You just choose a command and you're done. The following list explains how a few commands — all members of the Select menu — work:

- **Hide Edges (⌘-H):** Get those marching ants out of my face! We're all grown-ups, right? Do we really need constant streams of marching ants to tell us what we've selected? We were there; we remember. My point is that although visible selection outlines can be helpful sometimes, they can just as readily impede your view of an image. When they annoy you, press ⌘-H.

- **Deselect (⌘-D):** You can deselect the selected portion of an image in three ways. You can select a different portion of the image; click anywhere in the image window with the rectangular marquee tool, the elliptical marquee tool, or the lasso tool; or choose Select ➪ None. Remember, though, when no part of an image is selected, the entire image is susceptible to your changes. If you apply a filter, choose a color-correction command, or use a paint tool, you affect every pixel of the foreground image.

 ↪ **Inverse (⌘-Shift-I):** Choose Select ⇨ Inverse to reverse the selection. Photoshop deselects the portion of the image previously selected and selects the portion of the image not selected. This way, you can begin a selection by outlining the portion of the image you want to protect, rather than the portion you want to affect.

Manually adding and subtracting

Ready for some riddles? When editing a portrait, how do you select both eyes without affecting any other portion of the face? Answer: By drawing one selection and then tacking on a second one. How do you select a doughnut and leave the hole behind? Answer: Encircle the doughnut with the elliptical marquee tool, and then use that same tool to subtract the center.

Photoshop enables you to whittle away at a selection, add pieces back on, whittle away some more, ad infinitum, until you get it exactly right. Short of sheer laziness or frustration, no reason exists why you can't eventually create the selection outline of your dreams:

 ↪ **Adding to a selection outline:** To increase the area enclosed in an existing selection outline, Shift-drag with one of the marquee or lasso tools. You also can Shift-click with the magic wand tool or Shift-click with one of the marquee tools when the Fixed Size option is active (as described back in the "Geometric selection outlines" section earlier in this chapter).

 ↪ **Subtracting from a selection outline:** To take a bite from an existing selection outline, press the Option key while using one of the selection tools.

Some of you long-time Photoshop users are probably sitting there with your mouths hanging open. "Option to subtract? How could Adobe do such a thing?" After six years of using the ⌘ key to subtract, this was my reaction. But like it or not, the change is set in stone. From this day on, you press the ⌘ key to get the move tool, and you use Option to subtract from a selection.

 ↪ **Intersecting one selection outline with another:** Another way to subtract from an existing selection outline is to Shift-Option-drag around the selection with the rectangular marquee, elliptical marquee, or lasso tool. You also can Shift-Option-click with the magic wand tool. Shift-Option-dragging instructs Photoshop to retain only the portion of an existing selection that also falls inside the new selection outline. I frequently use this technique to confine a selection within a rectangular or elliptical border.

Although the old ⌘-key tasks have switched to Option, Photoshop 4 hasn't entirely abandoned faithful users of previous versions. The program now presents you with special cursors to show you what you're doing. Say you've selected part of an image and the lasso tool is active. When you press the Shift key, Photoshop appends a little plus sign to the lasso cursor to show you you're about to add. When you press Option, you see a little minus sign. Press Shift and Option to get an × for intersect. Keeping an eye on your cursors will make the transition easier.

Using Shift and Option like a pro

The expanded roles of the Shift and Option keys in adding, subtracting, and intersecting selection outlines can interfere with your ability to take advantage of other functions of the selection tools. For example, when no portion of an image is selected, you can Shift-drag with the rectangular marquee tool to draw a square. But after a selection is active, Shift-dragging adds a rectangle — not a square — to the selection outline.

The trick is to learn when to press the Shift and Option keys. Sometimes you must press the key before you begin your drag, sometimes you press the key after you begin the drag, but before you release. For example, to add a square to a selection outline, Shift-drag, release Shift while keeping the mouse button pressed, and press Shift again to snap the rectangle to a square. The same goes for adding a circle with the elliptical marquee tool.

A few other techniques follow that you'll do well to master. They sound pretty elaborate, I admit, but with a little practice, they become second nature (so does tightrope walking, but don't let that worry you):

- ☞ To subtract a square or circle from a selection, Option-drag, release Option, press Shift, drag until you get it right, release the mouse button, and then release Shift.

- ☞ To add a rectangle or ellipse and draw from the center outward, Shift-drag, release Shift, press the Option key, and hold Option until after you release the mouse button. You can even press the spacebar during the drag to move the marquee around, if you like.

- ☞ To subtract a marquee drawn from the center outward, Option-drag, release Option, press Option again, and hold the key down until after you release.

- ☞ What about drawing a straight-sided selection with the lasso tool? To add a straight-sided area to an existing selection, Shift-drag with the tool for a short distance. With the mouse button still down, release Shift and press the

Option key. Then click around as you normally would while keeping the Option key down.

- To subtract a straight-sided area, Option-drag with the lasso, release Option, press Option again, and click around with the tool.

If you can't manage the last two lasso-tool techniques, then switch to the polygonal lasso instead. In fact, the reason Adobe provided the polygonal lasso tool was to accommodate folks who don't want to deal with pressing the Option key seven times during a single drag.

Adding and subtracting by command

Photoshop provides several commands under the Select menu that automatically increase or decrease the number of selected pixels in an image according to numerical specifications. The commands in the Select ➪ Modify submenu work as follows:

- **Border:** This command selects an area of a specified thickness around the perimeter of the current selection outline and deselects the rest of the selection. For example, to select a 6-point-thick border around the current selection, choose Select ➪ Modify ➪ Border, enter 6 into the Width option box, and press Return. But what's the point? After all, if you want to create an outline around a selection, you can accomplish this in fewer steps by choosing Edit ➪ Stroke. The Border command, however, broadens your range of options. You can apply a special effect to the border, move the border to a new location, or even create a double outline effect by first applying Select ➪ Modify ➪ Border, and then Edit ➪ Stroke.

- **Smooth:** This command rounds off the sharp corners and weird anomalies in the outline of a selection. When you choose Select ➪ Modify ➪ Smooth, the program asks you to enter a Sample Radius value. Photoshop smoothes out corners by drawing little circles around them, and the Sample Radius value determines the radius of these circles. Larger values result in smoother corners.

The Smooth command is especially useful in combination with the magic wand. After you draw one of those weird, scraggly selection outlines with the wand tool, use Select ➪ Modify ➪ Smooth to smooth off the rough edges.

- **Expand and Contract:** Both of these commands do exactly what they say, either expanding or contracting the selected area by 1 to 16 pixels. For example, if you want an elliptical selection to grow by 8 pixels, choose Select ➪ Modify ➪ Expand, enter 8, and call it a day. These are extremely useful commands I'll refer to several times throughout the book.

Both Expand and Contract have a flattening effect on a selection. To round things off, apply the Smooth command with a Sample Radius value equal to the number you just entered into the Expand Selection or Contract Selection dialog box. You'll end up with a pretty vague selection outline, but what do you expect from automated commands?

In addition to the Expand command, Photoshop provides two older commands — Grow and Similar — that increase the area covered by a selection outline. Both commands resemble the magic wand tool in that they measure the range of eligible pixels by way of a Tolerance value. In fact, the commands rely on the same Tolerance value found inside the Magic Wand Options palette. If you want to adjust the impact of either command, therefore, you must first select the magic wand icon in the toolbox:

- **Grow:** Choose Select ⇨ Grow to select all pixels that both neighbor an existing selection and resemble the colors included in the selection, in accordance with the Tolerance value. In other words, Select ⇨ Grow is the command equivalent of the magic wand tool. If you feel constrained because you can only click on one pixel at a time with the wand tool, you may prefer to select a small group of representative pixels with a marquee tool, and then choose Select ⇨ Grow to initiate the wand's magic. (If you're familiar with previous versions of Photoshop, be aware that the old ⌘-G keyboard shortcut has been reassigned to Layer ⇨ Group with Previous.)

- **Similar:** Another member of the Select menu, the Similar command works just like the Grow command except the pixels needn't be adjacent to one another. When you choose Select ⇨ Similar, Photoshop selects any pixel that falls within the tolerance range, regardless of its location in the foreground image.

One of the best applications for the Similar command is to isolate a complicated image that's set against a consistent background whose colors are significantly lighter or darker than the image. Consider Figure 11-8, which features a dark and ridiculously complex foreground image set against a continuous background of medium- to light-brightness values. Although the image features sufficient contrast to make it a candidate for the magic wand tool, I would never in a million years recommend using that tool; too many of the colors in the foreground image are discontinuous. The following steps explain how to separate this image using the Similar command in combination with a few other techniques I've described thus far.

STEPS   Isolating a Complex Image Set Against a Plain Background

Step 1.   Use the rectangular marquee tool to select some representative portions of the background. In Figure 11-8, I selected the lightest and darkest portions of the background along with some representative shades in between. Remember, you make multiple selections by Shift-dragging with the tool.

Figure 11-8
Before choosing Select ➪ Similar, select a few sample portions of the background so Photoshop has something on which to base its selection range.

Step 2.   **Double-click on the magic wand tool icon to display the Tolerance option box.** For my image, I entered a Tolerance value of 16, a relatively low value, in keeping with the consistency of the background. If your background is less homogenous, you may want to enter a higher value. Make certain the Anti-aliased check box is turned on.

Step 3.   **Choose Select ➪ Similar.** Photoshop should select the entire background. If Photoshop fails to select all the background, choose Edit ➪ Undo (⌘-Z) and use the rectangular marquee tool to select more portions of the background. You may also want to increase the Tolerance value in the Magic Wand Options palette. If Photoshop's selection bleeds into the foreground image, try reducing the Tolerance value.

Step 4.   **Choose Select ➪ Inverse.** Or press ⌘-Shift-I. Photoshop selects the foreground image and deselects the background.

Step 5.   **Modify the selection as desired.** If the detail you want to select represents only a fraction of the entire image, Shift-Option-drag around the portion of the image you want to retain using the lasso tool. In Figure 11-9, I Shift-Option-dragged with the polygonal lasso tool to draw a straight-sided outline around the selection.

Figure 11-9
Shift-Option-drag with the polygonal lasso tool to
intersect the area you want to select with a straight-
sided outline.

Step 6. **Congratulations, you've isolated your complex image.** Now you can filter your image, colorize it, or perform whatever operation inspired you
to select this image in the first place. For myself, I wanted to superim-
pose the image onto a different background. To do so, I copied the
image to the Clipboard (⌘-C), opened the desired background image,
and then pasted the first image into place (⌘-V). The result, shown in
Figure 11-10, still needs some touching up with the paint and edit tools,
but it's not half bad for an automated selection process.

Whenever you introduce a selection into another image — by copying and
pasting or by dragging the selection and dropping it into another image window — Photoshop 4 automatically assigns the selection to a new layer. This
is a great safety mechanism, which prevents you from permanently affixing
the selection to its new background. But this also means you can't save the
image in a file format other than the native Photoshop format without first
flattening the image. For the big, new story on layers, read Chapter 13.

Figure 11-10
The completed selection super-imposed onto a new background.

Softening selection outlines

You can soften a selection in two ways. The first method is *antialiasing*, introduced in the "Rasterizing an Illustrator or FreeHand file" section of Chapter 4. Antialiasing is an intelligent and automatic softening algorithm, which mimics the appearance of edges you'd expect to see in a sharply focused photograph.

Where did the term *antialias* originate? Well, to *alias* an electronic signal is to dump essential data, thus degrading the quality of a sound or image. Antialiasing boosts the signal and smoothes the rough spots in a way that preserves the overall quality.

When you draw an antialiased selection outline in Photoshop, the program calculates the hard-edged selection at twice its actual size. The program then shrinks the selection in half using bicubic interpolation (described in the "General preferences" section of Chapter 2). The result is a crisp image with no visible jagged edges.

The second softening method, *feathering,* is more dramatic. Feathering gradually dissipates the selection outline, giving it a blurry edge. Photoshop accommodates partially selected pixels; feathering fades the selection both inward and outward from the original edge.

You can specify the number of pixels affected either before or after drawing a selection. To feather a selection before you draw it, double-click on the marquee or lasso tool icon and enter a value into the Feather option box in the Options palette. To feather a selection after drawing it, choose Select ⇨ Feather. Or press the new keyboard shortcut, ⌘-Shift-D. (Why D for feather? Because it Dissipates the selection, naturally.)

The Feather Radius value determines the approximate distance over which Photoshop fades a selection, measured in pixels in both directions from the original selection outline. Figure 11-11 shows three selections lifted from the image at the bottom of the figure. The first selection is antialiased only. I feathered the second and third selections, assigning Feather Radius values of 4 and 12, respectively. As you can see, a small feather radius makes a selection appear fuzzy; a larger radius makes it fade into view.

The math behind the feather

A few eagle-eyed readers have written to ask me why feathering blurs a selection outline more than the number of pixels stated in the Feather Radius value. A radius of 4 pixels actually affects a total of 20 pixels: 10 inward and 10 outward. The reason revolves around Photoshop's use of a mathematical routine called the *Gaussian bell curve*, which exaggerates the distance over which the selection outline is blurred.

Figure 11-12 demonstrates the math visually. The top-left image shows a hard-edged elliptical selection filled with white against a black background. To its right is a side view of the ellipse, in which black pixels are short and white pixels are tall. (Okay, so it's a really a graph, but I didn't want to scare you off.) Because no gray pixels are in the ellipse, the side view has sharp vertical walls.

The bottom-left image shows what happens if I first feather the selection with a radius of 4 pixels and then fill it with white. The side view now graphs a range of gray values, which taper gradually from black to white. See those gray areas on the sides (each labeled Radius)? Those are the pixels that fall into the 8-pixel diameter, measured 4 pixels in and out from the original selection outline. These gray areas slope in straight lines.

The rounded areas of the side view — painted black — are the Gaussian bell curves. These are appended onto the radius of the feather to ensure smooth transitions between the blurry edges and the selected and deselected pixels. Programs that do not include these extra Gaussian curves, such as Corel Photo-Paint for Windows, end up producing ugly feathered selections that appear to have sharp, incongruous edges.

Figure 11-11
Three clones selected with the elliptical marquee tool. The top image is antialiased and not feathered; the next is feathered with a radius of 4 pixels; and the third is feathered with a radius of 12 pixels.

If exact space is an issue, you can count on the Feather command affecting about 2.7 times as many pixels as you enter into the Feather Radius option box, both in and out from the selection. That's a total of 5.4 times as many pixels as the radius in all.

If this is more than you wanted to know, cast it from your mind. Feathering makes the edges of a selection fuzzy — 'nuff said.

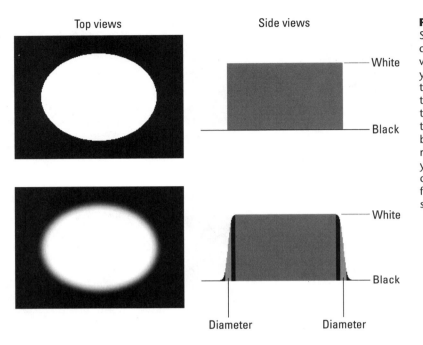

Top views   Side views

White

Black

White

Black

Diameter   Diameter

Figure 11-12
Some graphic demonstrations of what happens when you feather a selection. Photoshop tapers the ends of the feathered selections (shown by the black areas, bottom right) to prevent your eye from easily detecting where the feathering starts and stops.

Putting feathering to use

You can use feathering to remove an element from an image while leaving the background intact, a process described in the following steps. The image described in these steps, shown in Figure 11-13, is a NASA photo of a satellite with the earth in the background. I wanted to use this background with another image, but to do so I first had to eliminate that satellite. By feathering and cloning a selection outline, I covered the satellite with a patch so seamless you'd swear the satellite was never there.

STEPS   Removing an Element from an Image

Step 1.   **Draw a selection around the element using the lasso tool.** The selection needn't be an exact fit; in fact, you want it rather loose, so allow a buffer zone of at least six pixels between the edges of the image and the selection outline.

Step 2.   **Drag the selection outline over a patch in the image.** Now that you've specified the element you want to remove, you must find a patch — that is, some portion of the image which will cover the element in a manner that matches the surrounding background. In Figure 11-14, the best match seemed an area just below and to the right of the satellite. To select this area, move the selection outline independently of the image merely by dragging it with the lasso tool. (New to Photoshop 4, dragging a selection with a selection tool moves the outline without affecting the pixels.) Make certain you allow some space between the selection outline and the element you're trying to cover.

Step 3. **Choose Select ⇨ Feather.** Or press ⌘-Shift-D. Enter a small value (8 or less) in the Feather Radius option box — just enough to make the edges fuzzy. (I entered 3.) Then press Return to initiate the operation.

Figure 11-13
Your mission, if you choose to accept it, is to remove the satellite by covering it up with selections cloned from the background.

Figure 11-14
After drawing a loose outline around the satellite with the lasso tool, I dragged the outline to select a portion of the background.

Step 4. **Clone the patch onto the area you want to cover.** Select the move tool by pressing the V key. Then Option-drag the feathered selection to clone the patch and position it over the element you want to cover, as shown in Figure 11-15. To align the patch correctly, choose Select ⇨ Hide Edges (⌘-H) to hide the marching ants, and then nudge the patch into position with the arrow keys.

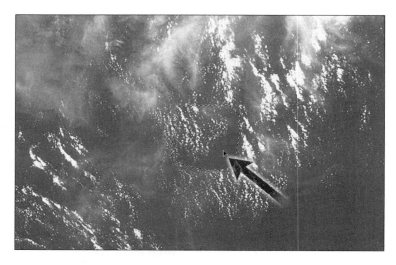

Figure 11-15
Next, I used the move tool to Option-drag the feathered selection over the satellite. Sadly, the patch was imperfect and required further adjustments.

Step 5. **Repeat as desired.** My patch was only partially successful. The upper left corner of the selection matches clouds in the background, but the lower right corner is dark and cloudless, an obvious rift in the visual continuity of the image. The solution: Try again. With the lasso tool, I drew a loose outline around the dark portion of the image and dragged it up and to the left as shown in Figure 11-16.

Step 6. **It's all déjà vu from here on out.** I chose Select ⇨ Feather, entered 6 into the Feather Radius option box — thus allowing the clouds a sufficient range to taper off — and pressed Return. I then selected the move tool and Option-dragged the feathered patch over the dark, cloudless rift. Finally, I nudged, nudged, nudged with the arrow keys, and voilà, no more satellite. Figure 11-17 shows $200 million worth of hardware vaporized in less than five minutes.

Figure 11-16
I used the lasso tool
to draw a new outline
around the dark,
cloudless portion of
the patch. Then I
dragged the outline
to a different spot in
the background.

Figure 11-17
I selected a new bit of
cloudy sky and placed
it over the formerly
cloudless portion of the
patch. Satellite? What
satellite?

Moving and Duplicating Selections

The previous steps showed how you can move either the selected pixels or the empty selection outline to a new location. Now it's time to examine these techniques in greater depth.

The new role of the move tool

In Photoshop 4, you *must* use the move tool to move the selected pixels. No longer is it acceptable to merely drag with the marquee, lasso, or wand tool, as in Version 3 and earlier. The move tool is no longer an elective feature; now it's your only option.

You can select the move tool at any time by pressing the V key (for mooV). The advantage of the move tool is that no chance exists of deselecting an image or harming the selection outline. Drag inside the selected area to move the selection; drag outside the selection to move the entire layer, selection included. I explain layers in more detail in Chapter 13.

To access the move tool on a temporary basis, press and hold the ⌘ key. The move tool remains active so long as ⌘ is pressed. This shortcut works when any tool except the hand or pen tool is active. Assign this shortcut to memory at your earliest convenience. Believe me, you'll spend a lot of time ⌘-dragging in Photoshop 4.

Previewing the move

If you just start in dragging (or ⌘-dragging) a selection, Photoshop displays the outline of the selected area during a move, as shown in the top image in Figure 11-18. But you can also preview the selected pixels in all their splendor as you move them, as shown in the bottom image in the figure. As you might expect, this slows down the screen refresh speed. This also prevents you from viewing the portion of the image behind the selection. But times occur when this capability comes in extremely handy.

To preview a selection as you move it, click and hold on the selection before you move the mouse. The watch cursor appears. The moment the cursor changes back to the standard move cursor — which may happen quickly if you're using a Power Mac system — you can start dragging.

Figure 11-18
You can drag a selection right off the bat to see only its outline (top) or you can press and hold the mouse button for a moment before beginning your drag to preview the selection (bottom).

Making precise movements

Photoshop provides three methods for moving selections in prescribed increments. In each case, the move tool is active, unless otherwise indicated:

  ↪ First, you can nudge a selection in one-pixel increments by pressing an arrow key on the keyboard, or in 10-pixel increments by pressing Shift with an arrow key. This technique is useful for making precise adjustments to the position of an image.

To nudge a selected area when the move tool is not active, press ⌘ with an arrow key. Press ⌘ and Shift to move in 10-pixel increments. Once the selection is floating — that is, after your first nudge — you can let up on the ⌘ key and just use the arrows (assuming a selection tool is active).

⤶ Second, you can press Shift during a drag to constrain a move to some 45-degree direction — that is, horizontally, vertically, or diagonally.

⤶ And third, you can use the Info palette to track your movements and to help locate a precise position in the image. To display the Info palette, choose Window ➪ Show Info, or press the F8 key. Figure 11-19 shows the Info palette as it appears in Photoshop 4. All eight items in the palette monitor movement, as follows:

- **X, Y:** These values show the coordinate position of your cursor. The distance is measured from the upper left corner of the image in the current unit of measure. The unit of measure in Figure 11-19 is pixels.

- **ΔX, ΔY:** These values indicate the distance of your move as measured horizontally and vertically.

- **A, D:** The A and D values reflect the angle and direct distance of your drag.

- **W, H:** These values reflect the width and height of your selection.

Figure 11-19
The Info palette provides a world of numerical feedback when you move a selection.

Cloning a selection

When you move a selection, you leave a hole in your image in the background color, as shown in the top half of Figure 11-20. If you prefer, instead, to leave the original in place during a move, you have to *clone* the selection — that is, create a copy of the selection without upsetting the contents of the Clipboard. Photoshop offers several different ways to clone a selection:

↪ **Option-dragging:** When the move tool is active, press the Option key and drag a selection to clone it. The bottom half of Figure 11-20 shows a selection that I Option-dragged three times. (Between clonings, I changed the gray level of each selection to make them more identifiable.)

↪ **⌘-Option-dragging:** If some tool other than the move tool is active, ⌘-Option-drag the selection to clone it. This is probably the technique you'll end up using most often.

Figure 11-20
When you move a selection, you leave a gaping hole in the selection's wake (top). When you clone an image, you leave a copy of the selection behind. Just to make a point, I cloned the selection in the bottom image three times.

↪ **Option-arrowing:** When the move tool is active, press Option in combination with one of the arrow keys both to clone the selection and to nudge it one pixel away from the original. If you want to move the image multiple pixels, Option-arrow the first time only. Then just nudge the clone using the arrow key alone. Otherwise, you'll create a bunch of clones you can't undo.

✎ **⌘-Option-arrowing:** If some other tool is active, press ⌘ and Option with an arrow key. Again, just press the Option key the first time, unless you want to create a string of clones.

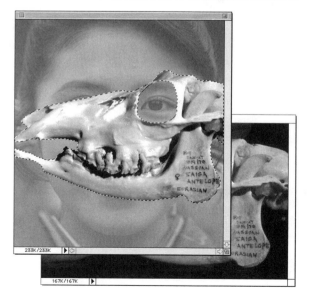

Figure 11-21
Use the move tool to drag a selection from one open window and drop it into another (top). This creates a clone of the selection in the receiving window (bottom).

✎ **Drag and drop:** Like just about every other program on the planet, Photoshop lets you clone a selection between documents by dragging it with the move tool from one open window and dropping it in another, as demonstrated in

Figure 11-21. As long as you manage to drop into the second window, the original image remains intact and selected in the first window. My advice: Don't worry about exact positioning during a drag and drop; first get it into the second window and then worry about placement.

⤳ **Shift-drop:** If the two images are exactly the same size — pixel for pixel — press the Shift key when dropping the selection to position it in the very same spot from which it came in the original image. This is called *registering* the selection.

⤳ **⌘-drag and drop:** Again, if some other tool than the move tool is selected, you must press the ⌘ key when you drag to move the selected pixels from one window to the other.

Moving a selection outline independently of its contents

After all this talk about the move tool and the ⌘ key, you might be wondering what happens if you just drag a selection with the marquee, lasso, or wand, as in the good old days. The answer is, you move the selection outline independently of the image. This technique serves as yet another means for manipulating inaccurate selection outlines. It also enables you to mimic one portion of an image inside another portion of the image or inside a completely different image window.

In the top image in Figure 11-22, I used the marquee tool to drag the skull outline down and to the right, so it only partially overlapped the skull. Note the image itself remains unaltered. I then lightened the new selection, applied a few strokes to set it off from its background, and gave it stripes, as shown in the bottom image. For all I know, this is exactly what a female Russian Saiga antelope looks like.

You can nudge a selection outline independently of its contents by pressing an arrow key when a selection tool is active. Press Shift with an arrow key to move the outline in 10-pixel increments.

The great news about the revised role of the selection tools is you can drag and drop empty selection outlines between images. Just drag the selection from one image and drop it into another, as demonstrated in the first example of Figure 11-21. The only difference is, only the selection outline gets cloned; the pixels remain behind. This is a great way to copy pixels back and forth between images. You can set up an exact selection in Image A, drag it into Image B with the marquee tool, move it over the pixels you want to clone, and ⌘-drag and drop the selection back into Image A. This is slick as hair grease, I'm telling you.

So remember, the selection tools now affect only the selection outline. The selection tools never affect the pixels themselves; that's the move tool's job.

Figure 11-22
Drag a selection with a selection tool to move the outline independently of its image (top). Wherever you drag the selection outline becomes the new selection (bottom).

Floating a selection

In Photoshop 4, floating selections are almost dead, but not quite. First, a *floating selection* is a selection that hovers above the surface of the image. The beauty of a floating selection is you can move it and apply fills using the Delete key, all without affecting the underlying image itself. Then you can mix the floating selection with the underlying image by adjusting the Opacity slider bar in the Layers palette. You can also select a blend mode from the pop-up menu in the upper left corner of the Layers palette.

In Photoshop 4, you can float a selection in one of two ways:

- **Move:** When you move a selection by ⌘-dragging it or pressing ⌘ with an arrow key, Photoshop floats the selection at its new location.

- **Clone:** Whether you clone a selection by ⌘-Option-dragging it or pressing ⌘ and Option in combination with an arrow key, Photoshop floats the cloned selection.

 Conversely, all the following techniques *defloat* a selection — that is, drop it in place — again making the image itself susceptible to changes. In Photoshop 4, this list has grown much longer:

- **Deselect:** Because a floating selection must remain selected to remain floating, choosing Select ➪ None (⌘-D) defloats a selection. Likewise, any operation that has the added effect of deselecting an image, such as selecting a different portion of the image, changing the canvas size, or choosing File ➪ Revert, defloats the selection.

- **Add to the selection:** If you add to a selection outline by pressing Shift while using any of the selection tools (or adding a path to a selection outline from the Make Selection dialog box, as I'll describe shortly), Photoshop defloats the image. You can subtract from a selection outline and intersect it, however, without defloating it.

- **Automatically adjusting the selection outline:** All the commands in the Select menu that affect the shape of a selection outline — including Inverse, Feather, Grow, Similar, and the commands in the Select ➪ Modify submenu — set down the selection. Like Shift-dragging with a selection tool, these commands add pixels to the selection outline, which invariably requires a defloat.

- **Paint or edit inside a selection:** If you so much as click in a selection with a paint or edit tool, Photoshop drops it.

- **Stroke the selection:** Photoshop automatically defloats a selection when you apply Edit ➪ Stroke.

- **Apply a filter or color correction:** One of my favorite things to do in previous versions of Photoshop was to float a selection, apply a filter, and then mix it with the underlying original to achieve a more subtle effect. Now, if you apply a filter or color correction to a floater, it drops. Phooey. Luckily, Photoshop 4 offers several workarounds, including the new Filter ➪ Fade command, which I discuss in Chapter 15.

- **Editing a mask:** Photoshop automatically defloats a selection when you switch to the quick mask mode, whether or not you edit the mask. For more information on this wonderful feature, read Chapter 12.

↪ **Layer ⇨ Defloat:** You can drop a selection by choosing Layer ⇨ Defloat, or by pressing the new keyboard equivalent, ⌘-E (for, "Eke, I just dropped my floater!").

 Why this new hostility toward floaters (who never did anyone any harm)? Adobe wants you to get in the habit of using layers. By taking away most of the advantages of floaters, you're left with no other choice. Layers are great, and they have many advantages over floaters (as you'll learn in Chapter 13). But I honestly see no reason why floaters had to be undercut so radically. Thanks for letting me get that off my chest.

If everything dropped a floater, there wouldn't be any use for them at all. Here are a few things you can do to leave your floater hovering in peace:

↪ **Move the floater:** You can move a floating selection by dragging it with the marquee, lasso, wand, or move tool. (No need for the ⌘ key once the selection is floating.) You can also nudge the floaters with the arrow keys, again sans ⌘.

↪ **Fill the floater:** Press Option-Delete to fill the floaters with the foreground color. Press ⌘-Delete to fill it with the background color. (Don't press Delete on its own, though — that'll just delete the floater.) Both Option-Delete and ⌘-Delete are great ways to establish drop shadows.

↪ **Subtract from the floater:** While a selection is floating, you can chip away portions of it by Option-dragging with a marquee tool or the lasso tool or by Option-clicking with the magic wand. The area around which you Option-drag (or on which you Option-click) disappears.

↪ **Intersect the floater:** Similarly, you can Shift-Option-drag with a marquee or lasso tool or Shift-Option-click with the magic wand tool to specify the portion of the selection you want to retain. Anything not included inside the Shift-Option-drag or Shift-Option-click disappears.

↪ **Transform the floater:** You can apply Photoshop 4's new Layer ⇨ Free Transform (⌘-T) to a floater without dropping it. This command lets you scale, rotate, slant, and distort a selection in one operation. I cover this and the other excellent transformation features in Chapter 13.

↪ **Change the Opacity:** As in previous versions of Photoshop, you can adjust the transparency of a floater by adjusting the Opacity slider bar or by pressing number keys. Press the 1 key for 10 percent, 2 for 20 percent, and so on, up to 0 for 100 percent. You can also press two numbers in a row to specify an exact Opacity value. Lower Opacity settings make the floater translucent, so you can see through to the pixels below.

◌➙ **Blend modes:** Select a blend mode from the pop-up menu at the top of the Layers palette to merge the floater with the underlying image in weird and wonderful ways. This topic is so huge, it takes all of Chapter 19 to get through it.

How to Draw and Edit Paths

Photoshop's path tools provide the most flexible and precise ways to define a selection short of masking. But, though a godsend to the experienced user, the path tools represent something of a chore to novices and intermediates. Most people take quite a while to become comfortable with the path tools because you must draw a selection outline one point at a time.

 If you're familiar with Illustrator's pen tool and other path-editing functions, you'll find Photoshop's tools are nearly identical. Photoshop doesn't provide the breadth of options available in Illustrator — you can't transform paths independently of an image or apply sophisticated path operations in Photoshop, for example — but the basic techniques are the same.

The following pages are designed to get you up and running with paths. I'll explain how you approach drawing a path, how you edit it, how you convert it to a selection outline, and how you stroke it with a paint or edit tool. All in all, you'll learn more about paths than you ever wanted to know.

Paths overview

In Photoshop 4, the path tools are now available in the toolbox, as shown in Figure 11-23. But the path management options — which let you convert paths to selections, fill and stroke paths, and save and delete them — still reside in the Path palette, also shown in the figure. Together, tools and palette options make up a fully functioning path-drawing environment, which rivals similar features provided by Illustrator or FreeHand.

Figure 11-23
The toolbox provides access to every one of Photoshop's path-drawing tools. To save and organize your paths, display the Paths palette by choosing Window ⇨ Show Paths.

How paths work

Paths differ from normal selections in that they exist on the equivalent of a distinct, object-oriented layer, which sits in front of the bitmapped image. This setup enables you to edit a path with point-by-point precision after you draw it to make sure it meets the exact requirements of your artwork. This also prevents you from accidentally messing up the image, as you can when you edit ordinary selection outlines. After creating the path, you convert it into a standard selection outline before using it to edit the contents of the image, as explained in the section "Converting and saving paths," later in this chapter.

The following steps explain the basic process of drawing a selection outline with the path tools. I explain each step in more detail throughout the remainder of this chapter.

STEPS   Drawing a Selection with the Path Tools

Step 1.   Draw the path. Use the pen tool to draw the outline of your prospective selection. You can select the pen tool by pressing the P key.

Step 2.   Edit the path. If the outline of the path requires some adjustment, reshape it using the other path tools. You can cycle through the tools by pressing P.

Step 3. **Save the path.** When you get the path exactly the way you want it, save the path in Photoshop by choosing the Save Path command from the Paths palette menu. Or you can double-click on the Work Path item in the scrolling list.

Step 4. **Convert the path to a selection.** You can make the path a selection outline by choosing the Make Selection command. Or press the Enter key when a path or selection tool is active.

That's it. After you convert the path to a selection, it works just like any of the selection outlines described earlier. You can feather a selection, move it, copy it, clone it, or apply one of the special effects described in future chapters. The path remains intact in case you want to edit it further or use it again.

Using the Paths palette tools

Before I get into my long-winded description of how you draw and edit paths, here is a quick introduction to the five path tools:

Pen: Use the pen tool to draw paths in Photoshop one point at a time. I explain this tool in detail in the following section. Press the P key to select the tool.

Arrow: This tool lets you drag points and handles to reshape a path. You can access the arrow tool when any other path tool is active by pressing and holding the ⌘ key. Or press the P key again to make the tool permanently active.

Insert point: Click on an existing path to add a point to it. You can access this function when the arrow tool is selected by ⌘-Option-clicking on a segment in the path. When the pen tool is active, Control-click.

Remove point: Click on an existing point in a path to delete the point without creating a break in the path's outline. To accomplish this when the arrow tool is selected, ⌘-Option-click on a point in a path. When the pen tool is active, Control-click.

Convert point: Click or drag on a point to convert it to a corner or smooth point. You also can drag on a handle to convert the point. Press Control to access the convert point tool when the arrow tool is selected. Press ⌘ and Control when the pen is selected. (Pressing Control and Option also works.)

The terms *point, smooth point,* and others associated with drawing paths are explained in the upcoming section.

Drawing with the pen tool

When drawing with the pen tool, you build a path by creating individual points. Photoshop automatically connects the points with *segments*, which are simply straight or curved lines.

All paths in Photoshop are *Bézier* (pronounced *bay-zee-ay*) *paths,* meaning they rely on the same mathematical curve definitions that make up the core of the PostScript printer language. The Bézier curve model allows for zero, one, or two levers to be associated with each point in a path. These levers, labeled in Figure 11-24, are called *Bézier control handles* or simply *handles.* You can move each handle in relation to a point, enabling you to bend and tug at a curved segment like a piece of soft wire.

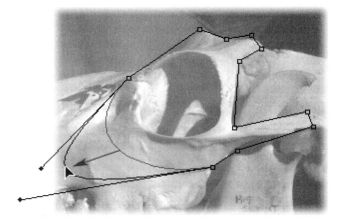

Figure 11-24
Drag with the pen tool to create a smooth point flanked by two Bézier control handles.

The following list summarizes how you can use the pen tool to build paths in Photoshop:

- **Adding segments:** To build a path, create one point after another until the path is the desired length and shape. Photoshop automatically draws a segment between each new point and its predecessor.

- **Closing the path:** If you eventually plan to convert the path to a selection outline, you need to complete the outline by clicking again on the first point in the path. Every point will then have one segment entering it and another segment exiting it. Such a path is called a *closed path* because it forms one continuous outline.

- **Leaving the path open:** If you plan to apply the Stroke Path command (explained later), you may not want to close a path. To leave the path open, so it has a specific beginning and ending, deactivate the path by saving it (choose the Save Paths command from the Paths palette menu). After you complete the save operation, you can click in the image window to begin a new path.

- **Extending an open path:** To reactivate an open path, click or drag on one of its endpoints. Photoshop draws a segment between the endpoint and the next point you create.

- **Joining two open paths:** To join one open path with another open path, click or drag on an endpoint in the first path, and then click or drag on an endpoint in the second.

  Points in a Bézier path act as little road signs. Each point steers the path by specifying how a segment enters it and how another segment exits it. You specify the identity of each little road sign by clicking, dragging, or Option-dragging with the pen tool. The following items explain the specific kinds of points and segments you can create in Photoshop. See Figure 11-25 for examples.

- **Corner point:** Click with the pen tool to create a *corner point,* which represents the corner between two straight segments in a path.

- **Straight segment:** Click at two different locations to create a straight segment between two corner points. Shift-click to draw a 45-degree-angle segment between the new corner point and its predecessor.

- **Smooth point:** Drag to create a *smooth point* with two symmetrical Bézier control handles. A smooth point ensures that one segment meets with another in a continuous arc.

- **Curved segment:** Drag at two different locations to create a curved segment between two smooth points.

- **Curved segment followed by straight:** After drawing a curved segment, Option-click on the smooth point you just created to delete the forward Bézier control handle. This converts the smooth point to a corner point with one handle. Then click at a different location to append a straight segment to the end of the curved segment.

- **Straight segment followed by curved:** After drawing a straight segment, drag from the corner point you just created to add a Bézier control handle. Then drag again at a different location to append a curved segment to the end of the straight segment.

- **Cusp point:** After drawing a curved segment, Option-drag from the smooth point you just created to redirect the forward Bézier control handle, converting the smooth point to a corner point with two independent handles, sometimes known as a *cusp point.* Then drag again at a new location to append a curved segment that proceeds in a different direction than the previous curved segment.

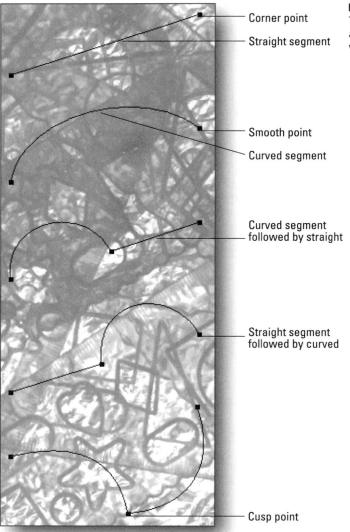

Corner point

Straight segment

Smooth point

Curved segment

Curved segment
followed by straight

Straight segment
followed by curved

Cusp point

Figure 11-25
The different kinds of points
and segments you can draw
with the pen tool.

Reshaping existing paths

As you become more familiar with the pen tool, you'll draw paths correctly the first
time around more frequently. But you'll never get it right 100 percent of the time or
even 50 percent of the time. From your first timid steps until you develop into a

seasoned pro, you'll rely heavily on Photoshop's ability to *reshape* paths by moving points and handles, adding and deleting points, and converting points to change the curvature of segments. Don't worry if you don't draw a path correctly the first time. The paths tools provide all the second chances you'll ever need.

Using the arrow tool

The arrow tool represents the foremost path reshaping function in Photoshop. After selecting this tool, you can perform any of the following functions:

- **Selecting points:** Click on a point to select it independently of other points in a path. Shift-click to select an additional point, even if the point belongs to a different path than other selected points. Option-click on a path to select all its points in one fell swoop. You can even marquee points by dragging in a rectangle around them. You *cannot,* however, apply commands from the Select menu, such as All or None, to the selection of paths.

- **Drag selected points:** To move one or more points in a path, select the points you want to move and then drag one of the selected points. All selected points move the same distance and direction. When you move a point while a neighboring point remains stationary, the segment between the two points shrinks, stretches, and bends to accommodate the change in distance. Segments located between two selected or deselected points remain unchanged during a move.

 You can move selected points in one-pixel increments by pressing arrow keys. If both a portion of the image and points in a path are selected, the arrow keys move the point only. Because paths reside on a higher layer, they take precedence in all functions that might concern them.

- **Drag a segment directly:** You also can reshape a path by dragging its segments. When you drag a straight segment, the two corner points on either side of the segment move as well. As illustrated in Figure 11-26, the neighboring segments stretch, shrink, or bend to accommodate the drag. When you drag a curved segment, however, you stretch, shrink, or bend that segment only, as demonstrated in Figure 11-27.

Figure 11-26
Drag a straight segment to move the segment and change the length, direction, and curvature of the neighboring segments.

Figure 11-27
Drag a curved segment to change the curvature of that segment only and leave the neighboring segments unchanged.

When you drag a curved segment, drag from the middle of the segment, approximately equidistant from both its points. This method provides the best leverage and ensures the segment doesn't go flying off in some weird direction you hadn't anticipated.

⤷ **Drag a Bézier control handle:** Select a point and drag either of its Bézier control handles to change the curvature of the corresponding segment without moving any of the points in the path. If the point is a smooth point, moving one handle moves both handles in the path. If you want to move a smooth handle independently of its partner, you must use the convert point tool, as discussed in the "Converting points" section later in this chapter.

⤷ **Clone a path:** To make a duplicate of a selected path, Option-drag it to a new location in the image window. Photoshop automatically stores the new path under the same name as the original.

⤷ **Deselect a path:** Click with the arrow tool outside any path to deselect all active paths. Because many options affect the selected path only, it's often a good idea to deselect the paths before choosing a command that you want to apply to *all* visible paths.

 Press and hold the ⌘ key to access the arrow tool temporarily when the pen tool or any of the path or edit tools are selected. When you release the ⌘ key, the cursor returns to the selected tool.

Adding and deleting points

The quantity of points and segments in a path is forever subject to change. Whether a path is closed or open, you can reshape it by adding and deleting points, which, in turn, forces the addition or deletion of a segment:

⤷ **Appending a point to the end of an open path:** If an existing path is open, you can activate one of its endpoints by either clicking or dragging on it with the pen tool, depending on the identity of the endpoint and whether you want the next segment to be straight or curved. Photoshop is then prepared to draw a segment between the endpoint and the next point you create.

⤷ **Closing an open path:** You also can use the technique I just described to close an open path. Just select one endpoint, click or drag on it with the pen tool to activate it, and then click or drag on the opposite endpoint. Photoshop draws a segment between the two endpoints, closing the path and eliminating both endpoints by converting them to *interior points,* which simply means the points are bound on both sides by segments.

⤷ **Joining two open paths:** You can join two open paths to create one longer open path. To do so, activate an endpoint of the first path, then click or drag with the pen tool on an endpoint of the second path.

⤷ **Inserting a point in a segment:** Select the insert point tool and click anywhere along an open or closed path to insert a point and divide the segment on which you click into two segments. Photoshop automatically inserts a corner or smooth point, depending on its reading of the path. If the point does not exactly meet your needs, use the convert point tool to change it.

 To access the insert or remove point tool, press ⌘ and Option when using the arrow tool. ⌘-Option-click on an existing segment to insert a point; ⌘-Option-click on a point to remove it. If the pen tool is active, press the Control key instead.

- **Deleting a point and breaking the path:** The simplest way to delete a point is to select it with the arrow tool and press either the Delete or Clear key. (You also can choose Edit ⇨ Clear, though why you would want to expend so much effort is beyond me.) When you delete an interior point, you delete both segments associated with that point, resulting in a break in the path. If you delete an endpoint from an open path, you delete the single segment associated with the point.

- **Removing a point without breaking the path:** Select the remove point tool and click on a point in an open or closed path to delete the point and draw a new segment between the two points that neighbor it. The remove point tool ensures no break occurs in a path.

- **Deleting a segment:** You can delete a single interior segment from a path without affecting any point. To do so, first click outside the path with the arrow tool to deselect the path. Then click on the segment you want to delete and press the Delete key. When you delete an interior segment, you create a break in your path.

- **Deleting a whole path:** To delete an entire path, select any portion of it and press the Delete key twice. The first time you press Delete, Photoshop deletes the selected point or segment and automatically selects all other points in the path. The second time you press Delete, Photoshop gets rid of everything it missed the first time around.

Converting points

Photoshop allows you to change the identity of an interior point. You can convert a corner point to a smooth point and vice versa. You perform all point conversions using the convert point tool as follows:

- **Smooth to corner:** Click on an existing smooth point to convert it to a corner point with no Bézier control handle.

- **Smooth to cusp:** Drag one of the handles of a smooth point to move it independently of the other handle, thus converting the smooth point to a cusp.

- **Corner to smooth:** Drag from a corner point to convert it to a smooth point with two symmetrical Bézier control handles.

- **Cusp to smooth:** Drag one of the handles of a cusp point to lock both handles back into alignment, thus converting the cusp to a smooth point.

 Press the Control key to temporarily access the convert point tool when the arrow tool is selected. Press both ⌘ and Control to access the convert point tool when the pen tool is active.

Filling paths

After you finish drawing a path and getting it exactly the way you want it, you can convert it to a selection outline — as described in the upcoming "Converting paths to selections" section — or you can paint it. You can either paint the interior of the path by choosing the Fill Path command from the Paths palette menu or you can paint the outline of the path by choosing Stroke Path.

The Fill Path command works much like Edit ➪ Fill. After drawing a path, choose the Fill Path command or Option-click on the fill path icon in the lower left corner of the palette (the one that looks like a filled circle). Photoshop displays a slight variation of the Fill dialog box discussed in Chapter 9, the only difference being the inclusion of two Rendering options. Enter a value into the Feather Radius option box to blur the edges of the fill, as if the path were a selection with a feathered outline. Select the Anti-aliased check box to soften slightly the outline of the filled area.

If one path falls inside another, Photoshop leaves the intersection of the two paths unfilled. Suppose that you draw two round paths, one fully inside the other. If you deselect both paths and then choose the Fill Path command, Photoshop fills only the area between the two paths, resulting in a letter *O*.

If the Fill Path command fills only part or none of the path, this is probably because the path falls outside the selection outline. Choose Select ➪ None (⌘-D) to deselect the image and then choose the Fill Path command again.

If you select one or more paths with the arrow tool, the Fill Path command changes to Fill Subpaths, enabling you to fill the selected paths only. The fill path icon also affects just the selected paths.

Painting along a path

Unlike the Fill Path command, which bears a strong resemblance to Edit ➪ Fill, the Stroke Path command is altogether different than Edit ➪ Stroke. Where Edit ➪ Stroke creates outlines and arrowheads, the Stroke Path command allows you to paint a brush stroke along the contours of a path. This may not sound like a big deal at first, but this feature enables you to combine the spontaneity of the paint and edit tools with the structure and precision of a path.

To paint a path, choose the Stroke Path command from the Paths palette menu to display the Stroke Path dialog box shown in Figure 11-28. In this dialog box, you can choose the paint or edit tool with which you want to *stroke* the path (which just means to paint a brush stroke along a path). Photoshop drags the chosen tool along the exact route of the path, retaining any tool or brush shape settings that were in force when you chose the tool.

Figure 11-28
Photoshop displays this dialog box when you choose the Stroke Path command while a tool other than a paint or edit tool is selected.

You can also display the Stroke Path dialog box by Option-clicking on the stroke path icon, the second icon at the bottom of the Paths palette (labeled back in Figure 11-23). If you prefer to bypass the dialog box, select a paint or edit tool, and then either click on the stroke path icon or simply press the Enter key on the numeric keypad. Instead of displaying the dialog box, Photoshop assumes you want to use the selected tool and strokes away.

If the path is selected, the Stroke Path command becomes a Stroke Subpath command. Photoshop then only strokes the selected path, rather than all paths saved under the current name.

The following steps walk you through a little project I created by stroking paths with the paintbrush and smudge tools. Figures 11-29 through 11-31 show the progression and eventual outcome of the image.

STEPS   Stroking Paths with the Paintbrush and Smudge Tools

Step 1.   **After opening a low-resolution version of a hurricane image, I drew the zigzag path shown in Figure 11-29.** As you can see, the path emits from the eye of the hurricane. I drew the path starting at the eye and working upward, which is important because Photoshop strokes a path in the same direction in which you draw it.

Step 2.   **I next saved the path.** I double-clicked on the Work Path name in the Paths palette, entered a name for my path, and pressed Return.

Step 3.   **I used the Brushes palette to specify three brush shapes.** Each one had a Roundness value of 40. The largest brush had a diameter of 16, the next largest had a diameter of 10, and the smallest had a diameter of 4.

Figure 11-29
I drew this path
starting at the eye of
the hurricane and
working my way
upward.

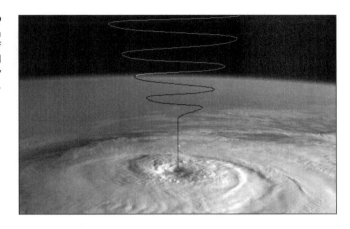

Step 4. **I double-clicked on the paintbrush tool to bring up the Paintbrush Options palette.** Then I set the Fade-out value to 400. Next, I selected the To Background radio button so Photoshop would draw gradient strokes between the foreground and background colors.

Step 5. **I stroked the path with the paintbrush three times using the Stroke Path command.** I changed the foreground and background colors for each stroke. The first time, I used the largest brush shape and stroked the path from gray to white; the second time, I changed to the middle brush shape and stroked the path from black to white; and the final time, I used the smallest brush shape and stroked the path from white to black. The result of all this stroking is shown in Figure 11-30.

Step 6. **Next, I created two clones of the zigzag path by Option-dragging the path with the arrow tool.** I pressed the Shift key while dragging to ensure the paths aligned horizontally. I then clicked in an empty portion of the image window to deselect all paths so they appeared as shown in Figure 11-30. This enabled me to stroke them all simultaneously in Step 9.

Figure 11-30
After stroking the
path three times
with the paintbrush
tool, I cloned the
path twice.

Step 7. **I created a 60-pixel version of my brush shape and reduced its Hardness value to 0 percent.** I then painted a single white spot at the bottom of each of the new paths. I painted a black spot at the bottom of the original path.

Step 8. **I selected the smudge tool.** Then I moved the Pressure slider bar in the Brushes palette to 98 percent and selected a brush shape with a radius of 16 pixels. At this setting, the tool has a tremendous range, but it eventually fades out.

Step 9. **I pressed Enter to apply the smudge tool to all three paths at once.** The finished image appears in Figure 11-31.

Figure 11-31
I stroked all three paths with the smudge tool set to 98 percent pressure to achieve this unusual extraterrestrial-departure effect. At least, I guess that's what it is. It could also be giant space slinkies probing the planet's surface. Hard to say.

If you're really feeling precise — I think they have a clinical term for that — you can specify the location of every single blob of paint laid down in an image. When the Spacing option in the Brush Options dialog box is deselected, Photoshop applies a single blob of paint for each point in a path. If this isn't sufficient control, I'm a monkey's uncle. (What a terrible thing to say about one's nephew!)

Converting and saving paths

Photoshop provides two commands to switch between paths and selections, both of which are located in the Paths palette menu. The Make Selection command converts a path to a selection outline; the Make Path command converts a selection to a path. And regardless of how you create a path, you can save it with the current image, which enables you not only to reuse the path but also to hide and display it at will.

Converting paths to selections

When you choose the Make Selection command or Option-click on the make selection icon (which looks like a dotted circle, as labeled back in Figure 11-23), Photoshop displays the dialog box shown in Figure 11-32. You can specify whether or not to antialias or feather the selection and to what degree. You can also instruct Photoshop to combine the prospective selection outline with any existing selection in the image. The Operation options correspond to the keyboard functions discussed in the "Manually adding and subtracting" section earlier in this chapter.

Figure 11-32
When you choose the Make Selection command, you have the option of combining the path with an existing selection.

Photoshop 4 offers several additional ways to convert a path to a selection outline, all of which are more convenient than the Make Selection command:

- **Press the Enter key:** As long as a path or selection tool is active, the Enter key converts the path to a selection.

- **⌘-click on the path name:** If some other tool is selected, you can ⌘-click on the name of a path in the Paths palette. The path need not be active.

- **Shift-Enter or ⌘-Shift-click:** To add the path to an existing selection, press Shift with one of the above techniques. You can press Shift-Enter. Or ⌘-Shift-click on a path name in the palette.

- **Option-Enter or ⌘-Option-click:** Naturally, if you can add, you can subtract. Just press the Option key with Enter or ⌘-clicking to subtract the path from the selection.

- **Shift-Option-Enter or ⌘-Shift-Option-click:** Now we're starting to get into some obscure stuff, but what's possible is possible. You select the intersection of a path and selection outline by pressing a whole mess of keys.

All of these wonderful techniques — most new to Photoshop 4 — have the added advantage of hiding the path when converting the path to a selection. This way, you have full, unobstructed access to your selection outline.

By contrast, the Make Selection command leaves the path on-screen in front of the converted selection. If you try to copy, cut, delete, or nudge the selection, you perform the operation on the path instead.

Converting selections to paths

When you choose the Make Paths command, Photoshop produces a single Tolerance option. Unlike the Tolerance options you've encountered so far, this one is accurate to 1/10 pixel and has nothing to do with colors or brightness values. Rather, it permits you to specify Photoshop's sensitivity to twists and turns in a selection outline. The value you enter determines how far the path can vary from the original selection. The lowest possible value, 0.5, ensures that Photoshop retains every nuance of the selection, but it can also result in overly complicated paths with an abundance of points. If you enter the highest value, 10, Photoshop rounds out the path and uses few points. If you plan on editing the path, you probably won't want to venture any lower than 2.0, the default setting.

Saving paths with an image

I mentioned at the beginning of the paths discussion that saving a path is an integral step in the path-creation process. You can store every path you draw and keep it on hand in case you decide later to select an area again. Because Photoshop defines paths as compact mathematical equations, they take up virtually no room when you save an image to disk.

You save one or more paths by choosing the Save Path command from the Paths palette menu or by simply double-clicking on the Work Path item in the scrolling list. After you perform the save operation, the path name appears in upright characters. A path name can include any number of separate paths. In fact, if you save a path and then set about drawing another one, Photoshop automatically adds that path in with the saved path. To start a new path under a new name, you first must hide the existing path. Or click on the new path icon — the little page at the bottom of the Paths palette — to establish an independent path.

To hide all paths, click in the empty portion of the scrolling list below the last saved path name. You can even hide unsaved paths in this way. If you hide an unsaved path and then begin drawing a new one, however, the unsaved path is deleted, never to return again.

Swapping Paths with Illustrator

Photoshop 4 can swap paths directly with Illustrator 6 (and later). (According to Macromedia, you'll also be able to do this with FreeHand 7.) All you must do is copy a path to the Clipboard and paste it into the other program. This special cross-application compatibility feature expands and simplifies a variety of path-editing functions. For example, suppose you want to scale and rotate a path:

- ☞ One way to pull off the feat is to duplicate the image (by choosing Image ⇨ Duplicate). Then scale the entire duplicated image using Image ⇨ Image Size and rotate it with Image ⇨ Rotate Canvas ⇨ Arbitrary. Next, drag the transformed path back into the original image.

- ☞ If you own Illustrator, however, a better way exists. Select the path in Photoshop with the arrow tool and copy it to the Clipboard (⌘-C). Then switch to Illustrator, paste the path, and edit it as desired. About 95 percent of Illustrator's capabilities are devoted to the task of editing paths — you have far more options at your disposal than in Photoshop. Then when you finish, copy the path again, switch to Photoshop, and paste.

When you paste an Illustrator path into Photoshop, the dialog box shown in Figure 11-33 appears offering you the option of rendering the path to pixels — just as you can render an Illustrator EPS document using File ⇨ Open — or keeping the path information intact. In other words, you can either turn the path into an image or bring it in as a path, which you can then use as a selection outline. If you want to save the path in the Paths palette, be sure to select the Paste As Paths option.

Figure 11-33
When pasting a path copied from Illustrator, Photoshop greets you with this dialog box.

Things can get pretty muddled in the Clipboard, especially when you're switching applications. If you copy something from Illustrator, but the Paste command is dimmed inside Photoshop, you may be able to force the issue a little. Inside Illustrator, press the Option key and choose Edit ⇨ Copy. This is intended to copy a PICT version of the path, but it sometimes has the added benefit of waking up the Clipboard to the fact that, yes indeed, something exists in here that Photoshop can use. (Computers are kind of slow sometimes. Every once in a while, you have to give them a kick in the pants.)

You can copy paths from Photoshop and paste them into Illustrator, regardless of the setting of the Export Clipboard check box in the Preferences dialog box. That option affects pixels only. Paths are so tiny that Photoshop always exports them.

Exporting to Illustrator

If you don't have enough memory to run both Illustrator and Photoshop at the same time, you can export Photoshop paths to disk and then open them in Illustrator. To export all paths in the current image, choose File ⇨ Export ⇨ Paths to Illustrator. Photoshop saves the paths as a fully editable Illustrator document. This scheme allows you to exactly trace images with paths in Photoshop and then combine those paths as objects with the exported EPS version of the image inside Illustrator. Whereas tracing an image in Illustrator can prove a little tricky because of resolution differences and other previewing limitations, you can trace images in Photoshop as accurately as you like.

 Unfortunately, Illustrator provides no equivalent function for exporting paths for use in Photoshop, nor can Photoshop open Illustrator documents from disk and interpret them as paths. This means the Clipboard is the only way to take a path created or edited in Illustrator and use it in Photoshop.

 Only about half of Photoshop users own Illustrator. Meanwhile, close to 90 percent of Illustrator users own Photoshop. That's why I've chosen to cover the special relationship between Illustrator and Photoshop in depth in Chapter 13 of my Illustrator book. Its prosaic title is *The Illustrator 6 Book* (1996, Peachpit Press). You'll find out more about using Photoshop with FreeHand in the *Macworld FreeHand 7 Bible* (1997, IDG Books Worldwide).

Retaining transparent areas in an image

When you import an image into Illustrator, QuarkXPress, or some other object-oriented program, the image comes in as a rectangle with opaque pixels. Even if the image appeared partially transparent in Photoshop — on a layer, for example — the pixels are filled with white or some other color in the receiving application. These same object-oriented applications, however, do allow you to mask away portions of an image you want to appear transparent by establishing a *clipping path*. Elements that lie inside the clipping path are opaque; elements outside the clipping path are transparent. Photoshop lets you export an image in the EPS format with an object-oriented clipping path intact. When you import the image into the object-oriented program, it appears premasked with a perfectly smooth perimeter, as illustrated by the clipped image in Figure 11-34.

Figure 11-34
I drew one path around the perimeter of the skull and another around the eye socket. After defining the paths as clipping paths, I exported the image in the EPS format, imported it into Illustrator, and set it against a black background for contrast.

The following steps explain how to assign a set of saved paths as clipping paths.

STEPS   **Saving an Image with Clipping Paths**

Step 1.   **Draw one or more paths around the portions of the image you want to appear opaque.** Areas outside the paths will be transparent.

Step 2.   **Save the paths.** Double-click on the Work Path name in the Paths palette, enter a name, and press Return. (Try to use a name that will make sense three years from now when you have to revisit this document and need to figure out what the heck you did.)

Step 3.   **Choose the Clipping Path command from the Paths palette menu.** Photoshop displays a dialog box that lets you select the saved paths you want to assign as the clipping path.

If you like, enter a value into the Flatness option box. This option permits you to simplify the clipping paths by printing otherwise fluid curves as polygons. The Flatness value represents the distance — between 0.2 and 100, in printer pixels — that the polygon may vary from the true mathematical curve. A higher value leads to a polygon with fewer sides. This means it looks chunkier, but it also prints more quickly. I recommend a value of 2 or 3. My technical editor, Ted Padova, who runs a service bureau in Ventura, CA, tells me you can go as high as 7 when printing to an imagesetter without seeing the straight edges. I strongly suspect, though, it depends on how much of a perfectionist you are.

Step 4. **Choose File ⇨ Save As and select Photoshop EPS from the Format pop-up menu.** The EPS Format dialog box (shown back in Figure 4-9 of Chapter 4) now includes a Clipping Path pop-up menu. As long as the proper path name appears in the menu — it will if you followed the previous step — you can press the Return key. An EPS image with masked transparencies is saved to disk.

 PageMaker is capable of handling clipping paths in the TIFF format. If you plan on placing the image in PageMaker, you can save the image in TIFF instead of EPS in Step 4.

Figure 11-35 shows an enhanced version of the clipped skull from Figure 11-34. In addition to exporting the image with clipping paths in the EPS format, I saved the paths to disk by choosing File ⇨ Export ⇨ Paths to Illustrator. Inside Illustrator, I used the exported paths to create the outline around the clipped image. I also used them to create the shadow behind the image. The white of the eyeball is a reduced version of the eye socket, as are the iris and pupil. The background features a bunch of flipped and reduced versions of the paths. This may look like a lot of work, but the only drawing required was to create the two initial Photoshop paths.

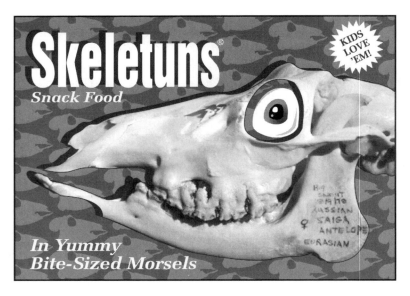

Figure 11-35
It's amazing what you can accomplish by combining scans edited in a painting program with smooth lines created in a drawing program.

 Be prepared for your images to grow by leaps and bounds when imported into Illustrator. The EPS illustration shown in Figure 11-35 consumes six times as much space on disk as the original Photoshop image saved in the TIFF format.

One more note of caution. When used in excess, clipping paths will present problems on the most sophisticated printing devices. You should only use a clipping path when it's absolutely necessary and cannot be avoided. If you want to place an image against a bitmapped background, for example, do it in Photoshop, not in QuarkXPress or PageMaker. This will invariably speed up printing and may mean the difference between whether or not a file prints successfully.

Creating Masks

CHAPTER 12

In This Chapter

- ➤ An introduction to masking
- ➤ Painting inside a selection outline
- ➤ Using the quick mask mode to modify selection outlines
- ➤ Drawing gradient selections in the quick mask mode
- ➤ Creating translucent gradient arrows
- ➤ Selecting images with the Color Range command
- ➤ Saving a selection outline to a mask channel
- ➤ Converting channels into selections
- ➤ Creating a highly accurate mask based on the image itself
- ➤ Selecting hair and other precarious details

Selecting Via Masks

Most Photoshop users don't use masks. If my personal experience is any indication, it's not just that masks necessarily seem complicated, it's that they strike most folks as being more trouble than they're worth. Like nearly everyone, when I first started using Photoshop, I couldn't even imagine a possible application for a mask. I've got my lasso tool and my magic wand. If I'm really in a rut, I can pull out my pen tool. What more could I possibly want?

Quite a bit, as it turns out. Every one of the tools I just mentioned is only moderately suited to the task of selecting images. The lasso tool lets you create free-form selections, but it can't account for differences in focus levels. The magic wand selects areas of color, but it usually leaves important colors behind, and the edges of its selection outlines often appear ragged and ugly. The pen tool is extremely precise, but it results in fairly mechanical outlines that may appear incongruous with the natural imagery they contain.

Masks offer all the benefits of the other tools. With them, you can create free-form selections and you can select areas of color, and they are amazingly precise. Masks also address all the deficiencies associated with the selection tools. They can account for different levels of focus, give you absolute control over the look of the edges, and are every bit as natural as the image itself.

In fact, a mask *is* the image itself. Masks use pixels to select pixels. Masks are your way of making Photoshop see what you see using the data inherent in the photograph. Masks permit you to devote every one of Photoshop's powerful capabilities to the task of creating a selection outline. They are without a doubt the most accurate selection mechanism available in Photoshop.

Masking defined

For those folks who aren't clear on what a *mask* is, let me take a moment to fill you in. A mask is a selection outline expressed as a grayscale image:

⮑ Selected areas appear white.

⮑ Deselected areas appear black.

⮑ Antialiased edges appear as gray pixels. Feathered edges are also expressed in shades of gray, from light gray near the selected area to dark gray near the deselected area.

Figure 12-1 shows two selection outlines and their equivalent masks. The top left example shows a rectangular selection that has been inverted (using Image ⮑ Adjust ⮑ Invert). Below it is the same selection expressed as a mask. Because the selection is hard-edged with no antialiasing or feathering, the mask appears hard-edged as well. The selected area is white and is said to be *unmasked*; the deselected area is black, or *masked*.

The top right example in Figure 12-1 shows a feathered selection outline. Again, I've inverted the selection so that you can better see the extent of the selection outline. (Marching ants can't accurately express softened edges, so the inversion helps show things off a little better.) The bottom right image is the equivalent mask. Here, the feathering effect is completely visible.

Figure 12-1
Two selection
outlines with
inverted interiors
(top) and their
equivalent masks
(bottom).

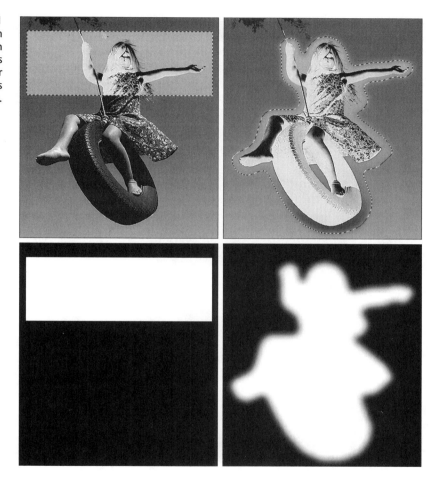

When you look at the masks along the bottom of Figure 12-1, you may wonder
where the heck the image went. One of the wonderful things about masks is that
they can be viewed independently of an image, as in Figure 12-1, or with an image,
as in Figure 12-2. In the second figure, the mask is expressed as a color overlay. By
default, the color of the overlay is a translucent red, like a conventional rubylith.
(To see the overlay in its full, natural color, see Color Plate 12-1.) Areas covered
with the rubylith are masked (deselected); areas that appear normal — without any
red tint — are unmasked (selected). When you return to the standard marching
ants mode, any changes you make to your image will affect only the unmasked
areas.

Now that you know roughly what masks are (it will become progressively clearer
throughout this chapter), the question remains, what good are they? Because a
mask is essentially an independent grayscale image, you can edit the mask using

any of the paint and edit tools discussed in Chapters 8 through 10, any of the filters discussed in Chapters 15 through 17, any of the color correction options discussed in Chapter 18, or just about any other function described in any other chapter. You can even use the selection tools, as discussed in the previous chapter. With all these features at your disposal, you can't help but create a more accurate selection outline in a shorter amount of time.

Figure 12-2
The masks from Figure 12-1 shown as they appear when viewed along with an image.

Painting and Editing inside Selections _____

Before we immerse ourselves in masking techniques, let's start with a warm-up topic, *selection masking*. When you were in grade school, perhaps you had a teacher who nagged you to color within the lines. (I didn't. My teachers were more concerned about preventing me from writing on the walls and coloring on the other kids.) At any rate, if you don't trust yourself to paint inside an image because you're afraid you'll screw it up, selection masking is the answer. Regardless of which tool you use to select an image — marquee, lasso, magic wand, or pen — you can paint or edit only the selected area. The paint can't enter the deselected (or *protected*) portions of the image, so you can't help but paint inside the lines. As a result, all selection outlines act as masks, hence the term *selection masking*.

Figures 12-3 through 12-6 show the familiar skull image subject to some pretty free-and-easy use of the paint and edit tools. (You think I ought to lay off the heavy metal or what?) The following steps describe how I created these images using a selection mask.

STEPS	Painting and Editing Inside a Selection Mask

Step 1. **I selected the slightly rotting skull of the enchanting Russian Saiga antelope.** You can see the selection outline in such golden oldies as Figures 11-18 and 11-20. If those figures are too remote, just look at the top example in Figure 12-3. For the record, I drew this selection outline using the pen tool.

Figure 12-3
After drawing a selection outline around the antelope skull (top), I inversed the selection and deleted the background (bottom).

Step 2. **I reversed the selection with the Inverse command.** I wanted to edit the area surrounding the skull, so I chose Select ⇨ Inverse (⌘-Shift-I) to reverse which areas were selected and which were not.

Step 3. **I pressed the ⌘-Delete key to fill the selected area with the background color.** In this case, the background color was white — as shown in the bottom half of Figure 12-3.

Step 4. **I painted inside the selection mask.** But before I began, I chose Select ⇨ Hide Edges (Command-H). This allowed me to paint without being distracted by those infernal marching ants. (In fact, this is one of the most essential uses for the Hide Edges command.)

Step 5. **I selected the paintbrush tool and expressed myself.** I selected the 21-pixel soft brush shape in the Brushes palette. With the foreground color set to black, I dragged the paintbrush around the perimeter of the skull to set it apart from its white background, as shown in Figure 12-4. No matter how sloppily I painted, the skull remained unscathed.

Figure 12-4
I painted inside the selection mask with a 21-pixel soft brush shape.

Step 6. **I next selected and used the smudge tool.** I set the Pressure slider bar inside the Smudge Tool Options palette to 80 percent by pressing the 8 key. I dragged from inside the skull outward 20 or so times to create a series of curlicues. I also dragged from outside the skull inward to create white gaps between the curlicues. As shown in Figure 12-5, the smudge tool can smear colors from inside the protected area, but it does not apply these colors until you go inside the selection. This is an important point to keep in mind, because it demonstrates that although the protected area is safe from all changes, the selected area may be influenced by colors from protected pixels.

Figure 12-5
Dragging with the smudge tool smeared colors from pixels outside the selection mask without changing the appearance of those pixels.

Step 7. **I double-clicked on the airbrush tool icon in the toolbox to display the Airbrush Options palette.** Then I selected the Fade check box and set the Fade value to 20, leaving the Transparent option selected in the pop-up menu. I then selected a 60-pixel soft brush shape and again dragged outward from various points along the perimeter of the skull. As demonstrated in Figure 12-6, combining airbrush and mask is as useful in Photoshop as it is in the real world.

Figure 12-6
I dragged around the skull with the airbrush to further distinguish it from its background. Pretty cool effect, huh? Well, if it's not your cup of tea, maybe you can track down a teenager who will appreciate it.

Working in the Quick Mask Mode

Selection masks give you an idea of what masks are all about, but they only scrape the surface. The rest of the discussions in this chapter revolve around using masks to define complex selection outlines.

The most straightforward environment for creating a mask is the *quick mask mode*. In the quick mask mode, a selection is expressed as a rubylith overlay. All the deselected areas in your image appear coated with red and the selected areas appear without red coating, just as shown in the middle examples of Color Plate 12-1. You can then edit the mask as desired and exit the mode to return to the standard selection outline. The quick mask mode is — as its name implies — expeditious and convenient, with none of the trappings or permanence of more conventional masks. It's kind of like a fast food restaurant — you use it when you aren't overly concerned about quality and you aim to get in and out in a hurry.

How the quick mask mode works

Typically, you'll want to at least rough out a selection with the standard selection tools before entering the quick mask mode. You can then concentrate on refining and modifying your selection inside the quick mask, rather than having to create the selection from scratch. (Naturally, this is just a rule of thumb. I violate the rule several times throughout this chapter, but only because the quick mask mode and I are such tight friends.)

To enter the quick mask mode, click on the quick mask mode icon, as I've done in Figure 12-7. Or just press the Q key. When I pressed Q after wreaking my most recent havoc on the extinct antelope skull, I got the image shown in Figure 12-7. The skull receives the mask because it is not selected. (In Figure 12-7, the mask appears as a light gray coating; on your color screen, the mask appears in red.) The area outside the skull looks just the same as it always did because it is selected and therefore not masked.

Notice that the selection outline disappears when you enter the quick mask mode. That's because it temporarily ceases to exist. Any operations that you apply affect the mask itself and leave the underlying image untouched. When you click on the marching ants mode icon (to the left of the quick mask mode icon) or again press the Q key, Photoshop converts the mask back into a selection outline and again allows you to edit the image.

Figure 12-7
Click on the quick mask mode icon (highlighted in the toolbox) to instruct Photoshop to temporarily express the selection as a grayscale image.

 If you click on the quick mask mode icon without seeing anything change on-screen, your computer isn't broken, it just means that you didn't have anything selected before you entered the mode. When nothing is selected, Photoshop allows you to edit the entire image; in other words, everything's selected. (Only a smattering of commands under the Edit, Layer, and Select menus require something to be selected before they work.) If everything is selected, the mask is white. Therefore, the quick mask overlay is transparent and you don't see any difference on-screen. This is another reason why it's better to select something before you enter the quick mask mode — so you get an immediate sense that you're accomplishing something.

Once in the quick mask mode, you can edit the mask in the following ways:

- **Subtracting from a selection:** Paint with black to add red coating and thus deselect areas of the image, as demonstrated in the top half of Figure 12-8. This means that you can selectively protect portions of your image by merely painting over them.

- **Adding to a selection:** Paint with white to remove red coating and thus add to the selection outline. You can use the eraser tool to whittle away at the masked area (assuming that the background color is set to white). Or you can swap the foreground and background colors so that you can paint in white with one of the painting tools.

Figure 12-8
After subtracting some of the selected area inside the eye socket by painting in black with the paintbrush tool (top), I feathered the outline by painting with white, using a soft 45-pixel brush shape (bottom).

- **Adding feathered selections:** If you paint with a shade of gray, you add feathered selections. You also can feather an outline by painting with black or white with a very soft brush shape, as shown in the bottom image in Figure 12-8.

- **Clone selection outlines:** You can clone a selection outline by selecting it with one of the standard selection tools and ⌘-Option-dragging it to a new location in the image, as shown in Figure 12-9. Although I use the lasso tool in the figure, the magic wand tool also works well for this purpose. To select an antialiased selection outline with the wand tool, set the tolerance to about 10 and be sure that the Anti-aliased check box is active. Then click inside the selection. It's that easy.

- **Transform selection outlines:** That's right, the quick mask mode provides a method for transforming a selection outline independently of its contents. Just enter the quick mask mode, select the mask using one of the standard selection tools, and transform it by choosing Layer ⇨ Free Transform or one of the commands from the Layer ⇨ Transform submenu. (I discuss these commands in a fair amount of detail in Chapter 13.)

Figure 12-9
To clone the eye socket selection, I lassoed around it (top) and ⌘-Option-dragged it (bottom).

These are just a few of the unique effects you can achieve by editing a selection in the quick mask mode. Others involve tools and capabilities I haven't yet discussed, such as filters and color corrections.

When you finish editing your selection outlines, click on the marching ants mode icon (just to the left of the quick mask mode icon) or just press the Q key again to return to the marching ants mode. Your selection outlines again appear flanked by marching ants, and all tools and commands return to their normal image-editing functions. Figure 12-10 shows the results of switching to the marching ants mode and deleting the contents of the selection outlines created in the last examples of the previous two figures.

Figure 12-10
The results of deleting the regions selected in the final examples of Figures 12-8 (top) and 12-9 (bottom). Kind of makes me want to rent *It's the Great Pumpkin, Charlie Brown*. I mean, who wouldn't give this antelope a rock?

As demonstrated in the top example of Figure 12-10, the quick mask mode offers a splendid environment for feathering one selection outline while leaving another hard-edged or antialiased. Granted, because most selection tools offer built-in feathering options, you can accomplish this task without resorting to the quick mask mode. But the quick mask mode lets you change feathering selectively after drawing selection outlines, something you can't accomplish with Select ➪ Feather. It also lets you see exactly what you're doing. Kind of makes those marching ants look piddly and insignificant, huh?

Changing the red coating

By default, the protected region of an image appears in translucent red in the quick mask mode, but if your image contains a lot of red, the mask can be difficult to see. Luckily, you can change it to any color and any degree of opacity that you like. To do so, double-click on the quick mask icon in the toolbox (or double-click on the Quick Mask item in the Channels palette) to display the dialog box shown in Figure 12-11.

↪ **Color Indicates:** Select the Selected Areas option to reverse the color coating — that is, to cover the selected areas in a translucent coat of red and view the deselected areas normally. Select the Masked Areas option (the default setting) to cover the deselected areas in color.

 You can reverse the color coating without ever entering the Quick Mask Options dialog box. Simply Option-click on the quick mask icon in the toolbox to toggle between coating the masked or selected portions of the image. The icon itself changes to reflect your choice.

Figure 12-11
Double-click on the quick mask mode icon to access the Quick Mask Options dialog box. You then can change the color and opacity of the protected or selected areas when viewed in the quick mask mode.

↪ **Color:** Click on the Color icon to display the Color Picker dialog box and select a different color coating. (If you don't know how to use this dialog box, see the "Using the Color Picker" section of Chapter 5.) You can lift a color from the image with the eyedropper after the Color Picker dialog box comes up, but you probably want to use a color that's not in the image so you can better see the mask.

↪ **Opacity:** Enter a value to change the opacity of the translucent color that coats the image. A value of 100 percent is absolutely opaque.

Change the color coating to achieve the most acceptable balance between being able to view and edit your selection and being able to view your image. For example, the default red coating shows up badly on my grayscale screen shots, so I changed the color coating to light blue and the Opacity value to 65 percent before shooting the screens featured in Figures 12-7 through 12-9.

Gradations as masks

If you think that the Feather command is a hot tool for creating softened selection outlines, wait until you get a load of gradations in the quick mask mode. There's simply no better way to create fading effects than selecting an image with the gradient tool.

Fading an image

Consider the Capitol building shown in Figure 12-12. Whether you care for the folks that reside inside — personally, I'm sick of all this cynicism about the government, but I'm happy to exploit it for a few cheap laughs — you have to admit, that's one beautiful building. Still, you might reckon that the House would be even more impressive if it were to fade into view out of a river of hot Hawaiian lava, like the one to the Capitol's immediate right. Well, you're in luck, because this is one of the easiest effects to pull off in Photoshop.

Figure 12-12
You can use the gradient tool in the quick mask mode to make the Capitol (left) fade out of the lava (right).

Switch to the quick mask mode by pressing the Q key. Then use the gradient tool to draw a linear gradation from black to white. (You can set the gradient style in the Gradient Tool Options palette to either Foreground to Background, or Black, White.) The white portion of the gradation represents the area that you want to select. I decided to select the top portion of the Capitol, so I drew the gradation from the top of the second tier to the top of the flag, as shown in the first example of Figure 12-13. Because the gradient line is a little hard to see, I've added a little arrow to show the direction of the drag. (To see the mask in full color, check out the first image in Color Plate 12-2.)

Figure 12-13
After drawing a linear gra-dation in the quick mask mode near the center of the image (left), I hid the image and applied the Add Noise filter with an Amount of 24 (right)

Banding can be a problem when you use a gradation as a mask. Therefore, to elimi-nate the banding effect, apply the Add Noise filter at a low setting several times. To create the right example in Figure 12-13, I applied Add Noise using an Amount value of 24 and the Uniform distribution option.

Notice in the right example of Figure 12-13 that I've hidden the image so only the mask is visible. As the figure shows, the Channels palette lists the *Quick Mask* in italics. This is because Photoshop regards the quick mask as a temporary channel. You can hide the image and view the mask in black and white by clicking on the eyeball in front of the color composite view, in this case RGB. Or just press the tilde key (~) to hide the image. Press tilde again to view mask and image together.

To apply the gradation as a selection, return to the marching ants mode by again pressing Q. I then ⌘-dragged the selected portion of the Capitol and dropped it into the lava image to achieve the effect shown in Figure 12-14. I could say something about Congress rising up from the ashes, but I have no idea what I'd mean by that. For the color version of this splendid image, see Color Plate 12-2.

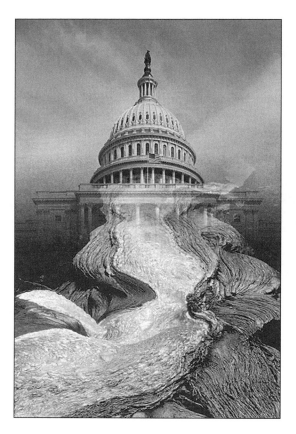

Figure 12-14
The result of selecting the top portion of the Capitol using a gradation mask, and then ⌘-dragging and dropping it into the lava image.

Applying special effects gradually

You also can use gradations in the quick mask mode to taper the outcomes of filters and other automated special effects. For example, I wanted to apply a filter around the edges of the Lincoln colossus that appears in Figure 12-15. I began by deselecting everything in the image (⌘-D) and switching to the quick mask mode. Then I brought up the Gradient Tool Options palette and selected the Foreground to Transparent option from the Gradient pop-up menu.

I pressed the D key to make the foreground color black and the background color white. Then I dragged with the gradient tool from each of the four edges of the image inward to create a series of short gradations that trace around the boundaries of the image, as shown in Figure 12-16. (As you can see, I've hidden the image so we're seeing the mask in black and white.) Because I've selected the Foreground to Transparent option, Photoshop adds each gradation to the last one.

Figure 12-15
This time around, my intention is to surround Lincoln with a gradual filtering effect.

Figure 12-16
Inside the quick mask mode, I dragged from each of the four edges with the gradient tool (as indicated by the arrows).

To jumble up the pixels in the mask, I applied Filter ➪ Noise ➪ Add Noise with an Amount value of 24. This is the effect that appears in Figure 12-16.

The only problem is that I want to select the outside of the image, not the inside. So I need the edges to appear black and the inside to appear white, just the opposite of what we see now. No problem. All I do is press ⌘-I (Image ➪ Adjust ➪ Invert) to invert the image. Inverting inside the quick mask produces the same effect as applying Select ➪ Inverse to a selection.

Finally, I switched back to the marching ants mode by again pressing Q. Then I applied Filter ➪ Render ➪ Clouds to get the atmospheric effect you see in Figure 12-17. Yes, he's Abe the Illusionist — Lincoln as you've never seen him before! Once he gets to Vegas, he'll wipe the floor with David Copperfield.

Figure 12-17
After switching back to the marching ants mode, I chose Filter ➪ Render ➪ Clouds to create the foggy effect shown here.

Notice the corners in the mask in Figure 12-16? These corners are rounded, but you can achieve all kinds of different corner effects with the gradient tool. For harsher corners, select the Foreground to Background option and set the brush mode to Lighten. For some *really* unusual corner treatments, try out the Difference and Exclusion brush modes. Very wild stuff.

Creating gradient arrows

A couple of sections ago, Figure 12-13 featured an upward-pointing arrow that faded into view with a dark halo around it. I could have created this arrowhead in a drawing program to get nice sharp points and smooth outlines. But I chose to create it in Photoshop so I could take advantage of two options that drawing programs don't offer: gradient lines and halos. Naturally, you can create both in the quick mask mode.

The following steps explain how to add cool fading arrows to any image, as demonstrated in Figures 12-18 and 12-19. The steps involve the quick mask mode, the gradient tool, the Fill command, and good old Delete.

STEPS   Creating Fading Arrows with Halos

Step 1.   **Save your image (⌘-S).** This is very important — you'll be reverting to the deleted image later.

Step 2.   **Deselect everything (⌘-D) and switch to the quick mask mode (Q).** The image should appear absolutely normal.

Step 3.   **Select the line tool (N) and press Return.** Adjust the line weight and arrowhead settings in the Line Tool Options palette to fit your needs. To create my first arrows (the ones that come inward from the corners in Figure 12-19), I set the Line Width value to 20 and the Width, Length, and Concavity values in the Arrowhead Shape dialog box to 400, 600, and 20 respectively.

Step 4.   **Press D to switch to the default colors.**

Step 5.   **Draw your line, which will show up in red.** If you don't get it right the first time — as is often the case with this tool — just press ⌘-Z and try again. The beauty of drawing a line in the quick mask mode is that you can edit it after the fact without damaging the image. (You could also do the same on a separate layer, but the quick mask mode affords you a little more flexibility in this specific exercise.)

Step 6.   **Select the gradient tool (G) and press Return.** Make sure that the Gradient option in the Options palette is set to Foreground to Background, the Type option is set to Linear, and the Opacity slider is set to 100 percent. Then choose Lighten from the brush mode's pop-up menu.

Step 7.   **Use the gradient tool to fade the base of the line.** Drag with the gradient tool from the point at which you want the line to begin to fade, down to the base of the line. Try to make the direction of your drag parallel to the line itself, thus ensuring a smooth fade. The first image in Figure 12-18 shows me in the progress of dragging along one of my arrows with the gradient tool. The small white arrow shows the direction of my drag. (The black line shows the actual cursor that you see on-screen.) The second image shows the result of the drag.

Figure 12-18
Drag from the point at which you want the arrow to begin fading to the base of the line (left) parallel to the line itself (indicated here by the white arrow) to fade the line out (right).

Step 8.   **Choose Image ⇨ Adjust ⇨ Invert (⌘-I).** This inverts the quick mask, thus making the arrow the selected area.

Step 9.   **Copy the quick mask to a separate channel.** Drag the *Quick Mask* item in the Channels palette onto the little page icon at the bottom of the palette to copy the quick mask to a permanent mask channel. You'll need it again.

Step 10.   **Press Q to switch back to the marching ants mode.** Your arrow appears as a selection outline.

Step 11.   **Expand the selection to create the halo.** Choose Select ⇨ Modify ⇨ Expand and enter the desired value, based on the size and resolution of your image. I entered 6 to expand the selection outline 6 pixels.

Step 12.   **Choose Select ⇨ Feather (⌘-Shift-D).** Enter the same value and press Return.

Step 13.   **Fill the selection with white for a light halo, or black for a dark one.** I wanted a white halo, so I pressed D to switch to the default foreground and background colors. Then I press ⌘-Delete to fill the selection with white.

Step 14.   **⌘-click on the Quick Mask Copy item in the Channels palette.** This regains your original arrow-shaped selection outline. (I explain channel masks in detail later in this chapter, but for now, just ⌘-click.)

Step 15.   **Press Shift-Delete to bring up the Fill dialog box.** Then select Saved from the Use pop-up menu to revert the portion of the image inside the arrows and press Return.

Step 16.   **Float the selection.** Press ⌘-Option-up arrow to nudge, clone, and float the selection, then press down arrow to nudge it back into place.

Change the foreground color to your favorite color and press Option-Delete to fill the selection.

Step 17. **Choose Multiply from the blend mode pop-up menu in the upper left corner of the Layers palette.** This burns the colored arrow into the image. Then adjust the Opacity slider to the desired level. I pressed the 4 key to change the Opacity to 40 percent.

After that, I just kept adding more and more arrows by repeating the process. Every once in a while I saved the image so that I could create arrows on top of arrows. Most notably, I saved the image before adding the last, big arrow that shoots up from the bottom. Then when I filled the arrow with the saved version, I brought back bits and pieces of a couple of the other arrows. (Had I not first saved the image, the arrow fragments behind the big arrow would have disappeared.)

Figure 12-19
I don't know whether this guy's in store for a cold front or what, but if you ever need to annotate an image with arrows, this gradient-arrowhead trick is certainly the way to do it.

Generating Masks Automatically

Another convenient method for creating a mask is the Color Range command under the Select menu. This command permits you to generate selections based on color ranges. You use the familiar eyedropper cursor to specify colors that should be considered for selection, and other colors that you want to rule out. It's a lot like the magic wand tool, except it permits you to select colors with more precision and change the tolerance of the selection on the fly.

Using the Color Range command

When you choose Select ⇨ Color Range, Photoshop displays the Color Range dialog box shown in Figure 12-20. Like the magic wand combined with the Similar command, Color Range selects areas of related color all across the image, whether the colors are immediate neighbors or not. You click in the image window to select and deselect colors, just as you do with the wand. But rather than adjusting a Tolerance value before you use the tool, you adjust a Fuzziness option any old time you like. Photoshop dynamically updates the selection according to the new value. Just think of it as the magic wand on steroids.

 So why didn't the folks at Adobe merely enhance the functionality of the magic wand rather than adding this strange command? The Color Range dialog box offers a preview of the mask — something a tool can't do — which is pretty essential for gauging the accuracy of your selection. And the magic wand is convenient, if nothing else. If Adobe were to combine the two functions, you would lose functionality.

Figure 12-20
The Color Range dialog box allows you to generate a mask by dragging with the eyedropper tool and adjusting the Fuzziness option.

Notice that when you move your cursor outside the Color Range dialog box, it changes to an eyedropper. Click with the eyedropper to specify the color on which you want to base the selection — which I call the *base color* — just as if you were using the magic wand. Alternatively, you can click inside the preview area, labeled in Figure 12-20. In either case, the preview area updates to show the resulting mask.

You can also do the following:

∽ **Add colors to the selection:** To add base colors to the selection, select the add color tool inside the Color Range dialog box and click inside the image window or preview area. You can also access the tool while the standard eyedropper is selected by Shift-clicking (just as you Shift-click with the magic wand to add colors to a selection). You can even Shift-drag with the eyedropper to add multiple colors in a single pass, something you can't do with the wand tool.

∽ **Remove colors from the selection:** To remove base colors from the selection, click with the remove color tool or Option-click with the eyedropper. You can also drag or Option-drag to remove many colors at a time.

 If adding or removing a color sends your selection careening in the wrong direction, just press ⌘-Z. Yes, the Undo command works inside the Color Range dialog box just as well as out of it.

∽ **Adjust the Fuzziness value:** This option resembles the Tolerance value in the Magic Wand Options palette in that it determines the range of colors that will be selected beyond the ones on which you click. Raise the Fuzziness value to expand the selected area; lower the value to contract the selection. A value of 0 selects the clicked-on color only. Unlike changes to Tolerance, however, changing the Fuzziness value adjusts the selection on the fly; no repeat clicking is required, as it is with the wand tool.

Fuzziness and Tolerance also differ in the kind of selection outlines they generate. Tolerance entirely selects all colors within the specified range and adds antialiased edges. If the selection were a mask, most of it would be white with a few gray pixels around the perimeter. By contrast, Fuzziness entirely selects only the colors on which you click and Shift-click and partially selects the other colors in the range. That's why most of the mask is expressed in shades of gray. The light grays in the mask represent the most similar colors; the dark grays represent the least similar pixels that still fall within the Fuzziness range. The result is a tapering, gradual selection that's much more likely to produce natural results.

∽ **Reverse the selection:** Select the Invert check box to reverse the selection, changing black to white and white to black. As when using the magic wand, it may be easier to isolate the area you don't want to select than the area you do want to select. When you encounter such a situation, select Invert.

∽ **Toggle the preview area:** Use the two radio buttons below the preview area to control the preview's contents. If you select the first option, Selection, you see the mask that will be generated when you press Return. If you select the Image option, the preview shows a reduced version of the image.

You can toggle between the two previews by pressing and holding the ⌘ key. My advice is to leave the option set to Selection and press the ⌘ key when you want to view the image.

✎ **Control the contents of the image window:** The Selection Preview pop-up menu at the bottom of the dialog box lets you change what you see in the image window. Leave the option set to None — the default setting — to view the image normally in the image window. Select Grayscale to see the mask on its own. Select Quick Mask to see the mask and image together. Select Black Matte or White Matte to see what the selection would look like against a black or white background.

Though they may sound weird, the Matte options allow you to get an accurate picture of how the selected image will mesh with a different background. Figure 12-21 shows Lincoln's head at top with the grayscale mask on the right. The mask calls for the shadows in Lincoln's face to be selected, with the highlights deselected. The two Matte views help you see how this particular selection looks against two backgrounds as different as night and day. Use the Fuzziness option in combination with Black Matte or White Matte to come up with a softness setting that will ensure a smooth transition.

✎ **Select by predefined colors:** Choose an option from the Select pop-up menu at the top of the dialog box to specify the means of selecting a base color. If you choose any option besides Sampled Colors, the Fuzziness option and eyedropper tools become dimmed to show they are no longer operable. Rather, Photoshop selects colors based on their relationship to a predefined color. For example, if you select Red, the program entirely selects red and partially selects other colors based on the amount of red they contain. Colors composed exclusively of blue and green are not selected.

The most useful option in this pop-up menu is Out of Gamut, which selects all the colors in an RGB or Lab image that fall outside the CMYK color space. You can use this option to select and modify the out-of-gamut colors before converting an image to CMYK.

✎ **Load and save settings:** Click on the Save button to save the current settings to disk. Click on Load to open a saved settings file.

When you define the mask to your satisfaction, click on the OK button or press Return to generate the selection outline. Although the Color Range command is more flexible than the magic wand, you can no more expect it to generate perfect selections than any other automated tool. Therefore, after Photoshop draws the selection outline, you'll probably want to switch to the quick mask mode and paint and edit the mask to taste.

Figure 12-21
Selecting an option from the
Selection Preview pop-up menu
changes the way the Color Range
command previews the selection in
the image window.

None

Grayscale

Black Matte

White Matte

If you learn nothing else about the Color Range dialog box, at least learn to use the Fuzziness option and the eyedropper tools. There are basically two ways to approach these options. If you want to create a diffused selection with gradual edges, set the Fuzziness option to a high value — 60 or more — and click and Shift-click only two or three times with the eyedropper. To create a more precise selection, enter a Fuzziness of 40 or lower and Shift- and Option-drag with the eyedropper until you get the exact colors you want.

Figure 12-22 shows some sample results. To create the left images, I clicked with the eyedropper tool once in Lincoln's face and set the Fuzziness to 160. To create the right images, I lowered the Fuzziness value to 20; then I clicked, Shift-clicked, and Option-clicked with the eyedropper to lift exactly the colors I wanted. The top examples show the effects of stroking the selections, first with 6-pixel white strokes, then with 2-pixel black ones. In the two bottom examples, I copied the selections and pasted them against an identical background of — what else? — the Lincoln Memorial. In all four cases, the higher Fuzziness value yields more generalized and softer results; the lower value results in a more exact but harsher selection.

Fuzziness: 160

Fuzziness: 20

Figure 12-22
After creating two selections with the Color Range command — one with a high Fuzziness value (left) and one with a low one (right), I alternately stroked the selections (top) and pasted them against a different background (bottom).

A few helpful Color Range hints

You can limit the portion of an image that Select ➪ Color Range affects by selecting part of the image before choosing the command. When a selection exists, the Color Range command masks only those pixels that fall inside it. Even the preview area reflects your selection. Try it and see.

You can also add or subtract from an existing selection using the Color Range command. Press the Shift key when choosing Select ➪ Color Range to add to a selection. Press the Option key when choosing Color Range to subtract from a selection.

If you get hopelessly lost when creating your selection and you can't figure out what to select and what to deselect, just click with the eyedropper tool to start over. This clears all the colors from the selection except the one you click on. Alternatively, you can press the Option key to change the Cancel button to a Reset button. Option-click on the button to return the settings inside the dialog box to those in force when you first chose Select ⇨ Color Range.

Creating an Independent Mask Channel

The problem with masks generated via the quick mask mode and Color Range command is that they're here one day and gone the next. Photoshop is no more prepared to remember them than it is a lasso or wand selection.

Most of the time, that's okay. You'll only use the selection once, so there's no reason to sweat it. But what if the selection takes you a long time to create? What if, after a quarter hour of Shift-clicking here and Option-dragging there, adding a few strokes in the quick mask mode, and getting the selection outline exactly right, a slight twitch pulses through your finger and you inadvertently double-click in the image window with the lasso tool? Good job — not only have you deselected the selection, you've eliminated your only chance to undo the deselection. To coin a euphemism from the world of women's lingerie, you're hosed.

For this reason, you'll probably want to back up your selection if you've spent any amount of time on it. Even if you're in the middle of creating the selection that you've been grinding at for quite a while, stop and take a moment to save it before all heck breaks loose. You wouldn't let a half an hour of image-editing go by without saving, and the rules don't change just because you're working on a selection.

Saving a selection outline to a mask channel

The following steps describe how to back up a selection to an independent *mask channel*, which is any channel above and beyond those required to represent a grayscale or color image. Mask channels are saved along with the image itself, making it a safe and sturdy solution.

STEPS   **Transferring a Selection to an Independent Channel**

Step 1.   **Convert the selection to a mask channel.** One way to do this is to choose Select ⇨ Save Selection, which allows you to save the selection as a mask. The dialog box shown in Figure 12-23 appears, asking you where you want to put the mask. In most cases, you'll want to save the mask to a separate channel inside the current image. To do so, make sure that the name of the current image appears in the Document pop-up menu and then select New from the Channel pop-up menu and press Return.

Figure 12-23
The Save Selection dialog box lets you convert your selection outline to a mask and save it to a new or existing channel.

If you have an old channel that you want to replace, select the channel's name from the Channel pop-up menu. The radio buttons at the bottom of the dialog box become available, allowing you to add the mask to the channel, subtract it, or intersect it. These radio buttons work just like the equivalent options that appear when you make a path into a selection outline (as discussed in the previous chapter), but they blend the masks together instead. The result is the same as if you were adding, subtracting, or intersecting selection outlines, except that it's expressed as a mask.

Alternatively, you can save the mask to a new document all its own. To do this, choose New from the Document pop-up menu and press Return.

Man, what a lot of options! If you just want to save the selection to a new channel and be done with it, you needn't bother with Select ▷ Save Selection. Just click on the make channel icon at the bottom of the Channels palette (labeled in Figure 12-23). Photoshop automatically creates a new channel, converts the selection to a mask, and places the mask in the channel.

Regardless of which of these many methods you choose, your selection outline remains intact.

Step 2.   **View the mask in the Channels palette.** To do so, click on the appropriate channel name in the Channels palette — presumably #2 if you're editing a grayscale image or #4 if you're working in the RGB or Lab mode. In Figure 12-23, I replaced the contents of a channel called Existing Mask, so this is where my mask now resides.

This step isn't the least bit mandatory. It just permits you to see your mask and generally familiarize yourself with how masks look. Remember, white represents selection, black is deselected, and gray is partial selection.

Step 3.   **Return to the standard image-editing mode by clicking on the first channel name from the Channels palette.** Better yet, press ⌘-1 if you're editing a grayscale image or ⌘-tilde (~) if the image is in color.

Step 4.   **Save the image to disk to store the selection permanently.** Only the PICT, TIFF, the World Wide Web formats GIF and PNG, and native Photoshop formats suffice for this purpose. And just the TIFF and native formats can handle more than four channels, both accommodating up to 24 channels in all. I generally use the TIFF format when saving images with masks — unless the image contains layers, in which case you have no choice but to save in the Photoshop format.

If you performed the steps in the "Creating gradient arrows" section earlier in this chapter, you know that you can also save a quick mask to its own channel for later use. But in case you missed those steps — or you're saving them for a special occasion — here's how it works. When you enter the quick mask mode, the Channels palette displays an item called *Quick Mask*. The italic letters show that the channel is temporary and will not be saved with the image. To clone it to a permanent channel, just drag the Quick Mask item onto the new channel icon at the bottom of the Channels palette (the little page labeled in Figure 12-23). Now save the image to the PICT, TIFF, or Photoshop format, and you're backed up.

Converting a mask to a selection

To later retrieve your selection, choose Select ➪ Load Selection. A dialog box nearly identical to the one shown in Figure 12-23 appears, except for the addition of an Invert check box. Select the document and channel that contains the mask you want to use. You can add it to a current selection, subtract it, or intersect it. Select the Invert option if you want to reverse the selected and deselected portions of the mask.

Want to avoid the Load Selection command? Just ⌘-click on the channel name in the Channels palette that contains the mask you want to use. (Note that this has changed in Photoshop 4 — you used to Option-click in Version 3.) For example, if I ⌘-clicked on the Existing Mask item in Figure 12-23, Photoshop would load the equivalent selection outline into the image window.

But wait, there's more:

- ↝ You can press ⌘-Option plus the channel number to convert the channel to a selection. For example, ⌘-Option-4 would convert the Existing Mask channel shown in the figure.

- ↝ You can also select the channel and click on the far left mask selection icon at the bottom of the Channels palette. But for my money, that takes too much effort.

- ↝ To add a mask to the current selection outline, Shift-⌘-click on the channel name in the Channels palette.

- ↝ ⌘-Option-click on a channel name to subtract the mask from the selection.

- ↝ And ⌘-Shift-Option-click to find the intersection.

You can convert color channels to selections as well as mask channels. For example, if you wanted to select the black pixels in a piece of scanned line art, you'd just ⌘-click on the first item in the Channels palette. This selects the white pixels; press ⌘-Shift-I (or choose Select ➪ Inverse) to reverse the selection to the black pixels.

Viewing mask and image

Photoshop lets you view any mask channel along with an image, just as you can view mask and image together in the quick mask mode. To do so, click in the first column of the Channels palette to toggle the display of the eyeball icon. An eyeball in front of a channel name indicates that you can see that channel. If you are currently viewing the image, for example, click in front of the mask channel name to view the mask as a translucent color coating, again as in the quick mask mode. Alternatively, if the contents of the mask channel appear by themselves on-screen, click in front of the image name to display it as well.

Using a mask channel is different from using the quick mask mode in that you can edit either the image or mask channel when viewing the two together. You can even edit two or more masks at once. To decide which channel you want to edit, click on the channel name in the palette. To edit two channels at once, click on one and Shift-click on another. All active channel names appear gray.

You can change the color and opacity of each mask independently of other mask channels and the quick mask mode. Click on the mask channel name to select one channel only and then choose the Channel Options command from the Channels palette menu. Or just double-click on the mask channel name. (This is not an option when you're editing a standard color channel.) A dialog box similar to the one shown back in Figure 12-11 appears, but this one contains a Name option box so that you can change the name of the mask channel. You can then edit the color overlay as described in the "Changing the red coating" section earlier in this chapter.

 If you ever need to edit a selection outline inside the mask channel using paint and edit tools, click on the quick mask mode icon in the toolbox. It may sound a little incestuous — like a play within a play, perhaps — but you can access the quick mask mode even when working within a mask channel. Just make sure that the mask channel color is different from the quick mask color so that you can tell what's going on.

Building a Mask from an Image

Okay, so far everything's been pretty straightforward. Now it's time to see how the professionals do it. This final section in the chapter explains every step required to create a mask for a complex image — updated especially for this edition of the book. Here's how to select the image you never thought you could select, complete with wispy little details like hair.

Take a gander at Figure 12-24 and you'll see what I mean. I chose this subject not for her good looks or her generous supply of freckles, but for that hair. I mean, just look at all that hair. Have you ever seen such a frightening image-editing subject in your life? Not only is this particular girl blessed with roughly 15 googol strands of hair, but every one of them is leaping out of her head at a different level of focus. Can you imagine selecting any one of them with the lasso? No way. Not only does the lasso tool lack sufficient accuracy to pull off this job, you'd be fit for an asylum by the time you finished. Furthermore, the hairs are too complex for the magic wand, and there are no definite edges for the Color Range command to latch onto.

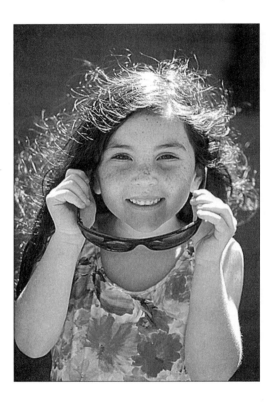

Figure 12-24
Have you ever wanted to select hair? Using masks — and a special technique I invented just for this purpose — you can.

So what's the solution? Manual masking. Though masking styles vary as widely as artistic style, there are a few tried and true formulas that work for everyone. First, you peruse the channels in an image to find the channel that will lend itself best to a mask. You're looking for high degrees of contrast, especially around the edges. Next, you copy the channel and boost the level of contrast using Image ⇨ Adjust ⇨ Levels. (Some folks prefer Image ⇨ Adjust ⇨ Curves, but Levels is more straightforward.) Then you paint inside the lines until you get the mask just the way you want it.

The only way to get a feel for masking is to try it out for yourself. The following steps explain exactly how I masked this girl and pasted her against a different background. The final result is so realistic, you'd think she was born there.

STEPS **Selecting a Monstrously Complicated Image Using a Mask**

Step 1. **Browse the color channels.** Press ⌘-1 to see the red channel, ⌘-2 for green, and ⌘-3 for blue. (This assumes you're working inside an RGB image. You can also peruse CMYK and Lab images. If you're editing a grayscale image, you only have one channel to choose from — Black.)

Figure 12-25 shows the three channels in my RGB image. Of the three, the red channel offers the most contrast between the hair, which appears very light, and the background, which appears quite dark.

Figure 12-25
Of the three color channels, the red channel offers the best contrast between hair and back-ground.

Red

Blue

Green

Step 2. **Copy the channel.** Drag the channel onto the little page icon at the bottom of the Channels palette. (I naturally copy the red channel.) Now you can work on the channel to your heart's content without harming the image itself.

Step 3. **Choose Filter ⇨ Other ⇨ High Pass.** The next thing you want to do is to force Photoshop to bring out the edges in the image so you don't have to hunt for them manually. And when you think edges, you should think filters. All of Photoshop's edge-detection prowess is packed into the Filter menu. There are several edge-detection filters available to you — Unsharp Mask, Find Edges, and many others that I'll discuss in Chapter 15 — but the best filter for finding edges inside a mask is Filter ⇨ Other ⇨ High Pass.

High Pass selectively turns an image gray. It may sound strange, but it's quite useful. The filter turns the non-edges completely gray while leaving the edges mostly intact, thus dividing edges and non-edges into different brightness camps, based on the Radius value in the High Pass dialog box. Unlike in most filters, a low Radius value produces a more pronounced effect than a high one, in effect locating more edges.

Figure 12-26 shows the original red channel on left with the result of the High Pass filter on right. I used a Radius of 10, which is a nice, moderate value. The lower you go, the more edges you find and the more work you make for yourself. A Radius of 3 is very accurate, but it'll take you an hour to fill in the mask. Granted, 10 is less accurate, but if you value your time, it's more sensible.

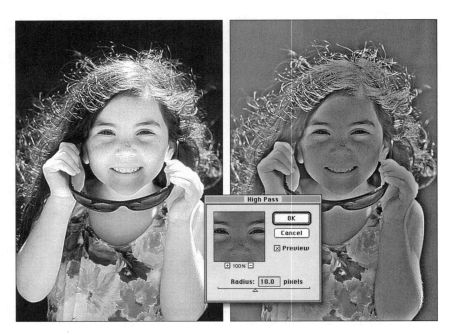

Figure 12-26
After copying the red channel (left), I apply the
High Pass filter with a Radius value of 10 to highlight
the edges in the image (right).

Step 4.   **Choose Image ⇨ Adjust ⇨ Levels (⌘-L).** After adding all that gray to the image, you need to follow it up by increasing the contrast. And the best command for enhancing contrast is Levels. Although I discuss this command in depth in Chapter 18, here's the short version: Inside the Levels dialog box, raise the first Input Levels value to make the dark colors darker, and lower the third Input Levels value to make the light colors lighter. (For now you can ignore the middle value.)

Figure 12-27 shows the result of raising the first Input Levels value to 110 and lowering the third value to 155. As you can see in the left-hand image, this gives me some excellent contrast between the white hairs and black background.

Just to demonstrate the importance of the High Pass command in these steps, I've shown what would happen if I had skipped Step 3 in the right-hand image in Figure 12-27. Here I've applied the very same Levels values as the left image, and yet the image is washed out and quite lacking in edges. Just look at that wimpy hair. It simply is not acceptable.

Figure 12-27
The results of applying the Levels command to
the mask after the High Pass step (left) and without
High Pass (right). As you can see, High Pass has a
pronounced effect on the edge detail.

Step 5. **Use the lasso tool to remove the big stuff that you don't need.** By way of High Pass and Levels, Photoshop has presented you with a complex coloring book. From here on out, it's just a matter of coloring inside the lines. To simplify things, get rid of the stuff you know you don't need. All you care about is the area where the girl meets her background — mostly hair and arms. Everything else goes to white or black.

For example, in Figure 12-28, I selected a general area inside the girl by Option-clicking with the lasso tool. Then I filled it with white by pressing ⌘-Delete. I also selected around the outside of the hair and filled it with black. At all times, I was very careful to stay about 10 to 20 pixels away from the hair and other edges; these I need to carefully brush in with the eraser.

Figure 12-28
To tidy things up a bit, I selected the general areas inside and outside the girl with the lasso tool and filled them with white or black (left). Then I painted inside the lines with the block eraser (right).

Step 6. **Erase inside the lines with the block eraser.** This is the most time-consuming part. You now have to paint inside the lines to make the edge pixels white (selected) or black (not). I like to use the block eraser, because it's a hard-edged block. See, Photoshop has already presented me with these lovely and accurate edges. I don't want to gum things up by introducing new edges with a soft paintbrush or airbrush. The block eraser is hard, you can easily see its exact boundaries, and it automatically adjusts as you zoom in and out — affecting fewer pixels at higher levels of magnification, which is just what you need. When working in a mask, the eraser always paints in the background color. So use the X key to toggle the background color between white and black.

The second example in Figure 12-28 shows the fruits of my erasing. As you can see, I had to make a few judgment calls and decide — sometimes arbitrarily — where the hair gets so thick that background imagery won't show through. You may even disagree with some of my eraser strokes. But you know what? It doesn't matter. Despite whatever flaws I may have introduced, my mask is more than accurate enough to select the girl and her unruly hair, as I'll soon demonstrate.

Step 7. **Switch to the color composite view.** Press ⌘-tilde (~). Or if you're working in a grayscale image, press ⌘-1. By the way, now is a very good time to save the image if you haven't already done so.

Step 8. **⌘-click on the mask channel to convert it to a selection.** This mask is ready to go prime time.

Step 9. **⌘-drag the selection and drop it into a different image.** Figure 12-29 shows the result of dropping the girl into a background of rolling California hills. Thanks to my mask, she looks as natural in her new environment as she did in her previous one. In fact, an uninitiated viewer might have difficulty believing that this isn't how she was originally photographed. But if you take a peak at Figure 12-24, you can confirm that Figure 12-29 is indeed an artificial composite. I lost a few strands of hair in the transition, but she can afford it.

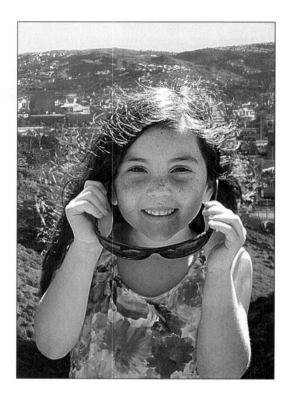

Figure 12-29
Thanks to masking, our girl has found a new life in southern California. Now she's ready to finally put those sunglasses on.

The grayscale Figure 12-29 looks great, but in all honesty, your compositions may not fare quite so well in color. When you get a chance, take a look at the first girl in Color Plate 12-3. Her hair is fringed with blue, an unavoidable holdover from her original blue background. The solution is to brush in the color from her new background. Using the paintbrush tool set to the Color brush mode, you can Option-click in the background to lift colors from the new background and then paint them into the hair. I also took the liberty of erasing a few of the more disorderly hairs, especially the dark ones above her head. (I used a soft paintbrush-style eraser, incidentally, not the block.) After a minute or two of painting and erasing, I arrived at the second girl in the color plate. Now if that isn't compositing perfection, I don't know what is.

Layers and Transformations

■ ■

In This Chapter

- ↠ Creating and cloning layers
- ↠ Floating the background layer
- ↠ Bringing layers forward and backward
- ↠ Using Photoshop's Matting commands
- ↠ Merging layers together
- ↠ Converting layers to selections
- ↠ Making drop shadows, halos, and spotlights
- ↠ Moving, scaling, and rotating layers
- ↠ Aligning images to grids and guides
- ↠ Using the Preserve Transparency option
- ↠ Working with layer masks
- ↠ Creating clipping groups
- ↠ Choosing Copy Merged and Paste Into

■ ■

Layers, Layers Everywhere _____

Layers are at once Photoshop's most overrated and most underused feature. On one hand — and let's be perfectly clear about this — they add absolutely no functionality to Photoshop. Anything you can accomplish with layers, you can also accomplish without layers. Photoshop artists have been devising fantastic compositions, applying all varieties of selections, and masking and blending images since the program was first released. Very wisely, in my opinion, Adobe has yet to make any feature exclusive to layers.

What layers add is flexibility. Because each layer in a composition is altogether independent of other layers, you can change your mind on a moment's notice. Consider Figure 13-1. Here I've compiled the ingredients for a very bad day at the doctor's office. (By golly, this may explain the reason for my chronic heartburn.) Each of the bits and pieces of hardware are located on a separate layer, all of which float above the surface of the background X-ray. Even though the pixels from the hardware blend with the X-ray and with each other, I can easily reposition and modify them as the mood strikes me. Photoshop automatically reblends the pixels on the fly.

To show what I mean, I've repositioned and transformed every single layer in the second example in Figure 13-1. The MO cartridge is smaller and rotated, the mess of chords hangs up instead of down, and the lock and key are just plain skewed. I can also exchange the order of the layers, merge layers together, and adjust their translucency until I keel over from sheer alternative overload.

Layers are also uniquely versatile. You can apply three levels of masking to layers — all of which can be in force simultaneously, if you like. You can move and transform multiple layers at a time. And, as I explain in Chapters 18 and 19, you can create a special kind of layer that adjusts the colors in the layers below it, and mix layers together using predefined mathematical calculations. Again, you can do it all without layers if you want, but with layers, the world becomes an infinitely editable place.

The basic way layers work remains the same in Photoshop 4 as it did in Version 3. The new Photoshop offers revised transformation capabilities — including numerical transformations — and you can align layers to guides and grids. But the biggest change is a matter of emphasis. Photoshop 4 forces you to use layers, where Photoshop 3 made it entirely optional. The type tool creates a new layer, dragging and dropping a selection with the move tool makes a new layer, the Paste command adds a new layer. Even Edit ⇨ Paste Into results in a new layer (now with an automatic layer mask). And as I mentioned in Chapter 11, many of the benefits of floating selections have been newly relegated to layers.

Photoshop 4 sticks layers in your face. And whether you like this change or not — I happen to think Adobe went a tad overboard — you can't argue with the logic. We should all use layers more often. Layers make it harder to make mistakes, they make it easier to make changes, and they expand your range of options. If a layer might help, there's very little reason not to add one. You may not appreciate having to use layers, but at least they're for your own good.

Figure 13-1
So that's what I did with my SCSI cable! Thanks to the flexibility of layers, you can arrange a bunch of images one way one moment (top) and quite differently the next (bottom). Layers permit you to modify a composition without sacrificing quality.

Sending a Selection to a Layer __

To its credit, Photoshop lets you establish a new layer in roughly a billion different ways. If you want to add a selected portion of one image to another image, the easiest method is to ⌘-drag the selection and drop it into its new home, as demonstrated in Figure 13-2. Photoshop makes you a new layer, lickety-split.

 Be sure to ⌘-drag or use the move tool. If you merely drag the selection with the marquee, lasso, or wand, you'll drop an empty selection outline into the new image window.

Figure 13-2
⌘-drag a selection and drop it into a different image
window to introduce the selection as a new layer.
As you can see in the Layers palette, the camera
becomes a new layer in front of the television.

When you drop the selection, your selection outline disappears. This is nothing to worry about. Now that the image resides on an independent layer, the selection outline is no longer needed. You can move the layer using the move tool — just as you would move a selection. You can even paint inside what was once the selection by selecting the Preserve Transparency check box in the Layers palette. I explain both the move tool and Preserve Transparency in greater detail throughout this chapter.

If you want to clone a selection to a new layer inside the same image window — useful when performing complex filter routines and color corrections — choose Layer ⇨ New ⇨ Layer Via Copy. Or just press ⌘-J (the keyboard shortcut for the dead-gone-dead Float command in Photoshop 3).

Other ways to make a layer

Those are just two of the many different ways to create a new layer in Photoshop. Here are a few others that you might want to be aware of:

- Copy a selection (⌘-C) and paste it into another image (⌘-V). Photoshop pastes the selection as a new layer.

- If you want to relegate a selection exclusively to a new layer, choose Layer ⇨ New ⇨ Layer Via Cut or press ⌘-Shift-J. Rather than cloning the selection, Layer Via Cut removes the selection from the background image and places it on its own layer.

- To create an empty layer — as when you want to paint a few brushstrokes without harming the original image — choose Layer ⇨ New ⇨ Layer. Or just click on the new layer icon at the bottom of the Layers palette (labeled in Figure 13-3).

- You can also convert a floating selection — one you've moved or cloned — to a new layer by clicking on the new layer icon. Or double-click on the *Floating Selection* item in the Layers palette. You can also press ⌘-Shift-J. (Both double-clicking and pressing ⌘-Shift-J display dialog boxes, asking you to name the image.)

 Incidentally, you can also create a new layer by choosing New Layer from the Layers palette menu. But this menu has become far less useful in Photoshop 4. As you can see in the wonderfully easy-to-follow Figure 13-3 — can you imagine a more illuminating piece of info art? — nearly all of the palette commands are duplicated in the Layer menu. The only unique palette command is Palette Options (circled in the figure), which lets you change the size of the thumbnails in front of the layer names.

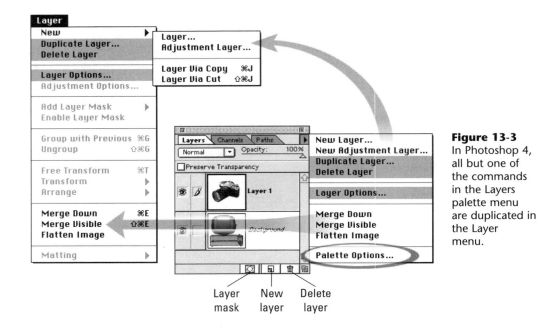

Figure 13-3
In Photoshop 4, all but one of the commands in the Layers palette menu are duplicated in the Layer menu.

When you choose either the Layer Via Copy or Layer Via Cut command, or click on the new layer icon, Photoshop automatically names the new layer for you. Unfortunately, the automatic names — Layer 1, Layer 2, and so on — are fairly meaningless and don't help to convey the contents of the layer. (Dammit, Photoshop, don't you know a camera when you see one?) If you want to specify your own name, press the Option key. Press ⌘-Option-J to clone the selection to a layer, press ⌘-Shift-Option-J to cut the selection, or Option-click on the new layer icon to create a blank layer. In any case, you'll see the dialog box shown in Figure 13-4. Enter a name for the layer and press Return. (You can ignore the other options in this dialog box for now.)

When converting a floating selection to a new layer, you can Option-double-click on the Floating Selection item to bypass the dialog box. So Option works both ways, forcing the dialog box some times and suppressing it others. The only time it produces no effect is when pasting or dropping an image. Too bad — I for one would get a lot of use out of it.

To rename a layer, just double-click on its name in the Layers palette. (You can also choose Layer ⇨ Layer Options, but what sane human being would go to all that effort?) Then enter a new name and whack that Return key.

Figure 13-4
Press the Option key to force
the display of the New Layer
dialog box, which lets you
name the new layer.

Figure 13-4
Press the Option key to force
the display of the New Layer
dialog box, which lets you
name the new layer.

New Layer	
Name: Louis, the 14th Layer	OK
Opacity: 100 % Mode: Normal ▼	Cancel
☐ Group With Previous Layer	
☐ (No neutral color exists for Normal mode.)	

Duplicating a layer

Cloning a layer isn't a simple matter of ⌘-Option-dragging, the way it is with a selection. (Again, I have to say, too bad. It really ought to be that easy.) Instead, you clone the layer and then reposition it in two separate operations.

To clone the active layer, you can choose Layer ➪ Duplicate Layer. But that's the sucker's way. The more convenient way is to drag the layer name that you want to clone onto the new layer icon at the bottom of the Layers palette.

To specify a name for the cloned layer, or to copy the layer into another image, Option-drag the layer onto the new layer icon. Always the thoughtful program, Photoshop displays the dialog box shown in Figure 13-5. You can name the cloned layer by entering something into the As option box. To jettison the layer to some other open image, choose the image name from the Document pop-up menu. Or choose New and enter the name for an entirely different image in the Name option box, as the figure shows.

Figure 13-5
You can duplicate the layer
into an entirely different
image by Option-dragging
the layer onto the new
layer icon in the Layers
palette.

Duplicate Layer	
Duplicate: Camera	OK
As: Camera	Cancel
Destination	
Document: *New* ▼	
Name: Layer on the Loose!	

Working with Layers _____

Regardless of how you create a new layer, Photoshop lists the layer along with a lit-tle thumbnail of its contents in the Layers palette. The layer appears gray to show that it's active. The little paintbrush icon in front of the layer name also indicates an active layer.

To the left of the paintbrush icon is a column of eyeballs, which invite you to tem-porarily hide and display layers. Click on an eyeball to hide the layer. Click where the eyeball used to be to bring it back and redisplay the layer. Whether hidden or displayed, all layers remain intact and ready for action.

 To view a single layer by itself, Option-click on the eyeball icon before the layer name to hide all other layers. Option-click in front of the layer again to bring all the layers back into view.

Switching between layers

You can select a different layer by clicking on its name in the Layers palette. This layer becomes active, permitting you to edit it. Only one layer may be active at a time in Photoshop — you can't Shift-click to select and edit multiple layers, I'm sorry to say.

 If your image contains several layers — like the one back in Figure 13-1 — it might prove inconvenient or even confusing to switch from one layer to another in the Layers palette. Luckily, Photoshop 4 offers a better way. With any tool, ⌘-Control-Option-click on an element in your composition to go directly to the layer that contains the element. For example, ⌘-Control-Option-clicking on the SCSI cable in Figure 13-1 would take me to the SCSI Cable layer.

Why ⌘-Control-Option-clicking? Here's how it breaks down:

- ⌘ gets you the move tool. (If the move tool is already selected, you don't have to press ⌘ — Control-Option-clicking would work just fine.)

- Control brings up the context-sensitive pop-up menu that I introduced back in Chapter 3. When you press Control and hold down the mouse button with the move tool — or ⌘-Control-click with any other tool — Photoshop dis-plays a pop-up menu that lists the layer the image is on and the background layer, as in Figure 13-6. Select the desired layer to go there.

- The Option key bypasses the pop-up menu and goes straight to the clicked layer.

Add them all up together, and you get ⌘-Control-Option-click.

Figure 13-6
⌘-Control-click on an image to view a pop-up menu. The menu lists the location of the image you've clicked and the Background layer.

Switching layers from the keyboard

You can also ascend and descend the layer stack from the keyboard:

- ⌦ **Option-]:** Press Option-right bracket to go to the next layer up in the stack. If you're already at the top layer, Photoshop takes you back around to the lowest one.

- ⌦ **Option-[:** Press Option-left bracket to go down a layer. If the background layer is active, Option-[takes you to the top layer.

- ⌦ **Shift-Option-]:** This takes you to the top layer in the image.

- ⌦ **Shift-Option-[:** This activates the background layer (or the lowest layer if there is no background).

Photoshop 3 users should note that every one of these shortcuts has changed in the new version. You used to press ⌘-bracket and ⌘-Shift-bracket. Now you use Option instead.

Understanding transparency

Although the selection outline disappears when you convert a selection to a layer, no information is lost. Photoshop retains every little nuance of the original selection outline — whether it's a jagged border, a little bit of antialiasing, or a feathered edge. Anything that wasn't selected is now transparent. The data that defines the opacity and transparency of a layer is called the *transparency mask.*

To see this transparency in action, click on the eyeball icon in front of the Background item in the Layers palette. This hides the Background layer and allows you to view the new layer by itself. In Figure 13-7, I've hidden the background TV from Figure 13-6 to view the camera on its own. The transparent areas are covered in a checkerboard pattern. Opaque areas look like the standard image, and translucent areas — where they exist — appear as a mix of image and checkerboard.

If the checkerboard pattern is hard to distinguish from the image, you can change the appearance of the pattern. Press ⌘-K and then ⌘-4 to go to the Transparency & Gamut panel of the Preferences dialog box. Then edit away (as explained back in Chapter 2).

Figure 13-7
When you hide the background layer, you see a checkerboard pattern that represents the transparent portions of the layer.

If you apply an effect to the layer while no portion of the layer is selected, Photoshop changes the opaque and translucent portions of the image but leaves the transparent region intact. For example, if you press ⌘-I (or choose Image ⇨

Adjust ⇨ Invert), Photoshop inverts the image but doesn't change a single pixel in the checkerboard area. If you click in the left column in front of the Background item to bring back the eyeball icon, you may notice a slight halo around the inverted image, but the edge pixels blend with the background image just as well as they ever did. In fact, it's exactly as if you applied the effect to a selection, as demonstrated in Figure 13-8. The only difference is that this selection is altogether independent of its background. You can do anything you want to it without running the risk of harming the underlying background.

Only a few operations affect the transparent areas of a layer, and most of these are limited to tools. You can paint on transparent pixels to make them opaque. You can clone with the rubber stamp, or smear pixels with the edit tools. But you can likewise send pixels back to transparency using the eraser. All of these operations change both the contents of the layer and the composition of the transparency mask.

 You can also fill all pixels by pressing Option-Delete for the foreground color or ⌘-Delete for the background color. To fill the pixels in a layer without altering the transparency mask, toss in the Shift key. Shift-Option-Delete fills the opaque pixels with the foreground color, while ⌘-Shift-Delete fills them with the background color. In both cases, the transparent pixels remain every bit as transparent as they ever were.

When a portion of the layer is selected, pressing plain old Delete gets rid of the selected pixels and makes them transparent, revealing the layers below.

Figure 13-8
Applying the
Invert command
to the camera
layer inverts just
the camera without affecting any
of the transparent
pixels. The TV
remains every bit
as visible as ever.

Modifying the background layer

At the bottom of the layer stack is the *background layer*, the fully opaque layer that represents the base image. The background image is as low as you go. Nothing can be slipped under the background layer, nor can pixels in the background layer be made transparent, unless you first convert the background to a floating layer.

To make the conversion, double-click on the *Background* item in the Layers palette. Then enter a name for the new layer — Photoshop suggests Layer 0 — and press Return. You can now change the order of the layer or erase down to transparency.

In Figure 13-9, I converted the background television to a layer. This particular image (from the PhotoDisc Object Series) included a predrawn path that encircled the TV. I ⌘-clicked on the path to convert it to a selection outline, and I pressed ⌘-Shift-I to reverse the selection. Finally, I pressed the Delete key to erase the pixels outside the TV, as the figure demonstrates.

Figure 13-9
After converting the TV image to a layer, I ⌘-clicked on the path, inversed the selection, and pressed the Delete key to reveal the transparent void below.

From this point on, I could reorder the camera and television layers, or add layers in back of the TV. I can also introduce a new background layer. (A program like QuarkXPress or PageMaker doesn't recognize Photoshop's transparency, so there's no point in leaving the background transparent. As I mentioned in Chapter 11, if you want to export transparency, you have to use a clipping path.)

To add a new background layer, Option-click on the new layer icon at the bottom of the Layers palette. When the New Layer dialog box appears, select the Background option from the Mode pop-up menu, as in Figure 13-10. Then press Return.

Figure 13-10
To add a new background layer, Option-click on the new layer icon and select the Background option from the Mode pop-up menu.

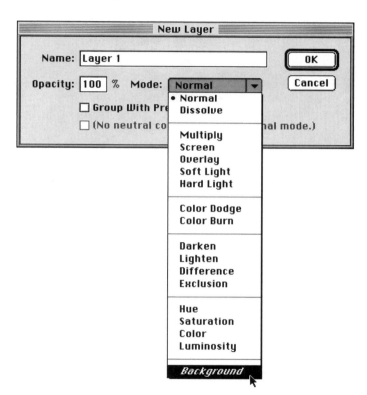

In Figure 13-11, I added a new background layer. I used the Add Noise and Emboss filters to create a paper texture pattern (as I explained back in Chapter 10). Then I added a drop shadow to match the contours of the TV. (To learn how to create drop shadows, read the "Drop Shadows, Halos, and Spotlights" section later in this chapter.)

Figure 13-11
I added a background layer behind the television and applied a paper texture and drop shadow to give my composition a little false depth.

Reordering layers

What good would layers be if you couldn't periodically change who's on top and who's on bottom? There are two ways to reorder layers in Photoshop 4. First, you can drag a layer name up or down in the scrolling list to move it forward or backward in layering order. The only trick is to make sure that the black bar appears at the point where you want to move the layer before you release the mouse button, as demonstrated in Figure 13-12.

You can even move floating selections by dragging them up and down in the palette. When you do, Photoshop automatically converts the floater to an independent layer. But don't miss that black bar, or Photoshop won't move a darn thing.

The second way to reorder layers — by choosing a command from the Layer ➪ Arrange submenu — is new to Photoshop 4. For example, choose Layer ➪ Arrange ➪ Bring Forward to move the active layer up one level; choose Layer ➪ Arrange ➪ Send to Back to move the layer to just above the background layer.

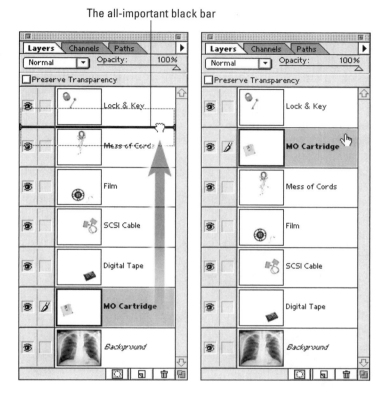

Figure 13-12
Drag the layer between two other layers to make the all-important black bar appear (left) to change the hierarchy of the layer (right).

You can move faster if you remember the following keyboard shortcuts (all of which perform different functions than they did in Photoshop 3):

- ⌘-Shift-]: Press ⌘-right bracket to move the active layer to the very top of the stack.

- ⌘-Shift-[: This shortcut moves the active layer to the bottom of the stack, just above the background layer.

- ⌘-]: This nudges the layer up one level.

- ⌘-[: This nudges the layer down.

You cannot reorder the background layer, nor may you move any other layer below the background, until first converting the background to a floating layer, as explained in the previous section.

Automated matting techniques

When you convert an antialiased selection to a layer, you sometimes take with you a few pixels from the selection's previous background. These "fringe pixels" can result in an unrealistic outline around your layer that cries out, "This image was edited by a hack." For example, Figure 13-13 shows a magnified detail from my original attempt at creating Figure 13-11. Although the selection outline was very accurate, I managed to retain a few white pixels around the edges, as you can see around the outline of the picture tube and arm that holds the tube.

Figure 13-13
This enlarged detail of the TV layer against the textured background shows the fringe pixels left over from the TV's original white background.

You can instruct Photoshop to replace the fringe pixels with colors from neighboring pixels by choosing Layer ⇨ Matting ⇨ Defringe. Enter the thickness of the perceived fringe in the Width option box to tell Photoshop which pixels you want to replace. To create the image shown in Figure 13-14, I entered a Width value of 1. But even at this low value, the effect is pretty significant, leaving gummy edges in its wake.

Photoshop provides two additional commands under the Layer ⇨ Matting submenu: Remove Black Matte and Remove White Matte. Frankly, it's unlikely that you'll have much call to use them, but here's the scoop:

- **Remove Black Matte:** This command removes the residue around the perimeter of a layer that was lifted from a black background.

- **Remove White Matte**: This command removed a white ring around a layer.

Figure 13-14
Here I used the Defringe command set to a
Width value of 1 to replace the pixels around
the perimeter of the layer with colors borrowed
from neighboring pixels.

Adobe tells me that these commands were designed specifically for compositing a
scene rendered in a 3D drawing program against a black or white background. But
for other purposes, they almost never work. For example, my television is a prime
candidate for Remove White Matte — it originated from a white background — and
yet it leaves behind more white pixels than the Defringe command set to its lowest
setting.

If you encounter unrealistic edge pixels and the automatic matting commands don't solve your problem, you may be able to achieve better results
by fixing the edges manually. First, switch to the layer that's giving you fits
and ⌘-click on its name in the Layers palette. This creates a tight selection
around the contents of the layer. (I tell you more about selecting layers in
the "Drop Shadows, Halos, and Spotlights" section later in this chapter.)
Then choose Select ⇨ Modify ⇨ Contract and enter the width of the fringe
in the Contract By option box. Next, choose Select ⇨ Feather (⌘-Shift-D)
and enter this same value into the Feather Radius option box. Finally, press
⌘-Shift-I to inverse the selection and press the Delete key to get rid of the
edge pixels.

Figure 13-15 shows the results of applying this technique to my television. (Figure
13-11 also shows the result at normal size.) By setting the Contract and Feather
commands to just 1 pixel, I've managed to remove the edges without harming the
layer itself. And the effect looks quite a bit better than that produced by the
Defringe command (see Figure 13-14).

Figure 13-15
Here I removed the edges manually using the Contract, Feather, and Inverse commands. It looks way better than anything Photoshop can do automatically.

Blending layers

Photoshop lets you blend layers with each other like no other program in the business. In fact, Photoshop does such a great job that it takes me an entire chapter — Chapter 19 — to explain these options in detail. I offer this section only by way of introduction, so you're at least aware of the basics. If you have bigger questions, then Chapter 19 is ready to tell all.

The Layers palette offers three basic ways to blend pixels between layers. None of these techniques changes so much as a pixel in any layer, so you can always go back and reblend the layers at a later date.

∾ **The Opacity slider bar:** Drag the Opacity slider triangle near the top of the Layers palette to change the opacity of the active layer or floating selection. If you reduce the Opacity value to 50 percent, for example, Photoshop makes the pixels on the active layer translucent, so that the colors in the layer mix evenly with the colors in the layer below.

If any tool other than a painting tool is active — including the selection and navigation tools — you can press a number key to change the Opacity value. Press 1 for 10 percent, 2 for 20 percent, up to 0 for 100 percent. Or you can enter a specific Opacity value by pressing two number keys in a row. For example, press 3 then 7 for 37 percent.

Figure 13-16
The blend mode pop-up menu
and the Opacity slider bar let you
mix layers together without making
any permanent changes to the pixels.

↬ **The blend mode pop-up menu:** Choose an option from the blend mode pop-up menu to mix every pixel in the active layer with the pixels below it according to one of several mathematical equations. For example, when you choose Multiply, Photoshop really does multiply the brightness values of the pixels and then divides the result by 255, the maximum brightness value. Blend modes use the exact same math as the brush modes covered in Chapter 8. But you can accomplish a lot more with blend modes, which is why I spend so much time examining them in Chapter 19.

↬ **Layer Options:** Choose Layer ➪ Layer Options or double-click on a layer name to display the Layer Options dialog box. This dialog box provides access to an Opacity value and a Mode pop-up menu, but it also offers a few unique functions. Using the Blend If slider bars, you can specify which colors are visible in the active layer and which colors show through from the layers behind it. You can also mix the colors using special fuzziness controls and change the slider bar settings for an individual color channel.

That's enough to prepare you for anything that I might throw at you between now and Chapter 19. But as I've mentioned four times now, Chapter 19 contains the whole story. (Oops, make that five mentions.)

Fusing several layers into one

Although layers are wonderful and marvelous creatures, they have their price. Layers expand the size of an image in RAM and ultimately lead to slower performance. And as explained in Chapter 4, you can save layered images in just one format, the native Photoshop format.

 Photoshop provides several methods for merging layers together (many new to Photoshop 4):

⤷ **Merge Down (⌘-E):** Choose Layer ➪ Merge Down to merge a layer with the layer immediately below it. When generating screen shots, I use this command fifty or sixty times a day. I paste the screen shot into the image window, edit the layer as desired, and then press ⌘-E to set it down. Then I can save the screen shot in any format I like.

 Merge Down is the answer to Defloat in Photoshop 4 In fact, when working with a floating selection, Merge Down changes to Defloat, and both commands share ⌘-E as a keyboard equivalent.

If the active layer is linked to other layers or part of a clipping group — two conditions I discuss later in this chapter — the Merge Down command changes to Merge Linked or Merge Group, respectively. Again, these commands use ⌘-E as a shortcut. Merge Down is forever changing to suit the situation.

⤷ **Merge Visible (⌘-Shift-E):** Choose the Merge Visible command to merge all visible layers into a single layer. If the layer is not visible — that is, no eyeball icon appears in front of the layer name — Photoshop doesn't get rid of it; the layer simply remains independent.

 To create a merged clone, press the Option key when applying either Layer ➪ Merge Down or Layer ➪ Merge Visible. Option-choosing Merge Down (or pressing ⌘-Option-E) clones the contents of the active layer into the layer below it. Option-choosing Merge Visible (or pressing ⌘-Shift-Option-E) copies the contents of all visible layers to the active layer.

 To copy the merged contents of a selected area, choose Edit ➪ Copy Merged, or press ⌘-Shift-C. You can then paste the selection into a layer, or make it part of a different image.

⤷ **Flatten Image:** This command, on the other hand, merges all visible layers and throws away the invisible ones. The result is invariably a single, opaque background layer. Photoshop does not give this command a keyboard shortcut because it's so dangerous. More often than not, you'll want to flatten an image incrementally using the two Merge commands.

A few of Photoshop's commands automatically flatten an image. For example, Photoshop has to flatten an image in order to switch color modes. So be sure to display all layers that you want to retain before choosing any of the commands from the Image ➪ Mode submenu.

Dumping layers

You can also merely throw a layer away, never to be seen again. Drag the layer name onto the trash icon at the bottom of the Layers palette. Or click on the trash icon to delete the active layer.

When you click on the trash icon, Photoshop displays an error message, asking you if you really want to toss the sucker. To give this error message the slip in the future, just Option-click on the trash icon.

Saving a flattened version of an image

Only one file format, the native Photoshop format, saves images with layers. If you want to save a flattened version of your image — that is, with all layers fused together into a single image — in some other file format, choose File ➪ Save a Copy and select the desired format from the Format pop-up menu. If you select any format other than Photoshop, the program selects and dims the Flatten Image check box in the lower left corner of the dialog box.

The Save a Copy command does not affect the image on-screen — all layers remain intact — nor does it change the name of the image in the title bar. It merely creates a flattened duplicate of the image on disk.

Drop Shadows, Halos, and Spotlights _____

A few sections back, I mentioned that every layer (except the background) includes a transparency mask that tells Photoshop which pixels are opaque, which are translucent, and which are transparent. And like any mask, Photoshop lets you convert the transparency mask for any layer — active or not — to a selection outline. In fact, you use the very same keyboard techniques that you use to convert paths to selections (as explained in Chapter 11) and channels to selections (Chapter 12):

↬ ⌘-click on a layer name to convert the transparency mask to a selection outline. (This replaces the old ⌘-Option-T shortcut offered by Photoshop 3).

↬ To add the transparency mask to an existing selection outline, ⌘-Shift-click on the layer name. The little selection cursor includes a plus sign to show you that you're about to add.

↬ To subtract the transparency mask, ⌘-Option-click on the layer name.

↬ And to find the intersection of the transparency mask and the current selection outline, ⌘-Shift-Option-click on the layer name.

If you're not sure you'll remember all these keyboard shortcuts, you can use Select ⇨ Load Selection instead. After choosing the command, select the italic *Transparency* item from the Channel pop-up menu. (You can even load a transparency mask from another open image if the image is exactly the same size as the one you're working in.) Then use the Operation radio buttons to merge the mask with an existing selection, as described in the "Converting a mask to a selection" section of Chapter 12.

Selection outlines exist independently of layers, so you can use the transparency mask from one layer to select part of another layer. For example, to select part of the background layer that exactly matches the contents of another layer, you'd merely press Shift-Option-[to descend to the background layer, then ⌘-click on the name of the layer that you want to match.

In fact, this is the very technique you use to create three of the most sought-after effects in image-editing — drop shadows, halos, and spotlights. So now that we've hit on the basics, let's look at a few real-life applications.

Drop shadows

In these first steps, I'll take the dolphin from Figure 13-17 and insert a drop shadow behind it. This might not be the exact subject to which you'll apply drop shadows — sea critters so rarely cast such shadows onto the water's surface — but it accurately demonstrates how the effect works.

Figure 13-17
A dolphin in dire need of a
drop shadow.

STEPS Creating a Drop Shadow

Step 1. **Select the subject that you want to cast the shadow.** In my case, I selected the dolphin by painting the mask shown in Figure 13-18 inside a separate mask channel. These days, I add a mask to nearly every image I create to distinguish the foreground image from its background. I converted the mask to a selection outline by ⌘-clicking on the mask name in the Channels palette and then pressing ⌘-tilde (~) to switch back to the composite view.

Figure 13-18
This mask separates the dolphin from its watery home.

Step 2.   **Send the image to a separate layer by pressing ⌘-J.** Now that the selection is elevated, you can slip in the drop shadow underneath it.

Step 3.   **Retrieve the selection outline for your new layer and apply it to the background layer.** To do this, ⌘-click on the new layer name (presumably Layer 1), then press Shift-Option-[to switch to the background layer. (Because I saved the mask to a separate channel, I could have alternatively ⌘-clicked on the Mask item in the Channels panel to retrieve the selection. Or I could have pressed ⌘-Option-4.)

Step 4.   **To create a softened drop shadow — indicative of a diffused light source — choose Select ⇨ Feather.** The Radius value you enter depends on the resolution of your image. I recommend dividing the resolution of your image by 20. When working on a 200 ppi image, for example, enter a Radius value of 10. My image is a mere 140 ppi, so I entered 7. Then press Return to soften the image.

Step 5.   **Press ⌘-J to send the feathered selection to a new layer.**

Step 6.   **Fill the feathered area with black.** If necessary, press D to make the foreground color black. Then press Shift-Option-Delete to fill just the area inside the transparency mask. A slight halo of dark pixels forms around the edges of the image.

Step 7.   **Press ⌘ with the arrow keys to nudge the shadow to the desired location.** In Figure 13-19, I nudged the shadow 12 pixels to the right.

Figure 13-19
A drop shadow nudged 12 pixels due right from
the dolphin head, which is situated on the layer above it.

Step 8. **Lower the Opacity setting.** If the shadow is too dark — black lacks a lit- tle subtlety — press M to make sure that a selection tool is active and then press a number key to change the opacity of the shadow. I typically press 7 for 70 percent. But I'm probably in a rut.

If you don't like a black drop shadow, you can make a colored one with only slightly more effort. Instead of filling the shadow with black in Step 6, select a different foreground color and press Shift-Option-Delete. For the best result, select a color that is the complimentary opposite of the color of your background. In Color Plate 13-1, for example, the background is blue, so I selected a reddish orange as the foreground color. Next, choose Multiply from the blend mode pop-up menu on the left side of the Layers palette. This burns the colors in the shadow into those in the image to cre- ate a darkened mix. Finally, press a number key to specify the opacity. (In the color plate, I again used 70 percent. I'm definitely in a rut.)

Photoshop 4 includes a predefined Drop Shadow script in the Actions palette. But it applies the drop shadow to the entire image, not just a select- ed area. If you anticipate that you'll be adding drop shadows a lot, you might want to create a script of your own using the above steps.

Halos

Creating a halo is very similar to creating a drop shadow. The only differences are that you have to expand the selection outline and fill the halo with white (or some other light color) instead of black. The following steps tell all.

STEPS **Creating a Downright Angelic Halo**

Step 1. **Follow Steps 1 through 3 of the previous instructions.** You'll end up with a version of the selected image on an independent layer and a matching selection outline applied to the Background image. (See, I told you that this was just like creating a drop shadow.)

Step 2. **Expand the selection outline.** Unlike a drop shadow, which is offset slightly from an image, a halo fringes the perimeter of an image pretty evenly. Therefore, you need to expand the selection outline beyond the edges of the image so that you can see the halo clearly. To do this, choose Select ⇨ Modify ⇨ Expand. You'll be greeted by an Expand By option box. Generally speaking, you want the expansion to match the size of your feathering so that the softening occurs outward. Therefore, I entered 7. (The maximum permissible value is 16; if you want to expand more than 16 pixels, you have to apply the command twice.)

Step 3. **Choose Select ⇨ Feather and enter the same value you entered in the Expand By option box.** Again, you decide this value by dividing the resolution of your image by 20 (or thereabouts).

Step 4. **Send the selection to a new layer.** Press ⌘-J.

Step 5. **Fill the halo with white.** Assuming the background color is white, press ⌘-Shift-Delete.

That's all there is to it. Figure 13-20 shows a particularly enlightened-looking dolphin set against a halo effect. I also drew a conventional halo above its head, added some sparklies, and even changed my finned friend's eye using the eyeball brush shape included in the Assorted Brushes document. I mean, if this aquatic mammal's not bound for glory, I don't know who is.

Figure 13-20
Few dolphins reach this level of spiritual awareness, even if you do set them off from their backgrounds using the halo effect. He kind of looks like one of the cast members from *Cocoon*, don't you think?

Incidentally, you don't have to create a white halo any more than you have to create a black drop shadow. In Step 5, set the background color to something other than white. Then select the Screen option from the blend mode pop-up menu in the Layers palette, thus mixing the colors and lightening them at the same time. If you don't like the effect, just select a different background color and press ⌘-Shift-Delete again. As long as the halo is floating, you can do just about anything you want and run no risk of harming the underlying original.

Spotlights

Now, finally, for the spotlight effect. I use spotlights about a billion times in this book to highlight some special option that I want you to look at in a palette or dialog box. I've gotten so many questions (from fellow authors mostly) on how to perform this effect that I've decided I might as well write it down once in the book and be done with it. So here goes.

STEPS   Shining a Spotlight on Something Inside an Image

Step 1.   **Draw an oval selection inside your image.** Obviously, the best tool for this purpose is the elliptical marquee tool. The selection represents the area where the spotlight will shine. If you don't like where the oval is located but you basically like its size and shape, drag the outline to a more satisfactory location.

Step 2.   **Choose Select ➪ Feather and enter whatever Radius value you please.** Again, you may want to follow the divide-the-resolution-by-20 rule, but feel free to use whatever value you like. (There's no such thing as a wrong Radius value.) To create Figure 13-21, I doubled my Radius value to 14 pixels to create a very soft effect.

Step 3.   **Press ⌘-Shift-I.** Most likely, you really want to darken the area outside the spotlight, not lighten the spotlight itself. So choose Select ➪ Inverse (⌘-Shift-I) to swap what's selected and what's not.

Step 4.   **Send the selection to a new layer.** That's ⌘-J, of course.

Step 5.   **Fill the transparency mask with black.** With the foreground color set to black, press Shift-Option-Delete.

Step 6.   **Lower the Opacity setting by pressing a number key.** To get the effect in Figure 13-21, I pressed 6 for 60 percent.

Figure 13-21
Create an elliptical selection, feather it, inverse it, layer it, fill it with black, and lower the opacity to create a spotlight effect like this one.

Actually, the image in Figure 13-21 isn't all that convincing. Although the steps above are fine for spotlighting flat images such as screen shots, they tend to rob photographs of a little of their depth. After all, in real life, the spotlight wouldn't hit the water in the exact same way it hits the dolphin. But there is a way around this. You can combine the oval selection outline with the mask used to select the foreground image, thereby eliminating the background from the equation entirely.

Assuming that your image has a mask saved in a separate channel, do this: After establishing the selection and feathering it (Steps 1 and 2), duplicate the mask channel so that you don't harm the original. (You do this by dragging the channel name onto the little page icon at the bottom of the Channels palette.) Then choose Select ➪ Save Selection. Inside the dialog box, select the duplicate mask channel from the Channel pop-up menu and then select the Intersect with Channel radio button. This creates a mask that retains only those selected areas that were selected both in the selection outline and the mask. ⌘-click on the revised mask in the Channels palette to convert it to a selection outline and switch to the composite view (⌘-tilde). Then perform Steps 3 through 6 above — that is, inverse the selection (⌘-Shift-I), send it to a layer (⌘-J), fill the transparency mask with black (Shift-Option-Delete), and change the opacity. Figure 13-22 shows this technique applied to a familiar character.

Figure 13-22
You can mix the feathered selection
with the contents of a mask channel
to limit the spotlighting effect to the
foreground character only.

 Sometimes, the darkness of the area around the spotlight appears sufficiently dark that it starts bringing the spotlighted area down with it. To
brighten the spotlight, inverse the selection (⌘-Shift-I) so that the spotlight
is selected again. Then apply the Levels command (⌘-L) to brighten the
spotlighted area. The Levels command is explained at length in Chapter 18.

Just for fun — what other possible reason would there be? — Color Plate
13-2 shows one result of combining the spotlight effect with the halo effect.
I filled the area outside the spotlight with a deep blue. (In this case, a similar color looked better than a complimentary one.) Then, using my original
mask, I sent the dolphin to a separate layer and created a yellowish, pinkish
halo behind it. Then, I used Edit ➪ Fill (Shift-Delete) to return the Background image to its original appearance — by selecting the Saved option
from the Use pop-up menu in the Fill dialog box — and inverted the background by pressing ⌘-I. (For the Saved option to work, the saved file must
contain a comparable layer.) An interestingly lit dolphin in a radioactive
bath is the result.

Moving and Aligning Layers ___

You can move an entire layer, or merely the selected portion of a layer, by dragging
inside the image window with the move tool. Drag inside a selection outline to
move just a selection, or drag outside the selection to move the entire layer.

As I mentioned in Chapter 11, you can temporarily access the move tool when some other tool is active by pressing the ⌘ key. To nudge a layer, press ⌘ with an arrow key. Press ⌘ and Shift together to nudge in 10-pixel increments.

If part of the layer disappears beyond the edge of the window, no problem. Photoshop saves even the hidden pixels in the layer, permitting you to later drag it into view. (This only works when moving *all* of a layer. If you move a selection beyond the edge of the image window, Photoshop clips the selection at the window's edge the moment you deselect it.)

If you ⌘-drag the background image — either when no portion of the image is selected or by dragging outside the selection outline — Photoshop automatically converts the background to a new layer (called Layer 0). The area revealed by the move appears as checkerboard transparency. Photoshop saves the hidden portions of the background image in case you ever decide to move the background back into its original position.

Photoshop 4 adds a new feature that speeds up layer movements. Select the move tool (by pressing the V key) and then press Return to display the Move Tool Options palette. You'll find a single Pixel Doubling check box. If you select this check box, Photoshop shows you a low-resolution proxy of the layer as you drag it (or ⌘-drag it) across the screen. You don't have to click and hold to preview the layer as you move it — because Photoshop has fewer pixels to display, it can preview the image right away. Give it a try.

Pixel Doubling has no effect when you ⌘-drag selections. It only works when you move entire layers.

Linking layers

Photoshop permits you to move multiple layers at a time. To do so, you have to establish a *link* between the layers you want to move and the active layer. Begin by selecting the first layer in the Layers palette that you want to link. Then click in the second column to the left of the other layer that you want to link. A chain link icon appears in front of each linked layer, as in Figure 13-23. This shows that the linked layers will move in unison when you ⌘-drag the active layer. (Note that this only works when nothing is selected. If a portion of the image is selected, the move tool moves only the selection on the active layer.) To break the link, click on a link icon, which hides it.

Dragging inside a selection outlines moves the selection independently of any linked layers. Dragging outside the selection moves all linked layers.

To link many layers at a time, drag up and down the link column. To unlink the active layer from all others, click on the paintbrush icon in the link column.

Figure 13-23
Click in the second column in the Layers palette to display or hide link icons. Here I've linked all layers except the background so I can ⌘-drag them in unison.

Link column

Link icons

Using guides

Photoshop 4's new grids and guides permit you to move selections and layers into alignment. Together with the move tool, grids and guides let you create rows and columns of image elements, and even align layers by their centers.

To create a guide, press ⌘-R (View ➪ Show Rulers) to display the horizontal and vertical rulers. Then drag a guideline from the ruler. At the top of Figure 13-24, you can see me dragging a horizontal guide down from the top ruler. Then ⌘-drag layers and selections in alignment with the guide. In the bottom portion of the figure, I've dragged the MO disk, film reel, and tape — each on different layers — so they snap into alignment at their centers. (The reel has some film hanging off it, which Photoshop considers in calculating the center.) You'll know when the layer snaps into alignment because the move cursor becomes hollow, like the labeled cursor in Figure 13-24.

Ruler

New guide

Snap cursor

Figure 13-24
Drag from one of the rulers to create a guide (top), then
⌘-drag each layer or selection into alignment (bottom).

Guides are pretty straightforward creatures. I mean, you don't have to study them rigorously for years to understand them — a couple of minutes are about all you need to master them. But there are a few hidden treats:

- ❧ You can show and hide all guides by pressing ⌘-semicolon (;), or by choosing the Hide (or Show) Guides command from the View menu. When the guides are hidden, layers and selections do not snap into alignment.

- ❧ You can turn on and off guide snappiness while the guides remain visible by pressing ⌘-Shift-semicolon (or choosing View ➪ Snap to Guides).

- ❧ As with all image elements in Photoshop 4, you can move a guide with the move tool. If some other tool is active, ⌘-dragging also works.

- ❧ To lock all guides so you can't accidentally move them while you're trying to ⌘-drag something else, press ⌘-Option-semicolon, or choose View ➪ Lock Guides. Press ⌘-Option-semicolon again to unlock all guides.

* When moving a guide, press the Shift key to snap the guide to the nearest ruler tick mark.

* To convert a horizontal guide to a vertical guide, or vice versa, press the Option key while moving the guide.

* To edit the color of the guides, ⌘-double-click on a guide to display the Guides & Grid panel of the Preferences dialog box. You can also change the guides from solid lines to dashed. (This is just for screen purposes, by the way. Guides don't print.)

* Like paths, Photoshop saves guides with any file format. If you export the image into another program, the guides are invisible.

* If you don't need your guides anymore, choose View ⇨ Clear Guides to delete them all in one housekeeping operation. (I wish I had a command like that built into my office — I'd just choose Maid ⇨ Clear Dust and be done with it.)

Setting up the grid

Photoshop also offers a grid, which is a regular series of snapping increments. You view the grid — and turn it on — by pressing ⌘-quote (") or choosing View ⇨ Show Grid. Turn the snapping forces of the grid on and off by pressing ⌘-Shift-quote or choosing View ⇨ Snap to Grid.

You edit the grid in the Guides & Grid panel of the Preferences dialog box (which you can get to by pressing ⌘-K and ⌘-6, or by ⌘-double-clicking on a guide). I explain how to use these options in the "Guides & Grid" section of Chapter 2. But, for the record, you enter the major grid increments in the Gridline Every option box, and the minor increments in the Subdivisions option box. For example, in Figure 13-25, I set the Gridline Every value to 50 pixels and the Subdivisions value to 5. This means a moved layer will snap in 10-pixel (50 pixels divide by 5) increments. Figure 13-25 also demonstrates each of the three Style settings.

Applying Transformations _____

Photoshop and other graphics have a habit of treating some kinds of edits differently than others. Edits that affect the geometry of a selection or layer are known collectively as *transformations*. These include scaling, rotating, flipping, slanting, and distorting. (Technically, moving is a transformation as well.) Transformations are special because they can affect a selection, a layer, multiple layers, or an entire image at a time.

Lines Dashed lines Dots

Figure 13-25
The three styles of grid with the Grid Preferences options shown at bottom.

Transforming the entire image

Photoshop 4 has radically overhauled its transformation capabilities, much for the better. Those transformation commands that affect the entire image are listed in the Image menu; those that affect layers and selections are found in the Layer menu. The following list explains how to apply transformations to every pixel in an image, regardless of whether the image is selected or not:

- **Scale:** To resize the image, use Image ⇨ Image Size. Because this command is one of the most essential low-level functions in the program, I covered it way back in Chapter 4.

- **Rotate:** To rotate the entire image, choose a command from the Image ⇨ Rotate Canvas submenu. To rotate an image scanned on its size, choose the 90° CW or 90° CCW command. (That's clockwise and counterclockwise, respectively.) Choose 180° to spin the image on its head. To enter some other specific value, choose Image ⇨ Rotate Canvas ⇨ Arbitrary.

To fix a scanned image that's slightly crooked, select the line tool and set the Line Width value in the Line Tool Options palette to 0. You can then display the Info palette and use the line tool as a measuring device. Because the line weight is 0, you don't do any damage to your image. When you figure out the proper angle, choose Image ⇨ Rotate Canvas ⇨ Arbitrary and enter it into the Angle option box.

Whenever you apply the Arbitrary command, Photoshop has to expand the canvas size to avoid clipping any of your image. This results in background-colored wedges at each of the four corners of the image. You'll either need to clone with the rubber stamp tool to fill in the wedges or clip them away with the crop tool.

   ↦ **Flip:** Choose Image ⇨ Rotate Canvas ⇨ Flip Horizontal to flip the image so left is right and right is left. To flip the image upside-down, choose Image ⇨ Rotate Canvas ⇨ Flip Vertical.

No command is specifically designed to slant or distort the entire image. In the unlikely event that you're keen to do such a thing, you'll have to link all layers and apply one of the commands under the Layer ⇨ Transform submenu, as explained in the next section.

Transforming layers and selections

To transform a layer or selection, you can apply one of the commands in the Layer ⇨ Transform submenu. There are nearly a dozen commands here, all of which you can explore on your own. I'm not copping out, it's just that it's unlikely that you'll use any of these commands on a regular basis. (The notable exception is Numeric, which I discuss in the following section.) It's not that these commands are bad, it's just that one command — Free Transform — is infinitely better.

Free Transform is one of the best enhancements in Photoshop 4. It lets you scale, flip, rotate, slant, distort, and move a selection or layer in one continuous operation. This one command makes it possible to get all of your transformations exactly right before pressing Return to apply the final changes.

To initiate the command, press ⌘-T or choose Layer ⇨ Free Transform. Photoshop surrounds the layer or selection with an eight-handle marquee. You are now in the Free Transform mode, which prevents you from doing anything except transform the image until you apply the operation or cancel it.

Here's how to work in the Free Transform mode:

   ↦ **Scale:** Drag one of the eight square handles to scale the image inside the marquee. To scale proportionally, Shift-drag a corner handle. To scale about the center, Option-drag a corner handle.

   ↦ **Flip:** You can flip the image by dragging one handle past its opposite handle. For example, dragging the left side handle past the right handle flips the image horizontally.

If you just want to perform a simple flip, it's generally easier to choose Layer ⇨ Transform ⇨ Flip Horizontal or Flip Vertical. Quite surprisingly, you can choose either command while working in the Free Transform mode.

↪ **Rotate:** To rotate the image, drag outside the marquee, as demonstrated in the first example in Figure 13-26. Shift-drag to rotate in 15-degree increments.

Figure 13-26
After pressing ⌘-T to initiate the Free Transform command, drag outside the marquee to rotate the layer (top). You can also ⌘-Option-drag a corner handle to move the opposite corner handle symmetrically.

↪ **Slant:** ⌘-drag a side handle (including the top or bottom handle) to slant the image. To constrain the slant — useful for producing perspective effects — ⌘-Shift-drag a side handle.

↪ **Distort:** You can distort the image by ⌘-dragging a corner handle. You can tug the image to stretch it in any of four directions.

To tug two opposite corner handles in symmetrical directions, ⌘-Option-drag either of the handles. I show this technique in the second example in Figure 13-26.

- **Perspective:** For a one-point perspective effect, ⌘-Shift-drag a corner handle. To move two points in unison, ⌘-Shift-Option-drag a corner handle.

- **Move:** Drag inside the marquee to move the image. This is useful when you're trying to align the selection or layer with a background image, and you want to make sure the transformations properly match up.

- **Undo:** To undo the last modification without leaving the Free Transform mode altogether, press ⌘-Z.

- **Zoom:** You can change the view size by choosing one of the commands in the View menu.

- **Apply:** Press Return to apply the final transformation and interpolate the new pixels. You can also double-click inside the marquee. (If the finished effect looks jagged, it's probably because you selected Nearest Neighbor from the Interpolation pop-up menu in the Preferences dialog box. To fix this problem, press ⌘-Z to undo the transformation, then press ⌘-K and select the Bicubic option. And press ⌘-T to start the transformation over again.)

- **Cancel:** To cancel the Free Transform operation, press the Escape key.

To transform a clone of a selected area, press Option when choosing the Free Transform command, or press ⌘-Option-T. This only works with selected areas — you can't clone an entire layer any more than you can by Option-dragging with the move tool.

Provided that no part of the image is selected, you can transform multiple layers at a time by linking them, as described in the "Linking layers" section earlier in this chapter. For example, I could have linked the TV and shadow layers to transform the two in unison back in Figure 13-26.

Numerical transformations

To track your transformations numerically, display the Info palette (F8) *before* applying the Free Transform command. Once you've initiated Free Transform, you can't change the visible palettes until you complete or cancel the operation.

Or, choose Layer ⇨ Transform ⇨ Numeric (⌘-Shift-T). You can apply this command while working in the Free Transform mode, or apply the entire transformation numerically by pressing ⌘-Shift-T at the outset. In any case, you get the dialog box shown in Figure 13-27. If you're in the middle of a

Free Transform operation, the dialog box reflects the changes you've made so far (except the distortions). Otherwise, Photoshop displays the last settings applied.

Figure 13-27
Press ⌘-Shift-T to transform a selection or layer numerically.

For the most part, this dialog box is pretty straightforward. Use the check boxes to decide which kinds of transformations you want to apply. (Skew is the same as slant, by the way.) The Relative check box controls whether a move is measured relative to the previous position of the element, or with respect to the absolute 0,0 coordinate (generally in the upper left corner of the image).

I imagine most folks will use this dialog box strictly for scaling and rotating. You'd have to have the spatial awareness of a NASA navigation system to be able to predict a numerical slant.

Masking and Layers

Layers offer special masking options unto themselves. You can paint inside the confines of a layer as if it were a selection mask; you can add a special mask for a single layer; or you can group multiple layers together and have the bottom layer in the group serve as the mask. Quite honestly, these are the kinds of thoughtful and useful functions that I've come to expect from Photoshop. Though they're fairly complicated to use — you really have to be on your toes once you start juggling layer masks — these functions provide new realms of opportunities.

Preserving transparency

You may have already noticed a little check box near the top of the Layers palette called Preserve Transparency. If not, the option appears spotlighted in Figure 13-28. When checked, it prevents you from painting inside the transparent portions of the layer.

Figure 13-28
The Preserve Transparency check box (upper right) lets you paint inside the layer's trans-parency mask with-out harming the transparent pixels.

Suppose I want to paint inside the girl shown in Figure 13-28. If this were a flat, non-layered image, I'd have to carefully draw a selection outline around her hair and arms, as I did back in Chapter 12. But there's no need to do this when using layers. Because the girl lies on a different layer than her background, a permanent selec-tion outline tells Photoshop which pixels are transparent and which are opaque. This is the transparency mask.

The first example in Figure 13-29 shows the girl on her own with background hid-den. The transparent areas outside the mask appear in the checkerboard pattern. When the Preserve Transparency option is turned off, you can paint anywhere inside the layer that you want. Selecting Preserve Transparency activates the trans-parency mask and places the checkerboard area off limits.

Figure 13-29
The layered girl as she appears on her own (left) and when airbrushed with the Preserve Transparency check box turned on (right).

The right image in Figure 13-29 shows what happens when I select Preserve Transparency and paint around the girl with the airbrush. (The foreground color is set to white.) Notice that no matter how much paint I may apply, none of it leaks out onto the background.

Though that enlightening discussion pretty well covers it, I feel compelled to share a few additional words about Preserve Transparency:

- You can turn Preserve Transparency on and off from the keyboard by pressing the standard slash character, /, right there on the same key with the question mark. This shortcut was available in Photoshop 3, but few folks knew about it.

- Don't forget that you can fill just the opaque pixels in a layer, whether Preserve Transparency is on or off. Use ⌘-Shift-Delete to fill with the background color, and Shift-Option-Delete to fill with the foreground color.

- The Preserve Transparency check box is dimmed when the background layer is active, because this layer is entirely opaque. There's no transparency to preserve, eh? (That's my impression of a Canadian explaining layer theory. It needs a little work, but I think I'm getting close.)

And finally, here's a question for all you folks who think you've pretty much got Photoshop mastered. Which of the brush modes (explained in Chapter 8) is the exact opposite of Preserve Transparency? The answer is Behind. If I were to turn off Preserve Transparency and select the Behind brush mode in the Airbrush Options palette, I'd paint exclusively outside the transparency mask, protecting the opaque pixels. So it follows that the Behind brush mode is dimmed when Preserve Transparency is turned on.

What this means is that Behind is not a true brush mode and should not be grouped with the brush modes. I trust this option will be presented more logically in a future version of Photoshop.

Creating layer-specific masks

In addition to the transparency mask that accompanies every layer (except the background), you can add a mask to a layer to make certain pixels in the layer transparent. Now, you might ask, "Won't simply erasing portions of a layer make those portions transparent?" The answer is yes, but when you erase, you delete pixels permanently. By creating a layer mask, you instead make pixels temporarily transparent. You can come back several months later and bring those pixels back to life again simply by adjusting the mask. Therefore, layer masks add yet another level of flexibility to a program that's already a veritable image-editing contortionist.

To create a layer mask, select the layer that you want to mask and choose Layer ⇨ Add Layer Mask ⇨ Reveal All. Or more simply, click on the layer mask icon at the bottom of the Layers palette, as labeled in Figure 13-30. A second thumbnail preview appears to the left of the layer name, also labeled in the figure. A heavy outline around the preview shows that the layer mask is active.

To edit the mask, simply paint in the image window. Paint with black to make pixels transparent. Because black represents deselected pixels in an image, it makes these pixels transparent in a layer. Paint with white to make pixels opaque.

In Photoshop 4, the default foreground and background colors for a layer mask are white and black, respectively. This ensures that painting with the paintbrush or airbrush makes pixels opaque, where painting with the eraser makes them transparent, just as you would expect.

Link icon   Layer mask thumbnail

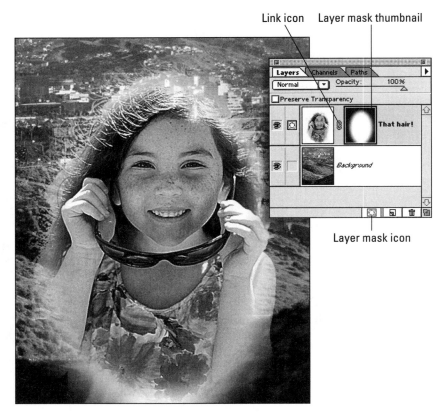

Layer mask icon

Figure 13-30
The black area in the layer mask (which you can see in the
thumbnail view, top right) translates to transparent pixels
in the layer itself.

In Figure 13-30, I created a feathered oval, inversed it, and filled it with black by
pressing ⌘-Delete. This results in a soft vignette around the layer. If I decide I've
gotten rid of too much of the hair, not to worry. I merely paint with white to bring it
back again.

Photoshop has really gone nuts in the layer mask department, adding lots of little
bells and whistles that make the function both convenient and powerful. Here's
everything you need to know:

    ➚ **Reveal Selection:** If you've selected some portion of your layer, Photoshop
        automatically converts the selection to a layer mask when you click on the
        layer mask icon at the bottom of the palette. The area outside the selection
        becomes transparent. (The corresponding command is Layer ⇨ Add Layer
        Mask ⇨ Reveal Selection.)

↪ **Hide Selection:** You can also choose to reverse the prospective mask, making the area inside the selection transparent and the area outside opaque. To do this, choose Layer ⇨ Add Layer Mask ⇨ Hide Selection. Or, better yet, Option-click on the layer mask icon in the Layers palette.

↪ **Hide everything:** To start off with a black mask that hides everything, choose Layer ⇨ Add Layer Mask ⇨ Hide All. Or press ⌘-D to deselect everything and Option-click on the layer mask icon.

 ↪ **View the mask:** Photoshop regards a layer mask as a layer-specific channel. You can actually see it listed in italics in the Channels palette. To view the mask on its own — as a black-and-white image — Option-click on the layer mask thumbnail in the Layers palette. Option-click again to view the image instead.

↪ **Layer mask rubylith:** To view the mask as a red overlay, Shift-Option-click on the layer mask icon. Or simply press the backslash key, \, just above Return.

 After you have both layer and mask visible at once, you can hide the mask by pressing \, or hide the layer and view just the mask by pressing the tilde key (~). So many alternatives!

↪ **Change the overlay color:** Double-click on the layer mask thumbnail to access the Layer Mask Display Options dialog box, which lets you change the color and opacity of the rubylith.

 ↪ **Turn off the mask:** You can temporarily disable the mask by Shift-clicking on the mask thumbnail. (You used to ⌘-click on the thumbnail in Photoshop 3, but this has changed for reasons that will become apparent in a moment.) A red X covers the thumbnail when it's disabled, and all masked pixels in the layer appear opaque. Shift-click again to put the mask in working order again.

↪ **Switch between layer and mask:** As you become more familiar with layer masks, you'll switch back and forth between layer and mask quite frequently, editing the layer one minute, editing the mask the next. You can switch between layer and mask by clicking on their respective thumbnails. The active item gets a heavy border.

 You can also switch between layer and mask from the keyboard. Press ⌘-tilde (~) to make the layer active. Press ⌘-\ to switch to the mask.

↪ **Link layer and mask:** A little link icon appears between the layer and mask thumbnails in the Layers palette. When the link icon is visible, you can move or transform the mask and layer as one. If you click on the link icon to turn it off, layer and mask move independently. (You can always move a selected region of the mask or layer independently of the other.)

↷ **Convert mask to selection:** As with all masks in Photoshop 4, you can convert a layer mask to a selection. To do so, just ⌘-click on the layer mask icon. Throw in the Shift and Option keys if you want to add or subtract the layer mask with an existing selection outline.

When and if you finish using the mask — you can leave it in force as long as you like — you can choose Layer ⇨ Remove Layer Mask. Or just drag the layer mask thumbnail to the trash icon. Either way, an alert box asks you if you want to discard the mask or permanently apply it to the layer. Click on the button that corresponds to your innermost desires.

Pasting inside a selection outline

In the new Photoshop, one command creates a layer mask automatically, and that command is Edit ⇨ Paste Into (⌘-Shift-V). Choose this command to paste the contents of the Clipboard into the current selection , so that the selection acts as a mask. Because Photoshop pastes to a new layer, it converts the selection into a layer mask. But here's the interesting part: By default, Photoshop turns off the link between layer and mask. This way, you can ⌘-drag the layer inside a fixed mask to position the pasted image, just as in the old days.

Once upon a time in Photoshop, there used to be a command named Edit ⇨ Paste Behind. (Or something like that. It might have been Paste in Back. My memory's a little hazy.) The command (whatever its name) pasted a copied image in back of a selection. But while the command is gone, its spirit lives on. Now you press the Option key when choosing Edit ⇨ Paste Into. Or just press ⌘-Shift-Option-V. Photoshop creates a new layer with an inverted layer mask, masking away the selected area.

Masking groups of layers

About now, you might be growing a little fatigued with the topic of layering masking. But one more option requires your immediate attention. You can group multiple layers into something called a *clipping group,* in which the lowest layer in the group masks the others. Where the lowest layer is transparent, the other layers are hidden; where the lowest layer is opaque, the contents of the other layers are visible.

Despite the similarities in name, a clipping group bears no relation to a clipping path. That is, it doesn't allow you to prepare transparent areas for import into QuarkXPress and the like.

In Photoshop 4, there are two ways to create a clipping group:

- ⌖ Option-click on the horizontal line between any two layers to group them into a single unit. Your cursor changes to the group cursor labeled in Figure 13-31 when you press Option; the horizontal line becomes dotted after you click. To break the layers apart again, just Option-click on the dotted line to make it solid.

- ⌖ Select the higher of the two layers that you want to combine into a clipping group. Then choose Layer ⇨ Group with Previous, or press ⌘-G. To make the layers independent again, choose Layer ⇨ Ungroup (⌘-Shift-G).

Figure 13-31
Option-click on the horizontal line between two layers to group them together.

Figures 13-31 and 13-32 demonstrate two steps in a piece of artwork I created for the February 1997 issue of *Macworld* magazine. I had already created some text on an independent layer using the type tool (the subject of the next chapter) and I wanted to fill the text with water. So I added a couple of photographs I shot of a swimming pool to a layer above the text, as shown in Figure 13-31. Then I combined text and pool images into a clipping group. Because the text was underneath the water, Photoshop masked the pool images according to the transparency mask assigned to the text. The result is a water pattern that exactly fills the type, as in Figure 13-32. (For a full-color version of these figures, see Color Plate 13-3.)

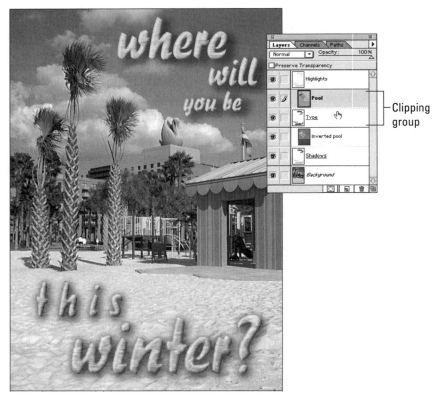

Figure 13-32
After combining pool water and type layers into a single clipping group, Photoshop applies the type layer's transparency mask to the pool layer.

If you're familiar with Illustrator, you may recognize this clipping group metaphor as a relative to Illustrator's clipping path. One object in the illustration acts as a mask for a collection of additional objects. In Illustrator, however, the topmost object in the group is the mask, not the bottom one. So much for consistency.

Amazing Text Stuff

■ ■

In This Chapter

- The advantages and disadvantages of bitmapped type
- Entering and editing type inside the Type Tool dialog box
- Specifying and measuring type size, leading, and spacing
- Editing text on an independent layer
- Selecting an image using the type mask tool
- Creating raised type and drop shadows
- Third-party plug-ins PhotoText and TypeCaster

■ ■

Type Basics

What I'm about to say is going to shake you to the very core. I'm warning you —
this is a biggie. You may want to sit down before you read any further. In fact, after
you sit down, you may want to strap yourself in. Maybe go ahead and soundproof
the room so that no one's alarmed when you scream, "Oh, no, it can't be true!" and
"Say it ain't so!"

(Ahem.) Type and graphics are the same thing.

There, there now. I understand. I reacted the same way when I heard the news. Dry
your eyes while I explain. You see, your computer treats each character in a word
as a little picture. The letter *O,* for example, is a big black oval with a smaller transparent oval set inside it. The only difference between a character of type and a
standard graphic is that you don't have to draw type; every letter is already drawn
for you. A font, therefore, is like a library of clip art you can access from the keyboard.

Qualities of bitmapped type

Now that you understand the realities of type, it should come as no surprise to learn that Photoshop treats type just like any other collection of pixels in an image. Type legibility is dependent upon the size and resolution of your image.

Figure 14-1, for example, shows four lines of type printed at equal sizes but at different resolutions. If these lines were printed at equal resolutions, each line would be twice as large as the line that precedes it. Hence, big type printed at a high resolution yields smooth, legible output, just as a big image printed at a high resolution yields smooth, detailed output. In fact, everything that you can say about an image is true of bitmapped type.

Type = Graphics
Type = Graphics
Type = Graphics
Type = Graphics

Figure 14-1
Four lines of type set in the TrueType font Geneva and printed at different resolutions.

You can create smooth, legible type in Photoshop only if you use TrueType fonts in combination with System 7 or 7.5, or if you use PostScript fonts with Adobe Type Manager (ATM) installed. To use a PostScript font, both the screen and printer version of the font must be installed on your machine.

The disadvantages of working with type in a painting program are obvious (but I'm going to tell them to you anyway). First, the resolution of the type is fixed. Rather than matching the resolution of printed text to that of your printer — a function provided by drawing, word processing, and desktop publishing programs, just to name a few — Photoshop prints type at the same resolution it prints the rest of the image.

In addition, after you add a line of type to an image, you can't go back and add and delete characters from the keyboard as you can in an object-oriented program. If you misspell a word or just want to rephrase some text, you must erase the offending characters or words and start over again. In terms of entering type, Photoshop is more likely to remind you of a typewriter and a bottle of correction fluid than a word processor.

But although the disadvantages of creating type in a painting program may initially hamper your progress, the advantages are tremendous. For example, you can do all of the following:

⤳ **Create translucent type:** Now that Photoshop 4 automatically creates type on a new layer, you can change the translucency of type more easily than ever using the Opacity slider bar in the Layers palette. By using this technique, you can merge type and images to create subtle overlay effects, as illustrated in the top example in Figure 14-2.

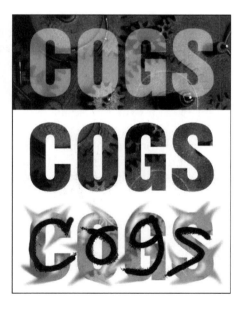

Figure 14-2
Examples of translucent white type (top), type used as a selection (middle), and type enhanced with painting and editing tools (bottom). On the whole, these effects are beyond the means of object-oriented programs.

⤳ **Use type as a selection:** Text is ultimately just another variety of selection outline. You can mask portions of an image (as I did back in Figure 13-32 of the last chapter) and even select elements and move, copy, or otherwise manipulate them using character outlines, as demonstrated in the middle example in Figure 14-2. I explore this option in detail in the upcoming "Character Masks" section.

⤳ **Customize characters:** You also can customize a character of type by converting it to a path, editing the path using the tools in the Paths palette, and converting it back to a selection outline. Only high-end drawing programs such as Illustrator, FreeHand, and Canvas match this capability.

↪ **Edit type as part of the image:** You can erase type, paint over type, smear type, fill type with a gradation, draw highlights and shadows, and create a range of special text effects that fall well outside the capabilities of an object-oriented program. The last example in Figure 14-2 is just one of the bazillion possibilities.

↪ **Trade images freely:** If you've ever traded documents over a network or otherwise tried to share a file created in a word processor or desktop publishing program with associates and coworkers, you know what a nightmare fonts can be. If other people's machines aren't equipped with the fonts you used in your document — which seems to be the case more often than not — your document looks awful on their screens. "What's wrong with this file you gave me?" "Why did you use *this* font?" And "I liked what you wrote in your report, but it is sure ugly!" are only a few of the responses you can expect. When you work with images, however, your font worries are over, because type in an image is bitmapped. Other users don't need special screen or printer fonts to view your images exactly as you created them. Mind you, I don't recommend that you use Photoshop as a word processor, but it's great for creating headlines and short missives that you want to fling about the office.

Using the type tool

In a drawing or desktop publishing program, the type tool typically serves two purposes: you can create text with the tool or you can edit the characters of existing text by highlighting them and either replacing characters or applying formatting commands. However, Photoshop doesn't allow you to reword or reformat text after you add it to an image.

To create text, select the standard type tool (the one that looks like a solid T) and click in the image window. In Photoshop 4, you can select the type tool from the keyboard by pressing the T key. Instead of producing a blinking insertion marker in the window, as other graphics programs do, Photoshop displays the Type Tool dialog box shown in Figure 14-3.

Expect to wait a few minutes before you use the type tool for the first time in Photoshop. You'll see a message saying, "Building a font menu. This may take five months or so. . ." (actually, it says "a minute or so" — it just seems like five months). Every program has to load font definitions before it permits you to create type. That's one of the reasons a program like Microsoft Word takes so long to launch. Photoshop waits to build its type library until you use the type tool, thus saving time for folks who never get around to creating type. If you do use the tool, Photoshop has to build the library only once per session.

Figure 14-3
To create type in Photoshop, enter it into the Type Tool dialog box, which appears after you click with the type tool. The bottom example shows the type as it appears in the image window.

Entering and editing type

At the bottom of the Type Tool dialog box is the text-entry box. You enter and edit the text you want to add to the current image into this box.

You can edit text up to the moment you add it to the image. To make your edits, first select the characters you want to change by dragging over them with the cursor. Then enter new text from the keyboard. To select a whole word, double-click on it. You can also cut, copy, and paste text by choosing commands from the Edit menu or using keyboard equivalents.

If the text you are typing reaches the right edge of the text-entry box, the word in progress automatically drops down to the next line. However, when you click on the OK button or press Enter on the keypad to exit the dialog box, all text appears on the same line unless you specifically entered carriage returns between lines (by pressing Return). Each carriage return indicates the end of one line and the beginning of the next, just as it does when you use a typewriter.

Get in the habit of pressing Enter rather than Return to exit the Type Tool dialog box. You can press Return to exit the dialog box when the Size, Leading, or Spacing option box is active, but the key inserts a carriage return when the text-entry box is active.

If your text doesn't look the way you anticipated after you exit the Type Tool dialog box, press ⌘-Z or click on the trash icon at the bottom of the Layers palette to delete the new layer. Then start the process over again by clicking with the type tool. When the Type Tool dialog box appears, your previous text is displayed in the text-entry box.

Formatting type

Photoshop formats *all* text entered into the text-entry box identically according to the specifications in the Type Tool dialog box. You can't select a single character or word in the text-entry box and format it differently than its deselected neighbors.

The formatting options in the Type Tool dialog box work as follows:

- **Font:** Select the typeface and type style you want to use from the Font pop-up menu. Alternatively, you can just select the plain version of the font, such as Times Roman or Helvetica Regular, and apply styles using the Style options.

- **Size:** Type size is measured either in points or pixels. You can select the desired measurement from the pop-up menu to the right of the Size option box, as shown in Figure 14-3. If the resolution of your image is 72 ppi, points and pixels are equal. However, if the resolution is higher, a single point may include many pixels. The resolution of Figure 14-3, for example, is 140 ppi, which is why the final text in the image (shown at bottom) is almost twice as large as the 72 ppi text in the dialog box. The moral? Select the points option when you want to scale text according to the image resolution; select pixels when you want to map text to an exact number of pixels in an image.

Type is measured from the top of its *ascenders* — letters like *b, d,* and *h* that rise above the level of most lowercase characters — to the bottom of its *descenders* — letters like *g, p,* and *q* that sink below the baseline. That's the way it's supposed to work, anyway. Characters from fonts in the Adobe Type Library, including those built into all PostScript laser printers and imagesetters, measure only 92 percent as tall as the specified type size.

The top two lines in Figure 14-4 contain 120-pixel type set in the Adobe versions of Times and Helvetica. All characters easily fit inside rectangular outlines that measure exactly 120 pixels tall. By contrast, the third and fourth lines of type are set in the TrueType fonts New York and Geneva. These characters are bursting their 120-point rectangular outlines at the seams.

Figure 14-4
From top to bottom, I formatted
these lines of type in the PostScript
versions of Times and Helvetica and
the TrueType versions of New York
and Geneva. The PostScript characters
fit inside their 120-point rectangular
outlines with room to spare; the
TrueType characters slightly overlap
their outlines.

- **Leading:** Also called line spacing, *leading* is the vertical distance between the baseline of one line of type and the baseline of the next line of type within a single paragraph, as illustrated in Figure 14-5. (You must separate lines of type manually by pressing the Return key in the text-entry box.) Leading is measured in the unit you selected from the Size pop-up menu. If you don't specify a leading value, Photoshop automatically inserts leading equal to 125 percent of the type size.

Figure 14-5
Leading is the dis-
tance between any
two baselines in a
single paragraph of
text created with the
type tool. Here, the
type size is 120 pixels
and the leading is 150
pixels.

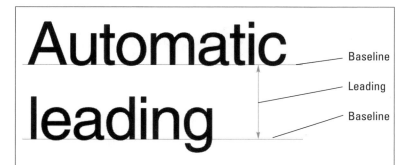

- **Spacing:** Each character in a font carries with it a predetermined amount of *side bearing* that separates it from its immediate neighbors. Although you can't change the amount of side bearing, you can insert and delete the overall amount of space between characters by entering a value into the Spacing option box. Enter a positive value to insert space; enter a negative value to delete space. The value is measured in the unit you selected from the Size pop-up menu.

◌◦ **Style:** Select one or more Style check boxes to specify the type styles you want to apply to your text. If you choose the plain version of a font, the Bold and Italic options call up the bold and italic PostScript or TrueType font definitions. If you apply the Bold option to a font that is already bold, such as Helvetica Bold or Helvetica Black (both shown in Figure 14-6), Photoshop makes the characters slightly heavier. If you apply the Italic option to a font that is already italicized, such as Helvetica Oblique (again, see Figure 14-6), Photoshop slants the characters even more.

1 Helvetica Regular

2 **Helvetica Regular Bold**

3 **Helvetica Bold**

4 **Helvetica Bold Bold**

5 **Helvetica Black**

6 **Helvetica Black Bold**

7 *Helvetica Regular Italic*

8 *Helvetica Oblique*

9 *Helvetica Oblique Italic*

Figure 14-6
Bolding a plain font produces the same result as choosing the bold version of the font (2 and 3), just as italicizing the plain style is the same as choosing an italicized font (7 and 8). But you can heighten the effects by applying styles to already stylized fonts (4, 6, and 9).

The Outline option produces unspeakably ugly results, as demonstrated by the top two examples in Figure 14-7. You can create a better outline style using Edit ⇨ Stroke. Press D and X to make the foreground color white. (You can also Option-click with the type tool to lift a color with the eyedropper if you like.) Then create your text using the Type Tool dialog box as usual, without selecting Outline, and press Enter when you're done. Press X to restore black as the foreground color, and press the / key to turn off Preserve Transparency. Finally, choose Edit ⇨ Stroke and enter the outline thickness of your choice. Figure 14-7 shows two stroked examples, one with a 1-pixel outline and the other with a 2-pixel outline.

The Shadow option produces equally unattractive results. To create attractive shadowed type, try out one of the techniques discussed in the "Character Masks" section of this chapter.

Figure 14-7
Photoshop's automated outline style, shown here when jagged (first) and antialiased (second), is nothing short of hideous. You can get better results by stroking the characters with 1-pixel or 2-pixel outlines (third and bottom).

- **Anti-aliased:** This Style option is special enough to mention separately. When you select Anti-aliased, Photoshop softens characters by slightly blurring pixels around the perimeter, as shown in Figure 14-8. Unless you want to create very small type or intend to match the resolution of your output device — printing a 300 ppi image to a 300 dpi printer, for example — select this check box. Photoshop takes longer to produce antialiased type, but it's worth it. Unless otherwise indicated, I created all figures in this chapter with the Anti-aliased check box selected.

Figure 14-8
The difference between 120-pixel type when the Anti-aliased option is selected (top line) versus deselected (bottom). Both examples were printed at 190 ppi.

Antialiased
Jagged as
all get out

- **Alignment:** Select one of these radio buttons to specify the way lines of type in a single paragraph align to the point at which you originally clicked with the type tool. Photoshop offers both horizontal and vertical alignment options. In my opinion, every one of the vertical options is a waste of time, particularly because you have no control over how the text aligns horizontally within the vertical columns. In Figure 14-9, for example, you can see how the characters in each vertical line are always aligned along their left edges. (Incidentally, I used capital letters to show off the vertical alignment options because vertically aligned lowercase letters always look bad, regardless of the program that creates them.)

Figure 14-9
A single paragraph of type shown as it appears if you select each of the six Alignment radio buttons. The I-beam cursor shows the point at which I clicked to display the Type Tool dialog box.

Here's how
text aligns

Here's how
text aligns

Here's how
text aligns

HT   T   T
E E   HE   E
R X   E X   X
E T   R T   HT
S   E   E
    A   S A   R
H L   H L   S A
O I   H I   H L
WG   O G   H I
 N   WN   O G
 S   S   WN
                        S

⤷ **Show:** The Type Tool dialog box can preview your settings for the Font, Size, and Style options. Select the Font check box at the bottom of the dialog box to preview font and type style; select the Size check box to preview type size. The size preview is always at 72 ppi, so the size is accurate only if you selected Pixels from the Size pop-up menu. That's why the text outside the dialog box back in Figure 14-3 is larger than the text inside the text entry area. Your settings for the Leading, Spacing, and Alignment options as well as the Anti-aliased check box are not reflected in the preview.

Manipulating type on a new layer

 After you confirm the contents of the Type Tool dialog box by clicking on the OK button or pressing Enter, Photoshop 4 places the type on a new layer. You can drag it up and down in the Layers palette, change the Opacity or blend mode, ⌘-drag the type to move it, transform the type by pressing ⌘-T, or perform any other operation that's applicable to a layer. Check out Chapter 13 for the full story.

Now that the type rests on a new layer, you can adjust the kerning without going through all the rigmarole associated with past versions of Photoshop. (Remember how you could ⌘-drag with the type tool to set down letters in Photoshop 3? That's gone in the new version.) Now you can merely select a letter with the marquee or lasso tool — don't use the magic wand, you'll mess up the edges — and press ⌘ with the left or right arrow tool to nudge the characters into more desirable positions. (Don't worry about selecting the characters perfectly — Photoshop automatically tightens the selection outlines around the characters once you start moving them.)

Photoshop 4 automatically activates the Preserve Transparency check box in the Layers palette for the new text layer. This way, you can paint inside the type without harming the character outlines, just as you could back in Version 3. In the top example of Figure 14-10, I dragged across the characters with the gradient tool; Photoshop automatically isolated the fill to the type. If you want to smear type (as back in Figure 14-2) or otherwise modify the area around the text, turn Preserve Transparency off. To create the bottom example in Figure 14-10, I first filled the characters with white by pressing ⌘-Delete. Then I pressed the / key to turn off Preserve Transparency, selected the Behind mode in the Airbrush Options palette, and airbrushed with black behind the letters.

Figure 14-10
To paint inside the letters (top), leave Preserve Transparency turned on. To paint in other portions of the layer (bottom), turn the check box off.

Another advantage to having text on a separate layer is that it never gets clipped. Have you ever created type that exceeded the boundary of the image? In the old days, Photoshop would clip away the offending characters the second you deselected or defloated it. So you'd have to delete the text and try again. Now you can simply increase the size of the canvas using Image ⇨ Canvas Size, or scale the text down with Free Transform (⌘-T). Either way, every character remains intact because the text resides on an independent layer.

Character Masks

 Photoshop 4 offers a second type tool. Known as the type mask tool, it creates character-shaped selection outlines. You can switch to the type mask tool by pressing the T key when the standard type tool is active. Or select the T with the dotted outline from the type tool pop-up in the toolbox.

Generally speaking, the type mask tool works like any other selection tool, except that you use the options in the Type Tool dialog box to create the character outlines. Click with the type mask tool to create a new selection outline. Shift-click to add the character outlines to an existing selection. Option-click to subtract from a selection, and Shift-Option-click to find the intersection.

The following sections demonstrate a few different ways to use this unusual new tool. Armed with these ideas, you should be able to invent enough additional type effects to keep you busy into the next millennia. Honestly, you won't believe the number of effects you can invent by screwing around with type outlines.

Filling type with an image

One of the most impressive and straightforward applications for text in Photoshop is to use the character outlines to select a portion of an image.

STEPS   Selecting Part of an Image Using Character Outlines

Step 1.   Open the image you want to mask.

Step 2.   Create your text. Select the type mask tool and click in the image window. Enter the text you want to use as a mask, format it as desired, and press Enter to display the type outlines in the image window. Large, bold characters work best. In Figure 14-11, I used the PostScript font Eras Ultra — an extremely bold type style — with a Size value of 260 and a Spacing value of negative 10.

Figure 14-11
The type mask tool produces character-shaped selection
outlines that you can use to lift portions of an image.

Step 3. **Drag the character outlines into position.** As with the other selection tools, dragging with the type mask tool moves just the selection outline without affecting the image itself.

Step 4. **Clone the selected portion of the image.** ⌘-Option-drag the selected characters to a new location, as demonstrated in Figure 14-12. Or you can ⌘-drag the selection and drop it into a different image window to set the text against a new background.

Figure 14-12
The result of
⌘-Option-
dragging the
selected
image to an
empty part
of the image
window.

Painting raised type

Instead of cloning the selected image or copying it to a different window, as suggested in Step 4 of the preceding section, you can paint around the character outlines to create a raised text effect, as illustrated in Figure 14-13.

Figure 14-13
Raised type created by painting with the dodge and airbrush tools around the perimeter of the character outlines.

To create this image, I carried out the first three steps described in the preceding section. I then prepared the characters by painting inside them with the dodge tool. I used a 65-pixel soft brush shape and selected Shadows from the brush modes pop-up menu (on the left side of the Brushes palette) to concentrate the lightening effect on the very dark areas in the image.

As shown in the top image in Figure 14-14, this helps set the letters apart from the rest of the image. To give the letters depth, I pressed D to set the foreground color to black; then I used the airbrush tool with a 35-pixel soft brush shape to apply shadows around the lower and right portions of each character, as shown in the middle row of Figure 14-14.

I next switched the foreground color to white and applied highlights around the upper and left portions of characters, which results in the image shown in the bottom row of Figure 14-14.

If you don't consider yourself an artist, you may find the prospect of painting around the edges of characters a little intimidating. But bear in mind that it's next to impossible to make a mistake. Because you're painting inside the selection, there's no danger of harming any portion of the image outside the character outlines. And if you mess up inside the selection, the problem is easily resolved.

If you look closely at the last image in Figure 14-14, for example, you can see that in applying white to the arch of the *a*, I accidentally got some on the right corner of the *e*. Hey, nobody's perfect. To fix the problem, all I need to do is select a smaller brush shape and paint over that area of the *e* with black.

Figure 14-14
After using the dodge tool to lighten the darkest pixels inside the letters (top), I painted in the shadows by airbrushing in black around the right and bottom edges of the letters (middle). Finally, I painted in the highlights by airbrushing in white around the left and top edges of the letters (bottom).

So if you make a mistake, press ⌘-Z or just keep painting. Give it a try. The process takes less than an hour and I bet you'll be pleasantly surprised with your results.

Feathering effects

You can feather text outlines just as you can feather other kinds of selections. In Figure 14-15, for example, I applied a Feather Radius value of 8 and pressed ⌘-Delete to fill the selection with white.

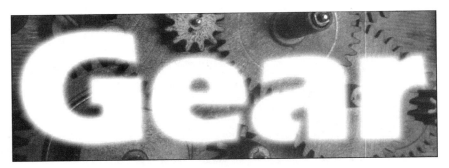

Figure 14-15
The result of feathering a text mask and filling it with white.

The following steps describe how to create a backlighting effect using Photoshop's feathering capability. Figure 14-16 shows the finished image. The text in the figure appears in front of a plain black background, but you can just as easily apply this technique to an image.

STEPS   Using Feathering to Backlight Text

Step 1. **Create a new image window large enough to accommodate a single line of large text.** I created an image 800 pixels wide by 300 pixels tall.

Step 2. **Fill the entire image with black.** Assuming default colors, press ⌘-A (Select ⇨ All) and Option-Delete.

Step 3. **Create your text using the type mask tool.** The text in the figure is set in 240-pixel Helvetica Inserat, a member of the Adobe Type Library.

Step 4. **Position and copy your text.** Drag the selection into the desired location in the image window and press ⌘-C.

Step 5. **Feather the selection.** Press ⌘-Shift-D, enter a number that's about equal to 1/20 the resolution of your image into the Feather Radius option box, and press Return. My resolution is about 180 ppi, so I entered 9. (Dividing by 20 isn't a hard and fast rule — you can use any value that works for your image.)

Step 6. **Press ⌘-Delete to fill the feathered selection with white.**

Step 7. **Press ⌘-V to paste the copied text.** As long as you don't deselect the feathered area, the new layer aligns with the feathered type below. Press ⌘-down arrow key to nudge the selection 3 to 5 pixels. The result appears in the top half of Figure 14-16.

Step 8. **For extra credit, stroke the type with the airbrush.** Set the foreground color to 50 percent black and then use the airbrush tool with the 100-pixel soft brush shape to paint a single line across the text. Because Preserve Transparency is on, you paint exclusively inside the characters.

This creates the effect of light seeping through a slightly open door, as shown in the bottom half of Figure 14-16.

Figure 14-16
You can create back-lit text by deleting a feathered version of a type mask and then pasting the original, unfeathered type in front (top). A slash of the airbrush gives it some depth (bottom).

Adding drop shadows

I already covered how to create drop shadows in the previous chapter, and it hasn't changed since then. Still, there are some minor differences, and drop shadows and text go together like ham and eggs, so we might as well take another look. This section examines two methods for adding drop shadows: one that involves changing the translucency of type (demonstrated in Figure 14-17); and another that relies on feathering (Figure 14-18).

The first steps work only if text and drop shadow are the same color. In the second set of steps, the text and background can be any colors.

STEPS   Creating Quick and Easy Hard-edged Drop Shadows

Step 1.   Create your text using the standard type tool. This technique involves filled type with no feathering, so it's easier to use the standard type tool. (You can use the type mask tool, but it turns out to be less convenient.) In Figure 14-17, I used an unusual typeface called Remedy Single from Emigre Graphics. It's a pretty wild font, so it lends itself well to this technique, which is by contrast quite simple.

Step 2. **Clone the new layer.** Drag the active layer name in the Layers palette onto the new layer icon at the bottom of the palette.

Step 3. **Nudge the shadow to offset it a few pixels.** To get the effect in Figure 14-17, I pressed ⌘-down arrow a few times and ⌘-right arrow a few more.

Step 4. **Press 4 on the keyboard.** This lowers the opacity of the cloned selection to 40 percent. Even though the translucent clone resides above the original type, it looks like a drop shadow because both layers of type are the same color.

Figure 14-17
I took two lines of type set in the font Remedy (yes, those lower characters are part of the font), cloned the type, and changed the opacity of the clone to 40 percent.

Step 5. **Press ⌘-Shift-[.** This step is optional — I didn't need it to achieve Figure 14-17. But if you want to paint inside the text or fill it with an image, you need to move the drop shadow in back of the text, which is what ⌘-Shift-left bracket will do.

The next steps describe a more functional, albeit slightly more complicated, drop shadow technique. The effect is illustrated in Figure 14-18.

STEPS   **Creating a Feathered Drop Shadow**

Step 1. **Create your type, this time using the type mask tool.** Figure 14-18 features my old standby, 240-pixel Helvetica Inserat. Drag the text to move it into the desired position.

Step 2. **Copy the selection to the Clipboard.** Even if your image window is empty, as mine was, this copies a bunch of white letters.

Step 3. **Feather the character outlines.** Use whatever Feather Radius value you like. I entered 8 because it reminded me of a pleasant year in my childhood and because it was roughly 1/20 of the resolution of the image.

Step 4. **Press Option-Delete to fill the feathered text with black.** The result is the first example of Figure 14-18. If you want to add a colored shadow to an image, send the selection to a new layer (⌘-J) and fill just the feathered characters with the foreground color (Shift-Option-Delete). Then select Multiply from the blend mode pop-up menu in the Layers palette and change the Opacity as desired. Whatever color you use, the feathered text is ready to serve as the drop shadow.

Figure 14-18
Feather the character outlines and fill them with black to create the drop shadow (top). Then paste the copied version of the text in front of the drop shadow (middle) and paint inside the characters (bottom).

Step 5. **Paste the copied text in front of the drop shadow.** ⌘-V results in a new layer.

Step 6. **Nudge the layer slightly off center from the shadow.** As always, press ⌘ with a few arrow keys. One possible result appears in the middle example of Figure 14-18. The text is white so you can see it clearly against the black shadow.

Step 7. **Turn on Preserve Transparency, and edit your text.** Photoshop doesn't activate Preserve Transparency automatically, because it doesn't know the layer contains text. You can then fill the selected type with a different color or gradation. Or paint inside the character. In the last example of Figure 14-18, I added a pattern with the rubber stamp tool (as discussed in Chapter 10). Then I painted in some wiggly lines with the airbrush tool.

Other Type Options

The type tool puts text on a new layer, and the type mask tool creates character-shaped selection outlines. But these are hardly the big text enhancements that many true-blue Photoshop users were hoping for. Word has it that Adobe plans to overhaul text fairly dramatically in Photoshop 5, but in the meantime, things haven't changed much since Photoshop's early days.

So what are your options? One option is to create your text in Illustrator, FreeHand, or some other drawing program, then drag and drop it into Photoshop. This way, you can keep the Illustrator or FreeHand file close at hand in case you need to edit the text in the future. Drawing programs also permit you to create type on a curve and other effects that are beyond Photoshop's capabilities.

If you don't own Illustrator or FreeHand — or if you're looking for an integrated solution that doesn't require you to leave Photoshop — then you might want to purchase a good third-party plug-in. The best all-around text creation plug-in is PhotoText, part of the $100 PhotoTools collection from Extensis. Shown in Figure 14-19, this is the only plug-in that lets you modify character spacing, expand or condense type, and apply multiple type styles from one central location inside Photoshop. You'll find a trial demonstration version of PhotoTools along with pricing and contact information on the CD-ROM in the back of this book.

Figure 14-19
PhotoText from Extensis serves as a fully functioning text-editing environment, complete with a preview of the image window.

Figure 14-20
TypeCaster lets you create 3D type inside Photoshop. But because TypeCaster doesn't permit you to hand-kern letters, you'll probably need to adjust the type manually on a separate layer.

If you want to create three-dimensional type effects inside Photoshop, the best solution is the $200 TypeCaster from Xaos Tools. To use the plug-in, you simply open a dialog box, enter some text, select a font, and modify the type in 3D space. You can rotate, scale, and adjust the depth of the extrusion. You can also apply and modify surface textures to the face, bevel, and extruded sides of the type, as demonstrated in Figure 14-20. Finally, you can assign and position light sources inside a separate dialog box. TypeCaster isn't perfect — live previews, individual character positioning, and letter warping would all go a long way — but it's an excellent addition to Photoshop.

Filters and Special Effects

V

Corrective Filtering

CHAPTER 15

In This Chapter

- ❖ An overview of corrective, destructive, and new effects filters
- ❖ Fading a filtered image with the original
- ❖ Fixing the focus of an image with Unsharp Mask
- ❖ Enhancing a grainy photograph using a custom edge mask
- ❖ Highlighting edges with the High Pass filter
- ❖ Creating glowing images with Gaussian Blur
- ❖ Creative uses for the Motion Blur, Wind, and Radial Blur filters
- ❖ Using the new Smart Blur filter
- ❖ Feathering a selection using Maximum and Gaussian Blur
- ❖ A complete guide to the filters in the Noise submenu
- ❖ Sharpening images with lots of compression artifacts
- ❖ Reducing moiré patterns in scanned images

Filter Basics

In Photoshop, *filters* enable you to apply automated effects to an image. Though named after photographer's filters, which typically correct lighting and perspective fluctuations, Photoshop's filters can accomplish a great deal more. You can slightly increase the focus of an image, introduce random pixels, add depth to an image, or completely rip it apart and reassemble it into a hurky pile of goo. Any number of special effects are made available via filters.

At this point, a little bell should be ringing in your head, telling you to beware of standardized special effects. Why? Because everyone has access to the same filters that you do. If you rely on filters to edit your images for you, your audience will quickly recognize your work as poor or at least unremarkable art.

Think of it this way: You're watching MTV. You should be watching VH1 with the rest of the old folks, but when you were flipping through the channels you got stuck on a Peter Gabriel video. Outrageous effects, right? He rides an imaginary roller coaster, bumper cars crash playfully into his face, fish leap over his head. You couldn't be more amused or impressed.

As the video fades, you're so busy basking in the glow that you neglect for a split second to whack the channel-changer. Before you know it, you're midway through an advertisement for a monster truck rally. Like the video, the ad is riddled with special effects — spinning letters, a reverberating voice-over slowed down to an octave below the narrator's normal pitch, and lots of big machines filled with little men filled with single brain cells working overtime.

In and of themselves, these special effects aren't bad. There was probably even a time when you thought that spinning letters and reverberating voice-overs were hot stuff. But sometime after you passed beyond preadolescence, you managed to grow tired of these particular effects. You've come to associate them with raunchy, local, car-oriented commercials. Certainly, these effects are devoid of substance, but more importantly, they're devoid of creativity.

This chapter and the two that follow, therefore, are about the creative application of special effects. Rather than trying to show an image subject to every single filter — a service already performed quite adequately by the manual included with your software — these chapters explain exactly how the most important filters work and offer some concrete ways to use them.

You'll also learn how to apply several filters in tandem and how to use filters to edit images and selection outlines. My goal is not so much to teach you what filters are available — you can find that out by tugging on the Filter menu — but how and when to use filters.

A first look at filters

You access Photoshop's special effects filters by choosing commands from the Filter menu. These commands fall into two general camps: "corrective" and "destructive."

Corrective filters

Corrective filters are workaday tools that you use to modify scanned images and prepare an image for printing or screen display. In many cases, the effects are subtle enough that the viewer won't even notice that you applied a corrective filter. As demonstrated in Figure 15-1 and Color Plate 15-1, these filters include those that change the focus of an image, enhance color transitions, and average the colors of neighboring pixels. You'll find these filters in the Filter ⇨ Blur, Noise, Sharpen, and Other submenus.

Figure 15-1

The gigantic head of 4th-century Roman emperor Constantine subject to four corrective filters, including one each from the Sharpen, Blur, Other, and Noise submenus (reading clockwise from upper left).

Unsharp Mask · Gaussian Blur

Median · High Pass

Many corrective filters have direct opposites. Blur is the opposite of Sharpen, Add Noise is the opposite of Median, and so on. This is not to say that one filter entirely removes the effect of the other; only reversion functions such as the Undo command provide that capability. Instead, two opposite filters produce contrasting effects.

Corrective filters are the subject of this chapter. Although they number fewer than their destructive counterparts, I spend more time on them because they represent the functions you're most likely to use on a day-to-day basis.

Destructive filters

The destructive filters produce effects so dramatic that they can, if used improperly, completely overwhelm your artwork, making the filter more important than the image itself. For the most part, destructive filters reside in the Filter ➪ Distort, Pixelate, Render, and Stylize submenus. A few examples of overwhelmed images appear in Figure 15-2 and Color Plate 15-2.

Wave

Figure 15-2
The effects of applying four destructive filters, one each from the Distort, Pixelate, Render, and Stylize submenus (clockwise from upper left). Note that Lens Flare is applicable to color images only, so I had to convert Constantine to the RGB mode before applying the filter.

Crystallize

Emboss

Lens Flare

Destructive filters produce way-cool effects, and many people gravitate toward them when first experimenting with Photoshop. But the filters invariably destroy the original clarity and composition of the image. Granted, every Photoshop function is destructive to a certain extent, but destructive filters change your image so extensively that you can't easily disguise the changes later by applying other filters or editing techniques.

Destructive filters are the subject of Chapter 16. Rather than explaining every one of these filters in detail, I try to provide a general overview.

Effects filters

 New to Photoshop 4 is a subset of destructive filters called the "effects" filters. These 47 filters come from the Gallery Effects collection, originally developed by Silicon Beach (the same folks responsible for the old SuperPaint), sold to Aldus Corporation (of PageMaker fame), and finally acquired by Adobe Systems. Not knowing what exactly to do with this grab bag of plug-ins, Adobe first added them to Illustrator 6 and has now made them part of Photoshop 4.

Frankly, I think Adobe should have sentenced Gallery Effects to the same grizzly fate as SuperPaint and a lot of other creaky old junk from the Aldus library. Although many of these filters are interesting — and a few might even be useful more than once or twice in a lifetime — they feel tacked on. They weren't developed to satisfy any specific user requirements; they were merely heaped on the Photoshop 4 pile to sweeten the deal.

Little about these filters has changed since Gallery Effects 1.5 came out in 1993. A couple of filters have been renamed — the old GE Ripple filter is now Ocean Ripple to avoid confusion with Photoshop's own Ripple filter. And one filter, GE Emboss, is gone, presumably because it detracted from the popular Filter ⇨ Stylize ⇨ Emboss. But Adobe hasn't bothered with any meaningful retooling. You can't raise or lower a GE dialog box value using the arrow keys, you can't switch applications when an effects dialog box is visible (both capabilities granted to other filters), and a few are dreadfully slow.

As a result, I devote only passing attention to the effects filters, explaining those very few that fulfill a real need. Of course, I encourage you to experiment and derive your own conclusions. After all, as Figure 15-3 illustrates, these filters do produce intriguing special effects. I mean, that Plaster effect is just plain cool. For the record, most of the effects filters reside in the Filter ⇨ Artistic, Brush Strokes, Sketch, and Texture submenus. A few have trickled out into other submenus, including Filter ⇨ Distort ⇨ Diffuse Glow, Glass, and Ocean Ripple; and Filter ⇨ Stylize ⇨ Glowing Edges.

Cutout

Angled Brushes

Patchwork

Plaster

Figure 15-3
The new "effects" filters come from Gallery Effects, a little toy surprise that Adobe accidentally acquired when it purchased Aldus Corporation. Here we see the impact of one filter each from the Filter ⇨ Artistic, Brush Strokes, Sketch, and Texture submenus (clockwise from upper left).

If your experimentation leads you to the same conclusion as me — that you can live through most days without the effects filters — you can turn them off to a save a whole lot of space in RAM that is better devoted to storing pixels. (Adobe once devised a special "piggy" plug-in to address the fact that the Gallery Effects were such RAM hogs.) All the effects filters are stored in the Effects folder inside the Plug-ins folder on your hard drive. Move the Effects folder out of the Plug-ins folder, and all 47 filters will be turned off.

How filters work

When you choose a command from the Filter menu, Photoshop applies the filter to the selected portion of the image. If no portion of the image is selected, Photoshop applies the filter to the entire image. Therefore, if you want to filter every nook and cranny of an image, press ⌘-D and then choose the desired command.

External plug-ins

Some filters are built into the Photoshop application. Others are external modules that reside in the Plug-ins folder. This allows you to add functionality to Photoshop by purchasing additional filters from third-party collections. Gallery Effects used to be such a collection. Others include PhotoTools from Extensis, Paint Alchemy from Xaos Tools, the Series collections from Andromeda, Eye Candy from Alien Skin, and Kai's Power Tools from MetaTools.

If you open the Plug-ins folder inside the Photoshop folder, you'll see that it contains several subfolders. By default, Photoshop places the filters in the Filters and Effects subfolders, but you can place additional filters anywhere inside the Plug-ins folder. Even if you create a new folder inside the Plug-ins folder and call it *No Filters Here*, create another folder inside that called *Honest, Fresh Out of Filters*, toss in one more folder called *Carpet Beetles Only*, and put every plug-in you own inside this latest folder, Photoshop sees through your clever ruse and displays the exact same filters you always see under their same submenus in the Filter menu. The only purpose of the subfolders is to keep things tidy, so that you don't have to look through a list of 6,000 files inside a single Plug-ins folder (like you did in the old days).

Previewing filters

For years, the biggest problem with Photoshop's filters was that none offered previews to help you predict the outcome of an effect. You just had to tweak your 15,000 meaningless settings and hope for the best. But today, life is much better. Photoshop 3 introduced previews, and Version 4 has made them commonly available to all but the most gnarly filters.

Photoshop offers two previewing capabilities:

➩ **Dialog box previews:** Labeled in Figure 15-4, the 100×100-pixel preview box is now a common feature to all filter dialog boxes. Drag inside the preview box to scroll the portion of the image you want to preview. Move the cursor outside the dialog box to get the square preview cursor (labeled in the figure). Click with the cursor to center the contents of the preview box at the clicked position in the image.

Click on the zoom buttons (+ and -) to reduce the image inside the preview box. You can even take advantage of the standard zoom tool by pressing ⌘-spacebar or Option-spacebar, depending on whether you want to zoom in or out.

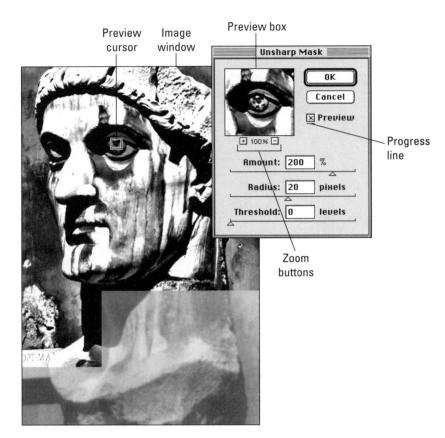

Preview cursor

Image window

Preview box

Unsharp Mask

OK

Cancel

☒ Preview

⊞ 100% ⊟

Amount: 200 %

Radius: 20 pixels

Threshold: 0 levels

Progress line

Zoom buttons

Figure 15-4
Most filter dialog boxes let you preview the effects of the filter both inside the dialog box and in the image window.

↪ **Image window previews:** Most corrective filters — as well as a couple of destructives like Mosaic and Emboss — also preview effects in the full image window. Just select the Preview check box to activate this function. While the effect is previewing, a blinking progress line appears under the check box. In Figure 15-4, for example, you can see that the bottom of the image still hasn't finished previewing, so the progress line strobes away. If you're working on a relatively poky computer, like a Mac II or Centris, you'll probably want to turn this check box off to speed up the pace at which the filter functions.

Incidentally, the Preview check box has no affect on the contents of the preview box. The latter continually monitors the effects of your settings, whether you like it or not.

Use the Preview check box to compare the before and after effects of a corrective filter in the image window. Turn it on to see the effect; turn it off to see the original image. You can also compare the image in the preview box by clicking in the box. Mouse down to see the old image; release to see the filtered image. It's like an electronic, high-priced, adult version of peek-a-boo. But not nearly as likely to induce giggles.

Even though a dialog box is on-screen and active, you can zoom and scroll the contents of the image window. ⌘-spacebar-click to zoom in, Option-spacebar-click to zoom out, and spacebar-drag to scroll. You can also choose commands from the View and Window menus. And feel free to switch applications.

 And one more tip: When you press the Option key, the Cancel button changes to a Reset button. Option-click on this button to restore the settings that appeared when you first opened the dialog box. (These are not necessarily the factory default settings; they are the settings you last applied to an image.)

Photoshop 4 enhanced the previewing capabilities of several destructive filters, including the likes of Filter ➪ Distort ➪ Ripple and Filter ➪ Stylize ➪ Wind. Even so, seven filters continue to offer no previews whatsoever: Radial Blur, Displace, Color Halftone, Extrude, Tiles, De-Interlace, and Offset. And of course, single-shot filters — the ones that don't bring up dialog boxes — don't need previews because there aren't any settings to adjust.

Reapplying the last filter

 To reapply the last filter used in the current Photoshop session, choose the first command from the Filter menu or simply press ⌘-F. If you want to reapply the filter subject to different settings, Option-choose the first Filter command or press ⌘-Option-F to redisplay that filter's dialog box.

Both techniques work even if you undo the last application of a filter. However, if you cancel a filter while in progress, pressing ⌘-F or ⌘-Option-F applies the last uncanceled filter.

Nudging numerical values

 In addition to entering specific numerical values inside filter dialog boxes, you can nudge the values using the up and down arrow keys. When working with percentage values, press an arrow key to raise or lower the value by 1. Press Shift-up or -down arrow to change the value in increments of 10.

If the value accommodates decimal values, it's probably more sensitive to the arrow key. Press an arrow for a 0.1 change; press Shift-arrow for 1.0.

As I mentioned earlier, these tricks don't work in some of the destructive filters dialog boxes, most notably those associated with old Gallery Effects filters.

Fading a filter

In many cases, you apply filters to a selection or image at full intensity — meaning that you marquee an area using a selection tool, choose a filter command, enter whatever settings you deem appropriate if a dialog box appears, and sit back and watch the fireworks.

What's so "full intensity" about that? Sounds normal, right? Well, the fact is, you can reduce the intensity of the last filter applied by choosing the Filter ⇨ Fade command or pressing ⌘-Shift-F. This command permits you to mix the filtered image with the original, unfiltered one. (This command also works with color corrections, as discussed in Chapter 18.)

As shown in Figure 15-5, the Fade dialog box provides you with the basic tools of image mixing — an Opacity value and a blend mode pop-up menu. To demonstrate the wonders of Filter ⇨ Fade, I've applied two particularly destructive Gallery Effects filters to the colossal marble head — Filter ⇨ Stylize ⇨ Glowing Edges and Filter ⇨ Sketch ⇨ Note Paper. In the second column of heads, I pressed ⌘-Shift-F and lowered the Opacity of the two effects to 30 percent. The right-hand images show the effects of two blend modes, Lighten and Overlay.

Glowing Edges   Lighten

Note Paper   30% Opacity   Overlay

Figure 15-5
Press ⌘-Shift-F to mix the filtered image with the unfiltered original. Now, is it me, or is Constantine on Note Paper the spitting image of Rambo? That's got to be keeping some art historian awake at night.

Creating layered effects

The drawback of the Fade command is that it's only available immediately after you apply a filter (or color correction). If you so much as modify a selection outline after applying the filter, the Fade command dims, only to return when you apply the next filter.

Therefore, you may find it more helpful to copy a selection to a separate layer (⌘-J) before applying a filter. This way, you can perform other operations, and even apply many filters in a row, before mixing the filtered image with the underlying original.

Filtering inside a border

And here's another reason to layer before you filter: If your image has a border around it — like the ones shown in Figure 15-6 — you don't want Photoshop to factor the border into the filtering operation. To avoid this, select the image inside the border and press ⌘-J to layer it prior to applying the filter. The reason is that most filters take neighboring pixels into consideration even if they are not selected. By contrast, when a selection floats, it has no neighboring pixels, and therefore the filter affects the selected pixels only.

Figure 15-6 shows the results of applying two filters discussed in this chapter — Unsharp Mask and Motion Blur — when the image is anchored in place and when it's layered. In all cases, the 2-pixel border was not selected. In the left examples, the Unsharp Mask filter leaves a high-contrast residue around the edge of the image, while Motion Blur duplicates the left and right edges of the border. Both problems vanish when the filters are applied to layered images, as seen on right.

Even if the area outside the selection is not a border per se — perhaps it's just a comparatively dark or light area that serves as a visual frame — layering comes in handy. You should always layer the selection unless you specifically want edge pixels to be calculated by the filter.

Figure 15-6
The results of applying two sample filters to images surrounded by borders. In each case, only the image was selected; the border was not. Layering the right examples prevented the borders from affecting the performance of the filters.

Undoing a sequence of filters

Okay, here's one last reason to layer before you filter. Copying an image to a layer protects the underlying image. If you just want to experiment a little, pressing ⌘-J is often more convenient than taking a snapshot or saving the image for possible reversion. After applying four or five effects to a floating image, you can undo all that automated abuse by Option-clicking on the trash icon at the bottom of the Layers palette. The underlying original remains unharmed.

Heightening Focus and Contrast_

If you've experimented at all with Photoshop, you've no doubt had your way with many of the commands in the Filter ➪ Sharpen submenu. By increasing the contrast between neighboring pixels, the sharpening filters enable you to compensate for image elements that were photographed or scanned slightly out of focus.

The Sharpen, Sharpen More, and Sharpen Edges commands are easy to use and immediate in their effect. However, you can achieve better results and widen your range of sharpening options if you learn how to use the Unsharp Mask and High Pass commands, which I discuss at length in the following pages.

Using the Unsharp Mask filter

The first thing you need to know about the Unsharp Mask filter is that it has a weird name. The filter has nothing to do with "unsharpening" — whatever that is — nor is it tied into Photoshop's masking capabilities. Unsharp Mask is named after a traditional film compositing technique (which is also oddly named) that highlights the edges in an image by combining a blurred film negative with the original film positive.

That's all very well and good, but the fact is most Photoshop artists have never touched a stat camera (an expensive piece of machinery, roughly twice the size of a washing machine, used by image editors of the late Jurassic, pre-Photoshop epoch). Even folks like me who used to operate stat cameras professionally never had the time to delve into the world of unsharp masking. In addition — and much to the filter's credit — Unsharp Mask goes beyond traditional camera techniques.

To understand Unsharp Mask — or Photoshop's other sharpening filters, for that matter — you first need to understand some basic terminology. When you apply one of the sharpening filters, Photoshop increases the contrast between neighboring pixels. The effect is similar to what you see when you adjust a camera to bring a scene into sharper focus.

Two of Photoshop's sharpening filters, Sharpen and Sharpen More, affect whatever area of your image is selected. The Sharpen Edges filter, however, performs its sharpening operations only on the *edges* in the image — those areas that feature the highest amount of contrast.

Unsharp Mask gives you both sharpening options. It can sharpen only the edges in an image or it can sharpen any portion of an image according to your exact specifications, whether it finds an edge or not. It fulfills the exact same purposes as the Sharpen, Sharpen Edges, and Sharpen More commands, but it's much more versatile. Simply put, the Unsharp Mask tool is the only sharpening filter you'll ever need.

When you choose Filter ⇨ Sharpen ⇨ Unsharp Mask, Photoshop displays the Unsharp Mask dialog box, shown in Figure 15-7, which offers the following options:

✐ **Amount:** Enter a value between 1 and 500 percent to specify the degree to which you want to sharpen the selected image. Higher values produce more pronounced effects.

Figure 15-7
Despite any conclusions you may glean from its bizarre name, the Unsharp Mask filter sharpens images according to your specifications in this dialog box.

✐ **Radius:** This option determines the thickness of the sharpened edge. Low values produce crisp edges. High values produce thicker edges with more contrast throughout the image.

✐ **Threshold:** Enter a value between 0 and 255 to control how Photoshop recognizes edges in an image. The value indicates the numerical difference between the brightness values of two neighboring pixels that must occur if Photoshop is to sharpen those pixels. A low value sharpens lots of pixels; a high value excludes most pixels from the running.

The preview options offered by the Unsharp Mask dialog box are absolutely essential visual aids that you're likely to find tremendously useful throughout your Photoshop career. Just the same, you'll be better prepared to experiment with the Amount, Radius, and Threshold options and less surprised by the results if you read the following sections, which explain these options in detail and demonstrate the effects of each.

Specifying the amount of sharpening

If Amount were the only Unsharp Mask option, no one would have any problems understanding this filter. If you want to sharpen an image ever so slightly, enter a low percentage value. Values between 25 and 50 percent are ideal for producing subtle effects. If you want to sharpen an image beyond the point of good taste, enter a value somewhere in the 300 to 500 percent range. And if you're looking for moderate sharpening, try out some value between 50 and 300 percent. Figure 15-8 shows the results of applying different Amount values while leaving the Radius and Threshold values at their default settings of 1.0 and 0, respectively.

Figure 15-8
The results of sharpening an image with the Unsharp Mask filter using eight different Amount values. The Radius and Threshold values used for all images were 1.0 and 0, respectively (the default settings).

If you're not sure how much you want to sharpen an image, try out a small value, in the 25 to 50 percent range. Then reapply that setting repeatedly by pressing ⌘-F. As you can see in Figure 15-9, repeatedly applying the filter at a low setting produces a nearly identical result to applying the filter once at a higher setting. For example, you can achieve the effect shown in the middle image in the figure by applying the Unsharp Mask filter three times at 50 percent or once at 250 percent. I created the top-row results in Figure 15-9 using a constant Radius value of 1.0. In the second row, I lowered the Radius progressively from 1.0 (left) to 0.8 (middle) to 0.6 (right).

50% twice   50% times three   50% times four

100%   250%   500%

Figure 15-9
Repeatedly applying the Unsharp Mask filter at 50 percent (top row) is nearly equivalent on a pixel-by-pixel basis to applying the filter once at higher settings (bottom row).

The benefit of using small values is that they allow you to experiment with sharpening incrementally. As the figure demonstrates, you can add sharpening bit by bit to increase the focus of an image. You can't, however, reduce sharpening incrementally if you apply too high a value; you must press ⌘-Z and start again.

Just for fun, Color Plate 15-3 shows the results of applying the Unsharp Mask filter to each of the color channels in an RGB image independently. In each case, the Amount value was set to 300 percent, and the Radius and Threshold values were set to their defaults (1.0 and 0). To heighten the effect, I applied the filter twice to each channel. The top row shows the results of applying the filter to a single channel; in the second row, I applied the filter to two of the three channels (leaving only one channel unfiltered). You can see how the filter creates a crisp halo of color around the rose. Sharpening the red channel creates a red halo, sharpening the red and green channels together creates a yellow halo, and so on. Applying the filter to the red and green channels produced the most noticeable effects because these channels contain the lion's share of the image detail. The blue channel contained the least detail — as is typical — so sharpening it produced the least dramatic results.

If you're a little foggy on how to access individual color channels, read Chapter 5. Incidentally, you can achieve similar effects by sharpening the individual channels in a Lab or CMYK image.

Setting the thickness of the edges

The Unsharp Mask filter works by identifying edges and increasing the contrast around those edges. The Radius value tells Photoshop how thick you want your edges. Large values produce thicker edges than small values.

The ideal Radius value depends on the resolution of your image and the quality of its edges:

- ↩ When creating screen images — such as Web graphics — use a very low Radius value such as 0.5. This results in terrific hair-line edges that look so crisp, you'll think you washed your bifocals.

- ↩ If a low Radius value brings out weird little imperfections — such as grain, scan lines, or JPEG compression artifacts — raise the value to 1.0 or higher. If that doesn't help, don't fret. I include two different sure-fire image fixing techniques later in this chapter, one designed to sharpen grainy old photos, and another that accommodates compressed images.

- ↩ When printing an image at a moderate resolution — anywhere from 120 to 180 ppi — use a Radius value of 1.0. The edges will look a little thick on-screen, but they'll print fine.

- ↩ For high-resolution images — around 300 ppi — try a Radius of 2.0. Because Photoshop prints more pixels per inch, the edges have to be thicker to remain nice and visible.

 If you're looking for a simple formula, I'd recommend 0.1 of Radius for every 15 ppi of final image resolution. That means 75 ppi warrants a Radius of 0.5, 120 ppi warrants 0.8, 180 ppi warrants 1.2, and so on. If you have a calculator, just divide the intended resolution by 150 to get the ideal Radius value.

You can of course enter higher Radius values — as high as 250, in fact. Higher values produce heightened contrast effects, almost as if the image had been photocopied too many times, generally useful for producing special effects.

But don't take my word for it; you be the judge. Figure 15-10 demonstrates the results of specific Radius values. In each case, the Amount and Threshold values remain constant at 100 percent and 0, respectively.

Original 0.5 1.0

1.5 2.5 5.0

10.0 50.0 100.0

Figure 15-10
The results of applying eight different Radius values, ranging from precise edges to very gooey.

Figure 15-11 shows the results of combining different Amount and Radius values. You can see that a large Amount value helps to offset the softening of a high Radius value. For example, when the Amount is set to 200 percent, as in the first row, the Radius value appears to mainly enhance contrast when raised from 0.5 to 2.0. However, when the Amount value is lowered to 50 percent, the higher Radius value does more to distribute the effect than boost contrast.

Figure 15-11
The effects of combining different Amount and Radius settings. The Threshold value for each image was set to 0, the default setting.

200%, 0.5   200%, 2.0   200%, 10.0

100%, 0.5   100%, 2.0   100%, 10.0

50%, 0.5   50%, 2.0   50%, 10.0

For those few folks who are thinking, "By gum, I wonder what would happen if you applied an unusually high Radius value to each color channel independently," you have only to gaze upon the wondrous Color Plate 15-4. In this figure, I again applied the Unsharp Mask filter to each channel and each pair of channels in the RGB rose image independently. But I changed the Amount value to 100 percent, the Radius value to a relatively whopping 10.0 pixels, and left the Threshold at 0. To make the splash more apparent, I applied the filter twice to each image. The colors now bound out from the rose, bleeding into the gray background by as much as 10 pixels, the Radius value. Notice how the color fades away from the rose, just as if I had feathered it? A high Radius value spreads the sharpening effect and, in doing so, allows colors to bleed. Because you normally apply the filter to all channels simultaneously, the colors bleed uniformly to create thick edges and high-contrast effects.

Recognizing edges

By default, the Unsharp Mask filter sharpens every pixel in a selection. However, you can instruct the filter to sharpen only the edges in an image by raising the Threshold value from zero to some other number. The Threshold value represents the difference between two neighboring pixels — as measured in brightness levels — that must occur for Photoshop to recognize them as an edge.

Suppose that the brightness values of neighboring pixels are 10 and 20. If you set the Threshold value to 5, Photoshop reads both pixels, notes that the difference between their brightness values is more than 5, and treats them as an edge. If you set the Threshold value to 20, however, Photoshop passes them by. A low Threshold value, therefore, causes the Unsharp Mask Filter to affect a high number of pixels, and vice versa.

In the top row of images in Figure 15-12, the high Threshold values result in tiny slivers of sharpness that outline only the most substantial edges in the woman's face. As I lower the Threshold value incrementally in the second and third rows, the sharpening effect takes over more and more of the face, ultimately sharpening all details uniformly in the lower right example.

Figure 15-12
The results of applying nine different Threshold values. To best show off the differences between each image, I set the Amount and Radius values to 500 percent and 2.0 respectively.

Using the preset sharpening filters

So how do the Sharpen, Sharpen Edges, and Sharpen More commands compare with the Unsharp Mask filter? First of all, none of the preset commands permit you to vary the thickness of your edges, a function provided by Unsharp Mask's Radius option. Secondly, only the Sharpen Edges command can recognize high-contrast areas in an image. And third, all three commands are set in stone — you can't adjust their effects in any way. Figure 15-13 shows the effect of each preset command and the nearly equivalent effect created with the Unsharp Mask filter.

Sharpen   Sharpen Edges   Sharpen More

100%, 0.5, 0   100%, 0.5, 5   300%, 0.5, 0

Figure 15-13
The effects of the three preset sharpening filters (top row) compared with the Unsharp Mask equivalents (bottom row). Unsharp Mask values are listed in the following order: Amount, Radius, Threshold.

Sharpening grainy photographs

Having completed my neutral discussion of Unsharp Mask, king of the Sharpen filters, I hasten to interject a little bit of commentary, along with a helpful solution to a common sharpening problem.

First, the commentary: While Amount and Radius are the kinds of superior options that will serve you well throughout the foreseeable future, I urge young and old to observe Threshold with the utmost scorn and rancor. The idea is fine — we can all agree that you need some way to draw a dividing line between those pixels that you want to sharpen and those that you want to leave unchanged. But the Threshold setting is nothing more than a glorified on/off switch that results in harsh transitions between sharpened and unsharpened pixels.

Consider the picture of pre-presidential Eisenhower in Figure 15-14. Like so many vintage photographs, this particular image of Ike is a little softer than we're used to seeing these days. But if I apply a heaping helping of Unsharp Mask — as in the second example in the figure — I bring out as much film grain as image detail. The official Photoshop solution is to raise the Threshold value, but the option's intrinsic harshness results in a pock-marked effect, as shown on the right. Photoshop has simply replaced one kind of grain with another.

Figure 15-14
The original Ike is a bit soft (left), a condition I can remedy with Unsharp Mask. Leaving the Threshold value set to 0 brings out the film grain (middle), but raising the value results in equally unattractive artifacts (right).

Soft

Sharpened, Threshold: 0

Sharpened, Threshold: 2.0

These abrupt transitions are quite out of keeping with Photoshop's normal approach. Paintbrushes have antialiased edges, selections can be feathered, the Color Range command offers Fuzziness — in short, everything mimics the softness found in real life. Yet right here, inside what is indisputably Photoshop's most essential filter, we find no mechanism for softness whatsoever.

While we wait for Photoshop to give us a better Threshold — one with a Fuzziness slider or similar control — you can create a better Threshold using a very simple masking technique. Using a few filters that I explore at greater length throughout this chapter and the next, you can devize a selection outline that traces the essential edges in the image — complete with fuzzy transitions — and leaves the non-edges unmolested. So get out your favorite old vintage photograph and follow along with these steps.

STEPS   Creating and Using an Edge Mask

Step 1.   Duplicate one of the color channels. Bring up the Channels palette and drag one of the color channels onto the little page icon. Ike is a grayscale image, so I duplicate the one and only channel.

Step 2.   **Choose Filter ➪ Stylize ➪ Find Edges.** As I explain in Chapter 16, the Find Edges filter automatically traces the edges of your image with thick, gooey outlines that are ideal for creating edge masks.

Step 3.   **Press ⌘-I, or choose Image ➪ Adjust ➪ Invert.** Find Edges produces black lines against a white background, but in order to select your edges, you need white lines against a black background. The Invert command reverses the lights and darks in the mask, as in the first example in Figure 15-15.

Find Edges, Invert

Find edge mask

Sharpened edges

Figure 15-15
I copy a channel, find the edges, and invert (left). I then apply a string of filters to expand and soften the edges (middle). After converting the mask to a selection outline, I reapply Unsharp Mask with winning results (right).

Step 4.   **Choose Filter ➪ Noise ➪ Median.** You need fat, gooey edges, and the current ones are a bit tenuous. To firm up the edges, choose the Median filter, enter a value of 2 (or thereabouts), and press Return.

Step 5.   **Choose Filter ➪ Other ➪ Maximum.** The next step is to thicken up the edges. The Maximum filter expands the white areas in the image, serving much the same function in a mask as Select ➪ Modify ➪ Expand serves when editing a selection outline. Enter 4 for the Radius value and press Return.

Step 6.   **Choose Filter ➪ Blur ➪ Gaussian Blur.** Unfortunately, the Maximum filter results in a bunch of little squares that don't do much for our cause.

You can merge the squares into a seamless line by choosing the Gaussian Blur command and entering 4, the same radius you entered for Maximum. Then press Return.

The completed mask is pictured in the second example of Figure 15-15. Though hardly an impressive sight to the uninitiated eye, you're looking at the perfect edge mask — soft, natural, and extremely accurate.

Step 7. **Return to the standard composite view**. Press ⌘-tilde (~) in a color image. Since I'm working in a grayscale image, I press ⌘-1.

Step 8. **Convert the mask to a selection outline**. ⌘-click on the mask name in the Channels palette. Photoshop selects the most essential edges in the image without selecting the grain.

Step 9. **Choose Filter ⇨ Sharpen ⇨ Unsharp Mask**. In the last example in Figure 15-15, I applied the highest permitted Amount value, 500 percent, and a Radius of 2.0.

Step 10. **Whatever values you use, make sure the Threshold is set to 0.** And always leave it at 0 from this day forward.

In case Figures 15-14 and 15-15 are a little too subtle, I include enlarged views of the great general's eyes in Figure 15-16. The top eyes show the result of using the Threshold value, the bottom eyes were created using the edge mask. Which ones appear sharper and less grainy to you?

Figure 15-16
Enlarged views of the last examples from Figures 15-14 (top) and 15-15 (bottom). A good edge mask beats the Threshold value every time.

Using the High Pass filter

The High Pass filter falls more or less in the same camp as the sharpening filters but is not located under the Filter ⇨ Sharpen submenu. This frequently overlooked gem enables you to isolate high-contrast image areas from their low-contrast counterparts.

Figure 15-17
The results of separating high- and low-contrast areas in an image with the High Pass filter set at eight different Radius values.

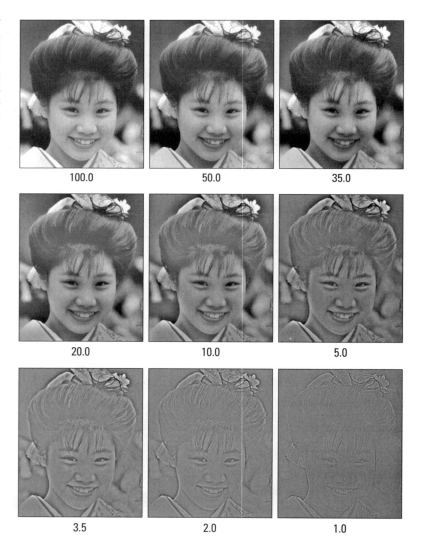

When you choose Filter ⇨ Other ⇨ High Pass, Photoshop offers a single option: the familiar Radius value, which can vary from 0.1 to 250.0. As demonstrated in Figure 15-17, high Radius values distinguish areas of high and low contrast only slightly.

Low values change all high-contrast areas to dark gray and low-contrast areas to a slightly lighter gray. A value of 0.1 (not shown) changes all pixels in an image to a single gray value and is therefore useless.

Applying High Pass to individual color channels

In my continuing series of color plates devoted to taking the simple beauty of a rose and abusing it but good, Color Plate 15-5 shows the results of applying the High Pass filter set to a Radius value of 10.0 to the various color channels. This application is actually a pretty interesting use for this filter. When applied to all channels at once, High Pass has an irritating habit of robbing the image of color in the low-contrast areas, just where the color is needed most. But when applied to a single channel, there's no color to steal. In fact, the filter adds color. For example, because there is almost no contrast in the black shadow of the rose, High Pass elevates the black to gray in each of the affected color channels. The gray in the red channel appears red, the gray in the red channel mixed with the gray in the green channel appears yellow, and so on. As a result, the filter imbues each image with a chalky glow.

 I enhanced the High Pass effect slightly in Color Plate 15-5 by increasing the contrast of each affected color channel using the Levels command. Using the three Input option boxes at the top of the Levels dialog box, I changed the first value to 65 and the third value to 190, thereby compressing the color space equally on both the black and white sides. Had I not done this, the images would appear a little more washed out. (Not a lot, but I figure that you deserve the best color I can deliver.) For detailed information on the Levels command, read Chapter 18.

Converting an image into a line drawing

The High Pass filter is especially useful as a precursor to Image ⇨ Adjust ⇨ Threshold, which converts all pixels in an image to black and white (again, covered in Chapter 18). As illustrated in Figure 15-18, the Threshold command produces entirely different effects on images before and after you alter them with the High Pass filter. In fact, applying the High Pass filter with a low Radius value and then issuing the Threshold command converts your image into a line drawing.

In the second row of examples in the figure, I followed Threshold with Filter ⇨ Blur ⇨ Gaussian Blur (the subject of the next section). I set the Gaussian Blur Radius value to 1.0. Like the Threshold option in the Unsharp Mask dialog box, the Threshold command results in harsh transitions; Gaussian Blur softens them to produce a more natural effect.

5.0 2.5 1.0

Threshold and Gaussian Blur

Opacity: 45%, Overlay mode

Figure 15-18
Several applications of the High Pass filter with low Radius values (top row), followed by the same images subject to Image ⇨ Adjust ⇨ Threshold and Filter ⇨ Blur ⇨ Gaussian Blur (middle). I then layered the second row onto the first and modified the Opacity and blend mode settings.

Why change your image to a bunch of slightly different gray values and then apply a command such as Threshold? One reason is to create a mask, as discussed at length in the "Building a Mask from an Image" section of Chapter 12. (In Chapter 12, I used Levels instead of Threshold, but both are variations on the same theme.)

You might also want to bolster the edges in an image. For example, to achieve the last row of examples in Figure 15-18, I layered the images prior to applying High Pass, Threshold, and Gaussian Blur. Then I monkeyed around with the Opacity setting and the blend mode to achieve an edge-tracing effect.

I should mention that Photoshop provides several automated edge-tracing filters — including Find Edges, Trace Contour, and the Gallery Effects acquisition, Glowing Edges. But High Pass affords more control than any of these commands and permits you to explore a wider range of alternatives. Also worth noting, several Gallery Effects filters — most obviously Filter ➪ Sketch ➪ Photocopy — lift much of their code directly from High Pass. Although it may seem at first glance a strange effect, High Pass is one of the seminal filters in Photoshop.

Blurring an Image

The commands under the Filter ➪ Blur submenu produce the opposite effects of their counterparts under the Filter ➪ Sharpen submenu. Rather than enhancing the amount of contrast between neighboring pixels, the Blur filters diminish contrast to create softening effects.

Applying the Gaussian Blur filter

The preeminent Blur filter, Gaussian Blur, blends a specified number of pixels incrementally, following the bell-shaped Gaussian distribution curve I touched on earlier. When you choose Filter ➪ Blur ➪ Gaussian Blur, Photoshop produces a single Radius option box, in which you can enter any value from 0.1 to 250.0. (Beginning to sound familiar?) As demonstrated in Figure 15-19, Radius values of 1.0 and smaller blur an image slightly; moderate values, between 1.0 and 5.0, turn an image into a rude approximation of life without my glasses on; and higher values blur the image beyond recognition.

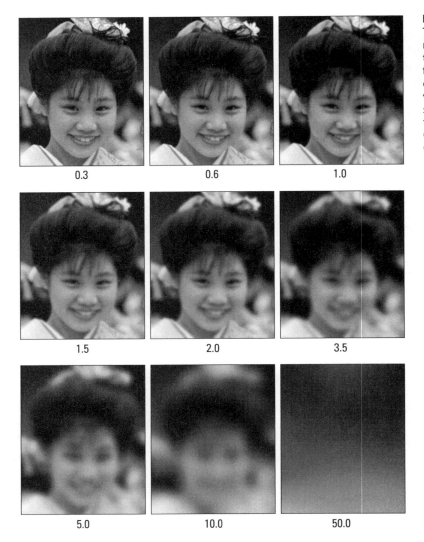

0.3 0.6 1.0

1.5 2.0 3.5

5.0 10.0 50.0

Figure 15-19
The results of blur-
ring an image with
the Gaussian Blur
filter using eight
different Radius
values, ranging from
slightly out of focus
to Bad Day at the
Ophthalmologist's
Office.

Applying the Gaussian Blur filter to a selection in the quick mask mode is
almost the exact equivalent of feathering the selection in the marching ants
mode. The only difference is that the Radius option in the Gaussian Blur
dialog box is accurate to 1/10 pixel, while its counterpart in the Feather dialog box accepts whole numbers only.

Moderate to high Radius values can be especially useful for creating that hugely amusing *Star Trek* Iridescent Female effect. This is the old *Star Trek*, of course. Captain Kirk meets some bewitching ambassador or scientist who has just beamed on board. He takes her hand in sincere welcome as he gives out with a lecherous grin and explains how truly honored he is to have such a renowned guest in his transporter room, and so charming to boot. Then we see it — the close-up of the fetching actress shrouded in a kind of gleaming halo that prevents us from discerning if her lips are chapped or perhaps she's hiding an old acne scar, because some cockeyed cinematographer smeared Vaseline all over the camera lens. I mean, what *wouldn't* you give to be able to recreate this effect in Photoshop?

Unfortunately, I don't have any images of actresses adorned in futuristic go-go boots, so Constantine cum Rambo will have to do in a pinch. The following steps explain how to make the colossal head glow as demonstrated in Figure 15-20.

STEPS: The Wondrous Kirk Myopia Effect

Step 1.   **Press ⌘-A to select the entire image.** If you only want to apply the effect to a portion of the image, be sure to feather the selection with a radius in the neighborhood of 5 to 8 pixels.

Step 2.   **Choose Filter ➪ Blur ➪ Gaussian Blur.** Enter some unusually large value into the Radius option box — say, 8.0 — and press Return. This blurs the cloned image only; the original image remains unchanged.

Step 3.   **Press ⌘-Shift-F to bring up the Fade dialog box.** To achieve the effects shown in Figure 15-20, I reduced the Opacity value to 70 percent, making the blurred image slightly translucent. This way, you can see the hard edges of the original image beneath the cloned image.

Step 4.   **You can achieve additional effects by selecting options from the Mode pop-up menu.** For example, I created the upper right example in the figure by selecting the Screen option, which uses the colors in the filtered image to lighten the original. I created the two bottom examples in the figure by applying the Darken and Lighten options.

Normal

Screen

Figure 15-20
After blurring the image, I chose
Filter ⇨ Fade Gaussian Blur and
changed the Opacity value to 70
percent. Then I applied the
labeled blend modes to alter the
image further.

Darken

Lighten

Color Plate 15-6 shows an image that's more likely to interest Captain Kirk. It shows a young agrarian woman subject to most of the same settings I applied earlier to Constantine. Again, I applied the Gaussian Blur filter with a Radius of 8.0. Then I used Filter ⇨ Fade Gaussian Blur to adjust the Opacity value and blend mode. The upper left image shows the Normal mode, but the upper right image shows the Luminosity mode. In this case, the Screen mode resulted in a washed-out effect, whereas Luminosity yielded an image with crisp color detail and fuzzy brightness values. As a result, there are some interesting places where the colors leap off her checkered dress. As in Figure 15-20, the bottom two images show the effects of the Darken and Lighten modes.

You know, though, as I look at this woman, I'm beginning to have my doubts about her and Captain Kirk. I mean, she has Scotty written all over her.

The preset blurring filters

Neither of the two preset commands in the Filter ➪ Blur submenu, Blur and Blur More, can distribute its blurring effect over a bell-shaped Gaussian curve. For that reason, these two commands are less functional than the Gaussian Blur filter. However, just so you know where they stand in the grand Photoshop focusing scheme, Figure 15-21 shows the effect of each preset command and the nearly equivalent effect created with the Gaussian Blur filter.

Figure 15-21
The effects of the two preset blurring filters (top row) compared with their Gaussian Blur equivalents (bottom row), which are labeled according to Radius values.

Blur

Blur More

0.3

0.7

Antialiasing an image

If you have a particularly jagged image, such as a black-and-white MacPaint file or a 256-color GIF file, there's a better way to soften the rough edges than applying the Gaussian Blur filter. The best solution is to antialias the image. How? After all, Photoshop doesn't offer an Antialias filter. Well, think about it. Back in the "Softening selection outlines" section of Chapter 11, I described how Photoshop antialiases a brushstroke or selection outline at twice its normal size and then reduces it by 50 percent and applies bicubic interpolation. You can do the same thing with an image.

Choose Image ⇨ Image Size and enlarge the image to 200 percent of its present size. Make sure that the Resample Image check box is turned on and set to Bicubic. (You can also experiment with Bilinear for a slightly different effect, but don't use Nearest Neighbor.) Next, turn right around and choose Image ⇨ Image Size again, but this time shrink the image by 50 percent.

The top left example in Figure 15-22 shows a jagged image subject to this effect. I used Image ⇨ Adjust ⇨ Posterize to reduce Moses to four colors. It's ugly, but it's not unlike the kind of images you may encounter, particularly if you have access to an aging image library. To the right is the same image subject to Gaussian Blur with a very low Radius value of 0.5. Rather than appearing softened, the result is just plain fuzzy.

Jagged original

Gaussian Blur, 0.5

Antialiased

Antialiased x 4

Figure 15-22
A particularly jagged image (top left) followed by the image blurred using a filter (top right). By enlarging and reducing the image one or more times (bottom left and right), I soften the pixels without making them appear blurry. The enlarged details show each operation's effect on the individual pixels.

However, if I instead enlarge and reduce the image with the Image Size command, I achieve a true softening effect, as shown in the lower left example in the figure, commensurate with Photoshop's antialiasing options. Even after enlarging and reducing the image four times in a row — as in the bottom right example — I don't make the image blurry, I simply make it softer.

Directional blurring

In addition to its everyday blurring functions, Photoshop provides two *directional blurring* filters, Motion Blur and Radial Blur. Instead of blurring pixels in feathered clusters like the Gaussian Blur filter, the Motion Blur filter blurs pixels in straight lines over a specified distance. The Radial Blur filter blurs pixels in varying degrees depending on their distance from the center of the blur. The following pages explain both of these filters in detail.

Motion blurring

The Motion Blur filter makes an image appear as if either the image or camera was moving when you shot the photo. When you choose Filter ⇨ Blur ⇨ Motion Blur, Photoshop displays the dialog box shown in Figure 15-23. You enter the angle of movement into the Angle option box. Alternatively, you can indicate the angle by dragging the straight line inside the circle on the right side of the dialog box, as shown in the figure. (You'll notice that the arrow cursor actually appears outside the circle. Once you begin dragging on the line, you can move the cursor anywhere you want and still affect the angle.)

Figure 15-23
Drag the line inside the circle to change the angle of the blur.

You then enter the distance of the movement in the Distance option box. Photoshop permits any value between 1 and 999 pixels. The filter distributes the effect of the blur over the course of the Distance value, as illustrated by the examples in Figure 15-24.

Mathematically speaking, Motion Blur is one of Photoshop's simpler filters. Rather than distributing the effect over a Gaussian curve — which one might argue would produce a more believable effect — Photoshop creates a simple linear distribution, peaking in the center and fading at either end. It's as if the program took the value you specified in the Distance option, created that many clones of the image, offset half the clones in one direction and half the clones in the other — all spaced 1 pixel apart — and then varied the opacity of each.

Original

50 pixels

100 pixels

150 pixels

200 pixels

300 pixels

Figure 15-24
A single black rectangle followed by five different applications of the Motion Blur filter. Only the Distance value varied, as labeled. A 0-degree Angle value was used in all five examples.

Using the Wind filter

The problem with the Motion Blur filter is that it blurs pixels in two directions. If you want to distribute pixels in one absolute direction or the other, try out the Wind filter, which you can use either on its own or in tandem with Motion Blur.

When you choose Filter ⇨ Stylize ⇨ Wind, Photoshop displays the Wind dialog box shown in Figure 15-25. You can select from three methods and two directions to distribute the selected pixels. Figure 15-26 compares the effect of the Motion Blur filter to each of the three methods offered by the Wind filter. Notice that the Wind filter does not blur pixels. Rather, it evaluates a selection in 1-pixel-tall horizontal strips and offsets the strips randomly inside the image.

Figure 15-25
Use the Wind filter to randomly distribute a selection in 1-pixel horizontal strips in one of two directions.

Figure 15-26
The difference between the effects of the Motion Blur filter (upper left) and the Wind filter (other three). In each case, I selected From the Right from the Direction radio buttons.

Motion Blur

Wind

Blast

Stagger

To get the best results, try combining the Motion Blur and Wind filters with a translucent selection. For example, to create Figure 15-27, I cloned the entire image to a new layer and applied the Wind command twice, first selecting the Stagger option and then selecting Blast. Next, I applied the Motion Blur command with a 0-degree angle and a Distance value of 30. I then set the Opacity option in the Layers palette to 80 percent and selected Lighten from the blend mode pop-up menu.

The result is a perfect blend between two worlds. The motion effect in Figure 15-27 doesn't obliterate the image detail, as the Wind filter does in Figure 15-26. And the motion appears to run in a single direction — to the right — something you can't accomplish using Motion Blur on its own.

Figure 15-27
The result of combining the Wind and Motion Blur filters with a translucent selection.

Radial blurring

Choosing Filter ➪ Blur ➪ Radial Blur displays the Radial Blur dialog box shown in Figure 15-28. The dialog box offers two Blur Method options: Spin and Zoom.

If you select Spin, the image appears to be rotating about a central point. You specify that point by dragging in the grid inside the Blur Center box (as demonstrated in the figure). If you select Zoom, the image appears to rush away from you, as if you were zooming the camera while shooting the photograph. Again, you specify the central point of the Zoom by dragging in the Blur Center box. Figure 15-29 features examples of both settings.

Figure 15-28
Drag inside the Blur Center grid to change the point about which the Radial Blur filter spins or zooms the image.

Figure 15-29
Four examples of the Radial Blur filter set to both Spin and Zoom, subject to different Quality settings (left and right). I specified Amount values of 10 pixels for the Spin examples and 30 for the Zooms. Each effect is centered about the right eye (your right, that is).

Spin, Draft   Spin, Best

Zoom, Draft   Zoom, Best

After selecting a Blur Method option, you can enter any value between 1 and 100 in the Amount option box to specify the maximum distance over which the filter blurs pixels. (You can enter a value of 0, but doing so merely causes the filter to waste time without producing an effect.) Pixels farthest away from the center point move the most; pixels close to the center point barely move at all. Keep in mind that large values take more time to apply than small values. The Radial Blur filter, incidentally, qualifies as one of Photoshop's most time-consuming operations.

Select a Quality option to specify your favorite time/quality compromise. The Good and Best Quality options ensure smooth results by respectively applying bilinear and bicubic interpolation (as explained in the "General preferences" section of Chapter 2). However, they also prolong the amount of time the filter spends calculating pixels in your image.

The Draft option *diffuses* an image, which leaves a trail of loose and randomized pixels but takes less time to complete. I used the Draft setting to create the left-hand images in Figure 15-29; I selected the Best option to create the images on the right.

Blurring with a threshold

The purpose of the new Filter ⇨ Blur ⇨ Smart Blur is to blur the low-contrast portions of an image while retaining the edges. This way, you can downplay photo grain, blemishes, and artifacts without harming the real edges in the image. (If you're familiar with Filter ⇨ Pixelate ⇨ Facet, then it may help to know Smart Blur is essentially a customizable version of that filter.)

Figure 15-30
The Smart Blur filter lets you blur the low-contrast areas of an image without harming the edges.

The two key options inside the Smart Blur dialog box are the Radius and Threshold slider bars. As with all Radius options, this one expands the number of pixels calculated at a time as you increase the value. Meanwhile, the Threshold value works just like the one in the Unsharp Mask dialog box, specifying how different two neighboring pixels must be to be considered an edge.

But the Threshold value has a peculiar and unexpected effect on the Radius. The Radius value actually produces more subtle effects if you raise the value beyond the Threshold. For example, take a look at Figure 15-31. Here we have a grid of images subject to different Radius and Threshold values. (The first value below each image is the radius.) In the top row of the figure, the 5.0 radius actually produces a more pronounced effect than its 20.0 and 60.0 cousins. This is because 5.0 is less than the 10.0 threshold, while 20.0 and 60.0 are more.

Figure 15-31
Combinations of different Radius (first number) and Threshold (second) values. Notice that the most dramatic effects occur when the radius is equal to about half the threshold.

5.0, 10.0   20.0, 10.0   60.0, 10.0

5.0, 30.0   20.0, 30.0   60.0, 30.0

5.0, 80.0   20.0, 80.0   60.0, 80.0

The Quality settings control the smoothness of the edges. The High setting takes more time than Medium and Low, but it looks smoother as well. (All of the effects in Figure 15-31 were set to High.) The two additional Mode options allow you to trace the edges defined by the Threshold value with white lines. Overlay Edges shows image and lines, while Edges Only shows just the traced lines. About the only practical purpose for these options is to monitor the precise effect of the Threshold setting in the preview box. Otherwise, the Edges options are clearly relegated to special effects.

Frankly, I'm not convinced that Smart Blur is quite ready for prime time. You already know what I think of the Threshold option, and it hasn't gotten any better here. Without control over the transitions between focused and unfocused areas, things are going to look pretty strange.

 The better way to blur low-contrast areas is to create an edge mask, as I explained back in the "Sharpening grainy photographs" section. Just reverse the selection by choosing Select ➪ Inverse and apply the Gaussian Blur filter.

Figure 15-32 shows how the masking technique compares with Smart Blur. In the first image, I applied Unsharp Mask with a Threshold of 20. Then I turned around and applied Smart Blur with a Radius of 2.0 and a Threshold of 20.0, matching the Unsharp Mask value. The result makes Ike look like he has dandruff coming out of every pore in his face.

In the second image, I created an edge mask — as explained in the "Creating and Using an Edge Mask" steps — and applied Unsharp Mask with a Threshold of 0. Then I pressed ⌘-Shift-I to reverse the selection and applied Gaussian Blur with a Radius of 2.0. The result is a smooth image with sharp edges that any president would be proud to hang in the Oval Office.

Figure 15-32
The difference between relying on Photoshop's automated Threshold capabilities (left) and sharpening and blurring with the aid of an edge mask (right). Despite the advent of computers, a little manual labor still wins out over automation.

Softening a selection outline

Gaussian Blur and other Blur filters are equally as useful when editing masks as they are when editing image pixels. As I mentioned earlier, applying Gaussian Blur to a mask has the same effect as applying Select ⇨ Feather to a selection outline. But Gaussian Blur affords more control. Where the Feather command affects all portions of a selection outline uniformly, you can apply Gaussian Blur selectively to a mask, permitting you to easily mix soft and hard edges within a single selection outline.

Another advantage to blurring a mask is that you can see the results of your adjustments on-screen, instead of relying on the seldom helpful marching ants. For example, suppose that you want to establish a buffer zone between a foreground image and its background. You've managed to accurately select the foreground image — how do you now feather the selection exclusively outward, so that no portion of the foreground image becomes selected? Although you can pull off this feat using selection commands like Expand and Feather, it's much easier to apply filters such as Maximum and Gaussian Blur inside a mask. But before I go any farther, I need to back up and explain how Maximum and its pal Minimum work.

Maximum and Minimum

Filter ⇨ Other ⇨ Maximum expands the light portions of an image, spreading them outward into other pixels. Its opposite, Filter ⇨ Other ⇨ Minimum, expands the dark portions of an image. In traditional stat photography, these techniques are known as *spreading* and *choking*.

When you are working in the quick mask mode or an independent mask channel, applying the Maximum filter has the effect of incrementally expanding the selected area, adding pixels uniformly around the edges of the selection outline. The Maximum dialog box presents you with a single Radius value, which tells Photoshop how many edge pixels to expand. Just the opposite, the Minimum filter incrementally decreases the size of white areas, which subtracts pixels uniformly around the edges of a selection.

Feathering outward from a selection outline

The following steps describe how to use the Maximum and Gaussian Blur filters to feather an existing selection outline outward so that it doesn't encroach on the foreground image.

STEPS	Adding a Soft Edge in the Quick Mask Mode

Step 1. **Select the foreground image.** As shown in Figure 15-33, my foreground image is the layered television that figured so heavily into Chapter 13. I convert the layer's transparency mask to a selection outline by ⌘-clicking on the layer's name in the Layers palette.

Step 2. **If you're working on a layer, switch to the background image.** The quickest route is Shift-Option-[.

Step 3. **Press Q to enter the quick mask mode.** You can create a new mask channel if you prefer, but the quick mask mode is more convenient.

Step 4. **Choose Filter ⇨ Other ⇨ Maximum.** Enter a Radius value to expand the transparent area into the rubylith. In Figure 15-33, I've entered the highest Radius value permitted, 10 pixels. After pressing Return, I decided this wasn't enough, so I press ⌘-Option-F to bring up the filter again, and further expanded the selection by 4 pixels.

Figure 15-33
The Maximum filter increases the size of the transparent area inside the quick mask mode, thereby expanding the selection outline.

Step 5. **Choose Filter ⇨ Blur ⇨ Gaussian Blur.** To ensure that you don't blur into the foreground image, enter a Radius value that's no more than half the value you entered into the Maximum dialog box. Altogether, I expanded the selection by 14 pixels, so I entered 7 into the Gaussian Blur dialog box. Photoshop blurs the transparent area, as shown in Figure 15-34.

Figure 15-34
Use the Gaussian Blur filter to soften the transparent area, thus feathering the selection outline.

Step 6. **Invert the mask by pressing ⌘-I.** So far, I've managed to select the TV, but I really want to edit the background. So I press ⌘-I to invert the mask and inverse the prospective selection.

Step 7. **Press Q to exit the quick mask mode.** Ah, back in the workaday world of marching ants.

Step 8. **Apply the desired effect.** I copied a zebra-skin pattern from another image. Then I chose Edit ⇨ Paste Into (⌘-Shift-V) to paste the pattern inside the selection. Photoshop created a new layer with layer mask. After ⌘-dragging the pattern into position, I applied the Overlay blend mode to achieve the effect shown in Figure 15-35.

Thanks to my expanded and softened selection outline, the stripes fade toward the television without ever quite touching it. As I said, you can achieve this effect using Select ⇨ Modify ⇨ Expand and Feather, but unless you have a special aversion to the quick mask mode, it's easier to be sure of your results when you can see exactly what you're doing.

Figure 15-35
I copied some zebra skin from one image window and pressed ⌘-Shift-V to paste it into my new selection.

Noise Factors

Photoshop offers four loosely associated filters in its Filter ⇨ Noise submenu. One filter adds random pixels — known as *noise* — to an image. The other three, Despeckle, Dust and Scratches, and Median, average the colors of neighboring pixels in ways that theoretically remove noise from poorly scanned images. But in fact, they function nearly as well at removing essential detail as they do at removing extraneous noise. In the following sections, I show you how the Noise filters work, demonstrate a few of my favorite applications, and leave you to draw your own conclusions.

Adding noise

Noise adds grit and texture to an image. Noise makes an image look like you shot it in New York on the Lower East Side and were lucky to get the photo at all because someone was throwing sand in your face as you sped away in your chauffeur-driven, jet-black Maserati Bora, hammering away at the shutter release. In reality, of course, a guy over at Sears shot the photo while you toodled around in your minivan trying to find a store that sold day-old bread. But that's the beauty of Noise. It makes you look cool, even when you aren't.

You add noise by choosing Filter ⇨ Noise ⇨ Add Noise. Shown in Figure 15-36, the Add Noise dialog box features the following options:

↪ **Amount:** Enter any value between 1 and 999 to specify the amount that pixels in the image can stray from their current colors. The value itself represents a color range rather than a brightness range. For example, if you enter a value of 10, Photoshop can apply any color that is 10 shades more or less green, more or less blue, *and* more or less red than the current color. Any value over 255 allows Photoshop to select random colors from the entire 16-million color spectrum. The higher you go above 255, the more likely Photoshop is to pick colors at opposite ends of the spectrum — that is, white and black.

Figure 15-36
The Add Noise dialog box enables you to specify the amount and variety of noise you want to add to the selection.

↪ **Uniform:** Select this option to apply colors absolutely randomly within the specified range. Photoshop is no more likely to apply one color within the range than another, thus resulting in an even color distribution.

↪ **Gaussian:** When you select this option, you instruct Photoshop to prioritize colors along the Gaussian distribution curve. The effect is that most colors added by the filter either closely resemble the original colors or push the boundaries of the specified range. In other words, this option results in more light and dark pixels, thus producing a more pronounced effect.

↪ **Monochromatic:** When working on a full-color image, the Add Noise filter distributes pixels randomly throughout the different color channels. However, when you select the Monochrome check box, Photoshop distributes the noise in the same manner in all channels. The result is grayscale noise. (This option does not affect grayscale images; the noise can't get any more grayscale than it already is.)

Figure 15-37 compares three applications of Gaussian noise to identical amounts of Uniform noise. Figure 15-38 features magnified views of the noise so that you can compare the colors of individual pixels.

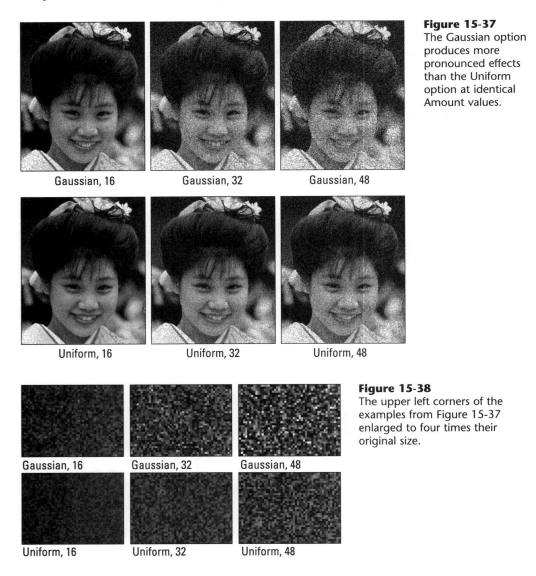

Gaussian, 16   Gaussian, 32   Gaussian, 48

Uniform, 16   Uniform, 32   Uniform, 48

Figure 15-37
The Gaussian option produces more pronounced effects than the Uniform option at identical Amount values.

Gaussian, 16   Gaussian, 32   Gaussian, 48

Uniform, 16   Uniform, 32   Uniform, 48

Figure 15-38
The upper left corners of the examples from Figure 15-37 enlarged to four times their original size.

Noise variations

Normally, the Add Noise filter adds both lighter and darker pixels to an image. If you prefer, however, you can limit the effect of the filter to strictly lighter or darker pixels. To do so, apply the Add Noise filter, then choose Filter ⇨ Fade Add Noise and select the Lighten or Darken blend mode. Or you can copy the image to a new layer, apply the filter, and merge the filtered image with the underlying original.

Figure 15-39 shows sample applications of lighter and darker noise. After copying the image to a separate layer, I applied the Add Noise filter with an Amount value of 100, and selected Gaussian. To create the upper left example in the figure, I selected Lighten from the blend mode pop-up menu. To create the right example, I selected the Darken mode. In each case, I added a layer of strictly lighter or darker noise while at the same time retaining the clarity of the original image.

Figure 15-39
You can limit the Add Noise filter to strictly lighter (left) or darker (right) noise by applying the filter to a layered clone. To create the rainy and scraped effects (bottom examples), I applied Motion Blur and Unsharp Mask to the noise layers.

Lighten   Darken

Motion Blur, Lighten   Motion Blur, Darken

To achieve the streaked noise effects in the bottom example of Figure 15-39, I applied Motion Blur and Unsharp Mask to the layered images. Inside the Motion Blur dialog box, I set the Angle value to -30 degrees and the Distance to 30 pixels. Then I applied Unsharp Mask with an Amount value of 200 percent and a Radius of 1. Naturally, the Threshold value was 0.

Chunky noise

My biggest frustration with the Add Noise filter is that you can't specify the size of individual specks of noise. No matter how you cut it, noise only comes in 1-pixel squares. It may occur to you that you can enlarge the noise dots in a layer by applying the Maximum or Minimum filter. But in practice, doing so simply fills in the image, because there isn't sufficient space between the noise pixels to accommodate the larger dot sizes.

Luckily, Photoshop provides several alternatives. One is the Pointillize filter, which adds variable-sized dots and then colors those dots in keeping with the original colors in the image. Though Pointillize lacks the random quality of the Add Noise filter, you can use it to add texture to an image.

To create the top left image in Figure 15-40, I chose Filter ⇨ Pixelate ⇨ Pointillize and entered 5 into the Cell Size option box. After pressing Return to apply the filter, I pressed ⌘-Shift-F and changed the Opacity value to 50 percent. The effect is rather like applying chunky bits of noise.

Pointillize, 50%

Halftone Pattern

Figure 15-40
The results of applying several different Add Noise-like filters, including Pointillize, Halftone Pattern, and Grain. A percentage value indicates that I modified the Opacity setting in the Fade dialog box.

Grain, Clumped

Speckled, 50%

The new Gallery Effects filters provide a few noise alternatives. Filter ⇨ Sketch ⇨ Halftone Pattern adds your choice of dot patterns, as shown in the upper right example in Figure 15-40. But like all filters in the Sketch submenu, it replaces the colors in your image with the foreground and background colors. Filter ⇨ Texture ⇨ Grain is a regular noise smorgasbord, permitting you to select from 10 different Grain Type options, each of which produces a different kind of noise. The bottom examples in Figure 15-40 show off two of the Grain options, Clumped and Speckled. I used Filter ⇨ Fade Grain to reduce the Opacity value for the Speckled effect to 50 percent.

Removing noise with Despeckle

Now for the noise removal filters. Strictly speaking, the Despeckle command probably belongs in the Filter ⇨ Blur submenu. It blurs a selection while at the same time preserving its edges — the idea being that unwanted noise is most noticeable in the continuous regions of an image. In practice, this filter is nearly the exact opposite of the Sharpen Edges filter.

The Despeckle command searches an image for edges using the equivalent of an Unsharp Mask Threshold value of 5. It then ignores the edges in the image and blurs everything else with the force of the Blur More filter, as shown in the upper left image in Figure 15-41.

Figure 15-41
The effects of the Despeckle filter (upper left) and Median filter. The numbers indicate Median filter Radius values.

Despeckle   Median, 1   3

5   10   16

Averaging pixels with Median

Another command in the Filter ⇨ Noise submenu, Median removes noise by averaging the colors in an image, one pixel at a time. When you choose Filter ⇨ Noise ⇨ Median, Photoshop produces a Radius option box, into which you can enter any value between 1 and 16. For every pixel in a selection, the filter averages the colors of the neighboring pixels that fall inside the specified radius — ignoring any pixels that are so different that they might skew the average — and applies the average color to the central pixel. As verified by Figure 15-41, large values produce the most destructive effects.

Normal   Screen

Figure 15-42
After applying the Median filter, I reversed the effect slightly using Filter ⇨ Fade Median. Although I varied the blend mode — as labeled beneath the images — the Opacity value remained a constant 70 percent.

Darken   Lighten

As with Gaussian Blur, you can achieve some very interesting and useful effects by backing off the Median filter with the Fade command. But rather that creating a *Star Trek* glow, Median clumps up details, giving an image a plastic, molded quality, as demonstrated by the examples in Figure 15-42. To create every one of these images, I applied the Median Filter with a Radius of 5 pixels. Then I pressed ⌘-Shift-F to display the Fade dialog box and lowered the Opacity value to 70 percent. The only difference between one image and the next is the blend mode.

Another difference between Gaussian Blur and Median is that Gaussian Blur destroys edges and Median invents new ones. This means you can follow up the Median filter with Unsharp Mask to achieve even more pronounced sculptural effects. I sharpened every one of the examples in Figure 15-42 using an Amount value of 150 percent and a Radius of 1.5

Sharpening a compressed image

Digital cameras are the hottest thing in electronic imaging. You can take as many images as you like, download them to your computer immediately, and place them into a printed document literally minutes after snapping the picture. By the end of this decade, I have little doubt that you — yes, *you* — will own a digital camera.

Unfortunately, the technology is still very young. Many brands take exceptional pictures, but most of these high-end devices cost $10,000 or more. Even the Polaroid PDC-2000 — the most affordable quality camera — costs more than $3,000. If you're hoping for a camera under $1,000, you'll have to make due with a consumer model like the Kodak DC50 or the Epson PhotoPC. Even if you pick up this book two years after I write it, and every one of these models has been discontinued, you can expect to pay $200 to $500 for a low-end model.

If you've ever used one of these cameras — it's only a matter of time, I assure you — you know how difficult it is to sharpen the photographs. Thanks to the stingy supply of pixels and the heavy-handed compression schemes (all based on JPEG), even the daintiest application of the Unsharp Mask filter can reveal a world of ragged edges and unsightly artifacts.

The solution is to firm up the detail and smooth out the color transitions by applying a combination of filters — Median, Gaussian Blur, and Unsharp Mask — to a layered version of the image. The following steps tell all.

If you own a digital camera, I encourage you to record these steps with the Actions palette, as explained in Chapter 3. This way, you can set Photoshop to open squads of images, batch process them, and save them in a separate folder, leaving you free to do something fun, like read more of this book.

STEPS   **Adjusting the Focus of Digital Photos**

Step 1.   **Select the entire image and copy it to a new layer.** That's ⌘-A, ⌘-J. Figure 15-43 shows the image that I intend to sharpen, a picture of a friend's child that I snapped with a DC40 (the predecessor to the earlier-mentioned DC50). His name, in case you're interested, is Cooper.

Figure 15-43
I captured this youthful fellow with a low-end digital camera equipped with a removable fish-eye lens. How innocent and happy he looks — obviously not a computer user.

Step 2.   **Choose Filter ⇨ Noise ⇨ Median.** After processing several thousand of these images, I've found that a Radius value of 2 is almost always the optimal choice. But if the image is particularly bad, 3 may be warranted.

Step 3.   **Choose Filter ⇨ Blur ⇨ Gaussian Blur.** Now that you've gummed up the detail a bit and rubbed out most of the compression, use the Gaussian Blur filter with a Radius of 1.0 to blur the gummy detail slightly. This softens the edges that the Median filter creates. (You don't want any fake edges, after all.)

Step 4.   **Choose Filter ⇨ Sharpen ⇨ Unsharp Mask.** All this blurring demands some intense sharpening. So apply Unsharp Mask with a maximum Amount value of 500 percent and a Radius of 1.0 (to match the Gaussian Blur radius). This restores most of the definition to the edges, as shown in Figure 15-44.

Figure 15-44
Thanks to Median, Gaussian Blur, and Unsharp Mask, Cooper is a much smoother customer. In fact, he's beyond smooth — he's a gummy kid.

Step 5. **Lower the layer's Opacity value.** By itself, the filtered layer is a bit too smooth. So mix the filtered floater with the underlying original with an Opacity value between 30 and 50 percent. I found that I could go pretty high — 45 percent — with Cooper. Kids have clearly defined details that survive filtering quite nicely.

Step 6. **Merge the image.** Press ⌘-E to send the layer down.

Step 7. **Continue to correct the image as you normally would.** The examples in Figure 15-45 show the difference between applying the Unsharp Mask filter to the original image (top) and the filtered mixture (bottom). In both cases, I applied an Amount value of 200 percent and a Radius of 1.0. The top photo displays an unfortunate wealth of artifacts — particularly visible in the magnified eye — while the bottom one appears smooth and crisp.

Figure 15-45
Here you can see the difference between sharpening a digital photograph right off the bat (top) and waiting to sharpen until after you've prepared the image with Median, Gaussian Blur, and Unsharp Mask (bottom).

These steps work well for sharpening other kinds of compressed imagery, including old photographs that you over-compressed without creating backups, and images that you've downloaded from the World Wide Web. If applying the Unsharp Mask filter brings out the goobers, try these steps instead.

Cleaning up scanned halftones

Photoshop offers one additional filter in the Filter ⇨ Noise submenu called Dust & Scratches. The purpose of this filter is to remove dust particles, hairs, scratches, and other imperfections that may accompany a scan. The filter offers two options, Radius and Threshold. As long as the offending imperfection is smaller or thinner than the Radius value and different enough from its neighbors to satisfy the Threshold value, the filter deletes the spot or line and interpolates between the pixels around the perimeter.

But like so many automated tools, this one works only when conditions are favorable. I'm not saying that you shouldn't ever use it — in fact, you may always want to give this filter the first crack at a dusty image. But if it doesn't work, don't get your nose out of joint. Just hunker down and eliminate the imperfections manually using the rubber stamp tool, as explained in the "Touching up blemishes" section of Chapter 10.

Now, as I say, Dust & Scratches was designed to get rid of gunk on a dirty scanner. But another problem that the filter may be able to eliminate is moiré patterns. These patterns appear when scanning halftoned images from books and magazines. See, any time you scan a printed image, you're actually scanning a collection of halftone dots rather than a continuous-tone photograph. In most cases, the halftone pattern clashes with the resolution of the scanned image to produce rhythmic and distracting moirés.

 When scanning published photographs or artwork, take a moment to find out if what you're doing is legal. It's up to you to make sure that the image you scan is no longer protected by copyright — most, but not all, works over 75 years old are considered free game — or that your noncommercial application of the image falls under the fair-use umbrella of commentary or criticism.

The Dust & Scratches filter can be pretty useful for eliminating moirés, particularly if you reduce the Threshold value below 40. But this also goes a long way toward eliminating the actual image detail, as shown in Color Plate 15-7. This figure features an image scanned from a previous issue of *Macworld* magazine. (Because I created the original image, *Macworld* probably won't sue me, but you shouldn't try it.)

The left half of Color Plate 15-7 shows the individual color channels in the image; the right half shows the full-color image. I've blown up a detail in each image so that you can better see the pixels in the moiré pattern.

The top example in the color plate shows the original scanned image with its awful moirés. (Actually, I've slightly exaggerated the moirés to account for any printing anomalies; but believe me, with or without enhancement, the image is a mess on-screen.) The middle example shows the same image subject to the Dust & Scratches filter with a Radius of 2 and a Threshold value of 20. The moirés are gone, but the edges have all but disappeared as well. I'm tempted to describe this artwork using adjectives like "soft" and "doughy," and them are fightin' words in the world of image-editing.

But what about that bottom example? How did I manage to eliminate the moirés *and* preserve the detail that is shown here? Why, by applying the Gaussian Blur, Median, and Unsharp Mask filters to individual color channels.

The first step is to examine the channels independently (by pressing ⌘-1, ⌘-2, and ⌘-3). You'll likely find that each one is affected by the moiré pattern to a different extent. In the case of this scan, all three channels need work, but the blue channel — the usual culprit — is the worst. The trick, therefore, is to eliminate the patterns in the blue channel and draw detail from the red and green channels.

To fix the blue channel, I applied both the Gaussian Blur and Median commands in fairly hefty doses. I chose Filter ⇨ Blur ⇨ Gaussian Blur and specified a Radius value of 1.5 pixels, rather high considering that the image measures only about 300 pixels tall. Then I chose Filter ⇨ Noise ⇨ Median and specified a Radius of 2.

The result was a thickly modeled image with no moirés but little detail. To firm things up a bit, I chose Filter ⇨ Sharpen ⇨ Unsharp Mask and entered 200 percent for the Amount option and 1.5 for the Radius. I opted for this Radius value because it matches the Radius that I used to blur the image. When correcting moirés, a Threshold value of 0 is almost always the best choice. A higher Threshold value not only prevents the sharpening of moiré pattern edges but also ignores real edges, which are already fragile enough as it is.

The green and red channels required incrementally less attention. After switching to the green channel, I applied the Gaussian Blur filter with a Radius of 1.0. Then I sharpened the image with the Unsharp Mask filter set to 200 percent and a Radius value of 0.5. In the red channel (⌘-1), I applied Gaussian Blur with a Radius value of 0.5. The gradual effect wasn't enough to warrant sharpening.

When you're finished, switch back to the RGB view (⌘-0) to see the combined result of your labors. (Or keep an RGB view of the image up on-screen by choosing Window ⇨ New Window.) The focus of the image will undoubtedly be softer than it was when you started. You can cure this to a limited extent by applying very discreet passes of the Unsharp Mask filter, say, with an Amount value of 100 percent and a low Radius value. Keep in mind that oversharpening may bring the patterns back to life or even uncover new ones.

One last tip: Always scan halftoned images at the highest resolution available to your scanner. Then resample the scan down to the desired resolution using Image ⇨ Image Size. This step by itself goes a long way toward eliminating moirés.

Full-Court Filtering

CHAPTER 16

In This Chapter

- ➖ Capsule descriptions of Photoshop's special effects filters
- ➖ Clever ways to use the Pixelate filters
- ➖ Putting the Mezzotint filter to good use
- ➖ Applying the edge-enhancement filters, including Emboss and Find Edges
- ➖ Creating metallic effects with Bas Relief, Plastic Wrap, and Chrome
- ➖ Exploring new worlds with the help of the distortion filters
- ➖ Designing specialized gradations and other abstractions
- ➖ How to change a picture's atmosphere using Clouds
- ➖ The complete inner workings of Lighting Effects

Destructive Filters

Corrective filters allow you to both eliminate flaws in an image and apply special effects. Destructive filters, on the other hand, are devoted solely to special effects. That's why this chapter is actually shorter than its predecessor, even though Photoshop offers nearly twice as many destructive filters as corrective counterparts. Quite simply, destructive filters are less frequently used and ultimately less useful.

Don't get me wrong — these filters are a superb bunch. But because of their more limited appeal, I don't explain each and every one of them. Rather, I concentrate on the ones that I think you'll use most often, breeze over a handful of others, and let you discover on your own the ones that I ignore.

A million wacky effects

Oh, heck, I guess I can't just go and ignore half of the commands under the Filter menu — they're not completely useless, after all. It's just that you aren't likely to use them more than once every lunar eclipse. So here are the briefest of all possible descriptions of these filters:

- **Color Halftone:** Located under the Filter ⇨ Pixelate submenu, this command turns an image into a piece of Roy Lichtenstein artwork, with big, comic-book halftone dots. While scads of fun, the filter is ultimately a novelty that takes about a year and a half to apply.

- **Fragment:** Ooh, it's an earthquake! This lame filter repeats an image four times in a square formation and lowers the opacity of each to create a sort of jiggly effect. You don't even have any options to control it. I guess I'm just missing the genius behind Filter ⇨ Pixelate ⇨ Fragment.

- **Lens Flare:** Found in the Render submenu, this filter adds sparkles and halos to an image to suggest light bouncing off the camera lens. Even though photographers work their behinds off trying to make sure that these sorts of reflections don't occur, you can go and add them after the fact. You can select from one of three Lens Type options, adjust the Brightness slider between 10 and 300 percent (though somewhere around 100 is bound to deliver the best results), and move the center of the reflection by dragging a point around inside the Flare Center box. You can also Option-click inside the preview to position the center point numerically.

 If you want to add a flare to a grayscale image, first convert it to the RGB mode. Then apply the filter and convert back to grayscale (like I did back in Figure 15-2). The Lens Flare filter is applicable to RGB images only.

Here's another tip suggested by my technical editor, Ted Padova. Prior to choosing Lens Flare, create a new layer, fill it with 50 percent gray, and apply the Overlay blend mode. After applying the filter, you can move it around and vary the Opacity as much as you like, giving you more control over the final effect. Heck, this is good advice for lots of filters.

- **Diffuse:** This single-shot filter under the Filter ⇨ Stylize submenu dithers the edges of color, much like the Dissolve brush mode dithers the edges of a soft brush. It's moderately useful, but not likely to gain a place among your treasured few.

- **Solarize:** Located in the Stylize submenu — as are the two filters that follow — Solarize is easily Photoshop's worst filter. It's really just a color-correction effect that changes all medium grays in the image to 50 percent gray, all blacks and whites to black, and remaps the other colors to shades in between. (If you're familiar with the Curves command, the map for Solarize looks like a pyramid.) It really belongs in the Image ⇨ Map submenu, or better yet, on the cutting room floor.

⌖ **Tiles:** This filter breaks an image up into a bunch of regularly sized but randomly spaced rectangular tiles. You specify how many tiles fit across the width and height of the image — a value of 10, for example, creates 100 tiles — and the maximum distance each tile can shift. You can fill the gaps between tiles with foreground color, background color, or an inverted or normal version of the original image. A highly intrusive and not particularly stimulating effect.

⌖ **Extrude:** The more capable cousin of the Tiles filter, Extrude breaks an image into tiles and forces them toward the viewer in three-dimensional space. The Pyramid option is a lot of fun, devolving an image into a collection of spikes. When using the Blocks option, you can select a Solid Front Faces option that renders the image as a true 3D mosaic. The Mask Incomplete Blocks option simply leaves the image untouched around the perimeter of the selection where the filter can't draw complete tiles.

Actually, I kind of like Extrude. For the sheer heck of it, Color Plate 16-1 shows an example of Extrude applied to one of the sharpened roses from Color Plate 15-4. I set the Type to Blocks, the Size to 10, the Depth to 30 and Random, with both the Solid Front Faces and Mask Incomplete Blocks radio buttons selected. Pretty great, huh? I only wish that the filter would generate a selection outline around the masked areas of the image so that I could get rid of anything that hadn't been extruded. It's a wonderful effect, but it's not one that lends itself to many occasions.

⌖ **Diffuse Glow:** The first of the Gallery Effects I mostly ignore, Filter ⇨ Distort ⇨ Diffuse Glow sprays a coat of dithered, background-colored pixels onto your image. Yowsa, let me at it.

⌖ **The Artistic filters:** As a rule, the effects under the Filter ⇨ Artistic submenu add a painterly quality to your image. Colored Pencil, Rough Pastels, and Watercolor are examples of filters that successfully emulate traditional mediums. Other filters — Fresco, Smudge Stick, and Palette Knife — couldn't pass for their intended mediums in a dim room filled with dry ice.

⌖ **The Brush Strokes filters:** I could argue that the Brush Strokes submenu contains filters that create strokes of color. This is true of some of the filters — including Angled Strokes, Crosshatch, and Sprayed Stroke. Others — Dark Strokes and Ink Outlines — generally smear colors, while still others — Accented Edges and Sumi-e — belong in the Artistic submenu. Whatever.

⌖ **The Sketch filters:** In Gallery Effects parlance, Sketch means color sucker. Beware, every one of these filters replaces the colors in your image with the current foreground and background colors. If the foreground and background colors are black and white, the Sketch filter results in a grayscale image.

Charcoal and Conté Crayon create artistic effects, Bas Relief and Note Paper add texture, and Photocopy and Stamp are stupid effects you could produce better and with more flexibility using High Pass.

To retrieve some of the original colors from your image after applying a Sketch filter, press ⌘-Shift-F to bring up the Fade dialog box and try out a few different Mode settings. Overlay and Luminosity are particularly good choices. In Color Plate 16-2, I applied the Charcoal filter with the foreground and background colors set to light blue and dark green. Then I used the Fade command to select the Overlay mode.

↪ **The Texture filters:** As a group, the commands in the Filter ⇨ Texture submenu are my favorite effects filters. Craquelure, Mosaic Tiles, and Patchwork apply interesting depth textures to the image. And Texturizer provides access to several scalable textures and permits you to load your own (so long as the pattern is saved in the Photoshop format), as demonstrated in Figure 16-1. The one dud is Stained Glass, which creates polygon tiles like Photoshop's own Crystallize filter, only with black lines around the tiles.

Burlap

Canvas

Sandstone

Random Strokes

Figure 16-1
Filter ⇨ Texture ⇨ Texturizer lets you select from four built-in patterns — including the first three shown here — and load your own. In the last example, I loaded the Random Strokes pattern included with Photoshop.

Certainly, there is room for disagreement about which filters are good and which are awful. After I wrote a two-star *Macworld* review about the first Gallery Effects collection back in 1992 — I must admit, I've never been a big fan — a gentleman showed me page after page of excellent artwork he had created with them. Recently, a woman showed me her collection of amazing Lens Flare imagery. I mean, here's a filter that just creates a bunch of bright spots, and yet this talented person was able to go absolutely nuts with it.

I guess the moral is that just because I consider a filter or other piece of software to be a squalid pile of unspeakably bad code doesn't mean that a creative artist can't come along and put it to remarkable use. But that's because *you* are good, not the filter. So if you're feeling particularly creative today, give the above filters a try. Otherwise, skip them with a clear conscience.

What about the others?

Some filters don't really belong in either the corrective or destructive camp. Take Filter ➪ Video ➪ NTSC Colors and Filter ➪ Other ➪ Offset, for example. Both are examples of commands that have no business being under the filter menu, and both could have been handled much better than they are.

The NTSC Colors filter modifies the colors in your RGB or Lab image for transfer to videotape. Vivid reds and blues that might otherwise prove very unstable and bleed into their neighbors are curtailed. The problem with this function is that it's not an independent color space; it's a single-shot filter that changes your colors and is done with it. If you edit the colors after choosing the command, you may very well reintroduce colors that are incompatible with NTSC devices and therefore warrant a second application of the filter. Conversion to NTSC — another light-based system — isn't as fraught with potential disaster as conversion to CMYK pigments, but it still deserves better treatment than this.

The Offset command moves an image a specified number of pixels. Why didn't I cover it in Chapter 11 with the other movement options? Because the command actually moves the image inside the selection outline while keeping the selection outline itself stationary. It's as if you had pasted the entire image into the selection outline and were now moving it around. The command is a favorite among fans of channel operations, a topic I cover in Chapter 19. You can duplicate an image, off-set the entire thing a few pixels, and then mix the duplicate and original to create highlight or shadow effects. But I much prefer the more interactive control of layering and nudging with the arrow keys. Nowadays, I imagine the Offset filter might find favor with folks who want to automate movements from the Actions palette.

Among the filters I've omitted from this chapter is Filter ⇨ Stylize ⇨ Wind, which is technically a destructive filter but is covered along with the blur and noise filters in Chapter 15. I discussed Filter ⇨ Render ⇨ Texture Fill in Chapter 10. And finally, for complete information on the Custom, Displace, and Filter Factory filters, stay tuned for Chapter 17.

As for the other filters in the Filter ⇨ Distort, Pixelate, Render, and Stylize submenus, read on to discover all the latest and greatest details.

Third-party filters

In addition to the filters provided by Photoshop, you can purchase all sorts of plug-in filters from other companies. In fact, Photoshop supports its own flourishing cottage industry of third-party solutions.

 The CD at the back of this book includes sample versions of some of my favorite filters. For complete information on the specific filters and the companies that provide them, read Appendix C. Many of the filters are demo versions of the shipping products, which means that you can see what they do but you can't actually apply the effects, or they only work for a limited period of time. I know, it's a drag, but these folks claim that they like to make money every once in a while, and I can't say that I blame them.

Also included on the CD is a feature article called "Top 20 Photoshop Plug-ins," which I wrote for the September 1996 edition of *Macworld* magazine. The article sums up my favorite filter packages, including both commercial and shareware products (some of which you'll find on the CD).

Two bits of information from the article don't apply to Photoshop 4: You no longer need PhotoNavigator since the Navigator palette is included with Version 4, and there's no sense in shelling out extra money for Gallery Effects. And naturally, some of the filters may have been updated by the time you read this.

The Pixelate Filters

The new Filter ⇨ Pixelate submenu features a handful of commands that rearrange your image into clumps of solid color:

- **Crystallize:** This filter organizes an image into irregularly shaped nuggets. You specify the size of the nuggets by entering a value from 3 to 300 pixels in the Cell Size option.

- **Facet:** Facet fuses areas of similarly colored pixels to create a sort of hand-painted effect.

- **Mosaic:** The Mosaic filter blends pixels together into larger squares. You specify the height and width of the squares by entering a value into the Cell Size option box.

- **Pointillize:** This filter is similar to Crystallize, except that it separates an image into disconnected nuggets set against the background color. As usual, you specify the size of the nuggets by changing the Cell Size value.

The Crystal Halo effect

By applying one of these filters to a feathered selection, you can create what I call a Crystal Halo effect, named after the Crystallize filter, which tends to deliver the most successful results. (For a preview of these effects, sneak a peek at Figure 16-2.) The following steps explain how to create a Crystal Halo, using the images in Figures 16-2 and 16-3 as an example.

STEPS   **Creating the Crystal Halo Effect**

Step 1.   **Select the foreground element around which you want to create the halo.** Then choose Select ⇨ Inverse to deselect the foreground element and select the background.

Step 2.   **Press Q to switch to the quick mask mode.**

Step 3.   **Choose Filter ⇨ Other ⇨ Minimum.** As I explained in Chapter 15, this filter allows you to increase the size of the deselected area around the foreground element. The size of the Radius value depends on the size of the halo you want to create. For my part, I wanted a 15-pixel halo. Unfortunately, the Radius option box in the Minimum dialog box can't accommodate a value larger than 10. So I entered 10 the first time. When Photoshop finished applying the filter, I pressed ⌘-Option-F to bring up the Minimum dialog box again and entered 5.

Step 4.   **Choose Filter ⇨ Blur ⇨ Gaussian Blur.** Then enter a Radius value 0.1 less than the amount by which you increased the size of the deselected area. In my case, I entered 14.9. This will cut into the image slightly, but hardly enough to be visible, as you can see in the left image in Figure 16-2.

Figure 16-2
Create a heavily feathered selection outline (left) and then apply the Crystallize filter to refract the feathered edges (right).

Step 5. **Choose Filter ⇨ Pixelate ⇨ Crystallize.** Enter a moderate value into the Cell Size option box. I opted for the value 12, just slightly larger than the default value. After pressing Return, you get something along the lines of the selection outline shown in the right image in Figure 16-2. The filter refracts the softened edges, as if you were viewing them through textured glass.

Step 6. **Switch back to the marching ants mode.** Then use the selection as desired. I merely pressed ⌘-Delete to fill the selection with white, as shown in the top left image in Figure 16-3.

You may find this technique particularly useful for combining images. You can copy the selection and paste it against a different background or copy a background from a different image and choose Edit ⇨ Paste Into to paste it inside the crystal halo's selection outline.

Figure 16-3 shows several variations on the Crystal Halo effect. To create the upper right image, I substituted Filter ⇨ Pixelate ⇨ Facet for Filter ⇨ Pixelate ⇨ Crystallize in Step 5. I also sharpened the result to increase the effect of the filter (which nevertheless remains subtle). To create the lower right image, I applied the Mosaic filter in place of Crystallize, using a Cell Size value of 8. Finally, to create the lower left image, I applied the Pointillize filter. Because Pointillize creates gaps in a selection, I had to paint inside Moses to fill in the gaps and isolate the halo effect to the background before returning to the marching ants mode.

Crystallize

Facet

Pointillize

Mosaic

Figure 16-3
Which aura will Moses don today? The images illustrate
the effects of applying each of four filters to a heavily
feathered selection in the quick mask mode and pressing
⌘-Delete.

Creating a mezzotint

A *mezzotint* is a special halftone pattern that replaces dots with a random pattern
of swirling lines and worm holes. Photoshop's Mezzotint filter is an attempt to emulate this effect. Although not entirely successful — true mezzotinting options can

only be properly implemented as PostScript printing functions, not as filtering functions — they do lend themselves to some pretty interesting interpretations.

The filter itself is straightforward. You choose Filter ➪ Pixelate ➪ Mezzotint, select an effect from the Type submenu, and press the Return key. A preview box allows you to see what each of the ten Type options looks like. Figure 16-4 shows off four of the effects at 230 ppi.

Medium dots

Coarse dots

Short lines

Long strokes

Figure 16-4
The results of applying the Mezzotint filter set to each of four representative effects. These line patterns are on par with the halftoning options offered when you select Mode ➪ Bitmap, as discussed back in Chapter 5.

To create Figure 16-5, I applied the Mezzotint filter set to the Long Lines effect. Then I used the Filter ⇨ Fade Mezzotint command to mix filtered and original images. I selected Overlay from the Mode pop-up menu and set the Opacity value to 40 percent. The result is a scraped image. (I've decreased the resolution of the image to 180 ppi so that you can see the effect a little more clearly.)

Figure 16-5
To get this effect, I chose Filter ⇨ Fade after applying the Mezzotint filter. Then I selected the Overlay mode and set the Opacity slider to 40 percent.

When applied to grayscale artwork, the Mezzotint filter always results in a black-and-white image. When applied to a color image, the filter automatically applies the selected effect independently to each of the color channels. Though all pixels in each channel are changed to either black or white, you can see a total of eight colors — black, red, green, blue, yellow, cyan, magenta, and white — in the RGB composite view. The upper left example of Color Plate 16-3 shows an image subject to the Mezzotint filter in the RGB mode.

If the Mezzotint filter affects each channel independently, then it follows that the color mode in which you work directly, and dramatically, affects the performance of the filter. For example, if you apply Mezzotint in the Lab mode, you again whittle the colors down to eight, but a very different eight — black, cyan, magenta, green, red, two muddy blues and a muddy rose — as shown in the top middle example of Color Plate 16-3. If you're looking for bright happy colors, don't apply Mezzotint in the Lab mode.

In CMYK, the filter produces roughly the same eight colors that you get in RGB — white, cyan, magenta, yellow, violet-blue, red, deep green, and black. However, as shown in the top right example of the color plate, the distribution of the colors is much different. The image appears much lighter and more colorful than its RGB counterpart. This happens because the filter has a lot of black to work with in the RGB mode but very little — just that in the black channel — in the CMYK mode.

The bottom row of Color Plate 16-3 shows the effects of the Mezzotint filter after using the Fade command to mix it with the original image. As in Figure 16-4, I chose Overlay from the Mode pop-up menu and set the Opacity value to 40 percent. These three very different images were all created using the same filter set to the same effect. Absolutely the only difference is color mode.

Edge-Enhancement Filters _____

The Filter ⇨ Stylize submenu offers access to a triad of filters that enhance the edges in an image. The most popular of these is undoubtedly Emboss, which adds dimension to an image by making it look as if it were carved in relief. The other two, Find Edges and Trace Contour, are less commonly applied, but every bit as capable and deserving of your attention.

Embossing an image

The Emboss filter works by searching for high-contrast edges (just like the Sharpen Edge and High Pass filters), highlighting the edges with black or white pixels, and then coloring the low-contrast portions with medium gray. When you choose Filter ⇨ Stylize ⇨ Emboss, Photoshop displays the Emboss dialog box shown in Figure 16-6. The dialog box offers three options:

- ⇨ **Angle:** The value in this option box determines the angle at which Photoshop lights the image in relief. For example, if you enter a value of 90 degrees, you light the relief from the bottom straight upward. The white pixels therefore appear on the bottom sides of the edges, and the black pixels appear on the top sides. Figure 16-7 shows eight reliefs lit from different angles. I positioned the images so that they appear lit from a single source.

Figure 16-6
Figure 16-6
The Emboss dialog box enables you to control the depth of the filtered image and the angle from which it is lit.

Figure 16-7
Reliefs lighted from eight different angles, in 45-degree increments. In all cases, the central sun image indicates the location of the light source. Height and Amount values of 1 pixel and 250 percent were used for all images.

↪ **Height:** The Emboss filter accomplishes its highlighting effect by displacing one copy of an image relative to another. You specify the distance between the copies using the Height option, which can vary from 1 to 10 pixels. Lower values produce crisp effects, as demonstrated in Figure 16-8. Values above 3 goop up things pretty good unless you also enter a high Amount value. Together, the Height and Amount values determine the depth of the image in relief.

TIP

The Height value is analogous to the Radius value in the Unsharp Mask dialog box. You should therefore set the value according to the resolution of your image — 1 for 150 ppi, 2 for 300 ppi, and so on.

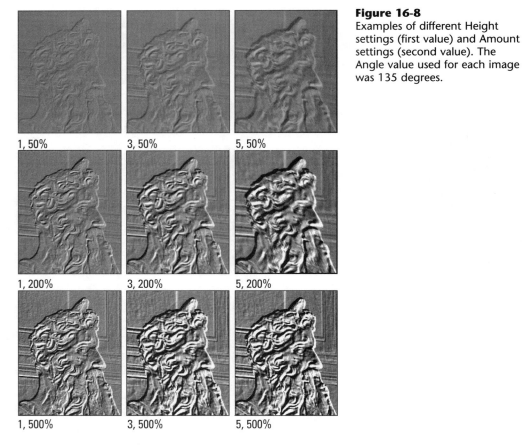

1, 50%   3, 50%   5, 50%

1, 200%   3, 200%   5, 200%

1, 500%   3, 500%   5, 500%

Figure 16-8
Examples of different Height settings (first value) and Amount settings (second value). The Angle value used for each image was 135 degrees.

↪ **Amount:** Enter a value between 1 and 500 percent to determine the amount of black and white assigned to pixels along the edges. Values of 50 percent and lower produce almost entirely gray images, as you can see in the top row of Figure 16-8. Higher values produce sharper edges, as if the relief were carved more deeply.

As a stand-alone effect, Emboss is only okey-dokey. It's one of those filters that makes you gasp with delight the first time you see it but never quite lends itself to any practical application after you become acquainted with Photoshop. But if you think of Emboss as an extension of the High Pass filter, it takes on new meaning. You can use it to edit selection outlines in the quick mask mode, just as you might use the High Pass filter. You also can use it to draw out detail in an image.

Figure 16-9 shows the result of using the Fade command immediately after applying the Emboss filter. First, I applied the Emboss filter at an Angle of 135 degrees, a Height of 2 pixels, and an Amount of 250 percent. Then I pressed ⌘-Shift-F to display the Fade dialog box. To create the left example, I selected Darken from the Mode pop-up menu. This added shadows to the edges of the image, thus boosting the texture without unduly upsetting the original brightness values. I selected the Lighten blend mode to create the right example. In both cases, I set the Opacity value to 70 percent.

Figure 16-9
After applying the Emboss filter, I used my old friend the Fade command to darken (left) and lighten (right) the image.

To create a color relief effect, apply the Emboss filter and then select the Luminosity option in the Fade dialog box. This retains the colors from the original image while applying the lightness and darkness of the pixels from the filtered selection. The effect looks something like an inked lithographic plate, with steel grays and vivid colors mixing together. An example of this effect at 80 percent Opacity appears in the first example of Color Plate 16-4.

The second example in that same color plate shows a more impressive — if less practical — technique. Rather than applying Luminosity, I chose the Difference mode inside the Fade dialog box. With its hard edges and vivid colors, this image looks like some impossible frame from an educational film on genetic engineering. I can just hear the narrator commenting, "Prom dates across America have perked up significantly since scientists discovered how to splice the red rose with a poppy."

Tracing around edges

 Photoshop 4 provides three filters that trace around pixels in your image to accentuate the edges, all located in the Filter ⇨ Stylize submenu. Long-time users will recognize Find Edges and Trace Contour. The new member of the team is the effects filter Glowing Edges.

- **Find Edges:** This filter detects edges similarly to High Pass. Low-contrast areas become white, medium-contrast edges become gray, and high-contrast edges become black, as in the labeled image in Figure 16-10. Hard edges become thin lines; soft edges become fat ones. The result is a thick, organic outline that you can overlay onto an image to give it a waxy appearance. To achieve the bottom left effect in the figure, I chose the Fade ⇨ Find Edges command and applied the Overlay mode and an 80 percent Opacity setting. She'll never get her hand off that canning jar as long as she lives.

- **Glowing Edges:** This Gallery Effects filter is a variation on Find Edges with two important differences: Glowing Edges produces an inverted effect, changing low-contrast areas to black and edges to white, as in the labeled image in Figure 16-10. It also displays a dialog box that lets you adjust the width, brightness, and smoothness of the traced edges. Glowing Edges is a great backup command. If you aren't satisfied with the effect produced by the Find Edges filter, choose the Glowing Edges command instead and adjust the options as desired. If you want black lines against a white background, press ⌘-I to invert the effect.

- **Trace Contour:** Illustrated on the right side of Figure 16-10, Trace Contour is a little more involved than the others and slightly less interesting. The filter traces a series of single-pixel lines along the border between light and dark pixels. Choosing the filter displays a dialog box containing three options: Level, Upper, and Lower. The Level value indicates the lightness value above which pixels are considered to be light and below which they are dark. For example, if you enter 128 — medium gray, as by default — Trace Contour draws a line at every spot where an area of color lighter than medium gray meets an area of color darker than medium gray. The Upper and Lower options tell the filter where to position the line — inside the lighter color's territory (Upper) or inside the space occupied by the darker color (Lower).

Find Edges Glowing Edges Trace Contour

Overlay, 80% Overlay, 60% Multiply, 100%

Figure 16-10
The top row of images demonstrates the effect of the three edge-tracing commands available from the Filter ⇨ Stylize submenu. After applying each command, I used the Fade command to apply the blend modes and Opacity values demonstrated in the bottom row.

Like Mezzotint, Trace Contour applies itself to each color channel independently and renders each channel as a 1-bit image. A collection of black lines surrounds the areas of color in each channel; the RGB, Lab, or CMYK composite view shows these lines in the colors associated with the channels. When you work in RGB, a cyan line indicates a black line in the red channel (no red plus full intensity green and blue becomes cyan). A yellow line indicates a black line in the blue channel, and so on. You get a single black line when working in the grayscale mode.

Creating a metallic coating

The edge-tracing filters are especially fun to use in combination with Filter ➪ Fade. I first got interested in playing with these filters after trying out the Chrome filter included with the first Gallery Effects collection. Now included with Photoshop as Filter ➪ Sketch ➪ Chrome, this filter turns an image into a melted pile of metallic goo. No matter how you apply Chrome, it completely wipes out your image and leaves a ton of jagged color transitions in its wake. It's really only useful with color images, and then only if you follow up with the Fade command and the Luminosity mode. Even then, I've never been particularly satisfied with the results.

But it got me thinking: How can you create a metallic coating, with gleaming highlights and crisp shadows, without resorting to Chrome? Find Edges offers a way. First, copy your image to a separate layer. Then apply the Gaussian Blur filter. A Radius value between 1.0 and 4.0 produces the best results, depending on how gooey you want the edges to be. Then apply the Find Edges filter. Because the edges are blurry, the resulting image is light; so I recommend you darken it using Image ➪ Adjust ➪ Levels (raise the first Input Levels value to 100 or so, as explained in Chapter 18). The blurry edges appear in the top left example in Figure 16-11.

To produce the bottom left image, I mixed the layer with the underlying original using the Overlay blend mode and an Opacity of 80 percent. The result is a shiny effect that produces a metallic finish without altogether destroying the detail in the image.

If you decide you like this effect, there's more where that came from. The second and third columns of Figure 16-11 show the results of applying Filter ➪ Sketch ➪ Bas Relief and Filter ➪ Artistic ➪ Plastic Wrap. After applying each filter, I choose Filter ➪ Fade, selected the Overlay mode, and set the Opacity value to 80 percent, repeating the effect I applied to the Gaussian Blur and Find Edges layer.

Color Plate 16-5 shows the same effects in color. Starting with an unedited construction worker, I went through the usual calisthenics of selecting and layering the image. Next, I applied Gaussian Blur (3.0 Radius) and Find Edges. The effect was too light, so I chose Image ➪ Adjust ➪ Levels and entered 128 into the first option box. Everything darker than medium gray went to black, uniformly strengthening the effect. The result is the full-color metallic coating shown in the second example in the top row of the color plate. To get the top right image, I merely selected Overlay from the blend mode pop-up menu in the Layers palette and changed the Opacity value to 80 percent.

Blur & Find Edges Bas Relief Plastic Wrap

Overlay, 80%

Figure 16-11
After applying Gaussian Blur and Find Edges to a layered
version of the image (top left), I composited the filtered
image with the original using the Overlay mode (bottom
left). The second and third columns show similar effects
achieved using the effects filters Bas Relief and Plastic
Wrap.

In the bottom row of Color Plate 16-5, I really went nuts. In each case, I applied one
of three effects filters —Bas Relief, Plastic Wrap, and the infamous Filter ⇨ Sketch
⇨ Chrome. And each time, I choose Filter ⇨ Fade, selected the Luminosity Mode,
and reduced the Opacity value to 80 percent.

Okay, okay, so Chrome still looks more metallic than the other effects, but it also
plays havoc with the detail. I'm willing to settle for a more subtle effect if it means I
can still recognize my subject when I'm finished.

Distortion Filters

For the most part, commands in the Distort submenu are related by the fact that they move colors in an image to achieve unusual stretching, swirling, and vibrating effects. They're rather like the transformation commands from the Layer menu in that they perform their magic by relocating and interpolating colors rather than by altering brightness and color values.

The distinction, of course, is that while the transformation commands let you scale and distort images by manipulating four control points, the Distort filters provide the equivalent of hundreds of control points, all of which you can use to affect different portions of an image. In some cases, you're projecting an image into a fun-house mirror; other times, it's a reflective pool. You can fan images, wiggle them, and change them in ways that have no correlation to real life, as illustrated in Figure 16-12.

Figure 16-12
This is your image (left); this is your image on distortion filters (right). Three filters, in fact: Spherize, Ripple, and Polar Coordinates.

Distortion filters are very powerful tools. Although they are easy to apply, they are extremely difficult to use well. Here are some rules to keep in mind:

  ✑ **Practice makes practical:** Distortion filters are like complex vocabulary words. You don't want to use them without practicing a little first. Experiment with a distortion filter several times before trying to use it in a real project. You may even want to write down the steps you take so that you can remember how you created an effect.

- **Use caution during tight deadlines:** Distortion filters are enormous time-wasters. Unless you know exactly how you want to proceed, you may want to avoid using them when time is short. The last thing you need when you're working under the gun is to get trapped trying to pull off a weird effect.

- **Apply selectively:** The effects of distortion filters are too severe to inflict all at once. You can achieve marvelous, subtle effects by distorting feathered and layered selections. Although I wouldn't call the image in Figure 16-12 subtle, no single effect was applied to the entire image. I applied the Spherize filter to a feathered elliptical marquee that included most of the image. I then reapplied Spherize to the eye. I selected the hair and beard and applied the Ripple filter twice. Finally, after establishing two heavily feathered vertical columns on either side of the image in the quick mask mode, I applied the Polar Coordinates filter, which reflected the front and back of the head. Turn the book upside down and you'll see a second face.

- **Combine creatively:** Don't expect a single distortion to achieve the desired effect. If one application isn't enough, apply the filter again. Experiment with combining different distortions.

- **Save your original:** Never distort an image until you save it. After you start down Distortion Boulevard, the only way to go back is File ⇨ Revert. And, as always, it's a good idea to layer the image before applying the filter so that you can delete it if you don't like the effect.

Distortion filters interpolate between pixels to create their fantastic effects. This means that the quality of your filtered images is dependent on the setting of the Interpolation option in the General Preferences dialog box. If a filter is producing jagged effects, the Nearest Neighbor option is probably selected. Try selecting the Bicubic or Bilinear option instead.

Reflecting an image in a spoon

Most folks take their first ventures into distortion filters by using Pinch and Spherize. Pinch maps an image onto the inside of a sphere or similarly curved surface; Spherize maps it onto the outside of a sphere. It's sort of like looking at your reflection on the inside or outside of a spoon.

You can apply Pinch to a scanned face to squish the features toward the center or apply Spherize to accentuate the girth of the nose. Figure 16-13 illustrates both effects. It's a laugh, and you pretty much feel as though you're onto something that no one else ever thought of before. (At least that's how I felt — but I'm easily amazed.)

Figure 16-13
Constantine does the popular throbbing facial dance — well, it was popular back in 300 AD — thanks to the Pinch (left) and Spherize (right) filters.

You can pinch or spherize an image using either the Pinch or Spherize command. As shown in Figure 16-14, a positive value in the Pinch dialog box produces a similar effect to a negative value in the Spherize dialog box. There is a slight difference between the spatial curvature of the 3D calculations: Pinch pokes the image inward or outward using a rounded cone — we're talking bell-shaped, much like a Gaussian model. Spherize wraps the image on the outside or inside of a true sphere. As a result, the two filters yield subtly different results. Pinch produces a soft transition around the perimeter of a selection; Spherize produces an abrupt transition. If this doesn't quite make sense to you, just play with one, try out the same effect with the other, and see which you like better.

Another difference between the two filters is that Spherize provides the additional options of allowing you to wrap an image onto the inside or outside of a horizontal or vertical cylinder. To try out these effects, select the Horizontal Only or Vertical Only options from the Mode pop-up menu at the bottom of the Spherize dialog box.

Figure 16-14
Both the Pinch and Spherize dialog boxes enable you to pinch or spherize an image. Pinch wraps on a rounded cone; Spherize wraps onto a sphere.

 Both the Pinch and Spherize filters are applicable only to elliptical regions of an image. If a selection outline is not elliptical in shape, Photoshop applies the filter to the largest ellipse that fits inside the selection. As a result, the filter may leave behind a noticeable elliptical boundary between the affected and unaffected portions of the selection. To avoid this effect, select the region you want to edit with the elliptical marquee tool and then feather the selection before filtering it. This softens the effect of the filter and provides a more gradual transition (even more so than Pinch already affords).

One of the more remarkable properties of the Pinch filter is that it lets you turn any image into a conical gradation. Figure 16-15 illustrates how the process works.

First, blur the image to eliminate any harsh edges between color transitions. Then apply the Pinch filter at full strength (100 percent). Reapply the filter several more times. Each time you press ⌘-F, the center portion of the image recedes farther and farther into the distance, as shown in Figure 16-15. After 10 repetitions, the face in the example all but disappeared.

Original   Gaussian blur, 5.0   Pinch, 100%

Pinch x 3   Pinch x 5   Pinch x 10, Radial Blur

Figure 16-15
After applying the Gaussian Blur filter, I pinched the image 10 times and applied the Radial Blur filter to create a conical gradation

Next, apply the Radial Blur filter set to Spin 10 pixels or so to mix the color boundaries a bit. The result is a type of gradation that you can't create using Photoshop's gradient tool.

You can also use the Spherize tool set to a negative Amount value to create a conical gradation. Color Plate 16-6 shows off the subtle differences between using the Pinch and Spherize filters for this purpose. The left examples were created with Pinch; the right examples with Spherize. The first row shows the effect of applying each filter twice set to 100 and –100 percent, respectively. The spherized face is larger, showing that the Spherize filter works more slowly. But it also grabs more edge detail. The second row shows the results of 12 repetitions of each filter. Though the two gradations are very similar, the spherized one contains a hundred or so extra streaks. In the last row, I mixed the gradation with the original image using different blend modes. The Soft Light mode was responsible for the alarming conical-sunburn effect on the left. I repeated the filter four times using the Screen mode to get the right image. "Look, ma, I had a sprinkler system installed on my helmet!"

Twirling spirals

The Twirl filter rotates the center of a selection while leaving the sides fixed in place. The result is a spiral of colors that looks for all the world as if you poured the image into a blender set to a very slow speed.

When you choose Filter ➪ Distort ➪ Twirl, Photoshop displays the Twirl dialog box, shown in Figure 16-16. Enter a positive value from 1 to 999 degrees to spiral the image in a clockwise direction. Enter a negative value to spiral the image in a counterclockwise direction. As you are probably already aware, 360 degrees make a full circle, so the maximum 999-degree value equates to a spiral that circles around approximately three times, as shown in the bottom right example in Figure 16-17.

Figure 16-16
The Twirl dialog box lets you create spiraling images.

The Twirl filter produces smoother effects when you use lower Angle values. Therefore, you're better off applying a 100-degree spiral 10 times rather than applying a 999-degree spiral once, as verified by Figure 16-17.

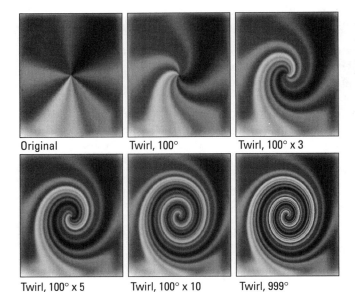

Original   Twirl, 100°   Twirl, 100° x 3

Twirl, 100° x 5   Twirl, 100° x 10   Twirl, 999°

Figure 16-17
The effects of applying the Twirl filter. Repeatedly applying the Twirl filter at a moderate value (bottom middle) produces a smoother effect than applying the filter once at a high value (bottom right).

In addition to creating ice-cream swirls like those shown in Figure 16-17, you can use the Twirl filter to create organic images virtually from scratch, as witnessed by Figures 16-18 and 16-19.

To create the images shown in Figure 16-18, I used the Spherize filter to flex the conical gradation vertically by entering 100 percent in the Amount option box and selecting Vertical Only from the Mode radio buttons. After repeating this filter several times, I eventually achieved a stalactite-stalagmite effect, as shown in the center example of the figure. I then repeatedly applied the Twirl filter to curl the flexed gradations like two symmetrical hairs. The result merges the simplicity of pure math with the beauty of bitmapped imagery.

Figure 16-18
You can create surprisingly
naturalistic effects using distortion
filters exclusively.

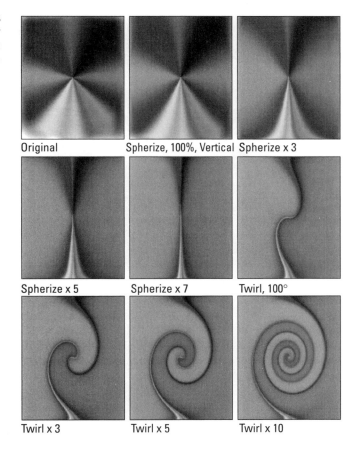

Original · Spherize, 100%, Vertical · Spherize x 3

Spherize x 5 · Spherize x 7 · Twirl, 100°

Twirl x 3 · Twirl x 5 · Twirl x 10

Figure 16-19 illustrates a droplet technique designed by Mark Collen. I took the liberty of breaking down the technique into the following steps.

STEPS   **Creating a Thick-liquid Droplet**

Step 1. **Press the D key.** As it has so many times in the past, the D key again restores the default foreground and background colors. Good effort, D key.

Step 2. **Select a square portion of an image.** Drag with the rectangular marquee tool while pressing the Shift key.

Step 3. **Drag inside the selection outline with the gradient tool.** Drag a short distance near the center of the selection from upper left to lower right, creating the gradation shown in the top left box in Figure 16-19.

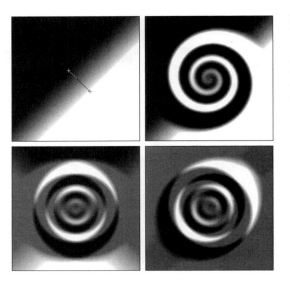

Figure 16-19
Though they appear as if they might be the result of the ZigZag filter, these images were created entirely by using the gradient tool, the Twirl filter, and a couple of transformations.

Step 4. **Choose the Twirl filter and apply it at –360 degrees so that the spiral moves counterclockwise.** To create the top right image in the figure, I applied the Twirl filter three times. Each repetition of the filter adds another ring of ripples.

Step 5. **Press ⌘-J to copy the selection to a layer.**

Step 6. **Choose Layer ⇨ Transform ⇨ Flip Horizontal.**

Step 7. **Lower the Opacity value to 50 percent.** Select the rectangular marquee tool, then press the 5 key. The result appears in the lower left example in Figure 16-19.

Step 8. **Choose Layer ⇨ Transform ⇨ Rotate 90° CW.** This rotates the layer a quarter turn, thus creating the last image in the figure. You can achieve other interesting effects by choosing Lighten, Darken, and others from the brush modes pop-up menu.

Now, if a few twirls and transformations can produce an effect this entertaining in black and white, just imagine what you can do in color. On second thought, don't imagine; check out Color Plate 16-7 instead. The first row in this eight-part color plate is nothing more than a color version of Figure 16-19, intended merely to set the scene. As you can see, I've created a gradation using two compementary colors, blue and yellow. In the fifth example (lower left), I apply the Difference blend mode to the Layer and return the Opacity setting to 100 percent. Next, I clone that layer and rotate it another 90 degrees clockwise to produce the sixth example. The Difference blend mode remains in effect for this cloned layer as well. Not satisfied, I clone that layer, rotate it another 90 degrees, and flip it horizontally. The result, also subject to Difference, is the seventh example. Then for the *coup de grâce*, I randomly apply the Twirl, Spherize, and ZigZag filters to the layers to mutate the concentric rings into something a little more interesting.

If that went a little fast for you, not to worry. More important than the specific effect is this general category of "distortion drawings." A filter like Pinch or Twirl permits you to create wild imagery without ever drawing a brushstroke or scanning a photograph. If you can do this much with a simple two-color gradation, just think of what you can do if you throw in a few more colors. Pixels are little more than fodder for these very powerful functions.

Creating concentric pond ripples

I don't know about you, but when I think of zigzags, I think of cartoon lighting bolts, wriggling snakes, scribbles — anything that alternately changes directions along an axis, like the letter *Z*. The ZigZag filter does arrange colors into zigzag patterns, but it does so in a radial fashion, meaning that the zigzags emanate from the center of the image like spokes in a wheel. The result is a series of concentric ripples. If you want parallel zigzags, check out the Ripple and Wave filters, described in the next section. (The ZigZag filter creates ripples and the Ripple filter creates zigzags. Go figure.)

When you choose Filter ➪ Distort ➪ ZigZag, Photoshop displays the ZigZag dialog box shown in Figure 16-20. The dialog box offers the following options:

- **Amount:** Enter an amount between negative and positive 100 in whole-number increments to specify the depth of the ripples. If you enter a negative value, the ripples descend below the surface. If you enter a positive value, the ripples protrude upward. Examples of three representative Amount values appear in Figure 16-21.

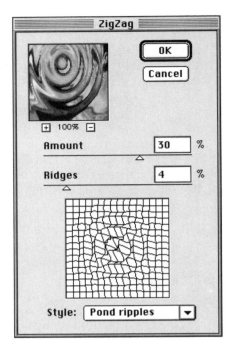

Figure 16-20
The ZigZag dialog box lets you add concentric ripples to an image, as if the image were reflected in a pond into which you dropped a pebble.

 co **Ridges:** This option box controls the number of ripples in the selected area and accepts any value from 1 to 20. Figure 16-22 demonstrates the effect of three Ridges values.

co **Pond Ripples:** This option is really a cross between the two that follow. It moves pixels outward and rotates them around the center of the selection to create circular patterns. As demonstrated in the top rows of Figures 16-21 and 16-22, this option truly results in a pond ripple effect.

co **Out From Center:** When you select this option, Photoshop moves pixels outward in rhythmic bursts according to the value in the Ridges option box. Because the gradation image I created in Figure 16-14 was already arranged in a radial pattern, I brought in Moses to demonstrate the effect of the Out From Center option, as shown in the second rows of Figures 16-21 and 16-22.

co **Around Center:** Select this option to rotate pixels in alternating directions around the circle without moving them outward. This is the only option that produces what I would term a zigzag effect. The last rows of Figures 16-21 and 16-22 show the effects of the Around Center option.

Figure 16-21
The effects of the ZigZag filter subject to three Amount values and the Pond Ripples, Out From Center, and Around Center settings. In all cases, the Ridges value was 5.

Pond Ripples

Amount = 10   50   100

Out From Center

10   50   100

Around Center

10   50   100

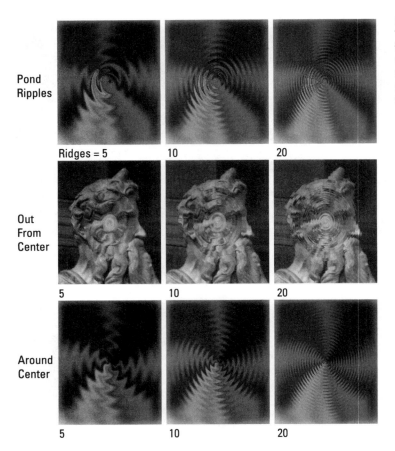

Pond Ripples

Ridges = 5   10   20

Out From Center

5   10   20

Around Center

5   10   20

Figure 16-22
The effects of the ZigZag filter using three Ridges values and each of the three radio button settings. In all cases, the Amount value was 20.

Creating parallel ripples and waves

Photoshop provides four means to distort an image in parallel waves, as if the image were lying on the bottom of a shimmering or undulating pool. Of the four, the ripple filters — which include Ripple, Ocean Ripple, and Glass — are only moderately sophisticated, but they're also relatively easy to apply. The fourth filter, Wave, affords you greater control, but its options are among the most complex Photoshop has to offer.

The Ripple filter

To use the Ripple filter, choose Filter ➪ Distort ➪ Ripple. Photoshop displays the Ripple dialog box shown in Figure 16-23. You have the following options:

- **Amount:** Enter an amount between negative and positive 999 in whole-number increments to specify the width of the ripples from side to side. Negative and positive values change the direction of the ripples, but visually speaking, they produce identical effects. The ripples are measured as a ratio of the Size value and the dimensions of the selection — all of which translates to, "Experiment and see what happens." You can count on getting ragged effects from any value over 300, as illustrated in Figure 16-24.

Figure 16-23
The Ripple filter makes an image appear as if it were refracted through flowing water.

- **Size:** Select one of the three options in the Size drop-down menu to change the length of the ripples. The Small option results in the shortest ripples and therefore the most ripples. As shown in the upper right corner of Figure 16-24, you can create a textured glass effect by combining the Small option with a high Amount value. The Large option results in the longest and fewest ripples.

You can create a blistered effect by overlaying a negative ripple onto a positive ripple. Try this: First, copy the selection. Then apply the Ripple filter with a positive Amount value — say, 300. Next, paste the copied selection and apply the Ripple filter at the exact opposite Amount value, in this case, –300. Press 5 to change the Opacity slider bar to 50 percent. The result is a series of diametrically opposed ripples that cross each other to create teardrop blisters.

Figure 16-24
The effects of combining three different Ripple filter Amount values with three different Size settings.

Ocean Ripple and Glass

The Ocean Ripple and Glass filters are gifts from Gallery Effects. Both filters emulate the effect of looking at an image through textured glass. These two distorters so closely resemble each other that they would be better merged into one. But where the effects filters are concerned, interface design is as fickle and transitory as the face on the cover of *Tiger Beat* magazine.

The Ocean Ripple and Glass dialog boxes appear joined at the hip in Figure 16-25. While the names and effects of the specific slider bars vary, the only real difference between the two filters is that Ocean Blur subscribes to a fixed ripple texture, and Glass lets you switch out the texture by selecting from a pop-up menu.

To guide you in your experimentations, Figure 16-26 shows the Pinch gradation subject to several Ocean Blur settings. The first number represents the Ripple Size value (listed first in the dialog box); the second number in the figure represents the Ripple Magnitude value. As you can see, you can vary the Size value with impunity. But raise the Magnitude value, and you're looking through sculpted glass.

Figure 16-25
The new Ocean Ripple and Glass effects filters are two birds of a feather, ultimately born from the same yoke.

Figure 16-26
Raising the Ripple Size value (first number in each pair) spreads out the effect, while raising the Ripple Magnitude (second number) adds more depth and contrast to the ripples.

But Ocean Blur and Glass emulate the effect of looking at an image through textured glass.

The Wave filter

Now that you've met the ripple family, it's time to ride the Wave. I could write a book on this filter alone. It wouldn't be very big, nobody would buy it, and I'd hate every minute of it, but you never know what a freelancer will do next. Keep an eye out for *Macworld Wave Filter Bible* at your local bookstore.

In the meantime, choose Filter ➪ Distort ➪ Wave (that's the easy part) to display the Wave dialog box shown in Figure 16-27. Photoshop presents you with the following options, which make applying a distortion almost every bit as fun as operating an oscilloscope:

> ➣ **Number of Generators:** Right off the bat, the Wave dialog box boggles the brain. A friend of mine likened this option to the number of rocks you throw in the water to start it rippling. One generator means that you throw in one rock to create one set of waves, as demonstrated in Figure 16-28. You can throw in two rocks to create two sets of waves (see Figure 16-29), three rocks to create three sets of waves, and all the way up to a quarryfull of 999 rocks to create, well, you get the idea. If you enter a high value, however, be prepared to wait a few years for the preview to update. If you can't wait, press ⌘-period, which turns off the preview until the next time you enter the dialog box.

Figure 16-27
The Wave dialog box enables you to wreak scientific havoc on an image. Put on your pocket protector, take out your slide rule, and give it a whirl.

Figure 16-28
The effect of three sets of Maximum Wavelength (first value) and Amplitude (second value) settings when combined with each of the three Type settings. The Number of Generators value was 1 in all cases.

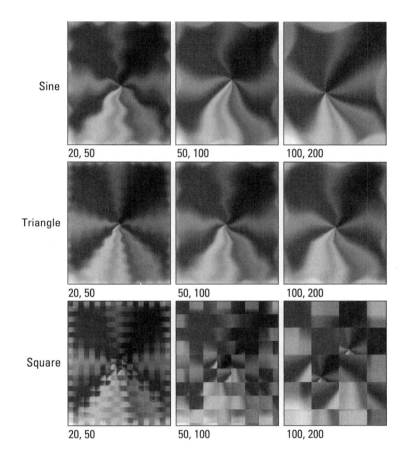

Sine

20, 50   50, 100   100, 200

Triangle

20, 50   50, 100   100, 200

Square

20, 50   50, 100   100, 200

✑ **Wavelength and Amplitude:** Beginning to feel like you're playing with a HAM radio? The Wave filter produces random results by varying the number and length of waves (Wavelength) as well as the height of the waves (Amplitude) between minimum and maximum values, which can range anywhere from 1 to 999. (The Wavelength and Amplitude options, therefore, correspond in theory to the Size and Amount options in the Ripple dialog box.) Figures 16-28 and 16-29 show examples of representative Wavelength and Amplitude values.

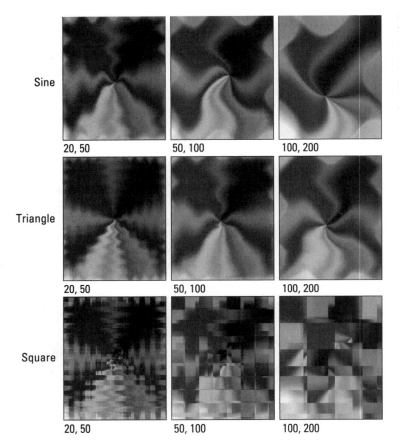

Figure 16-29
The only difference between these images and their counterparts in Figure 16-28 is that the Number of Generators value used for all images was 2.

- **Scale:** You can scale the effects of the Wave filter between 1 and 100 percent horizontally and vertically. All the effects featured in Figures 16-28 and 16-29 were created by setting both Scale options to 15 percent.

- **Undefined Areas:** The Wave filter distorts a selection to the extent that gaps may appear around the edges. You can either fill those gaps by repeating pixels along the edge of the selection, as in the figures, or by wrapping pixels from the left side of the selection onto the right side and pixels from the top edge of the selection onto the bottom.

- **Type:** You can select from three kinds of waves. The Sine option produces standard sine waves that rise and fall smoothly in bell-shaped curves, just like real waves. The Triangle option creates zigzags that rise and fall in straight lines, like the edge of a piece of fabric cut with pinking shears. The Square option has nothing to do with waves at all, but rather organizes an image into a series of rectangular groupings, reminiscent of Cubism. You might think of this option as an extension of the Mosaic filter. Figures 16-28 and 16-29 demonstrate all three options.

∽ **Randomize:** The Wave filter is random by nature. If you don't like the effect you see in the preview box, click on the Randomize button to stir things up a bit. You can keep clicking on the button until you get an effect you like.

Distorting an image along a curve

The Distort command, which isn't discussed elsewhere in this book, creates four corner handles around an image. You drag each corner handle to distort the selected image in that direction. Unfortunately, you can't add other points around the edges to create additional distortions, which can be very frustrating if you're trying to achieve a specific effect. If you can't achieve a certain kind of distortion using Image ⇨ Effects ⇨ Distort, the Shear filter may be your answer.

Shear distorts an image along a path. When you choose Filter ⇨ Distort ⇨ Shear, you get the dialog box shown in Figure 16-30. Initially, a single line that has two points at either end appears in the grid at the top of the box. When you drag the points, you slant the image in the preview. This plus the fact that the filter is named Shear — Adobe's strange term for skewing (it appears in Illustrator as well) — leads many users to dismiss the filter as nothing more than a slanting tool. But in truth, it's more versatile than that.

Figure 16-30
Click on the grid line in the left corner of the Shear dialog box to add points to the line. Drag these points to distort the image along the curve.

You can add points to the grid line simply by clicking on it. A point springs up every time you click on an empty space in the line. Drag the point to change the curvature of the line and distort the image along the new curve. To delete a point, drag it off the left or right side of the grid. To delete all points and return the line to its original vertical orientation, click on the Defaults button.

The Undefined Areas options work just as they do in the Wave dialog box (described in the preceding section). You can either fill the gaps on one side of the image with pixels shoved off the opposite side by selecting Wrap Around or you can repeat pixels along the edge of the selection by selecting Repeat Edge Pixels.

Changing to polar coordinates

The Polar Coordinates filter is another one of those gems that a lot of folks shy away from because it doesn't make much sense at first glance. When you choose Filter ⇨ Distort ⇨ Polar Coordinates, Photoshop presents two radio buttons, as shown in Figure 16-31. You can either map an image from rectangular to polar coordinates or from polar to rectangular coordinates.

All right, time for some global theory. The first image in Figure 16-32 shows a stretched detail of the world map included in the default System 7 Scrapbook file. Though a tad simplistic, this map falls under the heading of a *Mercator projection,* meaning that Greenland is all stretched out of proportion, looking as big as the United States and Mexico combined.

Figure 16-31
In effect, the Polar Coordinates dialog box lets you map an image onto a globe and view the globe from above.

Figure 16-32
The world from the equator up expressed in rectangular
(left) and polar (right) coordinates.

The reason for this has to do with the way different mapping systems handle longitude and latitude lines. On a spherical globe, lines of latitude converge at the poles. On a Mercator map, they run absolutely parallel. Because the Mercator map exaggerates the distance between longitude lines as you progress away from the equator, it likewise exaggerates the distance between lines of latitude. The result is a map that becomes infinitely enormous at each of the poles.

When you convert the map to polar coordinates (by selecting the Rectangular to Polar radio button in the Polar Coordinates dialog box), you look down on it from the extreme north or south pole. This means that the entire length of the top edge of the Mercator map becomes a single dot in the exact center of the polar projection. The length of the bottom edge of the map wraps around the entire perimeter of the circle. The second example in Figure 16-32 shows the result. As you can see, the Rectangular to Polar option is just the thing for wrapping text around a circle.

If you select the Polar to Rectangular option, the Polar Coordinates filter produces the opposite effect. Imagine for a moment that the conical gradation shown in the upper left corner of Figure 16-33 is a fan spread out into a full circle. Now imagine closing the fan, breaking the hinge at the top, and spreading out the rectangular fabric of the fan. The center of the fan unfolds to form the top edge of the fabric, and what was once the perimeter of the circle is now the bottom edge of the fabric. Figure 16-33 shows two examples of what happens when you convert circular images from polar to rectangular coordinates.

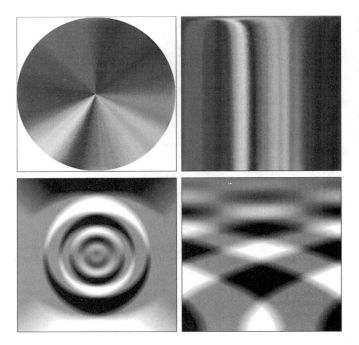

Figure 16-33
Two familiar circular images (left) converted from polar to rectangular coordinates (right). The top example is simple enough that you can probably predict the results of the conversion in your head. The lower example looks cool, but you'd need a brain extension to predict the outcome.

The Polar Coordinates filter is a great way to edit gradations. After drawing a linear gradation with the gradient tool (as discussed in Chapter 9), try applying Filter ⇨ Distort ⇨ Polar Coordinates with the Polar to Rectangular option selected. (Rectangular to Polar just turns it into a radial gradation, sometimes with pretty undesirable results.) You get a redrawn gradation with highlights at the bottom of the selection. Press ⌘-F to reapply the filter to achieve another effect. You can keep repeating this technique until jagged edges start to appear. Then press ⌘-Z to go back to the last smooth effect.

Distorting an image inside out

The following exercise describes how to achieve a sizzling Parting of the Red Sea effect. Though it incorporates several distortion filters, the star of the effect is the Polar Coordinates filter, which is used to turn the image inside out and then convert it back to polar coordinates after flipping it upside down. No scanned image or artistic talent is required. Rumor has it that Moses puts in a guest appearance in the final image.

This effect is the brainchild of Mark Collen, easily the most authoritative distortion expert I've had the pleasure of knowing. I already mentioned his name in this chapter, in connection with the "Creating a Thick-liquid Droplet" steps. To be perfectly honest, I probably should have mentioned him more than that, because many of the ideas conveyed in this chapter were based on long, expensive telephone conversations with the guy.

At any rate, Figures 16-34 through 16-39 show the progression of the image through the following steps, starting with a simplistic throwback to Dada (the art movement, not the family member) and continuing to the fabled sea rising in billowing streams. Color Plate 16-8 shows one of Mark's most vivid images, which was created in part using many of the techniques from the steps below. Obviously, Mark used a couple of other filtering and nonfiltering techniques to create his image, but gee whiz folks, you can't expect the guy to share everything he knows in one fell swoop. He has to make a living, after all.

STEPS   The Parting of the Red Sea Effect

Step 1.   **Draw some random shapes in whatever colors you like.** My shapes appear against a black background in Figure 16-34, but you can use any shapes and colors you like. To create each shape, I used the lasso tool to draw the outline of the shape and pressed Option-Delete to fill the lassoed selection with the foreground color. The effect works best if there's a lot of contrast between your colors.

Figure 16-34
Draw several meaningless shapes with the lasso tool and fill each with a different color.

Step 2.   **Choose Image ⇨ Rotate Canvas ⇨ 90° CCW.** In Step 3, you'll apply the Wind Filter to add streaks to the shapes you just created, as shown in Figure 16-35. Because the Wind filter creates horizontal streaks only, and your goal is to add vertical streaks, you must temporarily reorient your image before applying the filter.

Step 3. **Choose Filter ⇨ Stylize ⇨ Wind.** Select Blast and From the Left and press Return. To randomize the image in both directions, choose the Wind filter again and select Blast and From the Right.

Step 4. **Choose Image ⇨ Rotate ⇨ 90° CW.** This returns the image to its original orientation.

Step 5. **Choose Filter ⇨ Blur ⇨ Motion Blur.** Enter 90 degrees into the Angle option and use 20 pixels for the Distance option. This blurs the image vertically to soften the blast lines, as in Figure 16-35.

Figure 16-35
The result of rotating the image a quarter turn, blasting it in both directions with the Wind filter, rotating it back into place, and applying the Motion Blur filter vertically.

Step 6. **Choose Filter ⇨ Distort ⇨ Wave.** Then enter the values shown in Figure 16-36 into the Wave option box. Most of these values are approximate. You can experiment with other settings if you like. The only essential value is 0 percent in the Vert. option box, which ensures that the filter waves the image in a horizontal direction only.

Step 7. **Choose Filter ⇨ Distort ⇨ Ocean Ripple.** I entered 15 for the Ripple Size and 5 for the Ripple Magnitude to get the effect shown in Figure 16-37.

Figure 16-36
Apply these settings from the Wave dialog box to wave the image in a vertical direction only.

Step 8. **Expand the canvas size.** To perform the next step, the Polar Coordinates filter needs lots of empty room in which to maneuver. If you filled up your canvas like I did, choose Image ⇨ Canvas Size and add 200 pixels both vertically and horizontally. The new canvas size, with generous borders, appears in Figure 16-37.

Figure 16-37
After applying the Ripple filter, use the Canvas Size command to add a generous amount of empty space around the image.

Step 9. **Choose Filter ➪ Distort ➪ Polar Coordinates.** So far, you've probably been a little disappointed by your image. I mean, it's just this disgusting little hairy thing that looks like a bad rug or something. Well, now's your chance to turn it into something special. Choose Filter ➪ Distort ➪ Polar Coordinates and select the Polar to Rectangular radio button. Photoshop in effect turns the image inside out, sending all the hairy edges to the bottom of the screen. Finally, an image worth waiting for.

Step 10. **Choose Image ➪ Rotate Canvas ➪ Flip Vertical.** This turns the image upside down. As I believe Hemingway said, the hair also rises, as shown in Figure 16-38. This step prepares the image for the next major polar conversion, due in the year 2096.

Figure 16-38
Convert the image from polar to rectangular coordinates to turn it inside out. Then flip it vertically to prepare it for the next polar conversion.

Step 11. **Use the rectangular marquee tool to select the central portion of the image.** Leave about 50 pixels along the top and bottom of the image deselected, as well as 100 pixels along both sides. Then feather the selection with a 15-pixel radius.

Step 12. **Press ⌘-F to reapply the Polar Coordinates filter using the same settings as before.** Okay, so it happened before 2096. How could I have known? The pixels inside the selection now billow into a fountain.

Step 13. **Add Moses to taste.** The finished image appears in Figure 16-39.

Figure 16-39
Marquee the central portion of the image with a heavily feathered selection outline, convert the selection from rectangular to polar coordinates, and put Moses into the scene. My, doesn't he look natural in his new environment?

Adding Clouds and Spotlights___

In a way, you can think of all five filters in the Filter ⇨ Render submenu as lighting filters. You can use Clouds and Difference Clouds to create a layer of haze over an image. Lens Flare creates light flashes and reflections (as I mentioned earlier). Lighting Effects lights an image as if it were hanging on a gallery wall. You can even use the unremarkable Texture Fill command to add an embossed texture to a piece lighted with the Lighting Effects filter. Together, these five suggest a new category called *creative filters*, but it's really too early to tell.

Creating clouds

If you've played with the Clouds filters at all, you probably thought, "Hmf," and gave them up for a screwy feature that Adobe's programmers decided to add in lieu of some meatier functions. Certainly these filters don't qualify as groundbreaking, but they're not at all bad and can yield some pretty entertaining results.

Clouds create an abstract and random haze of color between the foreground and background colors. Difference Clouds works exactly like layering the image, applying the Clouds filter, and selecting the Difference blend mode in the Layers palette.

Why on earth should this filter make special provisions for a single blend mode? Because you can create cumulative effects. Try this: Select blue as the foreground color and then choose Filter ⇨ Render ⇨ Clouds. Ah, just like a real sky, huh? Now choose Filter ⇨ Render ⇨ Difference Clouds. It's like some kind of weird Halloween motif, all blacks and oranges. Press ⌘-F to repeat the filter. Back to the blue sky. Keep pressing ⌘-F over and over and notice the results. A pink cancer starts invading the blue sky; a green cancer invades the orange one. Multiple applications of the Difference Clouds filter generate organic oil-on-water effects.

To strengthen the colors created by the Clouds filter, press Shift when choosing the command. This same technique works when using the Difference Clouds filter as well. In fact, I don't know of any reason *not* to Shift-choose these commands, unless you have some specific need for washed-out effects.

Color Plate 16-9 shows some pretty entertaining applications of the Clouds filters. With the foreground and background colors set to blue and orange respectively, I applied the Clouds filter to a layered copy of the rose image. For maximum effect, I Shift-chose the filter to create the top left image in the color plate. I then Shift-chose the Difference Clouds filter to create the purple montage in the figure, and pressed ⌘-F ten times to achieve the top right image. Looks to me like I definitely have something growing in my Petri dish.

Yeah, so really groovy stuff, right? Shades of "Purple Haze" and all that. But now that I've created this murky mess, what the heck do I do with it? Composite it, of course. The bottom row of Color Plate 16-9 shows examples of mixing each of the images from the top row with the original rose. In the left example, I chose the Overlay option from the blend mode pop-up menu in the Layers palette. In the middle example, I chose the Screen mode. And in the last example, I chose Hue. This last one is particularly exciting, completely transforming the colors in the rose while leaving the gray (and therefore unsaturated) background untouched. Without a mask, without anything but a rectangular marquee, I've managed to precisely color the interior of the rose.

Lighting an image

Photoshop is definitely venturing into 3D drawing territory with the Lighting Effects filter. This very complex function allows you to shine lights on an image, color the lights, position them, focus them, specify the reflectivity of the surface, and even create a surface map. In many ways, it's a direct lift from Fractal Design Painter. But whereas Painter provides predefined paper textures and light refraction effects that bolster the capabilities of its excellent tool, Photoshop offers better controls and more lighting options.

 The Lighting Effects filter is applicable exclusively to RGB images. And your computer has to be equipped with an FPU math coprocessor, which rules out using the filter on most PowerBooks.

When you choose Filter ⇨ Render ⇨ Lighting Effects, Photoshop displays what is easily its most complex dialog box, as shown in Figure 16-40. The dialog box has two halves: One in which you actually position light with respect to a thumbnail of the selected image, and one that contains about a billion intimidating options. Between you and me, I think Adobe could have done a better job, but the dialog box is functional.

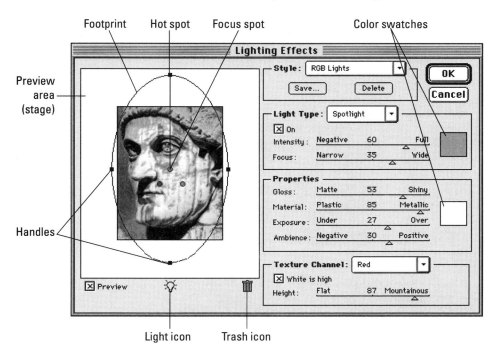

Figure 16-40
The Lighting Effects dialog box enables you to light an image as if it were hanging in a gallery, or lying on a floor, or perhaps resting too near a hot flame.

No bones about it, this dialog box is a bear. The easiest way to apply the filter is to choose one of the predefined lighting effects from the Style pop-up menu at the top of the right side of the dialog box, see how it looks in the preview area, and — if you like it — press Return to apply the effect.

But if you want to create your own effects, you'll have to work a little harder. Here are the basic steps involved in creating a custom effect.

STEPS   Lighting an Image

Step 1.   **Drag from the light icon at the bottom of the dialog box into the preview area to create a new light source.** I call this area the *stage* because it's as if the image is painted on the floor of a stage and the lights are hanging above it.

Step 2.   **Select the kind of light you want from the Light Type pop-up menu.** It's just below the Style pop-up menu. You can select from Directional, Omni, and Spotlight:

   ☞   Directional works like the sun, being a general, unfocused light that hits a target from an angle.

   ☞   Omni is a bare light bulb hanging in the middle of the room, shining in all directions from a center point.

   ☞   And Spotlight is a focused beam that is brightest at the source and tapers off gradually.

Step 3.   **Specify the color of the light by clicking on the top color swatch.** You can also muck about with the Intensity slider bar to control the brightness of the light. If Spotlight is selected, the Focus slider becomes available. Drag the slider toward Narrow to create a bright laser of light; drag toward Wide to diffuse the light and spread it over a larger area.

Step 4.   **Move the light source by dragging at the *focus point* (the colored circle in the stage).** When Directional or Spotlight is selected, the focus point represents the spot at which the light is pointing. When Omni is active, the focus point is the actual bulb. (Don't burn yourself.)

Step 5.   **If Directional or Spotlight is active, you can change the angle of the light by dragging the *hot spot*.** The hot spot represents the location in the image that's liable to receive the most light. When you use a Directional light, the hot spot appears as a black square at the end of a line joined to the focus point. The same holds true when you edit a Spotlight; the confusing thing is that there are four black squares altogether. The light source is joined to the focus point by a line, the three *handles* are not.

To make the light brighter, drag the hot spot closer to the focus point. Dragging the hot spot away from the focus point dims the light by increasing the distance that it has to travel. It's like putting a flashlight in the living room when you're in the garage — the light gets dimmer as you move farther away from it.

Step 6. **With Omni or Spotlight in force, you can edit the elliptical footprint of the light.** When Omni is in force, a circle surrounds the focus point. When editing a Spotlight, you see an ellipse. Either way, this shape represents the *footprint* of the light, which is the approximate area of the image affected by the light. You can change the size of the light by dragging the handles around the footprint. Enlarging the shape is like raising the light source. When the footprint is small, the light is close to the image, so it's concentrated and very bright. When the footprint is large, the light is high above the image, so it's more generalized.

When editing the footprint of a Spotlight, Shift-drag a handle to adjust the width or height of the ellipse without affecting the angle. To change the angle without affecting the size, ⌘-drag a handle.

Step 7. **Introduce more lights as you see fit.**

There are a bunch of different techniques you can take advantage of as you add and subtract lights from the stage. Press the Tab key to switch from one light to the next. You can duplicate a light in the stage by Option-dragging its focus point. To delete the active light, just press the Delete key. Or if you prefer, you can drag the focus point onto the trash can icon at the bottom of the dialog box.

Step 8. **Change the Properties and Texture Channel options as you see fit.** I explain these in detail after the steps.

Step 9. **If you want to save your settings for future use, click on the Save button.** Photoshop invites you to name the setup, which then appears as an option in the Style pop-up menu. If you want to get rid of one of the presets, select it from the pop-up menu and click on the Delete button.

Step 10. **Press Return to apply your settings to the image.**

That's almost everything. The only parts I left out are the Properties and Texture Channel options. The Properties slider bars control how light reflects off the surface of your image:

⌐ **Gloss:** Is the surface dull or shiny? Drag the slider toward Matte to make the surface flat and nonreflective, like dull enamel paint. Drag the slider toward Shiny to make it glossy, as if you had slapped on a coat of lacquer.

✎ **Material:** This option determines the color of the light that reflects back off the image. According to the logic employed by this option, Plastic reflects back the color of the light; Metallic reflects the color of the object itself. If only I had a bright, shiny plastic thing and a bright, shiny metal thing, I could check to see if this logic holds true in real life (like maybe that matters).

✎ **Exposure:** I'd like this option better if you could vary it between Sun Block 65 and Melanoma. Unfortunately, the more prosaic titles are Under and Over — exposed, that is. This option controls the brightness of all lights like a big dimmer switch. You can control a single selected light using the Intensity slider, but the Exposure slider offers the added control of changing all lights in the stage area and the ambient light (described next) together.

✎ **Ambience:** The last slider allows you to add *ambient light,* which is a general, diffused light that hits all surfaces evenly. First, select the color of the light by clicking on the color swatch to the right. Then drag the slider to cast a subtle hue over the stage. Drag toward Positive to tint the image with the color in the swatch; drag toward Negative to tint the stage with the swatch's opposite. Keep the slider set to 0 — dead in the center — to cast no hue.

The Texture Channel options let you treat one channel in the image as a *texture map*, which is a grayscale surface in which white indicates peaks and black indicates valleys. (As long as White is High is selected, that is. If you deselect that option, everything flips, and black becomes the peak.) It's as if one channel has a surface to it. By selecting a channel from the pop-up menu, you create an emboss effect, much like that created with the Emboss filter, except much better because you can light the surface from many angles at once, and it's in color to boot.

Choose a channel to serve as the embossed surface from the pop-up menu. Then change the Height slider to indicate more or less Flat terrain or huge Mountainous cliffs of surface texture.

Color Plate 16-10 shows an image lit with a total of five spotlights, two from above and three from below. In the first example, I left the Texture Channel option set to None. In the second example, I selected the green channel as the surface map. And in the third example, I filled a separate mask channel with a bunch of white and black dollops using Filter ➪ Pixelate ➪ Pointillize, then I selected the mask from the Texture Channel pop-up menu in the Lighting Effects dialog box. The result is a wonderfully rough paper texture.

Constructing Homemade Effects

■ ■

In This Chapter

➡ The mathematics behind the Custom filter

➡ More than 70 unique sharpening, blurring, edge-detection, and embossing effects

➡ An in-depth analysis of the Displace filter

➡ A look at Photoshop's predefined displacement maps

➡ How to apply custom gradations and textures as displacement maps

➡ A tour of the immensely powerful but complicated Filter Factory

➡ Create your own fully-functioning filter that rotates channels independently

■ ■

Creating a Custom Effect

If my wife were here right now, she might be tempted to say something diplomatic like, "Deke, dear, I think that our guests are growing a teeny bit tired of the subject of filters. Perhaps this would be a good time to move on to a new subject." To which I would respond, "Nonsense! Folks love to listen to me drone on and on about filters. I can't imagine anything more intriguing, can you? Speaking of which, is there any beer left in this house? (Urp.)" Whether you share my fascination with filters or not, don't get up and go home just yet, because I've yet to tell you about three very important filters — Custom, Displace, and the Filter Factory — that permit you to create your own, custom-tailored special effects.

Fully understanding the Custom and Displace filters requires some mathematical reasoning skills — and even if you're a math whiz, you'll probably have occasional difficulty predicting the outcomes of these filters. Using the Filter Factory requires flat-out programming skills. If math isn't your bag, if number theory clogs up your synapses to the extent that you feel like a worthless math wimp, by all means don't put yourself through the torture. Skip all the mathematical background in this chapter and read the "Applying Custom Values" and "Using Displacement Maps" sections to try out some specific, no-brainer effects.

 If you have no desire to learn the Filter Factory, you can experiment with some filters that I programmed using this plug-in. On the CD-ROM at the back of this book, you'll find several fully functioning filters, all of which include interactive slider bars and previews. If you copy the filters to your Plug-ins folder and launch Photoshop, you'll see my filters in the Filter ⇨ Tormentia submenu. (These filters torment your image in a demented way, hence *Tormentia*. I also considered *Tormento*, but that sounds like something you'd put on your pizza.) I explain what the filters do and how they work in Appendix C.

On the other hand, if you're not scared silly of math and you want to understand how to eventually create effects of your own, read on, you hearty soul.

The Custom filter

The Custom command enables you to design your own *convolution kernel*, which is a variety of filter in which neighboring pixels get mixed together. The kernel can be a variation on sharpening, blurring, embossing, or a half dozen other effects. You create your filter by entering numerical values into a matrix of options.

When you choose Filter ⇨ Other ⇨ Custom, Photoshop displays the dialog box shown in Figure 17-1. It sports a 5 × 5 matrix of option boxes followed by two additional options, Scale and Offset. The matrix options can accept values from negative to positive 999. The Scale value can range from 1 to 9,999, and the Offset value can range from negative to positive 9,999. The dialog box includes Load and Save buttons so that you can load settings from disk and save the current settings for future use.

Like most of Photoshop's filters, the Custom filter also includes a constantly updating preview box, which you'll have lots of time to appreciate if you decide to try your hand at designing your own effects. Select the Preview check box to view the effect of the kernel in the image window as well.

Figure 17-1
The Custom dialog box lets you design your own convolution kernel by multiplying the brightness values of pixels.

Here's how the filter works: When you press the Return key to apply the values in the Custom dialog box to a selection, the filter passes over every pixel in the selection, one at a time. For each pixel being evaluated — which I'll call the PBE, for short — the filter multiplies the PBE's current brightness value by the number in the center option box (the one that contains a 5 in Figure 17-1). To help keep things straight, I'll call this value the CMV, for *central matrix value.*

The filter then multiplies the brightness values of the surrounding pixels by the surrounding values in the matrix. For example, Photoshop multiplies the value in the option box just above the CMV by the brightness value of the pixel just above the PBE. It ignores any empty matrix option boxes and the pixels they represent.

Finally, the filter totals the products of the multiplied pixels, divides the sum by the value in the Scale option, and adds the Offset value to calculate the new brightness of the PBE. It then moves on to the next pixel in the selection and performs the calculation all over again. Figure 17-2 shows a schematic drawing of the process.

Perhaps seeing all of this spelled out in an equation will help you understand the process. Then again, perhaps not — but here it comes anyway. In the following equation, NP stands for *neighboring pixel* and MV stands for the corresponding matrix value in the Custom dialog box.

New brightness value = (((PBE × CMV) + (NP1 × MV1) + (NP2 × MV2) + . . .) ÷ Scale) + Offset

Luckily, Photoshop calculates the equation without any help from you. All you have to do is punch in the values and see what happens.

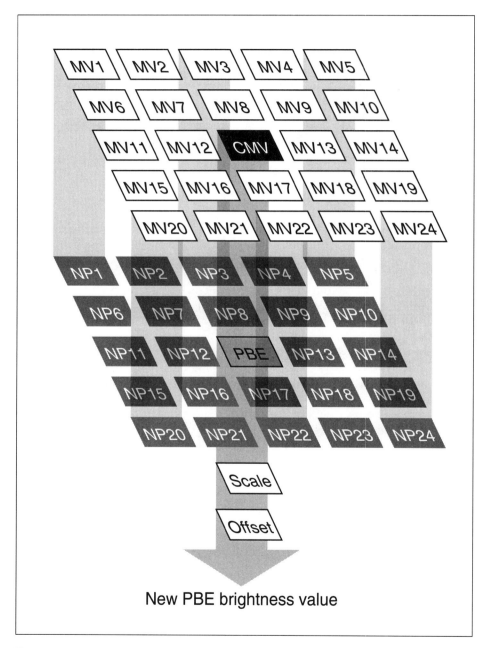

Figure 17-2
The Custom filter multiplies each matrix value by the
brightness value of the corresponding pixel, adds the
products together, divides the sum by the Scale value,
adds the Offset value, and applies the result to the pixel
being evaluated.

Custom filter advice

Now obviously, if you go around multiplying the brightness value of a pixel too much, you end up making it white. And a filter that turns an image white is pretty darn useless. The key, then, is to filter an image and at the same time maintain the original balance of brightness values. To achieve this, just be sure that the sum of all values in the matrix is 1. For example, the default values in the matrix shown back in Figure 17-1 are 5, –1, –1, –1, and –1, which add up to 1.

If the sum is greater than 1, use the Scale value to divide the sum down to 1. Figures 17-3 and 17-4 show the results of increasing the CMV from 5 to 6 and then to 7. This raises the sum of the values in the matrix from 1 to 2 and then to 3.

In Figure 17-3, I entered the sum into the Scale option to divide the sum back down to 1 (any value divided by itself is 1, after all). The result is that Photoshop maintains the original color balance of the image while at the same time filtering it slightly differently. When I did not raise the Scale value, the image became progressively lighter, as illustrated in Figure 17-4.

Figure 17-3
Raising the Scale value to reflect the sum of the values in the matrix maintains the color balance of the image.

If the sum is less than 1, increase the CMV until the sum reaches the magic number. For example, in Figure 17-5, I lowered the values to the left of the CMV and then above the CMV by 1 apiece to increase the sharpening effect. To ensure that the image did not darken, I also raised the CMV to compensate. When I did not raise the CMV, the image turned black, as shown in Figure 17-6.

Figure 17-4
Raising the sum of the matrix values without counterbalancing it in the Scale option lightens the image.

Figure 17-5
Raising the CMV to compensate for the lowered values in the matrix maintains the color balance of the image.

Although a sum of 1 provides the safest and most predictable filtering effects, you can use different sums, such as 0 and 2, to try out more destructive filtering effects. If you do, be sure to raise or lower the Offset value to compensate. For some examples, see the "Non-1 variations" section.

Figure 17-6
Lowering the sum of the matrix values without counterbalancing them with the CMV darkens the image.

Applying Custom Values_____

The following sections show you ways to sharpen, blur, and otherwise filter an image using specific matrix, Scale, and Offset values. It is my sincere hope that by the end of the Custom filter discussions, you not only will know how to repeat my examples, but also how to apply what you've learned to design special effects of your own.

Symmetrical effects

Values that are symmetrical both horizontally and vertically about the central matrix value produce sharpen and blur effects:

- **Sharpening:** A positive CMV surrounded by symmetrical negative values sharpens an image, as demonstrated in the first example of Figure 17-7. Figures 17-3 through 17-6 also demonstrate varying degrees of sharpening effects.

- **Blurring:** A positive CMV surrounded by symmetrical positive numbers — balanced, of course, by a Scale value as explained in the preceding section — blurs an image, as demonstrated in the second example of Figure 17-7.

- **Blurring with edge-detection:** A negative CMV surrounded by symmetrical positive values blurs an image and adds an element of edge-detection, as illustrated in the last example of the figure. These effects are unlike anything provided by Photoshop's standard collection of filters.

Figure 17-7
Symmetrical values can result in sharpening (left), blurring (middle), and edge-detection (right) effects.

Sharpening

The Custom command provides as many variations on the sharpening theme as the Unsharp Mask filter. In a sense, it provides even more, for whereas the Unsharp Mask filter requires you to sharpen an image inside a Gaussian radius, you get to specify exactly which pixels are taken into account when you use the Custom filter.

To create Unsharp Mask-like effects, enter a large number in the CMV and small values in the surrounding option boxes, as demonstrated in Figure 17-8. To go beyond Unsharp Mask, you can violate the radius of the filter by entering values around the perimeter of the matrix and ignoring options closer to the CMV, as demonstrated in Figure 17-9.

Figure 17-8
To create severe sharpening effects, enter a CMV just large enough to compensate for the negative values in the matrix.

Figure 17-9
To heighten the sharpening effect even further, enter negative values around the perimeter of the matrix.

You can sharpen an image using the Custom dialog box in two basic ways. First, you can enter lots of negative values into the neighboring options in the matrix and then enter a CMV just large enough to yield a sum of 1. This results in radical sharpening effects, as demonstrated throughout the examples in Figures 17-8 and 17-9.

Second, you can tone down the sharpening by raising the CMV and using the Scale value to divide the sum down to 1. Figures 17-10 and 17-11 show the results of raising the CMV to lessen the impact of the sharpening effects performed in Figures 17-8 and 17-9.

Figure 17-10
To sharpen more subtly, increase the central matrix value and then enter the sum into the Scale value.

Figure 17-11
When you soften the effect of radical sharpening, you create a thicker, higher contrast effect, much as when raising the Radius value in the Unsharp Mask dialog box.

Blurring

The philosophy behind blurring is very much the same as that behind sharpening. To produce extreme blurring effects, enter lots of values or high values into the neighboring options in the matrix, enter 1 into the CMV, and then enter the sum into the Scale option. Examples appear in Figure 17-12. To downplay the blurring, raise the CMV and the Scale value by equal amounts. In Figure 17-13, I used the same neighboring values as in Figure 17-12, but I increased the CMV and the Scale value by 3 apiece.

Figure 17-12
To create severe blurring effects, enter 1 for the CMV and fill the neighboring options with 1s and 2s.

Figure 17-13
To blur more subtly, increase the central matrix value and the Scale value by equal amounts.

Edge-detection

Many of you are probably beginning to get the idea by now, but just in case you're the kind of person who believes that friends don't let friends do math, I'll breeze through it one more time in the venue of edge-detection. If you really want to see those edges, enter 1s and 2s into the neighboring options in the matrix and then enter a CMV just *small* enough — it's a negative value, after all — to make the sum 1. Examples appear in Figure 17-14 for your viewing pleasure.

To lighten the edges and bring out the blur, raise the CMV and enter the resulting sum into the Scale option box. The first example in Figure 17-15 pushes the boundaries between edge-detection and a straight blur.

Figure 17-14
To create severe edge-detection effects, enter a negative CMV just small enough to compensate for the positive values in the matrix.

Figure 17-15
To blur the edges, increase the central matrix value and then enter the sum into the Scale value.

Non-1 variations

Every image shown in Figures 17-7 through 17-15 is the result of manipulating matrix values and using the Scale option to produce a sum total of 1. Earlier in this chapter, I showed you what can happen if you go below 1 (black images) or above 1 (white images). But I haven't shown you how you can use non-1 totals to produce interesting, if somewhat washed-out, effects.

The key is to raise the Offset value, thereby adding a specified brightness value to each pixel in the image. By doing this, you can offset the lightening or darkening caused by the matrix values to create an image that has half a chance of printing.

Lightening overly dark effects

The first image in Figure 17-16 uses nearly the exact same values used to create the extreme sharpening effect in the last image of Figure 17-8. The only difference is that the CMV is 1 lower (8, down from 9), which in turn lowers the sum total from 1 to 0.

The result is an extremely dark image with hints of brightness at points of high contrast. The image looks okay on-screen — actually, it looks pretty cool because of all those little star-like sprinkles in it — but it's likely to fill in during the printing process. If the first image in Figure 17-16 looks like anything but a vague blob of blackness, it's a credit to the printer of this book. Most printers who didn't have a giant publisher breathing down their necks would have kissed this image good-bye, and rightly so. It's too darn dark.

Figure 17-16
Three examples of sharpening effects with sum totals of 0. I lightened the images incrementally by entering positive values into the Offset option box.

To prevent the image from filling in and to help head off any disputes with your printer, lighten the image using the Offset value. Photoshop adds the value to the brightness level of each selected pixel. A brightness value of 255 equals solid white, so you don't need to go too high. As illustrated by the last example in Figure 17-16, an Offset value of 100 is enough to raise most pixels in the image to a medium gray. Figure 17-17 shows the results of lightening an overly dark edge-detection effect using the Offset value.

Figure 17-17
Three examples of edge-detection effects with sum totals of 0, lightened incrementally by using progressively higher Offset values.

Darkening overly light effects

You also can use the Offset value to darken filtering effects with sum totals greater than 1. The images in Figures 17-18 and 17-19 show sharpening and edge-detection effects whose matrix totals amount to 2. On their own, these filters produce effects that are too light. However, as demonstrated in the middle and right examples in the figures, you can darken the effects of the Custom filter to create high-contrast images by entering a negative value into the Offset option box.

Figure 17-18
Three examples of sharpening effects with sum totals of 2. I darkened the images incrementally by entering negative values into the Offset option box.

Figure 17-19
Three examples of edge-detection effects with sum totals of 2, darkened incrementally with progressively lower Offset values.

Using extreme offsets

If a brightness value of 255 produces solid white and a brightness value of 0 is solid black, why in blue blazes does the Offset value permit any number between negative and positive 9,999, a number 40 times greater than solid white? The answer lies in the fact that the matrix options can force the Custom filter to calculate brightness values much darker than black and much lighter than white. Therefore, you can use a very high or very low Offset value to boost the brightness of an image in which all pixels are well below black or diminish the brightness when all pixels are way beyond white.

Figure 17-20 shows exaggerated versions of the sharpening, blurring, and edge-detection effects. The sum totals of the matrixes are –42, 54, and 42, respectively. Without some help from the Offset value, each of these filters would turn every pixel in the image black (in the case of the sharpening effect) or white (blurring and edge-detection). But as demonstrated in the figure, using enormous Offset numbers brings out those few brightness values that remain. The images are so polarized that there's hardly any difference between the three effects, except that the first image is an inverted version of the other two. The difference is even less noticeable if you lower the Opacity of the effect using Filter ⇨ Fade, as demonstrated in the second row of examples in Figure 17-20.

Other custom effects

By now, I hope that you understand what an absolute trip the Custom filter can be, provided that you immerse yourself in the old adventurous spirit. Quite honestly, I could keep showing you ways to use the Custom filter for another 20 or 30 pages. But then my publisher would come unglued because I'd never finish the book, and you'd miss the pleasure of discovering variations on your own.

Nonetheless, you're probably wondering what happens if you just go absolutely berserk, in a computer-geek sort of way, and start entering matrix values in unusual or even arbitrary arrangements. The answer is that as long as you maintain a sum total of 1, you achieve some pretty interesting and even usable effects. Many of these effects will be simple variations on sharpening, blurring, and edge-detection.

Figure 17-20
You can create high-contrast effects by exaggerating all values in the matrix and then compensating by entering a very high or very low Offset value (top row). When you back off the effect using Filter ➪ Fade Custom (bottom row), these dramatic effects are barely discernible.

Directional blurs

Figure 17-21 shows examples of entering positive matrix values all in one row, all in a column, or in opposite quadrants. As you can see, as long as you maintain uniformly positive values, you get a blurring effect. However, by keeping the values lowest in the center and highest toward the edges and corners, you can create directional blurs. The first example resembles a slight horizontal motion blur, the second looks like a slight vertical motion blur, and the last example looks like it's vibrating horizontally and vertically.

Figure 17-21
Enter positive matrix values in a horizontal formation (left) or vertical formation (middle) to create slight motion blurs. By positioning positive values in opposite corners of the matrix, you create a vibrating effect (right).

Directional sharpening

To selectively sharpen edges in an image based on the angles of the edges, you can organize negative and positive matrix values into rows or columns. For example, to sharpen only the horizontal edges in an image, fill the middle row of matrix options with positive values and the rows immediately above and below with negative values, as demonstrated in the left example in Figure 17-22. Similarly, you can sharpen only the vertical edges by entering positive values in the middle column and flanking the column on left and right with negative values, as shown in the middle example in the figure. In the last example, I arranged the positive values along a diagonal axis to sharpen only the diagonal edges.

Figure 17-22
Arrange positive values in a row (left), column (middle), or along a diagonal axis (right) to sharpen horizontal, vertical, and diagonal edges exclusively.

You even can combine directional sharpening with directional blurring. Figure 17-23 shows the first example from Figure 17-22 blurred both horizontally and vertically. To blur the image horizontally, as in the middle example of Figure 17-23, I added positive values to the extreme ends of the middle row, thereby extending the range of the filter and creating a sort of horizontal jumbling effect. To blur the image vertically, as in the final example of the figure, I added positive values to the ends of the middle column.

Figure 17-23
The image from Figure 17-22 (left) blurred horizontally (middle) and vertically (right).

Embossing

So far, we aren't going very nuts, are we? Despite their unusual formations, the matrix values in Figures 17-21 through 17-23 still manage to maintain symmetry. Well, now it's time to lose the symmetry, which typically results in an embossing effect.

Figure 17-24 shows three variations on embossing, all of which involve positive and negative matrix values positioned on opposite sides of the CMV. (The CMV happens to be positive merely to maintain a sum total of 1.)

Figure 17-24
You can create embossing effects by distributing positive and negative values on opposite sides of the central matrix value.

This type of embossing has no hard and fast light source, but you might imagine that the light comes from the general direction of the positive values. Therefore, when I swapped the positive and negative values throughout the matrix (all except the CMV), I approximated an underlighting effect, as demonstrated by the images in Figure 17-25.

In truth, it's not so much a lighting difference as a difference in edge enhancement. White pixels collect on the side of an edge represented by positive values in the matrix; black pixels collect on the negative-value side. So when I swapped the locations of positive and negative values between Figures 17-24 and 17-25, I changed the distribution of white and black pixels in the filtered images.

Embossing is the loosest of the Custom filter effects. As long as you position positive and negative values on opposite sides of the CMV, you can distribute the values in almost any way you see fit. Figure 17-26 demonstrates three entirely arbitrary arrangements of values in the Custom matrix. Figure 17-27 shows those same effects downplayed by raising the CMV and entering the sum of the matrix values into the Scale option box.

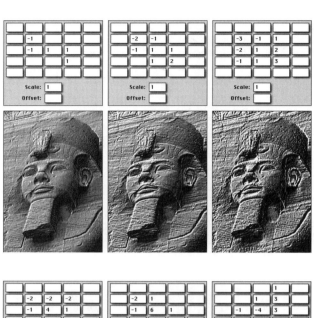

Figure 17-25
Change the location of positive and negative matrix values to change the general direction of the light source.

Figure 17-26
You can create whole libraries of embossing effects by experimenting with different combinations of positive and negative values.

Incidentally, the main advantage of using the Custom filter rather than using Filter ⇨ Stylize ⇨ Emboss to produce embossing effects is that Custom preserves the colors in an image while Emboss sacrifices color and changes low-contrast portions of an image to gray. Color Plate 17-1 shows the matrix values from the first example of Figure 17-26 applied to a color image. It also shows examples of other Custom effects, including variations on sharpening and edge-detection.

Figure 17-27
To emboss more subtly, increase the central matrix value and the Scale values by equal amounts.

If you become enthralled with convolution kernels and you feel compelled to explore them in more detail, you may want to check out a $200 plug-in called KPT Convolver from MetaTools. Although steeply priced, it permits you to explore convolutions using a more intuitive interface and without using any math. Convolver doesn't do anything that you can't already do with the Custom filter, it can simultaneously apply different convolutions to separate color channels, and it permits you to investigate filtering possibilities that you aren't likely to discover on your own.

Displacing Pixels in an Image

Photoshop's second custom effects filter is Filter ⇨ Distort ⇨ Displace, which enables you to distort and add texture to an image by moving the colors of certain pixels in a selection. You specify the direction and distance that the Displace filter moves colors by creating a second image called a *displacement map,* or *dmap* (pronounced *dee-map*) for short. The brightness values in the displacement map tell Photoshop which pixels to affect and how far to move the colors of those pixels:

- **Black:** The black areas of the displacement map move the colors of corresponding pixels in the selection a maximum prescribed distance to the right and/or down. Lighter values between black and medium gray move colors a shorter distance in the same direction.

- **White:** The white areas move the colors of corresponding pixels a maximum distance to the left and/or up. Darker values between white and medium gray move colors a shorter distance in the same direction.

↝ **Medium gray:** A 50 percent brightness value, such as medium gray, ensures that the colors of corresponding pixels remain unmoved.

Suppose that I create a new image window the same size as the scan of the Egyptian temple carving that I've used about sixty times now in this chapter. This new image will serve as the displacement map. I divide the image into four quadrants. As shown in the middle example of Figure 17-28, I fill the upper left quadrant with black, the lower right quadrant with white, and the other two quadrants with medium gray. (The arrows indicate the direction in which the quadrants will move colors in the affected image. They do not actually appear in the dmap.)

When finished, I save the dmap to disk in the native Photoshop format so that the Displace filter can access it. I then return to the Egyptian carving image, choose Filter ⇨ Distort ⇨ Displace, edit the settings as desired, and open the dmap from disk. The result is the image shown in the last example of Figure 17-28. In keeping with the distribution of brightness values in the dmap, the colors of the pixels in the upper left quadrant of the carving image move rightward, the colors of the pixels in the lower right quadrant move to the left, and the colors in the upper right and lower left quadrant remain intact.

Figure 17-28
The Displace filter moves colors in an image (left) according to the brightness values in a separate image, called the displacement map (middle). The arrows indicate the direction that the map moves colors in the image (right).

A dmap must be a color or grayscale image, and you must save the dmap in the native Photoshop file format. The Displace command does not recognize PICT, TIFF, or any of the other non-native (albeit common) file formats. Who knows why? Those programmers move in mysterious ways.

At this point, you likely have two questions: How do you use the Displace filter, and why in the name of all that is good would you possibly want to? The hows of the Displace filter are covered in the following section. To discover some whys — which should in turn help you dream up some whys of your own — read the "Using Displacement Maps" section later in this chapter.

Displacement theory

Like any custom filtering effect worth its weight in table salt — an asset that has taken something of a nose dive in the recent millennium — you need a certain degree of mathematical reasoning skills to predict the outcome of the Displace filter. Though I was a math major in college (well, actually, I double-majored in math and fine arts, and I must admit to paying the lion's share of attention to the latter), I frankly was befuddled by the results of my first few experiments with the Displace command. Don't be surprised if you are as well. With some time and a modicum of effort, however, you can learn to anticipate the approximate effects of this filter.

Direction of displacement

Earlier, I mentioned — and I quote — "The black areas of the displacement map move . . . colors . . . to the right and/or down . . . the white areas move. . .colors. . . to the left and/or up." Yikes, talk about your fragmented quotations. I think I'll sue! Anyway, the point is, you may have wondered to yourself what all this "and/or" guff was all about. "Is it right or is it down?" you may have puzzled, and rightly so.

The truth is that the direction of a displacement can go either way. It's up to you. If you like right, go with it. If you like down, don't let me stop you. If you like both together, by all means, have at it.

Beginning to understand? No? Well, it works like this: A dmap can contain one or more color channels. If the dmap is a grayscale image with one color channel only, the Displace filter moves colors that correspond to black areas in the dmap both to the right *and* down, depending on your specifications in the Displace dialog box. The filter moves colors that correspond to white areas in the dmap both to the left and up.

Figure 17-29 shows two examples of an image displaced using a single-channel dmap, which appears on the left side of the figure. (Again, the arrows illustrate the directions in which different brightness values move colors in the affected image. They are not part of the dmap file.) I displaced the middle image at 10 percent and the right image at 20 percent. Therefore, the colors in the right image travel twice the distance as those in the middle image, but all colors travel the same direction. (The upcoming section "The Displace dialog box" explains exactly how the percentage values work.)

Figure 17-29
The results of applying a single-channel displacement map (left) to an image at 10 percent (middle) and 20 percent (right).

However, if the dmap contains more than one channel — whether it's a color image or a grayscale image with an independent mask channel — the first channel indicates horizontal displacement, and the second channel indicates vertical displacement. All other channels are ignored. Therefore, the Displace filter moves colors that correspond to black areas in the first channel of the dmap to the right and colors that correspond to white areas to the left. (Again, this depends on your specifications in the Displace dialog box.) The filter then moves colors that correspond to the black areas in the second channel downward and colors that correspond to white areas upward.

Figure 17-30 shows the effect of a two-channel dmap on our friend the pharaoh. The top row shows the appearance and effect of the first channel on the image at 10 percent and 20 percent. The bottom row shows the appearance and effect of the second channel.

Figure 17-30
The horizontal (top row) and vertical (bottom row) results of applying a two-channel displacement map (left column) to an image at 10 percent (middle) and 20 percent (right).

Brightness value transitions

If you study Figure 17-30 for any length of time, you'll notice a marked stretching effect around the edges of the image, particularly around the two right images. This is an effect you want to avoid.

The cause of the effect is twofold: First, the transition from gray to black and gray to white pixels around the perimeter of the dmap is relatively quick, especially compared with the gradual transitions in the central portion of the image. Second, transitions — reading from left to right, or top to bottom — produce a more noticeable effect when they progress from light to dark than from dark to light. The reason for this is that these transitions follow the direction of Photoshop's displacement algorithm. (I know, when I throw in a word like *algorithm,* everybody's eyes glaze over, but try to stick with me.)

For example, in the light-to-dark transition on the left side of the first-channel dmap in Figure 17-30, one gray value nudges selected colors slightly to the right, the next darker value nudges them an extra pixel, the next darker value another pixel, and so on, resulting in a machine-gun displacement effect that creates a continuous stream of the same colors over and over again. Hence, the big stretch.

Get it? Well, if not, the important part is this: To avoid stretching an image, make your dmap transitions slow when progressing from light to dark and quick when progressing from dark to light. For example, in the revised dmap channels shown in the left column of Figure 17-31, the gray values progress slowly from gray to black, abruptly from black to gray to white, and then slowly again from white to gray. Slow light to dark, fast dark to light. The results are smoother image distortions, as demonstrated in the middle and right columns of the figure.

Figure 17-31
Changing the speeds of color transitions in the two-channel displacement map (left column) created smoother image distortions at both the 10 percent (middle) and 20 percent (right) settings.

The Displace dialog box

When you choose Filter ⇨ Distort ⇨ Displace, Photoshop displays the Displace dialog box. ("Displays the Displace" is the modern equivalent of "Begin the Beguine," don't you know.) As shown in Figure 17-32, the Displace dialog box provides the following options:

➣ **Scale:** You can specify the degree to which the Displace filter moves colors in an image by entering percentage values into the Horizontal Scale and Vertical Scale option boxes. At 100 percent, black and white areas in the dmap each have the effect of moving colors 128 pixels. That's 1 pixel per each brightness value over or under medium gray. You can isolate the effect of a single-channel dmap vertically or horizontally — or ignore the first or second channel of a two-channel dmap — by entering 0 percent into the Horizontal or Vertical option box respectively.

Figure 17-33 shows the effect of distorting an image exclusively horizontally (top row) and vertically (bottom row) at each of three percentage values: 5 percent, 15 percent, and 30 percent. In each case, I used the two-channel dmap from Figure 17-31.

Figure 17-32
Use these options to specify the degree
of distortion, how the filter matches the
displacement map to the image, and
how it colors the pixels around the
perimeter of the selection.

Figure 17-33
The results of applying the Distort
filter exclusively horizontally (top
row) and exclusively vertically (bottom row) at 5 percent (left column),
15 percent (middle), and 30 percent
(right).

✐ **Displacement Map:** If the dmap contains fewer pixels than the image, you
can either scale it to match the size of the selected image by selecting the
Stretch to Fit radio button or repeat the dmap over and over within the
image by selecting Tile. Figure 17-34 shows a small two-channel dmap that
contains radial gradations. In the first column, I stretched the dmap to fit the
image. In the second column, I tiled the dmap. To create both examples in
the top row, I set the Horizontal Scale and Vertical Scale values to 10 percent.
To create the bottom-row examples, I raised the values to 50 percent.

Figure 17-34
Using a small, two-channel dmap (offset top left), I stretched the dmap to fit (left column) and tiled it (right column) at 10 percent (top row) and 50 percent (bottom row).

⊸ **Undefined Areas:** These radio buttons let you tell Photoshop how to color pixels around the outskirts of the selection that are otherwise undefined. By default, the Repeat Edge Pixels radio button is selected, which repeats the colors of pixels around the perimeter of the selection. This can result in extreme stretching effects, as shown in the middle example of Figure 17-35. To instead repeat the image inside the undefined areas, as demonstrated in the final example of the figure, select the Wrap Around option.

The Repeat Edge Pixels setting was active in all displacement map figures prior to Figure 17-35. In these cases, I frequently avoided stretching effects by coloring the edges of the dmap with medium gray and gradually lightening or darkening the brightness values toward the center.

Figure 17-35
After creating a straightforward, single-channel displacement map (left), I applied the filter subject to two different Undefined Areas settings, Repeat Edge Pixels (middle) and Wrap Around (right).

After you finish specifying options in the Displace dialog box, press Return to display the Open dialog box, which allows you to select the displacement map saved to disk. Only native Photoshop documents show up in the scrolling list.

Using Displacement Maps _____

So far, all the displacement maps demonstrated involve gradations of one form or another. Gradient dmaps distort the image over the contours of a fluid surface, like a reflection in a fun-house mirror. In this respect, the effects of the Displace filter closely resemble those of the Pinch and Spherize filters described in the last chapter. But the more functional and straightforward application of the Displace filter is to add texture to an image.

Creating texture effects

Figure 17-36 shows the results of using the Displace filter to apply nine of the patterns from the Displacement Maps folder inside the Plug-ins folder. Color Plate 17-2 shows the effects of applying four of the patterns to color images. Introduced in Chapter 10, this folder contains repeating patterns that Adobe designed especially with the Displace filter in mind.

As shown in the figure and color plate, most of these patterns produce the effect of viewing the image through textured glass — an effect known in high-end graphics circles as *glass refraction*. Those few patterns that contain too much contrast to pass off as textured glass — including Fragment layers, Mezzo effect, and Schnable effect — can be employed to create images that appear as if they were printed on coarse paper or even textured metal.

To view each of the textures from the Displacement Maps folder on its own, see Figure 10-14 in the "How to create patterns" section of Chapter 10. Like Figure 17-36, Figure 10-14 is labeled so that you can easily match texture and effect.

When using a repeating pattern — including any of the images inside the Displacement Maps folder — as a dmap, be sure to select the Tile radio button inside the Displace dialog box. This repeats the dmap rather than stretching it out of proportion.

Figure 17-36
These are examples of applying nine patterns from the Displacement Maps folder with the Displace filter at 10 percent horizontally and vertically.

12-sided

Crumbles

Fragment layers

Mezzo effect

Random strokes

Rectangular tiles

Schnable effect

Streaks pattern

Twirl pattern

I also explained in Chapter 10 that you can create your own textures from scratch using filtering effects. I specifically described how to create a stucco texture by applying the Add Noise filter three times in a row to an empty image and then using the Emboss filter to give it depth. (See the "Using filters" item in the "How to create patterns" section.) This texture appears in the first example of Figure 17-37. I applied the texture at 2 percent and 10 percent to create the windblown middle and right examples in the figure.

Figure 17-37
After creating a stucco texture with the Add Noise and Emboss filters (left), I applied the texture as a displacement map at 2 percent (middle) and 10 percent (right).

The stucco pattern is only one of an infinite number of textures that you can create using filters. In fact, stucco is a great base texture on which to build. For example, to create the wavy texture that starts off the first row of Figure 17-38, I softened the stucco texture by applying the Gaussian Blur filter with a 0.3-pixel radius. I then applied the Ripple filter twice with the Large option selected and an Amount value of 100. That's all there was to it.

To create the second texture in the figure, I applied the Crystallize filter at its default Cell Size value of 10. Believe me, I could go on creating textures like this forever, and more importantly, so could you. The images in the second and third columns of Figure 17-38 show the results of applying the textures with the Displace filter at 2 percent and 10 percent respectively.

Figure 17-38
After creating two textures with the Add Noise, Emboss, and Ripple filters (first column), I applied the textures as displacement maps at 2 percent (middle) and 10 percent (right).

In the final analysis, any pattern you design for use with the rubber stamp tool is equally applicable for use with the Displace filter. Furthermore, of the two options — rubber stamp and Displace — the latter is more likely to yield the kind of textured effects that will leave your audience begging, pleading, and scraping for more.

Displacing an image onto itself

I throw this technique in just for laughs. Personally, I can't get enough of *Dr. Strangelove*. That's why I call this the *Make My Day at the Atomic Café* effect. Warning: This effect features simulated melting Egyptian carvings. If you find them unnerving, you have a very soft stomach.

The Make My Day at the Atomic Café effect involves nothing more than using an image as its own displacement map. First, make sure that the image you want to distort is saved to disk in the native Photoshop format. Then choose Filter ➪ Distort ➪ Displace, specify the desired settings, and select the version of the image saved to disk. Figure 17-39 shows three applications of this effect, once applied at 10 percent exclusively horizontally, the next at 10 percent vertically, and the last at 10 percent in both directions.

Figure 17-39
See Egypt, have a blast. Here I applied the pharaoh image as a displacement map onto itself at 10 percent horizontally (left), 10 percent vertically (middle), and 10 percent in both directions.

As a variation, save the image in its original form. Then choose Image ➪ Map ➪ Invert (⌘-I) and save the inverted image to disk under a different name. Open the original image and use the Displace filter to apply the inverted image as a displacement map. Figure 17-40 shows some results.

Figure 17-40
The results of applying an inverted version of the pharaoh as a displacement map onto the original image at 10 percent horizontally (left), 10 percent vertically (middle), and 10 percent in both directions.

If you really want to blow an image apart, apply Horizontal Scale and Vertical Scale values of 50 percent or greater. The first row of Figure 17-41 shows a series of 50 percent applications of the Displace filter. I took the liberty of sharpening each image to heighten the effect. In the second row, I applied the filter to floating selections and changed the translucency of each filtered image to 10 percent. In this way, I retained the detail of the original image while still managing to impart a smidgen of sandblasting.

Figure 17-41
The results of displacing the pharaoh image with itself at 50 percent horizontally, 50 percent vertically, and 50 percent in both directions (top row), followed by the same effects applied to highly translucent floating selections (bottom row).

Using the Filter Factory

If you've made it this far through the chapter, I just want to say one thing about the Filter Factory: It's incredibly powerful and capable of doing far, far more than any filter I've described so far. But it's also difficult to use — so difficult, in fact, that it makes everything I've discussed in the previous pages look incredibly easy and transparently obvious. The Filter Factory tests the capabilities of the most experienced Photoshop user.

 Before you can use Filter Factory, you must install the Filter Factory plug-in in your Plug-ins folder. The Filter Factory is included only on the Photoshop CD-ROM and does not install during the normal installation process. See Appendix A for more information.

Choose Filter ⇨ Synthetic ⇨ Filter Factory to display the Filter Factory dialog box, shown in Figure 17-42. By any account, I think this has to be the scariest dialog box ever put before a Photoshop user. Yours is probably even more scary. The R option box contains a little *r*, the G option box contains a little *g*, and the B option box contains a little *b*. Throw in a few arbitrarily named slider bars, and you have the perfect formula for striking terror in the unsuspecting image-editor's heart.

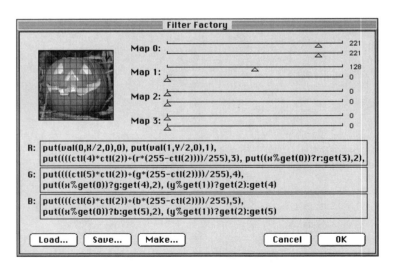

Figure 17-42
The Filter Factory dialog box containing the formulas for adding a series of grid lines to an image. The formula in the R option box is partially cut off because it's too long to fit on two lines.

 If the command is dimmed, it's because you're not in the RGB mode. Like the Light Flare and Lighting Effects filters, Filter Factory is applicable to RGB images only.

Now I need to make something perfectly clear: There's no way I can describe every nuance of programming a custom filter with the Filter Factory in less than 100

pages. So to keep the story short and sweet, I'll explain the most important functions and variables, walk you through the process of creating a moderately amusing effect, and show you how to save your work as a fully functioning filter. If you're serious about using the Filter Factory, I suggest that you also read the sparse PDF documentation that Adobe includes on its CD. It isn't the kind of thing you simply read through and ingest immediately, and some of the formulas are inaccurate (in my version, anyway), but it at least lists all the variables, operators, and functions permitted in the programming language. You may also want to load the settings that I've included on my CD and study my work. If you find a useful operation, feel free to copy it and paste it into a filter of your own. It's not stealing; it's research.

How the Factory works

To use this filter, you enter formulaic *expressions* into the R, G, and B option boxes. Each option box represents what you're doing to the red, green, or blue color channel. You can also integrate the slider bars at the top of the dialog box into your formulas. When you convert the formulas into a filter, you can specify which slider bars to include in the filter's own dialog box, enabling the user to modify the settings. You don't have to use the slider bars, but without them you get a single-shot filter like Photoshop's Sharpen More or Facet effects.

The Load and Save buttons enable you to load formulas from disk or save them for later use or editing. If you've had a long hard day and it's time to go home — or you're already home and you want to go to bed — don't forget to save the formulas to disk. Every time you restart Photoshop, the Filter Factory reverts to its original useless values of *r, g,* and *b*.

The Make button creates a filter (as I'll discuss more later). The problem is, you can't open a filter with the Filter Factory once you've created it. So if you ever want to modify a setting or two — and believe me, you will — be sure to save the settings separately using the Save button. I recommend saving filter and settings under the same name in different folders to eliminate as much confusion as possible.

The expressions

Like the Custom filter, the Filter Factory evaluates each pixel in each channel one at a time and then finishes up by sending a new brightness value to that pixel. So in the following discussions, I'll take advantage of that same acronym I used earlier in this chapter — PBE, to indicate the *pixel being evaluated*.

You change the brightness of the PBE using three kinds of expressions — *variables*, *operators*, and *functions*. Here's the scoop on each.

Variables

There are two kinds of values that you can enter into a Filter Factory option box — hard and fast numbers, such as 3 and 17, and *variables*. The latter are single letters that represent values that are forever changing. The *r* that first appears in the R option box, for example, represents the brightness value that currently occupies the PBE in the red channel. So by entering *r* in the R option box, you tell Photoshop to change the red PBE to its current color, which is no change whatsoever. It's just Adobe's way of creating a clean slate for you to work in.

All variables reset to a new value every time the filter advances from one pixel to the next. The most important variables are as follows:

- ∞ **r, g, and b:** The brightness value currently assigned to the PBE in the red channel is *r*. The green value of the PBE is *g*; the blue value is *b*. Why the heck would you want access to any of these values? Why, to mix them, of course. For example, if you enter *(r*g)/255* in the R option box — that's all you have to enter — you multiply the red value by the green value, divide the result by 255, and put the result in the filtered red channel. The final product is identical to copying the contents of the green channel, pasting it onto the red channel, and choosing the Multiply overlay mode. Try it out and see.

- ∞ **c:** This variable represents the brightness value of the PBE in the current channel, whatever that may be. In the R option box, *c* is identical to *r*. So the equation *(c*g/255)* means *(r*g/255)* in the R channel and *(b*g/255)* in the B channel.

- ∞ **x and y:** The horizontal coordinate of the PBE is saved to *x*. This value is measured in pixels from the left edge of the image. The vertical coordinate is *y*, as measured from the top of the image. These values are useful for shifting pixels around or mixing neighboring pixels together (as you can with the Custom command).

- ∞ **X and Y:** The total width of the image is *X*, the total height is *Y*. So *X–x* calculates the distance from the PBE to the right edge.

You can also use other variables: The letter *m,* for example, measures the distance from the PBE to the exact center of the image, and *d* is the angle from the PBE to the center pixel (measured from 0 to 1,024, so that 255 is equivalent to 90 degrees). But *r, g, b, c, x, y, X,* and *Y* are the ones you'll use most often.

Pinch

Spherize

Color Plate 16-6
The results of using the Pinch (left column) and Spherize (right column) filters to create conical gradations. By time I captured the first row of images, I had repeated each filter twice. By the second row, I had repeated each filter 12 times. I then mixed the Pinched gradation with the original image using the Soft Light blend mode (bottom left). I cloned the spherized gradation a few times and applied the Screen mode to each (bottom right).

×2

×12

Gradation

Twirl ×3

Flip Horizontal

Rotate 90° CW

Difference

Rotate 90° CW

Rotate and Flip

and more…

Color Plate 16-7
These two rows of images show a step-by-step experiment in abstract imagery. Starting with a two-color gradation, I convert it to a spiral with Filter⇨Distort⇨ Twirl. Then I copy the spiral to a layer, flip it, rotate it (top right), apply the Difference mode to achieve the orange image (bottom left). I clone the layer again and rotate it, then I clone a third time and rotate and flip the layer. The final image is the result of tweaking each layer with another distortion filter, including Twirl, Spherize, and ZigZag.

Color Plate 16-8
In this piece, titled Knowing Risk, distortion expert Mark Collen combines a variety of distortion filtering effects to create a surrealistic landscape. The cat, the book, the mongoose, and the twigs are the only scanned images.

Clouds

Difference Clouds

× 10

Overlay

Screen

Hue

Color Plate 16-9
The top row shows the results of Shift-choosing the Clouds filter (left), Shift-choosing Difference Clouds (middle), and pressing ⌘-F ten times in a row (right). I then took each of the images from the top row and mixed it with the rose using one of three blend modes (labeled above bottom row). You can create clouds, haze, and imaginative fill patterns with the Clouds filters.

Color Plate 16-10
Here I used the Lighting Effects filter to assign a total of five white spotlights, two pointing down from above and three pointing up from below. The bumpy surfaces of the second and third images are the results of texture maps. To create the right image, I used the green channel as the texture. In the bottom image, I used a pattern created with the Pointillize filter.

Color Plate 17-1
Color versions of four Custom filter effects, including (clockwise from upper left) mild sharpening, offset sharpening, edge-detection, and full-color embossing.

Color Plate 17-2
Examples of applying four patterns from the Displacement Maps folder with the Displace filter, including (clockwise from upper left) Crumbles, Streaks pattern, Mezzo effect, and Twirl pattern.

R:1, G:2, B:3

R:80, G:85, B:90

R:240, G:230, B:250

Color Plate 17-3
The top rows shows three different applications of the Rotator filters with the Red, Green, and Blue slider bars set to various positions. The Distorto option was set to 0. In the bottom examples, I added a cranked up Distorto value to each of the rotations above.

Distort = 10

Distort = 40

Distort = 140

Color Plate 17-4
Applications of six of the seven filters I created in Filter Factory that you'll find on the CD-ROM. Each filter has between 3 and 6 sliders, so there are all sorts of variations you can create.

Channel Mixer

Color Creep

Crisscross

Full Channel Press

Noise Blaster

SuperInvert

RGB Lab CMYK

Color Plate 18-1
The results of applying the Invert command to a single image in each of the three color modes. I inverted all channels in the RGB and Lab images and all but the black channel in the CMYK image.

Color Plate 18-2
Here I administered the High Pass filter with a Radius of 3.0, and then applied Threshold separately to each color channel within the three color modes. To smooth the jagged edges, I resampled each image up to 200 percent and then back down to 50 percent using the Image Size command. Then I repeated the process.

RGB Lab CMYK

Luminosity Hard Light Hue

Color Plate 18-3
After cloning the image to a new layer, I applied the High Pass filter and the Posterize command. Then I mixed the layer and the underlying original by choosing each of three overlay modes from the Layers palette. All effects were created with Opacity settings of 100 percent. To make things more colorful, I gave the saturation a healthy boost using the Hue/Saturation command.

Color Plate 18-4

You can downplay the colors in selected portions of an image by applying Desaturate to covert the pixels to gray values (top left). You can then use Filter➪Fade to reduce the Opacity setting and bring back some colors (top right). Alternatively, you can Invert the selection, choose Filter➪Fade, select the Color blend mode, and lower the Opacity value to 50 percent (bottom left). Raising the Opacity increases the presence of inverted colors (bottom right).

Desaturate

Fade to 50%

Invert and fade to 50%

Invert and fade to 70%

Uncorrected

RGB

Lab

CMYK

Color Plate 18-5

Starting with the uncorrected pumpkin image (top left), I applied Image➪Adjust➪Auto Levels to it in each of the three color modes. The command is really designed for RGB images and tends to mess up CMYK images (lower right). As you folks who live outside Love Canal are probably aware, few pumpkins are fire-engine red.

Master, −40°   Master, +20°   Master, +60°

Cyan only, −40°   Cyan only, +20°   Cyan only, +60°

Master, −90°   Master, +90°

Master, −50   Master, +50

Blue areas, 120°   Blue areas, −60°
Other, −50°   Other, 110°

All but cyan   Cyan and blue, −100
and blue, −100   All others, +50

Fuzziness, 40

Fuzziness, 200

Color Plate 18-9
These images show the results of correcting images with two of Photoshop's more specialized color commands, Replace Color (top row) and Selective Color (bottom row). The Replace Color command lets you adjust colors while at the same time modifying which pixels are affected and which are not with the help of a Fuzziness option. The Selective Color command adjusts the amount of CMYK ink assigned to predefined color ranges.

Red to violet, Relative

Red to violet and
black to white, Absolute

Color Plate 18-10
The effects of applying each of the thumbnails offered in the Variations dialog box to the familiar pumpkin. In each case, the slider bar was set to its default setting of midway between Fine and Coarse with the Midtones radio button selected.

More Green

Lighter

More Yellow

More Cyan

Original

More Red

More Blue

Darker

More Magenta

Color Plate 18-11
Starting with a rather typically washed out image that I shot with a Kodak DC50 (top), I copied the image to a new layer and boosted the saturation with the Hue/Saturation command (second). Then I applied the Median and Gaussian Blur commands and mixed the layer with the underlying original using the Color blend mode and an Opacity value of 70 percent (third). Finally, I used Median, Gaussian Blur, and Unsharp Mask to sharpen the image (bottom).

Original digital photo

Increase saturation to +80

Median, Gaussian Blur, and Color mode

Final sharpened image

Color Plate 18-12

The celebrated Virginian states-man before (left) and after (right) I corrected him with the Levels command. The white histograms superimposed on Jefferson's chest show the original and corrected distribution of brightness values. The colored histograms illustrate the corrections made to the individual red, green, and blue channels.

Color Plate 18-13

You can use the Curves dialog box to apply gradations as color maps. In the top row, I copied the famous Roman to a new layer, blurred him silly, and applied each of three gradients (saved to disk by ⌘-Option-clicking on the Save button in the Gradient Editor dialog box). Then I mixed the images with their underlying originals using the Color blend mode.

Chrome

Blue, Red, Yellow

Spectrum

Color blend mode

Color Plate 18-14
The results of using the Curves command to lighten the colors in the red channel (left), increase the level of contrast in the green channel (middle), and apply an arbitrary color map to the blue channel (right).

Color Plate 18-15
These images illustrate one way to use adjustment layers to correct the colors in a flat image. After observing that my original image was way too dark (left), I created a new adjustment layer and used the Curves command to lighten the image (middle). I then added two additional layers to increase the saturation levels with Hue/Saturation and correct the brightness levels of the topiary animal with Levels (right).

Normal | Dissolve | Difference

Multiply | 50% Normal | Exclusion

Screen | Color Dodge | Hue

Overlay | Color Burn | Saturation

Soft Light | Darken | Color

Hard Light | Lighten | Luminosity

Overlay | Soft Light | Color Dodge | Hue

Leaf in front

Woman in front

Charcoal

Hard Light

Color

Difference

Original

Soft Light

Color Dodge

Luminosity

Color Plate 19-3
Each column of images shows a progression in which I sandwiched an image filtered with the Charcoal effect (top left) between two originals (bottom left). Each image in the top row shows the filtered image interacting with the original background layered according to the labeled blend mode. The bottom images show the results of adding the top layer of the sandwich and applying another blend mode. For example, applying Difference to the filtered layer and Luminosity to the top layer creates the bottom right effect.

Color Plate 19-4
The top rows the results of a series of corrective and destructive filters, each of which go a long way toward destroying the detail in my image. But when I insert the filter effect in between two copies of the original image, and then apply the Difference blend mode to the middle and top layers, I bring back much of the detail, as shown in the bottom row. No other technique restores detail quite like a tasty Difference sandwich.

Unsharp Mask   Motion Blur   Lens Flare   Find Edges

Difference sandwich

Color Plate 19-5
For the purpose of comparison, the first image shows the result of compositing an RGB image onto itself using the Hard Light mode. Other examples show the different effects you can achieve by duplicating the image, converting it to the Lab mode, and then mixing it with the original RGB image using the Apply Image command, again set to Hard Light.

RGB on RGB

Lab on RGB

Lightness on RGB

Inverted b on RGB

Mask Channel

Hard Light

Color Plate 19-6
After creating a separate mask channel (top left), I used this mask to protect the sky in the target image. Though I used the Apply Image command to apply several compositing effects to the Capitol building, none affected the sky so long as the Mask check box was selected.

Screen

Inverted Difference

Original

System (Macintosh)

System (Windows)

Color Plate 20-1
Examples of a 24-bit image (top left) downgraded using the Indexed Color command. I applied the fixed palettes from the Macintosh and Windows operating systems in the upper middle and right examples. I used the Adaptive option to create the bottom row of images. As you can see, the Adaptive option produces reasonably good results, even at low-color settings.

Adaptive, 8 bits/pixel

Adaptive, 6 bits/pixel

Adaptive, 4 bits/pixel

None, 94K

Pattern, 105K

Diffusion, 118K

Color Plate 20-2
Here I reduced the image from Color Plate 20-1 using each of three different Dither options — None, Pattern, and Diffusion. Beside each option name is the size of the file when saved in the GIF format. As you can see, GIF is better suited to compressing an image when no dithering is involved.

Operators

Operators include arithmetic signs, such as plus and minus, as well as relational symbols, such as < and >. They also include logical operations. For example, *?* tells the Filter Factory to complete the following operation only if the previous expression holds true, and if it is false, complete the operation after the colon (:). For example, the expression *x<(X/2)?r:g* means that if the PBE is inside the left side of the image, color it with the red channel value. If not, color it with the green value. The following are the most important operators:

- **+, -, *, and /:** These symbols stand for plus, minus, multiply, and divide. The Filter Factory always handles multiply and divide operations before plus and minus operations. So the equation *4+8/2* equals 8, not 6.

- **%:** Use the percentage sign to retain the remainder from a division equation. For example, *11%4* equals 3.

- **(and):** Parentheses tell the Filter Factory to complete the equation inside the parentheses before completing others. The equation *(4+8)/2* equals 6 because 4 and 8 are added before dividing by 2.

- **<, >, <=, and >=:** These symbols mean less than, greater than, less than or equal to, and greater than or equal to. All four are used primarily within conditional operations like the one I mentioned at the beginning of this section.

- **==, =!:** Two equal signs in a row mean "equal to." An equal sign and an exclamation point mean "not equal to." Again, use these inside conditional operations.

- **?:** Here's the conditional operation, as I explained earlier.

Again, these aren't all the possible operators, just the best of. But I should mention one additional operator: The comma separates phrases in an expression, sort of like a period separates sentences. The phrase after the final comma is the one that the Filter Factory applies to the PBE. All previous phrases are used for calculation purposes only. You can see how this works in the step-by-step example that's coming up right after the discussion of functions.

Functions

All functions are composed of three letters followed by numbers, variables, and equations inside parentheses. For example, *abs(x–X)* finds the absolute value of the equation inside the parentheses, which means that you get a positive result whether the answer to the equation is positive or negative. (Because negative brightness values simply become black, this can be useful.)

Rather than simply listing the functions, I'll explain them in groups. First, there are the two functions that use holding cells. In typical programming, you store the results of incremental equations in variables, but in the Filter Factory, variables are used by the filter only. You get ten numbered cells, ranging from 0 to 9. The two functions that work with cells are *put*, to place a number inside a cell, and *get*, to retrieve it. It's sort of like copying and pasting with ten tiny Clipboards. The expression *put(r+b,0)* puts the result of the equation *r+b* into cell 0. Conversely, *put(r+b,1)* puts it in cell 1, and so on. The expression *get(0)/2* would retrieve the result of *r+b* and divide it by 2.

The function *src* retrieves information about a specific pixel in your image. For example, *src(x+5,y+5,0)* returns the brightness of the pixel five pixels to the right and five pixels down from the PBE. What is that last *0* for? That tells the function to get the value from the red channel. The green channel is *1*, the blue channel is *2*, mask channels are *3* through *9*.

Similar to *src, rad* finds out the brightness value of a pixel in a certain channel based on its distance and direction from the center of the image. For example, if you enter *rad(d–16,m–16,0)* into the red channel, you rotate the contents of the channel 16 increments (about 6 degrees) counterclockwise and distort its center outward. The upcoming step-by-step example uses this function.

The function *rnd* generates a random number between two extremes, which is great for creating noise. The expression *rnd(r,g)* generates a random value between the red brightness value of the PBE and the green brightness of the PBE.

Evaluating the sliders

These next functions — *ctl* and *val* — get their own headline because they're so important. They evaluate how a user of your filter sets the slider bars. The function *ctl* simply retrieves the setting of a specified slider bar. There are eight slider bars in all, numbered 0 to 7 from top to bottom. (The sliders labeled Map 0 are therefore sliders 0 and 1; Map 1 includes sliders 2 and 3; and so on.) Each slider can be adjusted from 0 to 255. So if the first slider bar is set to 128, the function *ctl(0)* retrieves the number 128. You can then change the impact of your filter by moving the slider in real time. For example, if you enter *r*ctl(0)/255* in the R option box, you multiply the red value of the PBE by the setting of the top slider divided by 255. This makes the red channel black when the slider is set to 0, normal when the slider is set to 255, and darker shades when set to any increment in between.

The *val* function evaluates the setting of a slider bar within a specified range. For example, *val(0,15,–15)* takes the setting of the top slider, translates it to 15 when it's at 0, and translates it to –15 when it's at 255. As you can see, this function lets you translate the data within any specified range, even making the low values high and vice versa. This is useful when you don't want the entire range of data from 0 to 255 to mess up the results of your equations.

Touring the factory

Okay, now for a little hands-on action. The steps will be short and straightforward, but the results are both useful and interesting. I encourage you to try these steps out. Even if you've been sitting there with your jaw hanging open throughout the entire chapter, even if you haven't the slightest idea what you're doing, you'll be able to create a fully functioning filter that is not included on the CD. Talk about your incentives.

STEPS   Creating a Filter inside the Factory

Step 1.   **Open an RGB image or convert some other image to the RGB mode.** This filter yields interesting results even when applied to grayscale images converted to RGB.

Step 2.   **Choose Filter ⇨ Synthetic ⇨ Factory.** Set all the slider bars back to 0, just in case somebody's been fooling around with them.

Step 3.   **Enter *rad(d–(4*ctl(0)),m,0)* into the R option box.** The first argument in the expression — *d-(4*ctl(0))* — subtracts four times the value of the top slider bar from the angle variable *d*. Why four times? Because the slider only offers 256 increments, and the filter measures a full circle in 1,024 increments — 256 times 4 equals 1,024, thus allowing you to translate the slider values to a full circle.

   Meanwhile, *d* is the angle of the current pixel from the center and *m* is the distance from the pixel to the center. So *rad(d–(4*ctl(0)),m,0)* tells the filter to lift the brightness from the pixel in a counterclockwise direction from the PBE. The result is that the red channel rotates in the opposite direction, clockwise. Drag the slider bar and you'll see that this is true.

Step 4.   **Insert the phrase *–ctl(4)/2* after the *m* so that the expression reads *rad(d–(4*ctl(0)),m–ctl(4)/2,0).*** You'll use the second and third slider bars — *ctl(1)* and *ctl(2)* — for rotating the other two channels. But I think that I'd like to use the fifth slider bar for distorting the image. Why not the fourth channel? Well, because the first three sliders are going to be devoted to rotation. The distortion slider will be logically different, so it might be nice to create a blank space between the rotation and distortion sliders. Not using slider four is the way to do it.

   By changing the expression to *rad(d–(4*ctl(0)),m–ctl(4)/2,0)*, you tell Photoshop to subtract half the value from the fourth slider from the distance-from-center variable, thus shoving the pixels outward as you drag the fifth slider bar (the top of the two labeled Map 2). Give it a try.

Step 5.   **Copy the R expression and paste it into G.** Select the entire expression in the R option box, copy it by pressing ⌘-C, tab to the G option box, and press ⌘-V to paste. Then change the *ctl(0)* function to *ctl(1)* and the final number after the comma from a *0* to a *1*, so that it reads *rad(d–(4*ctl(1)),m–ctl(4)/2,1)*. Now the expression takes rotation data from the second slider bar and lifts its colors from the green channel. The result is a rotating green channel.

Step 6. **Tab to the B option box and press ⌘-V again.** Change *ctl(0)* to *ctl(2)* and change the final *0* to a *2*. The result is *rad(d–(4*ctl(2)),m–ctl(4)/2,2)*. Just to make sure that you haven't fallen behind, Figure 17-43 shows all three expressions exactly as they should appear.

Figure 17-43
These three expressions let you rotate the three color channels independently using the first three slider bars and distort the image using the fifth slider.

Step 7. **Click on the Save button and save your settings to disk.** You may want to use the name *Rotator.afs* to show that it's a Filter Factory file. (For some reason, *afs* is the accepted suffix for settings files.)

Step 8. **Adjust the sliders to set the defaults.** Before you turn this sucker into its own filter, you need to be sure that the sliders are set how you want them to appear by default. Every time you open the new filter for the first time during a Photoshop session, these slider values will appear as they do now. You may want to set all sliders to 0 so that the user starts from square one, but it's completely up to you.

Step 9. **Click on the Make button to convert your code into a filter.** Clicking on Make displays the dialog box shown in Figure 17-44. Enter the submenu in which you want the filter to appear in the Category option box. If you want it to appear with the rest of the *Photoshop Bible* filters, enter

Tormentia. Enter the name of the filter, Rotator, in the Title option box. Then enter copyright and author information in the next two option boxes. (Go ahead, give yourself credit. You've earned it.)

Category:	Tormentia
Title:	Rotator
Copyright:	©1996 Deke McClelland Macworld Photoshop Bible
Author:	Deke McClelland

☐ Map 0   Map 0:
☐ Map 1   Map 1:
☐ Map 2   Map 2:
☐ Map 3   Map 3:

Red Twist: ☒ Control 0
Green Spin: ☒ Control 1
Blue Whirl: ☒ Control 2
Control 3: ☐ Control 3
Distorto: ☒ Control 4
Control 5: ☐ Control 5
Control 6: ☐ Control 6
Control 7: ☐ Control 7

[Cancel] [OK]

Figure 17-44
Click on the Make button to display this dialog box, which lets you name your filter, assign it to a submenu, and select the slider bars that you want to appear in the final dialog box.

Step 10. **Select a Control check box for every slider you want to appear in your final filter.** The Control check boxes along the right side represent the slider bars inside the Filter Factory dialog box. Select the check boxes for Control 0, Control 1, Control 2, and Control 4. Then name them appropriately. My suggested names appear in Figure 17-44, but they may be a little too clever for your tastes.

Watch out: The Filter Factory allows you to select any of the slider check boxes, whether they were used in your formulas or not. If you're not careful, you can activate a slider bar that has no function.

Step 11. **When you're finished, press Return.** You're asked to specify the location of the filter. To keep things tidy, you'll probably want to put it in the Filters folder inside the Plug-ins folder, but anywhere in the Plug-ins folder is okay. Click on the Cancel button to escape the Filter Factory dialog box.

Step 12. **Quit Photoshop and relaunch it.** Open an RGB image — like the Filter Factory itself, any filter you create in the factory is applicable to RGB images only — and choose your newest command, Filter ⇨ Tormentia ⇨ Rotator. The dialog box should look something like the one shown in Figure 17-45. Notice the gaps between the Blue Whirl and Distorto sliders. Nice logical grouping, huh? Feel free to drag the controls and apply the filter as much as you want. It's alive!

Figure 17-45
The new Rotator filter complete with its four slider bars.

To see a demonstration of your powerful new filter, check out Color Plate 17-3, in which I applied the filter six times at various settings. The top row shows the effect of rotating the channels to different degrees with the Distorto option set to 0. The bottom row shows the same rotation values, but with the Distorto slider turned up to various volumes. It's not the most practical filter on earth, but it's diverting. You might even find something to do with it.

By the way, those sliders have a tendency to move around after you finish dragging them. It's very irritating. If you're interested in achieving an exact value, click at the location where you want to move the slider triangle. The triangle jumps in place. Then click, click, click to get it right where you want it.

If you want practical filters, check out the ones I've included on the CD. Most are much more complicated than the one you created in the steps, but they all use the variables, operators, and functions described in this chapter. Open the settings files to take a look at my code. (Just click on the Load button inside the Filter Factory dialog box.) To whet your appetite, take a look at Color Plate 17-4, which shows all but one of the filters applied to the pumpkin. (The one that wouldn't fit is Ripping Pixels, which creates a random value between the brightness of the pixel in one channel and that of one of the other channels, creating a highly customizable noise effect.) These are only sample applications, most of them using the default slider bar settings. Obviously, jillions of other variations are possible. Have loads of fun.

Corrections, Composites, and the Web

VI

PART

Mapping and Adjusting Colors

In This Chapter

- ➡ Mapping colors with Invert, Equalize, Threshold, and Posterize
- ➡ Using Threshold and Posterize in combination with the High Pass filter
- ➡ Converting a selection to gray values using the Desaturate command
- ➡ Rotating colors around the color wheel using Hue/Saturation
- ➡ Editing saturation levels to prepare an RGB image for CMYK conversion
- ➡ Colorizing grayscale images
- ➡ Correcting colors with Replace Color, Selective Color, and Variations
- ➡ Increasing the saturation of a heavily compressed image
- ➡ Using the Levels and Curves commands
- ➡ Boosting brightness and contrast levels
- ➡ Drawing arbitrary color maps for psychedelic effects
- ➡ Correcting multiple layers at a time with adjustment layers

What Is Color Mapping?

Color mapping is just a fancy name for shuffling colors around. For example, to map Color A to Color B simply means to take all the A-colored pixels and convert them to B-colored pixels. Photoshop provides several commands that enable you to map entire ranges of colors based on their hues, saturation levels, and, most frequently, brightness values.

Color effects and corrections

Why would you want to change colors around? For one reason, to achieve special effects. You know those psychedelic horror movies that show some guy's hair turning blue while his face turns purple and the palms of his hands glow a sort of cornflower yellow? A grayscale version of this very effect appears in the second example of Figure 18-1. Although not the most attractive effect by modern standards — you may be able to harvest more tasteful results if you put your shoulder to the color wheel — psychedelic qualifies as color mapping for the simple reason that each color shifts incrementally to a new color.

But the more common reason to map colors is to enhance the appearance of a scanned image or digital photograph, as demonstrated in the third example in Figure 18-1. In this case, you're not creating special effects — you're just making straightforward color adjustments, known in the biz as *color corrections*. Scans are never perfect, no matter how much money you spend on a scanning device or a service bureau. They can always benefit from tweaking and subtle adjustments, if not outright overhauls, in the color department.

Figure 18-1
Nobody's perfect, and neither is the best of scanned photos (left). You can modify colors in an image to achieve special effects (middle) or simply fix the image with a few well-targeted color corrections (right). Too bad Photoshop hasn't delivered on its promised Remove Excessive Jewelry filter.

Keep in mind, however, that Photoshop can't make something from nothing. In creating the illusion of more and better colors, most of the color-adjustment operations that you perform actually take some small amount of color *away* from the image. Somewhere in your image, two pixels that were two different colors before you started the correction change to the same color. The image may look 10 times better, but it will in fact be less colorful than when you started.

It's important to keep this principle in mind because it demonstrates that color mapping is a balancing act. The first nine operations you perform may make an image look progressively better, but the tenth may send it into decline. There's no magic formula, unfortunately. The amount of color mapping you need to apply varies from image to image. But if you follow my usual recommendations — use the commands in moderation, know when to stop, and save your image to disk before doing anything drastic — you should be fine.

Photoshop 4 offers a new color correction option that ensures you can never make a mistake. You can now add a special layer of color correction information that affects all layers below it. Known as "adjustment layers," this is quite possibly Version 4's best enhancement. For more information about adjustment layers, read the "Adjustment Layers" section near the end of this chapter.

The good, the bad, and the wacky

Photoshop 4 stores all of its color mapping commands — numbering 14 in all — under the Image ⇨ Adjust submenu. These commands fall into three basic categories:

- ◦ Commands such as Invert and Threshold are quick-and-dirty color mappers. They don't fix images, but they can be useful for creating special effects and adjusting masks.

- ◦ Brightness/Contrast and Color Balance are true color correction commands, but they sacrifice functionality for ease of use. If I had my way, these commands would be removed from the Image ⇨ Adjust submenu and thrown in the dust heap.

- ◦ The third, more complicated variety of color correction commands provide better control, but they take a fair amount of effort to learn. Levels, Curves, and Hue/Saturation are examples of color correcting at its best and most complicated.

This chapter contains little information about the second category of commands for the simple reason that some of them are inadequate and ultimately a big waste of time. There are exceptions of course — Auto Levels is a decent quick fixer, and Variations offers deceptively straightforward sophistication — but Brightness/

Contrast and Color Balance are frankly beneath contempt. They are as liable to damage your image as fix it, making them quite dangerous in a dull, pedestrian sort of way. I know because I spent my first year with Photoshop relying exclusively on Brightness/Contrast and Color Balance, all the while wondering why I couldn't achieve the effects I wanted. Then, one happy day, I spent about a half an hour learning Levels and Curves, and the quality of my images skyrocketed. So wouldn't you just rather learn it right in the first place? I hope so, because the dye is set.

Quick Color Effects

Before we get into all the high-end gunk, however, I'll take a moment to explain the first category of commands, all of which happen to occupy one of the lower sections in the Image ➪ Adjust submenu. These commands — Invert, Equalize, Threshold, and Posterize — produce immediate effects that are either difficult to duplicate or not worth attempting with the more full-featured commands.

Invert

When you choose Image ➪ Adjust ➪ Invert (⌘-I), Photoshop converts every color in your image to its exact opposite, just as in a photographic negative. As demonstrated in Figure 18-2, black becomes white, white becomes black, fire becomes water, good becomes evil, Imelda Marcos goes barefoot, and the brightness value of every primary color component changes to 255 minus the original brightness value.

Figure 18-2
An image before the advent of the Invert command (left) and after (right).

Original   Invert

Image ⇨ Adjust ⇨ Invert is just about the only color mapping command that retains every single drop of color in an image. (The Hue/Saturation command also retains colors under specific conditions.) If you apply the Invert command twice in a row, you arrive at your original image.

When you're working on a full-color image, the Invert command simply inverts the contents of each color channel. This means that the command produces very different results when applied to RGB, Lab, and especially CMYK images. Color Plate 18-1 shows the results of inverting a single image in each of these modes. The RGB and Lab images share some similarities, but you'll find all kinds of subtle differences if you study the backgrounds and the basic colors of the faces.

Inverting in CMYK is much different. Typically, the Invert command changes much of a CMYK image to black. Except in very rare instances — such as in night scenes — the black channel contains lots of light shades and very few dark shades. So when you invert the channel, it becomes extremely dark. To reverse this effect, I inverted only the cyan, magenta, and yellow channels in the right example of Color Plate 18-1. (I did this by inverting the entire image and then going to the black channel — ⌘-4 — and pressing ⌘-I again.) Though this approach is preferable to inverting the black channel, it prevents the blacks in the hair and shadows from turning white (which would be the only portions even remotely light had I inverted the black channel as well).

Just so you know, when I refer to applying color corrections in the CMYK mode, I mean applying them after choosing Mode ⇨ CMYK Color. Applying corrections in the RGB mode when Mode ⇨ CMYK Preview is active produces the same effect as when CMYK Preview is not selected; the only difference is that the on-screen colors are curtailed slightly to fit inside the CMYK color space. You're still editing inside the same old red, green, and blue color channels, so the effects are the same.

As I mentioned back in Chapter 12, inverting the contents of the mask channel is the same as applying Select ⇨ Inverse to a selection outline in the marching ants mode. In fact, this is one of the most useful applications of the filter. If you're considering inverting a color image, however, I strongly urge you to try out the SuperInvert filter that I created for the CD. It permits you to invert each channel independently and incrementally. Any setting under 128 lessens the contrast of the channel; 128 makes it completely gray; and any value over 128 inverts it to some degree.

Equalize

Equalize is the smartest and at the same time least useful of the Image ⇨ Adjust pack. When you invoke this command, Photoshop searches for the lightest and darkest color values in a selection. Then it maps the lightest color in all the color channels to white, maps the darkest color in the channels to black, and distributes the remaining colors to other brightness levels in an effort to evenly distribute pixels over the entire brightness spectrum. This doesn't mean that any one pixel will actually appear white or black after you apply Equalize; rather, that one pixel in at least one channel will be white and another pixel in at least one channel will be black. In an RGB image, for example, the red, green, or blue component of one pixel would be white, but the other two components of that same pixel might be black. The result is a higher contrast image with white and black pixels scattered throughout the color channels.

If no portion of the image is selected when you choose Image ⇨ Adjust ⇨ Equalize, Photoshop automatically maps out the entire image across the brightness spectrum, as shown in the upper right example of Figure 18-3. However, if you select a portion of the image before choosing the Equalize command, Photoshop displays a dialog box containing the following two radio buttons:

- **Selected Area Only:** Select this option to apply the Equalize command strictly within the confines of the selection. The lightest pixel in the selection becomes white, the darkest pixel becomes black, and so on.

- **Entire Image Based on Area:** If you select the second radio button, which is the default setting, Photoshop applies the Equalize command to the entire image based on the lightest and darkest colors in the selection. All colors in the image that are lighter than the lightest color in the selection become white, and all colors darker than the darkest color in the selection become black.

The bottom two examples in Figure 18-3 show the effects of selecting different parts of the image when the Entire Image Based on Area option is in force. In the left example, I selected a dark portion of the image, which resulted in over-lightening of the entire image. In the right example, I selected an area with both light and dark values, which boosted the amount of contrast between highlights and shadows in the image.

The problem with the Equalize command is that it relies too heavily on some pretty bizarre automation to be of much use as a color correction tool. Certainly, you can create some interesting special effects. But if you'd prefer to automatically adjust the colors in an image from black to white regardless of the color mode and composition of the individual channels, choose Image ⇨ Adjust ⇨ Auto Levels (⌘-Shift-L). If you want to adjust the tonal balance manually and therefore with a higher degree of accuracy, the Levels and Curves commands are tops. I explain all of these commands at length later in this chapter.

Figure 18-3
An image before (top left) and after (top right) applying the Equalize command when no portion of the image is selected. You can also use the brightness values in a selected region as the basis for equalizing an entire image (bottom left and right).

Original

Equalize

Equalize based on selection

Threshold

I touched on the Threshold command a couple of times in previous chapters. As you may recall, Threshold converts all colors to either black or white based on their brightness values. When you choose Image ⇨ Adjust ⇨ Threshold, Photoshop displays the Threshold dialog box shown in Figure 18-4. The dialog box offers a single option box and a slider bar, either of which you can use to specify the medium brightness value in the image. Photoshop changes any color lighter than the value in the Threshold option box to white, and changes any color darker than the value to black.

Histogram

Figure 18-4
The histogram in the Threshold dialog box shows the distribution of brightness values in the selection.

The dialog box also includes a graph of all the colors in the image — even if only a portion of the image is selected. This graph is called a *histogram*. The width of the histogram represents all 256 possible brightness values, starting at black on the left and progressing through white on the right. The height of each vertical line in the graph demonstrates the number of pixels currently associated with that brightness value. Therefore, you can use the histogram to gauge the distribution of lights and darks in your image. It may seem weird at first, but with enough experience, the histogram becomes an invaluable tool, permitting you to corroborate the colors that you see on-screen.

Generally speaking, you achieve the best effects if you change an equal number of pixels to black as you change to white (and vice versa). So rather than moving the slider bar to 128, which is the medium brightness value, move it to the point at which the area of the vertical lines to the left of the slider triangle looks roughly equivalent to the area of the vertical lines to the right of the slider triangle.

The upper left example in Figure 18-5 shows the result of applying the Threshold command with a Threshold Level value of 120 (as in Figure 18-4). Although this value more or less evenly distributes black and white pixels, I lost a lot of detail in the dark areas.

As you may recall from my "Using the High Pass filter" discussion in Chapter 15, you can use Filter ⇨ Other ⇨ High Pass in advance of the Threshold command to retain areas of contrast. In the upper left image in Figure 18-5, I applied the High Pass filter with a radius of 1.0 pixel, followed by the Threshold command with a value of 125. In the two bottom images, I first chose an effects filter — Filter ⇨ Artistic ⇨ Watercolor on the left and Filter ⇨ Sketch ⇨ Bas Relief on the right — then I applied High Pass with a radius of 1.0 pixel followed by the Threshold command.

Figure 18-5
By itself, the Threshold command tends to deliver flat results (top left). To better articulate the detail, apply High Pass and other filters prior to choosing Threshold.

Threshold only   High Pass first

Watercolor and High Pass   Bas Relief and High Pass

If the Threshold effects in Figure 18-5 are a bit austere, first clone the image to a layer and then mix the layer with the underlying original. Figure 18-6 shows all the effects from Figure 18-5 applied to layers subject to the Overlay blend mode and 50 percent Opacity. In each example, the translucent selection helps to add contrast and reinforce details in the original image.

Figure 18-6
The Threshold operations from Figure 18-5 applied to separate layers, blended with the Overlay mode and an Opacity value of 50 percent.

You can compare the before and after effects of any color correction command that includes a Preview check box in its dialog box by turning the check box off and then mousing down on the title bar. If the Video LUT Animation option in the Display & Cursors panel of the Preferences dialog box is active (as by default), turning the Preview check box off causes Photoshop to apply the Threshold settings to the entire screen. Unfortunately, Photoshop applies the effect separately to each color channel, creating a series of brightly colored areas that bear little resemblance to the actual black-and-white effect. To get a realistic picture of your image, leave the Preview check box turned on.

If you want to achieve a colorful Threshold effect like the one that appears when using Video LUT Animation, try applying the Threshold command independently to each color channel. In an RGB image, for example, press ⌘-1 and then apply Image ⇨ Adjust ⇨ Threshold. Then press ⌘-2 and repeat the command, and press ⌘-3 and do it again. Color Plate 18-2 shows examples of what happens when I apply High Pass (with a Radius of 3.0) and Threshold to independent color channels in the RGB, Lab, and CMYK modes. To soften the transitions and avoid trapping problems, I resampled each image up and down a couple of times, as described back in the "Antialiasing an image" section of Chapter 15.

Posterize

The Posterize command is Threshold's rich cousin. Whereas Threshold boils down an image into two colors only, Posterize can retain as many colors as you like. However, you can't control how colors are mapped, as you can when you use Threshold. The Posterize dialog box does not provide a histogram or slider bar. Instead, Posterize automatically divides the full range of 256 brightness values into a specified number of equal increments.

To use this command, choose Image ⇨ Adjust ⇨ Posterize and enter a value into the Levels option box. The Levels value represents the number of brightness values that the Posterize command retains. Higher values result in subtle color adjustments; lower values produce more dramatic effects. The first example in Figure 18-7 shows an image subject to a Levels value of 8.

By now, you may be thinking, "By golly, if Posterize is so similar to Threshold, I wonder how it works when applied after the High Pass filter?" Well, you're in luck, because this is exactly the purpose of the second example in Figure 18-7. Here I chose the High Pass filter and entered 3.0 for the Radius. Then I applied the Posterize command with the same Levels value as before (8).

Figure 18-7
An image subject to the Posterize command with a Levels value of 8 (left). You can retain more detail in an image by applying the High Pass filter before using Posterize (right).

Posterize   High Pass first

Now, just in case you've tried this same effect on your full-color image and thought, "Yech, this looks terrible — half the color just disappeared," the key is to apply High Pass and Posterize to a layered version of the image and then mix the effect with the underlying original. Color Plate 18-3 shows the results of applying the High Pass filter with a Radius of 3.0 and the Posterize command with a setting of 8 to the layered clone and then compositing layer and underlying original using each of three overlay modes from the Layers palette. The Luminosity option applies only the lights and darks in the layered image, allowing the colors in the underlying image to show through; Hard Light strengthens the light and dark shades; and Hue applies the colors from the layer with the saturation and brightness values from the original. After flattening each image, I increase the saturation of the colors using Image ⇨ Adjust ⇨ Hue/Saturation (⌘-U), which I discuss in an upcoming section.

Quick Corrections

Photoshop offers two quick-correctors under the Image ⇨ Adjust submenu that I want to discuss before entering into the larger world of advanced color correction. Both are single-shot commands that alter your image without any dialog boxes or special options. The first, Desaturate, sucks the saturation out of a selection and leaves it looking like a grayscale image. The second, Auto Levels, automatically increases the contrast of an image according to what Photoshop deems to be the ideal brightness values.

Sucking saturation

There's little reason to apply the Desaturate command to an entire image; you can just as easily choose Image ⇨ Mode ⇨ Grayscale to accomplish the same thing and dispose of the extra channels that would otherwise consume room in memory and on disk. I know of only two reasons to sacrifice all colors in the RGB mode:

- You want to retain the option of applying RGB-only filters, such as Lens Flare, Lighting Effects, and anything created with the Filter Factory.

- You intend to downsize the colors using Image ⇨ Mode ⇨ Indexed Colors and save the final image in the GIF format for use on the World Wide Web (as I discuss in Chapter 20).

But mostly, you'll use Desaturate to rob color from discrete selections or independent layers, neither of which the Grayscale mode can accommodate. For example, in Color Plate 18-4, I used Select ⇨ Color Range to select all of the pumpkin except the eyes and mouth and a few speckly bits here and there. (I could have used the quick mask mode to tweak the selection and get it just right, but it didn't strike me as particularly important in this case.) I then applied Image ⇨ Adjust ⇨ Desaturate (⌘-Shift-U) to achieve the first example. To create the top right pumpkin, I chose

Filter ⇨ Fade Desaturate and changed the Opacity value to 50 percent, bringing back some of the original colors from the full-color original and achieving an only slightly desaturated pumpkin.

In case you missed that last paragraph, you can use Filter ⇨ Fade (⌘-Shift-F) to back off the effects of any command under the Image ⇨ Adjust submenu. As always, the Fade command is available immediately after you apply the color correction; if you so much as alter a selection outline, Fade goes dim.

Desaturate isn't the only way to suck colors out of an image. You can also invert the colors and mix them with their original counterparts to achieve a slightly different effect. The bottom row of Color Plate 18-4 shows what I mean. In the lower left example, I applied Invert (⌘-I) to my same Color Range selection. Then I pressed ⌘-Shift-F, changed the Opacity setting to 50 percent, and — here's the important part — selected Color from the Mode pop-up menu.

Note that the inverted and mixed colors are slightly different than the desaturated tones in the pumpkin above. When set to the Color blend mode, the colors in the inverted image should theoretically cancel out the colors in the underlying original. However, the Invert command doesn't change the saturation of the pixels, so the saturation of the inverted and original pixels are the same. As a result, some colors from the underlying image are allowed to show through, as the bottom left image shows.

The bottom right example shows what happened when I changed the Opacity to 70 percent, thus favoring the inverted colors. Why'd I do that? Maybe I just like blue pumpkins. Or more likely, I had a fourth spot to fill in the figure, and a blue pumpkin seemed like the guy to fill it.

By the way, you might be wondering why Adobe selected ⌘-Shift-U as the keyboard shortcut for Desaturate. Well, Desaturate is actually a renegade element from the Hue/Saturation command, which lets you raise and lower saturation levels to any degree you like. The shortcut for Hue/Saturation is ⌘-U — for *hUUUUe,* don't you know — so Desaturate is ⌘-Shift-U.

Auto contrast correction

Image ⇨ Adjust ⇨ Auto Levels (⌘-Shift-L) goes through each color channel and changes the lightest pixel to white, changes the darkest pixel to black, and stretches out all the shades of gray to fill out the spectrum. In Figure 18-8, I started with a drab and murky image. But when I applied Auto Levels, Photoshop pumped up the lights and darks, bolstering the contrast. Although I would argue that the corrected image is too dark, it's not half bad for an automated, no-brainer command that you just choose and let rip.

Figure 18-8
A grayscale image before (left) and after (right) applying the Auto Levels command.

Unlike the Equalize command, which considers all color channels as a whole, Auto Levels looks at each channel independently. So as with the Invert command, the active color mode has a profound effect on Auto Levels. Color Plate 18-5 shows our friendly jack o' lantern prior to color corrections, followed by the same image corrected with Auto Levels in the RGB, Lab, and CMYK modes. Quite frankly, the RGB image is the only one that's acceptable. The Lab image is far too orange, and the CMYK image is too dark, thanks to the exaggeration of the black channel. Auto Levels has also darkened the cyan channel, turning the pumpkin a bright red that one rarely sees in today's sincere pumpkin patches.

Like Invert, Equalize, and other automatic color mappers, Auto Levels is designed specifically for use in the RGB mode. If you use it in CMYK, you're more likely to achieve special effects than color correction.

The Auto Levels command serves the same purpose and produces the same effect as the Auto button in the Levels dialog box. You shouldn't really rely on either. What you *should* do is read the rest of this chapter and learn about the bigger and better color correction commands.

Hue Shifting and Colorizing _____

The following sections cover commands that are specifically designed to change the distribution of colors in an image. You can rotate the hues around the color spectrum, change the saturation of colors, adjust highlights and shadows, and even tint an image. Two of these commands — Hue/Saturation and Selective Color — are applicable exclusively to color images. The other two — Replace Color and

Variations — can be applied to grayscale images, but are not the best solutions. Although both permit you to select specific ranges of brightness values that you want to edit, they apply their corrections with less finesse than either the Levels or Curves commands, both of which are discussed toward the end of the chapter.

Before I go any further, I should mention one awesome little bit of advice. Remember that ⌘-Option-F redisplays the last filter dialog box so that you can tweak the effect? Well, a similar shortcut is available when you're applying color corrections. Press the Option key when choosing any of the commands described throughout the rest of this chapter to display that command's dialog box with the settings last applied to the image. If the command has a keyboard equivalent, just add Option to restore the last settings. ⌘-Option-U, for example, brings up the Hue/Saturation dialog box with the settings you last used.

Using the Hue/Saturation command

The Hue/Saturation command provides two functions. First, it enables you to adjust colors in an image according to their hues and saturation levels. You can apply the changes to specific ranges of colors or modify all colors equally across the spectrum. And second, the command lets you colorize images by applying new hue and saturation values while retaining the core brightness information from the original image.

This command is perfect for colorizing grayscale images. I know, I know, Woody Allen wouldn't approve, but with some effort, you can make Ted Turner green with envy. Just scan him and change the Hue value to 140 degrees.

When you choose Image ⇨ Adjust ⇨ Hue/Saturation (⌘-U), Photoshop displays the Hue/Saturation dialog box, shown in Figure 18-9. Before I explain how to use this dialog box to produce specific effects, let me briefly introduce the options:

    ↪ **Master:** Select the Master option to adjust all colors in an image to the same degree. If you prefer to adjust some colors in the image differently than others, select one of the color radio buttons along the left side of the dialog box. In the RGB and CMYK modes, the dialog box offers the R (Red), Y (Yellow), G (Green), C (Cyan), B (Blue), and M (Magenta) options, as shown in Figure 18-9. In the Lab mode, two radio buttons bite the dust, leaving Y (Yellow), G (Green), B (Blue), and M (Magenta), each of which represents an extreme end of the *a* or *b* spectrum.

    You can specify different slider bar settings for every one of the color ranges. For example, you might select R (Red) and move the Hue slider triangle to +50 and then select Y (Yellow) and move the Hue triangle to -30. All radio buttons are dimmed when you select the Colorize check box.

Figure 18-9
The Hue/Saturation dialog box enables you to adjust the hues and saturation values in a color image or colorize a grayscale image.

⤷ **Hue:** The Hue slider bar measures colors on the 360-degree color circle, as explained back in the "HSB" section of Chapter 5. When the Master radio button is selected, you can adjust the Hue value from negative to positive 180 degrees.

When one of the other color radio buttons is active in the RGB or CMYK mode, the Hue value can vary from negative to positive 60 degrees, because each of the colors is 60 degrees from either of its neighbors in the color wheel. (Red is 60 degrees from yellow, which is 60 degrees from green, and so on.) When a color radio button is active in the Lab mode, the Hue value can vary from negative to positive 90 degrees, thanks to Lab's specialized color organization.

Regardless of mode, letters appear at either end of the Hue slider when any option except Master is selected. The letters indicate the effect of moving the slider triangle in either direction. For example, if you select R (Red), the letters *M* and *Y* flank the slider, indicating that a negative value maps red pixels toward magenta, while a positive value maps red pixels toward yellow.

⤷ **Saturation:** Normally, the Saturation value can vary from negative to positive 100. The only exception occurs when the Colorize check box is active, in which case saturation becomes an absolute value, measured from 0 to 100.

Photoshop precedes positive values in the Hue, Saturation, and Lightness option boxes with plus signs (+) to show that you are adding to the current color attributes of the pixels. When you select Colorize, the plus signs disappear from all but the Lightness value because hue and saturation become absolute values that you apply to pixels rather than adding to or subtracting from existing pixel colors.

⤷ **Lightness:** You can darken or lighten an image by varying the Lightness value from negative to positive 100.

 However, because this value invariably changes *all* brightness levels in an image to an equal extent — whether or not Colorize is selected — it permanently dulls highlights and shadows. Therefore, you'll most likely want to avoid this option like the plague and rely instead on the Levels or Curves command to edit brightness and contrast.

⤷ **Sample:** This color swatch serves as a guidepost. Really, it's pretty redundant, because you can monitor the effects that your settings have on an image by selecting the Preview check box. But if you want to see the impact of your settings on one color in particular, you can isolate it by clicking on that color in the image window with the eyedropper cursor. (The cursor automatically changes to an eyedropper when you move it outside the Hue/Saturation dialog box and into the image window.)

⤷ **Load/Save:** As in all the best color correction dialog boxes, you can load and save settings to disk in case you want to reapply the options to other images. These options are especially useful if you find a magic combination of color-correction settings that accounts for most of the color mistakes produced by your scanner.

⤷ **Colorize:** Select this check box to apply a single hue and a single saturation level to the entire selection, regardless of how it was previously colored. All brightness levels remain intact, though you can adjust them incrementally using the Lightness slider bar (a practice that I do *not* recommend, as I mentioned earlier).

⤷ **Preview:** Select the Preview check box to continually update the image every time you adjust a setting.

 You can restore the options in the Hue/Saturation, Levels, and Curves dialog boxes to their original settings by Option-clicking on the Reset button (the Cancel button changes to Reset when you press the Option key). Or simply press ⌘-Option-period or ⌘-Escape.

Adjusting hue and saturation

All right, now that you know how the options work, it's time to give them a whirl. One caveat before I launch into things: Grayscale figures won't help you one whit in understanding the Hue/Saturation options, so I refer you a few times to three color plates. You may want to take a moment to slap a Post-it note on the page that contains Color Plates 18-6, 18-7, and 18-8 before you begin reading so that you can easily flip back and forth between text and figures.

Changing hues

When the Colorize check box is inactive, the Hue slider bar shifts colors in an image around the color wheel. It's as if the pixels were playing a colorful game of musical chairs, except that none of the chairs disappear. If you select the Master radio button and enter a value of +60 degrees, for example, all pixels stand up, march one sixth of the way around the color wheel, and sit down, assuming the colors of their new chairs. A pixel that was red becomes yellow, a pixel that was yellow becomes green, and so on. The top row of Color Plate 18-6 shows the result of applying various Hue values to a single image. Note that in each case, all colors in the image change to an equal degree.

 As long as you select only the Master option and edit only the Hue value, Photoshop retains all colors in an image. In other words, after shifting the hues in an image +60 degrees, you can later choose Hue/Saturation and shift the hues -60 degrees to restore the original colors.

If you select any radio button other than Master, the musical chairs metaphor breaks down a little. All pixels that correspond to the color you select move to the exclusion of other pixels in the image. The pixels that move must, well, sit on the non-moving pixels' laps, meaning that you sacrifice colors in the image.

For example, I edited the images in the second row of Color Plate 18-6 by applying Hue values while the C (Cyan) radio button only was selected. (In other words, I didn't apply Hue changes in combination with any other radio button.) All pixels that included some amount of cyan shifted to new hues according to the amount of cyan that the pixels contained; all non-cyan pixels remained unchanged. Despite the fact that the Hue values in each column of the color plate are identical, the colors in the horse changed less dramatically when C (Cyan) was selected than when I used the Master option. Even the pixels in the primarily cyan areas contain trace amounts of blue, which is excluded from the C (Cyan) hue adjustments.

Changing saturation levels

When I was a little kid, I loved watching my grandmother's television, because she kept the Color knob cranked at all times. The images appeared to leap off the screen, like they were radioactive or something. Way cool. Well, the Saturation option works just like that Color knob. I don't recommend that you follow my grandmother's example and send the saturation for every image through the roof, but it can prove helpful for enhancing or downplaying the colors in an image. If the image looks washed out, try adding saturation; if colors leap off the screen so that everybody in the image looks like they're wearing neon makeup, subtract saturation.

 Just as the Saturation option works like the Color knob on a TV set, the Hue value serves the same purpose as the Tint knob, and the Lightness value works like the Brightness knob. It looks like your mother was wrong when she told you that sitting on your behind and staring at the TV wasn't going to teach you anything.

The top row of Color Plate 18-7 shows the results of applying Saturation values when the Master option is selected. As you can see, all colors in the image fade or fortify equally. However, by applying the Saturation values to specific color options only, you can selectively fade and fortify colors, as demonstrated in the second row of the color plate. The lower left image in the color plate shows the result of selecting each color radio button — except C (Cyan) and B (Blue) — in turn and lowering the Saturation to -100, which translates to no saturation whatsoever, or all grays. Only grays, cyans, and blues are left. In the lower right image, I lowered the Saturation for C (Cyan) and B (Blue) to -100 and raised the saturation of all other colors to +50, thus eliminating the image's most prominent colors and enhancing the remaining weaker ones.

The Saturation option is especially useful for toning down images captured with low-quality scanners that exaggerate certain colors. Back in the early years, I used to work with a model that would digitize flesh tones in varieties of vivid oranges and red. I couldn't for the life of me figure out how to peel the colors off the ceiling until I tried the Saturation option in the Hue/Saturation dialog box. By selecting the R (Red) radio button and dragging the slider down to about -50, I was usually able to eliminate the problem. You can, too.

Correcting out-of-gamut colors

Another common use for the Saturation option is to prepare RGB images for process-color printing. As I explained in Chapter 5, many colors in the RGB spectrum are considered out of gamut, meaning that they fall outside the smaller CMYK color space. Photoshop now provides a means for recognizing such colors while remaining inside the RGB color space. Choose View ⇨ Gamut Warning (⌘-Shift-Y) to color all out-of-gamut colors with gray (or some other color that you specify using the Preferences command). The pixels don't actually change to gray; they just appear gray on-screen as long as the command is active. To turn View ⇨ Gamut Warning off, choose the command again.

How do you eliminate such problem colors? Well, you have three options:

❧ Let Photoshop take care of the problem automatically when you convert the image by choosing Image ➪ Mode ➪ CMYK Color. This tactic is risky, because Photoshop simply cuts off colors that are outside the gamut and converts them to their nearest CMYK equivalents. What was once an abundant range of differently saturated hues becomes abruptly flattened, like some kind of cruel buzz haircut. Choosing View ➪ CMYK Preview (⌘-Y) while working in the RGB color space gives you an idea of how dramatic the buzz can be. Sometimes the effect is hardly noticeable, in which case no additional attention may be warranted. Other times, the results can be disastrous.

❧ Another method is to scrub away with the sponge tool. In Chapter 8, I discussed how much I dislike this alternative, and despite the passage of 10 chapters, I haven't changed my mind. Although it theoretically offers selective control — you just scrub at areas that need attention until the gray pixels created by the Gamut Warning command disappear — the process leaves too much to chance and frequently does more damage than simply choosing Image ➪ Mode ➪ CMYK Color.

❧ The third and best solution involves the Saturation option inside the Hue/Saturation dialog box.

No doubt that last item comes as a huge surprise, given that I decided to broach the whole out-of-gamut topic in the middle of examining the Saturation option. But try to scoop your jaw up off the floor long enough to peruse the following steps, which outline the proper procedure for bringing out-of-gamut colors back into the CMYK color space.

STEPS   Eliminating Out-of-Gamut Colors

Step 1. **Create a duplicate of your image to serve as a CMYK preview.** Choose Image ➪ Duplicate to create a copy of your image. Then choose View ➪ CMYK Preview or press ⌘-Y. This image represents what Photoshop will do with your image if you don't make any corrections whatsoever. It's good to have around for comparative purposes.

Step 2. **Return to your original image and choose Select ➪ Color Range.** Then select the Out Of Gamut option from the Select pop-up menu and press Return. You have now selected all the nonconformist anti-gamut pixels throughout your image. These radicals must be expunged.

Step 3. **To monitor your progress, choose View ➪ Gamut Warning to display the gray pixels.** Oh, and don't forget to press ⌘-H to get rid of those pesky ants.

Step 4. **Press ⌘-U to display the Hue/Saturation dialog box.**

Step 5. **Lower the saturation of individual color ranges.** Don't change any settings while Master is selected; it's not exacting enough. Rather, experiment with selecting individual color radio buttons and lowering the Saturation value. The Hue slider can sometimes be useful as well. Every time you see one of the pixels change from gray to color, it means that another happy pixel has joined the CMYK pod. You may want to shout, "It's pointless to resist the invasion of the gamut snatchers!" and laugh mockingly just to make your work more entertaining.

 Keep an eye on the duplicate image in the CMYK preview mode. If you edit a color in your original image and render it less colorful than the CMYK preview, it means that you're doing damage you could avoid by simply choosing Image ➪ Mode ➪ CMYK Color. For example, if you drag the Saturation slider down to -35 for Y (Yellow) and notice that the revived pixels in the original image have become noticeably less colorful than their counterparts in the duplicate, nudge the slider back up to brighten the colors. If you can't seem to find an equitable solution, try selecting a different color radio button and editing it. Or try nudging the Hue slider and see what happens. Be patient, it takes a little time.

Step 6. **When only a few hundred sporadic gray spots remain on-screen, click on the OK button to return to the image window.** Bellow imperiously, "You may think you have won, you little gray pixels, but I have a secret weapon!" Then choose Image ➪ Mode ➪ CMYK Color and watch as Photoshop forcibly thrusts them into the gamut.

Mind you, the differences between your duplicate image and the one you manually turned away from the evil empire of RGB excess will be subtle, but they may prove enough to produce a better looking image with a wider range of colors.

 If the Hue/Saturation command doesn't seem to be working out, try using the Variations command or the Levels and Curves commands, as explained later in this chapter. The Variations command goes so far as to display the out-of-gamut pixels inside its previews and hide its gamut warning as colors come into the fold.

Avoiding gamut-correction edges

The one problem with the previous steps is that the Color Range command selects only the out-of-gamut pixels without even partially selecting their neighbors. As a result, you desaturate out-of-gamut colors while leaving similar colors fully saturated, an effect that can produce visual edges in an image.

One solution is to insert a step between Steps 2 and 3 in which you do the following: Change the Tolerance value in the Magic Wand Options palette to, say, 12. Next, choose Select ⇨ Similar, which expands the selected area to incorporate all pixels that fall within the Tolerance range. Finally, choose Select ⇨ Feather and enter a value that's about a quarter of the Tolerance value — in this case, 3.

This solution isn't perfect — ideally, the Color Range option box wouldn't dim the Fuzziness slider when you choose Out Of Gamut — but it does succeed in partially selecting a few neighboring pixels without sacrificing too many of the out-of-gamut bunch.

Colorizing images

When you select the Colorize check box in the Hue/Saturation dialog box, the options in the dialog box perform differently. Returning to that wonderful musical chairs analogy, the pixels no longer walk around a circle of chairs; they all get up and go sit in the same chair. Every pixel in the selection receives the same hue and the same level of saturation. Only the brightness values remain intact to ensure that the image remains recognizable.

The top row of Color Plate 18-8 shows the results of shifting the hues in an image in two different directions around the color wheel. In each case, the Colorize option is turned off. The second row shows similar colors applied separately to the blue and non-blue portions of the image using the Colorize option. (I selected these regions using the Color Range command.) The colors look similar within each column in the color plate. However, the Hue values are different in the shifted images than those in the colorized images because the shifted colors are based on relative adjustments while the colorized changes are absolute.

In most cases, you'll only want to colorize grayscale images or bad color scans because colorizing ruins the original color composition of an image. You'll probably also want to lower the Saturation value to somewhere in the neighborhood of 50 to 80. All the colors in the second-row images in Color Plate 18-8 er on the high side, with Saturation values of 80.

To touch up the edges of a colorized selection, change the foreground color to match the Hue and Saturation values that you used in the Hue/Saturation dialog box. You can do this by choosing the HSB Sliders command from the Color palette menu, and entering the values into the H and S option boxes. Set the B (Brightness) value to 100 percent. Then select the paintbrush tool and change the brush mode in the Paintbrush Options palette to Color. And paint away.

Shifting selected colors

The Replace Color command allows you to select an area of related colors and adjust the hue and saturation of that area. When you select Image ⇨ Adjust ⇨ Replace Color, you get a dialog box much like the Color Range dialog box. Shown in Figure 18-10, the Replace Color dialog box varies in only a few respects: It's missing the Select and Selection Preview pop-up menus and it offers three slider bars, taken right out of the Hue/Saturation dialog box.

In fact, this dialog box works exactly as if you were selecting a portion of an image using Select ⇨ Color Range and editing it with the Hue/Saturation command. There is no functional difference whatsoever. The Replace Color and Color Range dialog boxes even share the same default settings. If you change the Fuzziness value in one, the default Fuzziness value of the other changes as well. It's like they're identical twins or something.

Figure 18-10
The Replace Color dialog box works like the Color Range dialog box described back in Chapter 12, with a few Hue/Saturation options thrown in.

So why does the Replace Color command even exist? Because it allows you to change the selection outline and apply different colors without affecting the image in any way. Just select the Preview check box to see the results of your changes on-screen, and you're in business.

The top row of Color Plate 18-9 shows two effects created by selecting an area and changing the Hue value to +148 and the Saturation value to -12 (as in Figure 18-10).

In the first example, I selected the pumpkin face by setting the Fuzziness value to 40 and clicking and Shift-clicking a few times with the eyedropper tool. In the right example, I clicked just once in the area behind the pumpkin and changed the Fuzziness to 200, the maximum setting. I was able to experiment freely without once leaving the dialog box or redrawing the selection outline.

 If you're not clear on how to use all the options in the Replace Color dialog box, read the "Generating Masks Automatically" section in Chapter 12. It tells you all about the eyedropper tools and the Fuzziness option.

Shifting predefined colors

The Selective Color command permits you to adjust the colors in CMYK images. You can use the command when working on RGB or Lab images, but because it permits you to adjust the levels of cyan, magenta, yellow, and black inks, Selective Color makes more sense in the CMYK color space.

 Frankly, I'm not very keen on this command. For general image-editing, the Variations command provides better control and more intuitive options. Adobe created the Selective Color command to accommodate traditional press managers who prefer to have direct control over ink levels rather than monkeying around with hue, saturation, and other observational color controls. If Selective Color works for you, great. But don't get hung up on it if it never quite gels. You can accomplish all this and more with the Variations command, described in the next section.

Choosing Image ➪ Adjust ➪ Selective Color brings up the dialog box shown in Figure 18-11. To use the dialog box, choose the predefined color that you want to edit from the Colors pop-up menu and then adjust the four process-color slider bars to change the predefined color. When the Relative radio button is selected, you add or subtract color, much as if you were moving the color around the musical chairs using the Hue slider bar. When you select Absolute, you change the predefined color to the exact value entered into the Cyan, Magenta, Yellow, and Black option boxes. The Absolute option is therefore very much like the Colorize check box in the Hue/Saturation dialog box.

If you examine it closely, you'll notice that the Selective Color dialog box is very much like the Hue/Saturation dialog box. You have access to predefined colors in the form of a pop-up menu instead of radio buttons, and you can adjust slider bars to alter the color. The key differences are that the pop-up menu lets you adjust whites, medium grays (Neutrals), and blacks — options missing from Hue/Saturation — and the slider bars are always measured in CMYK color space.

The bottom row of Color Plate 18-9 includes two examples that show how this dialog box works. To create the first, I chose Red from the Colors pop-up menu and dragged the Cyan slider bar all the way up to +100 percent and the Yellow slider all the way to -100 percent. I also selected the Relative radio button, which retains a lot of pink in the pumpkin's face. To create the second example, I reapplied the same colors but selected the Absolute radio button, making the entire pumpkin purple. I also chose Black from the Colors pop-up menu and dragged the Black slider to -100 percent.

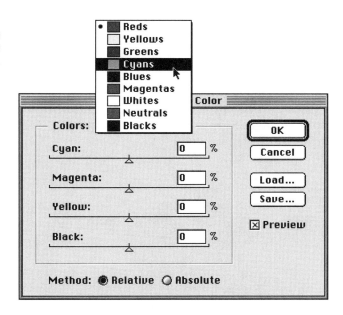

Figure 18-11
Select a predefined color from the Colors pop-up menu and adjust the slider bars to change that color.

As I mentioned at the outset, the Selective Color command produces the most predictable results when you're working on a CMYK image. When you drag the Cyan slider triangle to the right, for example, you're actually transferring brightness values to the cyan channel. However, you have to keep an eye out for a few anomalies, particularly when editing Black. In the CMYK mode, areas of your image that appear black include not only black, but also shades of cyan, magenta, and yellow, resulting in what printers call a *rich black* (or *saturated black*). Therefore, to change black to white, as I did in the lower right example of Color Plate 18-9, you have to set the Black slider to -100 percent and also set the Cyan, Magenta, and Yellow sliders to the same value.

Using the Variations command

The Variations command is at once Photoshop's most essential color correction function and its funkiest:

↩ On one hand, you can adjust hues and luminosity levels based on the brightness values of the pixels. This gives you a selective degree of control unmatched by Hue/Saturation. You can also see what you're doing by clicking on little thumbnail previews (see Figure 18-12), which takes much of the guesswork out of the correction process.

↩ On the other hand, the Variations dialog box takes over your screen and prevents you from previewing corrections in the image window. Furthermore, you can't see the area outside of a selection, which proves disconcerting when making relative color adjustments.

Variations is therefore best suited to correcting an image in its entirety. Here's how it works: To infuse color into the image, click on one of the thumbnails in the central portion of the dialog box. The thumbnail labeled More Cyan, for example, shifts the colors toward cyan. The thumbnail even shows how the additional cyan will look when added to the image. In case you're interested in seeing how these thumbnails actually affect a final printed image in the CMYK color space, check out Color Plate 18-10.

Figure 18-12
Click on the thumbnails to shift the colors in an image; adjust the slider bar in the upper right corner to change the sensitivity of the thumbnails; and use the radio buttons to determine which part of an image is selected.

Now notice that each thumbnail is positioned directly opposite its complementary color. More Cyan is across from More Red, More Blue is across from More Yellow, and so on. In fact, clicking on a thumbnail not only shifts colors toward the named color but away from the opposite color. For example, if you click on More Cyan and then click on its opposite, More Red, you arrive at the original imag

 Although this isn't exactly how the colors in the additive and subtractive worlds work — cyan is not the empirical opposite of red — the colors are theoretical opposites, and the Variations command makes the theory a practicality. After all, you haven't yet applied the color to the image, so the dialog box can calculate its adjustments in a pure and perfect world. Cyan and red ought to be opposites, so for the moment, they are.

To control the amount of color shifting that occurs when you click on a thumbnail, move the slider triangle in the upper right corner of the dialog box. Fine produces very minute changes; Coarse creates massive changes. Just to give you an idea of the difference between the two, you have to click on a thumbnail about 40 times when the slider is set to Fine to equal one click when it's set to Coarse.

The radio buttons at the top control which colors in the image are affected. Select Shadows to change the darkest colors, Highlights to change the lightest colors, and Midtones to change everything in between.

 In fact, if you're familiar with the Levels dialog box — as you will be when you read "The Levels command" section later in this chapter — the first three radio buttons have direct counterparts in the slider triangles in the Levels dialog box. For example, when you click on the Lighter thumbnail when the Highlights option is selected in the Variations dialog box, you perform the same action as moving the white triangle in the Levels dialog box to the left — that is, you make the lightest colors in the image even lighter.

The Saturation radio button lets you increase or decrease the saturation of colors in an image. Only one thumbnail appears on either side of the Current Pick image — one that decreases the saturation, and another that increases it. The Variation command modifies saturation differently than Hue/Saturation — where Hue/Saturation will push the saturation of a color as far as it will go, Variation attempts to modify the saturation without changing overall brightness values. As a result, an image saturated with Hue/Saturation will look lighter than one saturated with Variations.

As you click on the options — particularly when modifying saturation — you may notice that weird colors spring up inside the thumbnails. These brightly colored pixels are gamut warnings, highlighting colors that exceed the boundaries of the current color space. For example, if you're working in the RGB mode, these colors extend beyond the RGB gamut. Although the colors won't actually appear inverted as they do in the dialog box, it's not a good idea to exceed the color space because it results in areas of flat color, just as when you convert between the RGB and CMYK spaces. To view the thumbnails without the weirdly colored pixels, turn off the Show Clipping check box. (Incidentally, this use of the word *clipping* — Photoshop's third, in case you're counting — has nothing to do with paths or masks.)

Enhancing colors in a compressed image

Now that you know every possible way to adjust hues and saturation levels in Photoshop, it's time to discuss some of the possible stumbling blocks. The danger of rotating colors or increasing the saturation of an image is that you can bring out some very unstable colors. Adjusting the hues can switch ratty pixels from colors that your eyes aren't very sensitive to — particularly blue — into colors that you're eye sees very well — reds and greens. Drab color can also hide poor detail, which becomes painfully obvious when you make the colors bright and vivid.

 Consider the digital photograph featured in Color Plate 18-11. Snapped in Copley Square in Boston with a Kodak DC50, the original image at the top of the color plate is drab and lifeless. If I used the Hue/Saturation command to pump up the saturation levels, a world of ugly detail rises out of the muck, as shown in the second example. (Obviously, I've taken the saturation a little too high, but only to demonstrate a point.) The detail would have faired no better if I had used the Variations command to boost the saturation.

Unstable colors may be the result of JPEG compression, as in the case of the digital photo. Or you may have bad scanning or poor lighting to thank. In any case, you can fix the problem using our friends the Median and Gaussian Blur commands, as I explain in the following steps.

 If you find yourself working with heavily compressed images on a regular basis, you may want to record steps with the Actions palette, as explained in Chapter 3. Unlike the "Adjusting the Focus of Digital Photos" steps back in Chapter 15, you won't want to apply these steps to every digital photograph you take — or even most of them — but they come in handy more often than you might think.

STEPS   Boosting the Saturation of Digital Photos

Step 1.   **Select the entire image and copy it to a new layer.** It seems like half of all Photoshop techniques begin with ⌘-A and ⌘-J.

Step 2.   **Press ⌘-U to display the Hue/Saturation dialog box.** Then raise the Saturation value to whatever setting you desire. Don't worry if your image starts to fall apart — that's the whole point of these steps. Pay attention to the color and don't worry about the rest. In the second example in Color Plate 18-11, I raised the Saturation to +80.

Step 3. **Choose Filter ➪ Noise ➪ Median.** As you may recall from the last module, Median is the preeminent JPEG image fixer. A Radius value of 4 or 5 pixels works well for most images. You can take it even higher when working with resolutions of 200 ppi or more. I used 5. This destroys the detail, but that's not important. The color is all that matters.

Step 4. **Choose Filter ➪ Blur ➪ Gaussian Blur.** As always, the Median filter introduces its own edges. And this is one case where you don't want to add any edges whatsoever. So blur the heck out of the layer. I used a Radius of 4.0, just 1 pixel less than my Median Radius value.

Step 5. **Select Color from the blend mode pop-up menu in the Layers palette.** Photoshop mixes the gummy, blurry color with the crisp detail underneath. I also lowered the Opacity to 70 percent to produce the third example in Color Plate 18-11.

My image was still a little soft, so I applied the digital-photo sharpening steps from Chapter 15. After flattening the image, I pressed ⌘-A and ⌘-J again to copy it to yet another new layer. (I could have also used ⌘-Shift-Option-E to copy the previous layers to a new one.) Then I applied the Median, Gaussian Blur, and Unsharp Mask filters, flattened the image one last time, and sharpened the image to taste. The finished result appears at the bottom of Color Plate 18-11. Although a tad bit too colorful — Boston's a lovely city, but it's not quite this resplendent — the edges look every bit as good as they did in the original photograph, and in many ways better.

Making Custom Brightness Adjustments

The Lighter and Darker options in the Variations dialog box are preferable to the Lightness slider bar inside the Hue/Saturation dialog box because you can specify whether to edit the darkest, lightest, or medium colors in an image. But neither command is adequate for making precise adjustments to the brightness and contrast of an image. Photoshop provides two expert-level commands for adjusting the brightness levels in both grayscale and color images:

  ➪ The Levels command, which is ideal for most color corrections, enables you to adjust the darkest values, lightest values, and midrange colors for the entire selection or independently within each color channel.

✑ The Curves command, which is great for creating special effects and correcting images that are beyond the help of the Levels command. Using the Curves command, you can map every brightness value in every color channel to an entirely different brightness value.

There seems to be a controversy brewing in the back rooms of some print houses and art shops over which command is better, Levels or Curves. Based on a few letters I've received over the years, it seems some folks consider Curves to be the better command, and Levels to be about as useful as Brightness/Contrast.

However, this is most certainly not the case. Levels permits you to enter numerical values, and it includes a histogram so that you can better gauge how your adjustments will affect the image. Meanwhile, Curves lets you map out more than three significant points (the Levels limit) on a graph. The point is, both commands have their advantages, and both offer practical benefits for intermediate and advanced users alike.

There's no substitute for a good histogram, so I prefer to use Levels for my day-to-day color correcting. If you can't quite get the effect you want with Levels, or you know that you need to map specific brightness values in an image to other values, then use Curves. The Curves command is the more powerful function, but it is also more cumbersome than Levels.

The Levels command

When you choose Image ➪ Adjust ➪ Levels (⌘-L), Photoshop displays the Levels dialog box shown in Figure 18-13. The dialog box offers a histogram, as explained in the "Threshold" section earlier in this chapter, as well as two sets of slider bars with corresponding option boxes and a few automated eyedropper options in the lower right corner. You can compress and expand the range of brightness values in an image by manipulating the Input Levels options and then mapping those brightness values to new brightness values by adjusting the Output Levels options.

Figure 18-13
Use the Levels dialog box to map brightness values in the image (Input Levels) to new brightness values (Output Levels).

The options in the Levels dialog box work as follows:

- **Channel:** Select the color channel that you want to edit from this pop-up menu. You can apply different Input Levels and Output Levels values to each color channel. However, the options along the right side of the dialog box affect all colors in the selected portion of an image regardless of which Channel option is active.

- **Input Levels:** Use these options to modify the contrast of the image by darkening the darkest colors and lightening the lightest ones. The Input Levels option boxes correspond to the slider bar immediately below the histogram. You map pixels to black (or the darkest Output Levels value) by entering a number from 0 to 255 into the first option box or by dragging the black slider triangle. For example, if you raise the value to 55, all colors with brightness values of 55 or less in the original image become black, darkening the image as shown in the first example of Figure 18-14.

  You can map pixels at the opposite end of the brightness scale to white (or the lightest Output Levels value) by entering a number from 0 to 255 into the last option box or by dragging the white slider triangle. If you lower the value to 200, all colors with brightness values of 200 or greater become white, lightening the image as shown in the second example of Figure 18-14. In the last example of the figure, I raised the first value and lowered the last value, thereby increasing the amount of contrast in the image.

One of my favorite ways to edit the Input Levels values is to press the up and down arrow keys. Each press of an arrow key raises or lowers the value by 1. Press Shift with an arrow key to change the value in increments of 10.

Figure 18-14
The results of raising the first Input Levels value to 55 (left), lowering the last value to 200 (middle), and combining the two (right).

⊸ **Gamma:** The middle Input Levels option box and the corresponding gray tri-angle in the slider bar (shown highlighted in Figure 18-15) represent the *gamma* value, which is the brightness level of the medium gray value in the image. The gamma value can range from 0.10 to 9.99, with 1.00 being dead-on medium gray. Any change to the gamma value has the effect of decreasing the amount of contrast in the image by lightening or darkening grays without changing shadows and highlights. Increase the gamma value or drag the gray slider triangle to the left to lighten the medium grays (also called *midtones*), as in the first and second examples of Figure 18-16. Lower the gamma value or drag the gray triangle to the right to darken the medium grays, as in the last example in the figure.

You can also edit the gamma value by pressing the up and down arrow keys. Pressing an arrow key changes the value by 0.01, while pressing Shift-arrow changes the value by 0.10. I can't stress enough how useful this technique is. I rarely do anything except press arrow keys inside the Levels dialog box anymore.

Figure 18-15
I highlighted the gamma options by selecting everything but the highlighted areas and applying the values shown above.

Figure 18-16
The results of raising (left and middle) and lowering (right) the gamma value to lighten and darken the midtones in an image.

↪ **Output Levels:** Use these options to curtail the range of brightness levels in an image by lightening the darkest pixels and darkening the lightest pixels. You adjust the brightness of the darkest pixels — those that correspond to the black Input Levels slider triangle — by entering a number from 0 to 255 into the first option box or by dragging the black slider triangle. For example, if you raise the value to 55, no color can be darker than that brightness level (roughly 80 percent black), which lightens the image as shown in the first example of Figure 18-17. You adjust the brightness of the lightest pixels — those that correspond to the white Input Levels slider triangle — by entering a number from 0 to 255 into the second option box or by dragging the white slider triangle. If you lower the value to 200, no color can be lighter than that brightness level (roughly 20 percent black), darkening the image as shown in the second example of Figure 18-17. In the last example of the figure, I raised the first value and lowered the second value, thereby dramatically decreasing the amount of contrast in the image.

You can fully or partially invert an image using the Output Levels slider triangles. Just drag the black triangle to the right and drag the white triangle to the left past the black triangle. The colors flip, whites mapping to dark colors and blacks mapping to light colors.

Figure 18-17
The result of raising the first Output Levels value to 55 (left), lowering the second value to 200 (middle), and combining the two (right).

- **Load/Save:** You can load and save settings to disk using these buttons.

- **Auto:** Click on the Auto button to automatically map the darkest pixel in your selection to black and the lightest pixel to white, just like Image ⇨ Adjust ⇨ Auto Levels. Photoshop actually darkens and lightens the image by an extra half a percent just in case the darkest and lightest pixels are statistically inconsistent with the rest of the image.

To enter a percentage of your own, Option-click on the Auto button (the button name changes to Options) to display the Auto Range Options dialog box shown in Figure 18-18. Enter higher values to increase the number of pixels mapped to black and white; decrease the values to lessen the effect. The first two examples in Figure 18-19 compare the effect of the default 0.50 percent values to higher values of 5.00 percent. (Strictly for comparison purposes, the last image in the figure demonstrates the effect of the Equalize command applied to the entire image.)

Figure 18-18
Option-click on the Auto button to change the extent to which Photoshop closes the range of black and white pixels.

Figure 18-19
The default effect of the Auto button (left), the effect of the Auto button after raising the Clip values (middle), and the effect of the Equalize filter (right).

0.50% Clips   5.00% Clips   Equalize

Any changes made inside the Auto Range Options dialog box also affect the performance of the Auto Levels command. At all times, the effects of the Auto button and Auto Levels command are absolutely identical.

↪ **Eyedroppers:** Select one of the eyedropper tools in the Levels dialog box and click on a pixel in the image window to automatically adjust the color of that pixel. If you click on a pixel with the black eyedropper tool (the first of the three), Photoshop maps the color of the pixel and all darker colors to black. If you click on a pixel with the white eyedropper tool (last of the three), Photoshop maps it and all lighter colors to white. Use the gray eyedropper tool (middle) to change the exact color on which you click to medium gray and adjust all other colors in accordance. For example, if you click on a white pixel, all white pixels change to medium gray and all other pixels change to even darker colors.

One way to use the eyedropper tools is to color-correct scans without a lot of messing around. Include a neutral swatch of gray with the photograph you want to scan. (If you own a Pantone swatch book, Cool Gray 5 or 6 is your best bet.) After opening the scan in Photoshop, choose the Levels command, select the gray eyedropper tool, and click on the neutral gray swatch in the image window. This technique won't perform miracles, but it will help you to more evenly distribute lights and darks in the image. You then can fine-tune the image using the Input Levels and Output Levels options.

☞ **Preview:** Select this option to preview the effects of your settings in the image window. The effect of turning Preview off depends on the setting of the Video LUT Animation check box in the Display & Cursors panel of the Preferences dialog box (⌘-K, ⌘-3). When Video LUT Animation is turned off, turning off Preview simply displays the image prior to choosing the Levels command. When Video LUT Animation is turned on, turning off Preview applies the Levels settings to the entire screen. Click and hold on the title bar to see the original image prior to the correction, release to again apply the settings to the entire screen.

I discussed why I hate Video LUT Animation back in Chapter 2 — it applies adjustments to both selected and deselected areas in an image alike, and the preview is inaccurate in the Lab and CMYK modes. But there is one good thing about Video LUT Animation:

With Video LUT Animation turned on and the Preview check box turned off, you can preview the exact pixels that will turn to black or white in the image window. Just Option-drag the black or white triangle in the Input Levels slider bar. When Option-dragging the black handle, all pixels that appear some color other than white will change to black. When Option-dragging the white handle, look for the pixels that are not black to change to white.

To give you a sense of how the Levels command works, the following steps describe how to improve the appearance of an overly dark, low-contrast image such as the first example in Color Plate 18-12. Thanks to natural lighting and the dark color of the stone, this statue of Thomas Jefferson is hardly recognizable. Luckily, you can bring out the highlights using Levels.

STEPS   Correcting Brightness and Contrast with the Levels Command

---

Step 1.   Press ⌘-L to display the Levels dialog box. The histogram for the Jefferson image appears superimposed in white in front of the great man's chest. As you can see, most of the colors are clustered together on the left side of the graph, showing that there are far more dark colors than light.

Step 2. **Press ⌘-1 to examine the red channel.** Assuming that you're editing an RGB image, ⌘-1 displays a histogram for the red channel. The channel-specific histograms appear below Jefferson, colorized for your viewing pleasure.

Step 3. **Edit the black Input Levels value as needed.** Drag the black slider triangle to below the point at which the histogram begins. In the case of Jefferson, you can see a spike in the histogram about a half pica in from the left side of the graph. I dragged the black triangle directly underneath that spike, changing the first Input Levels value to 14, as you can see in the red histogram on the right side of Color Plate 18-12.

Step 4. **Edit the white Input Levels value.** Drag the white slider triangle to below the point at which the histogram ends. In the color plate, the histogram features a tall spike on the far right side. This means a whole lot of pixels are already white. I don't want to create a flat hot spot, so I leave the white triangle alone.

Step 5. **Edit the gamma value.** Drag the gray triangle to the gravitational center of the histogram. Imagine that the histogram is a big mass, and you're trying to balance the mass evenly on top of the gray triangle. Because my histogram is weighted too heavily to the left, I had to drag the gray triangle far to the left, until the middle Input Levels value changed to 2.40, which represents a radical shift.

Step 6. **Repeat Steps 2 through 5 for the green and blue channels.** Your image probably has a significant preponderance of red about it. To fix this, you need to edit the green and blue channels in kind. The graphs on the right side of Color Plate 18-12 show how I edited my histograms. Feel free to switch back and forth between channels as much as you like to get everything just right.

Step 7. **Press ⌘-tilde (~) to return to the composite RGB histogram.** Once you get the color balance right, you can switch back to the composite mode and further edit the Input Levels. I typically bump up the gamma a few notches — to 1.2 or so — to account for dot gain.

You may notice that your RGB histogram has changed. Although the histograms in the individual color channels remain fixed, the composite histogram updates to reflect the red, green, and blue modifications. I've superimposed the updated histogram in white on the corrected Jefferson on the right side of Color Plate 18-12. As you can see, the colors are now better distributed across the brightness range.

Step 8. **Press Return to apply your changes.** Just for fun, press ⌘-Z a few times to see the before and after shots. Quite the transformation, eh?

If you decide after looking at the before and after views that you could do a better job, undo the color correction. Then press ⌘-Option-L to bring up the Levels dialog box with the previous settings intact. Now you can take up where you left off.

The Curves command

If you want to be able to map any brightness value in an image to absolutely any other brightness value — no holds barred, as they say at the drive-in movies — you want the Curves command. When you choose Image ⇨ Adjust ⇨ Curves (⌘-M), Photoshop displays the Curves dialog box, shown in Figure 18-20, which offers access to the most complex and powerful color correction options on the planet.

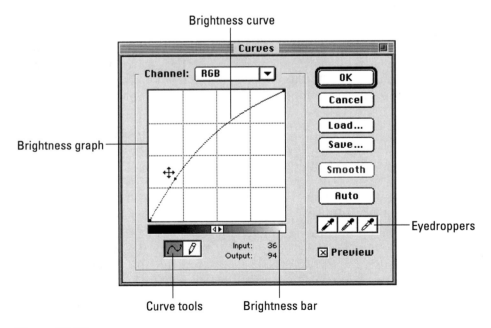

Figure 18-20
The Curves dialog box lets you distribute brightness values by drawing curves on a graph.

Quickly, here's how the options work:

- **Channel:** Surely you know how this option works by now. You select the color channel that you want to edit from this pop-up menu. You can apply different mapping functions to different channels by drawing in the graph below the pop-up menu. But, as is always the case, the options along the right side of the dialog box affect all colors in the selected portion of an image regardless of which Channel option is active.

- **Brightness graph:** The brightness graph is where you map brightness values in the original image to new brightness values. The horizontal axis of the graph represents input levels; the vertical axis represents output levels. The *brightness curve* charts the relationship between input and output levels. The lower left corner is the origin of the graph (the point at which both input and output values are 0). Move right in the graph for higher input values, up for higher output values. Because the brightness graph is the core of this dialog box, upcoming sections explain it in more detail.

- **Brightness bar:** The brightness bar shows the direction of light and dark values in the graph. When the dark end of the brightness bar appears on the left, colors are measured in terms of brightness values, in which case the colors in the graph proceed from black on the left to white on the right, as demonstrated in the left example of Figure 18-21. Therefore, higher values produce lighter colors. This is my preferred setting, because it measures colors in the same direction as the Levels dialog box.

  If you click on the brightness bar, white and black switch places, as shown in the second example of the figure. The result is that Photoshop measures the colors in terms of ink coverage, from 0 percent of the primary color to 100 percent of the primary color. Higher values now produce darker colors. If you click on the brightness bar in the process of drawing a curve, the curve automatically flips so as to retain any changes you made, as the figure illustrates.

Figure 18-21
Click on the brightness bar to change the way in which
the graph measures color: by brightness values (left)
or by ink coverage (right).

co **Curve tools:** Use the curve tools to draw the curve inside the brightness
graph. Click in the graph with the point tool (on the left, selected by default)
to add a point to the curve. Drag a point to move it. To delete a point, drag it
outside the boundaries of the graph. The pencil tool (on the right) enables
you to draw free-form curves simply by dragging inside the graph, as shown
in Figure 18-22.

You can draw straight lines with the pencil tool by clicking at one location
in the graph and Shift-clicking at a different point, just as you can when
using the real pencil tool in the image window.

co **Input/Output numbers:** The input and output numbers monitor the location
of your cursor in the graph according to brightness values or ink coverage,
depending on the setting of the brightness bar.

☞ **Load/Save:** Use these buttons to load and save settings to disk.

Figure 18-22
Use the pencil tool to draw free-form lines in the brightness graph. If the lines appear rough, you can soften them by clicking on the Smooth button.

Okay, here's *the* weirdest tip in all of Photoshop. It's not very practical, but it's about as wild as you can get. You can use a gradation as a Curves map. First, click on the Edit button in the Gradient Tool Options palette, select one of the more garish gradients, like Spectrum. Then ⌘-Option-click on the Save button to save the gradient as a Curves file. Open the file in the Curves dialog box, and stand back and watch the fireworks.

In the psychedelic Color Plate 18-13, I cloned Constantine to a new layer and applied a heavy dose of Gaussian Blur. Then I used the Curves command to apply one of three gradients. In the bottom row, I mixed each of the fantastic images with its underlying original using the Color blend mode.

☞ **Smooth:** Click on the Smooth button to smooth out curves drawn with the pencil tool. Doing so leads to smoother color transitions in the image window. This button is dimmed except when you use the pencil tool.

☞ **Auto:** Click on this button to automatically map the darkest pixel in your selection to black and the lightest pixel to white. Photoshop throws in some additional darkening and lightening according to the Clip percentages, which you can edit by Option-clicking on the button.

☞ **Eyedroppers:** Photoshop actually permits you to use a fourth eyedropper from the Curves dialog box. If you don't select any eyedropper tool (or you click in the graph to deselect the current eyedropper) and move the cursor out of the dialog box into the image window, you get the standard eyedropper cursor. Click on a pixel in the image to locate the brightness value of that pixel in the graph. A circle appears in the graph, and the input and output numbers list the value for as long as you hold down the mouse button, as shown in the first example in Figure 18-23.

The other eyedroppers work as they do in the Levels dialog box, mapping pixels to black, medium gray, or white. For example, the second image in Figure 18-23 shows the white eyedropper tool clicking on a light pixel, thereby mapping that value to white, as shown in the highlighted portion of the graph below the image. You can further adjust the brightness value of that pixel by dragging the corresponding point in the graph, as demonstrated in the last example of the figure.

∞ **Preview:** Select this option to preview your settings in the image window.

Figure 18-23
Use the standard eye-dropper cursor to locate a color in the brightness graph (left). Click with one of the eyedropper tools from the Curves dialog box to map the color of that pixel in the graph (middle). You then can edit the location of the point in the graph by dragging it (right).

Continuous curves

All discussions in the few remaining pages of this chapter assume that the brightness bar is set to edit brightness values (in which case the gradation in the bar lightens from left to right). If you set the bar to edit ink coverage (the bar darkens from left to right), you can still achieve the effects I describe, but you must drag in the opposite direction. For example, if I tell you to lighten colors by dragging upward, you drag downward. In a backward world live the ink coverage people.

When you first enter the Curves dialog box, the brightness curve appears as a straight line strung between two points, as shown in the first example of Figure 18-24, mapping every input level from white (the lower left point) to black (the upper right point) to an identical output level. If you want to perform seamless color corrections, the point tool is your best bet because it enables you to edit the levels in the brightness graph while maintaining a continuous curve.

To lighten the colors in the selected portion of the image, click near the middle of the curve with the point tool to create a new point and then drag the point upward, as demonstrated in the second example of Figure 18-24. To darken the image, drag the point downward, as in the third example.

Figure 18-24
Create a single point in the curve with the point tool (left) and then drag it upward (middle) or downward (right) to lighten or darken the image evenly.

Create two points in the curve to boost or lessen the contrast between colors in the image. In the first example of Figure 18-25, I created one point very near the white point in the curve and another point very close to the black point. I then dragged down on the left point and up on the right point to make the dark pixels darker and the light pixels lighter, which translates to higher contrast.

In the second example of the figure, I did just the opposite, dragging up on the left point to lighten the dark pixels and down on the right point to darken the light pixels. As you can see in the second image, this lessens the contrast between colors, making the image more gray.

In the last example in Figure 18-25, I bolstered the contrast with a vengeance by dragging the right point down and to the left. This has the effect of springing the right half of the curve farther upward, thus increasing the brightness of the light pixels in the image.

Figure 18-25
Create two points in the curve to change the appearance of contrast in an image, whether by increasing it mildly (left), decreasing it (middle), or boosting it dramatically (right).

Arbitrary curves

You can create some mind-numbing color variations by adjusting the brightness curve arbitrarily, mapping light pixels to dark, dark pixels to light, and in-between pixels all over the place. In the first example of Figure 18-26, I used the point tool to achieve an arbitrary curve. By dragging the left point severely upward and the right point severely downward, I caused dark and light pixels alike to soar across the spectrum.

If you're interested in something a little more subtle, try applying an arbitrary curve to a single channel in a color image. Color Plate 18-14, for example, shows an image subject to relatively basic color manipulations in the red and green channels, followed by an arbitrary adjustment to the blue channel.

Although you can certainly achieve arbitrary effects using the point tool, the pencil tool is more versatile and less inhibiting. As shown in the second example of Figure 18-26, I created an effect that would alarm Carlos Castaneda just by zigzagging my way across the graph and clicking on the Smooth button.

Figure 18-26
Arbitrary brightness curves created using the point tool (left) and the pencil tool (right).

In fact, the Smooth button is an integral part of using the pencil tool. Try this little experiment: Draw a bunch of completely random lines and squiggles with the pencil tool in the brightness graph. As shown in the first example of Figure 18-27, your efforts will most likely yield an unspeakably hideous and utterly unrecognizable effect.

Next, click on the Smooth button. Photoshop automatically connects all portions of the curve, miraculously smoothing out the color-mapping effect and rescuing some semblance of your image, as shown in the second example of the figure. If the effect is still too radical, you can continue to smooth it out by clicking additional times on the Smooth button. I clicked on the button twice more to create the right image in Figure 18-27. Eventually, the Smooth button restores the curve to a straight line.

Figure 18-27
After drawing a series of completely random lines with the pencil tool (left), I clicked on the Smooth button once to connect the lines into a frenetic curve (middle) and then twice more to even out the curve, thus preserving more of the original image (right).

Adjustment Layers

Every one of the commands I've discussed in this chapter is applicable to a single layer at a time. If you want to correct the colors in multiple layers, you have to create a special kind of layer called an *adjustment layer*. New to Photoshop 4, adjustment layers are layers that contain mathematical color correction information. The layer applies its corrections to all layers below it, without affecting any layers above.

You can create an adjustment layer in one of two ways:

- ↝ Choose Layer ⇨ New ⇨ Adjustment Layer.

- ↝ ⌘-click on the new layer icon at the bottom of the Layers palette.

Either way, Photoshop displays the New Adjustment Layer dialog box shown in Figure 18-28. This dialog box contains the standard Name, Opacity, and Mode options that accompany any kind of layer. But you also get a Type pop-up menu, which offers some of Photoshop's most important color correction commands. Select the kind of color correction that you want to apply from the menu, and press Return.

Figure 18-28
The New Adjustment
Layer dialog box, as it
appears normally
(top) and with Type
pop-up menu
unfurled (bottom).

Photoshop then displays the dialog box for the selected correction (unless you choose Invert, which does not offer a dialog box). Change the settings as desired and press Return as you normally would. The completed color correction appears as a new layer in the Layers palette. In Figure 18-29, for example, I've added a total of three adjustment layers. Photoshop marks adjustment layers with half-black circles so that you can readily tell them apart from image layers.

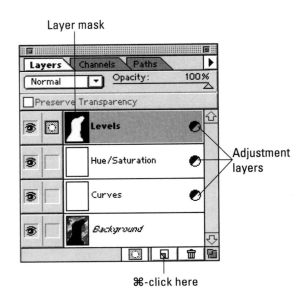

Layer mask

⌘-click here

Adjustment layers

Figure 18-29
Here I've created three layers of color correction in front of a single background image.

The advantages of layer-based corrections

Now at this point, you might think, "Big whoop. You can apply corrections to multiple layers. That doesn't seem like such a great feature." Not only would that be an unkind assessment of adjustment layers — hey, computer code has feelings too — but an inaccurate assessment as well. I've said before that this is Photoshop 4's most important new feature, and here's why:

↪ **Forever editable:** So long as the adjustment layer remains intact — stored in the native Photoshop format, of course — you can edit the color correction over and over again without damaging the underlying pixels. Unlike standard color corrections, which make permanent alterations to selected pixels, adjustment layers are temporary in nature. On the slightest whim, you can double-click on the layer name in the palette to bring up the color correction dialog box, complete with the settings that are currently in force. Tweak the settings as the mood hits you and press Return to make changes on the fly. You can't get any more flexible than this.

↪ **Flexible layer masking:** You can also adjust the affected area to your heart's content. An adjustment layer covers the entire image like an adjustable wall-to-wall carpet. You modify the affected area by painting inside the layer. The layer doesn't contain any pixels of its own, so painting in an adjustment layer changes its layer mask. Paint with black to remove the correction from an area, use white to paint the correction back in.

In fact, if a selection is active when you create a new adjustment layer, Photoshop automatically creates a layer mask according to the selection outline. For example, in Color Plate 18-15, I selected the topiary dinosaur before creating the Levels layer. Photoshop thoughtfully converted my selection into a mask, as labeled in Figure 18-29. And like any layer mask, I can edit it well into the future without any adverse side effects.

- **Reorder your corrections:** As with any layers, you can shuffle adjustment layers up and down in stacking order. For example, if you decide you don't want the correction to affect a specific layer, just drag the adjustment layer to a level in the Layers palette below the layer you want to exclude. If you're juggling multiple adjustment layers, as in Figure 18-29, you can shuffle the adjustment layers to change the order in which they're applied. You can even use the standard keyboard shortcuts, ⌘-[and ⌘-].

- **Fade corrections:** You can fade a standard color correction right after you apply it using Filter ⇨ Fade. But you can fade a correction applied with an adjustment layer any old time. Just change the Opacity and blend mode settings in the Layers palette.

- **Correct with blend modes:** Some folks prefer to correct overly light or dark images using blend modes. Take an image, copy it to a new layer, and apply the Multiply mode to darken the layer or Screen to lighten it. The problem with this trick is that it increases the size of the image in memory. Duplicating the image to a new layer requires Photoshop to double the size of the image in RAM.

Adjustment layers permit you to apply this same technique without adding pixels to RAM. Create a new adjustment layer with the Levels option selected. After the Levels dialog box comes up, press Return to ignore it. Now select Multiply or Screen from the blend mode pop-up menu in the Layers palette. The adjustment layer serves as a surrogate duplicate of the layers below it, mocking every merged pixel. And it doesn't add so much as a K to the file size. It's an image-editing miracle — layers without the pain.

Correcting a flat image using layers

Although many artists will use this new feature to edit multilayer compositions, adjustment layers are equally applicable to flat photos. Originally printed in the February, 1996 issue of *Macworld* magazine, Color Plate 18-15 shows how I corrected an image shot with a Polaroid PDC-2000 using a total of three color corrections, layered one on top of the other. (Much of this text also comes from that same article.) At first glance, the original photo on the left side of the color plate is a textbook example of what happens if you ignore backlighting. But as you have probably figured out by now, an image that appears black may actually contain several thousands of colors just itching to get out. Adjustment layers make it easier than ever to free these colors and make them fully visible to the world.

Because my image was in such rotten shape, I decided to start with the expert Curves command. I ⌘-clicked on the new layer icon and selected Curves from the Type pop-up menu. Then I used the pencil tool in the Curves dialog box to draw a radical upswing on the left side of the graph, dramatically lightening the blacks right out of the gate. I clicked on the Smooth button a few times to even out the color transitions, as demonstrated in the second example in Color Plate 18-15.

All this lightening resulted in some very washed-out colors (a typical side effect), so I created a second adjustment layer using the Hue/Saturation command. By raising the Saturation value, I quickly breathed a little enthusiasm into these tired old hues — a sufficient amount, in fact, to make it clear how soft the focus was. So I went back to the original image layer and applied the Unsharp Mask filter. Had it not been for the advent of adjustment layers, I would have either had to sharpen the image before color correcting it, making it impossible to accurately gauge the results, or sharpen the image after correcting, which might bring out compression artifacts and other undesirable anomalies. With adjustment layers, however, I can sharpen and correct at the same time, giving no operation precedent over the other.

The hedge monster remained a little dark, so I selected it with the Color Range command and then created a third adjustment layer for the Levels command. Using Levels, I quickly enhanced the brightness and contrast of the green beast, bringing him out into the full light of day. As I mentioned earlier, Photoshop automatically generated a layer mask for my selection, which appears as a tiny white silhouette in the Layers palette.

To be fair, I should mention that adjustment layers are not an original invention for Photoshop. Just as Painter/X2 offered bitmapped layers more than a year before Photoshop, Live Picture introduced correction layers two years prior to the arrival of Photoshop 4. Live Picture's layers also permit you to temporarily sharpen, blur, and distort underlying pixels, three operations that are currently beyond Photoshop's reach. My guess is that Photoshop will continue to grow in this direction in the future. The day you can apply filters with adjustment layers is the day the feature will be complete.

The Wonders of Blend Modes

19

In This Chapter

- Modifying the Opacity value

- Using blend modes to mix the active layer with the ones behind it

- Discussions of the new blend modes, Color Dodge, Color Burn, and Exclusion

- Opposite blend modes: Overlay and Hard Light, Color and Luminosity

- Sandwiching a heavily filtered image between two unfiltered originals

- Fading pixels according to brightness values from the Layer Options dialog box

- The advantages and disadvantages of channel operations

- Mixing same-sized images with the Apply Image command

- Using the Add and Subtract blend modes

- Modifying selection outlines and masks using the Calculations command

---

Mixing Images Together _____

There must be 50 ways to combine and compare differently colored pixels in Photoshop. So far, we've seen how you can smear and blur pixels into each other, select pixels using other pixels, layer pixels in front of pixels, compare a pixel to its neighbors using automated filters, and map the colors of pixels to other colors. Any time that you edit, mask, composite, filter, or color correct an image, you're actually breeding the image with itself or with other images to create a new and unique offspring.

This chapter explores the final and ultimate experiment in Photoshop's great genetics laboratory. *Blend modes*, also called *calculations*, permit you to mix the color of a pixel with that of every pixel in a straight line beneath it. A single blend mode is as powerful as a mask, a filter, and a color map combined, and best of all, it's temporary. So long as one image remains layered in front of another, you can replace one calculation with another as easily as you change a letter of text in a word processor.

To appreciate the most rudimentary power of blend modes, consider Figure 19-1. The first image shows a terrestrial thrill seeker composited in front of the Apollo crew's old stomping grounds. Both layers are as opaque as if you had cut them out with scissors and glued them together. (Granted, you'd have to be *very* skilled with scissors.) The antialiased edges of the parachute mix slightly with the moon pixels below them. But beyond that, every pixel is a digital hermit, steadfastly avoiding interaction.

The second image in Figure 19-1 paints a different picture. Here I've created several clones of the parachute and moon and mixed them together using Photoshop's considerable array of calculation capabilities. Although I used just two images, I composited them onto 10 layers, only one of which — the background layer — was fully opaque. I don't know if it's moon men invading earth or the other way around, but whatever it is, it wouldn't have been possible without blend modes and their ilk.

Figure 19-1
Layers permit you to combine images from different sources (left), but blend modes permit you to mix images together to create intriguing if sometimes unexpected interactions (right).

Photoshop gives you three ways to mix images:

> ◌ **The Layers palette:** Whether you're working with a floating selection or an independent layer, you can combine the floater with underlying pixels using the Opacity slider and blend mode pop-up menu, both members of the Layers palette. Figure 19-2 shows these two illustrious items in the context of the layers list for Figure 19-1. To learn everything there is to know about the Opacity slider and blend mode pop-up menu, read the next section.

Figure 19-2
The list of layers in the Invasion Moon composition, with blend mode pop-up menu proudly displayed on the right.

> ◌ **The Blend If sliders:** You can double-click on a layer name in the Layers palette to display the Layers Options dialog box. Many of the options in this dialog box are found elsewhere, but the two slider bars at the bottom are unique. They allow you to drop colors out of the active layer and force colors to show through from layers below. This is one of Photoshop's oldest, finest, and least used features, as I discuss later in the "Dropping Out and Forcing Through" section.

> ◌ **Channel operations:** The so-called channel operations permit you to combine two open images of identical size, or one image with itself. Photoshop offers two commands for this purpose, Image ⇨ Apply Image and Image ⇨

Calculations. Unusually complex and completely lacking in sizing and placement functions, these commands provide access to two unique blend modes named Add and Subtract. Simply put, unless a technique involves the Add or Subtract mode, or you want to clone two images into a third image window, you can mix images with greater ease, flexibility, and feedback using the Layers palette. For more on this lively topic, see the "Using Channel Operation Commands" section later in this chapter.

Blend modes are not Photoshop's most straightforward feature. There may even come a time when you utter the words, "Blend modes are stupid." They demand a generous supply of experimentation, and even then, they'll fool you. I was a math major in college (with a double-major in art), so I well understand the elementary arithmetic behind Photoshop's calculations. And yet, despite roughly a decade of experience with blend modes in Photoshop and other programs, I am frequently surprised by their outcome.

The key, therefore, is to combine a basic understanding of how blend modes and other compositing features work with your natural willingness to experiment. Sometime when you don't have a deadline looming over your head, take some multilayered composition you have lying around and hit it with a few calculations. Even if the end result is a disaster that you wouldn't share with your mother, let alone a client, you can consider it time well spent.

Using Opacity and Blend Modes_

This is not the first time in this book that I've touched on the Opacity slider or the blend mode pop-up menu. And given that the Layer palette's blend modes mimic the brush modes — both in name and in function — that I discussed in "The 18 paint tool modes" section near the end of Chapter 8, we're covering some familiar territory. But you'll soon find that there's a significant difference between laying down a single color with a brush, and merging the hundred or so thousand colors that inhabit a typical layer. This difference is the stuff of the following pages.

 Incidentally, both the Opacity and blend mode options are dimmed when working on the background layer, or in a single-layer image. There's nothing underneath, so there's no point in mixing.

Changing the Opacity setting

The Opacity slider is the easiest of the layer mixers to understand. It permits you to mix the active layer with the layers below in prescribed portions. It's sort of like mixing a drink. Suppose you pour one part vermouth and four parts gin into a martini glass. (Any martini enthusiast knows that's too much vermouth, but bear with me on this one.) The resulting beverage is 1/5 vermouth and 4/5 gin. If the vermouth were a layer, you could achieve the same effect by setting the Opacity to 20 percent. This implies that 20 percent of what you see is vermouth and the remaining 80 percent is underlying gin.

When any selection or navigation tool is active, you can change the Opacity setting for a layer or floating selection from the keyboard. Press a single number key to change the Opacity in 10-percent increments. That's 1 for 10 percent, 2 for 20 percent, up to 0 for 100 percent — in order along the top of your keyboard — just as it has been since the olden days. But, aye, here's the new rub. In Photoshop 4, you can press two keys in a row to specify an exact two-digit Opacity value. Yes, I know, I already mentioned this in Chapter 13, but it bears repeating.

The shy and retiring Behind and Clear

After that enlightening bit of repetitious information, it's time to move onto the more complicated realm of blend modes. There are in fact 19 blend modes in all. But most of the time, you only see 17. The two that you're missing are Behind and Clear, and they are available only after establishing a floating selection on a layer.

Try this: Create a layer and put some stuff on it. To better see the effects of the Behind and Clear modes, make sure that some portion of the layer is transparent, and that the layer looks different than its background. Then select part of the layer and press ⌘-Option-arrow key. (Any arrow key will do.) You now have a floating selection on a layer. Check out the blend mode pop-up menu in the Layers palette, and there you will find Behind and Clear in the third and fourth positions.

Just like the Behind mode available for brushes, the Behind blend mode lets you tuck the floating selection behind the opaque portions of the active layer. In other words, the floating selection is allowed to fill the transparent and translucent areas of the active layer only.

As I mentioned in Chapter 13, Behind is the opposite of Preserve Transparency. So if the Preserve Transparency check box is turned on, Behind has no effect.

The Clear mode uses the floating selection to cut a hole in the active layer. It's like having a little hole that you can move around independently of the pixels, without danger of harming them.

You know that scene in *Yellow Submarine* where the Fab Four are making fun of that poor little marsupial dude with the long, mustard-colored nose? After they finish labeling him a "Nowhere Man" — hey, give him a break, guys, maybe his priorities are just different — the creature announces that he has a hole in his pocket. He then takes it out, puts it on the floor, and it becomes a hole in the floor. Later, the holes multiply — I can't remember why — and all the guys sail through the holes while singing some other song that has nothing to do with the plot, which was already in awfully short supply. Granted, it's a pointless movie — just as this is a pointless analogy — but the concept is absolutely the same as Photoshop's Clear mode. Clear turns a floating selection into a portable hole in the active layer.

This feature is especially useful for clipping holes into a layer using character outlines. Create some text with the type mask tool, press ⌘-Option-arrow to float the text, and convert it to a bunch of holes by choosing the Clear mode. If you suddenly become concerned that you've lost part of the layer, don't panic. Just choose the Normal mode, and the original pixels come back into play.

The remaining 17 blend modes

The remaining 17 blend modes are available whether you're editing a layer or a floating selection. But it seems like a lot of excess verbiage to keep saying "layer or floating selection" over and over again, so any time I say "layer" in the following list, you'll know that I mean both.

Also, when I allude to a little something called a *composite pixel*, I mean the pixel color that results from all the mixing that's going on in back of the active layer. For example, your document may have hoards of layers with all sorts of blend modes in effect, but as long as you work on, say, layer 23, Photoshop treats the image formed by layers 1 through 22 as if it were one flattened image filled with a bunch of static composite pixels.

As you read through this plethora of blend mode descriptions, you can check out examples of the blend modes in Color Plate 19-1. Here we have a bunch of layered photographs of Saturn composited against the stormy gaseous planet of Jupiter. Though the planets aren't to scale — I understand that both bodies are several times larger than this book, for example — they do a fair job of showing the effects of the various blend modes.

- **Normal:** In combination with an Opacity setting of 100 percent, this option displays every pixel in the active layer normally regardless of the colors of the underlying image. Figure 19-3 shows a banner that has been positioned on a single layer composited in front of a stucco texture created on the Background layer. The blend mode in force is Normal. (The drop shadow, incidentally, is merely an artistic embellishment that exists on the background layer.)

When you use an Opacity of less than 100 percent, the color of each pixel in the active layer is averaged with the composite pixel in the layers behind it according to the Opacity value.

Figure 19-3
An active layer containing the banner image and drop shadow subject to the Normal blend mode and an Opacity setting of 100 percent.

- **Dissolve:** This option specifically affects feathered or softened edges. If the active layer is entirely opaque with hard edges, this option has no effect. If the selection is antialiased, the effect is generally too subtle to be of much use. The Dissolve option randomizes the pixels in the feathered portion of an active layer, as shown in the top example of Figure 19-4. It also randomizes pixels of hard- or soft-edged selections when the Opacity value is set below 100 percent, as shown in the second example in the figure.

- **Multiply:** To understand the Multiply and Screen modes, you have to use a little imagination. So here goes: Imagine that the active layer and the underlying image are both photos on transparent slides. The Multiply mode produces the same effect as holding those slides up to the light, one slide in front of the other. Because the light has to travel through two slides, the outcome is invariably a darker image that contains elements from both images. An example of the Multiply blend mode appears in Figure 19-5.

Figure 19-4
The Dissolve option applied to an opaque floating selection with heavily feathered edges (top) and to a second selection set to 40 percent opacity (bottom).

Figure 19-5
The Multiply blend mode produces the same effect as holding two overlapping transparencies up to the light. It always results in a darker image.

↪ **Screen:** Still have those transparent slides from the Multiply analogy? Well, place them both in separate projectors and point them at the same screen and you'll get the same effect as Screen. Rather than creating a darker image, as you do with Multiply, you create a lighter image, as demonstrated in Figure 19-6 and Color Plate 19-1.

You can use the Screen blend mode to emulate film that has been exposed multiple times. Ever seen Thomas Eakin's pioneering *Jumping Figure*, which shows rapid-fire exposures of a naked man jumping from one location to another? Each shot is effectively screened onto the other, lightening the film with each and every exposure. The photographer was smart enough to limit the exposure time so as not to overexpose the film; likewise, you should only apply Screen when working with images that are sufficiently dark so that you avoid overlightening.

Figure 19-6
The Screen mode produces the same effect as shining two projectors at the same screen. It always results in a lighter image.

- **Overlay, Soft Light, and Hard Light:** You just can't separate these guys. All three multiply the dark colors in the active layer and screen the light colors into the composite pixels in the layers below. But they apply their effects to different degrees. Overlay favors the composite pixels while Hard Light favors the layered pixels. (In fact, the two are direct opposites.) Soft Light is a washed out version of Hard Light that results in a low-contrast effect.

  Figure 19-7 shows all three blend modes applied to a single banner layer on the left. I then duplicated the banner layer with blend mode still in force to get the effects on the right. As these examples demonstrate, the modes effectively tattoo one image onto the image behind it. Even after multiple repetitions of the banners in the figure, the stucco texture still shows through, as if the banner were appliquéd on.

  I recommend starting with the Overlay mode any time you want to mix both the active layer and the layers behind it to create a reciprocal blend. By this, I mean a blend that mixes the colors evenly without eliminating any of the detail in either layer. After you apply Overlay, vary the Opacity to favor the composite pixels. I've said it before and I'll say it again, Overlay is Photoshop's most practical blend mode, the one you should always try first.

  If you can't quite get the effect you want at lower Opacity settings, switch to the Soft Light mode and give that a try. On the other hand, if the Overlay mode at 100 percent seems too subtle, switch to Hard Light. You can even clone the layer to darn well emblazon the layer onto its background, as in the bottom right image in Figure 19-7.

Figure 19-7
The results of the Overlay, Soft Light, and Hard Light blend modes as they appear when applied to a single floating banner image (left) and a second layer of the banner image (right).

Overlay

Soft Light

Hard Light

 ↪ **Color Dodge:** When you apply the Color Dodge mode, each color in the layer becomes a brightness value multiplier. Light colors like white produce the greatest effect and black produces no effect. As a result, Color Dodge is Photoshop's most dramatic whitening agent, the equivalent of applying bleach to colored fabric. When applied to the banner layer in Figure 19-8, it exaggerates the stucco texture, resulting in a rougher effect than either Screen or the upcoming Lighten.

Figure 19-8
Color Dodge uses the active layer to bleach the pixels in the layer below. There is nothing subtle about this effect.

 ⊛ **Color Burn:** If Color Dodge is bleach, then Color Burn is charcoal dust. It uses the colors in the active layer to reduce brightness values, resulting in a radical darkening effect. Like Color Dodge, the Color Burn mode creates a chalky effect when applied to the banner in Figure 19-9. You may also want to sneak a peek at Color Plate 19-1, which illustrates that both Color Dodge and Color Burn saps the colors out of your images more surely than any other blend modes. If you want a high-contrast stamping effect, these are the blend modes to use.

Figure 19-9
Color Burn seers an image charcoal black. No other darkening mode is this gritty or severe.

⊛ **Darken:** When you select this option, Photoshop applies colors in the active layer only if they are darker than the corresponding pixels below. Keep in mind that Photoshop compares the brightness levels of pixels in a full-color image on a channel-by-channel basis. So although the red component of a pixel in the active layer may be darker than the red component of the underlying composite pixel, the green and blue components may be lighter. In this case, Photoshop would assign the red component but not the green or blue, thereby subtracting some red and making the pixel slightly more turquoise. Compare the predictable grayscale example in Figure 19-10 to its more challenging color counterpart in Color Plate 19-1.

Figure 19-10
The same active layer subject to the Darken blend mode. Only those pixels in the selection that are darker than the pixels in the underlying stucco texture remain visible.

⮞ **Lighten:** If you select this option, Photoshop applies colors in the active layer only if they are lighter than the corresponding pixels in the underlying image. Again, Photoshop compares the brightness levels in all channels of a full-color image. Examples of the Lighten blend mode appear in Figure 19-11 and Color Plate 19-1.

Figure 19-11
Our friend the active layer subject to the Lighten blend mode. Only those pixels in the selection that are lighter than the pixels in the underlying stucco texture remain visible.

⮞ **Difference and Exclusion:** The Difference mode was available in Photoshop 3, but Exclusion is new to Version 4. Even so, the two are kindred blending spirits.

Difference inverts lower layers according to the brightness values in the active layer. White inverts the background absolutely, black inverts it not at all, and all the other brightness values invert it to some degree in between. As a result, the stucco shows through the black areas of the lion heads in Figure 19-12, while the light areas of the banner have inverted the texture nearly to black.

Exclusion works just like Difference, except for one, er, difference. Shown in the second example of Figure 9-12, Exclusion sends medium colored pixels to gray, creating a lower contrast effect, just as Soft Light is a low-contrast version of Hard Light.

One of my favorite uses for the Difference and Exclusion modes is to create a *Difference sandwich*, in which you sandwich a filtered version of an image between two originals. I explain this technique and others in the upcoming section "Sandwiching a filtered image."

Figure 19-12
When you apply the Difference mode (top), white pixels invert the pixels beneath them, while black pixels leave the background untouched. The Exclusion mode (bottom) performs a similar effect, but instead of inverting medium colors, it changes them to gray.

Difference

Exclusion

- **Hue:** The Hue mode and the following three blend modes make use of the HSL color model to mix colors between active layer and underlying image. When you select Hue, Photoshop retains the hue values from the active layer and mixes them with the saturation and luminosity values from the underlying image. An example of this mode appears in the right column of Color Plate 19-1.

 I don't include grayscale figures for the Hue, Saturation, Color, and Luminosity blend modes for the simple reason that these modes affect color images only. In fact, all four options are dimmed when editing a grayscale image.

- **Saturation:** When you select this option, Photoshop retains the saturation values from the active layer and mixes them with the hue and luminosity values from the underlying image. This mode rarely results in anything but very subtle effects, as demonstrated by the bright orange Saturn in Color Plate 19-1. You'll usually want to apply it in combination with some other blend mode. For example, after applying a random blend mode to a layer, you might duplicate the layer and then apply the Saturation mode to either boost or downplay the colors, much like printing a gloss or matte coating over the image.

- **Color:** This option combines hue and saturation. Photoshop retains both the hue and saturation values from the active layer and mixes them with the luminosity values from the underlying image. Because the saturation portion of the Color mode has such a slight effect, Color frequently produces an almost identical effect to Hue. For example, the Hue and Color versions of Saturn in Color Plate 19-1 are very similar, with the former appearing only slightly less bright than the latter.

- **Luminosity:** The Luminosity blend mode retains the lightness values from the active layer and mixes them with the hue and saturation values from the underlying image. An example of this mode appears in the lower right corner in Color Plate 19-1. Here Saturn appears every bit as clearly defined as the Normal example in the upper left corner, but it assumes the orange color of its Jupiterian background. So just as the Color mode uses the layer to colorize its background, the Luminosity mode uses the background to colorize the layer.

Blend mode madness

Remember that scene in *Amadeus* where Mozart is telling the king about some opera or other he's writing — "Marriage of Franz Joseph Haydn" or something like that — and he's bragging about how many folks he has singing on stage at the same time? Remember that scene? Oh, you're not even trying. Anyway, you can do that same thing with Photoshop. Not with melody or recitative or anything like that, but with imagery. Just as Mozart might juggle several different melodies and harmonies at once, you can juggle layers upon layers of images, each filtered differently and mixed differently with the images below it.

Predicting the outcome of these monumental compositions takes a brain the magnitude of Mozart's. But screwing around with different settings takes no intelligence at all, which is where I come in.

The hierarchy of blend modes

The most direct method for juggling multiple images is "sandwiching." By this I mean placing a heavily filtered version of an image between two originals. This technique is based on the principal that most blend modes — all but Multiply, Screen, Difference, and Exclusion — change depending on which of two images is on top.

For example, Figure 19-13 shows two layers, A and B, and what happens when I blend them with the Overlay mode. When the leaf is on top, as in the third example, the Overlay mode favors the woman; but when the woman appears on the top layer, the Overlay mode favors the leaf.

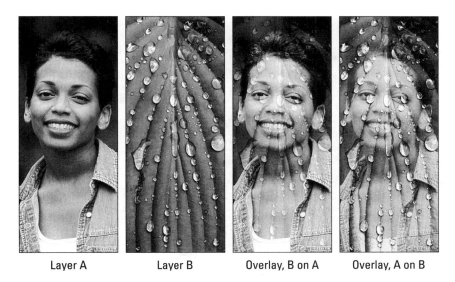

| Layer A | Layer B | Overlay, B on A | Overlay, A on B |

Figure 19-13
After establishing two layers, woman and leaf, I placed
the leaf on top and applied Overlay to get the third image.
Then I switched the order of the layers and applied the
Overlay mode to the woman to get the last image.

As I mentioned earlier, the Overlay mode always favors the lower layer. Its opposite, Hard Light, favors the active layer. Therefore, I could have achieved the exact effect shown in the third example of Figure 19-13 by placing the leaf underneath and setting the woman layer to Hard Light. Flip-flop the layers and apply Hard Light to the leaf to get the last example.

Other blend modes have opposites as well. Take the Normal mode, for example. When you apply Normal, whichever image is on top is the one that you see. However, if you change the Opacity, you reveal the underlying image. At 50 percent Opacity, it doesn't matter which image is on top. The color of every pair of pixels in both images is merely averaged. So an inverse relationship exists. If the filtered image is on top, an Opacity setting of 25 percent produces the same effect as if you reversed the order of the images and changed the Opacity to 75 percent.

The other obvious opposites are Color and Luminosity. If I were to position the green leaf in front of the woman and apply Color, the woman would turn green. The very same thing would happen if I placed the woman in front and applied Luminosity.

The moral of this minutia is that the order in which you stack your layers is as important as the blend modes you apply. Even filters that have no stacking opposites — Soft Light, Color Dodge, Hue, and others — will produce different effects depending on which layer is on top. Just for your general edification, Figure 19-14 and possibly more enlightening Color Plate 19-2 show a few examples.

Soft Light   Color Dodge   Color Burn

B on A

A on B

Figure 19-14
Examples of a few additional blend modes with the leaf on the front layer (top row) and the woman in front (bottom row).

Sandwiching a filtered image

When you sandwich a filtered image between two originals — which, as you may recall, is what all this is leading up to — you can lessen the effect of the filter and achieve different effects than those I discussed in Chapter 15. Layers and blend modes give you the flexibility to experiment as much as you want and for as long as you please.

In Color Plate 19-3, I copied the woman's face to a new layer, then I applied Filter ⇨ Sketch ⇨ Charcoal with the foreground color set to dark purple and the background color set to green. The top row of images in the color plate show what happened when I used three different blend modes — Hard Light, Color, and Difference — to mix the Charcoal image with the underlying original.

I next cloned the background layer and moved it above the Charcoal layer, so that the filtered image resided between two originals, creating a sandwich. The originals are the bread of the sandwich, and the Charcoal layer is the meat (or the eggplant, for you vegetarians). The bottom row demonstrates the effects of applying each of three blend modes to the top slice of bread, which interacts with the blend mode applied to the Charcoal meat shown above. For example, in the second column, I applied the Hard Light mode to the filtered image to achieve the top effect. Then I created the top layer and applied the Soft Light mode to get the bottom effect.

Creating a Difference sandwich

Ask your local deli guy, and he'll tell you that everyone has a favorite sandwich. Where blend modes are concerned, my favorite is the Difference sandwich. By applying Difference to both the filtered layer and the cloned original on top, you effectively invert the filter into the original image, and then reinvert the image to create a more subtle and utterly unique effect.

Figure 9-15 and Color Plate 19-4 show a small sampling of the several thousand possible variations on the Difference sandwich theme. In the top rows of both figures, I've vigorously applied a series of standard filters — so vigorously, in fact, that I've pretty well ruined the image. But no fear. By stacking it on top of the original, cloning the original on top of it, and applying the Difference mode to both layers, you can restore much of the original image detail, as shown in the bottom examples of the two figures. (I corrected the colors of the images by adding an adjustment layer on top of the sandwich, but otherwise you see the effects in their raw form.)

 A few notes about the Difference sandwich. First of all, the effect doesn't work nearly so well if you start reducing the Opacity values. Second, try using the Exclusion mode instead of Difference if you want to lower the contrast. And finally, Difference is one of those few blend modes that produces the same effect regardless of how you order the layers. This means you can filter either the middle layer or the bottom layer in the sandwich and get the exact same effect. But the top layer must be the original image.

Gaussian Blur   Radial Blur   High Pass

Filtered image

Inside sandwich

Figure 19-15
Three different filtering effects as they appear on their own (top row) and when inserted into a Difference sandwich (bottom row).

Dropping Out and Forcing Through

When you double-click on a layer name in the Layers palette, Photoshop displays the Layer Options dialog box shown in Figure 19-16. In addition to permitting you to name a layer, change the Opacity value, and do some other stuff that I've already covered in this book, you can drop out pixels in the active layer and force through pixels from lower layers according to their brightness values.

This feature has gone through more changes than a chameleon. In Photoshop 2.0, the Paste Controls dialog box was designed specifically to accommodate pasted images. In Photoshop 2.5, the Composite Controls dialog box was the only way to apply blend modes. Photoshop 3.0 did away with this dialog box for floating selections and made it exclusively applicable to layers. In Version 3.0.5, it once again became available for floaters (mostly because I complained, I think — no one else seemed to care). And now in Photoshop 4.0, floating selections are once again out of the picture. Sometimes I miss those old days.

Figure 19-16
When editing a layer, you
can access a dialog box of
options to selectively mix the
colors in the active layer with
the colors in the image
below.

After that bit of unnecessary nostalgia, let me take this opportunity to announce that the Layer Options dialog box offers the following eight options, which have changed little over time:

- **Name:** Use this option box to change the layer name that appears in the Layers palette.

- **Opacity:** The Opacity option box enables you to specify the translucency of the active layer. This option works identically to the Opacity slider bar in the Layers palette.

- **Mode:** Here's where you select one of the 17 blend modes you could already access in the Layers palette pop-up menu.

- **Group with Previous Layer:** Select this option to combine the active layer and the one below it into a clipping group, as discussed in the "Masking groups of layers" section of Chapter 13. I ignored this option in Chapter 13 because it's easier to simply Option-click on the horizontal line between the two layers to convert them to a clipping group.

- **Blend If:** Select a color channel from the Blend If pop-up menu to apply the effects of the slider bars beneath the menu to one color channel independently of the others. When the Gray option is active, as it is by default, your changes affect all color channels equally. (To my knowledge, this is the only instance where Gray means all color channels; elsewhere, Gray means a gray composite, just like Gray ought to mean.) Just for the record, the Opacity value and Mode option affect all channels regardless of the color channel you select from Blend If.

- **This Layer:** This slider bar lets you exclude ranges of colors according to brightness values in the active layer. When you exclude colors by dragging the black triangle to the right or the white triangle to the left, the colors disappear from view.

✎ **Underlying:** This slider forces colors from the underlying layers to poke through the active layer. Any colors not included in the range set by the black and white triangles cannot be covered and are therefore visible regardless of the colors in the active layer.

✎ **Preview:** Select the Preview check box to continually update the image window every time you adjust a setting.

The slider bars are far too complicated to explain in a bulleted list. To find out more about these options as well as the Blend If pop-up menu, read the following sections.

Color exclusion sliders

Drag the triangles along the This Layer slider bar to abandon those pixels in the active layer whose colors fall within a specified range of brightness values. You can abandon dark pixels by dragging the left slider triangle or light pixels by dragging the right slider triangle. Figure 19-17 shows examples of each. To create the top example, I dragged the left slider bar until the value immediately to the right of the *This Layer* label read 50, thereby deleting pixels whose brightness values were 50 or less. To create the bottom example, I dragged the right slider triangle until the second value read 180, deleting pixels with brightness values of 180 or higher.

Drag the triangles along the Underlying slider bar to force pixels in the underlying image to show through if they fall within a specified brightness range. To force dark pixels in the underlying image to show through, drag the left slider triangle; to force light pixels to show through, drag the right slider triangle.

To achieve the effect in the top example in Figure 19-18, I dragged the left slider triangle until the value immediately to the right of the *Underlying* label read 120, forcing the pixels in the stucco pattern that had brightness values of 120 or lower to show through. In the second example, I dragged the right slider triangle until the second value read 180, uncovering pixels at the bright end of the spectrum.

Figure 19-17
The results of moving the left This Layer slider triangle to 50 (top) and, after Option-clicking on the Reset button, dragging the right slider triangle to 180 (bottom).

Figure 19-18
The results of moving the left Underlying slider triangle to 120 (top) and then resetting the left triangle back to 0 and moving the right triangle to 180 (bottom).

Fuzziness

The problem with abandoning and forcing colors with the slider bars is that you achieve some pretty harsh color transitions. Both Figures 19-17 and 19-18 bear witness to this fact. Talk about your jagged edges! Luckily, you can soften the color transitions by abandoning and forcing pixels gradually over a fuzziness range, which works much like the Fuzziness value in the Color range dialog box, leaving some pixels opaque and tapering others off into transparency.

To taper off the opacity of pixels in either the active layers or the underlying image, Option-drag one of the triangles in the appropriate slider bar. The triangle splits into two halves, and the corresponding value above the slider bar splits into two values separated by a slash, as demonstrated in Figure 19-19.

Figure 19-19
Option-drag a slider triangle to split it in half. You can then specify a fuzziness range across which brightness values will gradually fade into transparency.

The left triangle half represents the beginning of the fuzziness range — that is, the brightness values at which the pixels begin to fade into or away from view. The right half represents the end of the range — that is, the point at which the pixels are fully visible or invisible.

Figures 19-20 and 19-21 show softened versions of the effects from Figures 19-17 and 19-18. In the top example of Figure 19-20, for example, I adjusted the range of the left This Layer slider triangle so that the value immediately to the right of the *This Layer* label read 30/70. The result is a much smoother effect than achieved in the top example in Figure 19-17. In the bottom example of Figure 19-20, I changed the range of the right This Layer slider triangle so that the second value read 120/230.

Figure 19-20
The results of adjusting the fuzziness range of the left This Layer slider triangle to 30/70 (top) and that of the right This Layer slider triangle to 120/230 (bottom).

In Figure 19-21, I applied fuzziness ranges with the Underlying slider. In fact, both examples in the figure are the result of applying the same value, 120/180, to opposite Underlying slider triangles. In the top example, all brightness values under 120 gradually extending to values up to 180 show through the active layer. In the second example, all brightness values above 180 gradually extending down to 120 show through. The resulting two images look very much like sand art. (The next thing you know, I'll be showing you how to create string art and black velvet Elvises.)

Color channel options

The options in the Blend If pop-up menu are applicable exclusively to the settings you apply using the This Layer and Underlying slider bars. When you work with a grayscale image, the Blend If pop-up menu offers one option only — Black — meaning that the Blend If option has no effect on grayscale editing. However, when you work in the RGB, CMYK, or Lab mode, the Layer Options dialog box enables you to abandon and force ranges of pixels independently within each color channel.

Figure 19-21
The results of adjusting the fuzziness range of both the left (top) and right (bottom) Underlying slider triangles to 120/180.

To do so, select a color channel from the Blend If pop-up menu and then set the slider triangles as desired. Each time you select a different Blend If option, the slider triangles retract to the positions at which you last set them for that color channel.

Using Channel Operation Commands

Image ⇨ Apply Image and Image ⇨ Calculations provide access to Photoshop's *channel operations*, which composite one or more channels with others according to predefined mathematical calculations. Although once hailed as Photoshop's most powerful capabilities, channel operations have been eclipsed by the standard and more accessible functions available from the Layers and Channels palettes. One day, I suspect Adobe will scrap Apply Image and Calculations altogether. But until that day, I will dutifully document them both.

The Apply Image and Calculations commands allow you to merge one or two identically sized images using 12 of the 17 blend modes discussed earlier plus two additional modes, Add and Subtract. In a nutshell, the commands duplicate the process of dragging and dropping one image onto another (or cloning an image onto a new layer), and using the blend mode and Opacity settings in the Layers palette to mix the two images together.

Although Apply Image and Calculations are more similar than different, each command fulfills a specific — if not entirely unique — function:

> ↪ **Apply Image:** This command takes an open image and merges it with the foreground image (or takes the foreground image and composites it onto itself). You can apply the command to either the full-color image or one or more of the individual channels.

> ↪ **Calculations:** The Calculations command works on individual channels only. It takes a channel from one image, mixes it with a channel from another (or the same) image, and puts the result inside an open image or in a new image window.

The primary advantage of these commands over other, more straightforward compositing methods is that they allow you to access and composite the contents of individual color channels without a lot of selecting, copying and pasting, cloning, floating, and layering. You also get two extra blend modes, Add and Subtract, which may prove useful on a rainy day.

The Apply Image and Calculations commands provide previewing options, so that you can see how an effect will look in the image window. But thanks to the share quantity of unfriendly options offered by the two commands, I suggest that you use them on a very occasional basis. The Calculations command can be a handy way to combine masks and layer transparencies to create precise selection outlines. And Apply Image is good for compositing images in different color models, such as RGB and Lab (as I explain in the "Mixing images in different color modes" section later in this chapter).

But if your time is limited and you want to concentrate your efforts on learning Photoshop's most essential features, then feel free to skip Apply Image and Calculations. I assure you, you won't be missing much.

The Apply Image command

Channel operations work by taking one or more channels from an image, called the *source*, and duplicating them to another image, called the *target*. When you use the Apply Image command, the foreground image is always the target, and you can select only one source image. Photoshop then takes the source and target, mixes them together, and puts the result in the target image. Therefore, the target image is the only image that the command actually changes. The source image remains unaffected.

When you choose Image ➪ Apply Image, Photoshop displays the dialog box shown in Figure 19-22. Notice that you can select from a pop-up menu of images to specify the Source, but the Target item — listed just above the Blending box — is fixed. This is the active layer in the foreground image.

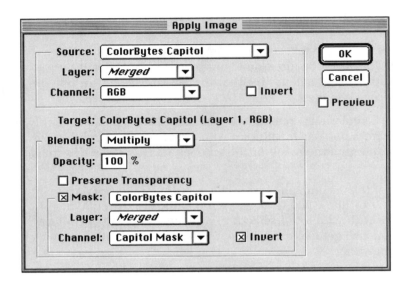

Figure 19-22
The Apply Image command lets you mix one source image with a target image and make the result the new target.

If this sounds a little dense, just think of it this way: The source image is the floating selection and the target is the underlying original. Meanwhile, the Blending options are the blend modes pop-up menu and Opacity slider in the Layers palette.

Using the Apply Image command is a five-step process. You can always simply choose the command and hope for the best, but you'll get the most use out of it if you do the following:

STEPS   Applying the Apply Image Command

Step 1.   **Open the two images that you want to mix.** If you want to mix the image with itself to create some effect, just open the one image.

Step 2.   **Make sure that the two images are exactly the same size, down to the last pixel.** Use the crop tool and Image Size command as necessary. (You don't have to worry about this step when mixing an image with itself.)

Step 3.   **Inside the target image, switch to the channel and layer that you want to edit.** If you want to edit all channels, press ⌘-tilde (~) to remain in the composite view.

When you're editing a single channel, I strongly advise you to display all channels on-screen. For example, after pressing ⌘-1 to switch to the red channel, click in front of the RGB item in the Channels palette to display the eyeball icon and show all channels. Only one channel is active, but all are visible. This way, you can see how your edits inside the Apply Image dialog box will affect the entire image, not just the one channel.

Step 4. **Select the portion of the target image that you want to edit.** If you want to affect the entire image, don't select anything.

Step 5. **Choose Image ⇨ Apply Image and have at it.**

Obviously, that last step is a little more difficult than it sounds. That's why I've put together the following list to explain how all those options in the Apply Image dialog box work:

⇨ **Source:** The Source pop-up menu contains the name of the foreground image as well as any other images that are both open and exactly the same size as the foreground image. If the image you want to merge is not available, you must not have been paying much attention to Step 2. Press Escape to cancel, then resize and crop as needed, choose Image ⇨ Apply Image, and try again.

⇨ **Layer:** This pop-up menu lists all layers in the selected source image. If the image doesn't have any layers, Background is your only option. Otherwise, select the layer that contains the prospective source image. Select Merged to mix all visible layers in the source image with the target image.

⇨ **Channel:** Select the channels that you want to mix from this pop-up menu. Both composite views and individual color and mask channels are included. Keep in mind that you'll be mixing these channels with the channels that you made available in the target image before choosing the command.

For example, if the target image is an RGB image shown in the full-color composite view, and you choose RGB from the Channel pop-up menu in the Apply Image dialog box, Photoshop mixes the red, green, and blue channels in the source image with the corresponding red, green, and blue channels in the target image. However, if you switched to the red channel before choosing Apply Image and then selected the RGB option, the program mixes a composite grayscale version of the RGB source image with the red channel in the target and leaves the other target channels unaffected.

⇨ **Selection, Transparency, and Layer Mask:** If a portion of the source image is selected, the pop-up menu offers a Selection option, which lets you apply the selection outline as if it were a grayscale image, just like a selection viewed in the quick mask mode. If you selected a specific layer from the Layer pop-up menu, you'll find a Transparency option that represents the transparency mask. If the layer includes its own layer mask, a Layer Mask option also appears.

None of the three options is particularly useful when you work in the composite view of the target image; you'll usually want to apply the Selection, Transparency, or Layer Mask option only to a single channel, as described in "The Calculations command" section toward the end of this chapter. (For an exception, see the upcoming tip.)

- **Invert:** Select this check box to invert the contents of the source image before compositing it with the target image. This option permits you to experiment with different effects. The last example in Color Plate 19-5, for example, shows one use for the Invert check box. I inverted the *b* channel before compositing it with the RGB image to create an early dawn effect.

- **Target:** You can't change this item. It merely shows which image, which channels, and which layers are being affected by the command.

- **Blending:** This pop-up menu offers access to 12 of the blend modes I discussed in "The remaining 17 blend modes" section earlier in this chapter. The Dissolve, Hue, Saturation, Color, and Luminosity options are missing. (Darken and Lighten have inexplicably been renamed Darker and Lighter, though they work just the same.) Two additional options, Add and Subtract, are discussed in the "Add and Subtract" section later in this chapter.

- **Opacity:** By now, I gather you're well aware of how this one works.

- **Preserve Transparency:** When you're editing a layer in the target image — that is, you activated a specific layer before choosing Image ➪ Apply Image — the Preserve Transparency check box becomes available. Select it to protect transparent portions of the layer from any compositing, much as if the transparent portions were not selected and are therefore masked.

- **Mask:** Select this option to mask off a portion of the source image. I already mentioned that you can specify the exact portion of the target image you want to edit by selecting that portion before choosing the Apply Image command. But you can also control which portion of the source image is composited on top of the target through the use of a mask. When you select the Mask check box, three new pop-up menus and an Invert check box appear at the bottom of the Apply Image dialog box. For complete information on these options, see the upcoming "Compositing with a mask" section.

- **Result:** If you press the Option key when choosing Image ➪ Apply Image, Photoshop appends one additional option — the Result pop-up menu — at the end of the Apply Image dialog box. This option lets you send the result of the operation to a separate image window, layer, or channel. This can be useful if you don't want to upset the contents of the foreground window, if you want to send the result to a separate layer for further compositing, or if you just want to edit a mask. (This last operation is generally made easier by the Calculations command, as described in the "Combining masks" section near the end of this chapter.)

One of my favorite reasons to Option-choose Apply Image is to convert a mask in one image to a selection outline in another image of equal size. You can accomplish this without the Apply Image command by converting the mask to a selection and then dragging and dropping it, but Apply Image lets you do it in one step.

Here's how it works: Go to the receiving image — the one you want to transfer the selection into — and Option-choose Apply Image. (Be sure that nothing in the image is already selected, or the Result pop-up menu will not appear.) Select the identically sized image that contains the mask from the Source pop-up menu, choose the mask channel name from the Channel pop-up menu, and choose Normal from the Blending menu. Then choose Selection from the Result pop-up menu and press Return.

Mixing images in different color modes

Throughout my laborious explanations of all those options in the Apply Image dialog box, I've been eagerly waiting to share with you the command's one truly unique capability. Image ➪ Apply Image is the only way to composite RGB and Lab images while leaving them set to their separate color modes. For example, you could mix the lightness channel from the Lab image with the red channel from the RGB image, the *a* channel with the green channel, and the *b* channel with the blue channel. By contrast, you'd have to composite the channels one at a time if there were no Apply Image command. (If you were to simply drag and drop a Lab image into an RGB image, Photoshop would automatically convert the image to the RGB color space, which results in a very different effect.)

To help make things a little more clear, Color Plate 19-5 shows four examples of an image composited onto itself using the Hard Light blend mode (which you select from the Blending pop-up menu, as I'll cover shortly). The first example shows the result of selecting the RGB image as both source and target. As always, this exaggerates the colors in the image and enhances contrast, but retains the same basic color composition as before.

The other examples in the color plate show what happened when I duplicated the image by choosing Image ➪ Duplicate, converted the duplicate to the Lab mode (Mode ➪ Lab Color), and then composited the Lab duplicate with the RGB original. To do this, I switched to the RGB image, chose Image ➪ Apply Image, and selected the Lab image from the Source pop-up menu. In the top right example, I chose Lab from the Channel pop-up menu to blend each of the Lab channels with one of the RGB channels — lightness with red, and so on. Though I stuck with the Hard Light blend mode, you can see that the effect is very different. In the bottom left example, I chose Lightness from the Channel pop-up menu, which mixed the lightness channel with all three RGB channels. And in the bottom right image, I chose *b* from the Channel pop-up menu and selected the Invert check box, which inverted the *b* channel before applying it.

 You cannot mix an entire CMYK image with an RGB or Lab image, because the images contain different numbers of channels. In other words, while you can mix individual channels from CMYK, RGB, and Lab images, you can't intermix the channels — cyan with red, magenta with green, and so on. In other words, CMYK does not appear as an option inside the Channel pop-up menu when you edit an RGB image. In other words. . . oh, nuts, that's enough of that.

Compositing with a mask

I said that I'd go into a little more depth about the Mask option in this section, and now it's time to owe up. All the Mask option does is provide a method for you to import only a selected portion of the source image into the target image. Select the Mask check box and choose the image that contains the mask from the pop-up menu on the immediate right. As with the Source pop-up menu, the Mask menu lists only those images that are open and happen to be the exact same size as the target image. If necessary, select the layer on which the mask appears from the Layer pop-up menu. Then select the specific mask channel from the final pop-up menu. This doesn't have to be a mask channel; you can use any color channel as a mask.

After you select all the necessary options, the mask works like so: Where the mask is white, the source image shows through and mixes in with the target image, just as if it were a selected portion of the floating image. Where the mask is black, the source image is absent, as if you had ⌘-dragged around that portion of the floating selection with the lasso or some other selection tool, leaving the target entirely protected. Gray values in the mask mix the source and target with progressive emphasis on the target as the grays darken.

If you prefer to swap the masked and unmasked areas of the source image, select the Invert check box at the bottom of the dialog box. Now, where the mask is black, you see the source image; where the mask is white, you don't.

The first example in Color Plate 19-6 shows a mask that I used to select the Capitol dome while protecting the sky. I prepared this mask and put it in a separate mask channel. In the other examples in the color plate, I again composited the RGB and Lab versions of the image — as in the previous section — using various blend modes. No matter how dramatically the Apply Image command affected the dome, the sky remained unscathed, thanks to the mask. If the Mask option had not been turned on, for example, the top right image in Color Plate 19-4 would have looked exactly like the corresponding image in Color Plate 19-3.

You can even use a selection outline or layer as a mask. If you select some portion of the source image before switching to the target image and choosing Image ⇨ Apply Image, you can access the selection by choosing — what else? — Selection from the Channel pop-up menu at the very bottom of the dialog box. Those pixels from the source image that fall inside the selection remain visible; those that do not are transparent. Use the Invert check box to inverse the selection outline. To use the boundaries of a layer selected from the Layer pop-up menu as a mask, choose the Transparency option from the Channel menu. Where the layer is opaque, the source image is opaque (assuming that the Opacity option is set to 100 percent, of course); where the layer is transparent, so too is the source image.

Add and Subtract

The Add and Subtract blend modes found in the Apply Image dialog box (and also in the Calculations dialog box) work a bit like the Custom filter that I discussed in Chapter 17. However, instead of multiplying brightness values by matrix numbers and calculating a sum, as the Custom filter does, these modes add and subtract the brightness values of pixels in different channels.

The Add option adds the brightness value of each pixel in the source image to that of its corresponding pixel in the target image. The Subtract option takes the brightness value of each pixel in the target image and subtracts the brightness value of its corresponding pixel in the source image. When you select either Add or Subtract, the Apply Image dialog box offers two additional option boxes, Scale and Offset. Photoshop divides the sum or difference of the Add or Subtract mode by the Scale value (from 1.000 to 2.000) and then adds the Offset value (from negative to positive 255).

If equations will help, here's the equation for the Add blend mode:

Resulting brightness value = (Target + Source) ÷ Scale + Offset

And here's the equation for the Subtract mode:

Resulting brightness value = (Target - Source) ÷ Scale + Offset

If equations only confuse you, just remember this: The Add option results in a destination image that is lighter than either source; the Subtract option results in a destination image that is darker than either source. If you want to darken the image further, raise the Scale value. To darken each pixel in the target image by a constant amount, which is useful when applying the Add option, enter a negative Offset value. If you want to lighten each pixel, as when applying the Subtract option, enter a positive Offset value.

Applying the Add command

The best way to demonstrate how these commands work is to offer an example. To create the effects shown in Figures 19-24 and 19-25, I began with the two images shown in Figure 19-23. The first image, Capitol Gray, is your everyday average grayscale image. The second image, Capitol Blur, took a little more work. I applied Filter ⇨ Other ⇨ Minimum to enlarge the dark regions of the image by a radius of 3 pixels and applied the Gaussian Blur filter with a radius of 6.0 pixels. I next used the Levels command to change the second Output Levels values to 140, thus uniformly darkening the image. (The Add and Subtract commands work best when neither target nor source contains large areas of white.) Finally, just for the sheer heck of it, I drew in some clouds and lightning bolts with the airbrush and smudge tools.

Figure 19-23
The target (left) and source (right) used to create the
effects shown in Figures 19-24 and 19-25.

After switching to the Capitol Gray image and choosing Image ⇨ Apply Image, I selected the Capitol Blur image from the Source pop-up menu. I was working with flat, grayscale images, so I didn't have to worry about the Layer and Channel options. I selected the Add option from the Blending pop-up menu and accepted the default Scale and Offset values of 1 and 0, respectively, to achieve the first example in Figure 19-24. Because the skies in both the target and source images were medium gray, they added up to white in the resulting image. The black areas in the source image helped prevent the colors inside the building from becoming overly light.

Figure 19-24
Two applications of the Add blend mode on the images
from Figure 19-23, one subject to Scale and Offset values
of 1 and 0 (left) and the other subject to values of 1.2 and
-60 (right).

Unfortunately, the image I created was a bit washed out. To improve the quality and
detail of the image, I changed the Scale value to 1.2 to slightly downplay the brightness values and entered an Offset value of -60 to darken the colors uniformly. The
result of this operation is the more satisfactory image shown in the second example
of Figure 19-24.

Applying the Subtract command

To create the first example in Figure 19-25, I selected the Subtract option from the
Blending pop-up menu, once again accepting the default Scale and Offset values of 1
and 0, respectively. This time, the sky turns pitch black because I subtracted the
medium gray of the Capitol Blur image from the medium gray of the Capitol Gray
image, leaving no brightness value at all. The building, however, remains a sparkling
white because most of that area in the Capitol Blur image is black. Subtracting black
from a color is like subtracting 0 from a number — it leaves the value unchanged.

The image seemed overly dark, so I lightened it by raising the Scale and Offset values. To create the second image in Figure 19-25, I upped the Scale value to 1.2, just
as in the second Add example, which actually darkened the image slightly. Then I
changed the Offset value to 60, thus adding 60 points of brightness value to each
pixel. This second image is more likely to survive reproduction with all detail intact.

Figure 19-25
Two applications of the Subtract command on the images
from Figure 19-23, one subject to Scale and Offset values of
1 and 0 (left) and the other subject to values of 1.2 and 60 (right).

The difference between Subtract and Difference

I've already shown examples of how the Difference mode inverts one image using the brightness values in another. But the math behind Difference is actually very similar to that behind Subtract. Like Subtract, the Difference option subtracts the brightness values in the source image from those in the target image. However, instead of treating negative values as black, as Subtract does, or allowing you to compensate for overly dark colors with the Scale and Offset options, Difference changes all calculations to positive values.

If the brightness value of a pixel in the target image is 20 and the brightness value of the corresponding pixel in the source image is 65, the Difference option performs the following equation: 20 - 65 = -35. It then takes the *absolute value* of -35 (or, in layman's terms, hacks off the minus sign) to achieve a brightness value of 35. Pretty easy stuff, huh?

Any divergence between the Subtract and Difference options becomes more noticeable on repeated applications. The top row of Figure 19-26, for example, shows the effect of applying the Subtract mode (left) versus the Difference mode (right). As before, I applied these commands to the Capitol Gray and Capitol Blur images from Figure 19-23.

As far as perceptible differences between the two images are concerned, the pixels that make up the bushes in the lower left corner of each image and those of the clouds along each image's right side are on the rebound in the Difference example. In effect, they became so dark that they are again lightening up. But that's about the extent of it.

In the second row of Figure 19-26, I applied the Subtract and Difference options a second time. Using the top left example in the figure as the target and the Capitol Blur image as the source, I achieved two very different results. When calculating the colors of the pixels in the sky, the Difference blend mode apparently encountered sufficiently low negative values that removing the minus signs left the sky ablaze with light. Everything dark is light again.

Figure 19-26
Repeated applications of the Subtract (left column) and
Difference (right column) commands.

The Calculations command

Though its options are nearly identical, the Calculations command performs a slightly different function than Apply Image. Rather than compositing a source image on top of the current target image, Image ➪ Calculations combines two source channels and puts the result in a target channel. You can use a single image for both sources, a source and the target, or all three. The target doesn't have to be the foreground image (although Photoshop previews the effect in the foreground image window). And the target can even be a new image. But the biggest difference is that instead of affecting entire full-color images, the Calculations command affects individual color channels only. Only one channel changes as a result of this command.

Choosing Image ⇨ Calculations displays the dialog box shown in Figure 19-27. Rather than explaining this dialog box option by option - I'd just end up wasting 35 pages and repeating myself every other sentence — I'll attack the topic in a little less structured fashion.

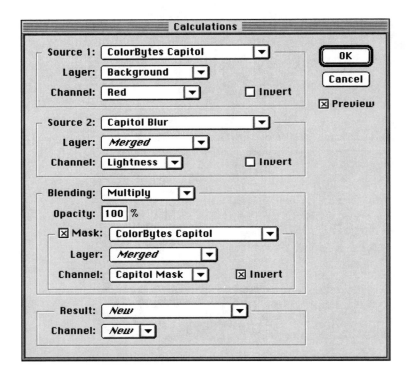

Figure 19-27
Use the Calculations command to mix two source channels and place them inside a new or existing target channel.

When you arrive inside the dialog box, you select your source images from the Source 1 and Source 2 pop-up menus. As with Apply Image, the images have to be exactly the same size. You can composite individual layers using the Layer menus. Select the channels you want to mix together from the Channel options. In place of the full-color options — RGB, Lab, CMYK — each Channel menu offers a Gray option, which represents the grayscale composite of all channels in an image.

The Blending pop-up menu offers the same 14 blend modes — including Add and Subtract — that are found in the Apply Image dialog box. But it's important to keep in mind how the Calculations dialog box organizes the source images when working with blend modes. The Source 1 image is equivalent to the source when using the Apply Image command (or the floating selection when compositing conventionally); the Source 2 image is equivalent to the target (or the underlying original). Therefore, choosing the Normal blend mode displays the Source 1 image. The Subtract command subtracts the Source 1 image from the Source 2 image.

Half of the blend modes perform identically regardless of which of the two images is Source 1 and which is Source 2. The other half — including Normal, Overlay, Soft Light, and Hard Light — produce different results based on the image you assign to each spot. But as long as you keep in mind that Source 1 is the floater — hey, it's at the top of the dialog box, right? — you should be okay.

 The only one that throws me off is Subtract, because I see Source 1 at the top of the dialog box and naturally assume that Photoshop will subtract Source 2, which is underneath it. Unfortunately, this is exactly opposite to the way it really works. If you find yourself similarly confused and set up the equation backwards, you can reverse it by selecting both Invert options. Source 2 minus Source 1 results in the exact same effect as an inverted Source 1 minus an inverted Source 2. (After all, the equation *(255 - Source 1) - (255 - Source 2)*, which represents an inverted Source 1 minus an inverted Source 2, simplifies down to *Source 2 - Source 1*. If math isn't your strong point, don't worry. I was just showing my work.)

As you can in the Apply Image dialog box, you can specify a mask using the Mask options in the Calculations dialog box. The difference here is that the mask applies to the first source image and protects the second one. So where the mask is white, the two sources mix together normally. Where the mask is black, you see the second source image only.

The Result options determine the target for the composited channels. If you select New from the Result pop-up menu, as in Figure 19-27, Photoshop creates a new grayscale image. Alternatively, you can stick the result of the composited channels in any channel inside any image that is the same size as the source images.

 If a dialog box full of 12-point Chicago type is too crowded and clunky for you, you can Option-choose Image ⇨ Calculations to display the text in 9-point Geneva. It's not the most exciting or useful function, but you may find it helpful.

Combining masks

As described for the Apply Image command, Selection, Transparency, and Layer Mask may be available as options from any of the Channel pop-up menus. But here they have more purpose. You can composite layer masks to form selection outlines, selection outlines to form masks, and all sorts of other pragmatic combinations.

Figure 19-28 shows how the Calculations command sees selected areas. Whether you're working with masks, selection outlines, transparency masks, or layer masks, the Calculations command sees the area as a grayscale image. So in Figure 19-28, the white areas are selected or opaque, and the black areas are deselected or transparent.

Figure 19-28
Two selections expressed as grayscale images (a.k.a. masks). The left image is the first source, and the right image is the second.

Source 1   Source 2

Assuming that I've chosen Image ⇨ Calculations and selected the images using the Source 1 and Source 2 options, the only remaining step is to select the proper blend mode from the Blending pop-up menu. Screen, Multiply, and Difference are the best solutions. The top row in Figure 19-29 shows the common methods for combining selection outlines. In the first example, I added the two together using the Screen mode, just as in the previous steps. In fact, Screening masks and adding selection outlines are exact equivalents. To subtract the Source 1 selection from Source 2, I inverted the former (by selecting the Invert check box in the Source 1 area) and applied the Multiply blend mode. To find the intersection of the two masks, I simply applied Multiply without inverting.

But the Calculations command doesn't stop at the standard three — add, subtract, and intersect. The bottom row of Figure 19-29 shows three methods of combining selection outlines that are not possible using keyboard shortcuts. For example, if I invert the Source 1 mask and combine it with the Screen mode, I add the inverse of the elliptical selection and add it to the polygonal one. The Difference mode adds the portion of the elliptical selection that doesn't intersect the polygonal one and subtracts the intersection. And inverting Source 1 and then applying Difference retains the intersection, subtracts the portion of the polygonal selection that is not intersected, and inverts the elliptical selection where it does not intersect. These may not be options you use every day, but they are extremely powerful if you can manage to wrap your brain around them.

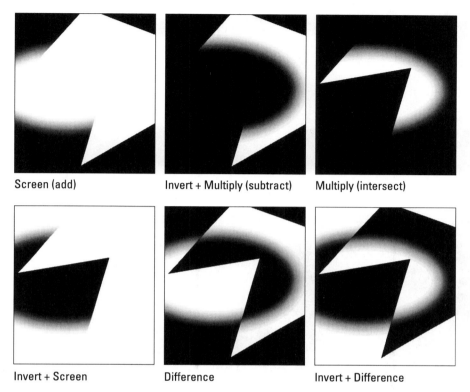

Screen (add)   Invert + Multiply (subtract)   Multiply (intersect)

Invert + Screen   Difference   Invert + Difference

Figure 19-29
Starting with the masks shown in Figure 19-28, I combined
them in traditional (top row) and nontraditional (bottom row)
ways using the Calculations command.

Depending on how well you've been keeping up with this discussion, you may be
asking yourself, "Why not apply Lighter or Add in place of Screen, or Darker or
Subtract in place of Multiply?" The reason becomes evident when you combine two
soft selections. Suppose that I blurred the Source 2 mask to give it a feathered edge.
Figure 19-30 shows the results of combining the newly blurred polygonal mask with
the elliptical mask using a series of blend modes. In the top row, I added the two
selection outlines together using the Lighter, Add, and Screen modes. Lighter results
in harsh corner transitions, while Add cuts off the interior edges. Only Screen does
it just right. The bottom row of the figure shows the results of subtracting the elliptical mask from the polygonal one by occasionally inverting the elliptical mask and
applying Darker, Subtract, and Multiply. Again, Darker results in sharp corners. The
Subtract mode eliminates the need to invert the elliptical marquee, but it brings the
black area too far into the blurred edges, resulting in an overly abrupt interior cusp.
Multiply ensures that all transitions remain smooth as silk.

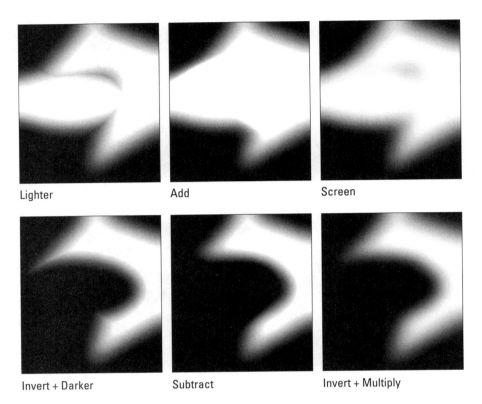

Lighter   Add   Screen

Invert + Darker   Subtract   Invert + Multiply

Figure 19-30
When adding softened selections (top row) and subtracting
them (bottom row), the Screen and Multiply modes provide
the most even and continuous transitions.

The reason for the success of the Screen and Multiply modes is that they mix colors together. Lighter and Darker simply settle on the color of one source image or the other — no mixing occurs — hence the harsh transitions. Add and Subtract rely on overly simplistic arithmetic equations — as I explained earlier, they really just add and subtract brightness values — which result in steep fall-off and build-up rates; in other words, there are cliffs of color transition where there ought to be rolling hills. Both Screen and Multiply soften the transitions using variations on color averaging that makes colors incrementally lighter or darker.

Creating Graphics for the Web

In This Chapter

- �» Accounting for differences between Mac and PC monitors
- �» Shrinking file sizes without sacrificing (too much) quality
- �» How and when to use the JPEG format
- �» Saving progressive JPEG images
- �» Indexing images down to their most essential colors
- �» Saving indexed images in the GIF format
- �» Using the GIF89a Export filter
- �» Everything you wanted to know about the PNG format

The World of Web Imagery

The Internet may well be the most chaotic, anarchic force ever unleashed on the planet. It has no boundaries, it has no unifying purpose, it is controlled by no one, and it is owned by everyone. It's also incomprehensibly enormous, larger than any single government or business entity on the planet. If the ten richest men in the world pooled their resources, they still couldn't purchase all the computers and cables that keep the Internet alive. In terms of pure size and volume, the Web makes the great thoroughfares of the Roman empire look like a paper boy's route.

As a result, it's impossible to get a bead on the World Wide Web. With several million hands in the pie, and several million more hands groping for a slice, the Web is as subject to casual comprehension as are the depths of the oceans, the infinity of the cosmos, or the meaning of life. And the Web mutates faster than any of those forces. Something just changed while you were reading the last sentence. An important new Web technology hit the market during the sentence you're reading now. It's enough to drive any sane human bonkers.

Fortunately, I'm not altogether sane, so I find the Web quite intriguing. Even so, whatever I write today will no doubt change by the time you read this. We may all have the Internet cabled into our homes, animation and video images may rule the day, and the Web as I presently know it may be stone cold dead. All of this will happen gradually, of course — even lightning-fast changes take some time to occur. And were a new technology to come along that combined the power of Java, the versatility of HTML, and the ease of use of a bar of soap, every one of the untold millions of Web content providers would continue to create their millions of different pages in millions of different ways. The most brilliant of technologies is forever mitigated by the willingness of humans to adapt to it.

I include the preceding by way of a disclaimer for the general thesis of this chapter, which is simply this: Bitmapped graphics rule the Web. Sure, text-based content, file libraries, and hyperlinks are the main stock and trade of the Internet, but the graphics are what make the Web intelligible and invite us to come back for more. Graphics have brought the masses to the Web, images account for 90 percent of all Web graphics, and Photoshop is the world's number one image editor. As a result, Photoshop has become as inextricably linked to the Web as Netscape Navigator, Adobe PageMill, RealAudio, and a hundred other programs. It's just another happy accident in Photoshop's unexpected runaway success.

The smaller, the speedier

If you have any experience with the Web, then you know that small images are speedy images. By "small," I don't mean small in physical size (although that often helps). I mean small in terms of disk space. A 20K image that fills your screen takes less time to download and display than a 50K file no larger than a sticky note. It's the act of getting the data through the cables and phone lines that takes the time; by comparison, the time it takes your browser software to interpret the data is insignificant.

Therefore, the main focus of this chapter is file size. How can you squish the finest graphics you're capable of creating into the smallest amount of disk space with the least amount of sacrifice? This is the single most important challenge facing Web artists today. And while the Web-wide world is certain to change by the time you read this, I have a sneaking suspicion that small and speedy will remain the watchwords for some time to come.

Preparing screen images

Many Web artists come from a background in print media, and while much of what you've learned while preparing printed photographs is equally applicable to online artwork, there are differences. Foremost among them, you never need worry about converting images to the CMYK color space. All Web graphics are RGB (or a subset of indexed colors or gray values). This is extremely good news, because it means that for once in the history of electronic publishing, what you see on-screen is really, truly what you're going to get.

Well, almost. Ignoring the differences in the ways people perceive colors and the variances in ambient light from one office or study to the next, there are measurable differences between monitors. Some monitors produce highly accurate colors, others — especially older screens —are entirely unreliable. But more importantly, some screens display images more brightly than others.

If you're a typical Macintosh user with an Apple-brand monitor, then you're cursed with a very bright screen. Apple monitors — and many non-Apple brands developed for the Mac — are calibrated to a gamma of 1.8. Meanwhile, most PC monitors are calibrated to 2.2, which is roughly equivalent to a standard television.

 Higher gamma values translate to darker displays because they indicate degrees of compensation. That is, an image has to be lightened only to 1.8 on the Mac to look as light as an image corrected to 2.2 on the PC.

Just because you use a Mac doesn't mean you have a light screen. Monitors from major PC brokers — including NEC, ViewSonic, and others — are usually calibrated to PC standards even when sold with Macs. Also, if you've calibrated your screen display using Photoshop's Gamma control panel or some other utility, then you may have already accounted for your overly light monitor. But if you own a standard Apple screen, and you've grown so accustomed to it that you look at PC monitors and think, "How can you see anything on this dim screen?" then you need to compensate for the inevitable brightness shift in your images.

Figure 20-1 shows a test image subjected to various brightness settings. The upper left example shows how the image looks when corrected for a typical Macintosh screen. The upper right example shows that very same image displayed on a typical PC monitor. Most of the folks who visit your Web page are seeing the darker of the two images.

The solution is to strike a compromise. Choose Image ⇨ Adjust ⇨ Levels (⌘-L) and raise the gamma (the middle Input Levels value) to between 1.2 and 1.25. Although the result will look a tad bit washed out on your screen, it'll look better on most monitors. The bottom two examples in Figure 20-1 show what happens when I raise the gamma to 1.25 and display the image on a Mac screen (left) and a PC screen (right). A little light on one, a little dark on the other, but ultimately an equitable compromise.

Corrected for Mac   Very dark for PC

Figure 20-1
Although most Web images are prepared on the Mac, they are more often viewed on PCs. Therefore, Mac users have to be aware that PC screens are typically darker.

Slightly light for Mac   Slightly dark for PC

More rules of Web imagery

Here are a few more items to remember when creating Web graphics:

- **Resolution doesn't matter:** Regardless of the Resolution value you enter into the Image Size dialog box, the Web browser displays one image pixel for every screen pixel (unless you specify an alternative image size in your HTML file). All that counts, therefore, is the pixel measurements — the number of pixels wide by the number of pixels tall.

∞ **GIF, JPEG, and PNG:** GIF and JPEG are the file formats of choice for Web graphics. GIF supports just 256 colors, so it's better for high-contrast artwork and text. JPEG applies lossy compression, so it's better for photographs and other continuous-tone images. The upstart format is PNG, which is essentially a 24-bit version of GIF designed for small full-color images that you don't want to compress.

∞ **Indexing colors:** Before you can save an image in the GIF format, you have to reduce the number of colors to 256 or fewer. Photoshop uses a technique called *indexing*, which reassigns colors according to a fixed index, which serves much the same purpose as the index in the back of this book.

∞ **Turn off image previews:** To keep your file sizes as small as possible, turn off the image previews. Go to the Saving Files panel of the Preferences dialog box (⌘-K, ⌘-2) and set the Image Previews option to Ask When Saving. Then when saving the image, turn off all Image Previews check boxes.

By recognizing which formats to use when, and how best to reduce colors, you can better ensure that visitors to your Web site will spend less time sitting on their hands and more time enjoying your site. I explain the fine points of the file formats and color indexing in the following sections.

Saving JPEG Images

When it comes to saving photographic images, no format results in smaller file sizes than JPEG. As explained in gory detail in Chapter 4, the JPEG format decreases the file size by applying a "lossy" compression scheme that actually redraws details in the image. Inside the JPEG Options dialog box, select lower Quality settings to put the screws to the image and squish it as low as it will go. But in doing so, you also sacrifice image detail. (Revisit the first color plate in this book, Color Plate 4-1, to see an example of JPEG compression at work.)

Just to show you how well the JPEG format works, Figure 20-2 shows a series of images saved in the JPEG and GIF formats, along with their file sizes. The original file consumed 62K in memory. Yet by lowering the Quality setting to Medium, I was able to get the file size down to 28K on disk. To accomplish similar savings using the GIF format, I had to reduce the color palette to 3 bits, or a mere 8 colors. (For the record, this same file saved in the PNG format consumed 63K on disk.) As you can plainly see in the enlarged details, applying JPEG compression has a less destructive effect on the appearance of the image than reducing the color palette.

JPEG

Maximum (8), 43K   High (6), 34K   Medium (3), 28K

GIF

8 bits/pixel, 71K   5 bits/pixel, 44K   3 bits/pixel, 26K

Figure 20-2
JPEG compression produces smaller file sizes with less
impact than reducing the color palette and saving in
GIF. The number in parentheses indicates the Quality
value entered into the JPEG Options dialog box.

When judging small differences in file size, be sure to select the file at the
Finder level and choose File ⇨ Get Info (⌘-I). Then check the Size item listed in bytes. For example, the Size item in Figure 20-3 reads *77K on disk
(64,471 bytes used)*. The value in parentheses is the true and accurate reading. The first value — in this case, 77K — is measured in drive blocks,
which are the smallest parcels of disk that the system can write to. This
makes for a misleading measurement that is invariably larger than the actual file size, and that grows in proportion to the capacity of the hard drive
(or drive partition). The value listed in the Size column inside a directory
window, and the value Photoshop shows in the Open dialog box, are likewise measured in drive blocks.

When you save a JPEG image, Photoshop displays the JPEG Options dialog box
shown in Figure 20-4. Here's how the options contained inside affect Web images:

Figure 20-3
To gauge the true size of a file, select it at the Finder level, press ⌘-I, and observe the value in parentheses. All other numbers lie.

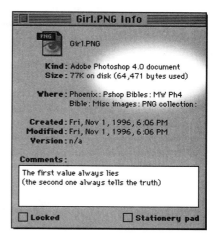

� **Image Options:** Use the Quality option to specify the amount of compression applied to your image. Lower values mean smaller file sizes and more JPEG compression gook. Many experts say Medium (3) is the best setting for Web graphics, but I think it looks pretty awful, especially on-screen. I prefer a Quality value of 5 or better.

Figure 20-4
Select the Baseline Optimized or Progressive radio button when saving a JPEG image for use on the Web.

⌘ **Format Options:** Most Web browsers support two variations on the JPEG format. The so-called *baseline* (or *sequentially displayed*) format displays images in line-by-line passes on-screen. The *progressive* JPEG format displays an image on-screen in multiple passes, permitting visitors to your page to get an idea of how an image looks right off the bat, without waiting for the entire image to arrive.

To save a baseline image for use on the Web, select Baseline Optimized. This format includes better Huffman encoding that makes the file even smaller than Baseline ("Standard"). You can generally reduce the file size by 5 to 10 percent using this option. Select the Progressive option to save an image that gradually appears on-screen in passes.

⌐ **Scans:** If you select the Progressive radio button, you can pick a number of passes from the Scans pop-up menu. A higher value results in a faster display of the initial image on your page, but it also takes longer to completely display on-screen because of all the incremental refreshing. A medium value of 4 is probably best, but it doesn't particularly matter.

There's a fair amount of debate over whether or not you should use progressive JPEG (and other incremental display options such as GIF interlacing). Certainly, some older Web browsers don't support progressive JPEG files, but that's not much of a problem these days. More controversial, some artists believe that progressive JPEGs are somehow tacky, because they have a rough appearance in the first few passes.

If that bothers you, and you don't want the viewer to see your image until it's in its final form, then select Baseline Optimized. But if you want my opinion, that would be doing your visitors a disservice. By providing an immediate, unfinished pass at your image, you're giving the viewer an early right of refusal. And that's what the Web's all about — providing the viewer with the tools of page customization and navigation. I mean, heck, guests can turn your graphics completely off if they want to. If you get too hung up on making your visitors see things your way, you'll go bonkers. Too many things are out of your control.

Preparing and Saving GIF Images

So much for JPEG, now on to GIF. The GIF format came into being during a time when only the super savvy owned 1200 Bps modems. It supports a maximum of 8 bits per pixel (256 colors), and it uses LZW compression, just like TIFF. GIF comes in two varieties, known by the snappy monikers 87a and 89a, with the latter supporting transparent pixels.

Frankly, GIF is getting a little long in the tooth. Most online pundits figure PNG will replace GIF in the next few years. But for the time being, GIF is an extremely popular and widely supported format. And despite its obvious limitations, it has its uses. GIF is a much better format than JPEG for saving high-contrast line art or text. Figure 20-5 shows two versions of the same image; the top image was saved in the JPEG format, and the bottom one was saved in GIF. As you can see, the JPEG compression utterly ruins the image. And I had to reduce the Quality setting to 0 — the absolute minimum — to get the file size down to 16K. Meanwhile, saving the image in the GIF format sacrificed no detail whatsoever and resulted in a file size of 18K. GIF's LZW compression is well suited to high-resolution artwork with large areas of flat color.

Figure 20-5
The JPEG format creates weird patterns in high-contrast images (top) and saves relatively little space on disk. Meanwhile, GIF keeps the sharp edges very much intact (bottom).

But before you can save a color image in the GIF format, you have to reduce the number of colors using Image ➪ Mode ➪ Indexed Color. The following section explains how this command works.

Incidentally, the Indexed Color command isn't the only way to decrease color palettes. If you find that the command doesn't quite meet your needs, then you may want to invest in a color management utility. The $400 DeBabelizer from Equilibrium is the absolute master of color reduction.
No other program does a better job of maintaining good color balance and smooth transitions. However, the program is expensive, and extraordinarily difficult to use — though Equilibrium is supposedly addressing the latter. Digital Frontiers provides a less expensive solution that is likely to address most people's needs. The $100 HVS Color lets you export low-color images directly out of Photoshop, while giving you control over gamma levels and color balance. The plug-in lacks GIF support and printed documentation, but it's a very handy tool.

Using the Indexed Color command

Choose Image ➪ Mode ➪ Indexed Color to display the dialog box shown in Figure 20-6. This command permits you to strip an image of all but its most essential colors. Photoshop then generates a color look-up table (or LUT) which describes the few remaining colors in the image. The LUT serves as an index, which is why the process is called "indexing."

For some reason, Photoshop doesn't let you index grayscale, Lab, or CMYK images. If the Indexed Color command is dimmed, choose Image ➪ Mode ➪ RGB to convert the image to the RGB mode and then choose Image ➪ Mode ➪ Indexed Color.

Don't expect to be able to edit your image after indexing it. Most of Photoshop's functions — including the gradient tool, all the edit tools, and the filters — refuse to work. Others, like feathering and the paintbrush and airbrush tools, don't work like they ought to. If you plan on editing an 8-bit image much in Photoshop, convert it to the RGB mode, edit it as desired, and then switch back to the indexed color mode when you're finished.

Now that I've gotten all the warnings and special advice out of the way, the following sections explain how to use the options inside the Indexed Color dialog box. Enjoy.

Specifying the palette

The first pop-up menu — Palette — tells Photoshop how to compute the colors in the look-up table. Most of the time, you'll want to select the Adaptive option, as in Figure 20-6. But just so you're prepared to be all you can be, the following list explains how each of the options works:

> ➥ **Exact:** If the image already contains fewer than 256 colors, the Exact option appears by default. This only occurs if you've created an extremely high-contrast image — such as a screen shot — or you're working from an image that originally started out as grayscale. If Exact is selected, just press Return and let the command do its stuff. No sense messing with a good thing.

✎ **System:** Photoshop 4 now offers two System options, which are used by the Macintosh and Windows operating systems. The only reason to use either of these options is if you want to add a bit of imagery to the system. For example, you always want to select the System (Macintosh) option when creating a wallpaper pattern, a custom file icon, or some other item that appears at the Finder level. Color Plate 20-1 shows examples of a 24-bit image downsized to the Mac and Windows system palettes.

✎ **Web:** Just to make things as confusing as possible, Netscape and other Web browsers include their own color palettes. This is a 216-color LUT that mostly includes colors found in both the Mac and Windows system palettes. If you're afraid that most of your guests own old 8-bit monitors, then Web might be the best choice. But I still argue in favor of Adaptive. The image will look far better on 16-bit and better monitors (which these days represents the majority), and it won't look that much worse on an 8-bit screen.

✎ **Uniform:** This is the dumbest option of them all. It merely retains a uniform sampling of colors from the spectrum. I've never heard of anyone finding a use for it — but as always, I welcome your suggestions.

✎ **Adaptive:** This option selects the most frequently used colors in your image, which typically delivers the best possible results. Because it ignores all system and Web palettes, images downsized with Adaptive look best on high-color monitors, as I mentioned above. To demonstrate just how much better they look, the bottom row of Color Plate 20-1 shows three images subject to the Adaptive palette at various Color Depth settings. Even with a mere 64 and 16 colors, the middle and right images look as good or better than the 256-color system-palette images above them.

You can influence the performance of the Adaptive option by selecting an area of your image before choosing the Indexed Color command. Photoshop will then favor the selected area when creating the palette. For example, when indexing the image in Color Plate 20-1 down to the 8-color palette (bottom right), I have to select the fellow's face to avoid losing all the flesh tones.

✎ **Custom:** Select this option to load a look-up table from disk. This is useful when creating multimedia content, but rarely serves any purpose for Web graphics. You can save a custom palette using Image ⇨ Mode ⇨ Color Table, as I explain in this chapter.

✎ **Previous:** This option uses the last look-up table created by the Indexed Color command. If you're trying to create a series of high-contrast graphics that you want to look as homogenous as possible, then this is the option to use. The Previous option is dimmed unless you have used the Indexed Color command at least once during the current session.

Color depth

Select a value from the Color Depth pop-up menu to specify the number of colors you want to retain in your image. Fewer colors results in smaller GIF files. I generally try 6 bits/pixel first, which results in 64 colors. If this looks okay, I press ⌘-Z and try 5 bits/pixel; if not, I press ⌘-Z and try 7 bits/pixel. It's all a matter of getting the colors as low as they can go without becoming ugly. The bottom row in Color Plate 20-1 shows examples of the same image with 256, 64, and 16 colors.

 Like all computer programs, Photoshop measures color in terms of *bit depth*. As I've mentioned several times in this book, an 8-bit image translates to 256 colors. Photoshop computes this figure by taking the number 2 and multiplying it by itself the number of times specified by the bit depth. 24-bit means 2 to the 24th power, which is 16 million; 4-bit means 2 to the 4th power, which is 16. You don't need to know this to select an option from a pop-up menu — Photoshop constantly keeps you apprised of the number of colors in the Colors option box — but sometimes it's nice to see what the program's up to.

Dither

Use the Dither pop-up menu to specify how Photoshop distributes the indexed colors throughout the image:

- **None:** If you select None, Photoshop maps each color in the image to its closest equivalent in the look-up table, pixel for pixel. This results in the harshest color transitions. But as I'll explain in a moment, it is frequently the preferable option.

- **Pattern:** This option is available only if you selected System (Macintosh) from the Palette options. But even then, avoid it like the plague, because it dithers colors in a geometric pattern. Look to the lower left example of Figure 20-7 and the middle image in Color Plate 20-2 for examples.

- **Diffusion:** The Diffusion option dithers colors randomly to create a naturalistic effect, as shown in the lower right example of Figure 20-7 and the last image in Color Plate 20-2.

After looking at Figure 20-7 and Color Plate 20-2, you might be inclined to think that Diffusion is the option of choice. Not necessarily. In most cases, None is the better option. First of all, None results in smaller GIF files (as Color Plate 20-2 shows). Because LZW is better suited to compressing uninterrupted expanses of color, harsh transitions mean speedier images. Second, if a guest views your page on an 8-bit monitor, the system will dither the image automatically (assuming you selected Adaptive from the Palette pop-up menu). System dithering on top of Diffusion dithering gets incredibly messy; system dithering on its own, however, is acceptable.

Figure 20-7
The results of converting an image (upper left) to the System palette using each of the three Dither options, None, Pattern, and Diffusion.

Original

None

Pattern

Diffusion

Editing indexed colors

As I said earlier, Adaptive is generally the best choice when creating Web graphics, because it scans each image for its most essential colors. But even the Adaptive option doesn't get things 100 percent right. On occasion, Photoshop selects some colors that look noticeably off base.

To replace all occurrences of one color in an indexed image with a different color, choose Image ⇨ Mode ⇨ Color Table. The ensuing Color Table dialog box, shown in Figure 20-8, enables you to selectively edit the contents of the LUT. To edit any color, click on it to display the Color Picker dialog box. Then select a different color and press Return to go back to the Color Table dialog box. Then press Return again to close the Color Table dialog box and change every pixel colored in the old color to the new color.

Figure 20-8
Use the Color Table dialog box to modify the colors in an indexed image.

The Color Table dialog box also enables you to open and save palettes and select predefined palettes from the Table pop-up menu. What the Color Table dialog box doesn't let you do is identify a color from the image. For example, if you're trying to fix a color in your image, you can't display the Color Table dialog box, click on the color in the image, and have the dialog box show you the corresponding color in the look-up table. The only way to be sure you're editing the correct color — and be forewarned, this is a royal pain in the behind — is to slog through the following steps, which begin before you choose Image ➪ Mode ➪ Color Table.

STEPS   Editing a Specific CLUT Color

Step 1.   **Use the eyedropper tool to click on the offending color in the image.** This makes it the foreground color.

Step 2.   **Click on the foreground color icon to display the specs for the color in the Color Picker dialog box.** Write down the RGB values on a handy piece of paper, the palm of your hand, or a bald friend's scalp. (Don't edit the color inside the Color Picker dialog box at this time. If you do, you just change the color without changing any pixel in the image associated with that color.) Press Escape to leave the dialog box.

Step 3.   **Choose Image ➪ Mode ➪ Color Table.**

Step 4.   **Click on a color that looks like it might be the right one.** After the Color Picker appears, compare the color's RGB numbers to those you wrote down. If they match, boy, did you ever luck out. Go ahead and edit the color as desired. If the RGB values don't match, press the Escape key to return to the Color Table dialog box and try again. And again. And again.

To create a *color ramp* — that is, a gradual color progression — drag rather than click on the colors in the palette to select multiple colors at a time. Photoshop then displays the Color Picker dialog box, enabling you to edit the first color in the ramp. After you select the desired color and press Return, the Color Picker reappears, this time asking you to edit the last color in the ramp. After you specify this color, Photoshop automatically creates the colors between the first and last colors in the ramp in even RGB increments.

Saving the completed GIF image

When it comes time to save your GIF image, you can save it in either the GIF87a or 89a format. To save a GIF87a image — where all pixels are opaque — choose File ⇨ Save and select the CompuServe GIF option from the Format pop-up menu. After you press Return, Photoshop presents you with two options, Normal and Interlaced. If you want the Web browser to display the image in incremental passes — similar to a progressive JPEG image — select the latter. Otherwise, select Normal.

On the other hand, if you want your GIF image to include transparent pixels, thereby permitting viewers to see through portions of the image to the Web page background pattern, you need to export the image to the GIF89a format. Choose File ⇨ Export ⇨ GIF89a Export to display the similarly named dialog box shown in Figure 20-9. Here you'll find an Interlace check box, which you can turn on or off as desired. There's also a Caption check box which lets you save a caption created with File ⇨ File Info. The only purpose for this is to let image cataloging programs search for the file by keywords. The caption does not appear in the HTML file.

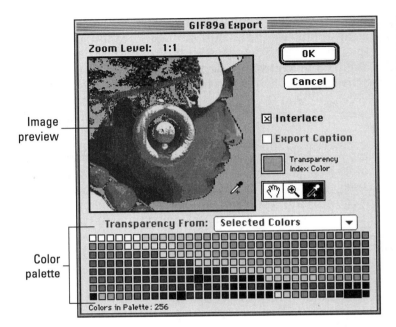

Figure 20-9
Click with the eyedropper cursor to make colors in the image transparent, as I have with the pixels outside the man's face.

All this is very well and good, but the real purpose of the GIF89a Export dialog box is to make pixels transparent:

- ↪ Click on a pixel in the image preview, or on one of the swatches in the color palette below, to make that color transparent. Keep clicking to add more transparent colors. Photoshop surrounds the transparent color swatches with heavy outlines.

- ↪ ⌘-click on a color to bring it back from transparency and return it to opacity again.

- ↪ You can scroll the preview by pressing the spacebar and dragging inside it. Zoom by ⌘-spacebar-clicking, and Option-spacebar-clicking.

- ↪ By default, Photoshop changes the transparent pixels to gray. But if gray is a popular color in your image, this may make it difficult to edit the image later. Because Photoshop has no method for expressing GIF transparency — the checkerboard method only works for native Photoshop files — the transparent pixels appear gray in color when you open and edit the image. So I recommend that you take the extra precaution of changing the transparent pixels to some way-out color, like bright yellow or green. To do this, click on the swatch labeled Transparency Index Color (just below the check boxes) and select a new color in the Color Picker.

If your image contains a mask channel, you can use the mask to define the transparent areas in the image. Just select the mask name from the Transparency From pop-up menu in the GIF89a Export dialog box. The black areas of the mask translate to transparency; the white areas are opaque. Keep in mind that GIF can handle just two levels of opacity — on and off, with no room for translucency. So if the mask includes gray pixels, the dark gray pixels become transparent and the light gray pixels become opaque.

For examples of transparent pixels, you might want to check out my site at http://www.dekemc.com. Every single graphic includes some transparent pixels, permitting the drop shadows and other gradual elements to blend in with the background.

Saving PNG Images

As I write this, the newest Web image format is the *Portable Network Graphics* format, or PNG (pronounced *ping*). Developed by a panel of independent graphics experts, PNG was designed specifically to outperform and ultimately replace GIF. It supports 24-bit and 48-bit images, it permits you to include mask channels for gradual transparency control, and — perhaps most importantly — PNG is not patented. Starting in 1995, Unisys, the developer of GIF, began to charge royalties to Web software developers. PNG, meanwhile, is free for all, which is why some folks claim PNG unofficially stands for "PNG, Not GIF."

PNG files are typically larger than comparable JPEG or GIF images because a PNG file does not include JPEG's lossy compression, and it can contain more colors than a GIF image. (The exception is when you save a grayscale or indexed PNG file, which is frequently smaller than the same file saved in GIF.) So PNG is generally best suited to small images — buttons and thumbnails — with fine details that you don't want mangled by JPEG compression.

Photoshop supports any RGB, grayscale, or indexed image in the PNG format. PNG doesn't support layers (of course), but it does permit you to include a single mask channel. Assuming the browser supports extra PNG channels, the mask defines the opacity and transparency of the image on the page. PNG graphics can even be translucent (as defined by gray areas in the mask channel), a terrific advantage over GIF and JPEG.

When you save a PNG image, Photoshop displays the dialog box shown in Figure 20-10. Here you can select the kind of interlacing and compression that you want to apply:

⤷ **Interlace:** The PNG format offers the strangely named "Adam7" interlacing. Adam7 draws your image on-screen in seven passes, drawing the image in blocks and filling in the pixels between blocks. If you want interlacing, select Adam7. If you don't, turn it off.

Figure 20-10
When saving a PNG file, Photoshop offers you some very peculiar options found nowhere else in the program.

⤷ **Filter:** These options permit you to specify the way in which Photoshop applies PNG's special *zlib* compression scheme. This particular scheme compresses data in blocks, and the Filter options let you specify the way in which the blocks are calculated. Even when armed with this knowledge, only one option, None, makes any sense. It turns off the compression. The other options permit you to tweak the compression for the minimum possible file size.

See, GIF's LZW compression can actually lead to an increase in file size in some cases. To avoid this, PNG gives you a sufficient number of compression options to ensure smaller files. You can certainly experiment with the options to see which one gives you the smallest results. But unless you're absolutely obsessed by small file size — we're talking about saving a few hundred bytes at most — just select Adaptive and let the compression do its magic without your help.

Before you rush out to save an image to the PNG format, however, you have to realize that support is thus far spotty. As I write this, none of the major HTML page-creation programs — including PageMill, Claris HomePage, Netscape Navigator Gold, and others — support PNG, and the major browser programs — Netscape and Microsoft Explorer — offer only limited support. (Netscape 3, for example, requires that you add a plug-in such as Siegel and Gale's PNG Live.) All this will change, of course. I imagine PNG support will become fairly universal by, say, the beginning of 1998. But in the meantime, PNG is more interesting than practical.

Appendixes

VII

PART

Appendix A:
Installing Photoshop 4

Appendix B:
Photograph Credits

Appendix C:
Using the CD-ROM

Installing Photoshop 4

The process of installing Photoshop is well documented in the user manual, and it's remarkably straightforward. So rather than waste valuable pages slogging through a step-by-step discussion, I'll touch on the few areas I think might prove helpful.

You install Photoshop 4 by running the Install Adobe Photoshop utility found on the CD-ROM included inside the box. Most folks already know this, but just to eliminate any confusion, I do *not* provide the Photoshop software on the CD-ROM included with this book. This book is intended to teach you how to use the software; you have to purchase the program itself from a software reseller. It costs roughly 15 times as much as this book, so you can see how it might be tough for us to include it.

After you run the Install program, a splash screen appears. Press Return to continue, and up pops the Install Adobe Photoshop dialog box. You can now simply click on the Install button to install the 40MB of programs, plug-ins, and extensions Adobe thinks you need to get the most out of Photoshop, but I for one prefer to wield a little more control over the prospective contents of my hard drive. Therefore, I recommend you choose the Custom Install option from the pop-up menu in the upper left corner of the dialog box. A scrolling list of check box options then fills the central portion of the dialog box. These options work as follows:

- **Adobe Photoshop 4.0 (select one):** Select just one of the first three check boxes to decide which version of Photoshop gets installed. If you own a Power Mac, select the Power Macintosh option. Otherwise, select the 68K option. Only select the Universal option if you want to install the "fat" version of Photoshop which is compatible with both kinds of Macs, but consumes more space on the hard drive.

- **Plug-ins (on):** This installs the many external filters, acquire modules, and export modules used by Photoshop. If you don't install this stuff, you miss out on half the program. If hard drive space is limited, go ahead and install, then open up the Plug-ins folder on your hard drive, locate the Effects folder, and throw it away. (See Chapters 15 and 16 for more information.)

- **Kodak Photo CD Support (on):** Select this option to enable Photoshop to open Photo CD images. I heartily recommend it.

🐝 **Sample Files (off):** These images permit you to complete Adobe's official tutorial for Photoshop. It's a fine tutorial, mind you, but you don't need no stinking tutorial. That's why you bought this book, right?

🐝 **Brushes & Patterns (on):** This installs a folder filled with custom brush shapes that you can load into the Brushes palette. I say install.

🐝 **Calibration (on):** Select this option to install the Gamma control panel, which lets you calibrate your monitor, as well as three images that you might want to display on-screen when performing the calibration. The operation is well documented in the manual. In theory, it's a good idea to calibrate your monitor, but in practice, it's a highly unreliable operation that rarely produces reliable results. Sadly, most commercial monitors are beyond accurate calibration. Still, you might as well give it a try — just don't put too much faith in what you see on-screen. (I explain color theory in detail in Chapter 5.)

🐝 **Color Palettes (on):** Select this option to install the custom color palettes from Pantone, Trumatch, and other companies discussed in Chapter 5. They're a must for creating duotones, and can be helpful in everyday image editing as well. Besides, they take up barely more than 100K. Go for it.

🐝 **Duotone Curves (off):** This option installs a whopping 2MB of files for creating duotones, tritones, and quadtones. If you don't anticipate creating such images — all covered in Chapter 7 — don't waste the disk space. If you do work with duotones, you'll find these predefined curve settings useful, but not essential. (If you select this option, make sure the Color Palettes option is selected as well.)

🐝 **Online Help (your call):** If you're new to Photoshop — and you probably are if you're reading this appendix — I recommend you go ahead and select this option. Although it consumes close to 14MB of disk space, the online help is quite useful. Once you install Photoshop and start up the program, you can access the help module by choosing Help Contents from the Help menu (the one that looks like a question mark on the right side of the screen).

🐝 **Adobe Type Manager (on):** Unlike the automated teller machines that spew money from your bank account, this ATM makes typefaces smooth on screen and is essential for creating text in Photoshop (as explained in Chapter A on the CD). Select this option to install ATM 3.9, which supports Power Mac acceleration, System 7.5, QuickDraw GX, and everything else on earth. Unless you've previously installed ATM 3.9 or later (as I write this, the newest version is 4.0), go for it.

🐝 **QuickTime (on):** Together, the QuickTime 2.1 system extension, Power Mac Plug, and Musical Instruments extensions take up 2MB of disk space. Unfortunately, you need QuickTime to view thumbnails inside the Open dialog box and to apply JPEG compression to PICT files. Bite the bullet and install (unless it's already installed on your hard drive).

∞ **Adobe Type Reunion (on):** This little system extension automatically organizes fonts into families inside all program menus and speeds up Photoshop's font loading process. Definitely install it.

∞ **SimpleText (off):** You probably already have SimpleText or TeachText — the former is an update to the latter — installed on your hard drive. In fact, if you're like most folks, you have several copies floating around. In fact, the darn thing is installed with your system software. Be smart, don't waste another 83K of space on your hard drive. Just say no to SimpleText.

∞ **Registration (your call):** This option installs a little utility that lets you register your copy of Photoshop with Adobe using your modem. Personally, I almost never register. Maybe I'm lazy, maybe I'm paranoid, maybe I figure my name's already on enough mailing lists. I don't really know what my problem is. But if you want to be apprised when new versions of Photoshop come out, then you have to let Adobe know where you are.

If you forget to install something, don't worry. You can always reinstall a single item later on. Just rerun the Install Adobe Photoshop utility, choose the Custom Install option from the upper left pop-up menu, and select the items that you want to install from the scrolling list. Then choose the Select Folder option from the pop-up menu in the Install Location area at the bottom of the dialog box. An Open dialog box will appear, allowing you to select the folder in which you previously installed Photoshop 4.

After you select the desired options, press the Return key to send the installation process on its merry way. You'll be instructed to swap disks every so often. Do the computer's bidding like a mindless automaton. Remember, you work for the computer now.

When the installation process is complete, the utility displays an alert box with three buttons, Restart, Quit, and Continue. You must restart the machine to load Adobe Type Manager, QuickTime, Type Reunion, and the Kodak Photo CD software. But I recommend that instead of restarting at this point, you click on the Quit button so you can change things around a little bit.

After you quit the Install program, search around for the new Adobe Photoshop 4 folder, which should be in the root directory of your primary hard drive. (In other words, just double-click on the hard drive icon in the upper left corner of your screen and you'll find it.) Move the folder as desired — inside an Applications folder, for example. Then open the folder and take a look at its contents. Along with the application icon and some other junk, you'll find the all-important Plug-ins and Goodies:

ॐ **Plug-ins:** This folder contains the plug-in files that you installed by selecting
the Plug-Ins and Kodak Photo CD Support items in the Install Adobe
Photoshop dialog box.

ॐ **Goodies:** The marvelous Goodies folder contains folders for Brushes &
Patterns, Calibration, and other items in the third grouping of check boxes
(depending on which items you chose to install).

Each folder contains several subfolders of its own, purely for organizational purposes. You can move things around if you like, so long as you don't move the files in
the Plug-ins folder out of that folder. (In other words, you can move a file from the
Filters folder in the Plug-ins folder to the Extensions folder inside that same folder,
but you shouldn't move the file outside the Plug-ins folder.) If you do, you'll prevent
that file from loading when you start up Photoshop, which will in turn make that
feature unavailable.

 Now open the Goodies folder and open the Calibration folder inside that. It
contains two items, the Separation Sources folder and the Gamma control
panel. Drag Gamma onto your System Folder. When you do, the operating
system requests permission to place Gamma in the Control Panels folder
automatically. Click on the OK button to make it so. (Optionally, you may
want to drag the Separation Sources folder out of the Calibration folder and
into the Goodies folder. Then drag the empty Calibration folder to the
Trash. After all, there's no sense in having a folder like Calibration that contains nothing but another folder.)

The Install utility doesn't necessarily install everything you may need to use
Photoshop. For example, included on the CD-ROM is a folder called Other Goodies.
Contained herein are several more folders, filled with predefined scripts for the
Actions palette (as covered in Chapter 3), predefined gradations (Chapter 9), and
textures for the Lighting Effects filter (Chapter 16).

Open up the Optional Plug-ins folder. The File Format and Export folders contain
plug-ins that support the Amiga IFF, Ham, MacPaint, and PixelPaint formats. I discuss all these items in Chapter 4. If you want to use them (not very likely), drag
them into the Plug-ins folder on your hard drive.

Then locate the Filter Factory folder. As described in Chapter 17, the Filter Factory
allows you to program your own custom filters. If you think there's even a slim
chance that you might like to learn how to use this wonderful but complex feature,
drag the Filter Factory folder into the Plug-ins folder on your hard drive.

Now open the Extensions folder inside the System Folder on your hard drive. Inside
you'll find at least two QuickTime files — QuickTime and QuickTime Musical
Instruments. If you're using a Power Mac, you'll also see a third file, QuickTime

PowerPlug. The 650K Musical Instruments file contains all kinds of instrument sounds that you can play using a MIDI file, but has nothing whatsoever to do with Photoshop. If multimedia isn't your bag, you can save 650K by deleting it, too.

Restart your computer to load QuickTime, ATM, Type Reunion, and Gamma into RAM. Then double-click on the Photoshop application to start using it. You'll be asked for a password. Enter PSW400R. . . ooh, you almost had me going there.

That's it. Now you're ready to start using the program, as described throughout the 20 chapters in this book.

Photograph Credits

The images used in this book came from all kinds of sources. The following list cites the figures or color plates in which a photograph appears. Following the figure number is the name of the photographer and the company from which the photo was licensed. In each case, the photographer holds the copyright. If the photograph comes from a CD collection, the product name appears in italics along with or instead of a photographer, and the company holds the copyright. If no company is listed, the photo was licensed from the photographer directly.

To all who contributed their photography, my heartfelt thanks.

Images	Photographer/Product	Company
Figures 2-2, 2-4, and 2-5	*Antistock*	Digital Stock
Figure 2-9	*Natural World*	Digital Stock
Figure 2-10	*V. 1, Business & Industry*	PhotoDisc
Figure 3-1	*Business & Commerce*	Digital Stock
Figure 4-1	*Urban Graffiti*	Digital Stock
Figure 4-9	*V. 11, Retro Americana*	PhotoDisc
Figure 4-17	*Urban Graffiti*	Digital Stock
Figure 4-24	*Urban Graffiti*	Digital Stock
Figures 4-26, 4-27, and 4-29	*Urban Graffiti*	Digital Stock
Figure 4-30	*V. 19, Agriculture*	PhotoDisc
Color Plate 4-1	*V. 9, Holidays & Celebrations*	PhotoDisc
Figures 5-7, 5-9, and 5-10	me, with a Polaroid PDC-2000	
Figures 6-2, 6-3, 6-4, and 6-6	*Water Sports*	Digital Stock
Color Plates 6-1 through 6-3	*Water Sports*	Digital Stock
Figure 7-5	*V. 11, Retro Americana*	PhotoDisc
Figure 7-6	Denise McClelland	
Figure 7-16	Mark Collen	
Color Plate 7-1	Mark Collen	
Figure 8-5	*Signature Series 16, Everyday People*	PhotoDisc
Figures 8-6 through 8-8, 8-29, and 8-30	Russell McDougal	
Figures 8-13 and 8-14	*V. 5, World Commerce & Travel*	PhotoDisc

Images	*Photographer/Product*	*Company*
Figure 8-15	*V. 12, Food & Dining*	PhotoDisc
Color Plate 8-1	*V. 12, Food & Dining*	PhotoDisc
Color Plate 8-2	*V. 5, World Commerce & Travel*	PhotoDisc
Color Plates 8-4 through 8-6	*Fine Art Series 1, European Paintings*	PhotoDisc
Figure 9-2	*V. 30, Contemporary Cuisine*	PhotoDisc
Figures 9-4, 9-11, 9-23, and 9-25 (dog)	*Object Series 18, Everyday Animals*	PhotoDisc
Figures 9-4, 9-11, 9-23, and 9-25 (hydrant)	me, with a Polaroid PDC-2000	
Figures 9-23 through 9-25 (fly)	*V. 8, Bugs & Butterflies*	MetaTools
Color Plate 9-1	*V. 30, Contemporary Cuisine*	PhotoDisc
Color Plate 9-3	*Signature Series 14, Cultural Arts*	PhotoDisc
Figures 10-2 through 10-5, 10-12, and 10-22	Denise McClelland	
Figures 10-6 and 10-7	Russell McDougal	
Figures 10-8 through 10-11	Michael Probst	Reuter
Figures 10-17 through 10-20	*V. 23, Far Eastern Business & Culture*	PhotoDisc
Figures 11-4, 11-18, 11-20 through 11-22, 11-24 through 11-27, 11-34, and 11-35	*V. 4, Technology & Medicine*	PhotoDisc
Figure 11-7	*V. 16, US Landmarks and Travel*	PhotoDisc
Figures 11-8 through 11-10	Russell McDougal	
Figures 11-11, 11-29 and 11-31	*V. 4, Technology & Medicine*	PhotoDisc
Figures 11-13 through 11-17	*V. 4, Technology & Medicine*	PhotoDisc
Figure 11-21 (face)	*V. 5, World Commerce & Travel*	PhotoDisc
Color Plate 11-1	*V. 16, US Landmarks and Travel*	PhotoDisc
Figures 12-1 and 12-2	*Sport & Leisure*	Digital Stock
Figures 12-3 through 12-10	*V. 4, Technology & Medicine*	PhotoDisc
Figures 12-12 through 12-14 (Capitol)	*Washington D.C.*	Digital Stock
Figures 12-12 and 12-14 (lava)	*Fire & Ice*	Digital Stock
Figures 12-15, 12-17, 12-20 through 12-22	*Washington D.C.*	Digital Stock
Figures 12-24 through 12-29	*Children & Teens*	Digital Stock
Color Plate 12-1	*Sport & Leisure*	Digital Stock
Color Plate 12-2 (Capitol)	*Washington D.C.*	Digital Stock
Color Plate 12-2 (lava)	*Fire & Ice*	Digital Stock
Color Plate 12-3 (girl)	*Children & Teens*	Digital Stock
Color Plate 12-3 (background)	*Southern California*	Digital Stock
Figure 13-1 (x-ray)	*V. 29, Modern Technologies*	PhotoDisc
Figures 13-1, 13-24, and 13-25	*Object Series 15, InfoMedia*	PhotoDisc

Images	Photographer/Product	Company
Figures 13-2, 13-6 through 13-9, 13-11, 13-13 through 13-15, 13-26	*Object Series 15, InfoMedia*	PhotoDisc
Figures 13-17, 13-19 through 13-22	*V. 6, Nature & the Environment*	PhotoDisc
Figures 13-28 through 13-30	*Children & Teens*	Digital Stock
Figures 13-31 and 13-32	me, with a Polaroid PDC-2000	
Color Plates 13-1 and 13-2	*V. 6, Nature & the Environment*	PhotoDisc
Color Plate 13-3	me, with a Polaroid PDC-2000	
Figures 14-2, 14-11 through 14-15	Carlye Calvin, *Sampler One*	Color Bytes
Figure 14-19	*Characters & Expressions*	Digital Stock
Figures 15-1 through 15-7, 15-20, 15-23, 15-25 through 15-27, 15-29, 15-30, 15-36, 15-39, 15-40, and 15-42	*Italy*	Digital Stock
Figures 15-8 through 15-13, 15-17 through 15-19, 15-21, 15-31, 15-37, and 15-41	*V. 23, Far Eastern Business & Culture*	PhotoDisc
Figures 15-14 through 15-16, and 15-32	*World War II*	Digital Stock
Figure 15-22	*V. 5, World Commerce & Travel*	PhotoDisc
Figures 15-33 through 15-35	*Object Series 15, InfoMedia*	PhotoDisc
Figure 15-35 (zebra pattern)	Nick Koudis, *Background Series 5, Wackgrounds*	PhotoDisc
Figures 15-43 through 15-45	me, with a Kodak DC40	
Color Plates 15-1 and 15-2	*Italy*	Digital Stock
Color Plates 15-3 through 15-5	*V. 9, Holidays & Celebrations*	PhotoDisc
Color Plate 15-6	*V. 5, World Commerce & Travel*	PhotoDisc
Figure 16-1	*Central Europe*	Digital Stock
Figure 16-2 through 16-5, 16-7 through 16-9, 16-12, 16-15, 16-21, 16-22, and 16-39	*V. 5, World Commerce & Travel*	PhotoDisc
Figures 16-6, 16-13, 16-14, 16-16, 16-23, 16-27, 16-30, and 16-40	*Italy*	Digital Stock
Figures 16-10 and 16-11	*V. 11, Retro Americana*	PhotoDisc
Color Plates 16-1 through 16-4, and 16-9	*V. 9, Holidays & Celebrations*	PhotoDisc
Color Plate 16-5 and 16-6	*V. 7, Business & Occupations*	PhotoDisc
Color Plate 16-8	Mark Collen	
Color Plate 16-10	*Antistock*	Digital Stock
Figures 17-1, 17-42, 17-43, and 17-45	*V. 9, Holidays & Celebrations*	PhotoDisc
Figures 17-3 through 17-31, and 17-33 through 17-41	*V. 5, World Commerce & Travel*	PhotoDisc
Color Plates 17-1 and 17-2	*Flowers*	Digital Stock

Images	*Photographer/Product*	*Company*
Color Plates 17-3 and 17-4	*V. 9, Holidays & Celebrations*	PhotoDisc
Figure 18-1	*V. 25, Government & Social Issues*	PhotoDisc
Figures 18-2, 18-3, 18-5 through 18-7, 18-14, 18-15, 18-17, 18-19, and 18-23 through 18-27	*V. 5, World Commerce & Travel*	PhotoDisc
Figures 18-8, 18-10, and 18-12	*V. 9, Holidays & Celebrations*	PhotoDisc
Color Plates 18-1 through 18-3, and 18-6 through 18-8	*Antistock*	Digital Stock
Color Plates 18-4, 18-5, 18-9, and 18-10	*V. 9, Holidays & Celebrations*	PhotoDisc
Color Plate 18-11	me, with a Kodak DC50	
Color Plate 18-12	*V. 25, Government & Social Issues*	PhotoDisc
Color Plate 18-13	*Italy*	Digital Stock
Color Plate 18-14	*V. 5, World Commerce & Travel*	PhotoDisc
Color Plate 18-15	me, with a Polaroid PDC-2000	
Figure 19-1 (parachute)	*Active Lifestyles 2*	Digital Stock
Figure 19-1 (moon)	*Space & Exploration*	Digital Stock
Figures 19-3 through 19-12, 19-17, 19-18, 19-20, and 19-21	Russell McDougal	
Figures 19-13 through 19-15 (woman)	*V.28, People, Lifestyles, & Vacations*	PhotoDisc
Figures 19-13 and 19-14 (leaf)	*V.26, Homes & Gardens*	PhotoDisc
Figures 19-23 through 19-26	Carlye Calvin, *Sampler One*	Color Bytes
Color Plate 19-1	*Space & Exploration*	Digital Stock
Color Plates 19-2 through 19-4	*V.28, People, Lifestyles, & Vacations*	PhotoDisc
Color Plate 19-2 (leaf)	*V.26, Homes & Gardens*	PhotoDisc
Color Plates 19-5 and 19-6	Carlye Calvin, *Sampler One*	Color Bytes
Figure 20-1	*V. 35, Business Today*	PhotoDisc
Figure 20-2	*Indigenous Peoples*	Digital Think
Figure 20-7	*V. 5, World Commerce & Travel*	PhotoDisc
Color Plates 20-1 and 20-2	*V. 5, World Commerce & Travel*	PhotoDisc
Backgrounds for all color plates	Nick Koudis, Jim Grant, The Studio Dog, Skan/9, *Background Series*	PhotoDisc

Using the CD-ROM

To access the images and documents included on the CD-ROM, start by inserting it into your CD-ROM drive. The CD icon, called Ph4.Bible CD-ROM, appears on your desktop. Double-click on the CD icon to open the CD-ROM. The window pops open and displays the following nine folders:

- **Gallery:** This folder contains original artwork that was created using Photoshop. The eight artists represented have a range of styles and techniques, and you can get some great ideas from looking at their images. These images are only for viewing purposes.

- **Images:** This folder contains both high-resolution and low-resolution images from stock photo agencies PhotoDisc and Digital Stock.

- **Filters:** There are two folders within this folder, one labeled Macintosh, and the second labeled Windows. Each contains Photoshop filters and demo software from a variety of vendors, including Extensis, Alien Skin, and Andromeda Software. The Tormentia filters described in Chapter 17 are also found here. To use any of these filters, drag them into the Plug-ins folder on your hard drive.

- **Macworld:** This folder contains two articles that were originally published in *Macworld* magazine.

- **DigThink:** This folder contains information from DigitalThink, a company that offers classes in Photoshop via the Web.

- **MultiMac:** This folder contains information from DayStar Digital about Macs that contain more than one CPU. Where Photoshop is concerned, these are the fastest Macs on the planet.

- **Acrobat:** This folder contains the items you need to install an Acrobat reader on your hard drive. The reader will let you read PDF files, including those from DayStar Digital and Extensis.

- **ImgSourc:** If you'd like to see a few more sample images, check out this folder. It contains some promotional pieces compiled by the technical editor of this book, Ted Padova.

- **Digimarc:** This folder contains information about an innovative new service that embeds an electronic copyright into any image. If you distribute a lot of images electronically, you may want to check it out.

Gallery

These folders contain images created by artists who use Photoshop as one of the tools of their trade. These images are provided as inspirational material only; they are not for commercial use and the artists retain all copyrights to their work.

To view these images, first start up Photoshop and then open the image inside Photoshop. A number of the artists have included Details files; check these out for information on how the images were created, the artists' thoughts about their work, and contact information. To access the Details files, just open them up in your favorite word-processor:

- **Jeff Brice:** Jeff is a Seattle-based digital artist/illustrator. He's worked for *Wired* Magazine, Adobe, Hewlett-Packard, Scribner, *Time*, *Newsweek*, Fidelity, J. P. Morgan, DEC, and many more editorial and corporate clients. Jeff tries to apply his background in fine arts to his illustration work. His work can be seen in the newly published "Mind Grenades" by Hardwired.

- **Steve Campbell:** Steve has been redefining and reinventing himself as a digital fine artist, having been twice selected to exhibit in Fractal Design's yearly Art Expo traveling gallery and winning prizes three years in a row in the MicroPublishing/Iris Digital Art contest, with awards ceremonies held yearly at Seybold, San Francisco. His work has been featured on the 1995 Adobe Graphics Sampler, and can also be seen in *Painting With Computers* from Rockport Publishing.

- **Christopher Ching:** Based in Manhattan, New York, Chris is an illustrator whose pictures are simple, conceptually distilled. Subtle Photoshop effects are an integral part of his illustration work.

- **Kevin Curry:** Kevin is an illustrator based in Albuquerque, New Mexico. His work has appeared in national publications, including *Macworld* and *PC World*.

- **Diane Fenster:** Cover artist Diane Fenster from Pacifica, California creates both fine art and illustration. Her style is an innovative combination of her own 35mm photography, video, still video and scanned imagery. Diane's fine art has been exhibited internationally and her images appear in numerous publications and CDs including the Aperture monograph "Metamorphoses: Photography In The Electronic Age." She is a guest lecturer at many seminars and conferences and her work was exhibited at the SIGGRAPH 95 Art & Design show. Her illustration style is an outgrowth of the explorations she has taken with her personal work and her commissions range from editorial to advertising to Web.

⊃ **Larry Goode:** Larry graduated from the University of Texas at Austin in 1985 with a BFA in Painting and Drawing. After working freelance at several Austin design firms he was hired as a designer for Fuller, Dyal and Stamper in 1987. At FD&S Larry started teaching himself the Macintosh and exploring Photoshop and other applications. In 1995, Larry joined forces with long-time friend and business associate Ranulfo Ponce to form Design Island, a four person design shop where the emphasis is on illustration, multimedia, and graphic design.

⊃ **Ranulfo Ponce:** Ponce is a partner in Design Island, a multi-talented corporation in the fields of graphic design, environmental graphics, multimedia, illustration, and World Wide Web page and site design. He studied technical illustration for five years with an additional 5 years' experience in graphic design, environmental graphics, and production. Ponce is also the driving force in the multimedia area of Design Island.

⊃ **Greg Vander Houwen:** Greg Vander Houwen is a principal in the computer graphics firm, Interact. He has a background in video, computers, photography and apple farming. His award-winning imagery has been shown internationally and his clients include Microsoft, Adobe, and Apple. He also lectures on image compositing, special FX, retouching, and illustration. He is an artist by nature, an illustrator by trade. He also enjoys philosophizing during an occasional lunar eclipse.

Images

The images folder contains two folders, named DigStock and PhotDisc:

⊃ **DigStock:** DigStock Corporation has provided us with a number of high-resolution images (pictured in Figure C-1), as well as several hundred low-resolution images. Every one of the images in the Hi-res folder comes from the figures of this book, permitting you to experiment with the very images you see on the printed page. Wow, talk about planning! To open any of the images, first start up Photoshop and then open the image inside the program. Digital Stock has provided these files to give you a feel for its extensive collection of stock photography. For a catalog containing thousands of images, follow the instructions in the text file, called FreeOffr. To read this file, open it in your favorite word-processor.

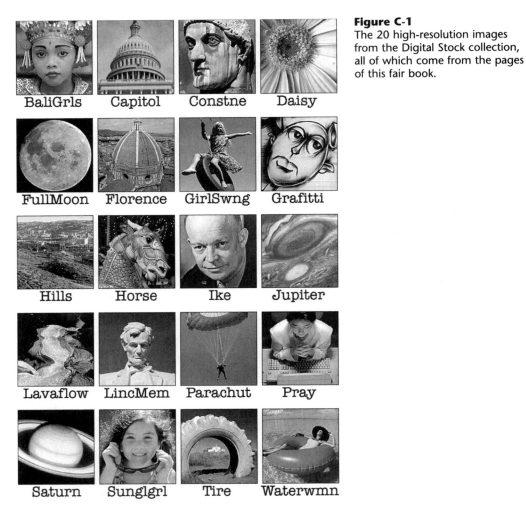

BaliGrls Capitol Constne Daisy

FullMoon Florence GirlSwng Grafitti

Hills Horse Ike Jupiter

Lavaflow LincMem Parachut Pray

Saturn Sunglgrl Tire Waterwmn

- **PhotDisc:** There are three folders in the PhotDisc folder. The first includes 20 high-resolution images that come from the book. See them again in Figure C-2. You can use these images to recreate the examples in the book, or to create your own effects. The folder called Low-res contains several thousand low resolution images from the company's extensive image library. Finally, the folder titled More contains information on the company, in the form of a Web page. To look at this file, you must have a World Wide Web browser such as Netscape Navigator or Internet Explorer. The images in the Hi-res folders from both Digital Stock and PhotoDisc include a limited-use license. You can use the images in your publications and original artwork, but you cannot sell or give away electronic versions of the files. The other images, including those in the Low-res folders, are for placement and experimentation only. You are not authorized to use them in artwork or post them electronically. If you are interested in using any of these images, you'll have to purchase the desired image directly from Digital Stock or PhotoDisc.

Figure C-2
The 20 high-resolution images from the PhotoDisc collection, which I have likewise featured in pivotal locations throughout the book.

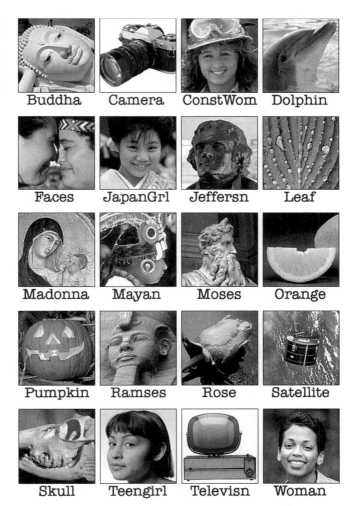

Buddha   Camera   ConstWom   Dolphin

Faces   JapanGrl   Jeffersn   Leaf

Madonna   Mayan   Moses   Orange

Pumpkin   Ramses   Rose   Satellite

Skull   Teengirl   Televisn   Woman

Filters

There are two folders here, one called Macintosh and the other Windows. All of the filters included in the Windows folder are also included in the Macintosh folder, so I'll explain the Windows contents first.

Windows (and Macintosh)

You can find the following plug-ins in both the Windows and Macintosh folders.

Alien Skin

Alien Skin has provided both Mac and Windows users with a demo version of Cutout, one of the 10 filters included in their plug-in collection, The Black Box 2. The demo is the same as the commercial version of Cutout, except that a splash screen appears every time the demo is run. Dismiss the splash screen by clicking on it. If you're a Mac user, you can install the demo by double-clicking on the icon labeled Install Cutout Demo 2.1. Windows users should run the file called Setup32.exe.

Andromeda

Andromeda Software has generously provided samples of their Series 1, Series 2, and Series 3 filters for both Macintosh and Windows users. They've also offered information on their newest filters, Series 4 and Velociraptor. For directions on installing these filters, please open the Read Me files included in each folder in your favorite word-processor:

- **Series 1:** This folder contains the Circular Multiple Images filter/plug-in, which is one of ten in the Andromeda Series 1 Photography Filters. The filter is fully operational. Try successive applications of the filter on the same image and vary Intensity (opacity) and Areas to create stunning kaleidoscopic effects.

- **Series 2:** The 3-D Demo filter in this folder has a fully operational interface and Preview Window, although the output (OK button) has been disabled. Use this filter to wrap your image on 3D surfaces; rotate and shade the image and surface and even view the surface from any angle.

- **Series 3:** The Series 3 Screens filter (which I awarded a rare five-star review in *Macworld* magazine) offers special effects screening for grayscale images. In this version, the interface and Preview windows are operational, but the output button has been disabled. For help getting started with this filter, check out the Quickstart tutorial included in the folder. You can use any word-processor to read the Quickstart file.

- **Series 4:** Series 4 Techtures is a product which lets you apply textures to images, while Velociraptor is a motion trails plug-in. These folders contain Read Me files which describe the filters, images created using the filters, and pictures of the filter interfaces.

Tormentia

This is a collection of eight filters that I created using the Filter Factory, explained in Chapter 17. To learn what each of these filters does, read the Torment.txt file included in the Tormentia folder. On Windows machines, this file is best opened in Microsoft Word. The strange looking characters are apostrophes that didn't translate properly. Sorry about that.

Macintosh (only)

You lucky Macintosh users will also find the following filters:

Extensis

This folder contains two files, a Read Me and Extensis' licensing agreement, as well as two folders, one named Software and one called Extensis Info. The Software folder includes demo versions of Extensis products including Intellihance 2.0.1, PhotoTools 1.0, and PhotoNavigator:

- **Intellihance:** This is an intelligent photo-correction plug-in that corrects images so simply even a child could use it. This demo lets you run Intellihance up to five times per session. You must quit and re-launch Photoshop if you wish to continue using Intellihance. You can run Intellihance on a total of 30 images before it fully expires. In order to install this software, double-click on the Intellihance installer.

- **PhotoTools:** Here is a collection of eight Photoshop plug-ins, including four modules for automatically creating commonly used special effects. PhotoTools also includes customizable toolbars and a special tips module chock full of Photoshop 4 insights by yours truly. (I've been told it's very helpful — but I should stop. I'm making me blush.) This demo version will function fully for 30 days, and then it'll poop out and die. To install it, double-click on the Install PhotoTools icon.

- **PhotoNavigator:** This bit of freeware allows you to quickly and accurately navigate your way around large images. It's a rather well-known secret that this filter was the inspiration for Photoshop 4's new Navigator palette. In fact, I only include PhotoNavigator so that you can compare it to the Navigator palette and say, "Well well!" or words to that effect. Feel free to give it to some poor slob that's still using Photoshop 3.

Extensis has also included demo versions of DrawTools (a collection of color, moving, and shaping plug-ins for Illustrator and FreeHand), PageTools (for PageMaker), QX-Tools 2.0 (for QuarkXPress), CyberPress (an HTML export XTension for QuarkXPress), and Fetch (an image-cataloging database).

Additionally, you can find information about all of Extensis' products in the folder named Extensis Info. Here you'll find an HTML file that you can read with your favorite browser and a PDF order form that you can open with Adobe Acrobat (included on this CD).

Chris' Filters

This collection of 25 filters is shareware. If you like them — and you're a good person — send the author, Chris Cox, a donation. His address is supplied in the Read Me file, which you can open in any word processor. On the other hand, if you like them and you're a horrible evil person, feel free to use them without paying Chris a penny. (Did I mention his poor sick mother?)

Colleen's PS Fun Pack

These plug-ins were created by Hugh Kawahara, who's distributing them as "charity-ware." If you like them, make a donation to your favorite charity. (Just think of the positive karma you'd generate if you did that!) To use these filters, drag the Colleen's PS Fun Pack folder to your plug-ins folder inside your Photoshop folder. The five filters, Kwick Mask, Modulate Doc, Rotate Color, Adjust Saturation, and Create BW create preview windows directly inside the image window. Documents inside the folder explain what each filter does; you can open these files inside any word-processor.

Garden Tools

This shareware collection by Paul Badger includes three filters, VectorGraph, Radar, and Lumpy Noise. VectorGraph, which appears in the Stylize menu, is a filter that maps the direction of shading. Radar, which appears in the Other menu, will create the effect of radial sweep radar on an image. Lumpy Noise, which appears in the Noise menu, adds noise with a specified grain size. These filters work both with and without a math coprocessor. If your Mac is a 68K machine with a math coprocessor, use the versions in the Math folder; if your Mac doesn't have a math coprocessor or is a Power Mac, use the versions in the No Math folder.

DataStream Imaging

This folder contains information about, as well as one filter from, WildRiverSSK. The included filter is DekoBoko, which in Japanese means convex/concave. This filter creates 3D-style frames. To install it, drag the file named WRSSK DekoBoko1.0e to the filters folder inside your Photoshop folder.

Macworld

This folder contains two articles originally published in the hallowed pages of the finest trade publication on Earth, *Macworld* magazine. The first, "Top 20 Photoshop Plug-Ins," was penned by me for the September, 1996 issue. The second article, "Copyright and the Visual Arts," comes from the October, 1996 issue of *Macworld*. Written by my very capable pal, Marjorie Baer, it explains copyright infringement and how to avoid it. You can open either article in your favorite Web browser.

DigThink

This folder (for Macintosh users only) contains HTML files from DigitalThink, a company that offers classes in Java, C++, and other topics over the World Wide Web. They also have a first-rate Photoshop class, authored by a guy named Deke. To learn more about this and other classes from DigitalThink, open the index.html document in your favorite Web program.

MultiMac

This folder (for Macintosh users only) contains information provided by DayStar Digital on the subject of multiprocessor Macs. Multiprocessing combines multiple CPU chips inside a single computer to accelerate the speed of the Mac's most complicated applications. Not surprisingly, the application that presently benefits the most from multiprocessing is Photoshop. To find out everything there is to know about the topic, open the MultiMac.html file in your favorite Web browser. Browse around to find Photoshop speed tests and technical information about multiprocessing. You can also learn more about DayStar Digital by opening the DayStar.pdf file in Acrobat.

Although DayStar invented multiprocessing on the Mac, it isn't the only company that sells multiprocessing computers. You can also buy multiprocessing models — sometimes at reduced rates — from Apple and Umax.

Acrobat

This folder contains everything you need to install the Acrobat reader, which will allow you to read the PDF files contained on the CD-ROM. To install the reader, double-click on the Acrobat Installer icon.

ImgSourc

This folder contains an Acrobat PDF file from my pal and technical editor Ted Padova at Image Source, a first-rate service bureau based out of Ventura, California. Open the PDF file with the Acrobat Reader to view a collection of images created and modified with Photoshop. The collection comes from the Ventura County Directory of Advertising Professionals. These 31 promotional images provide a nice contrast to the artistic images in the Gallery folder.

Digimarc

Photoshop 4 supports a digital watermarking feature called PictureMarc from a company called Digimarc. PictureMarc lets you embed special copyright information into any image that you distribute electronically. The embedding modifies the pixels in your image, but it's designed to be invisible, or as near to invisible as possible. People who look at your artwork can then view the copyright information by simply choosing a command, but they cannot eliminate the copyright as they might if you had entered it into the File Info dialog box.

The one tickle is that you have to register with Digimarc before you can take advantage of this service. And while Adobe has officially endorsed the PictureMarc service, I haven't decided what I think of it. So rather than writing it up in the pages of the book, I've instead chosen to include these HTML pages from Digimarc and let you investigate it for yourself.

Cross Platform Notes

Macintosh users should ignore the Autorun.inf and Ph4bible.ico files. These files are there strictly for Windows, so don't bother trying to open them. Similarly, Windows users should ignore the Icon_ files. These are there for the Mac folks.

Index

Numbers and Symbols

⌘ key, 68
3M Rainbow dye-sublimation printer, 207
8-bit monitor, 54–55
32-bit images, 122
256-color monitors, 54

•A•

absolute full screen control, 36
Acrobat Exchange, 121
Action Options dialog box, 95
actions
  how long it took, 22
  waiting until completion of, 34
Actions palette, 12, 68–89
  applying commands to images, 92
  Batch command, 97
  Button Mode command, 95–96
  circular record icon, 91
  deleting commands from scripts, 95
  icons, 90
  Insert Menu Item command, 94
  Insert Stop command, 94
  lack of power of, 92
  new script icon, 91
  similarities with Commands palette, 90
  viewing, 90
Actual Pixels View (⌘-

Option-0) keyboard shortcut, 40, 55
actual-pixels view, 40
ADCT (Adaptive Discrete Cosine Transformation), 132
Add blend mode, 741–744
add lasso cursor, 28
add marquee cursor, 27
Add Noise dialog box, 553
Add Noise filter, 296, 553–555
  custom pattern creation, 328
  eliminating gradient banding, 295
  limiting effect of, 554–555
add palette selection cursor, 33
Add Path to Selection (Shift-Enter) keyboard shortcut, 391
add polygonal lasso cursor, 28
add type mask cursor, 30
add wand cursor, 28
additive primary model. See RGB (red, green, blue) color model
Adjust Auto Levels (⌘-Shift-L) keyboard shortcut, 172
adjusting control handles, 31
adjustment layers, 14
  advantages, 707–708
  correcting flattened images, 708
  layer masks, 13
Adobe Acrobat, 121
Adobe Dimensions, 50
Adobe PageMaker, 9
Adobe PageMill, 10

Adobe Persuasion, 9
Adobe Photoshop 4.0 Prefs file, 47, 48
Adobe Premiere, 9, 127–129
Adobe's online Web site
  accessing, 17
  hot link to, 12
advanced transformation capabilities, 13
After Effects, 9
airbrush cursor, 31
airbrush eraser tool, 72
Airbrush Options palette Fade check box, 405
airbrush tool, 24, 31, 240, 263, 405
  color, 158
  soft brush shape, 242–243
airbrushing, 242
aligning
  channels, 198
  layers, 467–469
  patterns, 325–326
alpha channels, 122
Amiga, 119
Angled Brushes filter, 512
annotating images, 63–65
ANPA (American Newspaper Publishers Association) color library, 180
Anti-aliased PICT dialog box, 145
antialiased lines, 242
antialiasing
  converting selection to layer, 452–453
  free-form selection outlines, 348
  images, 123, 539–541
  low-resolution images, 216
  selection outlines, 361
  type, 491

Credits

**Senior Vice President
and Group Publisher**
Brenda McLaughlin

Director of Publishing
Walt Bruce

Acquisitions Editor
Nancy Dunn

Marketing Manager
Melisa M. Duffy

Executive Managing Editor
Terry Somerson

Development Editor
Amy Thomas

Copy Editors
Katharine Dvorak
Peggy Watt

Technical Editor
Ted Padova

Editorial Assistants
Sharon Eames
Annie Sheldon

Production Director
Andrew Walker

Supervisor of Page Layout
Craig A. Harrison

Project Coordinator
Ben Schroeter

Layout and Graphics
Laura Carpenter
Kurt Krames
Andreas F. Schueller
Mark Schumann
Dale Smith
Elsie Yim

Quality Control Specialist
Mick Arellano

Proofreader
Mary C. Oby

Indexer
Sharon Hilgenberg

Production Administration
Tony Augsburger
Todd Klemme
Jason Marcuson
Christopher Pimentel
Leslie Popplewell
Theresa Sánchez-Baker
Melissa Stauffer

Book Design
Beth Jenkins

About the Author

A contributing editor to *Macworld* magazine, Deke McClelland also writes for *Publish*. He has authored more than 30 books on desktop publishing and the Macintosh computer, and his work has been translated into more than 20 languages. Deke also hosts "Digital Gurus," a syndicated TV show about personal computing, from his home base in Colorado. He started his career as artistic director at the first service bureau in the United States.

McClelland won a Society of Technical Communication Award in 1994, an American Society for Business Press Editors award in 1995, and the Ben Franklin award for Best Computer Book in 1989. He also won the prestigious Computer Press Association Award in 1990, 1992, and 1994, and was runner-up in 1995.

Deke is author of IDG Books Worldwide's *CorelDRAW! 5 For Dummies*, *CorelDRAW! 7 For Dummies* (spring 1997), *Macworld FreeHand 5 Bible*, *Macworld FreeHand 7 Bible* (winter 1997), *PageMaker 6 For Windows For Dummies*, and *Photoshop 4 For Dummies* (winter 1997). He is also author of *The Illustrator 6 Book* (Peachpit Press).

IDG BOOKS WORLDWIDE, INC.

<u>END-USER LICENSE AGREEMENT</u>

<u>Read This</u>. **You should carefully read these terms and conditions before opening the software packet(s) included with this book ("Book"). This is a license agreement ("Agreement") between you and IDG Books Worldwide, Inc. ("IDGB"). By opening the accompanying software packet(s), you acknowledge that you have read and accept the following terms and conditions. If you do not agree and do not want to be bound by such terms and conditions, promptly return the Book and the unopened software packet(s) to the place you obtained them for a full refund.**

1. <u>License Grant</u>. IDGB grants to you (either an individual or entity) a nonexclusive license to use one copy of the enclosed software program(s) (collectively, the "Software") solely for your own personal or business purposes on a single computer (whether a standard computer or a workstation component of a multiuser network). The Software is in use on a computer when it is loaded into temporary memory (i.e., RAM) or installed into permanent memory (e.g., hard disk, CD-ROM, or other storage device). IDGB reserves all rights not expressly granted herein.

2. <u>Ownership</u>. IDGB is the owner of all right, title, and interest, including copyright, in and to the compilation of the Software recorded on the disk(s)/CD-ROM. Copyright to the individual programs on the disk(s)/CD-ROM is owned by the author or other authorized copyright owner of each program. Ownership of the Software and all proprietary rights relating thereto remain with IDGB and its licensors.

3. <u>Restrictions on Use and Transfer</u>.

    (a) You may only (i) make one copy of the Software for backup or archival purposes, or (ii) transfer the Software to a single hard disk, provided that you keep the original for backup or archival purposes. You may not (i) rent or lease the Software, (ii) copy or reproduce the Software through a LAN or other network system or through any computer subscriber system or bulletin-board system, or (iii) modify, adapt, or create derivative works based on the Software.

    (b) You may not reverse engineer, decompile, or disassemble the Software. You may transfer the Software and user documentation on a permanent basis, provided that the transferee agrees to accept the terms and conditions of this Agreement and you retain no copies. If the Software is an update or has been updated, any transfer must include the most recent update and all prior versions.

4. **Restrictions on Use of Individual Programs.** You must follow the individual requirements and restrictions detailed for each individual program in Appendix C, "About the CD-ROM," of this Book. These limitations are contained in the individual license agreements recorded on the disk(s)/CD-ROM. These restrictions may include a requirement that after using the program for the period of time specified in its text, the user must pay a registration fee or discontinue use. By opening the Software packet(s), you will be agreeing to abide by the licenses and restrictions for these individual programs. None of the material on this disk(s) or listed in this Book may ever be distributed, in original or modified form, for commercial purposes.

5. **Limited Warranty.**

   (a) IDGB warrants that the Software and disk(s)/CD-ROM are free from defects in materials and workmanship under normal use for a period of sixty (60) days from the date of purchase of this Book. If IDGB receives notification within the warranty period of defects in materials or workmanship, IDGB will replace the defective disk(s)/CD-ROM.

   (b) **IDGB AND THE AUTHORS OF THE BOOK DISCLAIM ALL OTHER WARRANTIES, EXPRESS OR IMPLIED, INCLUDING WITHOUT LIMITATION IMPLIED WARRANTIES OF MERCHANTABILITY AND FITNESS FOR A PARTICULAR PURPOSE, WITH RESPECT TO THE SOFTWARE, THE PROGRAMS, THE SOURCE CODE CONTAINED THEREIN, AND/OR THE TECHNIQUES DESCRIBED IN THIS BOOK. IDGB DOES NOT WARRANT THAT THE FUNCTIONS CONTAINED IN THE SOFTWARE WILL MEET YOUR REQUIREMENTS OR THAT THE OPERATION OF THE SOFTWARE WILL BE ERROR FREE.**

   (c) This limited warranty gives you specific legal rights, and you may have other rights which vary from jurisdiction to jurisdiction.

6. **Remedies.**

   (a) IDGB's entire liability and your exclusive remedy for defects in materials and workmanship shall be limited to replacement of the Software, which may be returned to IDGB with a copy of your receipt at the following address: Disk Fulfillment Department, Attn: *Building Web Commerce Servers*, IDG Books Worldwide, Inc., 7260 Shadeland Station, Ste. 100, Indianapolis, IN 46256, or call 1-800-762-2974. Please allow 3-4 weeks for delivery. This Limited Warranty is void if failure of the Software has resulted from accident, abuse, or misapplication. Any replacement Software will be warranted for the remainder of the original warranty period or thirty (30) days, whichever is longer.

(b) In no event shall IDGB or the author be liable for any damages whatsoever (including without limitation damages for loss of business profits, business interruption, loss of business information, or any other pecuniary loss) arising from the use of or inability to use the Book or the Software, even if IDGB has been advised of the possibility of such damages.

(c) Because some jurisdictions do not allow the exclusion or limitation of liability for consequential or incidental damages, the above limitation or exclusion may not apply to you.

7. **U.S. Government Restricted Rights.** Use, duplication, or disclosure of the Software by the U.S. Government is subject to restrictions stated in paragraph (c) (1) (ii) of the Rights in Technical Data and Computer Software clause of DFARS 252.227-7013, and in subparagraphs (a) through (d) of the Commercial Computer—Restricted Rights clause at FAR 52.227-19, and in similar clauses in the NASA FAR supplement, when applicable.

8. **General.** This Agreement constitutes the entire understanding of the parties and revokes and supersedes all prior agreements, oral or written, between them and may not be modified or amended except in a writing signed by both parties hereto which specifically refers to this Agreement. This Agreement shall take precedence over any other documents that may be in conflict herewith. If any one or more provisions contained in this Agreement are held by any court or tribunal to be invalid, illegal, or otherwise unenforceable, each and every other provision shall remain in full force and effect.

We're the Best Way to Learn Photoshop. Just Ask Deke.

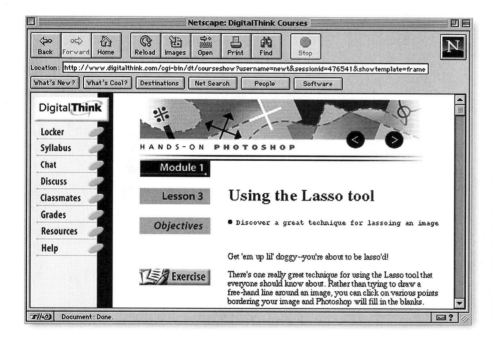

DigitalThink courses are taught completely over the Web and let you learn what you want, when you want.

Deke McClelland, author of *The MacWorld Photoshop 4.0 Bible,* is on the World Wide Web with **Hands-On Photoshop,** an all new online course from DigitalThink.

DigitalThink is the only Adobe-authorized source for online training. Our courses teach you how to get the most out of Adobe Photoshop, program with Java, and a ton of other useful stuff.

Learn anytime you want, from wherever you have a Web connection. DigitalThink courses give you live tutors, chat sessions with experts, interactive quizzes, discussion boards, and more.

If you can't get online, you can still sample DigitalThink's learning environment. Deke has included a lesson from **Hands-On Photoshop** on his CD-ROM in the back of this book.

Not convinced? Come to the DigitalThink site at **http://www.digitalthink.com** to take a FREE course on how to search the Net. Then sign up for **Hands-On Photoshop** at a 10% discount.

DigitalThink. Simply the best way to learn Adobe Photoshop. Just ask Deke.

www.digitalthink.com

12 Free Photo CD Scans...

Not All Photo CD Scans Are Created Equal

Quality, excellent service and support... just a few of the reasons Photoshop users, artists, designers, photographers, and publishers from around the United States choose PALMER'S for their Photo CD scanning. Your image is taken seriously whether you need one scan or thousands.

Introduce yourself to the PALMER'S difference. We'll scan 12 negatives or slides for free* (a $36 value) with an order of $36 (12 Repro scans) or more. That's it! You'll find PALMER'S is America's premier Photo CD service.

P A L M E R ' S

MOUNTAIN VIEW
650 Castro Street
415 969 1950
415 969 1956 *fax*

SACRAMENTO
2313 C Street
916 441 3305
916 441 1157 *fax*

SMART SOLUTIONS
800 735 1950
pcd@palmers.com

Name _____

Company _____

Address _____

City _____

State/Zip _____

How did you hear about us? _____

Title _____

Telephone _____

Fax _____

Business Type _____

Scans Per Month _____

*This offer is good for **35mm film** and **one time only**, although pass it along to your friends.
(does not include disc and offer subject to change)

IDG

IDG BOOKS WORLDWIDE REGISTRATION CARD

RETURN THIS
REGISTRATION CARD
FOR FREE CATALOG

Title of this book: Macworld® Photoshop® 4 Bible

My overall rating of this book: ☐ Very good [1] ☐ Good [2] ☐ Satisfactory [3] ☐ Fair [4] ☐ Poor [5]

How I first heard about this book:

☐ Found in bookstore; name: [6] _____

☐ Advertisement: [8] _____

☐ Word of mouth; heard about book from friend, co-worker, etc.: [10] _____

☐ Book review: [7] _____

☐ Catalog: [9] _____

☐ Other: [11] _____

What I liked most about this book:

_____

_____

What I would change, add, delete, etc., in future editions of this book:

_____

_____

Other comments:

_____

Number of computer books I purchase in a year: ☐ 1 [12] ☐ 2-5 [13] ☐ 6-10 [14] ☐ More than 10 [15]

I would characterize my computer skills as: ☐ Beginner [16] ☐ Intermediate [17] ☐ Advanced [18] ☐ Professional [19]

I use ☐ DOS [20] ☐ Windows [21] ☐ OS/2 [22] ☐ Unix [23] ☐ Macintosh [24] ☐ Other: [25]_____ (please specify)

I would be interested in new books on the following subjects:
(please check all that apply, and use the spaces provided to identify specific software)

☐ Word processing: [26] _____

☐ Data bases: [28] _____

☐ File Utilities: [30] _____

☐ Networking: [32] _____

☐ Other: [34] _____

☐ Spreadsheets: [27] _____

☐ Desktop publishing: [29] _____

☐ Money management: [31] _____

☐ Programming languages: [33] _____

I use a PC at (please check all that apply): ☐ home [35] ☐ work [36] ☐ school [37] ☐ other: [38] _____

The disks I prefer to use are ☐ 5.25 [39] ☐ 3.5 [40] ☐ other: [41]_____

I have a CD ROM: ☐ yes [42] ☐ no [43]

I plan to buy or upgrade computer hardware this year: ☐ yes [44] ☐ no [45]

I plan to buy or upgrade computer software this year: ☐ yes [46] ☐ no [47]

Name: _____ Business title: [48] _____ Type of Business: [49] _____

Address (☐ home [50] ☐ work [51]/Company name: _____

Street/Suite# _____

City [52]/State [53]/Zipcode [54]: _____ Country [55] _____

☐ **I liked this book!** You may quote me by name in future
IDG Books Worldwide promotional materials.

My daytime phone number is _____

IDG BOOKS

THE WORLD
COMPUTI
KNOWLED

YES!
Please keep me informed about IDG's World of Computer Knowledge.
Send me the latest IDG Books catalog.